Social Security Disability and the Legal Professional

The West Legal Studies Series

Your options keep growing with West Legal Studies
Each year our list continues to offer you more options for every area of the law to meet your course or on-the-job reference requirements. We now have over 140 titles from which to choose in the following areas:

- Administrative Law
- Alternative Dispute Resolution
- Bankruptcy
- Business Organizations/Corporations
- Civil Litigation and Procedure
- CLA Exam Preparation
- Client Accounting
- Computer in the Law Office
- Constitutional Law
- Contract Law
- Criminal Law and Procedure
- Document Preparation
- Environmental Law
- Ethics
- Family Law
- Federal Taxation
- Intellectual Property
- Introduction to Law
- Introduction to Paralegalism
- Law Office Management
- Law Office Procedures
- Legal Research, Writing, and Analysis
- Legal Terminology
- Paralegal Employment
- Real Estate Law
- Reference Materials
- Torts and Personal Injury Law
- Will, Trusts, and Estate Administration

You will find unparalleled, practical support
Each book is augmented by instructor and student supplements to ensure the best learning experience possible. We also offer custom publishing and other benefits such as West's Student Achievement Award. In addition, our sales representatives are ready to provide you with dependable service.

We want to hear from you
Our best contributions for improving the quality of our books and instructional materials are feedback from the people who use them. If you have a question, concern, or observation about any of our materials, or you have a product proposal or manuscript, we want to hear from you. Please contact your local representative or write us at the following address:

West Legal Studies, 5 Maxwell Drive, Clifton Park, NY 12065-2919

For additional information point your browser at
www.WestLegalStudies.com

Social Security Disability and the Legal Professional

Jeffrey Scott Wolfe
Lisa B. Proszek

THOMSON
DELMAR LEARNING™

Australia Canada Mexico Singapore Spain United Kingdom United States

WEST LEGAL STUDIES

Social Security Disability and the Legal Professional
by Jeffrey Scott Wolfe and Lisa B. Proszek

Business Unit Executive Director:
Susan L. Simpfenderfer

Senior Acquisitions Editor:
Joan M. Gill

Developmental Editor:
Alexis Breen Ferraro

Editorial Assistant:
Lisa Flatley

Executive Production Manager:
Wendy A. Troeger

Production Manager:
Carolyn Miller

Production Editor:
Matthew J. Williams

Executive Marketing Manager:
Donna J. Lewis

Channel Manager:
Nigar Hale

Cover Design:
TDB Publishing Services

Printed in the United States
1 2 3 4 5 XXX 06 05 04 03 02

For more information contact Delmar Learning, 5 Maxwell Drive, Clifton Park, NY 12065-2919

Or find us on the World Wide Web at
www.thomsonlearning.com or
www.WestLegalStudies.com

Library of Congress
Cataloging-in-Publication Data
Wolfe, Jeffrey Scott
Social security disability and the legal professional / Jeffrey Scott Wolfe and Lisa B. Proszek.
p. cm.
Includes index.
ISBN 0-7668-2115-3
1. Disability evaluation—Law and legislation—United States. 2. Insurance, Disability—Law and legislation—United States. 3. Social security—Law and legislation—United States. 4. Attorney and client—United States.
I. Proszek, Lisa B. II. Title

KF3649.W65 2002
344.73'023—dc21 2002019299

NOTICE TO THE READER

Publisher does not warrant or guarantee any of the products described herein or perform any independent analysis in connection with any of the product information contained herein. Publisher does not assume, and expressly disclaims, any obligation to obtain and include information other than that provided to it by the manufacturer.

The reader is notified that this text is an educational tool, not a practice book. Since the law is in constant change, no rule or statement of law in this book should be relied upon for any service to any client. The reader should always refer to standard legal sources for the current rule or law. If legal advice or other expert assistance is required, the services of the appropriate professional should be sought.

The Publisher makes no representation or warranties of any kind, including but not limited to, the warranties of fitness for particular purpose or merchantability, nor are any such representations implied with respect to the material set forth herein, and the publisher takes no responsibility with respect to such material. The publisher shall not be liable for any special, consequential, or exemplary damages resulting, in whole or part, from the readers' use of, or reliance upon, this material.

CONTENTS

PREFACE

Each year, hundreds of thousands of Americans find themselves in the midst of the disability appeals process, wending their way through complex administrative procedures, undergoing medical and psychological testing, and ultimately appearing before a federal Administrative Law Judge. Hundreds of thousands more drop out of the system, never pursuing the multilevel appellate process. The purpose of this work is to provide insight into the complexities of this adjudicatory process.

This text is not intended as a definitive reference on the case law underlying the Social Security Act or the regulations governing disability under Title II and Title XVI of the Act. Instead, it is a useful tool to help those unfamiliar with the process make their way through the heart of disability adjudication: the administrative hearing before a federal Administrative Law Judge.

The work is directed toward those who would serve as representatives, reaching out to others, less fortunate, rendering a public service and exemplifying the highest of American ideals. Those, who stand for the underdog, who call out to the ill and the infirm, can do no less. The system is not as daunting as it seems.

In the end, this work is for all who may encounter the disability appeals process. Written in a plain-English style and designed to be accessible, we hope it becomes a bright light revealing the intricacies of a complex system, so important to millions of Americans.

INTRODUCTION

Welcome to virtual learning. No, this isn't a computer, and no keyboard or daunting series of electronic instructions await. Instead, we have adopted the virtual reality concept, bringing to life the reality of professional practice before the Social Security Administration and the Office of Hearings and Appeals.

Professional service stands among the highest of individual endeavors, and no more so than in the representation of individuals before the Social Security Administration. There, individuals, often at the end of their personal resources, stand in great need; and the professional service rendered makes a tangible, if not immediate, difference in the lives so touched. In the spirit of time-honored professional service, we have designed this text to operate on multiple levels:

1. As an experiential guide with *narrative scenarios* to use as a template for client interactions;
2. With interactive checklists in the form of *Front of Your Mind Questions and Considerations;* and
3. With cross-references to a traditional legal analyses of pertinent statutes, regulations, and case law in the form of *A Trip to the Hard Drive* sections.

This work is deliberately structured to facilitate readability without sacrificing discussion of critical, factual, and legal issues necessary to a practical understanding of applicable law and effective practice. We want the legal professional, whether a lawyer, paralegal, or legal assistant, to understand and apply key legal issues in the successful representation of clients before the Social Security Administration generally, and the Office of Hearings and Appeals specifically.

NARRATIVE SCENARIOS

The *narrative scenarios* set the stage for the presentation of both legal issues and practice suggestions. As experiential guides, the narrative scenarios take the reader through the course of a client encounter at each stage of representation, beginning with first contact. Each scenario is preceded by highlights of the section contents, and centers on Chris, the prototypical representative. Chris is aided, at times, by Steve, the prototypical lawyer. The headings, Back to Chris, signal a new narrative scenario.

FRONT OF YOUR MIND QUESTIONS AND CONSIDERATIONS

What should you ask a client and why? *Front of Your Mind Questions and Considerations* provide real-world practice suggestions and investigative guides to prompt the reader through critical, factual issues at each stage of representation. General areas of practice are highlighted at the beginning of each section.

A TRIP TO THE HARD DRIVE

The Tenth Circuit Court of Appeals once described the Social Security disability regulatory scheme as second only to the Internal Revenue Code in its complex undertakings. Law and medicine, Social Security statutes, regulations, and case law must be carefully analyzed to be effectively applied. *A Trip to the Hard Drive* takes readers through the legal issues that define the critical, factual issues at selected stages of representation. Applicable statutory and regulatory law are explored.

USING THE TEXT

Approach this practice area with positive confidence. As a legal professional—lawyer, paralegal, or legal assistant—you already have the required tools to understand the legal and factual issues necessary to successfully represent your client before the Social Security Administration and the Office of Hearings and Appeals.

To help you effectively translate legal and factual issues into real-time representation, the text is structured to mirror the professional client relationship from start to finish. The first chapter brings the reader face to face with the "what-do-I-do-now" questions when a legal professional meets a client for the first time regarding a Social Security disability claim, and later chapters deal with issues such as collecting fees once the case is won.

Each chapter is a self-contained unit, which can be read alone or in conjunction with preceding chapters. To address factual issues, turn to the *Front of Your Mind Questions and Considerations* within a given chapter. To find pertinent regulations or suggested legal arguments, simply take *A Trip to the Hard Drive.* Finally, the Appendices include glossaries as well as other information, including a compilation of significant Social Security Rulings.

WHAT IF . . . ? SAMPLE PROBLEMS

Sample problems give the material in a chapter a practical context. At the end of each substantive chapter, sample problems pose problems and provide answers.

MEET CHRIS

Chris is our gender-neutral hypothetical representative. Through Chris's eyes we explore various questions and dilemmas. Chris takes us through each step of the disability appeals process, confronts the questions we all have, strives to learn and asks all the right questions. Through Chris we learn what it takes to be a representative.

DISCLAIMER

The opinions and material set forth herein are solely those of the authors and do not represent the views, policies, opinions or positions of the U.S. Government, the Social Security Administration, the Office of Hearings and Appeals, its personnel, or any of its various components. Any errors are solely those of the authors. Any resemblance to an actual person, claim, or event depicted in the narrative scenarios, sample problems, exemplar documents, exhibits, and decisions is coincidental; they are not intended to represent any person, claim, or event.

It should be noted, however, that government forms and other similar documents, as shown, for example, in the glossaries and other materials throughout the text and in the Appendices,[1] are freely available to the public either in hard copy or on the Internet, and are used to supplement the authors' work, and do not otherwise represent any official endorsement of this work by the federal government or the Social Security Administration, its personnel, or its components.

[1]**Appendices A, C, and D are available public documents. The material in Appendix B is used with the kind permission of Judge Paul Conaway of Denver, Colorado. All rights to the material in Appendix B remain with Judge Conaway.**

ACKNOWLEDGMENTS

The authors would like to extend their appreciation to the following reviewers for providing valuable feedback throughout the review process:

Deborah Kukowski
Minnesota State University Moorhead
Moorhead, MN

Jeffrey S. Rubel
University of Cincinnati Clermont
Batavia, OH

Teresa L. Conaway
Pillissippi State Technical College
Knoxville, TN

Bob Diotalevi
The College of West Virginia
Beckley, WV

Jeffrey Scott Wolfe
Lisa B. Proszek
Tulsa, Oklahoma

Dedication

To my wife, Sue, without whom this could not have been completed,
who endured countless nights without me as I labored onward.
Her never ending patience, love, and support
buoyed me as I strove to finish.
You are truly the best.

and

To my parents, Captain Malcolm and Elaine Wolfe of San Diego,
for your love and
unyielding belief in me.

—Jeff

1

CHAPTER ONE

The Administrative Determination

HIGHLIGHTS

- Understanding the administrative judicial system

CHRIS

"Chris, I've got to run to court," exclaimed Steve, one of the firm's lawyers, rushing out the front door of the small law office. "The judge just called on the *Jones* case. We've got a discovery problem," he called out over his shoulder, shrugging on his blue blazer as he headed to the elevator.

"Wait!" called Chris, looking aghast at the lawyer's retreating back. "We've got a new case coming in . . . ," Chris's voice trailed off as the office door shut silently behind the disappearing lawyer.

Now what do I do? thought Chris, looking at the wall clock. The new client was due in less than two hours. Less than two hours and no lawyer. *Great. What now? Call the client?—Maybe he has not left yet! Maybe I can cancel. . . .*

Chris replaced the receiver with a sigh. No answer. Mr. Carson had already left. Time to get ready. Chris turned to the master calendar, pulling the thin file they had started on Mr. Carson. Social Security disability. Disability? Was that like worker's comp? No, no, that was a state program. Social Security disability was federal. Chris knew that much.

Okay. Stay calm. You can do an interview. You've done it before for all sorts of cases—family law, automobile accidents, small claims—how different can this be?

But how? Chris despaired. *Social Security? What was that all about? Was it like a private disability insurance program? Or, was it something different altogether?*

FRONT OF YOUR MIND QUESTIONS AND CONSIDERATIONS, 1.1

INTRODUCTION TO SOCIAL SECURITY DISABILITY

The first thing Chris must understand about Social Security disability is the underlying public policy on which the program is grounded. As one court aptly noted, "Participation in the social security system is a non-contractual social welfare benefit."[1] "The goal of social security is to replace a worker's lost earnings."

Legislative history is equally informative. When amending the Social Security Act in 1980, the Senate (in Senate Report 96-987, 96th Cong., 2nd Sess.), commenting on the bill (H.R. 5295), which became the act of 1980, stated in part:

> **The disability program exists to provide a continuing source of monthly income to those whose earnings are cut off because they have suffered a severe disability.**

Within this stated public policy two key issues are immediately apparent:

- Earnings are cut off; and
- The individual has suffered a "severe disability."

So Chris knows two important points. But what else must be known? Clearly, the legal standards by which disability is determined. But before the legal standards are discussed, Chris must first understand the administrative adjudicatory system through which disability claims are decided. Understanding the procedure is as valuable as knowing the law. Indeed, one without the other leaves Chris in a vacuum. To be successful, Chris must understand *both* how the system works *and* what the legal issues and requirements are.

An effective initial disability interview requires an understanding of the legal mechanics of the disability determination system. Chris will not know how good Mr. Carson's case is without understanding both the legal system within which the case will be decided *and* the law that will be applied.

One fact stands out when considering the jurisprudence of the administrative decision-making system. Unlike legal actions in the courts, applying for and obtaining disability benefits is *not* an adversarial process, though many, during the proceedings, think otherwise.

Take *A Trip to the Hard Drive* to explore the legal mechanics of the system.

BACK TO CHRIS

Chris looked at the wall clock, then back at the thin folder. *What now?* Chris thought, *I know Social Security disability is a federal, not a state, program. I know the purpose of Social Security is to replace lost earnings. Is that all I've got to know—Mr. Carson doesn't have a job and can't work?* Instinctively, Chris knew there was more to learn. Nothing could be as easy as that. Chris started the computer. Time to access the hard drive.

A TRIP TO THE HARD DRIVE, 1.1

Take *A Trip to the Hard Drive* to learn more about the Social Security Administration, one of the world's most complex administrative agencies.

INTRODUCTION TO THE SOCIAL SECURITY ADMINISTRATION

The Social Security Act (the "Act") was passed in 1935 as part of President Franklin Roosevelt's New Deal legislation. Its original purpose was to provide working Americans a safety net from the economic instabilities of the Great Depression. The Act first provided for a national tax to fund an old age retirement program, incentives for the states to set up unemployment insurance programs, and grants to the states to provide financial assistance to destitute citizens.

In the 1950s, a disability insurance benefit program was added for workers who became disabled and unable to work before reaching the eligible age for retirement benefits. In the 1970s, a Supplemental Security Income benefits program was added for disabled citizens who had little or no work experience to qualify them for disability insurance benefits and who had not yet reached retirement age. The Social Security Act and subsequent amendments created five different benefit programs:

1. Old Age Retirement Insurance;
2. Survivor's Insurance;
3. Disability Insurance;
4. Supplemental Security Income; and
5. Medicare.

The Social Security Administration operates and manages the first four of these programs. Medicare benefits are administered by the Health Care Financing Administration, a separate government agency.

The Social Security Administration was part of the Department of Health and Human Services until March 1995 when it became an independent agency of the federal government.

Headquartered in Baltimore, Maryland, the Social Security Administration (SSA) has evolved into a vast bureaucratic entity with an operational hierarchy extending across the nation. For administrative ease, SSA divides the United States into ten regions. Each region is headed by a Regional Commissioner who oversees the administration of Social Security programs within that region.

Within each region, numerous Field Offices (formerly called District Offices) are located in selected cities. They handle the local business of the area with the Social Security Administration. Field offices typically serve as the initial contact between the general public and the Social Security Administration. The Field Offices issue Social Security numbers; take applications for retirement, disability, and supplemental security income benefits; and provide earnings records to wage earners on request. These functions also can be handled by a toll-free telephone call to one of SSA's tele-service centers.

The Social Security Account Number

The nine digit Social Security account number (SSN) is the lynchpin to SSA's management of the four benefit programs. Although this number has become virtually a universal means of identifying individuals for other government agencies such as the Internal Revenue Service and private businesses, Social Security numbers are issued by SSA in order to track an individual's earnings as reported to the SSA by employers. The Social Security Administration maintains records of a wage earner's earnings in order to determine whether the wage earner has worked long enough, and at a certain level of compensation, to receive insurance credits. The insurance credits are essential to determine eligibility for every benefit program handled by SSA, except for Supplemental Security Income (SSI) benefits, which do not depend on an individual's work history. Insurance credits are discussed more fully in Chapters 3 and 4.

Processing a Claim for Disability Benefits through the Social Security Administration's Hierarchy

A decision-making hierarchy has evolved within the Social Security Administration for disability claims. When an application for disability insurance benefits (DIB) or Supplemental Security Income benefits (SSI) is filed by a claimant, a permanent claims file is set up for the applications and related paperwork.

As part of that paperwork, the claimant furnishes the names and addresses of doctors and facilities that provided medical treatment for the claimant's alleged disabling condition(s). Generally, copies of the claimant's medical records are obtained by SSA from doctors and facilities and used as evidence to support or deny the disability benefits.

Here, the claims determination process takes on a strange jurisdictional twist. The benefits claim application is filed with a Field Office or teleservice center, both of which are operated by the federal government and staffed by federal employees who are part of the Social Security Administration. But once the application is made and the medical evidence is obtained, the permanent claims file and the medical evidence are sent to a state agency for the initial determination. The state agency, frequently termed the Disability Determination Service, or DDS, makes the first or "initial" determination as to the claimant's disability, applying pertinent Social Security (federal) regulations.

Back to Chris

"Hey," Chris blurted. "What's the DDS again?" *Too many acronyms,* Chris thought, vaguely wondering if the DDS had something to do with dentistry.

Steve returned from court in time to hear Chris' question.

"Let's look," said Steve, booting up the hard drive.

A TRIP TO THE HARD DRIVE, 1.2

Take *A Trip to the Hard Drive* to explore the state agency role in disability determination.

THE STATE DISABILITY DETERMINATION SERVICE'S INITIAL DETERMINATION

If a state opts to make the initial disability determination, it forms a state DDS.[2] Each state has a DDS staffed by state employees. The DDS employs evaluation teams, composed of disability evaluation specialists (called Disability Examiners, or DE's) and medical consultants (physicians and psychologists, called MCs). No lawyers or legal specialists work at the DDS. Review by the evaluation team is based solely on a paper record with little or no in-person contact with the claimant. After conducting a review of the medical and non-medical evidence, the team issues the initial decision regarding disability.[3] The claimant receives a standardized notice of the decision, which may briefly detail the various medical records reviewed and provide a very brief statement as to why the determination of disability or nondisability was made.

Nationally, the number of persons annually applying for benefits is staggering. In 1998, 2,559,985 persons filed initial applications for DIB and/or SSI. Of those applications, the state agencies granted 739,595 (31%) at the initial determination step. The state agencies denied 1,766,389 (69%) of the applications at the initial determination.

RECONSIDERATION BY THE STATE DISABILITY DETERMINATION SERVICE

If a claimant receives an unfavorable decision, he or she can file a request for reconsideration, again handled by the state DDS, but this time by an evaluation team other than the team that made the first determination. When applying for reconsideration, the claimant may submit additional medical evidence, and the assigned DDS team may ask the claimant to undergo a consultative examination (CE) by a physician or psychologist. The DDSs contract with private physicians or psychologists to perform these examinations. The purpose of the CE is to document and provide additional information about the claimant's medical condition.

On submission of new medical evidence (from the claimant or as a result of a consultative examination or both), the DDS team issues a second, or "reconsidered" decision. This second decision is often referred to as the "*recon determination,*" and is a required second step, even though the state agency rarely reverses itself. In 1998, for example, of the 1,766,389 denials issued at the initial decision stage, only 860,156 (49%) requested reconsideration of the initial decision. The state agencies issued unfavorable decisions on 748,335 (87%) of the requests for reconsideration filed. Because of this telling statistic, the Social Security Administration has announced plans to begin phasing out the reconsideration stage in favor of a protracted and more intense initial evaluation by the DDS.

APPEAL TO SOCIAL SECURITY'S OFFICE OF HEARINGS AND APPEALS

After the DDS makes its decision at the reconsideration stage,[4] if the claimant wishes further review of an unfavorable decision, the claim file and medical evidence are returned to the federal administrative venue for further proceedings before the Social Security Administration's Office of Hearings and Appeals (OHA). The claimant can file a request for a hearing before an Administrative Law Judge (ALJ) within sixty days of receipt of the unfavorable "recon" decision. Although OHA is part of the Social Security Administration, federal Administrative Law Judges who preside over the hearings are viewed as, and generally act as, independent decision makers without political or administrative influence.[5]

The first face-to-face encounter between a claimant and a decision maker occurs at the OHA level. Although the issues considered by the Administrative Law Judge are generally those previously decided unfavorably to the claimant, the Administrative Law Judge also can review any favorable part of a DDS determination. The Administrative Law Judge can also make an adverse redetermination of previously decided issues. The Administrative Law Judge, of course, must notify the claimant if any other new issues affecting the claim for benefits are being reconsidered.

Although the details of the hearing process are discussed in later chapters, a brief description is beneficial for introductory purposes. The hearing is closed to the public. Usually an Administrative Law Judge, the claimant, and the representative or attorney are present. The proceeding is tape-recorded, and a hearing assistant, also present, marks exhibits, takes notes, and runs the tape recorder. Witnesses may testify to the disabling conditions. Expert witnesses, such as medical experts who specialize in the claimant's medical condition and vocational experts may be called by the administration to offer testimony. Their specialized knowledge may assist the Administrative Law Judge in determining issues about the claimant's disability. The hearings are nonadversarial, because no representative or attorney represents the administration at the hearing to contest the medical evidence or the claimant's testimony. After a hearing, an Administrative Law Judge issues a written decision explaining the resolution of the issues in the claimant's case.

The number of benefit applications paid (i.e., reversed) by Administrative Law Judges is significant. In 1995, of 748,335 denials of requests for reconsideration, 493,133 (66%) requests for hearing were filed. Of that number, Administrative Law Judges granted (reversed, or awarded) benefits in 305,742 cases (62%) and denied benefits (affirmed the DDS) in 113,420 cases (23%). These statistics vary, of course, each year.

BACK TO CHRIS

"So what happens after a hearing? Where does the case go then? It's not over there, is it?"

Steve shook his head, pointing at the computer screen.

A TRIP TO THE HARD DRIVE, 1.3

THE APPEALS COUNCIL

If the claimant receives an unfavorable decision from the Administrative Law Judge, the final stop in this administrative process is an appeal to the Appeals Council. The Appeals Council (AC) is located in Falls Church, Virginia, and handles all appeals from Administrative Law Judges across the nation. Administrative appeals judges (AAJs) and their staffs review the evidence, including the tape-recorded hearing testimony and any comments and arguments made by the claimant or representative regarding errors the Administrative Law Judge may have made in the decision. Appeal is initiated by filing (mailing) a Request for Review to the Appeals Council. Practice procedures are discussed at length in Chapter 17.

The AAJ generally decides which of four possible actions should be taken on a case. The AAJ may remand the decision back to the same or another Administrative Law Judge for further action (typically the development of evidence). The AAJ may issue a decision in the case, reversing the Administrative Law Judge on both favorable and unfavorable parts of the decision. The AAJ may dismiss the Request for Review or dismiss the Request for Hearing (if the AAJ finds that the Administrative Law Judge should have dismissed the Request for Hearing). Or, the AAJ may deny the Request for Review, making the Administrative Law Judge's decision the final decision of the Commissioner of the Social Security Administration, for purposes of further appeal.

Of the 113,420 decisions issued by Administrative Law Judges who denied disability benefits, 51,405 (45%) Requests for Review were filed in 1995. The Appeals Council remanded 12,337 (24%) to the Administrative Law Judges, affirmed 37,525 (73%) of the Administrative Law Judge denials, and reversed (paid) 1,542 (3%) of the Administrative Law Judge denials.

If the AC issues an unfavorable decision, or denies the Request for Review, the claimant can take the case to the U.S. federal district courts. No appeal can be taken from an AC dismissal of the case or from an AC denial of review of an Administrative Law Judge dismissal under the SSA regulations. If an appeal is taken from the AC, the claimant must file a civil action in a local federal district court, naming the Commissioner of the Social Security Administration as the defendant. Here again, only the paper record is reviewed. There is no opportunity for the claimant to testify in the federal court proceeding. An unfavorable decision from the district court may be appealed to the regionally appropriate U.S. Circuit Court of Appeals, and eventually to the U.S. Supreme Court. Figure 1–1 shows the progression of appeals possible in Social Security disability benefits claims.

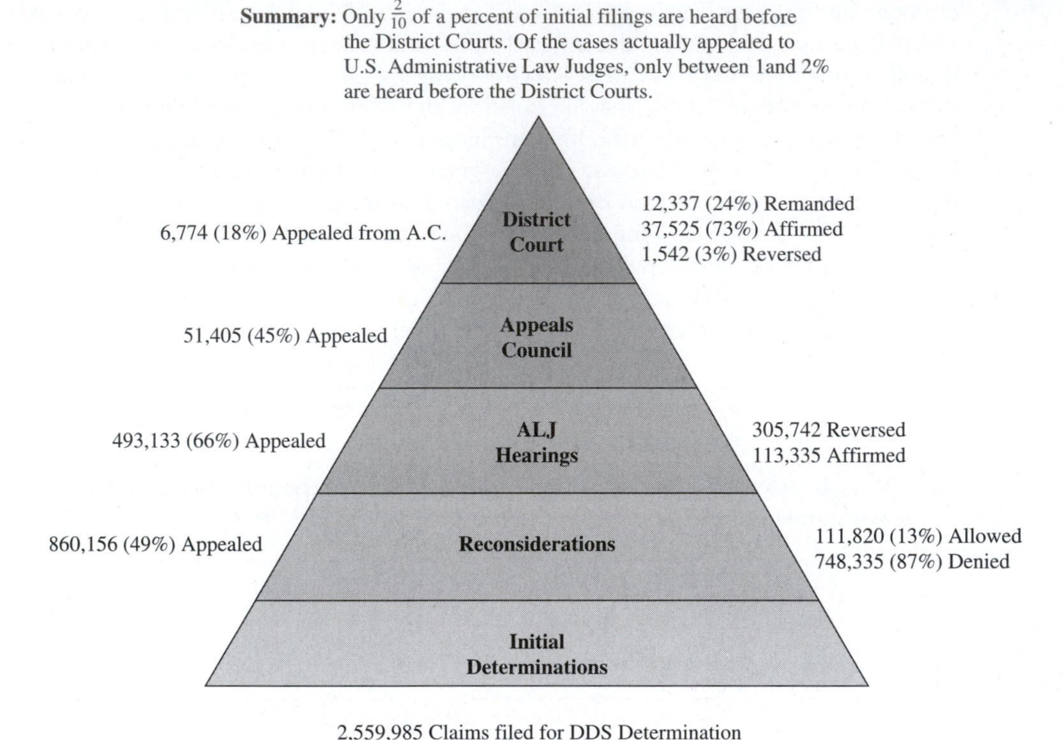

Figure 1–1 **Disability Hearings and Appeals in Context**

BACK TO CHRIS

Wait a minute! Chris thought hurriedly, suddenly puzzled. *If this is a federal agency, there must be a body of laws and regulations that govern Mr. Carson's claim, or, if he's coming to us before beginning the process, that will tell me how to get his case started.* Chris sighed, looking at the materials displayed on the hard drive, determined to deliver quality services.

"Okay," Chris muttered, "time to take the rest of the plunge. I'll assume that I'm in on this from the very beginning. Now, I need to know where to look to tell me what happens next."

Chris looked at the computer, and clicked on the research materials. A strange excitement began to take hold.

A TRIP TO THE HARD DRIVE, 1.4

As the genesis for the Social Security regulatory scheme, the Social Security Act should be the starting point for legal research. The Act is found at Title 42 of the U.S. Code, from sections 301 through 1397e. Three of the programs dealing with insured status (retirement insurance, disability insurance, and survivors' insurance) are covered in Title II of the Social Security Act. Title XVI covers the SSI program.

Many issues are not specifically addressed by the act. The Commissioner of Social Security issues regulations, administrative policies, and guidelines to provide statutory interpretations. As with other government agencies, the Commissioner publishes notices of proposed regulations in the *Federal Register* and receives public comment on proposed regulations. After receiving public comment, the Commissioner issues final or amended regulations, or the proposed regulations may be withdrawn.

Social Security regulations are codified at Title 20 of the Code of Federal Regulations (C.F.R.). Title 20, Part 404 contains the regulations pertaining to the insured programs under Title II of the Act, namely the retirement insurance, disability insurance, and survivors' insurance programs. Part 416 contains the regulations pertaining to SSI. The regulations are numbered sequentially. A citation such as Title 20 C.F.R. § 404.1520 directs you to C.F.R. Title 20, Part 404, subsection 1520. Because the SSI program's disability requirements are basically the same as the disability insurance programs and because it is not uncommon for applications for the two disability programs to be filed at the same time by a claimant (called concurrent applications by SSA [SSDC]), the same language at § 404.1520 can be found in Part 416 at § 416.920. Citation to the applicable part, however, is necessary if your claimant has applied only for Title II benefits or only for Title XVI benefits; you cannot casually cite regulations under any part of Title 20 when your client has not applied for those particular benefits.

The Social Security Administration also issues Rulings (SSRs or Social Security Rulings) designed to interpret aspects of the programs it administers. The Rulings are numbered sequentially, with the first two numbers signifying the year the Ruling was issued. For example, Ruling 96-2p was the second ruling issued in 1996; it deals with the consideration or weight to be given to a treating physician's opinion in disability benefits decisions. The Rulings become effective on publication in the *Federal Register.* The Rulings are binding on all components of SSA. They are not, however, binding on the courts.

Acquiescence Rulings (ARs) are issued by SSA when decisions from the federal circuit courts of appeal affect SSA policies. Acquiescence Rulings are only in effect and binding in the states within that circuit court's jurisdiction. These Rulings clarify how SSA applies the circuit court's decision within the states comprising that circuit. Acquiescence Rulings are numbered according to the year they are issued, then sequentially, with the circuit court number in parentheses. Thus, Acquiescence Ruling (AR) 96-5(8) indicates the fifth Acquiescence Ruling issued in 1996, issued in response to a decision from the Eight Circuit Court of Appeals.

The issuance of Acquiescence Rulings by SSA highlights a peculiarity of this area of the law. As previously discussed, the federal district courts and circuit courts of appeals adjudicate and issue decisions in appeals brought by claimants on unfavorable decisions issued by Administrative Law Judges or the Appeals Council. These federal court decisions are useful in interpreting the Social Security Act and SSA's regulations, rulings, and policy statements. Reading and analyzing Social Security decisions from local district and circuit courts is valuable in enhancing skills and understanding of the issues in Social Security disability cases.

However, according to the SSA's policy, a federal circuit court decision's interpretation of the Social Security Act or regulations is *not* binding on SSA decision makers at any level of the agency adjudication process *until* the SSA determines how the circuit court's decision conflicts with SSA's internal interpretation of the act or its regulations. SSA then issues instructions in an Acquiescence Ruling as to how agency adjudicators are to apply that circuit decision in the relevant states within that circuit. In issuing Social Security Ruling 96-1p, SSA cited its commitment to a "uniform and consistent adjudication necessary in the administration of a national program" as grounds for not following circuit court interpretations of Social Security regulations and rulings, until SSA had the opportunity to examine the case for potential conflict and issue an Acquiescence Ruling on it. The practical meaning of SSA's nonacquiescence policy is that, although a circuit court decision may have handed down a decision last week that exactly addresses an issue in a disability claim, the SSA adjudicators who review the decision can choose not to follow the decision's resolution of the issue as precedent. In fact, representatives have reported that, when informing an Administrative Law Judge of a new circuit court decision affecting a case, an Administrative Law Judge informed the representative that the circuit court decision was not binding on him! This, of course, is not the case in Social Security appeals in the federal, district, and circuit courts of appeals, where knowledge and citation of federal case law is expected.

Another peculiarity of this practice is that the Federal Rules of Civil Procedure or the Federal Rules of Evidence (or state law counterparts) do *not* apply at the administrative proceedings. Instead, internal guidelines, operating instructions, and policy statements are provided in two SSA publications. The *Program Operations Manual System* (*POMS*) is a large, multivolume handbook containing operating instructions and policy provisions used in processing claims within the administration. *POMS* is primarily used by district offices, the DDS's, and others in the Social Security Administration. The *Hearings, Appeals and Litigation Law Manual* (*HALLEX*) is a two-volume, paper-bound manual that provides procedures for carrying out administration policies, and guidance for processing and adjudicating claims at OHA, the Appeals Council, and the civil action level. *POMS* and *HALLEX* do not have the force of law and usually are not cited in decisions, except when a policy or procedure is not covered in the Social Security Act, or the regulations or rulings.

These are the basic tools to use when starting to research Social Security legal issues. In later chapters, other materials are discussed as aids to researching medical or vocational issues.

BACK TO CHRIS

"I've got a headache!" Chris sighed, pushing back from the desk and stretching. "Too many acronyms! How can I keep track of all this stuff?"

Uh-oh . . . the wall clock.

Mr. Carson was due in less than thirty minutes.

Still, Chris found the blizzard of letters and acronyms dizzying. He thought, *There must be some way to get a grip on this!*

FRONT OF YOUR MIND QUESTIONS AND CONSIDERATIONS, 1.2

Learning the intricacies of the Social Security administrative appeals process requires an understanding of an array of multiletter acronyms.

SPEAKING A NEW LANGUAGE: "ACRONYM-ESE"

The bureaucratic tendency to develop and speak a shorthand jargon for frequently used terms does not exclude the Social Security Administration. Many abbreviations and acronyms have been used in this chapter for the different SSA organizational components. Social Security employees and those who regularly deal with the SSA speak an unfamiliar language laced with acronyms and undecipherable abbreviations. To understand and develop fluency in "acronym-ese," commonly used acronyms appear in parentheses in this text, following the term being *acronymized.* A glossary of important and frequently used terms and acronyms appears in Appendix A.

Unfortunately, the Social Security acronyms are not the only new language to be mastered in this practice. Medical records, particularly physicians' treatment notes, are also filled with acronyms and abbreviations. Some of the more common medical abbreviations are provided in Appendix A.

BACK TO CHRIS

"What if . . . " Chris muttered aloud, ruminating on Murphy's law, "whatever could go wrong, usually did. . . . "

WHAT IF . . . ? SAMPLE PROBLEMS

WHAT IF . . .

What if, when Mr. Carson arrived, he had already started the process and had received an initial determination from the state DDS that denied him benefits?

Answer: ***You could represent Mr. Carson at the reconsideration stage.***

Explanation

1. The first question is, *When* was the initial determination issued? If it was issued within sixty days, you can mail or hand carry a request for reconsideration to the state agency.
2. The next question is, What medical records did the state agency rely on in making their initial determination? Ask Mr. Carson. Has he seen other doctors? Other medical providers (hospitals, emergency rooms, therapists, or clinics)? If so, gather these records and include them with Mr. Carson's request for

reconsideration. Even if you cannot get them in time, submit a list of the records and make a formal request that the DDS try to get them, or, alternately, send Mr. Carson for a consultative examination to document the other doctors' assessments.

3. Remember, even though Mr. Carson is at the reconsideration stage, the rate of favorable decisions is low so you must think about the records needed to make an effective appeal before an Administrative Law Judge. Keep trying to get Mr. Carson's records yourself!

WHAT IF . . .

What if Mr. Carson has missed the deadline for filing a request for reconsideration? Is that the end of his claim?

Answer: ***No, not at all. You may still file (mail or hand carry) the request for reconsideration, and ask that SSA accept the late filing anyway, setting forth a good reason for the delay. At the same time, you can file a new application for disability benefits, in effect starting over again. This works without a problem for Title II disability insurance benefits; but not for SSI benefits. As discussed in greater detail later, SSI benefits begin on the date of the filing of the application (or, no earlier than your first formal contact with SSA.) Refiling for SSI benefits potentially means foregoing several months of benefits.***

Explanation

1. Federal regulation provides for "reopening and revising decisions and determinations." See Title 20 C.F.R. § 404.987. Reopening may be done at SSA's own initiative; or, you may request reopening (in effect, a waiver) of the sixty day deadline, *if you've got a good reason.*
2. Title 20 C.F.R. § 404.988 sets forth "conditions for reopening," including clerical errors by Social Security and "good cause." Good cause is defined at Title 20 C.F.R. § 404.989 and includes submission of "new and material evidence."
3. Because the administrative procedures at the DDS do not have the force and effect of a court decision, nothing precludes the claimant from refiling. However, once an Administrative Law Judge enters a decision, the doctrine of "administrative finality" becomes effective, and, unless reversed and/or remanded by the Appeals Council or a federal court, the Administrative Law Judge's decision stands as final. Note, however, that even in the face of a denial from the Administrative Law Judge, nothing prevents you from (1) refiling anew, (2) filing a request for review before the Appeals Council, *and* (3) asking the judge to reconsider the decision—all at the same time. *See, for example,* Title 20 C.F.R. § 404.992, which provides for a "revised decision" by an Administrative Law Judge, setting forth procedures for implementing a revised decision.

---

[1] *Buccheri-Bianca v. Heckler,* 768 F.2d 1152 [10th Cir. 1985].

[2] See Title 20 C.F.R. § 404.1613, which provides in part that

> *A state agency will make determinations of disability with respect to all persons in the State except those individuals whose cases are in a class specifically excluded by our written guidelines. A determination of disability made by the State is the determination of the Commissioner.*

[3] A favorable decision is reviewed by the Disability Quality Branch (DQB), a federal watchdog arm of the Social Security Administration, whose purpose is to monitor and report on the programmatic integrity of the DDS. Interestingly, before a favorable decision can be sent to the claimant, the DQB must approve it as "programmatically" supported before issuance. If the DQB fails to approve it, a denial decision is reached, notwithstanding an otherwise favorable DDS decision.

[4] If the Social Security Administration eliminates the reconsideration stage, appeals will go from the DDS initial determination directly to the Office of Hearings and Appeals.

[5] The late Professor Bernard Schwartz aptly captured the role of the administrative judiciary:

> *Perhaps the greatest accomplishment of the APA [Administrative Procedure Act] has been this elevation of the federal hearing officer to the status of administrative judge, vested even with the dignity of the judicial title. The importance of the Administrative Law Judge corps set up by the APA has been emphasized by the Supreme Court itself. In Butz v. Economou, [438 U.S. 478 (1978)], the Court went out of its way to discuss "the role of the modern . . . Administrative Law Judge," which the Court said is "functionally comparable to that of a judge."*

32 *Tulsa L. Journal* 203, 211 (Winter 1996).

2

CHAPTER TWO

Service as a Representative in Social Security Disability Claims and Appeals

HIGHLIGHTS

- ❑ Acting as a representative in Social Security disability claims and appeals

CHRIS

Chris looked up as Steve rushed past the law library door.

"Hey, what's the rush Steve?" asked Chris, following the young lawyer into his office.

"The judge finally set some deadlines in the Jones case," the lawyer said heatedly. "I'm going to be eating, drinking, and sleeping the Jones case for the next two months!"

Chris inhaled sharply. "What about Mr. Carson's Social Security claim? He called from the hospital emergency room forty-five minutes ago. He was being treated for chest pains."

Chris suddenly felt relieved and anxious. Relieved that Mr. Carson wouldn't be coming in immediately, and anxious about Steve's availability. Surely now he would handle Mr. Carson? Wouldn't he?

The lawyer looked up from his desk, tossing his coat aside. "Carson canceled?"

Chris nodded. "For today. I rescheduled his interview appointment for the first of next week, if he's feeling well enough."

The lawyer rummaged through his briefcase. "You'll just have to take on Mr. Carson's case, Chris. I won't have time now, with this Jones thing heating up."

"I—I can't," Chris stammered, "I've never done anything like this kind of law and besides . . . ."

"Aww, you can do it," the young lawyer said, his head bent over a pile of pleadings. "You don't have to be a lawyer to represent people in Social Security cases. Besides, Mr. Carson is a friend of my in-laws and doesn't know where else to go for help on his claim. He seems pretty sick; he hasn't worked in awhile and probably simply needs someone to walk him through the process. Just do the best you can, OK?"

Chris backed out of the office, dazed by the sudden inheritance of the Carson case.

"OK, I've got less than a week to figure this Social Security stuff out," Chris muttered grimly, walking back to the law library. "Before Mr. Carson comes in, I've got to know what I'm supposed to do as his new representative."

As Chris began to explore the realities of representation in this odd system of administrative jurisprudence a strange excitement began to set in.

I could be an income producing resource for the firm, he thought.[1]

FRONT OF YOUR MIND QUESTIONS AND CONSIDERATIONS, 2.1

Several questions come immediately to mind.

- ❑ Who is a *representative* under federal regulations? Is this simply another word for *lawyer?*
  - ■ Are there rules that govern representation?
  - ■ Does one pass a test or become licensed or a member of something like a bar association?
- ❑ What does one do as a representative?

Some of these questions have seemingly straightforward answers, but none are easily answered in one or two sentences. Representation of another, taking responsibility for another, is a solemn undertaking. Representatives' actions can stand between the claimant and life, or, failing adequate representation, illness and demise. In such an undertaking, no easy answers are possible; each case is unique. However, there are several important principles to keep in mind.

For example, in the foregoing scenario, Chris has been given two incorrect presumptions about service as a representative in a Social Security disability case. First, a representative is *not* simply someone who processes the forms and paperwork involved in making a disability claim. The representative takes an active role, indeed, a proactive role, assisting the claimant in obtaining evidence, making certain all necessary information is provided on the claimant's behalf, and serving as the claimant's advocate with the Social Security Administration generally, and DDS and OHA specifically, both in writing and orally, at a hearing.

Second, a representative can be either a lawyer or a nonlawyer. Within the Administration, *representative* has come to mean *nonlawyer,* whereas attorneys are simply referred to as such. Technically, however, under governing regulations, both are representatives.

Regardless of whether a representative is an attorney or a nonlawyer, Social Security disability claims have become complex, specialized areas of the law that demand as much study of the pertinent law and knowledge of the facts of a particular case as any other form of litigation. The declared nonadversarial character of these administrative proceedings should not lull a representative into a sense that he or she must simply monitor the process and let the SSA adjudicators and their staffs do most of the work to develop the case.

Just the opposite is true. While the proceedings before the DDS and ultimately OHA are non-adversarial in the sense that the process is aimed at determining eligibility for an "entitlement" program, the question being whether the claimant is *entitled* to benefits, and not whether he or she can "trump" the government's case; or otherwise prevail in a clash of conflicting proofs; the representative is required to be persuasive in marshaling the evidence and presenting the client's case. Yes, we said *client,* because whether the representative is an attorney or a nonlawyer, the obligations to the claimant are fiduciary in nature.

Take *A Trip to the Hard Drive* for further information.

A TRIP TO THE HARD DRIVE, 2.1

This trip explores the requirements for service as a representative before the Social Security Administration.

WHO MAY SERVE AS A REPRESENTATIVE

A unique feature of practice before the Social Security Administration is that nonlawyers as well as attorneys may represent a claimant in proceedings. Title 42, § 406(a)(1) of the U.S. Code provides that "other persons, other than attorneys" may represent "claimants before the Commissioner of Social Security." An attorney is subject to the requirements of admission to practice law in a state, before the U.S. Supreme Court, or before one of the lower federal courts. Indeed, before a lawyer may be admitted to practice in a federal court, he or she must first be admitted to practice in one of the fifty states or the District of Columbia. Admission carries with it an oath of office, with attendant obligations to the court, the client, and the profession. Hence, the public is deemed to be protected, and the relationship between a lawyer and a client is regarded as unique, placing the lawyer in a fiduciary relationship (a relationship of special trust) with a client.

What about a nonlawyer who holds himself or herself out as having a special knowledge and skill in administrative proceedings? Are there any rules governing such individuals?

A nonlawyer may serve as a representative, appearing and representing a claimant before the Social Security Administration subject only to two fundamental requirements. First, the nonlawyer must be generally known to have a good character and reputation. Second, the nonlawyer must be capable of giving valuable help to the claimant in connection with the claim.[2] Both attorneys and non-attorneys are subject to the additional requirement that they not be disqualified or suspended from acting as a representative in dealing with the Social Security Administration and that no law prohibits them from acting as a representative.[3]

APPOINTMENT AS A REPRESENTATIVE

To be appointed as a representative, a written notice of appointment must be signed by the claimant and filed with the Social Security Administration. The administration provides an Appointment of Representative form for this purpose—Form SSA-1696-04; (see Figure 2–1). This form is more commonly known as the "1696" form.

The 1696 validates the representative's right to perform a variety of tasks in service to the claimant. In dealing with the Administration, you may be asked several times, "Where is your 1696?" which, in essence, is a request for proof that you have authority from the claimant to act in his or her behalf. Appointment as a representative, however, can also be made in another written document, such as a letter, a contract for representation by the claimant, or a fee agreement.[4]

If a representative is not an attorney, he or she must indicate acceptance of the appointment in writing and file the acceptance with SSA. The 1696 form has a specific place on it for a representative to indicate acceptance of the appointment. No similar requirement is made of attorneys to accept an appointment in writing. Like lawyers, the status of a nonlawyer representative is personal. Thus, only named individuals may be appointed as representatives. A specific person must serve in that capacity. So, although an attorney or representative may work in a law firm or be affiliated with an organization dedicated to serving others, such as a legal aid society, the law firm or organization cannot itself be named as the representative. Effectively, representatives are not interchangeable. The appointment is personal, as is the relationship.

After filing written documentation of an appointment as a representative, the Social Security Administration confirms the appointment in writing. It is important to file an appointment as representative with the administration as soon as it is completed. In general, the Administration prefers dealing with representatives who are knowledgeable about its regulations and the claims process, rather than unrepresented claimants, for whom the Administration must take extra precautions to guarantee due process.

HAVING REPRESENTATIVE STATUS

A representative (lawyer or nonlawyer) is entitled, and, arguably, required, to perform a variety of functions on behalf of a client, for which payment may be authorized if the claimant is successful. Payment for services as a representative from the Administration cannot be authorized unless a 1696 or other written authorization of appointment is in the claim file and in SSA's computer records. Fees and their calculations are discussed later. Figure 2–1 depicts an exemplar "1696."

After filing the notice of appointment with SSA, a representative is authorized to act on the claimant's behalf and may obtain the same information on the claim available to the claimant.[5] The representative may review and copy the claimant's file. The representative may be present, either with or without the claimant, at any interview, conference, or hearing with SSA personnel. The representative may engage in research and obtain evidence from the claimant's medical care providers and submit that evidence to SSA to prove the disability claim. Once on record, the representative receives notices and copies of any action that SSA takes on the claim for benefits, including determinations and decisions, and copies of any requests for information or evidence on the claimant's condition from the SSA.[6] A representative may not make an application for benefits on behalf of a client. Only the interested individual can make such a claim.[7]

Social Security Administration

Form Approved
OMB No. 0960-0527

Please read the back of the last copy before you complete this form.

Name (Claimant) **(Print or Type)**	Social Security Number
Wage Earner (If Different)	Social Security Number

Part I **APPOINTMENT OF REPRESENTATIVE**

I appoint this person, ____ ,
(Name and Address)

to act as my representative in connection with my claim(s) or asserted right(s) under:

☐ Title II (RSDI) ☐ Title XVI (SSI) ☐ Title IV FMSHA (Black Lung) ☐ Title XVIII (Medicare Coverage) ☐ Title VIII (SVB)

This person may, entirely in my place, make any request or give any notice; give or draw out evidence or information; get information; and receive any notice in connection with my pending claim(s) or asserted right(s).

☐ I am appointing, or I now have, more than one representative. My main representative is ____ .
(Name of Principal Representative)

Signature (Claimant)	Address
Telephone Number (with Area Code)	Date

Part II **ACCEPTANCE OF APPOINTMENT**

I, ______________________________ , hereby accept the above appointment. I certify that I have not been suspended or prohibited from practice before the Social Security Administration; that I am not disqualified from representing the claimant as a current or former officer or employee of the United States; and that I will not charge or collect any fee for the representation, even if a third party will pay the fee, unless it has been approved in accordance with the laws and rules referred to on the reverse side of the representative's copy of this form. If I decide not to charge or collect a fee for the representation, I will notify the Social Security Administration. (Completion of Part III satisfies this requirement.)

☐ I am an attorney. ☐ I am not an attorney. (Check one.)

Signature (Representative)	Address	
Telephone Number (with Area Code)	Fax Number (with Area Code)	Date

Part III (Optional) **WAIVER OF FEE**

I waive my right to charge and collect a fee under sections 206 and 1631(d)(2) of the Social Security Act. I release my client (the claimant) from any obligations, contractual or otherwise, which may be owed to me for services I have provided in connection with my client's claim(s) or asserted right(s).

Signature (Representative)	Date

Part IV (Optional) **ATTORNEY'S WAIVER OF DIRECT PAYMENT**

I waive only my right to direct payment of a fee from the withheld past-due retirement, survivors, disability insurance or black lung benefits of my client (the claimant). I do not waive my right to request fee approval and to collect a fee directly from my client or a third party.

Signature (Attorney Representative)	Date

Form **SSA-1696-U4** (6-2001) EF (8-2001) **(See Important Information on Reverse)** **FILE COPY**
Prior Editions May Be Used

Figure 2–1 **Appointment of Representative Form 1696**

BACK TO CHRIS

Whew! Being a representative seemed just like being a lawyer. You actually got to, well there was no other word for it, advocate on behalf of your client. How could that happen? How could someone act like a lawyer and not be one?

A vague fear edged into Chris's consciousness. What was it?

Unauthorized practice of law! That's what it was. How can someone sign a fee agreement with a client, appear before a judge, make oral arguments, collect evidence, and question witnesses and not be prosecuted for unauthorized practice of law?

Worriedly, Chris slid his mouse to the research icon on the hard drive.

A TRIP TO THE HARD DRIVE, 2.2

Take *A Trip to the Hard Drive* and explore the boundaries of practice as a representative.

UNAUTHORIZED PRACTICE OF LAW

Many states prosecute individuals who are not lawyers, but who, nevertheless, perform services as lawyers. Conviction for such activity (known as UPL or the unauthorized practice of law) usually results in fines and jail time.

Chris's apprehension (although rightly based on the perception that a nonlawyer is, for all intents and purposes, acting no differently than a lawyer) is, nevertheless, misplaced. A nonlawyer's activity before the Social Security Administration is authorized by federal laws and regulations as noted earlier. A nonlawyer is simply that; his or her activity, which is lawyerlike, is not illegal. Federal law preempts state statutes regulating the practice of law.[8]

Federal law is limited. Nonlawyers recognized as representatives by the Social Security Administration may practice only before the Social Security Administration and its various appellate components, including administrative law judges. Thus, once a final appeal has been heard before the Appeals Council, a nonlawyer, to prosecute a client's case before the courts, must pass the client on to a member of the bar who is authorized and admitted to practice before the federal courts.

Chris's activity as a nonlawyer is authorized by federal laws and regulations. Federal statute preempts state law so he cannot be prosecuted for unauthorized practice of law. As a nonlawyer, continued status as a representative depends wholly on compliance with federal regulations governing the conduct of representatives.

BACK TO CHRIS

Still, Chris thought, *what is it I really can do? What am I supposed to do?* A lead weight suddenly took roost in the pit of Chris' stomach. *What if I blow it? What if I really don't know what to do....*

Chris sat back heavily, thinking hard. *How must I act if I really am going to represent Mr. Carson to the best of my ability?*

Thinking furiously, Chris felt as if steam were pouring out of his ears for all the office to see. Several questions and considerations came immediately to mind.

FRONT OF YOUR MIND QUESTIONS AND CONSIDERATIONS, 2.2

To be successful, a lawyer or representative must know how to *advocate* a client's case. But, what is *advocacy?* At its heart, advocacy is the effective advancement of a client's interests within the bounds of ethical and lawful behavior. Within the trial venue, including proceedings before administrative law judges, advocacy means *persuasion.* The ultimate question in such a setting is, How can I persuade the decision maker to decide my client's case in my favor? The following issues must be addressed at the beginning of representation:

1. What must I persuade the decision maker to find? What does my client actually want? Surprisingly, many lawyers, when defining a client's legal position, automatically assume that the client wants a specific result, one mandated by the legal position taken. Lawyers may neglect to ask the client what he or she actually wants to achieve.
2. Once I know what my client really wants, what must the decision maker find to be true to find in my client's favor? This is an often-overlooked paradigm shift, critically important to effective advocacy. Put another way, what would persuade a judge to find in the claimant's favor? This process requires that you put yourself in the judge's shoes, then step back into your own and prepare accordingly. It is an effective way of understanding and presenting your client's case.
3. Have I obtained all the information I can from my client? His or her family? Friends? Do not assume anything. Do not assume that your client is able to fully and completely relate his or her complete medical history. Beware of assumptions made by clients. Imagine a client who believes he or she is disabled as a result of back problems while suffering from severe bouts of depression. You never hear about the depression because your client thinks you only need to hear about the perceived physical disability and he or she does not associate the depression with the inability to work.
4. Have I obtained all of my client's medical records? Do not assume that certain records are not necessary because they do not relate to the disability claim. Many judges will (a) want the entire medical record for the claimed disability period and (b) think you are trying to hide something if you do not produce all the medical records.
5. Once you have decided what your client wants, obtained all the information from him or her, and secured all the medical records for the pertinent period, you must plan, organize, and present your case. In other words, having gotten all the details together, how do you assemble them so the end result is an effective (i.e., persuasive) presentation?
6. Given the level of activity described in items 1 through 5, what rules govern a representative's conduct?

Take *A Trip to the Hard Drive* to find out.

A TRIP TO THE HARD DRIVE, 2.3

How must a representative behave in representing persons before the Social Security Administration? Take *A Trip to the Hard Drive* to learn.

INTRODUCTION

Each representative must decide how to act in prosecuting an appeal before the Office of Hearings and Appeals, which annually addresses more than 500,000 administrative appeals. Attorneys must abide by minimum standards of conduct established by state Rules of Professional Responsibility. The Rules of Professional Responsibility generally govern the conduct of a lawyer engaging in advocacy before various tribunals, including federal administrative proceedings before the Office of Hearings and Appeals of the Social Security Administration. The rules help guide ethical decisions, providing approved pathways through complex questions often raising potentially conflicting choices. The rules flow directly from the licensure of attorneys by the state.

No certification or licensure, however, exists for nonlawyer representatives. Are nonlawyer representatives then free to act as they wish, with no consequences or responsibility, either to their clients or the judges before whom they appear?

The answer is no, they are not. Since 1980, the Social Security Administration had promulgated but a single brief regulation addressing rules of conduct for representatives. Effective September 3, 1998, however, a new regulation took effect, superceding the prior regulation.[9] The new regulation "provides enforceable standards governing aspects of practice, performance and conduct for all persons who act as claimant's representatives."[10] Specifically, the expanded regulation was adopted by the Social Security Administration as final rules to "establish standards of conduct and responsibility for persons serving as representatives and further define . . . expectations regarding their obligations to those they represent and to . . . [the Social Security Administration]"[11]

THE REPRESENTATIVE AS A FIDUCIARY

According to the newly enacted regulatory scheme, a representative is a *fiduciary.* For lawyers, this is nothing new. For nonlawyers, there are an entirely different set of responsibilities for and obligations to the client. Newly revised section 404.1740(a) provides in part:

> **All attorneys or other persons acting on behalf of a party seeking a statutory right or benefit shall, in their dealings with us, faithfully execute their duties as agents and fiduciaries of a party.**[12]

In effect, the newly expanded regulations give the nonlawyer representative a status already held by attorneys—fiduciary, someone in a position of trust.[13] However, the regulatory term for *fiduciary* is *bidirectional,* which represents a critical distinction from the concept of fiduciary as an attorney. As a fiduciary under the regulations, a representative owes a high degree of competence to both the claimant and the agency in order to promote a nonadversarial proceeding before the administrative law judge. Indeed, the requirement is that a representative "shall, in their dealings with *us*" act as "fiduciaries." Figure 2–2 describes the representative's role.

A critical component is the duty to provide competent assistance. Integral to providing competent assistance are the requirements that representatives be "forthright in their dealings" and "act with reasonable promptness to obtain information and evidence" to support their claims.[14] Thus, fiduciary expectations under the regulations are, perhaps, little different from expectations of attorneys as officers of the court. As a practical matter, this means that unfavorable as well as favorable evidence must be produced by the representative (i.e., the representative must produce *all* the medical evidence, not only the records he or she deems favorable). Lawyers have the same obligation when informing the court of pertinent law and legal precedent. Attorneys cannot shade the law; they cannot omit legal precedent that is unfavorable to their clients. An attorney's fiduciary obligation to the court, as an officer of the court, is to advise the court of all the law.

The imposition of a bidirectional fiduciary duty, one in which the representative owes a duty of trust both to the client and to the agency, promotes the nonadversarial nature of the proceedings. Theoretically, both the representative and the judge should be trying to determine if there is a factual and legal basis for entitlement to benefits. It is not an adversarial contest in which the representative is trying to beat the judge in order to win the case.

THE REQUIREMENT OF COMPETENCY

Significantly, expanding the regulation is directly related to further regulating the conduct of representatives to ensure adequate representation of members of the public who appear as claimants, recognizing "the increased participation of compensated representatives in the adjudicative process."[15] According to the Social Security Administration, "we are publishing these rules to improve the efficiency of our administrative process and to ensure that claimants receive competent services from their representatives. *While we recognize that most representatives do a conscientious job in assisting their clients, our experience has convinced us that there are suf-*

"All attorneys or other persons acting on behalf of a party seeking a statutory right or benefit shall, in their dealings with us, faithfully execute their duties as agents and fiduciaries of a party."

- This Means that the Representative shall:
  - ➛ Be forthright in dealing with the Social Security Administration;
  - ➛ Be prompt in his or her actions; and
  - ➛ Act with a high degree of competency.

Figure 2–2 The Representative as Fiduciary

ficient instances of questionable conduct to warrant promulgation of additional regulatory authority."[16] Concerning representative competency, the expanded regulation requires

> **A representative shall provide competent assistance to the claimant and recognize the authority of the Agency to lawfully administer the process.**[17]

The newly expanded rules establish "an affirmative duty of competency," requiring "that a representative know the significant issue(s) in a claim and have a working knowledge of the applicable provisions of the [Social Security] Act, the regulations and the [Social Security] Rulings."[18]

Lawyers and nonlawyers are both required to have the minimum skills and knowledge necessary to effectively represent their clients.[19] Representatives must, therefore, prepare themselves as well as be prepared. Not only must representatives generally possess the requisite adversarial skills to effectively represent their clients but they must also be knowledgeable about the specific facts and law pertaining to the case at hand. According to the newly expanded rules, it is unacceptable simply to attend an administrative hearing and expect the federal administrative law judge to do the majority of the work in developing the record.[20]

Competency is defined throughout the new regulations, including a requirement that representatives

1. Be forthright in their dealings with the Administration and with the claimant;[21]
2. Act with reasonable promptness to obtain information and evidence;[22]
3. Assist the claimant in complying with SSA's requests;[23] and
4. Act with reasonable diligence and promptness in representing a claimant.[24]

Competent representation

> **requires the knowledge, skill, thoroughness and preparation reasonably necessary for the representation.** ***This includes knowing the significant issue(s) in a claim and having a working knowledge of the applicable provisions of the Social Security Act . . . the regulations and the Rulings.***[25]

In effect, representatives, lawyers and nonlawyers alike, are required to know the law and the facts of their clients' cases. This is the only way can they actually provide valuable service to their clients.

BACK TO CHRIS

"So, what does that mean in terms of actual conduct by a representative? What does a representative do to be good?" Chris asked.

"Good question, Chris." Steve leaned back against the door frame. "Let's talk about some attributes of a good representative."

A TRIP TO THE HARD DRIVE, 2.4

Take *A Trip to the Hard Drive* to learn about the attributes of a good, or effective, representative.

REPRESENTATIVES SHOULD BE PROMPT

The new regulations require the representative to

> **Act with reasonable promptness to obtain the information and evidence that the claimant wants to submit in support of his or her claim. . . .**[26]

Figure 2–3 presents the new regulations that are, in effect, the ethical standards required of representatives.

New Regulations—20 CFR § 404.1740
- Shall provide competent assistance to the claimant
- Shall be forthright in their dealings
- Act with reasonable promptness to obtain information and evidence
- Assist the claimant in complying with requests for information or evidence about . . . any other factors showing how the claimant's impairments affect his ability to work

Figure 2–3 **New Regulations Are Effectively Ethics Standards**

The requirement of promptness is repeated throughout the newly expanded regulation, requiring, among other things, that a representative "assist the claimant in complying, *as soon as practicable,* with our requests for information or evidence at any stage of the administrative decisionmaking process in his or her claim."[27] Thus, administrative orders that require the submission of additional medical evidence ten days before a scheduled administrative hearing may find the weight of regulatory authority behind them—in effect defining what is "reasonable."

Specifically, the representative is to "act with reasonable diligence and promptness in representing a claimant," including "prompt and responsive answers to requests from the Agency for information pertinent to the processing of the claim."[28]

Indeed, among the "prohibited actions" are those that "through . . . actions or omissions, unreasonably delay or cause to be delayed, without good cause . . . the processing of a claim at any stage of the administrative decisionmaking process."[29]

AN AFFIRMATIVE DUTY TO PROVIDE ALL MATERIAL EVIDENCE

The ethical dilemma sometimes faced by counsel regarding the selection of evidence to be presented now appears to be answered. Title 20 C.F.R. § 404.1740(b)(1) provides that counsel must bring

> **to our attention everything that shows that the claimant is disabled or blind, and to assist the claimant in furnishing medical evidence that the claimant intends to personally provide and other evidence that we can use to reach conclusions about the claimant's medical impairment(s) and, if material to the determination of whether the claimant is blind or disabled, its effect upon the claimant's ability to work on a sustained basis.**

Where some question previously existed about the representative's obligation to submit all evidence regardless of whether such information was detrimental to the ultimate issue of disability, there now appears to be an affirmative obligation to so act. Advocates, stressing the obligation to act "zealously" on behalf of a client, often felt constrained not to supply medical information that might support a finding contrary to that which would result in the award of benefits. Thus, selective submissions of medical records has not been uncommon. The newly expanded regulation appears, however, to require submission of "everything that shows that the claimant is disabled . . . and other evidence that we can use to reach conclusions about the claimant's medical impairments."

Reading the first part of § 404.1740(b)(1) alone, an argument could be made that the standard has not changed—that representatives are still free to supply information only insofar as it tends to show disability. However, on reading the complete sentence, it is evident that all evidence affecting the ultimate conclusion is to be tendered.

From a jurisprudential perspective, the newly expanded regulation is consistent with the notion that the administrative appeal before the administrative law judge is nonadversarial. Instead of adversarial submissions (i.e., "putting your best evidentiary foot forward"), the advocate is required to supply all "material" information bearing on the ultimate determination.

In the context of the administrative hearing, the new regulation arguably establishes a baseline requirement that the representative be knowledgeable about the hearing, the procedures surrounding the process, and the individual case being prosecuted. Understanding these requirements necessarily requires careful consideration of the issues that define competency within the hearing generally and as regards representation specifically. Each is discussed in turn.

A Representative's Scope of Action before the Judge

At an initial, or recon determination before the DDS, personal appearances are rare. The overwhelming majority of advocacy takes place on paper, and, occasionally, by telephone. Once the case is appealed to a federal administrative law judge, the fundamental tenor of the proceedings changes. It is within this transformed venue that the representative is most needed and, is likely most effective. No longer is the determination based only on paper records. Instead, a full evidentiary presentation is possible. "At the hearing you may appear in person, submit new evidence, examine the evidence used in making the determination or decision under review and present and question witnesses."[30]

Because the decision by the judge is not solely limited to a paper review, the claimant's credibility when testifying becomes a key factor affecting the final decision.[31] In this, the administrative appeals hearing is no different from an appearance in a court of law.

However, there are fundamental differences between the administrative proceeding and one in the courts. Understanding the essential differences between the two proceedings is a necessary first step in attaining competency in the administrative appeal, as defined in the newly adopted regulation. One difference is simply the fact that the government, having previously denied the claim administratively (by the action of the DDS), does not appear at the hearing. The only present party is the claimant.

At an actual hearing, only the judge, the claimant, the representative, and other witnesses are present. The government does not appear as a party.[32] The administrative hearing before the administrative law judge is thus a single-party proceeding, and as such, becomes an entirely different kind of hearing from that of the traditional two-party contest.

The issue at a hearing concerns entitlement to benefits, not prevailing over an opposing litigant. Rather than contest an opponent's evidence or contradict an opposing legal theory, the representative in the administrative venue must focus on demonstrating entitlement to benefits. The issue is not one of triumph over an opponent so much as it is winning by presentation of evidence and testimony required under the *Five Step Sequential Evaluation* by which such claims are decided.[33]

Unlike the formality of a proceeding in the courts, hearings before an administrative law judge are not governed by the Federal Rules of Civil Procedure, or the Federal Rules of Evidence.[34] Indeed, the only evidentiary standard in the governing regulations is materiality. Pragmatically, almost any evidence may be offered and received—the only questions are whether, at the end of the proceeding, disability was established in accordance with the requirements of the *Five Step Sequential Evaluation* and whether the judge properly considered the evidence.

At the hearing, evidence is presented in the form of medical records and reports. Testimony is given by the claimant and others, including vocational witnesses and medical experts. The order of the proceedings is largely at the discretion of the administrative law judge.[35] Some judges undertake inquiry of the claimant at the outset of a hearing, because they believe effective development of the administrative record depends on direct examination by the presiding judicial officer. Others, deferring to the representative, will only ask clarifying questions after the representative has concluded his or her examination.

Regardless of whether the judge inquires initially or whether the representative takes the lead, effective examination throughout the proceeding depends on an understanding of applicable law generally, and the facts of the case specifically. To know one without the other, either the law or the facts, is detrimental to effective representation. As law professors are wont to say: *The law gives life to the facts and the facts to the law.*

Understanding the law enables the effective representative to emphasize facts critical to a favorable decision. Complete knowledge of the facts enables the representative to make an effective argument to the administrative law judge that the legal requirements for disability have been met. Both are necessary for an effective presentation at a hearing.

THE REPRESENTATIVE, IN SUMMARY

It is not enough to know how the administrative process works or to be generally proficient in administrative procedure without specific proficiency in the facts of the case.

Anecdotal tales abound of representatives who meet their clients minutes before a hearing, only to be surprised during the proceeding by learning the client earned income while allegedly "disabled." Similarly, a representative who fails to meet with a client before a hearing should not be surprised to learn of "new" medical evidence. Effective advocacy requires careful preparation well in advance of standing before a judge.[36] The essence of competence is professionalism, as illustrated in Figure 2–4.

Representatives who fall into the trap of thinking that Social Security appeals are all the same fail in their fiduciary duties. Representation requires proactive measures on behalf of a client to maximize the opportunity for success. Waiting until the last possible minute, expecting the agency or the judge to prepare the case for you, not only is a disservice to the client but is violative of the new regulations governing representative conduct and the standards of responsibility.

Even a cursory review of the administrative appeals process leads to the inevitable conclusion that the majority of case development, that is, the procurement of medical records and reports, should primarily be undertaken by the representative, not by the administrative law judge. Faced with more than 550,000 national case filings, 1,060 U.S. administrative law judges will not be as effective as the individual representative in obtaining critical records before an administrative hearing.

"Competent representation requires the knowledge, skill, thoroughness and preparation reasonably necessary for the representation."[37] Preparation for a hearing requires adequate marshaling of the evidence. The evidence should be organized to meet the specific issues of the case. A file should be organized based on the *Five Step Sequential Evaluation,* and evidence should be maintained so that it is readily accessible to the representative during the proceeding and in accordance with the *Five Step Sequential Evaluation.*

Thus, evidence of work should be filed separately from medical evidence. The medical evidence, in turn, should be compiled to address the legal theory of recovery. Is the claimant entitled to benefits because the condition meets the requirement of federal regulation, and, if so, what medical records demonstrate the condition? Is the claimant entitled to benefits because he or she cannot return to past work, and, because of that same condition, is unable to perform other, less demanding employment? What medical records demonstrate an inability to work at the heavier exertional level? Such records should be carefully maintained and summarized for ready reference during the proceeding.

Thoroughness is akin to completeness. A record that contains chronological gaps cannot generally support an award, especially if the record ends well before the hearing and disability remains an issue through the administrative proceeding.[38] The effective representative considers the case through the eyes of the decision maker. How will the judge view this? Have I presented the evidence in such a manner as to clearly communicate my theory of recovery? Is it understandable? These are the questions which, if carefully weighed, can change the advocate's perspective, creating a perceptual distance that empowers the representative to see the case from the judge's viewpoint. Only then can the representative fully be prepared to meet the expectations of the judge.

The effective representative tries to ask the same hard questions as the decision maker—but the questions are not asked at the hearing; they are asked well in advance. Such inquiry enables an understanding of the weak points of a case, then the difficult questions may be realistically addressed at the hearing. Federal regulation authorizes the representative to engage in a number of activities on behalf of a client, as shown in Figure 2–5.

Professionalism Demands
- Preparation
- Presence
- Effective Presentation

Figure 2–4 **Competent Professionalism**

Professionalism—20 C.F.R. § 404.1710
A Representative May:
- Obtain information
- Submit evidence
- Make statements about facts and law
- Make any request or give notice
- Represent the claimant before an Administrative Law Judge

Figure 2–5 **Activities of a Representative**

BACK TO CHRIS

They are the same as lawyers, Chris marveled, overwhelmed by the potential magnitude of the undertaking that Steve deferred to him. *Can I do this?* he wondered.

Standing, Chris set out to find Steve.

"Steve?" Chris stood in the young lawyer's doorway, feeling guilty at disturbing the lawyer. Mounds of books teetered on the once-immaculate desk.

"Yeah?" Steve said, not glancing up but flipping slowly through a legal encyclopedia.

"Can I ask you about something?"

"Now?"

"Well, I thought, because I was starting to examine the Carson case, you might share some tips on how to actually present a case in person." Chris suddenly felt nervous, anticipatory.

Steve sighed, leaned back, and stretched. "Okay. I guess that's only fair since I foisted the case off on you anyway."

"Thanks. I've been reading about the Social Security appeals system and about representatives. They do the same thing as lawyers."

Steve grimaced, then shrugged. "You're right. And the judges will expect you to act the same as well. You don't get any breaks because you're a 'nonlawyer' representative."

"That's what I thought."

"So, what do you want to know?"

Chris hesitated. Steve didn't need to spend too much time. "Can you give me some general principles so I can learn how to present Mr. Carson's case?"

Steve thought for a moment, then brightened. "I know just the thing," he declared. "Something one of my law school professors preached."

Chris waited expectantly.

"The three P's," Steve said, his enthusiasm building.

"The three P's," Chris echoed.

"Yes! Preparation, presentation, and presence," Steve replied, ticking off each with a raised finger. "Let me tell you what they mean."

FRONT OF YOUR MIND QUESTIONS AND CONSIDERATIONS, 2.3

The essence of professional practice as a representative involves a synergy of factors as described in this section.

PREPARATION

To be an effective representative requires preparation. Preparation requires spending time with the client, with others, and with yourself. Initially, an effective representative plans the first meeting with the client. A careful interview reveals critical information about the client and the medical condition and treatment.

Preparation requires a thorough understanding of the administrative adjudicatory system, as well as the specific law related to the client's case. To be an effective representative, nonlawyers must learn fundamental legal skills, including the following:

1. How the federal court system works, including knowing in which circuit court of appeals the hearing will take place;
2. How to look up legal issues in a legal encyclopedia or use computer-aided legal search programs;
3. How to look up cases in a "reporter"—a compilation of cases that includes trial and appellate decisions handed down by various (in this case, federal) courts;
4. How to cite case law;
5. How to cite federal regulations; and
6. How to apply the law to the facts of a case.

In disability appeals, it is essential to know the five-step Sequential Evaluation Process (SEP) by which these claims are decided. A judge may want to know the legal theory of the client's claim and expect a brief analysis of the facts. What does the client suffer from and what is the regulatory basis for disability? Does the condition meet or medically equal a listed impairment? Is the claimant's "residual functional capacity" so limited as to preclude competitive employment (applying the medical–vocational guidelines)? To merely answer, *my client is disabled and cannot work,* is insufficient. It simply suggests that you are not prepared and do not know either the legal basis for disability or the facts of the case to support such a determination.

It is necessary to know the facts of the case. This means knowing the details of your client's medical history (diagnosis dates, treating and consulting physicians, hospitalization dates, and so on), as well as being able to tell the judge where the pertinent medical information is located in the file. The judge should not have to sift through medical documents to find support for your argument.

You must identify critical facts that support the case. One effective, yet simple, method is to list exhibits, with a brief summary of each, so you can make ready reference to them as necessary. Make a note for yourself next to each exhibit reference as a reminder of why each exhibit supports your client's case (i.e., what the *value* of the evidence is). Do not simply rely on your memory. Murphy's law has a bad habit of coming true just when you're trying to make a persuasive presentation. Be prepared!

Finally, submit a written distillation (call it a "brief" if you wish) of your legal theory and the supporting exhibits and facts at the outset of the proceeding so the judge can follow the presentation. For example, giving the judge an intelligently compiled list of exhibits (such as similar issues grouped together) will help persuade the judge of the efficacy of the case. At the conclusion of the hearing, make a brief closing statement. Refer to the exhibits and weave the testimonial facts in with those on paper.

PRESENTATION

An effective argument and an effective case must be well presented. It is not sufficient to stand up, ask a set of prepared questions of your client, and sit down. Unfortunately, many representatives use "go-by's" (lists of questions they ask start to finish regardless of the nature of a case). Such lack of individual tailoring communicates volumes to the judge—most of it negative. Using a rote list of questions suggests a lack of preparation, stealing the effectiveness of a presentation. This is most noticeable to the judge when an answer to a rote question naturally lends itself to a follow-up inquiry, such as *why is that?* only to be met with silence as the representative moves on to the next question on the list. Nothing communicates lack of interest in *what* the client is actually saying more than this. Regardless of the legal issues, hearings are human endeavors. They should be persuasive presentations, not obligatory marches by representative and client. You must act as if you are convinced of the case, which means tailoring the presentation to the individual case.

Indeed, you can be the most prepared representative ever but fail because you did not effectively present your client's case. With this in mind, what are the key ingredients to an effective presentation?

First, identify for the judge the legal theory on which the claim is based. Focus the judge's attention on the specific line of inquiry necessary for a favorable decision. The expression, *never walk into a committee meeting empty handed,* is relevant here. If you simply say *my client is disabled,* you risk misinterpretation. Circumscribe the issue; direct the judge's attention toward a specific goal.

Second, begin with a strong point. You want to build your case to be sure the judge will reasonably conclude that the evidence supports your theory. If the heart of your case lies with your claimant, start there, then bring in a corroborating witness (a family member, friend, or former employer.) If, however, your client does not make a good witness (for example, if he or she cannot follow a line of questioning), begin with another witness, explaining your client's deficits, then present your client, illustrating and corroborating the first witness's testimony.

Third, carefully consider the order of presentation of multiple witnesses, or, if only the claimant will testify, the order of the questions asked. Some basic principles are important to remember. Always end on a positive note. End your inquiry (you cannot control the judge's) with facts that support the essential premise that your client is unable to engage in competitive work.

Fourth, build your case. Building your case requires an explanation of why your client claims disability. Having a client simply say, *I can't work,* is not persuasive. A discussion about the activities the client was able to do prior to the onset of disability, followed by an explanation of why those same activities can no longer be pursued, will be more persuasive than simply telling the judge what your client can't do. Show connections between a client's symptoms and activity levels. Group related questions together. Do not simply begin the examination by asking the client how far he can walk or how much weight she can lift—those are facts that need to be related to symptoms.

Fifth, let the judge get to know the claimant before getting to the heart of the case. Design your presentation so that the judge believes the client. Explain the progression of your clients disability; link impairments with symptoms, symptoms with limitations, and limitations with the inability to perform work or worklike activity.

Sixth, organize the facts. In an effective presentation, critical evidence is presented persuasively. If your client has suffered a sequence of steadily more grievous conditions, one after the other, a chronological description of the events leading to the current condition may be the most persuasive way to present the case.

However, if your client's present inability to work is a result of a cumulation of ailments, essentially unrelated to one another, a transactional description of the condition may be appropriate for presenting the case. For example, suppose in 1982 your client suffered a back injury that prevented him from working for six months, but eventually he was able to return to do work that was less strenuous. Suppose ten years later, he lost several fingers on his right, dominant hand. After a period of recuperation, he again returned to work, but five years later suffered depression, which prevents him from meeting people, working with others, accepting criticism from supervisors, and so on. If you tried to present the case chronologically, you would cover lots of time that the client worked, even at less demanding occupations. It would be more effective to make a *transactional* presentation, beginning with the diagnosis of depression and the resulting limitations. Then, when the question becomes, *Why can't he work alone?* the logical response is that he does not have the exertional capacity for that kind of work, given the limitations that existed earlier.

Finally, remember that an evidentiary presentation need not be boring. Photographs or other demonstrative exhibits can be persuasive. Look for opportunities to present visuals, but remember that the judge cannot "play doctor" and reach medical conclusions.

PRESENCE

Presence involves the combination of *preparation* and *presentation* and is more than either. It may be described as *poise, style,* or *panache.* A representative may be well prepared, render an effective presentation, and nevertheless lack presence. In simple terms, a representative's presence is the catalyst that turns a good presentation into *persuasive advocacy.*

A representative's presence before a judge as the advocate for a client is communicated by appearance, presentation, and demeanor. At the most basic level, persuasive advocacy demands respect for the proceeding, the judge and, ultimately, the claimant. Respect is manifested in a variety of ways.

Physically, presence is reinforced with a positive posture. Stand straight. Don't slouch. Refrain from unnecessary movement when examining witnesses. Voice reveals attitude. Speak at an appropriate rate. Speaking too quickly loses the witness, and perhaps the judge. Avoid repeating questions. Speaking too slowly sounds rehearsed.

Modulate your voice, such that the tone is respectful and the volume understandable. Avoid speaking in monotone. Nothing conveys disinterest more quickly than monotonic presentations. Speech patterns should communicate the message—*I believe in this, my client's cause.*

Eye movements are also noticeable. Make good eye contact with the judge during the opening address or when answering questions. Do not roll your eyes at a judge's question or at a client's response.

Refrain from negative comments about doctors—they appear self-serving. Accept medical evidence for what it is—unless you have evidence to the contrary. Then argue the facts as they appear on paper. To criticize a consultative examiner without any extrinsic evidence to support the criticism leads the judge to ponder Shakespeare's admonition: *Thou dost protest too much!*

Do not show undue emotion on behalf of your client or others. Do not act defensively toward a judge or an expert witness. Always be courteous. Do not raise your voice or start an argument with an expert. Maintain decorum appropriate for a formal legal proceeding. Although these proceedings have been described as "informal," that appellation refers simply to the legal fact that the Federal Rules of Evidence and Federal Rules of Civil Procedure do not apply—not to the actual decorum expected of you or your client.

Dress the part. You only have one opportunity to make a first impression. Representatives in casual attire unconsciously communicate the same message—this is not a serious affair. Similarly, do not communicate to your client that he or she should dress as if afflicted. In most cases, the opposite reaction occurs. A judge may think, *Has the claimant not enough respect for the proceeding as not even to attempt to dress decently?* Why do claimants arrive in torn or tattered T-shirts? Certainly, for some that may be all they have, but consider the overall effect. How will your client's presence affect the judge? Should your client dress in a certain way? Or spend $10 or $20 to buy a new T-shirt? Only the representative can answer the question; but everything communicates in the hearing, whether it's speaking or not. Nonverbal communication can be as powerful as the spoken word.

Finally, act with confidence but not arrogance. Do not demand. Do not argue. Be sure to have a complete record; conduct yourself professionally and with attention to detail.

BACK TO CHRIS

Chris felt a renewed excitement. These were the visions of lawyering one only dreamed of, not having gone to law school. Amazing! *I can be a bona fide member of the firm, with my own clients and cases!*

Then a dark tendril of fear crept into view. *Murphy's law! Oh no!*

WHAT IF . . . ? SAMPLE PROBLEMS

WHAT IF . . .

What if Mr. Carson wants a "real" lawyer?

Discussion

Mr. Carson is, of course, entitled to select his own representative—a lawyer or a nonlawyer representative. However, the key issue in either instance, is whether the representative knows (is competent in) Social Security law and practice. This is a highly specialized field of practice and simply being a member of the bar does not automatically mean competency in this area of practice. Both lawyers and nonlawyer representatives are held to the same standards of conduct under the new Social Security regulation found at Title 20 C.F.R. § 404.1740. Indeed, in response to comments that the standards were superfluous in the face of state licensing and the Rules of Professional Responsibility, SSA responded

> **Bar rules differ in language and format among the fifty states . . . . As the administrator of a national program, however, SSA should not be expected or required to apply local rules, or local interpretations of the rules, to problems that require national uniformity. . . .**
>
> **Therefore, it is essential to provide rules that will govern the conduct of non-attorneys who practice before us. Moreover, it is only fair and equitable to hold all representatives who practice before us to the same standards.[39]**

Answer: ***Explaining to Mr. Carson that nonlawyers are regarded as equally capable under governing federal regulations may be sufficient to allay his concerns about nonlawyers.***

WHAT IF . . .

What if Mr. Carson decides at the last moment that he does not want a representative but a hearing is already scheduled? Is permission to withdraw from the case required as would be for a lawyer in federal court?

Discussion

The answer is straightforward. A claimant or a representative may withdraw at any time. SSA's response to comments to the new rule change are helpful:

> SSA's decisionmaking process is nonadversarial and informal and claimants do not require representation. The decision to have a representative is the claimant's and SSA neither encourages nor discourages representation. A claimant may revoke the appointment of a representative at any time. Likewise, a representative may withdraw from representing a claimant at any time....
>
> If a claimant still desires representation after his or her representative withdraws, we will allow the individual time to secure a new representative before we adjudicate the claim.

Answer: A representative or attorney may withdraw at any time without obtaining permission. A letter indicating such withdrawal, should, however, be made a part of the administrative record. Furthermore, even though a lawyer or representative withdraws, a claim may still be made for a pro rate fee.

---

[1]An immediate ethical issue is raised in the course of the dialogue. Rule 1.1 of the A.B.A.s *Model Rules of Professional Responsibility* requires that a lawyer not accept a case he or she is not competent to handle. No such affirmative duty applies to nonlawyers practicing before the Social Security Administration's Office of Hearings and Appeals. Instead, Title 20 C.F.R. § 404. 1740 (2000) requires all representatives to provide "competent assistance," an expression of the statutory mandate that a representative provide "good and valuable assistance" to the claimant. No affirmative duty is imposed *not* to take a case, otherwise. Indeed, as discussed more fully in Chapter 2, "competent representation" is defined as having "the knowledge, the skill, thoroughness and preparation reasonably necessary for the representation (Title 20 C.F.R. § 404.1740[b][3][i]). The scenario is not intended to suggest that these types of cases should be taken regardless of one's competency in the substantive and practice area but is merely intended to prepare for the "What do I do now?" questions the situation poses. As such, it is an interactive instructional device and not a suggested method of practice; although, it is, unfortunately, a scenario based on a real experience of which the authors are aware.

[2]Title 42 U.S.C. § 406(a)(1) limits "other persons, other than attorneys" to individuals "of good moral character and in good repute, possessed of the necessary qualifications to enable them to render such claimants valuable service, and otherwise competent to advise and assist such claimants in the presentation of their cases."

[3]Title 20 C.F.R. § 404.1705(a)(2) and § 404.1705(a)(3).

[4]Title 20 C.F.R. § 404.1707.

[5]Title 20 C.F.R. § 404.1710.

[6]Title 20 C.F.R. § 404.1715.

[7]Title 20 C.F.R. § 404.1710(b).

[8]See, for example, *Sperry v. State of Florida,* 373 U.S. 379 (1963), wherein the state of Florida sought to enjoin a nonattorney registered to practice before the U.S. Patent Office from preparing and prosecuting patent applications in Florida because he was not a member of the Florida bar. The Supreme Court held that the federal government has preemptive powers over states' legislative and judicial authorities when acting under federal regulation. These same principles apply to practice before the Social Security Administration.

[9]Until the adoption of these expanded regulations, only a single regulation addressed the conduct of lawyers before Social Security's Office of Hearings and Appeals. Title 20 C.F.R. § 404.1740 generally proscribed fraud, the collection of a fee "in excess of that allowed," or the "presentation of any false statement, representation or claim."

[10]62 *Federal Register* 352 (January 3, 1997).

[11]63 *Federal Register* 149 (August 4, 1998).

[12]Title 20 C.F.R. § 404.1740(a)(1999).

[13]See Title 20 C.F.R. § 404.1740(a).

[14]Ibid.

[15]62 *Federal Register* 353 (January 3, 1997).

[16]Ibid. Emphasis added.

[17]Title 20 C.F.R. § 404.1740(a)(1999).

[18]Title C.F.R. § 404.1740(b)(3)(i).

[19]Ibid.

[20]Administrative law judges have a continuing duty to ensure that the record before them is developed. Although this duty may diminish in the face of a claimant who is represented, it never fully disappears.

[21]Title 20 C.F.R. § 404.1740(a)(2) (1999).

[22]Title 20 C.F.R. § 404.1740(b)(1) (1999).

[23]Title 20 C.F.R. § 404.1740(b)(2) (1999).

[24]Title 20 C.F.R. § 404.1740(b)(3)(ii) (1999).

[25]Title 20 C.F.R. § 404.1740(b)(3)(i) (1999).

[26]Title 20 C.F.R. § 404.1740(b)(1).

[27]Title 20 C.F.R. § 404.1740(b)(2). Furthermore, Title 20 C.F.R. § 404.1740(c)(4) specifically describes as a "prohibited action" conduct by counsel, either "by his or her own actions or omissions [that] unreasonably delay or cause to be delayed without good cause . . . the processing of a claim. . . .

[28]Title 20 C.F.R. § 404.1740(b)(3)(ii) (1999).

[29]Title 20 C.F.R § 404.1740(c)(4).

[30]Ibid.

[31]For example, the judge's decision may ultimately turn on whether claimant's subjective pain is as great as he or she says it is when testifying. Medical records documenting on-going complaints of severe pain are more likely to corroborate such testimony, as opposed to records which merely describe pain as mild or intermittent.

[32]The administrative hearing is thus described as nonadversarial because of the lack of an opponent at the hearing itself. Some, however, have charged that the proceeding retains its adversarial flavor, because the judge must affirmatively develop the record, and evidence contrary to that produced by the claimant. See, for example, *Richardson v. Perales,* 402 U.S. 389, 91 S.Ct. 1420, 28 L.Ed.2d 842 (1971).

[33]See the following discussion for a more thorough discussion of the *Five Step Sequential Analysis* by which Social Security cases are decided. Briefly, Title 20 C.F.R. § 404.1520(a), which sets forth the five-step sequential evaluation process for disability determination, provides as follows.

Step 1 asks whether the claimant is engaging (or has engaged during the alleged period of disability) in "substantial gainful activity." If not, *step 2* asks whether the claimant suffers from a severe impairment. The term *severe* means a medically determinable (medically diagnosed and documented) condition that has lasted for twelve months or more (or is reasonably expected to last twelve months or more or a condition that will result in death) and that is reasonably likely to produce the disabling condition. *Step 3* of the evaluation asks whether the impairment meets or medically equals the requisites of a "listed impairment." Listed impairments are found in the fourteen categories of impairments cataloged in the federal regulations and include specific medical findings. If a claimant's impairment does not per se meet the requisites of a medical listing, the question then becomes whether the impairment is equivalent in severity to that listed. Prevailing regulations require the testimony of a medical expert to establish equivalence. If the impairment does not meet or equal a listed impairment, the next inquiry concerns an assessment of the claimant's limitations (i.e., what is the claimant able to do in spite of an impairment; and, conversely, what is he or she unable to do because of the impairment?). Once limitations are established (i.e., once the claimant's "residual functional capacity" or "RFC" has been formulated), the question becomes, can the claimant, in view of the limitations, return to past work (*step 4*)? If not, can he or she perform other work within the regional or national economy (*step 5*)? The vocational issues are addressed through the testimony of a "vocational expert" ("VE"), called on to attend the hearing by the administrative law judge, and paid an expert fee for his the appearance. If the claimant cannot return to past work and cannot perform other work, then, as a matter of law, he or she is "disabled."

[34]See Title 20 C.F.R. § 404.950(c), which provides that evidence may be received "even though the evidence would not be admissible in court under the rules of evidence."

[35]See Title 20 C.F.R. § 404.944, which provides, in part, "The administrative law judge may decide when the evidence will be presented and when the issues will be discussed."

[36]Even meeting with a client a week before a hearing is likely inadequate. At a minimum two, if not three, meetings should be scheduled with the client. The first introductory meeting may be required solely to outline the issues; the second meeting to verify necessary medical records; and the third, just before the hearing, to review the case before making the formal presentation to the administrative law judge.

[37]Title 20 C.F.R. § 404.1740(b)(3)(i).

[38]In some cases, however, the individual's coverage under the Social Security Act expires before the hearing; the question then becomes whether the individual can be found to be disabled on or before the last date of coverage by the Act, regardless of the date of the hearing or the date of the actual application.

[39]62 *Federal Register* 352 (January 3, 1997).

Chapter Three

Social Security Disability Programs—Eligibility Requirements for Title II Disability Insurance Benefits Claims

Highlights

- Ensured status
- Auxiliary benefits

Chris

While going through Mr. Carson's file, Chris noticed two application forms. One was for Title II disability Insurance benefits, but the other was for Title XVI Supplemental Security Income benefits.

My first research session indicated that the Social Security Administration manages four different programs, Chris recalled. *So, Mr. Carson is applying for two different benefits at the same time? Can he do that?*

What's the difference between the Title II and the Title XVI program benefits? Are we really prosecuting two separate cases for different benefits? Chris wondered, walking to the library.

Front of Your Mind Questions and Considerations, 3.1

Why are there two programs for disability benefits from the same government agency? Why not have only one program, with one set of rules and one application? The answer to these questions, as well as Chris's questions, lies in the historical progression of the Social Security Act. Recall, from Chapter 1, that the Act was originally envisioned as a retirement insurance program, in which employers and employees, or self-employed wage earners, would pay a percentage of the employee's earnings into a federally managed trust fund. At the designated retirement ages of sixty-two or sixty-five, the wage earner could elect to retire and receive a monthly stipend from the federally managed trust fund, based on the amount of earnings the wage earner and employers paid into the trust fund on behalf of the employee.

The "safety net" aspects of the Act are evident in the ensuing amendments to Title II. The Act was amended in 1954 to provide survivors' benefits to designated family members of a wage earner who died before reaching age sixty-two. In 1956, the Act was amended to permit a wage earner who suffered a medical disability that prevented gainful activity to "freeze" his earnings record, so he would not lose credits for earnings contributed to the trust fund during prior years of employment. In 1957, the Act was again amended to permit a disabled wage earner to draw on earnings "credits" and receive a monthly stipend during a period of medical disability, without jeopardizing retirement insurance benefits due at age sixty-two. The amendment also permitted the disabled wage earner's family members to receive auxiliary benefits as compensation for the income lost by the wage earner who cannot work.

In 1972, Title XVI was added to the Act to provide a new program for Supplemental Security Income (SSI) benefits. These benefits were added in the belief that every person in the United States was entitled to a basic minimum standard of living, regardless of past work record. Essentially, SSI is a welfare program, requiring no earnings record of contributions to the Title II trust fund, but requiring that the recipient of these benefits be over age sixty-five, blind or disabled, and have little or no income or financial resources to provide for basic needs. Because there is no requirement of an earnings record or payment into the trust fund, disabled children can receive SSI benefits, as long as their parents meet the limited income and resources requirements.

Although the requirements for DIB and SSI are different, the definition of *disability* and the means for proving a disability exists are the same for both programs. A disabled wage earner who qualifies for Title II DIB benefits can apply for SSI benefits on the same disability alleged in the Title II DIB application. Two separate applications, one under each program, must be filed with the Social Security Administration. The two applications may be filed at the same time, and in Social Security's terms are considered *concurrent* applications. When the two applications are received, the local Field Office sets up two separate file folders, one for each program's application and jurisdictional documents. The two files are physically kept together as the wage earner's disability claims go through the adjudicative process.

In this chapter, we examine the basic requirements for a wage earner's entitlement to Title II disability insurance benefits and auxiliary benefits the wage earner's family members may be entitled to, based on the wage earner's earnings record. In Chapter 4, we address the requirements for SSI benefits, and contrast those requirements with those for DIB.

Back to Chris

OK, thought Chris, Mr. Carson can file two applications at the same time. But does he meet the requirements to receive disability insurance benefits? Does he have enough of these "credits?" How will I know if he's paid enough into the trust fund?

A Trip to the Hard Drive, 3.1

Take *A Trip to the Hard Drive* to discover the requirements for coverage under Title II of the Social Security Act.

Introduction to Disability Insurance Benefits

The Disability Insurance Benefits (DIB) program in Title II has two features. DIB actually refers to the monthly cash benefits paid to the disabled wage earner and the auxiliary benefits paid to the wage earner's family members. The wage earner may also establish a period of disability (POD), which includes the disability "freeze" concept of Title II. The freeze preserves the amount of disability or retirement insurance benefits and survivors' benefits accrued on the wage earner's earnings record. It does so by excluding the time the wage earner is disabled from the determination of insurance credits or the amount of benefits. The POD is automatically considered part of the DIB application, and the adjudication of the DIB application determines entitlement to both DIB cash benefits and a POD.

The safety net offered by Title II programs for retired and disabled wage earners, their spouses and children, as well as the survivors of deceased wage earners, is extensive, judging by the numbers of lives affected by these programs. In December 1998, forty-four million persons were receiving some type of Title II benefits, with the majority of benefits being paid to retired workers, as illustrated in Figure 3-1.

In 1998, 1.6 million new awards of Title II benefits were made to retired wage earners, and 0.6 million awards were made to disabled wage earners. Figure 3-2 shows the percentage of Title II benefits made to the three categories of benefit recipients in 1998.

As these figures illustrate, retirement insurance benefits (RIB) make up the majority of the Title II benefits awarded. However, because of the fairly straightforward requirements for RIB, representatives typically

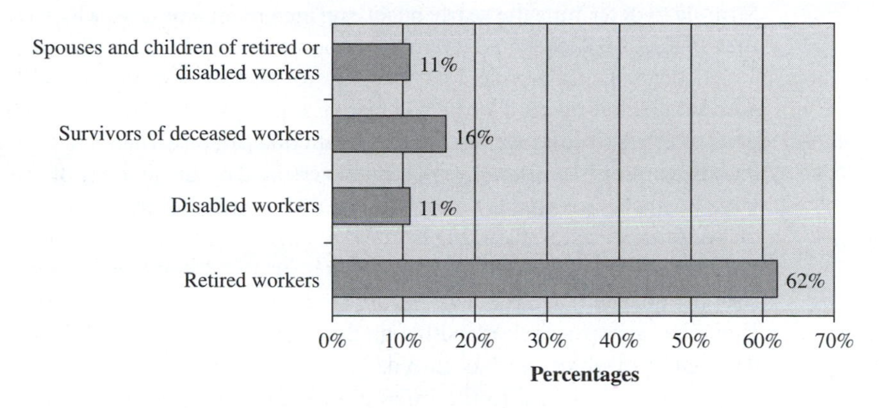

Figure 3–1 **Types of Beneficiaries Receiving Title II Benefits, December 1998**
Source: Social Security Administration

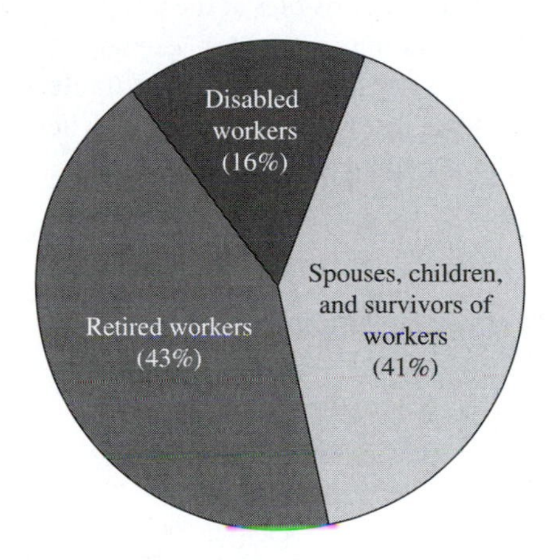

Figure 3–2 **Title II Benefit Awards, 1998**
Source: Social Security Administration

handle few cases involving RIB entitlement issues. Of such cases, most involve issues about whether the wage earner had sufficient credits, or payments, into the trust fund. DIB claims also involve consideration of whether the claimant paid into the trust fund sufficiently to have enough credits for such benefits. The number of credits is what gives the wage earner insured status to qualify for Title II benefits.

The Need for "Insured" Status

The premise underlying Title II RIB and DIB programs is truly that of insurance: think of an individual's years of paying into the trust fund from payroll deductions in the form of Federal Insurance Contributions Act (FICA) taxes as a sort of premium paid to maintain the insurance. To be entitled to RIB or DIB benefits, the wage earner must be "insured." "Insured status" depends on the quarters of coverage that have been acquired as a result of gainful, "covered" employment. "Covered" employment is employment for which FICA taxes have been paid, either by the employer or by the wage earner, if self-employed.

A "quarter of coverage" is based on one of four calendar year quarters (i.e., the three-month time periods that end on March 31, June 30, September 30, or December 31). A wage earner is credited with a quarter of coverage for each calendar quarter employed and earning above a specified amount. If a wage earner is employed for a full calendar year, four quarters of coverage are credited. Before 1978, a wage earner had to earn at least $50 in wages or be credited with at least $100 in self-employment income each calendar quarter to earn a quarter of coverage. Since 1978, quarters of coverage are credited based on specified yearly increments of covered earnings credited to the calendar year. In 1978, for example, the increment amount was set at $250. A wage earner had to earn four times that increment ($250.00, or at least $1000 in covered employment) in order to acquire four quarters of coverage for calendar year 1978. The Social Security Administration uses a formula to determine the yearly qualifying increment amounts, which are then published in the *Federal Register.* Figure 3-3 shows the increment amounts needed for each year since 1978.

If the wage earner has total earnings for the calendar year equal to at least four times the increment amount for that year, she or he will receive a quarter of coverage for each of the four calendar year quarters. Four quarters of coverage are the maximum that can be earned in a year, even if an individual's earnings exceed this amount. A quarter of coverage is credited on the first day of the quarter in which it is assigned. The wage earner is thus credited with a full quarter of coverage from the first day of the quarter, even if he or she dies or otherwise stops working before the calendar quarter actually ends. Quarters of coverage are somewhat flexible in their assignment to the calendar quarters. However, a quarter of coverage may not be credited for a calendar quarter that has not yet begun. A quarter of coverage may not be credited for the calendar quarter *following* a wage earner's death, although the deceased will receive a full quarter of coverage credit for the calendar quarter in which death occurred.

Earnings reported to the Internal Revenue Service with payment of FICA taxes are recorded in the SSA's computer system. The SSA keeps track of every wage earner's covered earnings and compiles a report to denote the calendar quarter for which each wage earner has earned coverage. These reports are frequently in a client's claims files at the Office of Hearings and Appeals, or a client can request the local field office to run a computer-generated "earnings query" for quarters of coverage. The quarters of coverage report generated by the Social Security computers looks similar to that shown in Figure 3–4. The ability to read these reports helps you to determine whether the client has the requisite types and amounts of coverage for Title II benefits.

Year	Amount Needed	Year	Amount Needed
1978	$250	1990	$540
1979	$260	1991	$570
1980	$290	1992	$590
1981	$310	1993	$590
1982	$340	1994	$620
1983	$370	1995	$630
1984	$390	1996	$640
1985	$410	1997	$670
1986	$440	1998	$700
1987	$470	1999	$740
1988	$500	2000	$780
1989	$520		

Figure 3–3 **Yearly Required Earnings Increments for Quarters of Coverage**

SSN: __________ **Unit:** ______ **Requestor:** ______________

Pre 1951 Earnings: 0.00 Total Earn:

Yr	Earnings	QC	Yr	Earnings	QC	Yr	Earnings	QC
77	0.00	NNNN	84	5200.62	CCCC	91	15437.98	CCCC
78	263.09	NNNC	85	7289.02	CCCC	92	20745.08	CCCC
79	1511.70	CCCC	86	9344.51	CCCC	93	28501.30	CCCC
80	1754.36	CCCC	87	10416.77	CCCC	94	30023.45	CCCC
81	2322.80	CCCC	88	12937.82	CCCC	95	1709.00	CCNN
82	2555.12	CCCC	89	1751.66	CCCN	96	0.00	NNNN
83	2963.75	CCCC	90	1954.11	NNCC			

Figure 3–4 **Sample SSA Earnings Record Query Showing Quarters of Coverage**

"FULLY" INSURED STATUS

A wage earner must have sufficient quarters of coverage to be "fully insured," and, therefore, entitled to disability insurance benefits. The maximum quarters of coverage needed is forty, but six quarters of coverage are required at a minimum. For the wage earner with less than the maximum number of quarters of coverage, to be considered fully insured, the wage earner must have one quarter of coverage for each calendar year after 1950, or for each year after the year in which the wage earner became twenty-one years of age. That year is then subtracted from the year that the wage earner either attains retirement age (sixty-two or older), dies, or becomes disabled. The following examples illustrate how fully insured status is calculated:

Example 1:

From year age 62 is attained	2000
<subtract>	(−)
year after 21st birthday (born in 1938)	1961
<equals>	39 quarters of coverage needed

Example 2:

From year of death	1998
<subtract>	(−)
year after 21st birthday (born in 1944)	1966
<equals>	32 quarters of coverage needed

Example 3:

From year disability began	1999
<subtract>	(−)
year after 21st birthday (born in 1963)	1985
<equals>	14 quarters of coverage needed

BACK TO CHRIS

"There's more, isn't there?" Chris asked resignedly. This kind of detail was daunting, but it had to be learned.

Steve smiled as he walked by. "Talking to yourself Chris?"

Chris grinned, "Just a little. Don't mind me! I can do this!"

A TRIP TO THE HARD DRIVE, 3.2

Learn more about insured status under Title II—take *A Trip to the Hard Drive.*

"CURRENTLY" INSURED

In addition to being fully insured, the wage earner must also be "currently insured" for DIB. For the period of forty quarters immediately preceding retirement, death, or disability, the wage earner must have at least twenty quarters of coverage in that forty-quarter period. This is the "20/40 rule." In other words, the wage earner must have worked steadily and fairly recently until death, disability, or ceasing to work. A wage earner's insured status will lapse if she or he stops working, dies or becomes disabled, and fails to earn quarters of coverage for twenty quarters (about five years). If the wage earner did not work steadily during the forty-quarter periods, the insured status lapse sooner than five years. The wage earner must be fully insured at the time of becoming eligible for retirement benefits or in the first full month of becoming disabled. Lapse in insured status means that the wage earner is not eligible for retirement benefits or disability insurance benefits.

For wage earners applying for disability insurance benefits, the date that the insured status lapsed becomes critical for establishing that disability began before that lapse date in order to be eligible for DIB. The field office can compute the wage earner's date last insured (DLI) as March 31, June 30, September 30, or December 31 of a particular year, based on a computation of the quarters of coverage and application of the 20/40 rule.

For a young wage earner who becomes disabled before the age of thirty-one, the 20/40 rule changes. The wage earner must then have quarters of coverage in at least half of the quarters since the quarter *after* the quarter in which the wage earner turned twenty-one years of age, and ending with the quarter of disability onset or death. If the number of quarters since age twenty-one is odd, the number of quarters is reduced by one. If the number of elapsed quarters is less than twelve, the young wage earner must have at least six quarters of coverage in the most recent twelve quarters of coverage. If the young wage earner has a previous period of disability, those quarters will not be counted unless the quarter is the first or last quarter of the period of disability and that quarter is a quarter of coverage. However, if it is to the individual's advantage, all quarters in the previous period of disability may be counted.[1]

If the young wage earner had a previous period of disability before turning thirty-one, and does not meet the 20/40 rule, he or she may still be insured for DIB in a subsequent quarter on becoming disabled again at or after age thirty-one, but the young wage earner must have been fully insured for the previous period of disability under the special age thirty-one rule. The young wage earner must also be fully insured, and have quarters of coverage in at least half of the calendar quarters in the period beginning with the quarter after the quarter she or he turns twenty-one.

Age Limits and Application

In addition to being fully and currently insured, the wage earner must meet other DIB entitlement requirements. The wage earner must be under age sixty-five, although this is not so much a requirement as common sense. At age sixty-five, the wage earner may receive full retirement benefits, so there is no advantage in claiming disability benefits after this age. A wage earner, however, can file an application for DIB after turning 65, if it can be shown that DIB would be entitled for the months before age sixty-five. The wage earner would then receive a retroactive payment of DIB for the period of disability established before the wage earner turned sixty-five.

The wage earner also must file an application for DIB benefits with the Social Security Administration. The application must be filed no later than twelve months after the month in which the disability ended. If the wage earner was prevented from filing the DIB application within that twelve-month period because of a physical or mental impairment, a period of no more than thirty-six months after the month in which his disability ended will be allowed to file the DIB application.[2]

The application date is critical, because DIB benefits are retroactive only for up to twelve months before the date of filing. In other words, the wage earner will receive retroactive DIB for no more than the twelve months prior to the date of filing the DIB application. This twelve-month limit on payment of retroactive benefits applies even though the wage earner has alleged that the disability began two to three years prior to the date of the DIB application. This retroactivity provision means that clients should not delay filing DIB applications and possibly losing retroactive benefits to which they would otherwise be entitled.

Waiting Period to Receive Benefits

A wage earner seeking DIB must meet a five-month waiting period requirement before receiving the cash benefits. The five-month waiting period is intended to provide time for most temporary disabilities to improve, to be corrected, or for definite signs of recovery to be manifested.

The waiting period must last five full, consecutive calendar months. If a disability is alleged to have begun in the middle of a month, the five-month waiting period will start the next full calendar month. The full calendar month requirement is enforced rigidly. For example, if a disabling injury caused the wage earner to stop working on January 15, the five-month waiting period begins on February 1 and lasts until June 30. If the disabling injury occurred on January 1, however, the five-month period would start on January 1 and last until May 30. If the disabling injury occurred on January 2, the five-month period starts on February 1 and lasts until June 30.

The five-month waiting period must begin with a month in which the wage earner was determined to be disabled *and* was insured for DIB. The Act and the regulations require that the five-month waiting period not begin earlier than the seventeenth month before the month in which the wage earner files the DIB application.[3] The seventeen-month limit links the five-month waiting period with the twelve-month retroactivity on payment of benefits. This calculation is illustrated in the following example:

A wage earner files for DIB in January 1999. She is found disabled beginning in June 1996. When does the waiting period start and what is the wage earner's first month of entitlement for DIB?

ANSWER:

The waiting period starts on August 1, 1997. Her first month of entitlement to DIB is January 1998 (twelve months of retroactivity). The five-month period is placed ahead of the twelve-month retroactivity requirement, making it August 1997. Because the wage earner established disability in June 1996, she had ample time for the operation of the five-month waiting period and twelve-month retroactivity limit.

In contrast, consider this second example of the operation of the seventeen-month requirement:

A wage earner files for DIB in January 1998. She alleges she became disabled beginning in January 1997, but is finally determined, based on the medical evidence, to have become disabled in July 1997. When does the waiting period start and what is the wage earner's first month of entitlement for DIB benefits?

ANSWER:

The waiting period starts in July 1997 as the first month she is found disabled. Her first month of entitlement to DIB would be December 1997.

PRESENCE OF OTHER INCOME AND RESOURCES AVAILABLE TO THE WAGE EARNER

Unlike Title XVI's SSI program, in order to receive DIB, the disabled wage earner is not obligated to disclose other sources of income or financial resources that are available. There are no limits to the amount of income or financial resources the wage earner claiming DIB can have available. However, if the wage earner files a concurrent application for SSI with a DIB application, the claimant's means of support will become a factor for consideration in the SSI application.

Additionally, workers' compensation benefits may offset DIB benefits paid. Many private, long-term disability insurers and other government disability programs, such as the Department of Veterans' Affairs disability payments, may reduce their benefits paid to a wage earner when DIB benefits from Social Security begin.

BACK TO CHRIS

"How are you coming with Mr. Carson's Social Security claim?" Steve asked, pausing at the door of Chris's office.

"Actually two claims," Chris said and looked up from the notes and interview questions outlined on the legal pad next to Mr. Carson's case file. "When Mr. Carson comes in next week, I'll go over his work record with him. After he signs the 1696 form, I can go to the Social Security Field Office and ask them to run an earnings query for him. I noticed Mr. Carson's wife's name was listed on his DIB application, so we'll discuss if his wife qualifies for auxiliary benefits on his earnings record. I guess his children are grown and wouldn't qualify for auxiliary benefits."

Steve frowned and looked at the DIB application. "I remember at one time Mr. Carson and his wife were guardians for one of their grandchildren. I don't know if that grandchild still lives with them. That's another question to ask Mr. Carson."

As Steve walked away, Chris jotted *"grandchild—?"* on the list of interview questions. *Maybe a grandchild is not eligible to receive auxiliary benefits,* thought Chris, even though the grandchild may still live with Mr. Carson. *Guess I'd better confirm that before Mr. Carson's appointment.*

Front of Your Mind Questions and Considerations, 3.2

Chris's research thus far indicates that the history of Title II amendments provided family members of a disabled wage earner with auxiliary benefits, which is intended to replace some of the income lost to the family when the wage earner is unable to work. The question then becomes, How extensive is the safety net provided by DIB to a wage earner's family? Chris is generally correct in assuming that adult, emancipated children of the wage earner are not eligible for auxiliary benefits. However, because the traditional concept of a nuclear family has broadened in the past decade to include blended and nontraditional families, who is now a "family" member eligible for auxiliary benefits?

A Trip to the Hard Drive, 3.3

Take *A Trip to the Hard Drive* to find out more about auxiliary benefits.

Auxiliary Benefits

The wage earner's earning record is not only crucial to establishing the wage earner's qualification for DIB benefits but also for providing a basis for additional benefit payments to family members. Eligibility for auxiliary benefits focuses on the relationship between the disabled wage earner and the particular family member. For a relationship defined by legal parameters, such as a legally valid marriage or adoption, the Social Security Administration will look to the state law in which the wage earner was domiciled, at the time of the application, for the criteria to determine the validity of the marriage or adoption.

In this section, we review the most common requirements for each family member who may be eligible for auxiliary benefits. However, in determining family relationships SSA has a number of exceptions and special case considerations that may apply to a nontraditional family member. Bear in mind, then, when considering auxiliary benefits to family members, the statutory requirements in Title 42 of the U.S. Code, as they pertain to the particular family member seeking auxiliary benefits, need to be reviewed.

Remember also that, in addition to meeting the criteria for eligibility to auxiliary benefits, each eligible family member must make a separate, written application to SSA to receive that particular auxiliary benefit. For example, in a disabled wage earner's family with three minor children (all under the age of eighteen), each minor child must make a separate application for child insurance benefits.

The wage earner's monthly DIB or RIB payment is the basis from which the amount of auxiliary benefits paid to family members is computed. The amount of the wage earner's monthly DIB or RIB payment is derived from a computation called the primary insurance amount, or PIA. The PIA is based on the wage earner's taxable earnings averaged over the wage earner's working lifetime. As an indicator of the monthly benefit the wage earner will receive, the wage earner's PIA can be calculated at the SSA Field Office when the DIB or RIB application is filed. In recent years, SSA has been providing every wage earner paying into the trust fund an estimate of the wage earner's PIA projected for the time of retirement, assuming that the wage earner will continue to earn approximately the same amount of taxable income until retirement.

Although DIB is intended to provide a safety net for the family members of a disabled or deceased wage earner, concern for the financial well-being of the trust fund causes some limitations on the amount of auxiliary benefit payments that beneficiaries may receive. For example, SSA does not allow "double-dipping" of benefits; a wage earner receiving DIB or RIB on his or her own earning record may not also receive spouse benefits when the wage earner's spouse is entitled to receive DIB or RIB benefits on the spouse's earnings record. SSA permits the wage earner and spouse to elect to receive benefits on one of the two earnings records, which provides the largest amount of benefit payment to both the wage earner and the spouse. In the discussion of auxiliary and survivor benefits that follows, a frequent requirement is that the spouse or widow cannot be entitled to a higher benefit payment on personal earnings records and still claim on the wage earner's earning record.

SSA also restricts the total amounts of benefits paid to a disabled wage earner and eligible family members on the wage earner's record under the "Family Maximum Rule." The wage earner's DIB or RIB benefits are not reduced, but auxiliary benefits to entitled family members are proportionately reduced, so that the total amounts of benefits paid to the wage earner and family members does not exceed a limit set by SSA.

In the following sections we consider eligibility requirements for auxiliary benefits for certain family relationships. We first examine auxiliary benefits for family members of a disabled wage earner, then auxiliary benefits for surviving family members of a deceased wage earner.

SPOUSE BENEFITS

For a spouse to receive auxiliary benefits, the spouse must be currently married to the disabled wage earner. The spouse must be age sixty-two or older, or caring for a minor child entitled to benefits on the wage earner's earnings record. If age sixty-two or older, the spouse also cannot be entitled to either disability or retirement benefits in an amount equal to or greater than one-half of the wage earners monthly disability payment on the spouse's own earnings record.[4]

State laws vary in their requirements for establishing a common-law marriage. If a marital relationship with a wage earner cannot be established under the pertinent state law, SSA recognizes that a spouse can establish the relationship requirement with the wage earner, if, under that state's law, the spouse would inherit a spouse's share of the wage earner's personal property if the wage earner were to die intestate. SSA also permits the claiming spouse to demonstrate what is called a "deemed" valid marriage. Under this concept, the claimant is deemed to be the spouse of the wage earner if he or she went through a marriage ceremony in good faith with the wage earner and if that would have resulted in a valid marriage except for some legal impediment. The spouse "deemed" to be so married must have been living in the same household with the wage earner at the time the spouse applied for auxiliary spouse benefits.[5]

A claimant spouse under age sixty-two must demonstrate that he or she is caring for the wage earner's minor or disabled adult child. Generally, the child "in care" must be living with the claimant spouse for at least six months prior to the benefits application, although there are exceptions to this rule for children who are mentally disabled and sixteen years of age or older. If the child in care becomes age sixteen, or is no longer entitled to child's benefits, a claimant spouse under age sixty-two is no longer entitled to spouse benefits.[6]

CHILD BENEFITS

Auxiliary benefits may be paid to a child of a disabled or retired wage earner if several requirements are met.[7] In addition to filing an application claiming entitlement to child benefits, the child must establish a relationship to the wage earner. Relationship encompasses not only natural children, but stepchildren, legally or equitably adopted children, grandchildren, and stepgrandchildren.[8] The relationship between the claimant child and the wage earner is determined by the laws of the state where the wage earner was domiciled when the child's application for benefits was filed, and generally uses the state's laws to determine whether the claimant could inherit a child's share of the wage earner's personal property if the wage earner were to die intestate. Even if the pertinent state law does not qualify the child, SSA has several tests that permit the claimant to qualify as the child of the wage earner entitled to benefits.

Thus, if the wage earner acknowledges in writing that the claimant is a son or daughter, or if a court decrees the wage earner to be the claimant's parent, or if a court orders the wage earner to contribute to the support of the claimant as the wage earner's child, SSA will recognize the claimant as the child of the wage earner. However, the written acknowledgment, court decree, or order must have been made prior to the wage earner's most recent period of disability or at least one year prior to the wage earner's entitlement to RIB. SSA will also accept any other evidence "satisfactory to the Commissioner" that the wage earner is the parent of the claimant child, and that the wage earner was living with or contributing to the claimant child's support at the time the application for child's benefits was filed.

In addition to establishing a relationship to the wage earner, the claimant child must also establish dependence on the wage earner. Proving dependency is governed, to some extent, by the child's relationship to the insured. The claimant child must provide evidence of living with the wage earner, receiving contributions from the wage earner, or receiving from the wage earner at least one-half of the claimant child's support.[9]

The claimant child is considered to be living with the wage earner if the child ordinarily lives in the same house with the wage earner and if the wage earner exercises, or has the right to exercise, parental control and authority over the child's activities. The wage earner is deemed to have "contributed to the support" of the claimant child if the wage earner provides personal goods or cash to provide shelter, food, routine medical care, and other ordinary or customary items needed for the child's maintenance, or if the wage earner provides services to the child that otherwise would have to be paid to another. The contributions must be made regularly and in a large enough amount to meet a significant part of the child's living costs. Thus, infrequent gifts or donations for a special purpose do not qualify as contributions for support.[10] If the wage earner contributes cash, goods, or services equaling or exceeding one-half of the child's ordinary living costs, with one-half or less of those costs provided by another, the claimant child is deemed to be dependent on the wage earner.

Grandchildren or stepgrandchildren of the wage earner may qualify for child's insurance benefits if the grandchild's natural or adoptive parents are deceased or disabled at the time the wage earner became entitled to DIB or RIB. The grandchild must be dependent on the wage earner for support, showing either that the wage earner lived with the grandchild before the grandchild turned eighteen years of age, or that the wage earner contributed at least one-half of the support for the grandchild.

The claimant child must be under the age of eighteen, or over eighteen and a full-time elementary or secondary school student. When the child turns eighteen, or stops full-time attendance at an elementary or secondary school, the child's benefits will cease. Child benefits are not paid to college students over eighteen.

If the claimant child is over eighteen, child's benefits as a disabled adult child (DAC) may be applied (or reapplied) for on the wage earner's earnings record. In addition to showing relationship to, and dependency on, the wage earner, the claimant child must also show that the disability occurred before age twenty-two, and that the claimant child is unmarried. If the claimant child marries anyone other than another DAC benefits recipient, DAC benefits will be lost.

BACK TO CHRIS

"What about former spouses?" Chris asked.

"Good question. Let's see," replied Steve.

A TRIP TO THE HARD DRIVE, 3.4

Auxiliary benefits apply to a variety of persons. Take *A Trip to the Hard Drive* to discover more.

EX-SPOUSES

Contrary to society's expectation that divorce severs all ties between the divorcing spouses, SSA permits an ex-spouse to claim auxiliary benefits under the earnings record of the formerly married wage earner. The ex-spouse must file an application for divorced spouse benefits and establish that he or she is not entitled to either RIB or DIB which equal or exceed one-half of the wage earner's monthly payment. In other words, the ex-spouse cannot be entitled to more monthly benefits on the ex-spouse's own earnings record than would be received based on the wage earner's earnings record.

Additionally, the ex-spouse must be sixty-two or older, even if the ex-spouse has a child in care who is eligible to receive child's benefits on the wage earner's records. The ex-spouse cannot be married at the time of the application. The ex-spouse must have been married to the wage earner for at least ten years before the date their divorce became final.

Auxiliary benefits paid to the ex-spouse are not counted in, and do not affect, the computations of the family maximum rule for the wage earner's current spouse and children.

WIDOW(ER)'S BENEFITS

If the wage earner was fully insured at the time of his or her death, the surviving spouse may file an application for benefits based on evidence that he or she is the widow or widower of the deceased wage earner. The claimant spouse must be able to show a relationship with the deceased that lasted at least nine months prior to the wage earner's death. The relationship with the wage earner is determined according to the laws of the state in which the wage earner was domiciled at the time of death. Other requirements include the following:

- The widow(er) must also be at least sixty years of age.
  - Alternatively, a widow(er) must be at least fifty years old, and under a disability that began not later than the earlier of the last day of the month before the attainment of age sixty, or seven years after the wage earner died, or seven years after the surviving spouse was last entitled to mother's, father's, or widow(er)'s benefits based on a disability (whichever comes later).
  - The disability must have continued during the full consecutive five-month waiting period.
  - The widow(er) must remain unmarried, unless the new marriage took place after the widow(er) became sixty years old, or the widow(er) is between the ages of fifty and sixty, and was under a disability at the time of the new marriage.

Surviving Child Benefits

Basically, the same criteria required for payment of child's benefits to the child of a disabled wage earner applies to a child of a deceased wage earner. The wage earner's acknowledgment of the child as the wage earner's under decree, or the court order requiring payment of child support must have been entered before the wage earner's death. SSA also requires evidence that the wage earner was either living with the child or contributing to the child's support when the wage earner died.

Back to Chris

"There's more?" asked Chris incredulously.

"There's more," nodded Steve.

"Ooh, boy."

"You said it Chris. Let's keep after it!"

A Trip to the Hard Drive, 3.5

Benefits extend to a variety of other persons, as well. Take *A Trip to the Hard Drive* to learn more.

Surviving Divorced Spouse Benefits

The same requirements of a valid marriage to the wage earner which lasted at least ten years before the date the divorce became final are applicable for surviving divorced spouses.[11]

Mother's and Father's Benefits

If, for some reason, the surviving spouse or ex-spouse of the deceased wage earner is not entitled to widow(er)'s or surviving divorced spouse benefits, an application may be filed for survivor's benefits based on the wage earner's earning records if the applicant can show that the wage earner's minor or disabled child is in her or his care, and that the child is entitled to child's benefits. The applicant must establish that a valid marriage to the wage earner existed under the state laws in which the deceased was domiciled at the time of death, and show that he or she is the mother or father of the child in care. Additionally, the applicant must be the widow(er) of the deceased wage earner and meet the nine-month duration of marriage requirement. The applicant cannot be entitled to widow(er) benefits or to RIB benefits on his or her own earnings record in an amount that is equal to or exceeds the full mother's or father's benefit amount. The applicant's mother's or father's benefits will terminate if the applicant remarries, unless the applicant marries another recipient of RIB, DIB, auxiliary benefits, or survivor's benefits.[12]

PARENT'S BENEFITS

The parents of a deceased wage earner may claim survivor benefits if they are age sixty-two or older and have not married since the death of the wage earner. The parent must prove a relationship to the wage earner as the natural or adopted parent, or as a stepparent who married the wage earner's natural or adoptive parent before the wage earner became sixteen years of age. The wage earner must have been contributing at least one-half of the parent's support at the time of the wage earner's death, or at the beginning of a period of disability that continued until the wage earner's death. The parent cannot be entitled to a monthly RIB payment that is larger than the amount received as a parent's benefit.[13]

LUMP SUM DEATH PAYMENT

A widow(er) of a wage earner who dies currently or fully insured may be entitled to a lump sum death payment (LSDP) of $255. The widow(er) must present evidence of a valid marriage under state law or a "deemed" valid marriage as discussed previously. The widow(er) must also show that he or she was living in the same household with the wage earner at the time of the wage earner's death. A temporary absence from the household for either the wage earner or the widow(er) will not defeat the "living in the same household" requirement, but the widow(er) must show that they customarily lived together as husband and wife in the same residence. The widow(er) must file for the LSDP benefit within two years of the wage earner's death.

If no widow(er) was living in the same household with the deceased wage earner, the LSDP may be paid to a claimant who is entitled to widow(er)'s benefits, mother's or father's benefits, or child's benefits. Again, the application for LSDP benefits must be filed within two years of death.[14]

A FINAL NOTE ABOUT AUXILIARY AND SURVIVOR'S BENEFITS

In the past fifty years, our society's traditional ideas of marriage and family have greatly changed. Our discussion of the requirements for auxiliary and survivor benefits primarily focused on the most common requirements for eligibility by SSA and any notable exceptions to those requirements that SSA recognizes. If a client's disability claim involves potential auxiliary benefit claimants among the client's family members, review the statutory requirements and regulatory requirements to ensure that all relationship, time frame, and support issues are resolved with the help of the client and provide appropriate documentation.

WHAT IF . . . ? SAMPLE PROBLEMS

WHAT IF . . .

Title 42 U.S.C. § 416(h) provides the dependency requirements for grandchildren to qualify for child's insurance benefits on the wage earner's record. What questions should Chris prepare for the interview with Mr. Carson concerning Mr. Carson's grandchild? What documents might be required for Mr. Carson to submit to SSA regarding his grandchild?

Answers: *Chris may begin by asking Mr. Carson who lives in the same household with him to establish whether the grandchild is still living with Mr. Carson. If Chris learns the grandchild is still living with Mr. Carson and his wife, he should then question Mr. Carson about the grandchild's age, how long the grandchild has lived with Mr. Carson, the circumstances and any legal consequences leading to that living arrangement, and who provides the majority of the grandchild's life necessities or covers such expenses.*

Necessary documentation that Mr. Carson may need to submit to SSA if he wishes to claim auxiliary benefits for his grandchild may include guardianship court orders, related custody decrees entered in the grandchild's parents' divorce action, and federal and state tax returns showing Mr. Carson's claim of the grandchild as a dependent.

WHAT IF . . .

What questions will Chris want to discuss with Mr. Carson regarding his wife and any auxiliary benefits to which Mrs. Carson might be entitled? What documents will Chris want Mr. Carson to begin assembling to submit to SSA regarding his wife?

Answer: With regard to Mr. Carson's wife, Chris will want to learn Mrs. Carson's age to determine if she meets the age 62 requirement. Chris will also want to generally learn Mrs. Carson's work history to determine if she may be entitled to benefits on her own earnings record, rather than spouse benefits on Mr. Carson's earnings record. Chris may also ask general questions about the Carson's date of marriage and performance of the marriage ceremony, only to ensure that there is no need to establish a common-law or "deemed" marriage situation for the Carsons.

Chris may advise Mr. Carson to find or obtain a copy of the marriage license to provide SSA. If the Carsons need to establish that a common-law marriage exists between them, Chris will need to research the pertinent law for the state in which the Carsons are domiciled and advise Mr. Carson of the necessary documents to establish such a marriage. For the Carsons to establish a "deemed" valid marriage recognized by SSA, Mr. Carson will need to provide a marriage license and documents establishing the "legal impediment" which prevented his marriage to Mrs. Carson from being legally valid. Mr. Carson will also need to demonstrate that Mrs. Carson is living in the same household with him at the time she applies for spouse benefits, if he is relying on a "deemed" marriage situation.

---

[1]See Title 20 C.F.R. § 404.130(f).

[2]See Title 20 C.F.R. §§ 404.320(b)(3), 404.322, and 404.621(d).

[3]See Title 42 U.S.C. § 423(c)(2) and Title 20 C.F.R. § 404.315(d).

[4]See generally, 20 C.F.R. §§ 404.330—404.333.

[5]See generally, 20 C.F.R. § 404.335.

[6]See generally, 20 C.F.R. §§ 404.348—404.349.

[7]See generally, 20 C.F.R. § 404.350.

[8]See generally, 20 C.F.R. §§ 404.354—404.359.

[9]See Title 20 C.F.R. §§ 404.361—404.365.

[10]See Title 20 C.F.R. § 404.366.

[11]C.F.R. § 404.336.

[12]See generally, 20 C.F.R. §§ 404.341—404.342.

[13]See generally, 20 C.F.R. §§ 404.370—404.374.

[14]See generally, 20 C.F.R. §§ 404.390—404.392.

4

Chapter Four

Social Security Disability Programs—Eligibility Requirements for Title XVI Supplemental Security Income Benefits Claims

Highlights

- ❑ SSI defined
- ❑ Income and resource requirements

Chris

Hitting the Save button, Chris prepared to print the short progress memo to Steve about Mr. Carson's Social Security disability claim. In clipping together the interview questions for Mr. Carson, however, Chris remembered that Mr. Carson had also filed an application for SSI benefits on the same day he filed for DIB under Title II.

I know a little about Title XVI from my research on DIB, thought Chris. *There's no need for the "insured status" with Title XVI, but I remember that there is some kind of limitation on what Mr. Carson can have as far as income and savings. I'd better look into what Mr. Carson will need to qualify for SSI, in case Steve has any questions about it.*

Front of Your Mind Questions and Considerations, 4.1

From the discussion of DIB benefits in Chapter 3, we learned that SSI benefits differ from DIB in several significant ways. First, SSI is a needs-based program, designed to assure a minimum level of income to aged, disabled, or blind individuals who have limited income and resources. Unlike DIB, entitlement to SSI is not based on a past history of employment, from which payment into a trust fund creates an "insured status." SSI benefits may be paid to eligible individuals, regardless of whether they have ever worked at all. Thus, even minor children, who meet the criteria for disability and limited income and resources, may receive SSI benefits in their own name, without relationship to a wage earner's earnings record.

SSI benefits are paid out of general revenue funds of the U.S. Treasury, rather than a trust fund. Essentially, SSI is a type of welfare program. However, neither SSA nor any other part of the federal government places any restrictions on SSI beneficiaries on their use of these benefits. Figure 4–1 shows the percentage by program of Social Security benefits recipients.

Unlike DIB, SSI is paid only to the individual applying for these benefits. Family members of the SSI beneficiary cannot receive auxiliary benefits. Similarly, when the SSI beneficiary dies, surviving family members do not receive survivor's benefits, as they would under Title II.

There is no five-month waiting period for SSI benefits, as for DIB benefits. SSI benefits are paid from the date of the claimant's application; however, there is no retroactivity for twelve-months as there is for DIB. Thus, even though the SSI applicant may allege and prove that a disability began at a date prior to the application, the applicant will only be paid benefits beginning with the date of application.

The definition of *disability* is the same for both programs, and the issue of disability is adjudicated at the same time when concurrent applications under both programs are filed by the same adult claimant. Additionally, a DIB applicant who finds that the PIA indicates a monthly benefit payment may be below the monthly income limits to qualify for SSI can later file an SSI application and have it "escalated" or raised to the level of adjudication where a DIB application is being considered. Figure 4-1 shows that, of the more than forty-eight million persons receiving Social Security payments in December 1998, most (41.9 million) received Title II benefits only, whereas 4.2 million received SSI benefits only, and 2.4 million received both Title II and SSI benefits.

A Trip to the Hard Drive, 4.1

Following is an overview of the SSI program.

Introduction

SSI benefits also provide a safety net to aged, blind, or disabled individuals of limited income in the United States. In December 1999, 1.308 million adults over the age of sixty-five and 4.377 million blind or disabled adults received SSI benefits from the federal government. In December 1999, 871,000 blind or disabled children received SSI benefits. Most SSI recipients receive benefits on the basis of disability; those over 65 are the second largest group receiving benefits. Only 1 percent of SSI benefits are awarded on the basis of blindness. Figure 4–2 shows the percentages of SSI recipients according to the basis on which benefits are awarded. More than 6.5 million persons received federally administered SSI payments in July 2000. The average federally administrated SSI monthly benefit payment is $377.00.

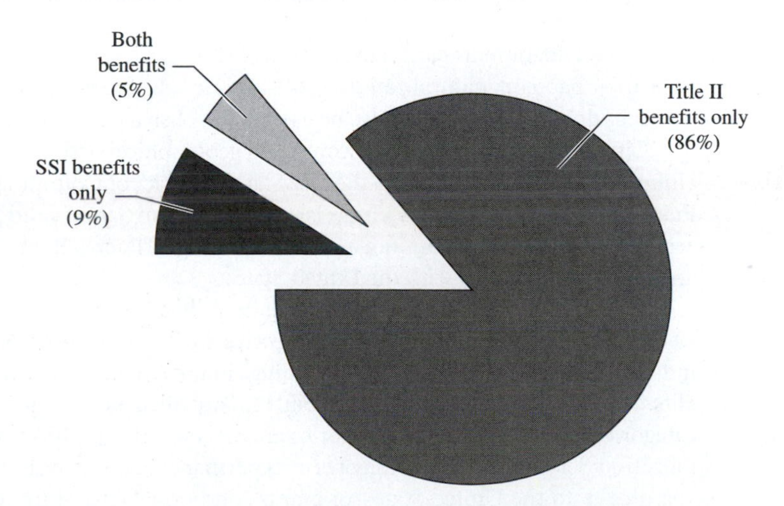

Figure 4–1 **Percentage by Program of Social Security Benefit Recipients**

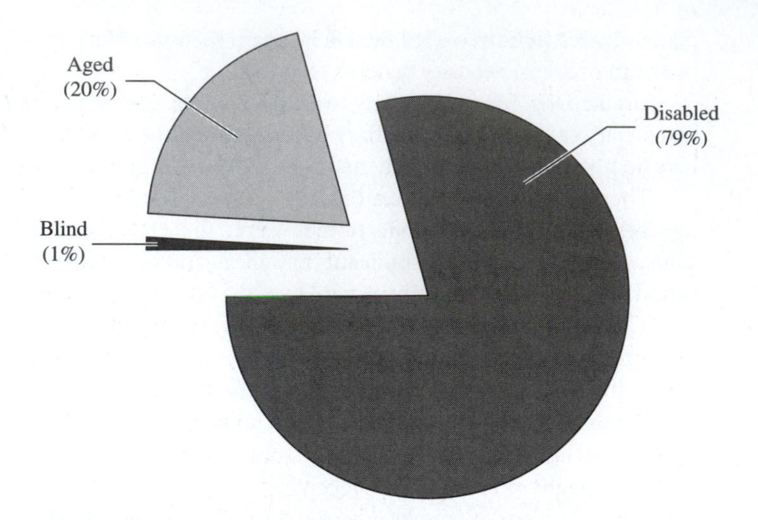

Figure 4–2 **Basis of Eligibility for SSI Recipients**

In addition to proving age over 65, disability, or blindness, an SSI applicant must also demonstrate a connection to the United States by proving citizenship and/or lawful residency in the United States. As noted previously, the applicant must also demonstrate income and resources below a specified limit as evidence that basic living needs cannot otherwise be met. We first consider the requirements of citizenship and residency, then the income and resource limitations for SSI eligibility.

CITIZENSHIP AND RESIDENCY IN THE UNITED STATES

SSI recipients must be American citizens or nationals who reside in the United States. Aliens lawfully admitted for permanent residence or permanently residing in the United States under color of law (i.e., have resided in the United States continuously since before January 1, 1972) may also receive SSI benefits.[1] The SSA defines "residency in the United States" as residing in one of the fifty states, the District of Columbia, or the Northern Mariana Islands.[2] Residency also includes being present in the United States for at least thirty consecutive days. If the SSI claimant or recipient leaves the United States, as geographically defined previously, for more than thirty days, SSI eligibility is forfeited. The claimant or recipient cannot regain SSI eligibility until the claimant establishes residency in the geographically defined U.S. for at least thirty consecutive days.[3]

Several documents can be used to establish U.S. citizenship, including birth certificates, religious records of birth or baptism, naturalization certificates, or U.S. passports. SSA's regulations at Title 20 C.F.R. 416.1610 list other documents that can also be used to establish a claimant's U.S. citizenship.

Citizenship is distinguished from SSA's geographical definition of residency. In terms of citizenship, the United States includes not only the fifty States, District of Columbia, and Northern Mariana Islands but also Puerto Rico, Guam, the U.S. Virgin Islands, American Samoa, and Swain's Island.[4] Thus, one may be a citizen of the United States, but not a resident if living in Puerto Rico, Guam, or the other named islands, which are typically associated with the United States.

Prior to 1996, noncitizens who were lawfully admitted for permanent residence and noncitizens who were residing under color of law could receive SSI benefits. In 1996, Congress enacted new requirements for individuals who were not "lawfully residing" in the United States in August 1996 in order to receive SSI benefits. The new laws restricted SSI eligibility to "qualified aliens" who met certain criteria in at least one of eight categories. Most of the eight categories are based on the applicant's status with the Immigration and Naturalization Service, which lawfully permits permanent residence in the United States, a "refugee," "asylee," or "parolee" into the United States, or grants conditional entry into the United States. A second criteria common to all eight categories is the "military exception," which is met if an alien has served in a branch of the U.S. military.

BACK TO CHRIS

Chris made a note to question Mr. Carson about his citizenship status. With Mr. Carson's recent health problems, it is unlikely that he has been out of the geographical United States for more than a month recently. But, he didn't want to assume that fact.

Chris then studied Mr. Carson's application for SSI benefits. Mr. Carson listed a 1988 American-made sedan, his home, two burial plots, and an insurance policy as his assets.

I don't get it, thought Chris. *I'm pretty sure Mr. Carson is eligible for DIB, and his wife will probably qualify for spouse benefits on his earnings records, too. So, why is Mr. Carson also applying for Title XVI benefits? What can he get from Title XVI benefits, that he wouldn't already have from DIB?*

Chris reached across the desk for the Code of Federal Regulations and found a clean page on the notepad.

FRONT OF YOUR MIND QUESTIONS AND CONSIDERATIONS, 4.2

Why should Mr. Carson file an SSI application if he can qualify for DIB benefits, and possible auxiliary spouse benefits for his wife? The answer to Chris's questions will be found in the information Chris obtains from Mr. Carson in their initial interview, supplemented by the information from the Field Office regarding Mr. Carson's work history and potential DIB monthly payment amounts.

When Title XVI was enacted in 1972, many of the supplemental assistance programs for individuals unable to provide for their basic life needs were handled by state-based programs. Each state determined the amounts to provide its citizens as supplemental assistance, and the federal government matched the state-determined amount. By the 1970s, significant disparities in the amounts various states provided their citizens prompted Congress to establish Title XVI and the SSI program as a federally administered assistance program providing a nationwide, uniform level of entitlement guidelines for supplemental income benefits for all recipients. States were given the option of providing some type of additional supplemental assistance to those receiving SSI benefits. Not all states, however, provide the supplementation assistance.

Each year SSA sets a basic federal benefit rate (FBR) as the maximum amount an individual or a married couple can have as "countable income" each month. In 2000, the FBR was $512 a month for an individual and $769 for an eligible couple. As we discuss in greater detail later, income includes monthly Social Security benefit payments, including DIB, RIB, and related auxiliary benefits. If the DIB and auxiliary benefits of an eligible couple are below $769 a month, and no other countable income is available to the couple, SSI benefits could be paid to the applicant to make up the difference between the monthly Title II benefits received and the $769 FBR. In essence, the SSI benefit raises the monthly Title II benefits to the $769 FBR cap.

As noted in Chapter 3, the wage earner's work history influences the amount of monthly DIB benefit. Chris's initial interview with Mr. Carson may reveal work history punctuated with gaps of no earnings because of illnesses, unemployment, or other reasons. Such a work history may suggest that Mr. Carson may need to file for SSI benefits, in addition to his DIB application, in order to obtain the additional benefits to bring his total monthly benefit to the current FBR limit amount.

A TRIP TO THE HARD DRIVE, 4.2

It is important to understand the specific requirements in terms of income and resources allowed and counted.

INCOME AND RESOURCE LIMITATIONS

Because it is a needs-based program, SSI focuses on the income and resources available to the applicant to meet basic life needs. Having income in excess of the SSI-specified limits precludes eligibility for SSI. An eligible SSI recipient's benefits may be reduced in proportion to the amount of income and resources available.

We examine first how SSA defines "income" and what limitations are placed on the amount of income available to an SSI applicant. We then consider how and what SSA defines as "resources" and the limitations as to what an SSI applicant can own as a resource.

WHAT IS INCOME?

SSA defines *income* as anything the individual receives in cash or in-kind that can be used to meet basic needs for food, shelter, and clothing.[5] Some items or services received by an SSI applicant cannot be used as, or used to obtain food, shelter, or clothing, and, thus, are not considered by SSA to constitute income. Examples include medical care and services, social services, income tax refunds, bills paid by another on behalf of the applicant, and weatherization assistance for an applicant's dwelling.[6]

SSA distinguishes between "earned" income and "unearned" income. This difference is important because SSA applies different exclusions to each type of income. Earned income may be paid in cash, such as wages from a job, self-employment income, commissions, bonuses, or severance pay. If wages are paid by the employer's provision of in-kind items such as food, clothing, or shelter, the value of those items is treated as the payment of wages. SSA counts not only the amount of wages the applicant receives monthly but also any amounts withheld from wages because of garnishment or repayment of a debt or other obligation. Net earnings from self-employment are counted on a taxable year basis, then divided by the number of months in the taxable year to determine the monthly wage.[7]

Other federal laws make it possible to exclude certain amounts from consideration in the monthly calculation of earned income. Sixty-five dollars of earned income in a month is always excluded. Up to $10 a month of earned income may be excluded if the income is infrequently or irregularly received from a single source and is paid only once in a calendar quarter, or if the income cannot be reasonably expected to be received. A monthly $20 general income exclusion is given to offset unearned income, but it may be applied to earned income if it is not used in that month. After these deductions have been taken, one-half of the remaining income is excluded.

Anything that is not earned income, SSA defines as "unearned" income. Unearned income can also be paid in cash or in-kind. Prime examples of unearned income are periodic payments from pensions or annuities, including Social Security benefits, private employment pensions, veterans benefits, workers' compensation, and unemployment benefits. Other examples of "unearned" income include alimony and support payments, dividends, interest, royalties, income from rentals, proceeds of life insurance policies, prizes and awards, and gifts and inheritances. Additionally, food, shelter, and clothing furnished to an applicant by another person are considered to be in-kind support and maintenance and are treated by SSA as unearned income.[8]

Generally, unearned income is counted either when it is received by the applicant or when the income is set aside for the applicant's use, whichever is earlier. The amount of income is not reduced by deducting personal income taxes. Some types of unearned income are not counted in determining eligibility for SSI benefits. These may include the value of food stamps; any portion of a grant or scholarship used for paying tuition, fees, or necessary educational expenses; certain housing subsidies; foster care payments for an ineligible child; or certain natural disaster or emergency assistance received. Also excluded as income may be one-third of support payments made to a child by an absent parent. Up to $20 a month in unearned income may not be counted, if that income is irregular or infrequent as defined previously for earned income.[9]

In-kind support and maintenance as unearned income includes food, shelter, or clothing given to or received by the applicant and paid for by another. Shelter may include not only rent or mortgage payments but also utility services, garbage collection services, and real property taxes. If the applicant is living in the household of another who provides both food and shelter to the applicant for an entire month, the applicant's FBR is reduced by one-third. This is the "one-third" reduction rule. When this rule is applied, the applicant cannot claim the benefit of the $20 general exclusion on unearned income. SSA applies the one-third reduction rule either fully or not at all. If the one-third rule is applied, SSA will not consider any other in-kind support or maintenance the applicant receives.[10]

The one-third rule does not apply if the applicant is living in the household of a spouse or minor child who supplies the in-kind support and maintenance, or if the applicant has an ownership interest in the home, is liable to the landlord for any part of the rental payment, or pays a pro rata share of the household and operating expenses of the home. The one-third rule also does not apply if the applicant lives in a noninstitutional care situation or if all members of the household receive public assistance.[11]

Effective Date	Individual	Couple
January 1, 1985	$1,600	$2,400
January 1, 1986	$1,700	$2,550
January 1, 1987	$1,800	$2,700
January 1, 1988	$1,900	$2,850
January 1, 1989 and after	$2,000	$3,000

Figure 4–3 **Limitations on Owned Resources**

Another issue of unearned income is that of "deeming." In certain situations, SSA will consider income of another person to be available to the SSI applicant for provision of basic living needs. This income will be "deemed" available for use by the applicant, regardless of whether it actually is available. SSA has identified three basic categories of persons whose income may be subject to deeming. First, an applicant who lives in the same household with a spouse not eligible for SSI will have a portion of the spouse's income deemed available to the applicant. Second, the income of a parent ineligible for SSI will be deemed available to a child in determining the child's SSI benefit amount. Third, income of the sponsor of a "qualified" alien is deemed available to the alien for three years after the alien is admitted to the United States for permanent residence. Figure 4–3 shows the increase in allowable, owned resources from January 1985.[12]

What Is a "Resource"?

SSA defines a "resource" as cash, liquid assets, or property that an individual or a spouse owns that could be converted to cash for support and maintenance. The individual or spouse must possess the right, authority, or power to liquidate the property for it to be considered a resource. If the property right has a legal restriction on it that prevents its sale or liquidation, the property is not considered a resource. Restricted, allotted land owned by an enrolled member of a Native American tribe is not a resource if the tribe member can not dispose of the land without the tribe's permission.[13]

According to SSA, resources are liquid or nonliquid. The criteria for liquidity is the ability to convert the property into cash within twenty days. Examples of liquid resources include cash or other property, such as stocks and bonds, mutual fund shares, promissory notes, mortgages, bank accounts, or life insurance policies. Property, such as automobiles, buildings, land, household goods, and livestock, are considered nonliquid resources because it usually takes more than twenty days to convert such property to cash. As with income, resources can be deemed to the applicant from a spouse, parent, sponsor, or essential person.[14]

SSA limits the amounts and types of resources that an applicant may have and be entitled to SSI benefits. Currently, an individual is limited to $2,000 and a married couple is limited to $3,000 in resources. Figure 4–3 shows the historical limits on resources. Resources are valued on a monthly basis. If a resource increases in value, its increased value is counted the next month. Similarly, a resource that decreases in value will have its decreased value counted the next month. Items received in cash or in-kind during a month are counted as income for the month in which they are received. If the applicant keeps the item, it is counted as a resource in the next month, unless it can be excluded.[15]

SSA permits certain resources to be excluded. The primary exclusion is the applicant's home and the land adjacent to it, regardless of its value. Household goods, personal property essential to self-support, and personal effects in which one's equity does not exceed $2,000 are also excludable. One automobile, whose current market value does not exceed $4,500 and which is used for necessary transportation, may be excluded. Life insurance policies, whose total face value does not exceed $1,500, may also be excluded. The applicant also may exclude burial spaces and designated burial funds that do not exceed $1,500.[16]

If the applicant has excess nonliquid resources, but would otherwise qualify for SSI benefits, SSA permits the applicant to dispose of those excess resources under certain restrictions. The applicant's liquid resources may not exceed an amount three times the monthly FBR or exceed one-fourth the total annual FBR.

The applicant must agree in writing to dispose of the excess resources at the current market rate value within nine months for real property or three months for personal property.[17]

However, an individual may be penalized if he or she disposes of resources at less than fair market value within a thirty-six-month period prior to filing the application for SSI benefits. The penalty is basically a loss of benefits for a number of months, which is calculated by dividing the uncompensated value of the disposed-of resource by the FBR. The penalty is not assessed if the applicant can positively show that the resources were disposed of for a purpose other than establishing SSI eligibility.[18]

BACK TO CHRIS

"Are there other things that affect eligibility for SSI benefits?" Chris asked Steve.

"Absolutely. Study further."

A TRIP TO THE HARD DRIVE, 4.3

Explore other factors affecting eligibility for SSI benefits—take *A Trip to the Hard Drive.*

OTHER FACTORS AFFECTING SSI ELIGIBILITY

SSI is a benefit of last resort. The SSI applicant must apply for all other public assistance benefits to which she or he may be entitled, including annuities, pensions, workers' compensation, and unemployment insurance benefits. SSI provides an applicant with written notice of potential eligibility for such other benefits and allows the applicant thirty days to file for those benefits. Failure to seek all other avenues of public assistance may cause the applicant to be deemed ineligible for SSI.[19]

Inmates housed for a full calendar month in a prison or other public institution are not eligible for SSI benefits. This prohibition does not extend to public institutions, such as a publicly operated community residence serving no more than sixteen residents or an emergency shelter for the homeless, although payments may be limited to no more than a total of six months.[20]

A FINAL NOTE ABOUT INCOME AND RESOURCE LIMITATIONS

An award of SSI benefits is not guaranteed for life. About every three years, SSA reviews the case of SSI recipients granted on the basis of disability for improvement in medical conditions. Nonmedical eligibility factors, including residence, income, and resource amounts are also redetermined, anywhere from one to six years, depending on the circumstances of each case.

SSA has acknowledged criticism from Field Office employees and from claimants and beneficiaries that the manner in which income and resources are counted and/or excluded in determining eligibility for SSI benefits is overly complex, time consuming, and difficult to administer. In late 2000, SSA issued a report in which it outlined possible options to simplify the needs-based determinations for SSI benefits qualification. Among its proposals for simplification in this area, SSA proposed estimating wages on a monthly basis by dividing the yearly income by twelve or by the amount of months actually worked, recognizing that workers paid on a weekly or biweekly basis may have greater earnings in months with three or more pay periods. SSA also is considering methods to simplify the calculation of resource exclusions, ranging from combining some of the current seventeen categories of exclusion to eliminating some exclusions and allowing higher amounts for resources owned per individual or couple. Lastly, in response to criticism that its investigation of in-kind support, maintenance situations, and living arrangements is intrusive and subjective, as well as discourages help from the claimant's or beneficiaries' family members, SSA is reexamining its consideration of in-kind maintenance and support, with the aim of reducing reporting requirements by the claimant and beneficiary.

Although these proposals for simplification may be several years from implementation, they show a positive movement away from the minutiae-focused determinations of whether a client meets the needs-based objectives of the SSI program. The Field Office employees known as claims representatives (CR's) will continue to be a representative's and a client's best source of information on the calculations of income and resources, even after simplification of these calculations is made by SSA.

WHAT IF . . . ? SAMPLE PROBLEMS

WHAT IF . . .

Given the statements in Mr. Carson's SSI application regarding ownership of a car, home, insurance policy, and two burial plots, can Chris determine if Mr. Carson's resources exceed the limits to qualify for SSI benefits? If not, what questions will Chris need to ask Mr. Carson about these resources?

Answer: Chris will need to ask Mr. Carson about the make and year of his car, to determine if the current market value exceeds the $4,500 limit allowed by SSA. Public libraries usually carry automobile value guides which will help Chris establish a current market value for Mr. Carson's car. Such information can also be obtained from the Internet. Chris and Mr. Carson will also have to determine if the life insurance policy's total face value is less than $1,500, which SSA allows to be excluded. Mr. Carson's house and burial plots are excluded as resources.
Although Mr. Carson's SSI application did not mention bank savings accounts, additional real property ownership, significant personal property worth more than $2000, or other resources, Chris would be wise to ask Mr. Carson about any other investments or resources the Carsons may have. Often, SSI benefits are awarded to a disabled claimant, but then are denied because a forgotten resource is discovered which takes the claimant out of the FBR limits.

WHAT IF . . .

Herman Jones was born in American Samoa on January 23, 1930. After living most of his life in Mexico City, Herman decided to take up skiing and other winter sports and moved to Crested Butte, Colorado, on December 1, 1994. He filed an application for SSI benefits on February 1, 1995. Assuming Herman meets the income and resource requirements, is he eligible for SSI benefits? If he is, what is the earliest date he can receive those benefits?

Answer: Herman was born in American Samoa, which makes him a "citizen" under SSA's definition. Although Herman has lived in Mexico City most of his life, he had resided in the United States (Colorado) for more than 30 consecutive days (December 1, 1994 to February 1, 1995) when he filed his SSI benefits application. Herman thus meets the citizenship and residency requirements for SSI benefits. Herman was 65 years old when he filed his SSI application, so he is eligible for benefits on that basis. He will receive benefits beginning the date of his application, February 1, 1995.

WHAT IF . . .

Loretta Campbell has received SSI benefits since 1999. On August 10, 2000, she received word that her brother, Lorenzo, was injured in a wind-sailing accident in Puerto Rico. Loretta immediately flew to Puerto Rico to take care of Lorenzo, spending the rest of August and all of September at his hospital bedside and then taking him to physical therapy. Loretta returned to her home in the United States on October 2, 2000 and notified her SSA local field office that she had returned from Puerto Rico. Will Loretta's SSI benefits be affected by her travel to, and stay in, Puerto Rico?

Answer: Loretta will lose her SSI eligibility because she did not reside (i.e., was not present) in the United States for 30 consecutive days in August and September 2000. While one can claim U.S. citizenship from being born in Puerto Rico, one's presence in Puerto Rico does not meet SSA's definition of residency in the United States.

WHAT IF . . .

May Knott applied for SSI benefits. Her home was appraised at $130,000 and her car is worth $4,000. She has a whole life insurance policy worth $1,500, and she maintains a checking account with less than $1,500 in it. Based on these resources, is May eligible to receive SSI benefits?

Answer: ***May Knott's home is excluded as a resource, no matter what its value. Her car's current market value is under the $4,500 limit set by SSA, and may be excluded as a resource. Her whole life insurance policy meets the $1,500 limit for exclusion as a resource. Assuming May has no other resources, her checking account of less than $1,500 is below the $2000 limitation on resources set by SSA for an individual. May's income and resources qualify her for SSI benefits; she must still prove a disability, blindness, or that she is over 65 to be entitled to receive SSI benefits.***

---

[1] 20 C.F.R. § 416.1600.
[2] 20 C.F.R. § 416.1613(c).
[3] 20 C.F.R. § 416.215.
[4] 20 C.F.R. § 416.1610.
[5] 20 C.F.R. § 416.1102.
[6] 20 C.F.R. § 416.1103.
[7] See, 20 C.F.R. §§ 416.1110, 416.1111 and 416.1112.
[8] See, 20 C.F.R. §§ 416.1120 and 416.1121.
[9] See, 20 C.F.R. §§ 416.1123, 416.1124.
[10] See, 20 C.F.R. § 416.1130.
[11] 20 C.F.R. §§ 416.1131, 416.1132 and 416.1133.
[12] 20 C.F.R. §§ 416.1160; 416.1161; 416.1163; 416.1165; 416.1166 and 416.1166a.
[13] 20 C.F.R. § 416.1201.
[14] See, 20 C.F.R. §§ 416.1201(b); 416.1202; 416.1203; 416.1204.
[15] See, 20 C.F.R. §§ 404.1205 and 404.1207.
[16] See, 20 C.F.R. §§ 416.1210; 416.1212; 416.1216; 416.1218; 416.1230; and 416.1231.
[17] See, 20 C.F.R. §§ 416.1240; 416.1242; 416.1244; and 416.1245.
[18] See, 20 C.F.R. § 416.1246.
[19] 20 C.F.R. § 416.210.
[20] 20 C.F.R. § 416.211.

5

CHAPTER FIVE

The Definition of Adult Disability for Title II and Title XVI Claims—The Five-Step Sequential Evaluation Process

HIGHLIGHTS

- Adult disability defined
- Introduction to the five-step sequential evaluation process

CHRIS

"Okay," Chris said finally. "I get the big picture, but there's more to this than simply filing a Request for Hearing after a state agency denial."

Chris's mirror image stared back impassively. No answers there.

"Okay, smartie. Now what?"

Chris' eyes wandered to the stack of books on the edge of the desk.

"I don't want to," Chris said aloud. It looked like too much work. Too much detail.

The would-be representative groaned, flopping back onto the ergonomic chair. "No, no, you gotta do this."

There really was no other choice. Think of Mr. Carson.

"So," Chris muttered finally, "I guess it's time to crack the books." Chris was determined. There would be no discouragement.

And there was none.

Chris opened the first book. "Okay," Chris said to no one in particular, "Let's get down to the legal standards."

Front of Your Mind Questions and Considerations, 5.1

The Five-Step Sequential Evaluation Process

The heart of any decision-making process is the *standard* by which decisions are made. In disability decision making, that standard is a five-step *sequential evaluation process,* the S-E-P. Understanding the five-step analytical process requires appreciation of the nature of the program itself. Social Security disability is a benefits entitlement program best viewed as an expression of societal concern for those unable to care for themselves. It is an act of charitable giving on a national scale designed to help the less fortunate. It ensures a minimum level of sustenance for those in need.

The concept of disability is subjective. Without an objective standard, the issue of disability can vary widely among individuals. For one person, the inability to perform a specific task may signify complete disability, whereas another may believe that disability applies only when one is on the death bed. Between these two extremes are a multitude of definitions of disability. The solution: a legal standard which takes into account both medical and vocational issues, founded on the premise that disability in American society is grounded in an ability to maintain a minimum level of sustenance through one's own efforts. Integral to any standard, however, is the requirement of fundamental fairness.

A subjective decision-making process, with the potential for widely varying standards, cannot, by definition, be fair. Therein lies the problem. How can societal concern be expressed for those among us unable to assist themselves if the standard is subjective? How are questions such as, "Why don't you show some character and live beyond your disease?" avoided? Implicit in such questioning is an underlying judgment: "You're exaggerating," or "You want something for nothing." Clearly, such comments, even if unspoken, are prejudicial.

How can this be overcome? How can prejudicial decision making be minimized?

Without established standards, or criteria by which decisions are made, prejudicial decision making is a foregone conclusion. Fortunately, the standard at the base of all governmental decision making is *fundamental fairness.* Thus, to offer disability benefits the government was required to develop an objective standard, neutral on its face, and fundamentally fair in its application. The result was the *five-step sequential evaluation process.*

Two descriptors stand out. First, the analysis is *sequential.* One may not proceed from one step to the next unless the determination in the prior step fails to resolve the issue. Second, the analysis is a *process.* It requires consideration of a number of discrete elements, ultimately legal in nature, involving both medical and vocational evidence. The sequential nature of the process and the process itself are discussed next.

The Sequential Nature of the Disability Determination Process

The five-step sequential evaluation process is founded on essential principles of public policy—the same principles that underlie the Social Security Act. If an individual is unable to maintain a minimum level of personal sustenance, society, through the mechanism of the Social Security Act, has determined not to allow this individual to suffer without resources. A minimum level of daily sustenance is provided, including financial and medical benefits.

It is important to understand this public policy in all its dimensions. For example, societal outreach is premised on an inability of the individual to function, not on the individual's volitional refusal. If one chooses not to engage in activity that will result in daily sustenance, society honors the freedom of that choice—but does not provide benefits.

Public policy echoes throughout the sequential analysis, recognizing essential prerequisites to the award of disability. These include

- Establishing presumptive monthly earnings that, if attained, preclude an award of benefits.
- Establishing a minimum level of functional impairment as a threshold on which a determination of disability is conditioned.
- Establishing presumptions of medical severity, such that the presence of specified symptoms is equivalent to a finding of functional disability.

- ❑ Linking the Department of Labor, *Dictionary of Occupational Titles* (*DOT*), and functional performance levels for competitive work (sedentary, light, medium, heavy, and very heavy work).
- ❑ Linking age, education, and skill level, such that the older an individual is, or the less education or skills one has, the more likely it is that he or she will be found to be disabled.
- ❑ Establishing a baseline standard for competitive work in American society of eight hours per day, five days per week, and linking the disability determination with a legal determination such work cannot be performed.
- ❑ Establishing a presumption that an individual's past work, if performed in the preceding fifteen years, is of sufficient recency as to allow the individual to perform it again, if the person retains the residual functional capacity for such work. Work beyond fifteen years is presumed not to be of sufficient recency to be able to be performed.

Careful review reveals that each step builds on the one before it, in somewhat logical sequence. For example, the first step in the process considers whether an individual is working (engaged in "substantial gainful activity"). If the individual is working, why explore the individual's medical condition, educational background, and vocational history if the essential public policy underlying the disability program is defeated in the first instance? If an individual is working at what is presumed to be a competitive level, why award public assistance?[1]

The second step in the sequential evaluation considers the severity of an impairment. The only question at this stage is whether the individual suffers from an impairment that has lasted or is expected to last at least twelve months or result in death which reasonably gives rise to limitations of function likely to affect the individual's ability to perform competitive work. This does not require an intense assessment of the claimant's precise limitations. It is sufficient for a step 2 analysis that there are, in fact, limitations affecting the claimant's ability to function competitively. It is not, however, necessary at this step to evaluate the actual degree of limitation.[2] Thus, it is presumed at this step that an impairment of at least twelve months duration (or one so grave as to result in death in less than twelve months) which reasonably gives rise to limitations of function *likely* to affect an individual's ability to perform competitive work is of sufficient severity as to merit further consideration as a basis for disability. The analysis then continues.

The third step in the sequential analysis takes the presumptions at the second step a step further. Having concluded that a medically diagnosed condition of sufficient severity exists, if sufficient symptoms are then found to be present, the inquiry need not proceed further. It is presumed, given a defined set of existing symptoms, that the diagnosed condition is so serious that its presence at this level precludes competitive work, *without any actual showing of what the individual is actually capable of doing (apart from a showing of existing symptoms.)* If an individual is found to have a condition of such gravity that the illness is attended by the set of defined symptoms and medical signs in Appendix 1 to subpart P (Listings of Impairments) to part 404 of Title 20, Code of Federal Regulations, then it may be presumed that the individual is entitled to "automatic disability."

Before moving to step 4, the individual's residual functional capacity (RFC) must be established. The Department of Labor's *Dictionary of Occupational Titles* (*DOT*) includes five categories of exertional work activity:[3]

1. Sedentary work;
2. Light work;
3. Medium work;
4. Heavy work; and
5. Very heavy work.

These categories are presumptive descriptions of an individual's functional capabilities. The ability to work, regardless of its nature, is ultimately affected by the ability to engage in various activities, classified as *exertional* or *nonexertional* activities. The ability to perform work is affected to a greater or lesser degree, depending on the individual's ability to perform a range of such exertional and nonexertional activities. More to the point, an individual's functional capability varies, depending on the inability to engage in specified exertional or nonexertional activities. It is this variation, and specifically the absence of a specific capability, or *limitation,* that ultimately defines the individual's capacity for different work categories (e.g., sedentary, light, medium, heavy, and very heavy work.)

Once an individual's limitations are established, the issue becomes, can a job that was done in the past fifteen years still be done? This issue invokes a different public policy standard from that of state Workers' Compensation. In a state Workers' Compensation claim, the question is generally limited to whether the injured individual is capable of performing the work done at the time of injury. Workers' Compensation seeks to compensate for an on-the-job injury, which necessarily limits recovery to the extent of the injury actually suffered while working. Social Security disability considers a broader issue. Regardless of whether the basis for disability is an injury or a disease and regardless of whether it was suffered on the job, the question is whether the individual can be competitively employed at any job within the scope of his or her capability?

This is, in effect, a two-part inquiry. The first part simply asks whether jobs that were once performed could again be performed, despite the individual's impairments and resulting limitations. The public policy issue is evident. If society declares an individual unable to perform competitive work in any of its myriad forms, should it not first consider those competitive jobs that the person once actually performed? In fairness to the person, a fifteen-year cutoff is a recency standard founded on the vocational assumption that a person will likely not retain knowledge and skills pertinent to a given job beyond that time.

Only when it is established that the individual cannot return to a past job is the question finally considered whether there are other, less demanding, competitive jobs the individual can perform. This too, is a manifestation of public policy. In a program founded on the premise that society must reach out to those unable to provide for themselves, the natural corollary is an inquiry as to whether, in the wide world of the local (i.e., regional) and national economies, there are, in fact, jobs the person could still perform at competitive levels, even at a reduced level of function? The premise is that society should not have to supply a minimum daily sustenance to an individual who is capable of working at a competitive level.

The policy has a subtle twist. The question is not whether there are actually jobs in the person's community that he or she could apply for and be hired. Instead, the question is whether there are significant numbers of jobs in the regional and national economies that the person could, *hypothetically,* perform. Many claimants have protested this formulation of public policy, asserting pragmatic realities. In most cases, the region is the state in which the person applying for benefits lives. Although it may be determined that 700 jobs exist that the person could hypothetically perform, there is no guarantee that (1) the jobs exist within commuting range of the claimant or (2) there are actual openings to be filled.

Why? Because to premise a disability determination on the existence of actual job openings would create a program constantly in motion, with a subjective, not an objective, standard. For example, in a given month, suppose a new plant opens, with two hundred or three hundred new jobs. When the plant is hiring, claimants would be unfairly denied benefits because of the large number of immediate openings at the new plant. Those applying for benefits after the hiring was complete, would, in effect, be judged by a different standard. The new plant jobs would no longer be open. Finally, as a practical matter, it would be difficult, if not impossible, to ascertain on a daily, weekly, or even monthly basis the status of current openings in a given city, much less a state. Vocational experts who testify in disability hearings would have to establish some means to assure themselves that their numbers were up to date and accurate. And even if they were, the standard thus established would be subjective, changing daily, and thus, fundamentally, unfair.

The underlying presumption, that an individual should be adjudicated disabled based on the inability to perform competitive work, seems firmly grounded in the fact that we live *and* work in a competitively capitalist society. Although we recognize and attempt to address the plight of those less fortunate, the standard is nevertheless the same—can the individual compete?

Back to Chris

"Wait a minute," Chris said aloud. "Why do I need to know this? I thought all I had to know was the five-step sequential analysis and that was that!" Chris pushed away from the desk, frustrated.

"Hey Chris?" Steve popped his head through the door.

"Hi Steve."

"You talking to yourself?"

"Just this Social Security business. It's difficult. Why do I have to know the rationale behind the five-step analysis anyway?"

Steve thought a moment. "How do you determine, in a capitalist economy, where work is a valued activity, who gets to have a 'bye' on working, with the blessing of society?"

Oh brother, Chris thought. "Thanks Steve, I guess I can handle it." Chris turned back to the desk.

Steve wasn't to be put off. "Wait. Think about it. If you don't have a job, you're unemployed. What does that make you?"

Guess I better play along. "Unless your significant other is working, or you're independently wealthy, you're a bum for not working."

"Right. But if society officially declares that you are unable to work—that is, you're given an accepted and valid reason for not working, a legal reason why you don't have a job—then you're not."

"Not what? A bum?"

"Exactly. Even though you're not working, you're OK. It's not your fault you can't work. You would if you could, but because your government declares you disabled, it's all right. No harm, no foul."

A light clicked on in Chris's head. "I get it. That's why it's important to understand the assumptions behind the disability decision. The determination that you are disabled carries with it more than simply a legal determination. It gives you a role and status within society as well."

"Right, but there's more."

"Such as?"

"Your client's emotional response. Their view of themselves."

"I don't get it."

"Chris, think about it. Your disability client has been raised and has functioned in a society where work is a measure of a person. Who you are as a person is, to some degree, defined by what you do."

"But if there is a legitimate reason for not working, then what is the problem?"

"It's not as simple as that. The inability to work is emotionally debilitating. It creates an exacerbating condition in which negative consequences increase."

"Negative consequences?"

"No money. Bills due. Spouses have to work. Kids going without. Perhaps even losing your home. All of this."

"I hadn't thought that far," Chris murmured, suddenly chastened.

"When you get a disability client, it's not a business transaction, it's a life. It's personal. For many, it's a tragedy in the most intimate way imaginable, and it's painful."

"By the time a person gets a disability decision, even if it's from the state agency, a good deal of time has passed. Waiting for a hearing before an administrative law judge can take one or two years from the first application, and it is probably longer since the applicant first wrestled with the realization that life could no longer go on as before."

"What you mean is that, even if the client gets a favorable decision, the damage is already done to the self-esteem."

"Right. This is especially the case in people who have worked and supported a family. It's like having your roots cut out from under you. Often, because of the disability, not only has the job suffered but also the ability to interact with others suffers. Participatory sports disappear. Socialization is reduced. Even church attendance is curtailed."

Chris let out a long low whistle of understanding. "So, I need to know this stuff?"

"You do. It will help you to look behind the facts and the law, and see your client in a broader light. All of us relate in a variety of ways. We are connected with our family, friends, co-workers and, in a very real way, through them, to society at large. If you begin eliminating those interactions, you begin to lose not only a sense of who you are but also where you belong."

Chris nodded. "I get it. Thanks. I guess I'll hit the books. Again."

FRONT OF YOUR MIND QUESTIONS AND CONSIDERATIONS, 5.2

So, what are the five steps in the sequential evaluation process?

THE FIVE STEPS OUTLINED

The five-step sequential evaluation process is the step-by-step process used by the Social Security Administration in determining disability with both administrative and medical components. Disability is an *administrative* or legal determination. Impairment is a *medical* determination. For Social Security purposes, an impairment is an anatomical or functional abnormality or loss. The existence of an impairment does not mean an individual is disabled. The sequential evaluation process was instituted to ensure that an assessment of the severity of an impairment is based on objective medical data evaluated fairly and correctly.

The five-step sequential analysis includes five discrete steps, as described by the Social Security Administration in its own literature.[4]

Step 1. **Is an individual engaging in substantial gainful activity (SGA)?**
When an individual is actually engaging in SGA, a finding is made that the individual is not disabled. This decision is made without consideration of either medical or vocational factors.

Step 2. **Does the individual have a severe impairment?**
A finding that the individual can engage in SGA may be justified on the basis of medical considerations alone when the degree of medically determinable impairment is found to be not severe. A not severe impairment exists when the medical evidence establishes only a slight abnormality that has no more than a minimal effect on the individual's physical or mental capacity to perform basic work-related functions. However, if the claimant has several impairments that individually would be considered not severe, the cumulative effect of all the impairments must be evaluated to determine if the overall condition is severe.

Step 3. **Does the individual have an impairment that meets or equals the Listing?**
A finding of disability is justified if the impairment is as severe or of an equivalent level of severity as one of the impairments contained in the Listing of Impairments. An individual who is not engaged in SGA and who has an impairment of the level of severity described in the Listing is considered unable to work by reason of the impairment alone.

For an impairment or a combination of impairments to be of equivalent severity to a listed impairment, the set of symptoms, signs, and laboratory findings in the medical evidence must be judged to be medically equivalent in severity to the set of symptoms, signs, and laboratory findings specified for the identified impairment.

Step 4. **Can the individual perform past relevant work?**
When a determination cannot be made on medical considerations alone, nonmedical factors must be considered. The claimant's residual functional capacity (RFC) is determined and compared to the physical and mental demands of the past relevant work.

Step 5. **Can the individual perform other work?**
When it is determined that the individual cannot perform past relevant work, RFC, age, education, past work experience, and transferable skills must be considered to determine if there is other less demanding work the individual can do.

BACK TO CHRIS

"Time out," Chris breathed. "How does this really work? I know there is a sequential evaluation, meaning one step is considered in sequence before moving to the next, but I need some real-world insight."

Chris thought for a long time before the epiphany hit.

"Ah! I see!" Chris drew a graph that looked like a huge V subdivided by horizontal lines, each representing one of the five steps.

"This makes more sense now."

FRONT OF YOUR MIND QUESTIONS AND CONSIDERATIONS, 5.3

OVERVIEW OF THE FIVE STEPS

The key issue in contemplating the effective operation of the five-step sequential evaluation process (SEP) is identification of the critical decision points in the five-step process. A decision point is a step where a grant or denial decision may be made by the adjudicator. The decision may be at the administrative level (by the state DDS) or before a federal administrative law judge, the Appeals Council, or the federal courts.

There are four points in the five-step sequential evaluation where an individual can be denied benefits, and there are three points where an individual can be granted benefits. Only one step holds potential for both a denial or a grant of benefits—step 5.

Benefits can be denied at steps 1, 2, 4, and 5. Benefits can be granted at steps 3 and 5. Although granting benefits may seem to take place only at two, and not three, steps, benefits can be approved in two ways at step 5. (This is discussed more fully later in the book.) Figure 5–1 illustrates the points in the five-step sequential analysis where benefits can be paid and where they can be denied.

At step 1, if an individual earns $780.00 or more a month,[5] it is presumed that he or she is engaged in substantial gainful activity and benefits will be denied. There are a variety of exceptions.

1. If an activity actually performed is not competitive in nature, such as working for a relative, getting paid regularly, but actually doing little or nothing to earn the money, the activity is not substantial and does not meet the SGA test. Both substantial *and* gainful activity are required to defeat an award of benefits.
2. All disabled persons are entitled to a trial work period (TWP) during which they are not penalized for attempting to return to work. Social Security regulations encourage no fault attempts to return to work, without placing disability status in jeopardy.[6] Every five years, a disabled individual is entitled to nine months in which to attempt to return to work without penalty. The time is cumulative and need not be consecutively worked.
3. All disabled persons are entitled to attempt work and, if unsuccessful, will not be penalized for the attempt. If an individual attempts to return to work, the work does not last longer than ninety days, and the work is terminated because of the claimed impairment, the attempt is classified as an unsuccessful work attempt, (UWA) for which no penalty is assessed, either in terms of disability in general, or as a trial work period.
4. If an individual is self-employed, an assessment must be made of the profitability of the activity, including such things as the cost of doing business. If it is not profitable, then the activity does not constitute SGA.

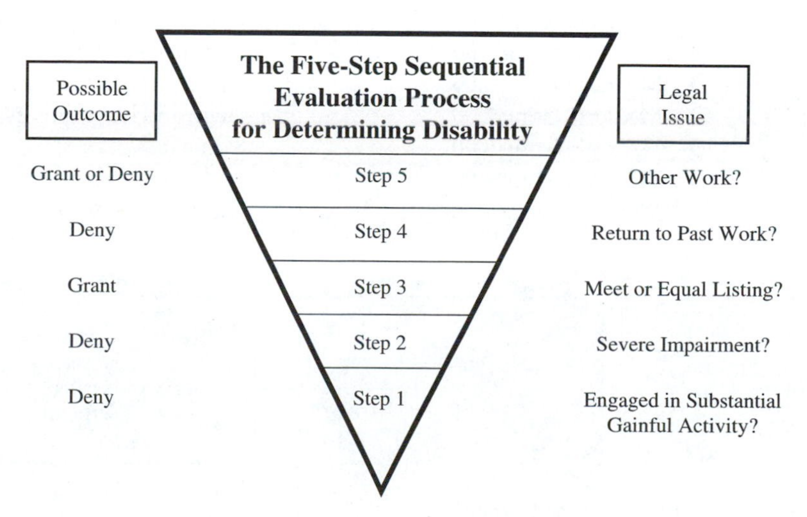

Figure 5–1 **The Five-Step Sequential Evaluation Process for Determining Disability**

5. In assessing whether work is gainful, the regulations require that the cost of equipping the individual with necessary medicines, assistive devices, and other requirements attendant to work must be taken into account and offset against actual earnings. If the net amount earned then falls below $780 per month the work activity is not gainful.

At step 2, if the individual is adjudged not to have a severe impairment, then the application for benefits is denied. The term *severe,* however, is not used in its commonsense meaning. Instead, it is a legal term that includes several discrete requirements.

1. For an impairment to be severe it must have lasted for at least twelve months, or (given the nature of the impairment) reasonably be expected to, or result in death. Impairments of shorter duration are considered nonsevere and do not constitute a basis for the award of disability benefits.
2. A severe impairment is medically determinable. It must have been diagnosed by a recognized medical source (physician, podiatrist, psychologist, or psychiatrist). Chiropractors are not recognized by the governing federal regulations as an acceptable or recognized source. Hypothetically, a record containing only chiropractic evidence will be adjudged as nonsevere.[7] A medically determinable impairment is one in which a recognized medical source has made a diagnosis that is supported by objective findings, either clinically or by medical testing (e.g., X-rays, laboratory studies, and so forth).
3. Finally, a severe impairment gives rise to limitations of function that must reasonably affect (limit) the individual's ability to engage in work-required activity. If an individual suffers from a hangnail, although medically diagnosable, and perhaps even meeting the time requirement, if no limitations of function actually arise that limit the individual's ability to engage in competitive work, the impairment is nonsevere and will not form the basis for the award of disability benefits.

Figure 5–2 describes the analytical process at step 2.

Step 3 is an opportunity to "pay the case." If the case is not payable (benefits awarded) at this step, the only consequence is passage to step 4 of the SEP. For an individual to qualify for an award of benefits at step 3, he or she must suffer from a severe impairment that "meets" or "equals" an impairment in the Listings of Impairments in the Appendix of subpart P of Title 20, Code of Federal Regulations. Social Security parlance or lingo refers to such an occurrence as "meets (or equals) the listing for [*fill in the blank with the impairment*]," or "meets (or equals) a listed impairment." If asked whether a claimant's condition (impairment) "meets a listing," the questioner is directing you to the Listings of Impairments in Appendix 1 of subpart P, Title 20, Code of Federal Regulations.

The Listing of Impairments addresses both adult and childhood impairments, and describes ailments and injuries in fourteen identified bodily systems. The adult listings are

- ❑ Medical Listing 1.00 — Musculoskeletal system
- ❑ Medical Listing 2.00 — Special senses and speech
- ❑ Medical Listing 3.00 — Respiratory system
- ❑ Medical Listing 4.00 — Cardiovascular system
- ❑ Medical Listing 5.00 — Digestive system
- ❑ Medical Listing 6.00 — Genito-urinary system
- ❑ Medical Listing 7.00 — Hemi and lymphatic system
- ❑ Medical Listing 8.00 — Skin
- ❑ Medical Listing 9.00 — Endocrine system
- ❑ Medical Listing 10.00 — [Reserved for future medical]

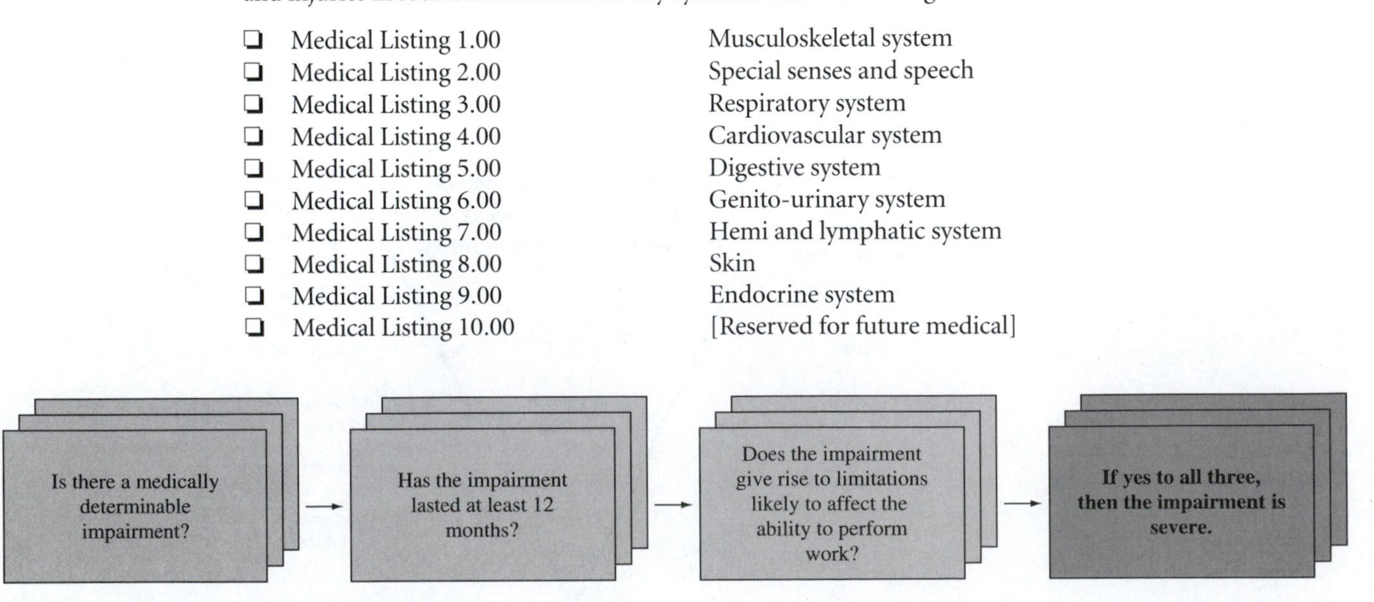

Figure 5–2 **Step 2: Is the Impairment Severe?**

❑ Medical Listing 11.00	Neurological
❑ Medical Listing 12.00	Mental disorders
❑ Medical Listing 13.00	Neoplastic diseases, malignant
❑ Medical Listing 14.00	Immune system

The childhood listings are

❑ Medical Listing 100.00	Growth impairment
❑ Medical Listing 101.00	Musculoskeletal system
❑ Medical Listing 102.00	Special senses and speech
❑ Medical Listing 103.00	Respiratory system
❑ Medical Listing 104.00	Cardiovascular system
❑ Medical Listing 105.00	Digestive system
❑ Medical Listing 106.00	Genito-urinary system
❑ Medical Listing 107.00	Hemic and lymphatic system
❑ Medical Listing 108.00	[Reserved for future medical]
❑ Medical Listing 109.00	Endocrine system
❑ Medical Listing 110.00	Multiple body systems
❑ Medical Listing 111.00	Neurological
❑ Medical Listing 112.00	Mental and emotional disorders
❑ Medical Listing 113.00	Neoplastic diseases, malignant
❑ Medical Listing 114.00	Immune system

Within each category are descriptions of specific injuries and illnesses. Each description includes specific symptoms, medical signs, and laboratory findings which, if present in their entirety (and lasting the required period of time), qualify the individual for disability. The award is based on a presumption of severity associated with the presence of a requisite constellation of symptoms, medical signs, and laboratory findings.

If each of the requisite symptoms are documented, either by credible testimony or medical records, demonstrating the presence of the symptoms, signs, and findings over the required time period, benefits are awarded.

If the symptoms, signs, and findings do not coincide with those required in the appropriate listing, the individual's condition may still be equivalent in medical severity to a listed impairment. This is called "equaling the listing." To equal a listing requires expert medical testimony or evidence from a treating physician received in close proximity to the DDS determination or hearing before an administrative law judge. The issue concerns whether the claimant's condition, while not producing exactly the same symptoms, needed signs, and laboratory findings as set forth in the Listing of Impairments, nevertheless equates in medical severity to the condition described in the Listing.

If, for example, the claimant suffers from a combination of impairments (i.e., multiple impairments), does the existence of the other impairments contribute to the severity of the primary impairment, which is close to meeting the requisites of a listing? And, if so, can the individual's condition be described as equivalent in severity because of the effect of the additional impairments? These are the questions that must be asked and that a medical expert or treating physician must answer. Step 3 is illustrated in Figure 5–3.

Step 4 of the five-step sequential evaluation requires an assessment of the individual's residual functional capacity (RFC). The term *residual functional capacity* refers to an assessment of what the individual can still do despite the impairments and resulting limitations and what can no longer be done because of them. Evaluation of

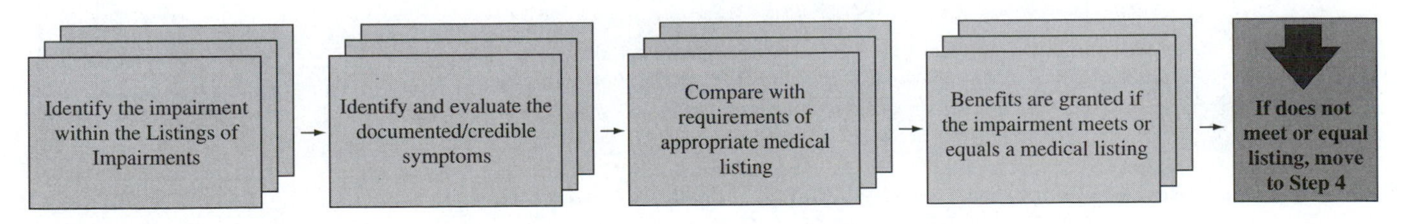

Figure 5–3 **Step 3: The Listings**

what the individual can and cannot do is expressed in terms of both exertional and nonexertional limitations of function. A limitation is simply an expression of capability.

If, for example, an individual is only capable of lifting ten pounds the individual is said to have a "lifting limitation" of no more than ten pounds. Similarly, if, because of carpal tunnel syndrome (a condition in which the nerve becomes entrapped in the wrist), an individual experiences pain after prolonged use of the hand, he or she is said to be limited in repetitive use of the hand or in the ability to engage in fine motor manipulation. The first example is an exertional limitation, whereas the second, even though still physical in nature, is nonexertional. Other nonexertional limitations include those caused by mental or emotional disorders, and medication side effects, among others. RFC is discussed in greater detail later in the text.

Once the individual's capability has been established, it needs to be determined whether, given the individual's limitations (both exertional and nonexertional), he or she can return to past relevant work performed within the past fifteen years? If the answer is *yes*, then, as a matter of public policy, the individual is considered not disabled. If the answer is *no*, the inquiry moves to step 5 of the sequential evaluation process. As such, step 4 is not a step in which benefits can be granted. Benefits can only be denied at step 4. Step 4 is illustrated in Figure 5–4.

Step 5 is the proverbial "two-edged sword," with potential to grant or deny. The issues at step 5 concern whether there are other, less demanding jobs—less demanding than the individual's past work—that the individual can perform. The resolution is found in the Medical–Vocational Guidelines, euphemistically called "the Grids." The Grids consist of three tables, each containing a set of rules by which disability is determined based on the claimant's exertional capability, age, education, and vocational skill. The following public policy principles guide outcomes on the Grids:

- The *less an individual is able to do exertionally,* the more likely he or she is to be found disabled;
- The *less skill* an individual has, the more likely he or she is to be found disabled;
- The *less education* an individual has, the more likely he or she is to be found disabled; and
- The *older* an individual is, the more likely he or she is to be found disabled.

The Grids are applicable in one of two ways:

- When the claimant has only exertional limitations, the result is directed by the applicable Grid rule; or
- In the presence of one or more nonexertional limitations (regardless of whether there are also exertional limitations), the Grids are used as a framework, meaning that a "not disabled" result otherwise directed by the applicable Grid rule is not followed because of the overriding effect of one or more nonexertional limitations.

When only exertional limitations are present, many jurisdictions do not require the testimony of vocational experts. However, when one or more nonexertional limitations are present, every jurisdiction requires vocational testimony. In the presence of nonexertional limitations, the Grid rules may not direct a determination, because, as discussed later in the text, the Medical–Vocational Guidelines do not consider the effect of nonexertional limitations. Figure 5–5 illustrates step 5.

Back to Chris

"Okay. I think I've got it. But I need to know the regs also. After all, the heart of the disability process is found in the regulations."

Chris turned to the books, starting with the Code of Federal Regulations.

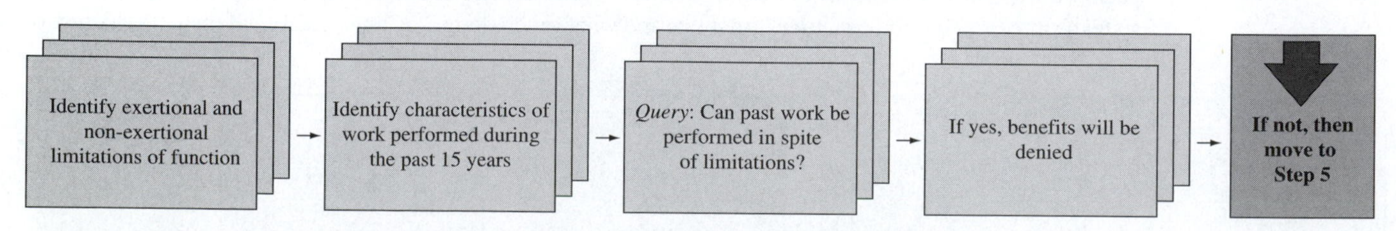

Figure 5–4 Step 4: Residual Functional Capacity—Ability to Perform Previous Work

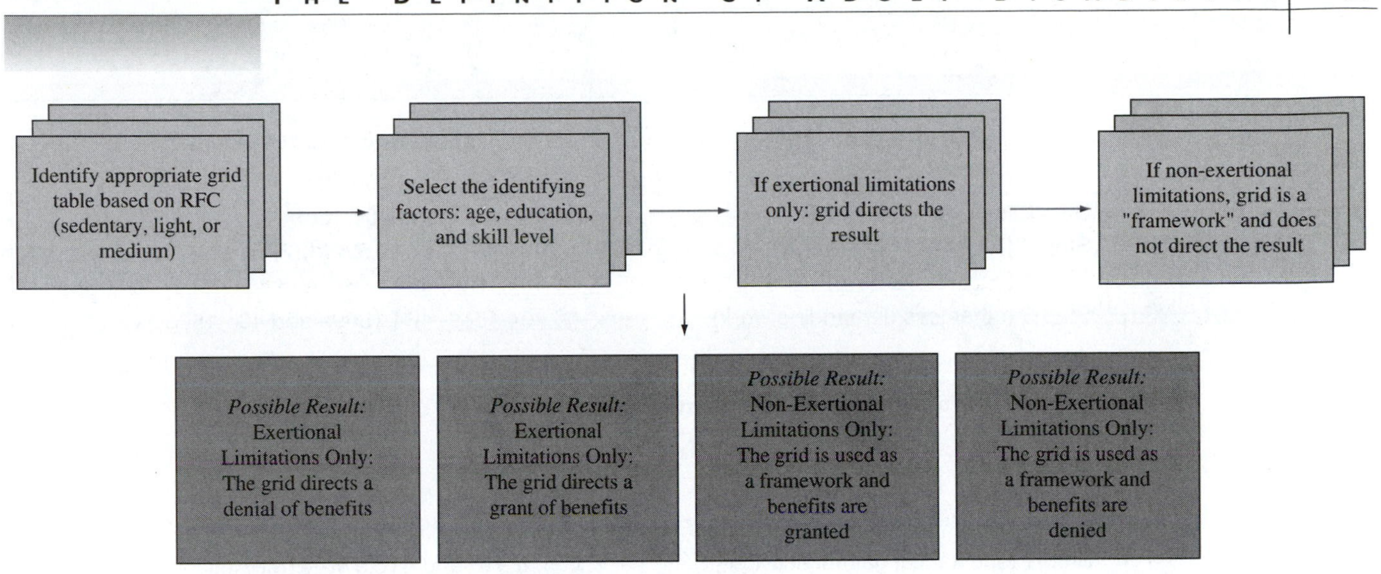

Figure 5–5 **Step 5: Other Jobs**

A Trip to the Hard Drive, 5.1

The five-step sequential analysis for claims made by an adult under Title II of the Social Security Act is set forth at Title 20 C.F.R. § 1520, which addresses an evaluation of disability in general. The sequential nature of the analysis is clearly established:

> **If we can find that you are disabled or not disabled at any point in the review, we do not review your claim further.[8]**

The five-step sequential analysis for adult SSI claims under Title XVI of the Social Security Act is found at Title 20 C.F.R. § 416.920 and mirrors that for claims made under Title II. Subsections §§ 404.1520 and 416.920 address each of the five steps:

❑ §§ 404.1520(b) and 416.920(b)	Step 1	Are you working?
❑ §§ 404.1520(c) and 416.920(c)	Step 2	You must have a severe impairment.
❑ §§ 404.1520(d) and 416.920(d)	Step 3	When your impairment(s) meets or equals a listed impairment in Appendix I.
❑ §§ 404.1520(e) and 416.920(e)	Step 4	Your impairment(s) must prevent you from doing past relevant work.
❑ §§ 404.1520(f) and 416.920(f)	Step 5	Your impairment(s) must prevent you from doing any other competitive work.

Each step is described and defined in greater detail at various sections within the regulations, as set forth in Figure 5–6. Similar related regulations are found for each of the sequential steps within the SSI or Title XVI regulations, as shown in Figure 5–7.

Back to Chris

Five steps, Chris thought. *Each one seems logical. At least, once you understand the reasons behind them. What was that? Oh, "public policy."*

Slowly Chris began to feel more comfortable with the material. *I can do this. I know I can.*

Part 404 Steps 1–5	Descriptive Regulation(s)
Step 1 (substantial gainful activity)	§§ 401.1510 and 404.1571–404.1576
Step 2 (severe impairment)	§§ 404.1508 and 404.1509
Step 3 (listing of impairments)	§§ 404.1511, 404.1529(d)(2) and (3)
Step 4 (past relevant work and RFC)	§§ 404.1545, 404.1565, and 404.1566–404.1568
Step 5 (other less demanding work)	§§ 404.1569–404.1569a and 404.1573

Figure 5–6 **Regulatory Basis for the 5-step SEP under Title II (Disability Insurance)**

Part 416 Steps 1–5	Descriptive Regulation(s)
Step 1 (substantial gainful activity)	§§416.910 and 416.971–416.976
Step 2 (severe impairment)	§§416.908 and 416.909
Step 3 (listings of impairments)	§§416.911, 416.929(d)(2) and (3)
Step 4 (past relevant work and RFC)	§§416.945, 416.965, and 416.966–416.968
Step 5 (other less demanding work)	§§416.969–416.969a and §416.973

Figure 5–7 **Regulatory Basis for the 5-step SEP under Title Sixteen (SSI)**

WHAT IF . . . ? SAMPLE PROBLEMS

WHAT IF . . .

What if your client has a severe impairment that meets a listed impairment at step 3 of the sequential evaluation process but is working full time, above SGA levels?

1. No problem. If the listing is met, work does not matter.
2. More information is needed about the job before a final conclusion can be reached.
3. More information is needed about the impairment before a final conclusion can be reached.
4. Case denied. Your client's working.

Discussion

If an individual is working at SGA levels, then the *sequential* nature of the analysis demands that that issue be considered first, at step 1 of the evaluation. Generally, an individual who is working at SGA levels is precluded from disability because the public policy underlying the program is defeated in the first instance—that is, a person who is working and able to support himself or herself does not need the support of a disability payment.

There are certain limited exceptions. If an individual is working at SGA levels he or she may be in the midst of a trial work period. This is defined at Title 20 C.F.R. § 404.1592 and is a no penalty provision. This section effectively operates to encourage people to try and return to work, even though disabled. The regulations consider it a chance "to test your ability to work and still be considered disabled."

The trial work period is only available, however, for a limited time within the period of disability. Specifically, an individual is entitled to nine months trial work without penalty. After the nine-month period the person may be found to no longer have a disability. During the nine-month period the individual is entitled to receive *both* the disability payment *and* the money earned from working. (See Title 20 C.F.R. § 404.1592.)

Answer: ***The correct answer is 1. You need more information about the job to reach the correct conclusion.***

- ❑ How long has the individual been working at SGA levels?
- ❑ Is work continuing, or did it end?

❑ Was there a period in which there was no work, followed by the present position?
❑ Or, is this simply an anticipatory filing? Is the person still working at an old job but anticipates becoming unable to do so in the near future? If so, disability cannot be granted, because it cannot be prospectively granted. If the individual has worked at this level for longer than nine months, the trial work period does not apply.

The other possibility is that the work may have been an unsuccessful work attempt. In order to so qualify, however, the work must already have ended when the application for disability is filed. Here, the work is ongoing, so an unsuccessful work attempt does not apply. An unsuccessful work attempt is an attempt to return to work, lasting no longer than ninety days, and ended as a result of the impairment(s) which underlie the claim for disability.

WHAT IF . . .

At what step of the five-step sequential evaluation process may an individual be found disabled if disability is alleged as a result of obesity?

1. Step 2: There is a severe impairment.
2. Step 3: Obesity meets a listing.
3. Steps 1 and 2.
4. Step 5: The individual's RFC, because of obesity, limits him or her to less than sedentary work, therefore, he or she is unable to engage in competitive work activity.

Discussion

Obesity, with the attendant symptoms was, until recently, an impairment in the Listing of Impairments (former Medical Listing 9.09). However, the Social Security Administration rescinded obesity as a listed impairment, determining instead, that obesity is a potentially severe impairment, giving rise to limitations of function, as other, severe impairments.

Because obesity is no longer a listed impairment the decision cannot be made at step 3. Proper evaluation requires an RFC at steps 4 and 5 because benefits cannot be granted at step 5 unless the judge determines that the individual cannot return to past relevant work at step 4. An individual who can perform at less than sedentary levels is generally not capable of competitive work; hence, likely to be awarded benefits.

Answer: 4.

WHAT IF . . .

What if your client meets a listing at step 3. Do you still have to formulate an RFC?

1. Absolutely. An RFC is the heart of any disability analysis; this is the only way to quantify the claimant's limitations.
2. Possibly. It depends on the nature of the listing being met. The listing itself may require you to quantify the claimant's limitations.
3. No. Meeting the listing at step 3 eliminates the need for a formal RFC assessment at step 4 because of the sequential nature of the analysis.
4. No. Meeting the listing results in a denial of benefits.

Discussion

The five-step analysis which undergirds the disability determination process is sequential in nature, meaning that one step proceeds only after the preceding step fails to yield a disposition. Thus, if the impairment is healed before twelve months have elapsed, the claim is denied as nonsevere—that is, the claimant does not suffer from a severe impairment—one that lasts twelve months or more. The case then ends at step 2.

Similarly, if it is determined that the claimant's condition is so grave as to be attended with each of the required symptoms necessary to meet a listed impairment, no functional analysis need be made. It is presumed, as a matter of public policy, that an individual suffering from an impairment with documented symptoms, medical signs, and laboratory findings as described within the regulations will, by definition, be functionally restricted to less than competitive work.

See Title 20 C.F.R. § 404.1520(a) (stating in part, "If we can find that you are disabled or not disabled at any point in the review, we do not review your claim further.")

Answer: *3*

---

[1]See 20 C.F.R. § 404.1520.

[2]Such an inquiry is appropriate and part of the analysis at step 4 (euphemistically, step 3.5) of the analysis.

[3]See Title 20 C.F.R. § 404.1567, which describes these "physical exertion requirements" within the regulations for Title II claims. Title 20 C.F.R. § 416.967 describes these same "physical exertion requirements" for Title XVI or SSI claims.

[4]What follows is a selection found in various SSA publications, descriptive of each of the five steps.

[5]Prior to the enactment of new regulations in January 2001, the presumptive earnings floor was $700 per month. Additionally, if a person were earning less than $300 per month, it was presumed they were not engaged in SGA. Earning between $300 and $700 per month was a gray area: whether earnings constituted SGA was made on a case-by-case basis. The January 2001 regulations eliminated the $300 presumption and the gray area by declaring that earning below $740 per month did not constitute SGA. The earnings limit was again raised to $740.00 per month in January 2002.

[6]Thus, during a trial work period a disabled individual who is receiving benefits may continue to receive benefits and the pay from the trial work.

[7]In all likelihood, however, such a record will require further development and will be referred to one or more consultative examiners (who are acceptable medical sources) because the presence of chiropractic evidence gives rise to a reasonable belief that there may be other, medically determinable impairment(s) present. Consultative examinations by physicians or psychologists approved by SSA (and scheduled through the state DDS) are paid for by SSA and can form the basis for an award. Consultative examinations (CEs) are also conducted when an individual cannot or has not been able to afford to see a doctor and thus has not longitudinal medical history or diagnosis.

[8]Title 20 C.F.R. § 404.1520(a).

6

CHAPTER SIX

Step 1: Substantial Gainful Activity

HIGHLIGHTS

- ❑ Definitions of substantial, gainful, and activity

CHRIS

Chris pressed the Open Door button just in time for Steve to squeeze into the elevator. "Thanks," wheezed Steve. "It would have taken another fifteen minutes for this elevator to get back to the ground floor. I need to get the exhibits for the Jones case and then go to the courthouse."

Hesitating slightly, Chris said, "I put a conflicts memo on your desk about a possible new client with a Social Security disability claim. Mr. Carson referred him to me."

Steve looked up from a file folder in surprise. "That's great! Mr. Carson must think you're doing a good job on his case."

Chris shrugged. "Mr. Fiske is a friend of Mr. Carson's, but his case may not be as good as Mr. Carson's. Mr. Fiske told me that he has gone back to work several times since his back injury, and he's working part time now. I thought people couldn't get benefits if they were working."

Steve nodded as they stepped out of the elevator. "The regulations call it 'substantial gainful activity.' But in all the Social Security claims I've heard about, the person had stopped working because of a medical condition. Substantial gainful activity wasn't really an issue in those cases."

"Well, it seems as if it will be in Mr. Fiske's case. I'll look up those regulations before Mr. Fiske stops in tomorrow on his way home from work to talk to me. I'll get more details from him then about his case," said Chris, heading for the coffee machine.

"Great!" Steve replied as he left for the courthouse.

FRONT OF YOUR MIND QUESTIONS AND CONSIDERATIONS, 6.1

Chris has recognized that, in applying for Social Security disability benefits, the applicant represents an inability to work because of a medical condition. Chris understandably views Mr. Fiske's part-time employment as inconsistent with his application for disability benefits.

But is all work activity prohibited in order to be entitled to disability benefits? What about someone, such as Mr. Fiske, who tries to work on a part-time basis? What about work for which a person receives little, or in the case of volunteer work, no money at all? What about a person who attempts to work after filing an application for DIB or SSI benefits, only to find in a matter of days, weeks, or even months, that their medical impairments prevent him or her from working at the pace an employer has set?

As Steve indicated, the key concept in which SSA addresses issues of work and disability is "substantial gainful activity" (SGA, in acronym-ese). As discussed in the previous chapter, the first step in the sequential evaluation process requires a determination of whether the applicant is engaged in SGA. If the applicant's work activity is determined to qualify as SGA, a decision can be issued denying the applicant disability benefits without going through the remaining steps of the sequential evaluation process. Thus, any work activity in which a client engages after filing a disability benefits application should be reviewed under SSA's guidelines for SGA prior to the hearing to avoid becoming a step 1 denial. Take A Trip to the Hard Drive to learn more about SGA.

A TRIP TO THE HARD DRIVE, 6.1

The first step in the sequential evaluation process concerns earnings within the claimed period of disability—that is, the time the claimant claims to be disabled. Explore the ramifications of monies received during this time with *A Trip to the Hard Drive.*

INTRODUCTION TO SUBSTANTIAL GAINFUL ACTIVITY (SGA)

Generally, SSA's regulations define SGA as work that is both substantial and gainful. However, further definitions of *substantial* and *gainful* are provided in the regulations to help determine what constitutes SGA. Substantial work activity involves significant physical or mental activities. Work may be considered substantial even if it is performed on a part-time basis or the individual does less, is paid less, or has less responsibility than in a previous job or occupation. Gainful is defined as work activity that is usually performed for pay or profit, regardless of whether profit is actually realized.

Certain activities generally are not considered SGA, such as taking care of one's personal needs; performing household tasks for oneself or family members; or engaging in hobbies, physical therapy, school attendance, or club meetings.

Activities an individual performs that result in income may be SGA, even though such activities are not within traditional concepts of work activity. Illegal activities, for example, may be considered SGA. The federal courts have upheld SSA's decisions that performance of criminal activity can constitute engaging in SGA. In *Dotson v. Sullivan* (813 F. Supp. 651 [C.D. Ill. 1992]), the U.S. District Court upheld the ALJ's determination that the claimant was "earning" approximately $5,600 a month based on his testimony that his drug habit cost him between $200 and $300 a day, which he supported by "hustling," begging, or stealing. The district court agreed with the ALJ's finding that the amount of income the claimant "earned" while "hustling" demonstrated that the claimant engaged in SGA. The district court affirmed the ALJ's denial of disability benefits at step 1 of the sequential evaluation process.

SSA uses the amount of monthly earnings received by a claimant as an objective measure of SGA. SSA regulations at Title 20 C.F.R. §§ 404.1574(b)(2) and 416.974(b)(2) provide guidelines for determining the amount of monthly earnings that constitute SGA. After 1989, earnings of more than $500 a month are deemed to be generally indicative of SGA. In 1999, SSA raised the SGA limit from $500 to $700 a month. In 2000, SSA proposed that an automatic adjustment be made to the SGA threshold amount based on any increase in the national average wage index. Beginning in January 2001, the SGA threshold amount is the larger of either the previous year's threshold amount or an increased amount based on the Social Security national average wage index. Thus, in 2001, the monthly SGA earnings limit increased to $740; and in 2002, to $780.

Currently, SSA's regulations at Title 20 C.F.R. §§ 404.1574(b)(3) and 416.974(b)(3) define any monthly income below $300 as not indicative of SGA. If an applicant's monthly earnings fall between $300 (not SGA presumption) and $780 (presumed SGA), the regulations provide that other factors must be considered in determining whether the applicant is engaging in SGA. First, it must be determined whether the applicant's work is comparable to that of unimpaired individuals in the community doing the same or similar work, including similar time, skills, energy, and responsibility. Second, is the work, though significantly less than that done by unimpaired individuals, worth the amount presumed to be consistent with SGA ($780 per month)?

In 2000, SSA eliminated the $300 floor indicative of not SGA. Any earnings below $780, or the yearly adjusted wage index amount will be considered not SGA.

In computing monthly earnings to evaluate SGA, SSA subtracts the reasonable costs to the applicant of certain items and services needed by the applicant to perform the work. These expenses are known as impairment-related work expenses (IRWE). For example, medication the applicant takes to prevent seizures may be subtracted from the applicant's amount of monthly earnings when calculating SGA as an IRWE.

If earnings vary from month to month and are below the earnings limit, the earnings are averaged over the actual period of time worked. If, for example, Mr. Fiske worked part time for five months, earning $650 the first month, but only $450 the remaining four months, Mr. Fiske's total earnings would be averaged over the five month period, resulting in average monthly earning of $490. Would Mr. Fiske be presumed to be engaged in SGA based on this amount of average earnings for the five-month period of part-time work?

If the applicant's work is subsidized or performed in a sheltered workshop, different guidelines apply to the amounts earned by the applicant. Of the applicant's total earnings, only the part of pay that is actually earned is considered; pay representing subsidized earnings is not considered SGA. Social Security ruling 83-33 provides additional guidance for determining how subsidized earnings are counted. The regulations at Title 20 C.F.R. §§ 404.1574(a)(3) and (b)(3) and Title 20 C.F.R. §§ 416.974(a)(3) and (b)(3) provide guidelines evaluating earnings for sheltered work. Typically, however, an applicant who is working in a sheltered workshop will have earnings below the regulatory guideline levels.

In evaluating whether an applicant's work activity can be presumed to be SGA, SSA considers several factors. One important consideration is whether the job requires the applicant's experience, education, and skill, and requires supervision of others. If the applicant's expertise contributes substantially to the operation of the business, SSA may regard the applicant as capable of performing SGA. Another factor SSA considers is how well the applicant performs the job. Does the applicant require special working conditions or special assistance from the employer to perform the job? If, because of the impairment, the applicant cannot perform the ordinary or simple tasks typically performed by others doing similar work without accommodations from the employer, SSA will likely consider the applicant's work not to be SGA. Similarly, if the applicant performs work with minimal duties that make little or no demands on the applicant and that are of little or no use to the employer or to the operation of the business, the applicant's work activity will likely not be considered SGA by SSA.

Self-Employed Work Activity as SGA

Because a self-employed individual generally has control over the manner in which they are paid and the amount of earnings they report to SSA, the agency takes a different approach to determining whether a self-employed applicant is engaging in SGA. In these cases, SSA considers such factors as the applicant's hours, skills, energy output, efficiency, duties, and responsibilities. SSA then compares those factors to those of unimpaired individuals in the same community in the same or similar business.

If SSA finds the applicant's use of time, skills, and responsibilities comparable to that of an unimpaired person within a similar business, SSA will conclude that the applicant is engaging in SGA. Even if the applicant's work activity is not comparable, if it is clearly worth the amount specified in the regulatory guidelines as indicative of SGA for employed individuals in its value to the business or when compared to the salary an employer would pay to an employee to do the kind of work performed by the applicant, SSA will conclude that the applicant is engaging in SGA.

In determining SGA, SSA also considers whether the applicant renders significant services and receives substantial income from the business. Significance of services is determined by the applicant's participation in the business. If the applicant operates the business alone, any services provided are considered significant. If more than one person is involved in the business, the applicant's services are deemed significant if she or he contributes more than one-half of the total time required to manage the business. The applicant's services are also considered significant if she or he provides management services for more than forty-five hours a month.

Substantial income includes net income from the business. Normal business expenses are deducted from gross income, followed by deductions of the reasonable value of unpaid help and impairment-related work expenses. The resulting amount derived from these calculations is considered substantial if it averages more than the amounts in the regulatory guidelines indicating SGA for employed persons. However, even if the resulting amount averages less than that specified in the regulatory guidelines for SGA, if the amount is either comparable to what it was before the applicant became disabled or to that earned by unimpaired persons in the same or similar business, SSA will consider the applicant engaging in SGA.

BACK TO CHRIS

Chris reviewed the notes from Mr. Fiske's telephone call scribbled on the legal pad. Mr. Fiske called to tell Chris that he and his employer had reached a mutual understanding to end Mr. Fiske's part-time job.

Mr. Fiske told Chris that even the limited amount of bending and stooping his employer had required of him had proved to be too much for his lower back. The employer believed that Mr. Fiske could not maintain even the slow pace allowed for him. Mr. Fiske reported that he had received his last paycheck and was trying to see his doctor because his lower back was so painful.

According to Chris's notes, Mr. Fiske had worked two months and one week, for twenty-five hours a week. Mr. Fiske promised to bring his paycheck stubs so Chris could determine whether Mr. Fiske's monthly earnings qualified as SGA.

It doesn't seem fair, thought Chris, *that Mr. Fiske at least tried to work, but his back pain kept him from doing even the easy duties assigned to him. His employer seems to have given Mr. Fiske every opportunity to keep working, but he couldn't because of the back pain. What if he has enough earnings to qualify as SGA? Will the brief amount of time Mr. Fiske worked short-circuit his disability claim?*

A TRIP TO THE HARD DRIVE, 6.2

Learn about work attempts with *A Trip to the Hard Drive.*

WHAT IF I TRY TO WORK?

Financial or other reasons may cause an applicant to try to resume work after filing for disability benefits. However, sometimes the applicant's impairment, the symptoms produced by the impairment, the side effects of prescribed medication, or the effects of a prescribed treatment regimen prevent the applicant from working more than a few days, a few weeks, or a few months. SSA recognizes these short-term efforts to work as unsuccessful work attempts (UWA). If the applicant continues to work but the level of earnings is below the SGA threshold, the work may still be considered UWA.

UNSUCCESSFUL WORK ATTEMPTS

The first step in establishing a UWA is whether there was a significant break in the continuity of the applicant's usual work activity. Typically, the applicant ceases usual employment for a period of time while coping with the effects, or the treatment, of an impairment. An applicant may believe that a medical condition has stabilized and that work activity may be resumed. In general, a break in continuity of work activity is considered significant if the applicant did not work for at least thirty days. A significant break in continuity of work activity may also be found if the applicant was forced to find another type of work or another employer because of an impairment.[1]

Second, a UWA is evaluated in terms of duration. A work attempt for three months or less, even though performed at the SGA level of earnings, is considered a UWA. A work attempt lasting from three to six months at the SGA level, however, requires evaluation of certain additional factors. SSA considers whether the work attempt was performed during a temporary remission of the impairment or under special conditions the employer permitted to enable the applicant to continue the work attempt. SSA also considers whether the applicant had frequent absences or otherwise performed unsatisfactorily during the work attempt because of the impairment. In almost all cases, a work attempt lasting longer than six months is not considered a UWA regardless of why the applicant stopped working.

In evaluating unsuccessful work attempts, remember that the applicant's impairment, and its related symptoms and limitations, must be the reason the applicant stopped working after such a short time. In Mr. Fiske's case, for example, he appears to have an impairment of degenerative disc disease of the lumbar spine. Mr. Fiske stopped working because the pain in his lower back was worsening, and his employer found that

Mr. Fiske could not keep up with the pace of work. If Mr. Fiske had been fired for reasons other than those related to his medical condition, such as theft or a security breach of information, it is unlikely that Mr. Fiske could claim his short period of employment as an unsuccessful work attempt.

TRIAL WORK PERIOD

An applicant who works longer than six months will unlikely be able to claim that period of employment as an unsuccessful work attempt but may be able to claim it as a trial work period even though work was performed at the SGA level of earnings. SSA introduced the trial work period in 1992 as a means of giving disabled individuals the opportunity to test their ability to work without fear of losing their disability benefits eligibility or having their benefit payments suspended.[2]

The trial work period is a nine-month period of work activity for an applicant who has not medically recovered from a disabling impairment. The nine months are not necessarily consecutive, but they do have to occur within a consecutive sixty-month period before the trial work period is considered completed. Any work performed in the nine-month trial period cannot be considered by SSA as evidence of the ability to perform SGA, thereby terminating disability benefits. However, SSA can consider other evidence, such as improved medical condition, occurring during the nine-month trial period as a reason to terminate benefits.

Only DIB applicants can claim a trial work period. The SSI benefit program does not permit its applicants to claim a trial work period. The trial work period cannot begin earlier than the first month of entitlement to DIB benefits or the month in which the DIB application is filed, whichever is later. The trial work period ends in the ninth month of trial work or in the month in which disability ceases, whichever is earlier. At the end of the ninth month, the applicant's case is reviewed to ascertain whether the disability is continuing.

A trial work month is any month in which earnings for employed applicants, or net earnings for self-employed applicants, are more than $200 for years after 1989. In January 2001, that limit was raised to $530 per month. In future years SSA will make annual changes to the limit based on the national average wage index.

Alternatively, a month in which a self-employed applicant works more than forty hours may be considered a trial work month. The work performed by the applicant does not have to be SGA in that month in order to be considered a trial work month. Work performed in the nine-month period must be for pay or profit; volunteer work, therapy, training, daily personal care, and household tasks are not considered work activity which triggers the running of the nine-month period. The work activity must be performed with some regularity over a reasonable amount of time to trigger the nine-month trial period.

The applicant is limited to one trial work period only during a given 60 month time. If the applicant had a previous period of disability, for which employment as a trial work period was claimed, a second trial work period in any subsequent period of disability cannot be claimed. Any work performed by the applicant in a subsequent period of disability can be used as evidence of the ability to engage in SGA.

However, SSA permits those who have completed their nine-month trial work period to continue to attempt to work with a fifteen-month reentitlement period. During those fifteen months, the DIB recipient can receive benefits for any month in which there is not SGA. If the DIB recipient stops working completely, the person can be reinstated and resume receiving monthly benefits without having to reapply.

SSA's policy has been that a claimant cannot claim a trial work period if she or he returns to work at the SGA level after filing an application for DIB but before being awarded those benefits. SSA has historically viewed the trial work period as available only to those claimants who were already receiving DIB when they attempted to go back to work. However, the federal courts have disagreed with SSA's interpretation of the statutory and regulatory provisions governing the start of a trial work period. Several courts have held that the trial work period can begin during the period of time the claimant was *entitled to* benefits but not actually *receiving* benefits.

Thus, a claimant who attempts to work after filing a DIB application, but before a final decision is issued on the entitlement to DIB benefits by SSA, may claim that work attempt as a trial work period. Moreover, the courts have held that SSA cannot consider any work performed in the nine-month trial work period as evidence of the claimant's ability to return to work when adjudicating whether the claimant is disabled. The courts, however, agree with SSA that the trial work period provisions do not apply to work the applicant performed before filing an application for DIB benefits.

BACK TO CHRIS

Chris stretched, a glimmer of something tickling his thoughts. *There was something about working, and I can't remember what it was.*

Somewhere an office door closed with a slam.

That's it! A closed period of disability. I need to find out what that is.

A TRIP TO THE HARD DRIVE, 6.3

Explore the significance of a closed period by taking *A Trip to the Hard Drive.*

CLOSED PERIOD OF DISABILITY

If a client continues to work after the trial work period has ended, or if a client has returned to work after filing an SSI application, he or she still may be entitled to disability benefits under Title II or Title XVI. It may be argued that a claimant is entitled to a closed period of disability, beginning on the date of the alleged onset of disability and ending with sufficient medical improvement in the condition, enabling the claimant to return to SGA by a particular date.

The closed period of disability claimed must be supported by medical evidence of disability and must have lasted at least twelve months. The advantage in claiming a closed period of disability, rather than simply dismissing the case, is that payment will be received for past due benefits for the closed period, and the accumulated quarters of coverage on the earnings record will be frozen so that insured status will not be lost for Title II by not having worked during the closed period.

BACK TO CHRIS

Something Mr. Fiske had said nagged at Chris. What was it? Then Chris remembered that Mr. Fiske had mentioned another job he had tried soon after his back surgery. Mr. Fiske tried to work as a telephone solicitor, calling people to sell subscriptions to a special-interest newspaper. Mr. Fiske had worked from his home and received $.50 for each subscription he sold over the phone. He worked four hours a day, five days a week, for four weeks, and sold 130 subscriptions in that time.

Mr. Fiske had been discouraged by how little he earned and was thinking of quitting, when the company publishing the newspaper went out of business and the owners left town. Mr. Fiske received only one "paycheck" and could not remember the small amount of that check. He was fairly sure that he had not received all he was owed when the company folded.

How can I find out what Mr. Fiske made on that job? Chris wondered. *The newspaper publisher is not available to ask, and I'll bet their records are not available either. It's probably not SGA, but I would like to make sure. Plus, Mr. Fiske has been taking that pain medication, which makes him drowsy. Maybe he is forgetting other work attempts he has made. How do I find that information?* Chris went to find Steve for some advice.

FRONT OF YOUR MIND QUESTIONS AND CONSIDERATIONS, 6.2

In Chapter 3, we discussed the use of the summary earnings report to verify if an applicant had enough quarters of coverage to qualify him or her for insured status for DIB benefits. We also learned that the applicant and representative can request the Field Office to run a query on the SSA databases, called a Summary Earnings Query (SEQY, see-quee), to generate that summary earnings report. The SEQY is also useful for identifying potential SGA issues for a client. Either the representative or the client can request the Field Office claims representatives to run a SEQY if the client's claim is at the initial or reconsideration stage. If the client's claim is at the Office of Hearings and Appeals, a SEQY may have already been run and placed in the case file in preparation for the ALJ's review of the case prior to the actual hearing. If so, the SEQY can be photocopied in the OHA case file. After obtaining the SEQY copy from either the Field Office or the OHA office, review it with the client to ensure all periods of employment are indicated by the annual earnings figures on the report.

But what if the client is like Mr. Fiske and may have several periods of attempted employment with small earnings for each period? The SEQY's totaled annual earning figures may or may not help your client identify all past work efforts.

SSA provides another report of the claimant's work history by year and employer for all earnings reported to SSA by the employers. This report is known as a Detailed Earnings Report and is generated from SSA databases using a Detailed Earnings Query (DEQY, dee-quee). An example of a DEQY is provided in Figure 6–1.

Thus, it is possible to discover the claimant's earnings even he or she cannot recall or otherwise be of assistance.

Detail Covered FICA Earnings and Employer Name and Address for Years Requested

RPYR	REO	EIN-SEI	LOAC NAME	EARNINGS	TOTAL COMP
0095		0000000	A Claimant	8665.07	8665.07
			Wage Total	8665.07	
			Employer Total	8665.07	
		EIN 000000			
		100 Main St.			
		Aroundtown, NY	00200-0000		
		1111	A Claimant	750.99	750.99
			Wage Total	750.99	
			Employer Total	750.99	
		EIN 11111			
		Giant Company			
		200 Main St.			
		Aroundtown, NY	00200-0000		
			95 Yearly Total 9416.06		
0096		0000000	A Claimant	9565.01	9565.01
			Wage Total	9565.01	
			Employer Total	9565.01	
		0000000 Big Company			
			96 Yearly Total 9565.01		
0097		2222	A Claimant	1027.86	1027.86
			Wage Total	1027.86	
			Employer Total	1027.86	
		EIN 2222			
		Super Company			
		300 Main St.			
		Aroundtown, NY	00200-0000		
		33333	A Claimant	65.41	65.41
			Wage Total	65.41	
			Employer Total	65.41	
		EIN 3333			
		Tiny Company			
		400 Main St.			
		Aroundtown, NY	00200-0000		
		44444	A Claimant	9611.54	9611.54
			Wage Total	9611.54	
			Employer Total	9611.54	
		EIN 44444			
		Good Company			
		500 Main St.			
		Aroundtown, NY	00200-0000		
			97 Yearly Total 10704.81		

Figure 6–1 **Sample SSA Detailed Earnings Query (DEQY)**

WHAT IF . . . ? SAMPLE PROBLEMS

WHAT IF . . .

Can Chris determine, based on the information provided by Mr. Fiske, whether Mr. Fiske's return to part-time work was SGA or an unsuccessful work attempt? What other information will Chris need from either Mr. Fiske or his ex-employer to be able to make that determination?

Answer: No. Chris will need to obtain Mr. Fiske's actual job description, including hours worked, tasks performed, and monies earned.

WHAT IF . . .

Mr. Accountant is fifty-five years old and had a major heart attack on September 15, requiring coronary artery bypass surgery. After several months of recuperation and physical therapy, he decided to file for Social Security benefits. He filed his Title II application on November 30. On December 10, Mr. Accountant returned to his office and worked five days a week, eight hours a day. During this time, however, Mr. Accountant experienced episodes of chest pain and shortness of breath, and he finally stopped working at his office on December 31.

On January 15, Mr. Accountant's old friend, Herbert Black, asked Mr. Accountant to help him during tax season and work part time preparing tax returns. Mr. Accountant was glad to help his old friend, provided he could take his two-hour nap each afternoon. From mid-January to mid-April, Mr. Accountant worked twenty-five hours a week and earned about $250 each week. After April 15, Mr. Black closed his office, bid his friend Mr. Accountant good-bye, and took his yearly trip to the Bahamas to recover from the stress of the tax season. On May 5, Mr. Accountant, and you, as his representative, received a notice to appear before the administrative law judge for a hearing on Mr. Accountant's claim for Title II disability benefits.

1. What will you argue is Mr. Accountant's disability onset date, and why?

Answer: The onset date is September 15. The return to work, arguably an UWA, began after the filing, and ceased within one month, because of symptoms related to the allegedly disabling impairment.

2. Is the period from December 10 to December 31, when Mr. Accountant worked at his job at his office, an unsuccessful work attempt?

Answer: Yes. It lasted less than 90 days, and work ceased because of symptoms related to the impairment.

3. Is the period from mid-January to mid-April, when Mr. Accountant prepared tax returns, an unsuccessful work attempt?

Answer: No. Mr. Accountant did not cease work because of symptoms related to his impairment. He stopped because Mr. Black closed the office after tax season.

4. What other information would you obtain when interviewing Mr. Accountant about his work activity after his disability application claim?

Answer: You need to know his earnings in December. In January you already know how much he worked, how much he made and that he needed special accommodations not otherwise given to regular employees (lying down to take a nap).

WHAT IF . . .

Ms. Baird works on an assembly line, soldering parts in electronic devices. She sustained a serious left leg fracture in an automobile accident on March 29, which required extensive reconstructive surgery on the lower portion of that leg. With a cast and crutches, Ms. Baird is able to return to her job on April 20. She is given a modified job assignment, which allows her to do some of her duties while sitting down and slightly elevating her left leg.

Ms. Baird performs her modified duties in this manner until May 10, when an undiagnosed injury to her right shoulder from the car accident is aggravated by the use of the crutches and prevents her from using her dominant right hand to reach and move the parts she is supposed to solder. Also, on May 10, X-rays reveal nonunion of the fractured leg. Ms. Baird is now scheduled for surgeries on her right shoulder and left leg. Her physician has advised her that she will need several months off from work for a good recovery from her surgeries. Ms. Baird's employer, who was in the middle of downsizing its workforce, laid off Ms. Baird on May 26.

1. What will you argue is Ms. Baird's disability onset date?

Answer: You can argue her onset is the date of the accident because she never returned to competitive work afterward.

2. How will you characterize the period from March 29 to April 20? From May 10 to May 26?

Answer: From March 29 to April 20 is a period of disability, provided her incapacity lasts 12 months from the date of the accident. From May 10 to May 26 is an UVW because Ms. Baird had to leave work because of symptoms related to her impairment and the work lasted less than 90 days.

WHAT IF . . .

Mr. Jones has been diagnosed with psychiatric problems, which make him unable to return to his previous job and prevent him from working with the general public, according to his treating psychiatrist. He is scheduled for his hearing with an administrative law judge. When you photocopy the DEQY in his case file at the Office of Hearings and Appeals, you discover that Mr. Jones's father, who owns a small company, has been claiming his son as an employee in order to provide Mr. Jones with funds until he is determined entitled to disability benefits. The amounts Mr. Jones has been "paid" may exceed the amount considered to be SGA.

In response to your phone call, Mr. Jones states that he never goes to the company plant other than to get his check and that he does not provide any service for the company.

What documentation or testimony will you need to take to the hearing to show that Mr. Jones's applications for benefits should not be denied at step 1?

Answer: The "best evidence" is the testimony of the father, describing the special arrangement he has to "pay" his son. Additionally, an unrelated employee from the plant can be offered to corroborate the father's testimony. Alternately, the testimony of the son, accompanied by an affidavit or declaration of the father explaining the circumstances can be offered. The key issue here is the failure of the son to actually earn the money by engaging in work or work-like activity. In reality, the father was making a gift of the salary.

[1]See 20 C.F.R. § 404.1574(c).

[2]See 20 C.F.R. § 404.1592.

7

Chapter Seven

Step 2: Severe Impairments and Basic Work Activities

Highlights

- ❑ Step 2 in the sequential evaluation
- ❑ Severe defined
- ❑ Impairment defined

Chris

Steve waved Chris over to the second seat at the small table. The coffee shop at noon was busy, but not crowded. David, the waiter, brought Chris a menu and acknowledged that the noon business was because of a waitstaff shortage, not because of an excess of customers.

"Sadie is out today," David said, waiting with pencil poised to take Chris's sandwich order. "She had a doctor's appointment today, but I don't think she will be working here much longer. Or anywhere else, for that matter. She's sixty years old, and her medical problems are catching up with her."

"Ham on rye. What's wrong with Sadie?" asked Steve, scanning the day's soup selections.

"Oh, you name it," shrugged David. "She's seeing the doctor today for her hands. They cramp up on her when she is trying to write the orders. She also has a problem with her back since she slipped and fell on the kitchen floor a couple of months ago. Her back 'catches' on her. Although she stopped smoking a couple of years ago, she wheezes. She has to stop and use the inhaler medicine her doctor gives her. I think she has a cataract in her right eye, too."

"Sadie won't qualify for retirement benefits at age sixty," Chris thought out loud. "Didn't she have to leave school when she was in the sixth grade to help her family?"

"Yeah," said David. "She's really worried about what she will live on until she's sixty-two."

"Give Sadie your card," prodded Steve. "Chris is helping some of our other clients with their Social Security disability benefits claims. Maybe Chris can help Sadie."

Chris handed a business card to David. "I would be glad to talk to Sadie, if she wants to. She can come to the office and bring any medical records or doctor's bills with her."

"I'll give Sadie your card," promised David.

Sadie called Chris the next day. Her doctor had diagnosed arthritis in her finger joints and right shoulder. The doctor recommended that Sadie stop working as a waitress; the constant use of her hands and shoulder aggravated the pain and other symptoms related to her arthritis.

"I would have lost my job anyway," lamented Sadie. "The cook couldn't read my writing on the order tickets, and I was dropping dishes when my hands started cramping and hurting so much."

Sadie agreed to go to the Field Office and file an application for disability benefits. Chris made an appointment to meet with Sadie about her disability case.

FRONT OF YOUR MIND QUESTIONS AND CONSIDERATIONS, 7.1

Chris knows Sadie stopped working because of her medical conditions. From the little Chris knows, Sadie seems to have several medical conditions that either prevent or hinder her from performing her duties as a waitress. At step 2 of the sequential evaluation process, Chris must determine if Sadie's medical conditions would be considered by SSA to be "severe." The question is then, what criteria does SSA use to determine if a medical condition is "severe" at step 2?

Recall from earlier discussions that step 2 is not a "pay" step; proving that a medical condition is "severe" does not qualify a claimant for benefits. However, step 2 *is* a "denial" step, because benefits can be denied if the claimant fails to demonstrate at least one medical condition that SSA considers "severe." The claimant and the representative can avoid a denial decision at step 2 by ensuring the case file contains all the pertinent medical records documenting the claimant's various impairments.

A TRIP TO THE HARD DRIVE, 7.1

Take *A Trip to the Hard Drive* to discover the difference among impairments, symptoms, and limitations.

DISTINGUISHING AMONG IMPAIRMENTS, SYMPTOMS, AND LIMITATIONS

In Chapter 5, we discussed the distinction that SSA makes among impairments, symptoms, and limitations. An *impairment* is a physical or mental medical condition or illness. To qualify for disability, SSA requires the claimant to demonstrate that a "medically determinable physical or mental impairment," resulting from anatomical, physiological, or psychological abnormalities that are demonstrable by medically acceptable clinical and laboratory diagnostic techniques.[1]

Impairments give rise to *symptoms*, manifestations of how the impairment affects the body, such as pain, numbness, dizziness, or shortness of breath. SSA describes a symptom as a "medical finding," with signs and laboratory findings. It is the claimant's "own description" of a physical or mental impairment, which in itself cannot establish the existence of a physical or mental impairment.[2] SSA defines *signs* as anatomical, physiological, or psychological abnormalities that can be observed independent of the claimant's statements.[3] An example of the difference is a muscle spasm; it can be described by the claimant (a symptom) but can also be observed by the physician (a sign). Signs must be apparent using medically acceptable clinical diagnostic techniques. Psychiatric signs are medically acceptable phenomena that indicate specific abnormalities of behavior, affect, thought, memory, orientation, and contact with reality. Psychiatric signs must also be apparent by observable facts that can be medically described and evaluated.

SSA defines *laboratory findings* as anatomical, physiological, or psychological phenomena that are apparent using medically acceptable laboratory diagnostic techniques, such as chemical tests, X-rays, and psychological tests. Other acceptable tests include electrophysical studies, such as electrocardiogram and electroencephalogram.[4]

Limitations are the way in which the symptoms affect how an individual performs physical or mental activities. Recall from Chapter 5 that SSA separates limitations into two categories: "exertional" and "nonexertional," according to an individual's ability to perform physical or mental work activities. "Exertional" limitations affect the individual's ability to meet the seven strength demands of jobs (sitting, standing, walking, lifting, carrying, pulling, and pushing). "Nonexertional" limitations include all other limitations that affect the individual's ability to perform nonstrength demands, such as postural, manipulative, environmental, and mental demands, inherent in a job.

Reviewing the distinctions between impairments, symptoms, and limitations is important before discussing severe impairments at step 2. Figure 7–1 illustrates the relationship among impairments, symptoms, and limitations. Some administrative law judges and federal courts confuse the three terms on occasion. Keeping the terms in mind when interviewing a client is helpful. Clients should be asked about each medical condition claimed, the treatment for each, and how each condition affects functioning in daily activities.

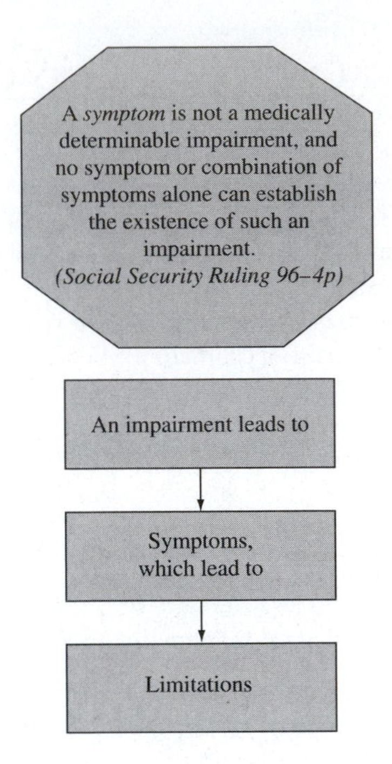

Figure 7–1 **Step 2: Impairments, Symptoms, and Limitations**

WHAT IS A "SEVERE" IMPAIRMENT?

SSA defines a "severe" impairment as one that "significantly limits" an individual's mental or physical ability to perform basic work activities.[5] SSA does not quantify the phrase "significantly limit." However, the impairment must prevent the claimant from performing at least one of the basic work-related functions.

The standard for assessing "severity" at step 2 is medical only. Vocational factors, such as age, education, and past work history, are considered at this step, but they are more important at step 5 of the sequential evaluation process. Even though we know Sadie is sixty years old and has only a sixth-grade education, those factors won't be considered at step 2 in determining whether Sadie's impairments are "severe."

In the past, the medical-only standard for assessing severity at step 2 could be abused by decision makers. They could reject disability claims for older individuals with limited education or work experience at step 2 rather than consider education and experience at step 5 of the sequential evaluation process. However, the federal courts believed it was unfair to stop the sequential analysis of disability at step 2. They found that step 2 was only a "de minimus," or threshold, showing of an impairment causing vocational limitations. In response to the court rulings, SSA issued Ruling 85-28, which stated that a finding of nonseverity should be made when "the evidence establishes only a slight abnormality which has no more than a minimal effect on a claimant's ability to do basic work activities." SSA also admonished its adjudicators to exercise "great care" at step 2 in finding an impairment not severe. Despite this ruling, the federal courts remained divided on the interpretation of a "severe" impairment.

The U.S. Supreme Court settled the controversy with its decision in *Bowen v. Yuckert* (482 U.S. 137 [1987]). The Supreme Court found that SSA's "severity" regulation was valid. The Court determined that if an impairment was not severe enough to limit in a significant way a claimant's ability to perform most jobs, then it would be unlikely that the impairment would prevent the claimant from engaging in substantial gainful activity. The Court upheld the Commissioner's authority to place the burden of demonstrating a determinable impairment on the claimant. The Court also found no need for SSA to consider vocational factors in determining "severity" at step 2.

More recently, SSA has provided further guidance regarding the interpretation of impairment "severity." Social Security Ruling 96-3p requires the ALJ to evaluate an individual's impairment(s) to assess their effects on the individual's performance of "basic work activities." The Ruling cautions ALJs that when the effect an impairment has on an individual's ability to perform basic work activities cannot be clearly determined, the

ALJ should move on to step 3 and the remaining steps of the sequential evaluation process until a determination regarding disability can be reached. Ruling 96-3p thus suggests that if the ALJ is doubtful about the severity of the alleged impairments, she or he should give the claimant the benefit of the doubt and continue with the sequential evaluation process, rather than simply denying benefits and dismissing the case at step 2 for lack of a severe impairment.

WHAT ARE "BASIC WORK ACTIVITIES?"

SSA defines "basic work activities" as the abilities and aptitudes necessary to perform most jobs.[6] SSA illustrates these activities with the following categories of examples:

- Physical functions, such as walking, standing, sitting, lifting, pushing, pulling, reaching, carrying, or handling;
- Capacities for speaking, seeing, or hearing;
- Understanding, carrying out, and remembering simple instructions;
- Use of judgment;
- Responding appropriately to supervision, co-workers, and usual work situations; and
- Dealing with changes in a routine work setting.

BACK TO CHRIS

"What if someone has more than one impairment?" Chris asked.

"Good question. You consider all of them. Let me explain further," answered Steve.

A TRIP TO THE HARD DRIVE, 7.2

A combination of impairments is different in cumulative effect than a single impairment. Take *A Trip to the Hard Drive* to further explore the significance of multiple impairments.

COMBINATION OF IMPAIRMENTS

In addition to assessing the severity of each impairment, the ALJ must also assess the impact of all impairments in combination on the claimant's ability to function.[7]

For example, a claimant may have a spinal impairment, or arthritis in one of the major weight-bearing joints, that causes pain when the claimant performs some physical "basic work activities." The claimant's pain could be relieved by certain prescribed pain medications, allowing the claimant to perform the difficult physical activities. The claimant may also be diagnosed with a digestive impairment, which can be controlled by diet and prescribed medication, and is considered a nonsevere impairment.

However, considering the two impairment together, it becomes clear that the claimant's digestive impairment prevents the claimant from taking the prescribed pain medications for the back or joint pain. Without the pain relief afforded by those medications, the claimant cannot perform the physical basic work activities.

When considering the effects of a combination of impairments, remember that the impairment must last twelve months.[8] If the claimant has two or more unrelated impairments, each lasting six months or less, the claimant cannot combine the two impairments' durations to meet the twelve months, showing a continuing disability. The duration requirement also may not be met if one of the combined impairments improves or is expected to improve within the twelve-month time period, so the combined effect of the two impairments is no longer "severe." Thus, in the preceding example, if the claimant's physicians prescribe a pain medication that improves the claimant's physical functioning without adversely affecting the digestive impairment, the claimant's combined impairments may not be considered "severe."

BACK TO CHRIS

Sadie called Chris to report that her doctor had taken a number of X-rays of her hands, elbows, shoulders, and knees. When Sadie asked the nurse about getting copies of her medical records, the nurse indicated that Sadie would have to sign a release in order to have the records sent to Chris and that Sadie would be charged for the cost of copying the medical records.

Chris outlined the situation for Steve. "I have a medical release form you can use. Let me get it from my forms file," Steve said, scanning through a disk on the computer. "But as far as paying for medical copies, I think Sadie is covered by our state's law, which prevents the doctor from charging more than $100 for copies of medical records. I'll find that citation for you."

"But what if copying Sadie's records costs more than $100?" Chris's forehead puckered in thought.

"I guess you should check that out." Steve retrieved the release form from the desktop printer. "Chris, this is where you need all your diplomatic skills in dealing with Sadie's doctors. Social Security gives particular attention to the records and the opinions of a treating physician. You have to make a good impression on Sadie's doctor; get him interested in helping both Sadie and you to prove her disability case. If the doctor is on your side, the cost of copying the medical records may not be insurmountable, or even an issue at all."

"Where should I start?" Chris asked, grabbing the note pad.

"First, have Sadie sign this release. Look up the state's law on charges for medical record copies. Here are the SSA regulations and Rulings about a treating physician's records. I can find you a letter and a request to a doctor I used for another case. You may be able to adapt them for Sadie's doctor." Steve piled papers and books on Chris's note pad and waved at Chris while reaching for the ringing telephone.

FRONT OF YOUR MIND QUESTIONS AND CONSIDERATIONS, 7.2

INTRODUCTION

At step 2, impairment(s) must be documented with medical records and physician's statements, explaining how the impairments affect the ability to function, not only at work but also in daily activities. At step 2 it must be shown that a client's impairment(s) are so severe that they significantly affect "basic work activities." The client's physician becomes an important ally to demonstrating the existence of a medical impairment and its severity.

The confidential nature of most medical records requires written authorization by the patient, allowing another person access to those records. A release form, signed by the patient, indicates that written assent. For liability reasons, most physicians insist on a signed release form before making medical records available. Figure 7–2 is an example of a standard release form.

For physical impairments, a physician may be willing to give the patient/claimant copies of the medical records for the claimant's legal representative. For mental impairments, however, most mental health care providers are not allowed by law to let the client see their own treatment records. The mental treatment medical record may be sent directly to the legal representative, with a cautionary note that the records not be shown to the claimant.

WHERE DO I OBTAIN MEDICAL RECORDS?

If a client is scheduled to appear before an administrative law judge after the DDS decision, there already will be a list of medical records considered by the DDS in both the "initial" and "reconsideration" notices of denial. This list, although usually incomplete at this time (because time has passed and the client has continued to seek medical assistance or the condition has worsened) is an excellent starting point.

I understand that my records are protected under the Federal and State Confidentiality regulations and cannot be released without my written consent unless otherwise provided for in the regulations. Federal regulations prohibit you from making any further disclosure of it without the specific written consent of the person to whom it pertains, or as otherwise permitted by such regulation. I also understand that I may revoke this consent (in writing) at any time unless action has already been taken based upon it and that in any event this consent expires 90 days from the date of signing. THE INFORMATION I AUTHORIZE FOR RELEASE MAY INCLUDE INFORMATION THAT COULD BE CONSIDERED INFORMATION ABOUT COMMUNICABLE OR VENEREAL DISEASES WHICH MAY INCLUDE, BUT ARE NOT LIMITED TO, DISEASES SUCH AS HEPATITIS, SYPHILIS, GONORRHEA, AND THE HUMAN IMMUNODEFICIENCY VIRUS, ALSO KNOWN AS ACQUIRED IMMUNE DEFICIENCY SYNDROME (AIDS).

Name: ______________________

Date of Birth: ______________________

Social Security Number: ______________________

I authorize the following person or agency

Name: ______________________

Address: ______________________

____

to release to______________________

the following information for the purpose of representation in a Social Security disability case:

____

____

____

______________ Date ______________________ Signature

Figure 7–2 **Sample Medical Release Form**

Obtain the names of all medical providers seen by the client, both before and during the claimed period of disability. Hospitals and other major medical providers usually have a medical records department. Physicians' offices often will have a separate administrator for medical records. Contact the medical records custodian by telephone, then send a formal written request with the medical release. Asking the client to follow up helps smooth the way, because medical providers sometimes do not cooperate when the law is involved.

Once a request for hearing has been filed with the Office of Hearings and Appeals, a subpoena can be requested of the administrative law judge. If a medical provider does not cooperate by providing medical records, a subpoena may be necessary to get them. Subpoenas must be requested well in advance of their need, as is discussed later in the book, though the regulations only specify five days before the actual hearing.[9] As a practical matter, it is unlikely such short notice will result in document production.

Finally, remember to ask the client for his or her records. Often, and surprisingly, people will maintain a copy of records.

BACK TO CHRIS

Chris lifted the water glass, staring at the ice.

"Hey Chris!" Steve walked into the break room. "You look lost in thought."

"I guess I am. How do you avoid mixing up step 2 with step 3 and even step 4?"

"You mean with the medical?"

"Yes."

"The bottom-line question at step 2 is whether the impairment(s) limit the person and the person's ability to function competitively."

"So a cut on the finger does not meet that level?"

"No. It's a matter of common sense, as well as law."

"Because of the twelve-month or death rule?"

Steve grabbed a bag of chips from the snack tray. "That's right. First, the impairment has to last at least twelve months, or be expected to, or result in death. If something has lasted that long, it is likely close to severe."

"That's a good point. I have been trying to determine how much medical information I really need to know."

"Well, it definitely helps to have a passing acquaintance with basic medical terms, some anatomy and the like. But your best bet is good medical dictionary and encyclopedia. That way, you can look up the terms directly and understand what they involve."

"Okay, but how do you really know whether an impairment is going to affect functioning?"

"It's common sense, supported by medical records and the client's testimony."

"I thought you would say something like that. So, there is no table, form, or guide that gives the answers?"

"No. Remember, we're dealing with human beings. Absolutes occur only in the most vague of ways. Diseases, injuries, and illnesses affect different people differently. Each case is unique."

"Thanks, Steve."

"Don't mention it, Chris. Time to get back to work."

WHAT IF . . . ? SAMPLE PROBLEMS

WHAT IF . . .

Jim broke his leg in June and had to quit his job as a welder. Surgery was performed in July and a rod was implanted. Because of complications, the rod was removed the following January. Jim had physical therapy in February and, despite some muscle wasting, was released to return to work without restrictions in May. Jim comes to you wanting to file a claim for a closed period of disability. What do you tell him?

1. You have a good case.
2. Because your claim did not last a full year and because you've been released without any restrictions from the injury, you do not have an actionable claim for benefits.
3. We can stretch it out a bit.
4. None of these suggestions would be good to tell Jim.

Answer: Applying the definition at step 2, the best answer is 2. Jim's injury did not last twelve months, and given that he has no remaining restrictions on the use of his leg, it can be said that the injury has fully resolved. The case cannot be stretched out and it would not be appropriate to lead Jim along. The medical records simply do not support it.

WHAT IF . . .

Does Sadie, whom Chris considered at the beginning of the chapter, have "severe impairments?"

Answer: *Sadie* does *have "severe impairments." For example, the fact that her hand cramps up so that she can no longer perform her job is likely the result of arthritis or perhaps even carpal tunnel syndrome. The hand cramp by itself is a symptom, which gives rise to a limitation; she can no longer engage in fine motor manipulation (e.g., write) with her hand. What is missing is the actual medical diagnosis. She will have to be seen by a doctor. Once her condition is diagnosed, and if the condition has lasted or is reasonably expected to last for twelve months, she will then have a "severe impairment" relating to her hand.*

In addition, Sadie likely suffers from a back problem that "catches" (the symptom) and a lung problem because she wheezes (also, a symptom). She needs to see a doctor so a diagnosis can be made. Each of these problems has the potential to restrict vocational activity, so, if diagnosed and reasonably likely to last twelve months, they too will be "severe impairments."

---

[1]Title 20 C.F.R. §§ 404.1508 and 416.908.
[2]Title 20 C.F.R. § 404.1528(a).
[3]Title 20 C.F.R. § 404.1528(b).
[4]Title 20 C.F.R. §§ 404.1528(c) and 416.928(c).
[5]Title 20 C.F.R. § 404.1520(c).
[6]See Title 20 C.F.R. § 404.1545(b).
[7]See Title 20 C.F.R. § 404.1523.
[8]See Title 20 C.F.R. § 404.1509.
[9]See Title 20 C.F.R. § 404.950(d).

8

CHAPTER EIGHT

Step 3: The Listings

HIGHLIGHTS

- ❑ Step 3 in the sequential evaluation
- ❑ The medical listings
- ❑ Use of a medical expert

CHRIS

"Step 3," Chris mused. "That's a pay step, isn't it?"

The offices were quiet over the lunch hour, bright, late morning sun shone through gleaming windows. A beautiful day.

"That's right. It's one of only two steps in the five-step sequential analysis in which the judge can grant benefits," Steve replied, gazing wistfully out the window.

"But it's mainly medical, right? We don't use vocational experts."

Steve smiled at the young advocate's enthusiasm. "You have been studying. That's absolutely correct."

"So that means doctors are involved."

Steve nodded, his attention was momentarily diverted by a bluejay twittering outside the second-story windows. "The makeup of the five-step sequential evaluation is really interesting. Once you get past the first two steps—that is, once you know that your client isn't working during the time he claims disability (or at least not at SGA levels) and once you know that the impairment is severe (it produces limitations reasonably likely to affect the ability to do competitive work), you get to this step."

"Why is that interesting?"

"Because the Social Security disability determination process is defined as a complex 'medical–legal' undertaking. At step 3 you encounter the medical side. At steps 4 and 5 you're dealing with the vocational side."

"That is interesting. First things first, then. We deal with the medical before the vocational?"

"The framers of the process look at it this way: If the medical problem is so severe, then we can *presume disability without the need to show actual vocational deficits.*"

"Can you show me?"

"Sure!"

FRONT OF YOUR MIND QUESTIONS AND CONSIDERATIONS, 8.1

INTRODUCTION

Step 3 of the five-step sequential evaluation process is straightforward in the regulations.

Title 20 C.F.R. § 404.1520(d) provides:

> **When your impairment(s) meets or equals a listed impairment in Appendix 1.**
> **If you have an impairment(s) which meets the duration requirement and is listed in Appendix 1 or is equal to a listed impairment(s) we will find you disabled without considering your age, education and work experience.**

Appendix 1 in the Code of Federal Regulations is actually Appendix 1 to subpart P of part 404 and is called the *Listing of Impairments.* In substance, Appendix 1 is simply what it purports to be. It is a list of thirteen bodily systems.[1] Each listing is designated by a specific section, euphemistically referred to as a "listing." The thirteen categories are

- ❑ 1.00 Musculoskeletal system
- ❑ 2.00 Special senses and speech
- ❑ 3.00 Respiratory system
- ❑ 4.00 Cardiovascular system
- ❑ 5.00 Digestive system
- ❑ 6.00 Genito-urinary system
- ❑ 7.00 Hemic and lymphatic system
- ❑ 8.00 Skin
- ❑ 9.00 Endocrine system
- ❑ 10.00 [Reserved]
- ❑ 11.00 Neurological
- ❑ 12.00 Mental disorders
- ❑ 13.00 Neoplastic diseases, malignant
- ❑ 14.00 Immune system

The regulations specifically describe the purpose of the "listings of impairments." If an individual suffers from an impairment with all of the symptoms, test results, and conditions or consequences as described in a particular listing, he or she will be considered disabled on medical grounds regardless of previous work experience, age, or education.[2]

As the regulations provide, if a client's impairment, together with the appropriate signs and laboratory findings, is actually listed in one of the thirteen categories of bodily systems within Appendix 1, the law presumes that the client's medical condition (the impairment) is "severe enough to prevent a person from doing any gainful activity."[3] As such, the regulations establish a set of medical–legal presumptions in each of the thirteen listed categories.

Once the medical diagnosis, signs, and laboratory findings are established—and match the diagnosis, signs, and laboratory findings in a medical listing—the assumption is

> **The claimant suffers from a condition, at such a level of severity so as to preclude, as a matter of medical fact, activity necessary to perform competitive work within the regional and national economies.**

In effect, the Social Security Administration, in promulgating the listings of impairments, is ascribing automatic disability to them. In doing so, the Social Security Administration is recognizing the debilitating effect of certain medical conditions once the condition reaches a specified level of severity. If a client's condition "meets a listing"—a phrase peculiar to this area of practice—then the client's impairment carries with it the diagnosis, medical signs, and laboratory findings set out for that disease, illness, or injury within the regulations (the listings).

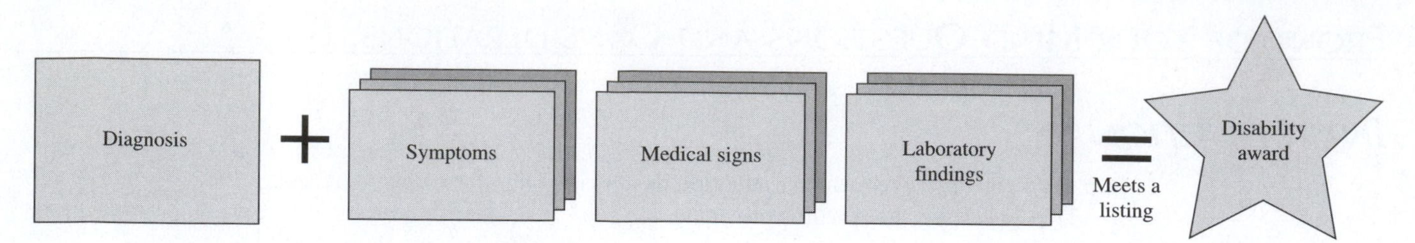

Figure 8–1 **Meeting a Listing Requires All Criteria Be Met**

To be found disabled at step 3 in the sequential evaluation, the client must demonstrate

- ❑ A diagnosis falling within one of the listed categories; and
- ❑ Evidence of the signs, symptoms, and laboratory findings as set out under the specified listing.

Figure 8–1 illustrates the requirements necessary to meet a listing.

MEETING THE LISTING

If a client's impairment meets the listing, his or her illness, disease, or injury carries a diagnosis that matches one of the thirteen categories of bodily systems in Appendix 1. Simply having the same diagnosis, however, is not sufficient. Title 20 C.F.R. § 404.1525(d) makes this clear:

> **We will not consider your impairment to be one listed in Appendix 1 solely because it has the diagnosis of a listed impairment.** ***It must also have the findings shown in the Listing of that impairment.*** **(Emphasis added)**

To actually meet the listing there must be medical documentation of the required medical signs, laboratory findings, and, where specified, the symptoms described. Only when the diagnosis, medical signs, laboratory findings, and any specified symptoms are present can the judge make the determination that a client is entitled to an award of disability at step 3. Remember, this determination is one of sufficiency of the evidence. The judge must find by a preponderance of the evidence (at least 51% for, 49% against) that a client's impairment meets the listing.

It is critical to be prepared to prove an assertion that a client's medical condition meets the listing—not simply by his or her assertion, but by medical records, reports, and, where appropriate, testimony.

BACK TO CHRIS

"Time out."

Steve looked up. "Question?"

Chris nodded vigorously. "Can you give me an example?"

"Of what it means to 'meet the listing?' "

"Please."

"OK. Look at Appendix 1." Steve flipped through the C.F.R., while Chris winced at the fine print. "Some of the most common ailments giving rise to disability applications are disorders of the back."

"Oh, my aching back?" Chris quipped.

"It's really serious."

"I know, I was only kidding."

"OK. But," Steve grinned, "it does get a little familiar after you get into a routine."

Chris relaxed.

"Here. Look at Medical Listing 1.04(C)."

Chris peered over Steve's shoulder. "Disorders of the Spine."

"Look at Section (C)."

"Other Vertebrogenic disorders?"

"It sounds complicated, but it's basically a 'catch-all' for all other back problems that aren't defined in the preceding sections."

"I see."

"Each listing begins with a diagnosis. In this case, a back disorder. What follows is a statement of required symptoms, medical signs, or laboratory findings."

"So you start with a diagnosis, then look for the confirming symptoms, signs, and laboratory findings?"

"Exactly. In this case, a series of symptoms are described that include a further durational requirement."

"Durational requirement?"

"The listing requires that the claimant's symptoms have lasted for at least three months, with the requirement that they be expected to last at least twelve months."

Chris looked at 1.04(C). "These are the symptoms, right?" Chris pointed at the C.F.R.

"Yes."

"So, in addition to a back disorder, the person must suffer pain, muscle spasm, and significantly limited motion in the spine?"

"That's not all. What word comes after 'significant limitation of motion in the spine?' "

"Oh, I see. The word is *and*."

"Correct. That means you have to look at the next sentence as well. That next sentence also contains required symptoms."

"You mean 'appropriate distribution of significant motor loss with muscle weakness and sensory and reflex loss?' "

"You have it!"

"That's a lot of symptoms."

"It's what the law requires for a person with a back injury to receive disability."

"Wow."

"Do you see how the listing works?"

"I think so. First you determine your client's diagnosis. Then you find the right listing. Then you see what the listing requires in the way of medical signs, symptoms, and laboratory findings."

"That's it."

FRONT OF YOUR MIND QUESTIONS AND CONSIDERATIONS, 8.2

To determine if a client's condition, whether an illness, disease, or injury, meets a listed impairment, first identify the appropriate listing. Sometimes, more than one listing may be applicable. Examine each carefully in light of the medical records.

Next, determine the specific requirements. What does the listing require in terms of

- ❑ Medical signs;
- ❑ Symptoms; and
- ❑ Laboratory findings?

Only if all the required elements are present, can you properly conclude that your client's impairment meets the listing. If even one element is missing, the listing cannot be met. Figure 8–2 depicts the analysis for determining whether an impairment meets a listing.

One of the critical variables in determining whether a client's condition meets a listing, are the medical records that support the diagnosis, signs, symptoms, and other medical findings. In assessing whether the client meets a listing, the judge must determine whether each of the criteria required in a specified listing can be documented throughout the claimed disability period. For example, if the client claims disability since 1996, but only received a formal diagnosis in 1999, and there were no previous related diagnoses, a finding

- ❑ Meeting a listing at step 3 means that your client has been diagnosed with an impairment that is subject to one of the listings in Appendix 1; and
- ❑ The impairment is documented by the same medical signs and laboratory findings set forth in the listing.
- ❑ This means that the condition has reached a specific level of severity, which is presumed to be disabling without discussing age, education, and past work experience (the vocational factors).
- ❑ Meeting a listing at step 3 focuses primarily on the medical evidence as controlling the outcome.
  1. Does your client have a diagnosis that matches an impairment in one of the thirteen listings?
  2. If so, are the medical signs and laboratory findings required by the listing present and documented?
  3. The only question remaining is that of the onset date—do the *documented* signs and laboratory findings arise at the time the claimant alleges disability, or, is there another point in time, perhaps later, where the required medical signs and laboratory findings are documented?

Figure 8–2 **Analysis of Meeting a Listing**

that the client meets the listing in 1996 cannot be made. The evidence dates only to 1999, not 1996. At best, the impairment may meet the listing in 1999, not 1996. Thus, it is important when determining whether an impairment meets the listing to examine the longitudinal basis for the claim. In effect, disability is found when it is supported by evidence of medical signs, symptoms, and findings. Allegations alone will not suffice without such evidence. A client may have stopped working, or taken other steps that directly or indirectly indicate a disabling condition, but until there is actual medical evidence of the impairment, showing that the requisite criteria are present, the individual cannot be said to meet the listing.

BACK TO CHRIS

"What kind of evidence is needed? I don't quite understand that part."

"There is no required *kind* of evidence. But, it is important to obtain *all* your client's medical records; not only the ones you think apply to the disability issue."

"Why?"

"Often, clients focus on one particular problem, minimizing other problems—sometimes not even mentioning them to you—when in reality, the unmentioned problem is as significant, or more so, than the condition they have focused on."

"So, what kind of records can I generally expect to find?"

"First, you want to find records that are as close in time to when your client alleges he or she first became disabled. Then continue getting records up to the time of the hearing. That way you establish a longitudinal record of treatment that coincides with the client's allegations."

"Like what?"

"Suppose a client quit work in June because of severe back pain. Hopefully, he or she saw the doctor about that time. If the doctor made a note, actually documenting severe back pain, your client's allegations are supported, and you can establish proof of the existence of pain at the time your client indicated. This also helps establish your client's credibility testifying about other pain." Steve reached over to an open Social Security file. "Here, look at this." Steve handed Chris a sample progress note (see Figure 8–3).

"It's a doctor's note."

"Right. Now look at the last entry. What do you see?"

"It says 'severe back pain.' That's the documentation you were talking about?"

"That's right." Steve tapped the paper. "What's the date?"

"June."

"Which means if your client quit the job in June because of back pain, you can document it with this Progress Note."

"But how do you know that the doctor actually found there was a problem?"

"You mean if the record merely repeats the patient's complaints?"

"Yes."

"You have to watch for that. The key thing in all medical records is what the *doctor* actually finds. What the patient says is important too, but if the doctor doesn't confirm it, then the record simply repeats the patient's allegations—with no proof that a problem actually exists."

"What about this record?"

"The doctor repeats the patient's complaints of severe back pain, but then does some additional testing. See where it says positive SLR?"

Chris nodded slowly.

"That's an objective test of referred pain—from the back to the legs. If the patient feels that kind of "referred" pain, there is a back problem."

"So, the reference in the note to "SLR" is confirmation of the claimant's subjective complaints?"

"Correct. And that generally is a plus for credibility."

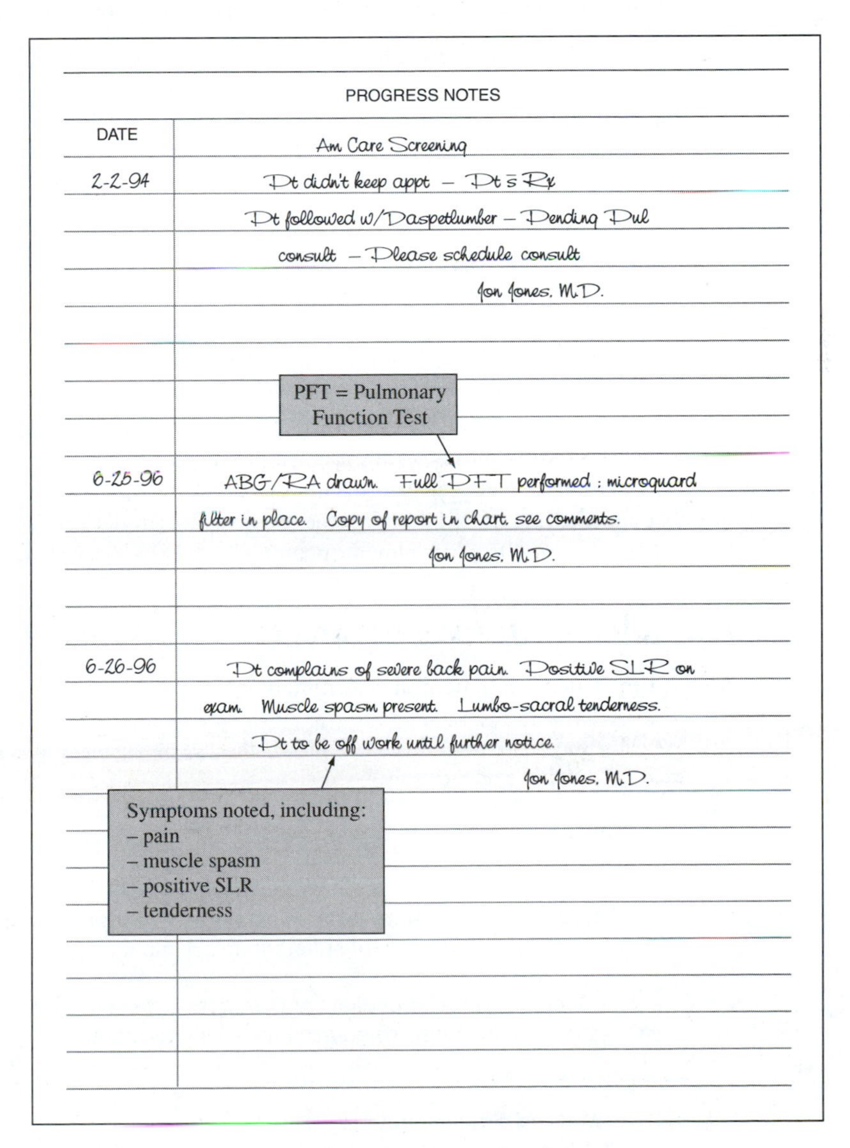

PROGRESS NOTES

DATE	
	Am Care Screening
2-2-94	Pt didn't keep appt – Pt s̄ Rx
	Pt followed w/Daspetlumber – Pending Pul
	consult – Please schedule consult
	Jon Jones, M.D.
6-25-96	ABG/RA drawn. Full PFT performed : microguard
	filter in place. Copy of report in chart. see comments.
	Jon Jones, M.D.
6-26-96	Pt complains of severe back pain. Positive SLR on
	exam. Muscle spasm present. Lumbo-sacral tenderness.
	Pt to be off work until further notice.
	Jon Jones, M.D.

Figure 8–3 **Sample Progress Note Indicating Back Pain**

FRONT OF YOUR MIND QUESTIONS AND CONSIDERATIONS, 8.3

EQUALING A LISTING OR MEDICAL EQUIVALENCE

The regulations recognize that people do not all fit into the defined categories in the Listings of Impairments. Each individual is unique. According to the regulations, if a given impairment is not accompanied by exactly the required medical signs, symptoms, and laboratory findings, the individual can be found disabled at step 3.

Title 20 C.F.R. § 1526 addresses *medical equivalence.* Medical equivalence is a means of evaluating the *medical severity* of an impairment and attributing the legal effect of "meeting a listing," even if the impairment does not present the same symptoms, medical signs, and laboratory findings required to "meet a listing." The key term is *medical severity.* Because the Listings are based on the assumption that a medical condition, if attended by specific symptoms, medical signs, and laboratory findings, gives rise to a presumption of disability, it is possible that an impairment or combination of impairments may also give rise to such a presumption, depending on the severity of the resulting condition. Even if the impairment is not found within the Listings of Impairments, a finding of disability can be made at step 3 if the resulting condition is "at least equal in severity and duration to the listed findings."[4]

There are two circumstances giving rise to a medical equivalency.

- ❑ The claimant's impairment may not be set forth (listed) in the Listings of Impairments; or
- ❑ The claimant may suffer from a combination of impairments, none of which individually rises to listing level, but all of which, taken together, result in a medical condition equivalent in medical severity to a listed impairment.

The process is straightforward. If an impairment is not otherwise included in the Listings of Impairments in Appendix 1, a similar impairment must be identified "to decide whether [the] impairment is medically equal."[5] The symptoms, medical signs, and laboratory findings can then be compared with "the symptoms, signs, and laboratory findings . . . as shown in the medical evidence . . . , with the medical criteria shown in the listed impairment."[6] If the symptoms, signs, and laboratory findings are "at least equal in severity" to the referenced listing, disability may be awarded.

Similarly, if a client suffers from *multiple impairments* the Social Security Administration "will review the symptoms, signs, and laboratory findings about [the] impairments to determine whether the combination of . . . impairments is *medically equal* to any listed impairment."[7] If, because of a combination of impairments, a client suffers from symptoms that are equivalent in severity to symptoms found in a listed impairment, disability may, again, be awarded. Figure 8–4 describes the circumstances under which an impairment may be found "medically equivalent in severity" to a listed impairment.

THE ROLE OF THE MEDICAL EXPERT AND/OR PHYSICIAN

Medical equivalence is a medical determination.

> **We will always base our decision about whether . . . impairment(s) is medically equal to a listed impairment on medical evidence only."[8]**

Medical equivalence may be addressed under two circumstances:
- First, where your client suffers from an impairment not otherwise listed;

Or,

- Second, where your client suffers from a combination of impairments, none of which individually meets or equals a listed impairment.

Figure 8–4 **Medical Equivalence**

Although the judge determines the sufficiency of the evidence, he or she may not determine medical equivalency. Judges are not medical experts—medical doctors, psychologists, or other approved medical sources. Only a medical doctor or psychologist is responsible for assessing comparative medical severity, testifying as medical experts:

> **We will also consider the medical opinion given by one or more medical or psychological consultants designated by the Commissioner in deciding medical equivalence.**

The legal question for the judge is whether the evidence supports the medical doctor's or psychologist's opinion as to medical equivalency. The representative's argument is twofold:

- ❏ The medical condition should be equivalent in medical severity to a listed impairment; and
- ❏ The evidence should support such a finding.

In the past, judges attempted to determine medical equivalency. The result was unsatisfactory. Judges were tempted to play doctor. Even today, despite the requirement that medical equivalency be determined by a qualified medical doctor or psychologist, judges are tempted. Case law is replete with the federal courts chastising administrative law judges for overstepping their "expertise" and making medical, not legal, decisions. As a result, most administrative law judges rely on a medical expert at the hearing to review written evidence, listen to testimony, and offer an opinion as to whether a claimant meets or equals a medical listing.

Generally, the administrative law judge will determine on prehearing review of the case that a particular medical expert is necessary to address the medical issues. The notice of hearing sets forth prospective witnesses, including medical and vocational experts. If a medical expert is needed to address step 3 or step 4 issues, a written request must be submitted to the judge. As a practical matter, such requests generally are not seen by the judge in time to actually schedule a medical expert for the hearing. Such letters are generally filed by the administrative staff in the case file and not brought to the judge's attention.

The remedy is to make personal contact with the case technicians who set the case for hearing. Then, make a formal written request. The personal contact ensures a reasonable possibility that a doctor can be found in time for the hearing, and the written request documents the record in the event the judge decides to go forward with the hearing without a medical expert.

Because a medical expert is needed to determine medical equivalency, careful attention must be paid to the doctor's testimony. The administrative law judge generally examines the medical witness before yielding the floor to the representative. The representative should ensure that a full, fair, and complete examination has been conducted; and that all the medical records have been explored. Following are significant touchstones in a medical expert's testimony:

- ❏ *The expert's qualifications.* Generally this is not an issue. Medical doctors and psychologists are screened by the Office of the Regional Chief Administrative Law Judge and approved to appear (and be paid by the federal government) based on their academic and professional qualifications. The real issue is specialization. It may be important to have a medical doctor present who is certified in a particular area of specialization. The problem is the availability of doctors. Doctors who testify in administrative hearings are volunteers. (They are paid, but not very much; and no one forces them to appear.) Unfortunately doctors in a given specialty often are not available. A potential remedy is to ask the client's treating physician to appear or participate in a brief teleconference with the representative and the judge.
- ❏ *Review of the medical record.* The medical expert must review the entire medical record before testifying. Administrative law judges become unhappy if a representative brings a stack of medical records to a hearing in which a medical expert is to testify. The hearing will likely be postponed, so the doctor can review the entire medical record. Surprising a doctor and judge with newly submitted records wastes time, not generally available in a high-volume hearing schedule. The judge will either "trail" the case to the end of the docket, postpone it, or proceed without reviewing the newly surfaced documents. This last course of action will probably enable an appeal or a denial, but the practical effect is a significant delay in the case (particularly in the administrative appeals process). Ensure that the doctor has reviewed the whole record. If the claimed time period is more than one year, make sure the doctor has addressed the entire time period or addressed your client's changing condition over time (especially where significant medical events occurred).

- *Substantive questions for the medical expert.* The examination of the medical expert is far from haphazard. Such examinations are methodical and energized by the force of the regulations. At step 3 of the sequential evaluation process, the primary concerns are with the medical listings. The medical expert's opinion becomes evidence the judge relies on to award benefits. Thus, the medical expert's testimony must be comprehensive. If the judge does not make appropriate inquiries, the representative must. Following are key areas of inquiry:

  1. Does the claimant suffer from a medically determinable impairment?
  2. If so, when was the diagnosis first made?
  3. What was the course of treatment, over time?
  4. What is the claimant's prognosis (future)?
  5. What listing most closely approximates the claimant's condition?
  6. Does the claimant's condition (impairment) meet (match) a listed impairment?
  7. Does the claimant suffer from multiple impairments? If so, repeat questions 1 through 4 for each impairment.
  8. If the claimant's impairment does not meet a listing, is the claimant's condition medically equivalent in severity to a listed impairment? Also consider the combination of all impairments.
  9. Ask the doctor to explain each response to questions 6 and 8, with specific references to exhibits in the administrative record (the case file).
  10. If the claimant's impairment(s) does not meet or equal a listing, what limitations as a result of the impairment(s) does the medical record support? This is important at step 4 and step 5, where the client's limitations (physical or mental) are considered in determining whether past work (step 4) or other, less demanding work (step 5) can be performed.

- *Examination tips.* The following tips should be considered when examining the medical expert:

  1. Address the client's condition with as much specificity as possible.
  2. Refer the doctor to actual exhibits in the administrative record; provide copies for review while asking questions.
  3. If a residual functional capacity evaluation or other document appears in the record that addresses physical or mental functional capacity, or that otherwise sets forth restrictions for the client, ask if the expert agrees with the assessment.
  4. Inquire into the doctor's thought processes. *Why* does he or she agree or disagree with the assessment?
  5. Ask the doctor what restrictions would normally attend an individual with the same or a similar diagnosis?
  6. Ask the doctor to verify subjective complaints, particularly as they relate to pain.
  7. Do not become angry or impatient with the doctor. Professionalism is paramount, even if you disagree with the expert's conclusions or findings. Use substance, not emotion to make your points.

STEP 3 STRATEGIES

To be effective at any step in the sequential evaluation process, the representative must be able to synthesize information, putting divergent facts together as part of a cohesive whole. At step 3, certain strategies are evident from the regulations.

Because opinions from medical practitioners are preeminent at step 3, it is important, where possible, to obtain opinions from the claimant's treating physician. Such opinions should specifically consider the language and requirements of the selected medical listing. They should not, however, be simple repetitions of the listing without analysis. A conclusory statement by the doctor to the effect that the claimant "meets Listing 1.04(C)" without analysis of why the listing is met is insufficient and cannot form the basis of a step 3 award.

To obtain a medical opinion from the doctor, the representative should provide the doctor with the following:

- A copy of the pertinent medical listing in its entirety;

- ❑ A statement of the time period for which the patient (the claimant) is claiming disability; and
- ❑ A simple rendition of the question to be answered (e.g., "Given Mr. Jones's diagnosis of a herniated disk at C5-C6, can you give us your opinion whether Mr. Jones's medical condition is *the same as* that in the attached federal regulation? Please be specific in your answer, because without a complete description of the patient's symptoms, clinical findings, and tests, the federal administrative law judge will not be able to adopt your opinion.")

A similar question can be asked for an opinion of medical equivalency. However, it is important to explain, as simply as possible, what medical equivalency means, and to share that explanation with the judge. This is to forestall a finding by the judge that the doctor was unfamiliar with the concept, discounting (and failing to adopt) the opinion.

Because an individual claimant can be afflicted with more than one impairment, it is important that the synergy of all impairments be fully explored. Often, doctors, in answering a question about "meeting a listing" fail to consider whether the claimant "equals" the listing. When addressing that question, the representative must urge consideration of the *combined effect* of all documented impairments. The combined effect of multiple impairments may be the equivalent of a single impairment in terms of overall severity.

For example, suppose the claimant is afflicted with a heart condition that does not, in itself, result in the level of fatigue required to meet the medical listing at 4.00. The claimant also suffers from diabetes, which is only partially controlled, resulting in bouts of lethargy and dizziness because of jumps in blood sugar levels. Neither impairment meets the appropriate listing, but, in combination, they are equivalent in severity to medical listing 4.02.

A clear strategy at step 3 is to integrate the effects of all documented impairments, ensuring that (1) the treating physician or (2) the medical expert fully consider these possibilities.

WHAT IF . . . ? SAMPLE PROBLEMS

WHAT IF . . .

What if your client suffers from a back condition and has documented symptoms that match Medical Listing 1.04 in every respect but one?

1. The impairment meets the listing because it is substantially the same as that in the regulations.
2. The impairment equals the listing because it is substantially the same as in the regulations.
3. Further case development is necessary.
4. The impairment *may* equal the listing depending on the testimony of a medical expert.

*Answer: **All criteria in a medical listing must be present and so found by the judge by a preponderance of the evidence at the hearing. Lacking even one criterion will negate a finding that the claimant's impairment meets the listing. Medical equivalency must be documented by a medical finding, generally by a medical expert at the hearing or by a treating physician who renders an opinion in light of the regulations. There is no standard such as "substantially the same as that set forth in the regulations." An opinion to the effect that the claimant's impairment "equals" a listing must be supported by a preponderance of the evidence over the course of the claimed period of disability. Simply because the evidence is "close" to a listing is not grounds for a conclusion of equivalency, and it is not a basis for further development of the evidence. The correct answer is 4, the claimant's impairment may equal a listing, depending on the testimony of a medical expert.***

WHAT IF . . .

Which of the following is true?

1. The evidence required for a determination that the claimant's impairment meets the listing generally must be collected and documented in a short time.
2. An individual claimant can only be found to meet or equal one listing at a time.

3. To meet or equal a listing, the evidence (medical records and so on) may be provided by diverse medical sources and need not be from a single doctor or health care provider.
4. Only impairments actually in the listing of impairments qualify as medical conditions leading to an award of disability at step 3.

Discussion

1. The evidence necessary to legally conclude that an individual meets or equals a listed impairment may be amassed over the claimed period of disability. However, depending on the nature of the impairment (for example, certain conditions do not appear overnight; they necessarily require time to develop) it takes time to determine that a listing is met or equaled. As a result, the actual point in time in which a person meets the listing may not occur until the last piece of evidence is documented. Conversely, a person may meet the listing at the inception of the diagnosis. Each situation is unique. The statement is false.
2. If an individual suffers from multiple impairments, a finding can be made that multiple listings are met or equaled. The statement is false.
3. Determining that an individual meets or equals a listing does not depend on medical evidence from a single source. Symptoms, medical signs, and laboratory findings are usually provided by multiple sources, including treating doctors, hospitals, consulting physicians, and Social Security consultative examinations (CEs), as well as observations from the DDS. All such evidence may be used to meet or equal a listed impairment. The statement is true.
4. If an individual suffers from an impairment that is not found in the Listing of Impairments, the judge may properly conclude that the claimant's condition, although not listed, is comparable in medical severity to a listed impairment. Generally, expert medical testimony, either from the treating doctor or a medical expert at the hearing, is necessary to support such a conclusion. The statement is false.

---

[1]There are actually fourteen listed categories, but category 10.00 is unassigned and is shown as "reserved" for a future medical condition, system, or impairment.

[2]Note, however, for children, under age eighteen, there is a separate set of medical listings immediately following the adult listings, denoted as the "one hundred numbers" (e.g., 101.00, 102.00, etc.). These are discussed more fully in Chapter 12, addressing childhood disability. See also Title 20 C.F.R. § 404.1525(b)(2).

[3]Title 20 C.F.R. § 404.1525(a)(2000).

[4]Title 20 C.F.R. § 1526(a)(2000).

[5]Ibid.

[6]Ibid.

[7]Ibid.

[8]Title 20 C.F.R. § 1526(b)(2000).

9

CHAPTER NINE

The Five Step Sequential Evaluation Process: Step "3 1/2"—Residual Functional Capacity

HIGHLIGHTS

- ❑ Formulating the claimant's residual functional capacity

CHRIS

Chris looked at the bewildering array of medical reports, hospital data, handwritten notes, and progress records.

"How do I figure this out?" He'd already been through the medical records and noted the appropriate symptoms, the dates of diagnosis, and the longitudinal history of Mr. Carson's illness, ultimately concluding that Mr. Carson's condition, that is, Chris made a mental correction, Mr. Carson's *impairments*, did not, either singly or in combination with each other meet or equal a listed impairment within the federal regulations (the so-called Listings).

"So, how do I figure out what the residual functional capacity is?"

Chris stared for a long moment at the file, the stacked medical records, the computer screen where the medical records were now cataloged. *I'm pretty well organized. Surely, I can think this through!*

"Time for the books—again!"

FRONT OF YOUR MIND QUESTIONS AND CONSIDERATIONS, 9.1

INTRODUCTION TO RESIDUAL FUNCTIONAL CAPACITY

Chris's dilemma is initially one of understanding, then of information retrieval, and then of marshaling the evidence into a persuasive presentation. At the center of the disability determination process is the definition of disability in the governing regulations. According to the regulations, the basic definition of disability is

> **the inability to do any substantial gainful activity by reason of any medically determinable physical or mental impairment which can be expected to result in death or which has lasted or can be expected to last for a continuous period of not less than 12 months.**[1]

The question obviously becomes, how do you determine whether someone can or cannot "do any substantial gainful activity?" The answer is found at what is euphemistically called step *Three-and-a-Half* of the five-step sequential evaluation process. The answer (naturally) is found in more government regulations:

To determine whether you are able to do . . . work we consider your *residual functional capacity* [RFC] and your age, education, and work experience.[2] (Emphasis added)

Thus, a determination of whether an individual can perform past work or other, less demanding competitive jobs depends on the actual capacity to do so, termed the residual functional capacity (RFC). This classification of function occurs against a baseline definition of physical and mental capability, drawn in large measure from the *Dictionary of Occupational Titles* (*DOT*). So defined, jobs are classified in five basic physical categories:

- ❑ Sedentary;
- ❑ Light;
- ❑ Medium;
- ❑ Heavy; and
- ❑ Very heavy.

Within each category are three levels of vocational achievement, or "skill levels." These describe work that is

- ❑ Unskilled;
- ❑ Semiskilled; or
- ❑ Skilled.

An individual's residual functional capacity is similarly classified. For example, if an individual has the physical capacity only for sedentary work, he or she is generally said to have the "residual functional capacity for sedentary work." In agency shorthand, this translates to "an RFC for sedentary." When an individual has only mental or nonexertional limitations, he or she is described as *being limited* in those ways. If an individual has, either through education or work experience, acquired certain skills, he or she may also be said to have the capacity for *semiskilled* or *skilled* work. An individual with no skills is said to be *unskilled.*

Assessment of an individual's RFC is not, however, a simple matter of categorizing individuals into an exertional category. Instead, the assessment involves a variety of factors, each of which must be supported by a preponderance of the evidence at a hearing before an Administrative Law Judge. Assessment of an individual's RFC is a conclusion about the person's *maximum remaining ability to perform sustained work activities.* It is not the least an individual can do, but the most. As such, the RFC embraces the following:

- ❑ What the individual can no longer do because of his or her impairment(s); and
- ❑ What the individual can still do, in spite of his or her impairment(s).[3]

This includes physical attributes as well as the ability to engage in unskilled, semiskilled, or skilled work. In Social Security parlance, the RFC is expressed generally:

In determining whether your physical or mental impairment or impairments are of a sufficient medical severity that such impairment or impairments could be the basis of eligibility under the law, *we will consider the combined effect of all of your impairments* without regard to whether any such impairment, if considered separately, would be of sufficient severity.[4] (Emphasis added)

Specifically, the Social Security Administration adjudges capacity to perform by the individual's ability to "meet certain demands of jobs."[5] These demands are called "basic work activities" and include

- ❑ Exertional activities

  1. Walking;
  2. Standing;
  3. Sitting;
  4. Pushing;
  5. Pulling;
  6. Carrying; and
  7. Lifting.

- ❑ Nonexertional activities
  1. Hearing;
  2. Seeing; and
  3. Communicating.
- ❑ Postural activities
  1. Climbing;
  2. Balancing;
  3. Stooping (bending the spine alone);
  4. Kneeling (bending the legs alone);
  5. Crouching (bending both the spine and the legs); and
  6. Crawling.
- ❑ Manipulative activities
  1. Reaching;
  2. Handling;
  3. Fingering; and
  4. Feeling.
- ❑ Mental activities
  1. Understanding, remembering, and carrying out instructions;
  2. Exercising appropriate judgment;
  3. Responding appropriately to supervision and co-workers; and
  4. Dealing with usual work settings and routine changes in the workplace.

In assessing an individual's residual functional capacity, the question ultimately becomes: How are each of the foregoing activities affected by the individual's impairment(s)? In real terms, the RFC is the individual's maximum remaining capability to do sustained work activities in an ordinary work setting on a regular and continuing basis. Social Security Ruling 96-8p defines "regular and continuing" as being performed five days per week, eight hours per day, or an equivalent work schedule.

BACK TO CHRIS

Now I'm getting confused. "Exertional" and "nonexertional" activities. "Exertional" and "nonexertional" limitations. Which is it? Jobs? No jobs? RFC?

Get ahold of yourself. Chris thought for a moment. *Think this through logically. Maybe you can draw it out.* Taking a deep breath Chris grabbed a pen and paper and started to diagram the process. Chris's diagram appears in Figure 9–1.

"What if I take out some things? I wonder." Chris drew a different diagram. The modified diagram appears in Figure 9–2.

Chris puzzled over the two drawings. *What's the diagram really of?*

A light suddenly dawned. "I get it. It's a diagram of what it takes to do different jobs. So, if I take away something—such as postural activities—that means that the *job* doesn't require those activities. That means that *a person* who couldn't do those activities could still do that particular job, because the job didn't require the ability to do postural activities."

Chris thought again for a long moment.

"If I were to diagram what a *person* could and could not do, then I would have an idea about what kinds of jobs they were capable of doing. All I'd have to do is match diagrams."

Chris drew yet another diagram showing a person's capabilities (see Figure 9–3).

Chris put the first and third drawings side-by-side. "They sure look similar," Chris exclaimed, knowing they would.

"So, if I take away some things a person can do, what's left? Let's see. How about postural activities? Let's eliminate the ability to do those."

Chris drew another diagram. Experimenting, Chris eliminated the ability to perform postural activities in Figure 9–4.

"Now that's interesting. If a person can't do certain activities, then she or he can't do jobs that require those activities."

Chris thought a moment. "Let's make it more straightforward. Suppose someone has a back injury and can't lift as much as before. Suppose the person is limited to lifting something less than ten pounds." Chris imposes a lifting limitation (see Figure 9–5).

"Then, suppose that the person worked as a delivery truck driver that required lifting at least twenty-five pounds. What then?"

The answer was suddenly obvious. If someone had to be able to lift at least twenty-five pounds, but could only lift up to ten pounds because of a back injury, the person couldn't do the job. The job required the ability to lift at least twenty-five pounds and the person couldn't do it. Simple.

"Surely, Chris murmured, it can't be as easy as that?"

Time to think about this some more. Maybe even hit the books. Chris suppressed a small groan and launched back into study.

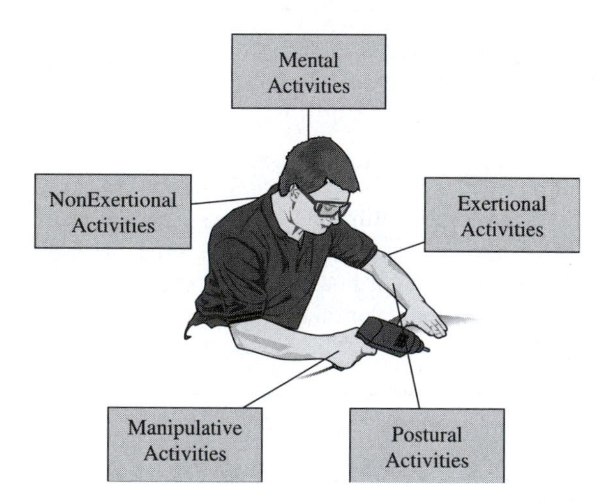

Figure 9–1 **Individual Jobs Require Performance of Different Activities**

Figure 9–2 **Sedentary Jobs**

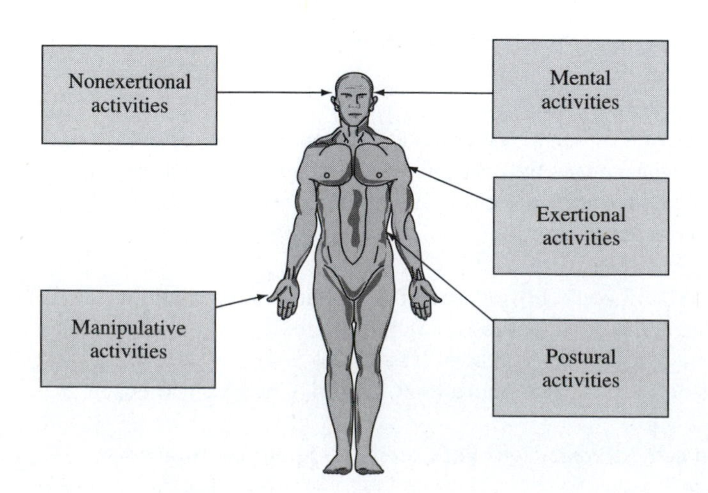

Figure 9–3 **Individual Capability for Work Requires Different Activities**

Figure 9–4 **An Inability to Engage in Postural Activities**

Suppose a person could only lift things that weighed less than 10 pounds.

How would that affect performance in certain jobs?

Figure 9–5 **Lifting Limitation**

FRONT OF YOUR MIND QUESTIONS AND CONSIDERATIONS, 9.2

Formulation of an individual residual functional capacity (RFC) is a multifaceted task. In effect, you paint a picture of the client, describing his or her ability to function in each of the defined areas. This mosaic becomes the definitional standard by which the client's ability to perform work is measured. It becomes the objective throughout the administrative proceeding. Much like a puzzle, evidence must be gathered to prove each of the allegations that comprise the client's limitations. As more fully discussed later, this evidence primarily consists of medical records, including doctors reports, hospital records, laboratory data, and similar information that reflects either the client's medical condition or vocational limitations. Figure 9–6 illustrates how the compilation of many records contributes to the description of the client's condition and resulting limitations.

Describing a client's capabilities is a challenge that demands concise expression. It is easy, however, to become confused. *Limitations* are functional attributes, not *symptoms.* Similarly, symptoms are not *impairments.* Each, however, is related. An impairment gives rise to symptoms, which, in turn produce limitations. The constellation of all limitations attributable to a medically documented impairment creates a picture of a client's capabilities for competitive work.

The Administrative Law Judge must be persuaded that an individual is so limited in what he or she can do that he or she cannot engage is competitive work and is thus entitled to disability benefits. One's capabilities are expressed as what one *can still do* or what one *can no longer do*—a positive or a negative—two sides to the same coin. Think of two basic categories of expression:

- ❑ An individual's exertional *limitations;* and
- ❑ An individual's nonexertional *limitations.*

Why use the term *limitations* and not *capabilities?* Why speak in terms of limitations of function? The answer is simple. First, the client seeks disability benefits. It is, therefore, consistent to consider curtailed capabilities as *limitations,* because a decision maker must be persuaded that the individual can no longer perform activities necessary to sustain competitive work. The goal is to focus the decision on what the client can no longer do, as opposed to what she or he can still do. The collective description of these limitations is the residual functional capacity (RFC). Describing what the client is left able to do—his or her "residual" capacity for work—is a direct function of the established limitations, and that is how it should be expressed.

Limitations must be a result of an impairment. Limitations not reasonably attributable to a medically determinable (diagnosed) condition (an impairment) don't count. Applicable regulations require this linkage, hence the legal determination. Limitations suffered by an otherwise healthy individual solely as a result of age (i.e., not suffering from a medically determinable impairment) are not recognized in the disability determination process. Limitations of function must be a result of an impairment, not simply a result of one's *body habitus,* or *natural bodily condition,* apart from illness, disease, or injury. As seen in Figure 9–7, the relationships and the distinctions among impairments, symptoms, and limitations are important to understanding the disability determination.

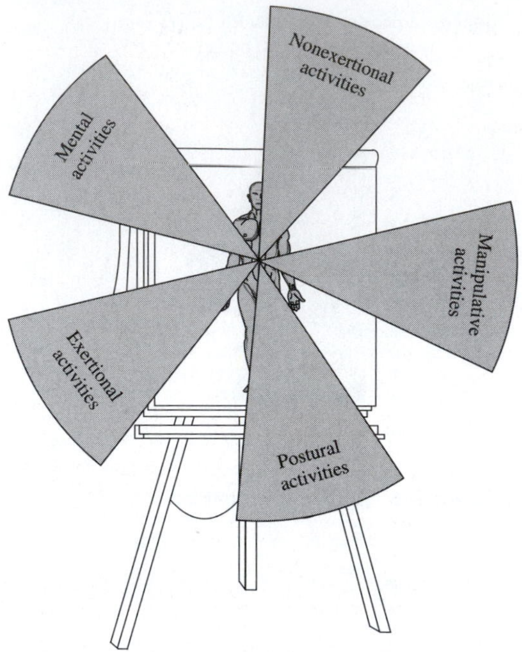

Effective representation requires the construction of a complete picture of your client's capabilities. Evidence must show the capability to engage in exertional, postural, mental, nonexertional, and manipulative activities.

Figure 9–6 **Many Records Contribute to the Description of a Client's Capabilities**

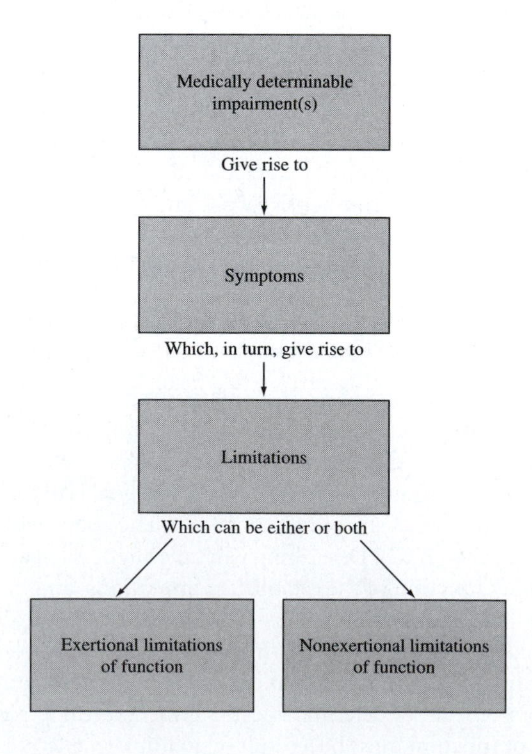

Figure 9–7 **Relationships among Impairments, Symptoms, and Limitations**

IMPAIRMENTS

An impairment is a medically diagnosed (determinable) condition. It must be documented by medical signs and laboratory findings. (See, Social Security Ruling 96-4p, Appendix B-1.) The medical signs and laboratory findings constitute the evidence that supports a representative's assertions. The regulations define acceptable medical sources from which evidence may be acquired. Acceptable medical sources include the following:

1. Licensed physicians;
2. Licensed osteopaths;
3. Licensed or certified psychologists;
4. Licensed optometrists; and
5. Persons authorized to send copies of summaries of hospital, clinical, sanatorium, medical institution, or health care facility medical records.[6]

The reports and records obtained from these acceptable medical sources constitute the evidence that supports a client's testimony. The reports and records contain, among other things, descriptions of the client's symptoms, the medical signs the doctor finds supportive (or not) of the symptoms, and the laboratory findings, that is objective medical tests in aid of diagnosis and treatment. Indeed, the regulations are clear about these issues. "Medical findings consist of *symptoms, signs,* and *laboratory findings.*"[7] In other words, the doctor should be able to document symptoms, and show the existence or severity of a disease, illness, or injury by means of signs and laboratory findings. This information is contained in medical records, reports, progress notes, and narrative summaries—all evidence that must be presented.

SYMPTOMS

Symptoms are defined as the patient's "own description of . . . [the] . . . physical or mental impairment."[8] A client's statements about what he or she is suffering is insufficient evidence to support a claim for disability without objective signs and laboratory findings. Objective evidence in the form of signs and laboratory findings that confirms the existence of an impairment can then be linked to the symptoms. Complaints of symptoms without evidence of an underlying impairment cannot form the basis for an award of disability.[9] Similarly, an underlying impairment that does not give rise to symptoms, and, therefore, to limitations of function, cannot be the basis for an award of disability.

MEDICAL SIGNS

Medical signs include objective evidence that support allegations of disabling symptoms, and, in turn, limitations of function. The regulations define signs as

> **anatomical, physiological, or psychological abnormalities which can be observed, apart from your statements (symptoms).[10]**

To be accepted, evidence of medical signs that support a client's symptoms must be "shown by medically acceptable clinical diagnostic techniques."[11] In other words, the clinical methods used by the doctor to demonstrate the validity of symptoms, such that signs of an underlying disease, illness, or injury are documented, must be recognized within the medical community as legitimate. A clinical method depends on a doctor's subjective observations, not laboratory data, which is different in the regulations (and in medical practice).

These standards apply in the diagnosis of mental disorders as well:

> **Psychiatric signs are medically demonstrable phenomena which indicate specific abnormalities of behavior, affect, thought, memory, orientation and contact with reality.[12]**

Because mental disorders are sometimes more difficult to diagnose, the regulations also require that

> **[t]hey must also be shown by observable facts that can be medically described and evaluated.[13]**

What this means in terms of actual signs depends, of course, on the nature of the underlying impairment, much like a physical impairment.

LABORATORY FINDINGS

Laboratory findings are objective, consisting of

> **anatomical, physiological, or psychological phenomena which can be shown by the use of medically acceptable laboratory diagnostic techniques. Some of these diagnostic techniques include chemical tests, electrophysiological studies (electrocardiogram, electroencephalogram, etc.) roetgenological studies (X-rays), and psychological tests.[14]**

Such tests are often performed by treating physicians or other medical professionals during a hospital stay, but they can also be performed by consultative examiners for the Social Security Administration, either prior to the state DDS determination or, before an Administrative Law Judge decides the case on appeal. Notably, a consultative examination can be requested at any point in the adjudicative process. When doing so, however, it is important to document the request and the basis for it. Simply asking for testing, or a specific test, without some medical basis in the record may be appropriate grounds for denial of the request. Note, however, some jurisdictions require such testing, even if the only basis for it is the client's own allegations, unsupported by medically documented signs or laboratory findings. This is especially true when a client has been unable to afford to see a doctor or receive medical care.

BACK TO CHRIS

Steve strolled into Chris' office. "Doing Ok?" he asked.

"Wow! This is a lot of stuff about impariments, symptoms, and limitations! Tell me why it's important—not only from a medical standpoint but also from a legal point of view. After all, that's what this is all about eventually—proving your case to a judge."

"Here goes," replied Steve, sliding a chair across from Chris.

FRONT OF YOUR MIND QUESTIONS AND CONSIDERATIONS, 9.3

WHY SYMPTOMS, SIGNS, AND LABORATORY FINDINGS ARE IMPORTANT

Symptoms, medical signs, and laboratory findings are evidentiary. A client's recitation of symptoms, both during testimony at a hearing and as recounted to a physician, constitute legal *evidence* of limitations. Medical signs, observed and recorded by a doctor, are potentially corroborative of the client's symptomology. Similarly, laboratory findings are tangible evidence of an impairment and, like observed signs, potentially corroborate the existence of symptoms giving rise to limitations. Thus, symptoms, medical signs and laboratory findings are crucially important. They are the basis of a case. They are the essence of what must be proved to win.

Symptoms, as experienced and related by the client, are often the only expression of a client's limitations. The client's expression of symptoms is generally the only way to describe his or her limitations.

Medical signs, however, are clinical observations by a doctor, and although not related by the client, can serve to corroborate his or her symptoms.

Laboratory findings are the proverbial icing on the cake. They are objective data potentially supportive not only of a client's description of symptoms but also of the doctor's observation of medical signs.[15] (See Figure 9–8.)

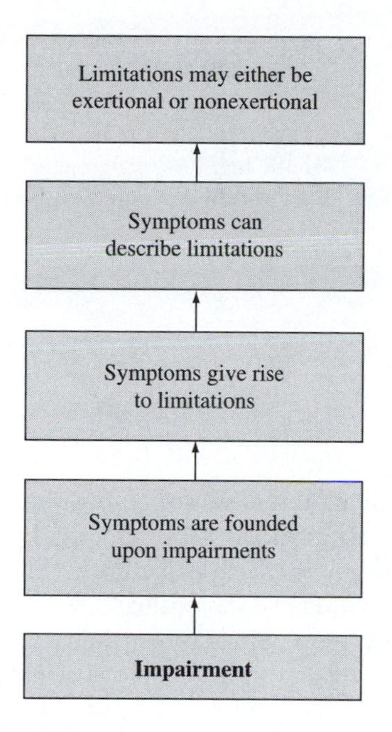

To persuade the judge of the existence of a disabling impairment, you must first prove the existence of an impairment, which produces symptoms which, in turn, gives rise to limitations of function, both exertional and nonexertional in nature.

Figure 9–8 **The Relationship among Impairments, Symptoms, and Limitations**

BACK TO CHRIS

Chris wished Steve hadn't had to go. This was still a lot of informatin to digest.

"Climb the ladder," Chris muttered, staring at the multilevel chart. "First I have to show an impairment. Got it." *An impairment is a medically documented (determinable) condition—a disease, illness, injury, or other bodily condition—that has lasted or is expected to last at least twelve months or result in death and that reasonably gives rise to limitations of function, which in turn prevent the individual from engaging in competitive work—eight hours a day, five days a week.*

"Whew! That's a mouthful!" Chris pondered the chart. "Then I have to show a limitation—No, symptoms next! Then limitations, either exertional or nonexertional."

I've got to organize this further. Let's see. How about if I make a chart of some commonly seen exertional and nonexertional limitations?

"Here goes something!" *I hope....*

FRONT OF YOUR MIND QUESTIONS AND CONSIDERATIONS, 9.4

EXERTIONAL LIMITATIONS

Exertional limitations describe what an individual cannot do in terms of

- ❑ Walking;
- ❑ Standing;
- ❑ Sitting;
- ❑ Pushing;
- ❑ Pulling;
- ❑ Lifting; and
- ❑ Carrying.[16]

The severity of a limitation is measured against vocational requirements for competitive work. *Sedentary* jobs, which are the least physically demanding work, require lifting "no more than 10 pounds at a time and occasionally lifting or carrying articles like docket files, ledgers, and small tools. . . . Jobs are sedentary if walking and standing are required occasionally. . . ."[17]

Light jobs are the next most physically demanding work. They involve "lifting no more than 20 pounds at a time with frequent lifting or carrying of objects weighing up to 10 pounds . . . a job is . . . in this category . . . requires a good deal of walking or standing, or . . . involves sitting most of the time with some pushing and pulling of arm or leg controls."[18]

Medium work is more demanding than sedentary or light work and "involves lifting no more than 50 pounds at a time with frequent lifting or carrying of objects weighing up to 25 pounds."[19]

Beyond medium work are *heavy* jobs, which involve "lifting no more than 100 pounds at a time with frequent lifting or carrying of objects weighing up to 50 pounds."[20]

Finally, *very heavy* jobs are those which require the worker to lift "objects weighing more than 100 pounds at a time with frequent lifting or carrying of objects weighing 50 pounds or more."[21]

Exertional limitations (arising as a result of a medically determinable impairment) that restrict an individual's ability to function potentially affect the extent to which an individual can perform physically, thus potentially limiting the type of job able to be performed. The regulations define basic work activities as including a range of physical functions

such as walking, standing, sitting, lifting, pushing, pulling, reaching, carrying or handling.[22]

When these functions are limited, they potentially restrict the type and numbers of jobs which the individual can perform. Figure 9–9 describes the requirements associated with the basic physical work activities

Physical Activity	Sedentary Requirement	Light Requirement	Medium Requirement	Heavy Requirement	Very Heavy Requirement
Sitting	6 of 8 hours	2 of 8 hours	2 of 8 hours	2 of 8 hours	2 of 8 hours
Standing and walking	2 of 8 hours	6 of 8 hours	6 of 8 hours	6 of 8 hours	6 of 8 hours
Lifting and carrying	Under 10 pounds frequently	10 pounds frequently, 20 pounds occasionally	25 pounds frequently, 50 pounds occasionally	50 pounds frequently, occasionally no more than 100 pounds	50 pounds frequently, occasionally more than 100 pounds

Figure 9–9 **Physical Requirements of Various Exertional Levels**

for the basic work activities of sitting, standing, walking, lifting, and carrying. These are the defining characteristics of the foregoing job categories. Limitations that affect these activities can dramatically affect the ability to perform work at a given physical (sedentary, light, medium, heavy, or very heavy) level.

Figure 9–10 describes sample limitations of function for each of the exertional functions.

Each defined exertional activity is subject to limitations. Figure 9–10 provides examples of what different limitations might be (and the list is far from complete). The actual limitation a judge might find, and the evidence might show, is a direct expression of the medical evidence. An acceptable limitation must be documented as (1) related to a medically determinable impairment and (2) actually existing over a twelve-month period or be expected to last twelve months. This parallels the requirement at step 2 that a severe impairment subsist for twelve months, result in death, or otherwise be reasonably expected to last for at least twelve months. Thus, limitations must "track" the impairment to which they are related.

Formulation of a "typical" residual functional capacity (RFC) is a process in which the representative must actively participate. Figure 9–11 is illustrative.

Exertional Function	Limitations Example 1	Limitations Example 2	Limitations Example 3	Limitations Example 4	Limitations Example 5
Sitting	Unable to sit for longer than 15 minutes at a time	Must elevate one or both legs above waist while seated	Must balance weight on right, dominant arm while seated	Must use restroom 5 times an hour, 5 minutes at a time	Can only sit 2 of 8 hours per day
Standing and walking	Cannot stand or walk	Can only stand or walk less than 5 minutes at a time	Ataxic (uneven) gait	Cannot walk on uneven surfaces	Can only stand and walk less than 6 hours per day
Lifting and carrying	Can lift less than 5 pounds	Can only lift with non-dominant, left arm	Cannot lift any weight frequently	Cannot lift above waist height	Can only lift up to 10 pounds
Handling—fine motor manipulation	Unable to use left hand for grasping	Two fingers on dominant right hand are stiff and cannot bend to grasp	Can only write or use dominant hand for 15 minutes at a time before having to rest for 30 minutes	Right dominant hand amputee	Bilateral carpal tunnel syndrome prevents repetitive motion of the hand and wrist
Reaching	Unable to reach overhead	Unable to reach to the side	Unable to reach to the front	Unable to reach above waist	Unable to reach above chest
Pushing and Pulling	Unable to push with lower extremities	Unable to pull with upper extremities	Only able to push with right leg	Only able to pull with left arm	Left leg amputee

Figure 9–10 **Exemplar Functional Limitations**

1st — The representative must prove the existence of an impairment, meeting the durational requirements

2nd — The representative must show that there are limitations that flow from the impairment and that these limitations restrict the claimant's ability to engage in competitive work

Figure 9–11 **Representatives Actively Participate in RFC Process**

BACK TO CHRIS

"So how do I actually prove the impairments and the limitations?" mused Chris aloud.

"With the medical evidence," Steve answered, standing against the doorjamb.

"Steve," Chris exclaimed. "I didn't see you there."

"It's late Chris. Is the Carson case bothering you?"

"Well . . . ."

"It's OK to admit it."

"It's not that it's bothering me. It's only that this process is a real challenge. First, it's academic. I have to learn about a whole legal system, something about legal procedure, then something about medicine, and then I have to actually do it!"

Steve smiled. "A little daunting?"

Chris offered a small smile. "A little."

"So what's the problem?"

"OK," Chris took a deep breath. "It's this: How do I actually prove a limitation, or even an impairment?"

"You mean at the hearing?"

"Right."

"Well, it's really not that difficult. Let me show you." Steve went to Chris's desk.

A TRIP TO THE HARD DRIVE, 9.1

Understanding the legal significance of medical records is vitally important. Take *A Trip to the Hard Drive* to learn more about applying this information in a legal setting.

PROVING THE EXISTENCE OF AN IMPAIRMENT AND RELATED LIMITATIONS

Case law is clear. The standard of proof required at a hearing before an Administrative Law Judge is a preponderance of the evidence.[23] In legal proceedings, this is not the lowest standard, but neither is it the highest. The hierarchy proceeds from lowest to highest:

1. Reasonable (belief);
2. Substantial evidence;
3. Preponderance of the evidence;
4. Clear and convincing evidence; and
5. Evidence beyond a reasonable doubt.

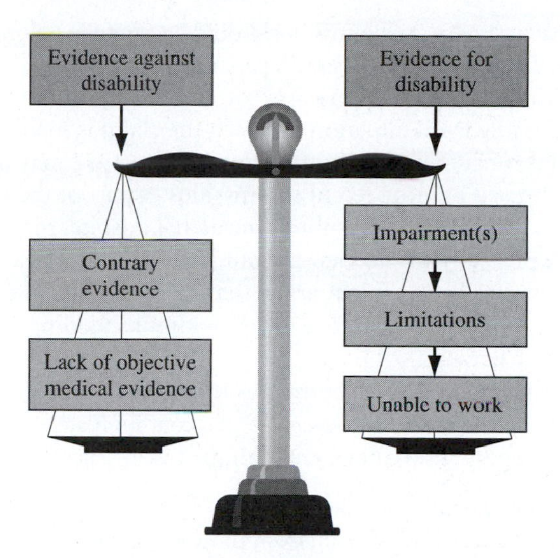

Figure 9–12 **Preponderance of the Evidence**

Preponderance of the evidence means the greater weight of the evidence. It is a question of weight on a scale: 51% versus 49%. Even tipping the scale by a mere percentage point is sufficient to meet the preponderance of the evidence standard. Thus, the task is to show the judge by a preponderance of the evidence that the client suffers from a severe impairment, from which reasonably arise limitations of function, which, in turn, prevent him or her from engaging in competitive work, five days per week, eight hours per day. Figure 9–12 diagrams the process.

In an administrative proceeding before the Social Security Administration, the formal rules of evidence otherwise applicable in a municipal, state, or federal court do not apply. For many, this brings a sigh of relief—"I don't have to memorize and know a bunch of new rules"—which is especially true for non-lawyer practitioners.[24] The downside is the absence of any standard that tells which evidence is acceptable and which is not. Fortunately, federal regulations offer some guidance.

Materiality

The only evidentiary standard at an administrative hearing before the Social Security Administration is materiality. The pertinent regulation provides, in part:

> **At the hearing, the Administrative Law Judge looks fully into the issues, questions you and the other witnesses, and accepts as evidence any documents *that are material* to the issues.[25]**

This means any document, medical record, information, report, or other written submission can be presented without regard to formal legal rules on hearsay, authenticity, or relevancy. Materiality is a broad standard, which allows the judge (and the representative) great latitude in accepting or submitting written materials.

Be careful, however. Do not assume, simply because a document is accepted, marked, and admitted as an exhibit to the administrative record, that it will be given equal consideration with other documents. Admission as a material exhibit does not require a judge to give it the same weight as other evidence. Thus, how much credence, or weight, a judge gives a document is up to the discretion of the judge. It must, nevertheless, be viewed in light of the record as a whole and given the credence appropriate to the nature of the document itself. This is discussed more fully later.

Given the absence of formal rules governing the submission of evidentiary records, it becomes far easier to submit records in support of the assertion of both an impairment and an RFC. The challenge is to be prepared: Be thorough, creative, and well organized—effectively present the case to prove the existence of an impairment and demonstrate by a preponderance of the evidence the resulting limitations.

Types of Evidence That Are Acceptable to Prove an Impairment

As a general matter, a representative is entitled to "state your case," to "present a written summary of your case, or to enter written statements about the facts and the law material to your case."[26] From a broad perspective this means that almost anything bearing on the issues then before the judge may be subject to written submission.

As a practical matter, however, submissions should be carefully tailored to meet the issues; they should not be part of a bombardment of paper. Too much paper may dilute the impact of significant individual reports, opinions, or other records critical to the case.

A classic example is the situation in which the claim is made for disability beginning in 2000. Medical evidence of a congenital condition dating back to 1972 may only be of marginal relevance and may be generally addressed in more recent submissions as part of the present medical history or summary. It would be a mistake to obtain and submit the actual hospital records, reports, and supporting data from 1972. The judge probably would view the old records as superfluous to the issue of disability in the year 2000, though technically one might argue that the earlier records are material. Such a submission only increases the size of the administrative record without shedding any real light on the issue of current disability benefits entitlement.

As noted earlier, an impairment must be supported by medical signs and laboratory findings. Records that establish both the diagnosis and the severity of the condition are important. Equally important are documents that establish the longevity and currency of the impairment. These issues address simple, but powerful questions:

- ❑ How long has the condition lasted?
- ❑ Is the claimant currently suffering from this condition?
- ❑ How severe was the condition over time?
- ❑ How severe is the condition now?

Once they are answered, these questions establish the nature, extent, and duration of the impairment; they also inform the Administrative Law Judge whether there has been improvement or worsening in the condition over time.

What documents accomplish these tasks? The list is varied. Every case will not have all of the following records, but the fact that such records may exist or can be obtained should always be kept in mind when formulating the nature, extent, and severity of the claimant's impairment.

- ❑ Medical records generally;
- ❑ Treating physician's reports;
- ❑ Treating physician's progress notes;
- ❑ Treating physician's opinion(s) about the diagnosis, symptoms, restrictions, treatment regimen, medication side effects, and prognosis;
- ❑ Physical and mental medical source statements (MSS) prepared by a treating physician, examining physician, or medical expert (the MSS is a form describing the various physical or mental limitations a person might have, as described by the physician). It is a form the Social Security Administration generates (see Figure 9–15);
- ❑ Hospital records;
- ❑ Emergency room records;
- ❑ Nursing home or other long-term care facility records;
- ❑ Prison records, including prison medical records;
- ❑ Veteran's Affairs (VA) records, including hospital, clinic, and in-patient alcohol and drug addiction treatment records;
- ❑ Consulting physicians' reports and testing;
- ❑ Physical therapy records and reports;
- ❑ Psychological and psychiatric reports and testing;
- ❑ Psychotherapy treatment records (such as at a mental health center);
- ❑ Consultative examination reports and records of consulting physicians retained by SSA to conduct a one-time examination of the claimant;
- ❑ Medical expert testimony offered by an expert witness at a hearing after review of all pertinent medical records;
- ❑ School testing, reports, academic records, and disciplinary reports or actions taken;
- ❑ Reports or statements from a teacher or school counselor; and
- ❑ Statements, declarations, or affidavits of lay people, including friends, co-workers, family, or others desiring to comment on the claimant's condition or ability to function.

Each of these records, if they exist in the case, holds potential for positive evidence that supports a claim for disability. Records can be obtained in several ways. Records a client is able to provide should be obtained first. These will likely lead to other doctors consulted or treatment received. Second, write to the health care provider (be it a hospital, other facility, or an individual doctor) and request their records.

Note: Many states now require health care providers to provide medical records to a patient pursuing workers' compensation or other disability claims free of charge. Check state law to determine if such is the case. If so, obtain a copy of the law and send it with the written request for records.

Note further: A client should have completed and signed an authorization form for release of medical records; include this with the request.

Finally, request that the Administrative Law Judge issue a subpoena if the records cannot be obtained otherwise. Title 20 C.F.R. § 404.950(d) provides that a subpoena may be issued "when it is reasonably necessary." Subpoenas may also be issued by a member of the Appeals Council. Subpoenas may require the "appearance and testimony of witnesses" or may require the "production of books, records, correspondence, papers, or other documents *that are material* to an issue at the hearing."[27]

When requesting a subpoena, do so in writing no later than at least five days before the hearing date. As a practical matter, the request must be received by the Administrative Law Judge at least five days before the scheduled hearing. In reality, a subpoena should be requested at the earliest opportunity if there is to be a reasonable expectation that a document will be produced, or a witness appear, at a scheduled hearing.

BACK TO CHRIS

"Doctors don't write for lawyers or representatives, do they?"

"Very perceptive question, Chris. You're right; the medical profession prepares records for their own use, generally not for legal purposes. You have to understand the import of the various records you receive."

"You mean, how they can be used to prove different parts of the five-step sequential analysis process?"

"Exactly. Let's look at it more closely, particularly as related to proving limitations."

A TRIP TO THE HARD DRIVE, 9.2

To learn more about how different documents can be used to prove a claimant's limitations, take *A Trip to the Hard Drive.*

TYPES OF EVIDENCE THAT ARE ACCEPTABLE TO PROVE A LIMITATION OR RFC

Like evidence of an impairment, the documents in which information may be found that describe a limitation or restriction, or the RFC generally, may be found in a variety of documents, virtually identical to those listed earlier:

- ❑ Medical records generally;
- ❑ Treating physician's reports;
- ❑ Treating physician's progress notes;
- ❑ Treating physician's opinion(s) about the diagnosis, symptoms, restrictions, treatment regimen, medication side effects, and prognosis;
- ❑ Physical and mental MSS; prepared either by a treating physician, examining physician, or medical expert;
- ❑ Hospital records;
- ❑ Emergency room records;
- ❑ Nursing home or other, long-term care facility records;
- ❑ Prison records, including prison medical records;
- ❑ Veteran's Affairs (VA) records, including hospital, clinic, and in-patient alcohol and drug addiction treatment records;
- ❑ Consulting physicians' reports and testing;
- ❑ Physical therapy records and reports;
- ❑ Psychological and psychiatric reports and testing;

- ❑ Psychotherapy treatment records (such as at a mental health center);
- ❑ Consultative examination reports and records of consulting physicians retained by SSA to conduct a one-time examination of the claimant;
- ❑ Medical expert testimony offered by an expert witness at a hearing after review of all pertinent medical records;
- ❑ School testing, reports, academic records, and disciplinary reports or actions taken;
- ❑ Reports or statements from a teacher or school counselor; and
- ❑ Statements, declarations, or affidavits of lay people, including friends, co-workers, family, or others desiring to comment on the claimant's condition or ability to function.

Health care providers (doctors, hospitals, or other entities) will not "speak" the specialized language of Social Security disability. Specific references to terms such as *RFC* or *limitation* will not likely be used by them. Representatives must carefully review all available records to ascertain whether a doctor has, in some way, suggested limits to a client's ability to function.

Sometimes a doctor's report is direct, specifically detailing a patient's restrictions or otherwise curtailing activities. These are limitations. Other times, the physician may be indirect, commenting that the patient "should not return to work," or using other, similar language. Such information must be gleaned from the record, isolated, correlated with the medical evidence of the impairment(s), and presented to the judge. Like the old gold rush miners in California, the myriads of sands must be sifted through to find the golden nuggets.

UNDERSTANDING THE HIERARCHY OF MEDICAL EVIDENCE

Although materiality is the essential standard by which the submission of evidence is judged, the regulations specify a hierarchy of medical evidence, such that evidence from one type of source may be given greater weight than evidence from another type of source.

Title 20 C.F.R.§ 404.1527(d) addresses how medical opinions are weighed and establishes a hierarchy:

- ❑ Evidence from a *treating doctor* is given controlling weight, because, as the regulation notes, "these sources are likely to be the medical professionals most able to provide a detailed, longitudinal picture of your medical impairment(s)";
- ❑ Evidence from an *examining doctor*, that is, a doctor who has examined the claimant but who is not a treating doctor, is considered after the treating doctor. Typically, an examining doctor is a consulting examiner (CE) who has been retained by the state DDS (the state agency) to examine the claimant on a one-time basis and prepare a report of the findings. However, nothing prevents the representative or the claimant from retaining an examining doctor to conduct a personal examination. (See Title 20 C.F.R. § 404.1527[d][1].)
- ❑ Evidence from a *nonexamining doctor* falls third in the ranks, behind the examining doctor. Typically, a nonexamining doctor is a physician who has reviewed the various medical records and reports but not actually examined the claimant. Such evidence is usually testimony from an expert witness. Again, nothing prevents the claimant or the representative from retaining a personal medical expert—though such persons are usually called by the Administrative Law Judge to appear in a difficult case. (See Title 20 C.F.R. § 404.1527[f]).

The significance of the foregoing hierarchy is self-evident. A treating physician generally trumps an examining physician, who generally trumps a nonexamining expert witness. However, in assessing the weight given, the regulations further provide that specific factors be considered, and, only then, may the hierarchy be followed in its essential form. These factors include the following:

- ❑ Length of treating relationship and frequency of examination;
- ❑ Nature and extent of treating relationship;
- ❑ Supportability (Are there clinical observations, medical signs, and laboratory findings that support the doctor's opinion?);
- ❑ Consistency (Is the opinion consistent with the record as a whole?);
- ❑ Specialization (Is the opinion offered from a specialist in a given field? If so, more weight will be accorded the specialist than someone who is not, all else being equal.).

Figure 9–13 diagrams the relationship of these various elements.

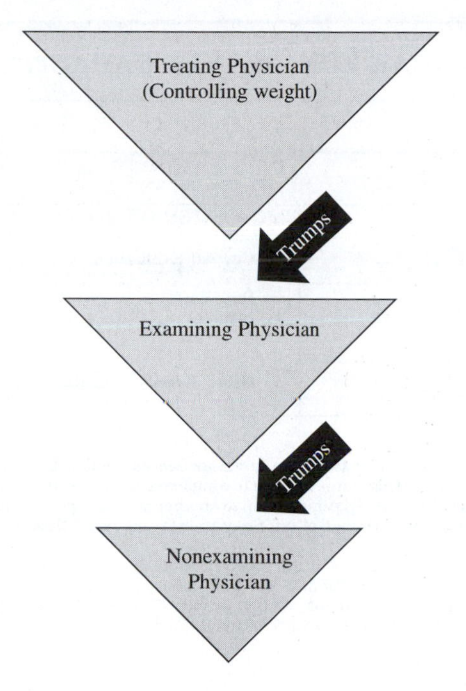

Figure 9–13 **Hierarchy of Medical Evidence**

BACK TO CHRIS

"Aren't there forms or something?"

"For the doctors to fill out?"

"Right. Something that lays out all the possible limitations."

"Absolutely." Steve scratched his head. "I think I've got some in my office. Let's go see."

And, not surprisingly, he did have some in his office.

A TRIP TO THE HARD DRIVE, 9.3

Take *A Trip to the Hard Drive* to learn more about the forms that describe both physical and mental limitations of function.

THE PHYSICAL RFC FORM (MEDICAL SOURCE STATEMENT)

The Social Security Administration uses standardized forms called medical source statements to express the opinion of a medical doctor or psychologist about a claimant's limitations. It is not an affidavit per se, because it is not sworn to, but it is a signed statement of the doctor expressing his or her opinions about the claimant. As such, it is similar to a declaration if offered in federal court, applying the Federal Rules of Evidence (FRE). Here, however, the FRE do not apply, hence there are generally no issues concerning authenticity or validity. The form, once signed and dated by a claimant's doctor, an examining doctor (CE), or a medical expert, is admissible into the administrative record. The judge ascertains how much weight the document will be given, depending on both who prepared the document and on the nature and quality of the supporting medical evidence.

Medical source statements (MSSs) are used throughout the country in various formats. Figures 9–14 through 9–16 show three formats.

FORM APPROVED
OMB NO. 0960-0431

RESIDUAL PHYSICAL FUNCTIONAL CAPACITY ASSESSMENT

CLAIMANT:

SOCIAL SECURITY NUMBER:

NUMBERHOLDER (IF CDB CLAIM):

PRIMARY DIAGNOSIS:

SECONDARY DIAGNOSIS:

OTHER ALLEGED IMPAIRMENTS:

RFC ASSESSMENT IS FOR:

☐ Current Evaluation

☐ Date Last Insured: ______ (Date)

☐ Date 12 Months After Onset: ______ (Date)

☐ Other (Specify): ______

Paperwork/Privacy Act Notice: The information requested on this form is authorized by Section 223 and Section 1633 of the Social Security Act. The information provided will be used in making a decision on this claim. Failure to complete this form may result in a delay in processing the claim. Information furnished on this form may be disclosed by the Social Security Administration to another person or governmental agency only with respect to Social Security programs and to comply with federal laws requiring the exchange of information between Social Security and other agencies.

TIME IT TAKES TO COMPLETE THIS FORM: We estimate that it will take you about 20 minutes to complete this form. This includes the time it will take to read the instructions, gather the necessary facts and fill out the form. If you have comments or suggestions on how long it takes to complete this form or on any other aspect of this form, write to the Social Security Administration, ATTN: Reports Clearance Officer, 1-A-21 Operations Bldg., Baltimore, MD 21235, and to the Office of Management and Budget, Paperwork Reduction Project (0960-0431), Washington, D.C. 20503.

I. LIMITATIONS:

For Each Section A - F

➡ Base your conclusions on **all evidence** in file (clinical and laboratory findings; symptoms; observations; lay evidence; reports of daily activities; etc.).

➡ Check the blocks which reflect your **reasoned judgment**.

➡ Describe how the **evidence substantiates your conclusions.** (Cite specific clinical and laboratory findings, observations, lay evidence, etc.).

➡ Ensure that you have requested:

- Apropriate treating and examining source statements regarding the individual's capacities (DI 22505.000ff. and DI 22510.000ff.) and that you have given appropriate **weight to treating source conclusions**. (See Section III.)
- Considered and responded to **any alleged limitations imposed by symptoms** (pain, fatigue, etc.) attributable, in your judgment, to a medically determinable impairment. Discuss your assessment of symptom - related limitations in the explanation for your conclusions in A - F below. (See also Section II.)
- Responded to all allegations of physical limitations or factors which can cause physical limitations.

➡ **Frequently** means occurring one-third to two-thirds of an 8-hour workday (cumulative, not continuous). **Occasionally** means occurring from very little up to one-third of an 8-hour workday (cumulative, not continuous).

FORM **SSA-4734-U8** (1/89)
Supersedes Forms SSA-4734-F4 (3-82)

Page 1

☐ Continued on Page 2

Figure 9–14 **Residual Physical Functional Capacity Assessment Generally Completed by a Physician**

A. EXERTIONAL LIMITATIONS

☐ None established. (Proceed to section B.)

1. **Occasionally** lift and/or carry (including upward pulling) (maximum)—when less than one-third of the time or less than 10 pounds, explain the amount (time/pounds) in item 6.

   ☐ less than 10 pounds
   ☐ 10 pounds
   ☐ 20 pounds
   ☐ 50 pounds
   ☐ 100 pounds or more

2. **Frequently** lift and/or carry (including upward pulling) (maximum)—when less than two-thirds of the time or less than 10 pounds, explain the amount (time/pounds) in item 6.

   ☐ less than 10 pounds
   ☐ 10 pounds
   ☐ 25 pounds
   ☐ 50 pounds or more

3. Stand and/or walk (with normal breaks) for a total of—

   ☐ less than 2 hours in an 8-hour workday
   ☐ at least 2 hours in an 8-hour workday
   ☐ about 6 hours in an 8-hour workday

   ☐ medically required hand-held assistive device is necessary for ambulation

4. Sit (with normal breaks) for a total of—

   ☐ less than about 6 hours in an 8-hour workday
   ☐ about 6 hours in an 8-hour workday

   ☐ must periodically alternate sitting and standing to relieve pain or discomfort. (If checked, explain in 6.)

5. Push and/or pull (including operation of hand and/or foot controls)—

   ☐ unlimited, other than as shown for lift and/or carry
   ☐ limited in **upper** extremities (describe nature and degree)
   ☐ limited in **lower** extremities (describe nature and degree)

6. Explain how and why the evidence supports your conclusions in item 1 through 5. Cite the specific facts upon which your conclusions are based.

FORM **SSA-4734-U8** (1-89) Page 2 ☐ Continued on Page 3

(continued)

6. Continue (NOTE: MAKE ADDITIONAL COMMENTS IN SECTION IV)

B. POSTURAL LIMITATIONS

☐ None established. (Proceed to section C.)

	Frequently	Occasionally	Never
1. Climbing—ramp/stairs —ladder/rope/scaffolds	☐	☐	☐
2. Balancing	☐	☐	☐
3. Stooping	☐	☐	☐
4. Kneeling	☐	☐	☐
5. Crouching	☐	☐	☐
6. Crawling	☐	☐	☐

7. When less than two-thirds of the time for frequently or less than one-third for occasionally, fully describe and explain. Also explain how and why the evidence supports your conclusions in items 1 through 6. Cite the specific facts upon which your conclusions are based.

FORM **SSA-4734-U8** (1-89) Page 3 ☐ Continued on Page 4

C. MANIPULATIVE LIMITATIONS

☐ None established. (Proceed to section D.)

	LIMITED	UNLIMITED
1. Reaching all directions (including overhead) →	☐	☐
2. Handling (gross manipulation) →	☐	☐
3. Fingering (fine manipulation) →	☐	☐
4. Feeling (skin receptors) →	☐	☐

5. Describe how the activities checked "limited" are impaired. Also, explain how and why the evidence supports your conclusions in item 1 through 4. Cite the specific facts upon which your conclusions are based.

D. VISUAL LIMITATIONS

☐ None established. (Proceed to section E.)

	LIMITED	UNLIMITED
1. Near acuity →	☐	☐
2. Far acuity →	☐	☐
3. Depth perception →	☐	☐
4. Accommodation →	☐	☐
5. Color vision →	☐	☐
6. Field of vision →	☐	☐

7. Describe how the faculties checked "limited" are impaired. Also explain how and why the evidence supports your conclusions in item 1 through 6. Cite the specific facts upon which your conclusions are based.

FORM **SSA-4734-U8** (1-89) Page 4 ☐ Continued on Page 5

(continued)

E. COMMUNICATIVE LIMITATIONS

☐ None established. (Proceed to section F.)

	LIMITED	UNLIMITED
1. Hearing →	☐	☐
2. Speaking →	☐	☐

3. Describe how the faculties checked "limited" are impaired. Also, explain how and why the evidence supports your conclusions in items 1 and 2. Cite the specific facts upon which your conclusions are based.

F. ENVIRONMENTAL LIMITATIONS

☐ None established. (Proceed to section II.)

	UNLIMITED	AVOID CONCENTRATED EXPOSURE	AVOID EVEN MODERATE EXPOSURE	AVOID ALL EXPOSURE
1. Extreme cold →	☐	☐	☐	☐
2. Extreme heat →	☐	☐	☐	☐
3. Wetness →	☐	☐	☐	☐
4. Humidity →	☐	☐	☐	☐
5. Noise →	☐	☐	☐	☐
6. Vibration →	☐	☐	☐	☐
7. Fumes, odors, dusts, gases, poor ventilation, etc. →	☐	☐	☐	☐
8. Hazards (machinery, heights, etc.) →	☐	☐	☐	☐

9. Describe how these environmental factors impair activities and identify hazards to be avoided. Also, explain how and why the evidence supports your conclusions in items 1 through 8. Cite the specific facts upon which your conclusions are based.

FORM **SSA-4734-U8** (1-89) Page 5 ☐ Continued on Page 6

9. Continue (NOTE: MAKE ADDITIONAL COMMENTS IN SECTION IV)

II. SYMPTOMS

For symptoms alleged by the claimant to produce physical limitations, and for which the following have not previously been addressed in section I, discuss whether:

A. The symptom(s) is attributable, in your judgment, to a medically determinable impairment.

B. The severity or duration of the symptom(s), in your judgment, is disproportionate to the expected severity or expected duration on the basis of the claimant's medically determinable impairment(s).

C. The severity of the symptom(s) and its alleged effect on function is consistent, in your judgment, with the total medical and nonmedical evidence, including statements by the claimant and others, observations regarding activities of daily living, and alterations of usual behavior or habits.

 ☐ Continued on Page 7

(continued)

Figure 9–14 **Residual Physical Functional Capacity Assessment Generally Completed by a Physician** ***(continued)***

III. TREATING OR EXAMINING SOURCE STATEMENT(S)

A. Is a treating or examining source statement(s) regarding the claimant's physical capacities in file?

☐ **Yes**

☐ **No (Includes situations in which there was no source or when the source(s) did not provide a statement regarding the claimant's physical capacities.)**

B. If yes, are there treating/examining source conclusions about the claimant's limitations or restrictions which are significantly different from your findings?

☐ **Yes**

☐ **No**

C. If yes, explain why those conclusions are not supported by the evidence in file. (Cite the source's name and the statement date.)

FORM **SSA-4734-U8** (1-89) Page 7

☐ Continued on Page 8

IV. ADDITIONAL COMMENTS:

MEDICAL CONSULTANT'S SIGNATURE:	MEDICAL CONSULTANT'S CODE:	DATE:

FORM **SSA-4734-U8** (1-89)

*U.S. GPO:1991-300-570

MEDICAL SOURCE STATEMENT OF ABILITY TO DO WORK-RELATED ACTIVITIES (PHYSICAL)

NAME OF INDIVIDUAL **SOCIAL SECURITY NUMBER**

To assist us in determining this individual's ability to do work-related activities, please give us your professional opinion of what the individual can still do despite his/her impairment(s). The opinion should be based on your findings with respect to medical history, clinical and laboratory findings (or lack thereof), diagnosis, prescribed treatment and response, expected duration and prognosis.

For each activity shown below:

(1) Check the appropriate block;

(2) Respond to the questions about the individual's ability to perform the activity; and

(3) Identify the factors (e.g., the particular medical signs, laboratory findings, or other factors described above) that support your assessment of any limitations.

IT IS VERY IMPORTANT TO DESCRIBE THE FACTORS THAT SUPPORT YOUR ASSESSMENT. WE ARE REQUIRED TO CONSIDER THE EXTENT TO WHICH YOUR ASSESSMENT IS SUPPORTED.

EXERTIONAL LIMITATIONS

1. Are **LIFTING/CARRYING** affected by the impairment? ☐ No ☐ Yes

If "yes" how many pounds can the individual lift and/or carry?
Frequently means occurring one-third to two-thirds of an 8-hour workday (cumulative, not continuous)
Occasionally means occurring from very little up to one-third of an 8-hour workday (cumulative, not continuous).

Occasionally lift and/or carry (including upward pulling)
(maximum)—when less than one-third of the time or less than 10 pounds, explain the amount (time/pounds) in item 5.

☐ less than 10 pounds
☐ 10 pounds
☐ 20 pounds
☐ 50 pounds
☐ 100 pounds or more

Frequently lift and/or carry (including upward pulling)
(maximum)—when less than two-thirds of the time or less than 10 pounds, explain the amount (time/pounds) in item

☐ less than 10 pounds
☐ 10 pounds
☐ 20 pounds
☐ 50 pounds
☐ 100 pounds or more

2. Are **STANDING and/or WALKING** affected by the impairment? ☐ No ☐ Yes

If "yes" how many hours total (with normal breaks) can the individual stand and/or walk?

☐ less than 2 hours in an 8-hour workday
☐ at least 2 hours in an 8-hour workday
☐ about 6 hours in an 8-hour workday
☐ medically required hand-held assistive device is necessary for ambulation

FORM HA-1151-test(4/99) Page 1

Figure 9–15 **Physical RFC Form**

3. Is **SITTING** affected by the impairment? ☐ No ☐ Yes

If "yes" how many hours total (with normal breaks) can the individual sit?

☐ less than about 6 hours in an 8-hour workday
☐ about 6 hours in an 8-hour workday
☐ must **periodically alternate sitting and standing** to relieve pain or discomfort. (If checked, explain in item 5.)

4. Is **PUSHING and/or PULLING** affected by the impairment? ☐ No ☐ Yes
(including operation of hand and/or foot controls)

☐ limited in **upper** extremities (describe nature and degree)
☐ limited in **lower** extremities (describe nature and degree)

5. What medical/clinical finding(s) support your conclusions in items 1–4 above?

POSTURAL LIMITATIONS

How often can the individual perform the following **POSTURAL** activities?
Frequently means occurring one-third to two-thirds of an 8-hour workday (cumulative, not continuous)
Occasionally means occurring from very little up to one-third of an 8-hour workday (cumulative, not continuous)

	Frequently	Occasionally	Never
1. Climbing—ramps/stairs/ladder/rope/scaffold	☐	☐	☐
2. Balancing	☐	☐	☐
3. Kneeling	☐	☐	☐
4. Crouching	☐	☐	☐
5. Crawling	☐	☐	☐

When less than two-thirds of the time for frequently or less than one-third for occasionally, fully describe and explain. What medical/clinical findings support your conclusions?

FORM HA-1151-test(4/99) Page 2

(continued)

MANIPULATIVE LIMITATIONS

Are the following **MANIPULATIVE** functions affected by the impairment?

	LIMITED	UNLIMITED
1. Reaching all directions (including overhead)	☐	☐
2. Handling (gross manipulation)	☐	☐
3. Fingering (fine manipulation)	☐	☐
4. Feeling (skin receptors)	☐	☐

5. Describe how the activities checked "limited" are impaired. What medical/clinical findings support your conclusions?

VISUAL/COMMUNICATIVE LIMITATIONS

Are the following functions affected by the impairment?

	LIMITED	UNLIMITED
1. Seeing	☐	☐
2. Hearing	☐	☐
3. Speaking	☐	☐

4. Describe how the faculties checked "limited" are impaired. What medical/clinical findings support your conclusions?

ENVIRONMENTAL LIMITATIONS

Are the following **ENVIRONMENTAL LIMITATIONS** caused by the impairment?

	LIMITED	UNLIMITED
1. Temperature Extremes	☐	☐
2. Noise	☐	☐
3. Dust	☐	☐
4. Vibration	☐	☐
5. Humidity/Wetness	☐	☐
6. Hazards (machinery, heights, . . .)	☐	☐
7. Fumes, odors, chemicals, gases	☐	☐

8. Describe how the environmental factors impair activities and identify hazards to be avoided. What medical/clinical findings support your conclusions?

Physician's Signature ______________ Medical Specialty ______________ Date ______________

FORM HA-1151-test(4/99) Page 3

Claimant's Name: ______________________________

SSN: ______________________________

Statement of Current Physical Abilities

Today, I am physically able to perform the following activities **in a typical 8-hour workday:**

1. Walk ____ minutes **at a time;** and ____ hours **in a workday.**
2. Stand ____ minutes **at a time;** and ____ hours **in a workday.**
3. Sit ____ minutes **at a time;** and ____ hours **in a workday.**
4. Push items weighing ____ **# occasionally;** and ____ **# frequently.**
5. Pull items weighing ____ **# occasionally;** and ____ **# frequently.**
6. Lift items weighing ____ **# occasionally;** and ____ **# frequently.**
7. Carry items weighing ____ **# occasionally;** and ____ **# frequently.**

["occasionally" means up to 1/3 of the time; "frequently" means from 1/3 to 2/3 of the time]

I have the following additional physical and/or mental restrictions and limitations:

Claimant's Signature ______________________ **Date:** __________

Figure 9–16 **Claimant's Own Statement of Limitations**

Although each of these forms differs in appearance, each contains selected common areas:

❑ ***Exertional limitations***

1. Lifting and carrying;
2. Sitting;
3. Standing and walking; and
4. Pushing and pulling.

❑ ***Postural limitations***

1. Climbing;
2. Balancing;
3. Kneeling;
4. Crouching; and
5. Crawling.

❑ ***Environmental limitations***

1. Temperature extremes;
2. Noise;
3. Dust;

4. Vibration;
5. Humidity;
6. Hazards (moving machinery, heights, etc.); and
7. Fumes, odors, chemicals, and gases.

Each form also asks the physician to support his or her findings with medical and clinical findings. The official form (HA-1151) addresses an additional area that is not covered in the unofficial forms:

- ***Visual/communicative limitations***

  1. Seeing;
  2. Hearing; and
  3. Speaking.

The unofficial forms include areas not covered by the official form:

- ***Exertional activity "at one time"***

  1. Sitting;
  2. Standing; and
  3. Walking.

- ***Repetitive movement***

  1. Use of feet for repetitive movement;
  2. Use of hands for repetitive movement;
     A. Grasping, and
     B. Fingering.

Each of these areas may be important, depending on the client's age, education, and past work experience. Thus, use of a given form may provide all necessary data. However, it may be critical to know about repetitive limitations or about a client's ability to see, hear, or speak. Each case is unique and must be evaluated according to the individual circumstances presented.

The lesson is straightforward. Do not simply use a form because it is available. Use the instrument that best addresses and describes the client's limitations. Do not be afraid to modify a form to suit a client's particular needs. Critical to any instrument, however, is its integrity.

- Do not prepare or submit a document that is misleading or, by omission, misrepresents the claimant's true status.
- A form should actually be completed by the signing medical professional.

Do not be tempted to complete the form yourself and then ask the doctor to sign the finished product. There is too great a chance that you, as a layperson, will provide contradictory information, giving rise to inquiry from the bench. You do not want to have to tell a judge that you, not the doctor, actually filled in the form, particularly if the judge later decides to conduct a telephone conference with the doctor, who inadvertently comments on the origin of the form.

- Finally, no additional information should be added after the signature, and the client should not write comments (or any other evidence) on it that may be submitted by a medical professional.

THE MENTAL RFC FORM (MEDICAL SOURCE STATEMENT)

Two essential *mental RFC* forms are used in assessing the nature and extent of limitations flowing from emotional or psychological impairments:

- The Mental MMS Statement; and
- The Psychiatric Review Technique Form (PRTF).

The mental MSS differs from the Psychiatric Review Technique Form in that the PRTF follows the prescribed regulations governing mental impairments. An exemplar copy appears in Figure 9–17.

Form Approved
OMB No. 0960-0413

PSYCHIATRIC REVIEW TECHNIQUE

Name | SSN

Assessment is For: ☐ Current Evaluation ☐ 12 Mo. After Onset: ____________

☐ Date Last Insured: ____________ ☐ Other: ____________ to ____________

Reviewer's Signature | Date

PRIVACY ACT NOTICE: The information requested on this form is authorized by section 223 and section 1633 of the Social Security Act. The information provided will be used in making a decision on this claim. Completion of this form is mandatory in disability claims involving mental impairments. Failure to complete this form may result in a delay in processing the claim. Information furnished on this form may be disclosed by the Social Security Administration to another person or governmental agency only with respect to Social Security programs and to comply with federal laws requiring the exchange of information between Social Security and another agency.

I. MEDICAL SUMMARY

A. Medical Disposition(s):

1. ☐ No Medically Determinable Impairment
2. ☐ Impairment(s) Not Severe
3. ☐ Meets Listing ____________ (Cite Listing and subsection)
4. ☐ Equals Listing ____________ (Cite Listing and subsection)
5. ☐ Impairment Severe But Not Expected to Last 12 Months
6. ☐ RFC Assessment Necessary (i.e., a severe impairment is present which does not meet or equal a listed impairment)
7. ☐ Referral to Another Medical Specialty (necessary when there is a coexisting nonmental impairment) (Except for OHA reviewers)
8. ☐ Insufficient Medical Evidence (i.e., a programmatic documentation deficiency is present) (Except for OHA reviewers)

B. Category(ies) Upon Which the Medical Disposition(s) is Based:

1. ☐ 12.02 Organic Mental Disorders
2. ☐ 12.03 Schizophrenic, Paranoid and other Psychotic Disorders
3. ☐ 12.04 Affective Disorders
4. ☐ 12.05 Mental Retardation and Autism
5. ☐ 12.06 Anxiety Related Disorders
6. ☐ 12.07 Somatoform Disorders
7. ☐ 12.08 Personality Disorders
8. ☐ 12.09 Substance Addiction Disorders

Form **SSA-2506-BK** (10-90)

Figure 9–17 **Psychiatric Review Technique Form Generally Completed by a Psychologist or Psychiatrist**

(continued)

II. REVIEWER'S NOTES (Except OHA reviewers. OHA reviewers should record the subject information in the body and findings of their decision.): A. Record below the pertinent signs, symptoms, findings, functional limitations, and the effects of treatment contained in the case, B. Remarks (any information the reviewer may wish to communicate which is not covered elsewhere in the form, e.g., duration situations).

We may also use the information you give us when we match records by computer. Matching programs compare our records with those of other Federal, State, or local government agencies. Many agencies may use matching programs to find or prove that a person qualifies for benefits paid by the Federal government. The law allows us to do this even if you do not agree to it.

Explanations about these and other reasons why information you provide us may be used or given out are available in Social Security Offices. If you want to learn more about this, contact any Social Security Office.

The **Paperwork Reduction Act of 1995** requires us to notify you that this information collection is in accordance with the clearance requirements of section 3507 of the Paperwork Reduction Act of 1995. We may not conduct or sponsor, and you are not required to respond to, a collection of information unless it displays a valid OMB control number.

TIME IT TAKES TO COMPLETE THIS FORM

We estimate that it will take you about 15 minutes to complete this form. This includes the time it will take to read the instructions, gather the necessary facts and fill out the form. If you have comments or suggestions on this estimate, write to the Social Security Administration, ATTN: Reports Clearance Officer, 1-A-21 Operations Bldg., Baltimore, MD 21235-0001. **Send only comments relating to our "time it takes" estimate to the office listed above. All requests for Social Security cards and other claims-related information should be sent to your local Social Security office, whose address is listed under Social Security Administration in the U.S. Government section of your telephone directory.**

Form **SSA-2506-BK** (10-90) **(2)**

III. DOCUMENTATION OF FACTORS THAT EVIDENCE THE DISORDER (COMMENT ON EACH BROAD CATEGORY OF DISORDER.)

A. 12.02 Organic Mental Disorders

☐ No evidence of a sign or symptom CLUSTER or SYNDROME which appropriately fits with this diagnostic category. (Some features appearing below may be present in the case but they are presumed to belong in another disorder and are rated in that category.)

☐ Psychological or behavioral abnormalities associated with a dysfunction of the brain . . . . as evidenced by at least one of the following:

PRESENT-ABSENT-INSUFFICIENT EVIDENCE

1. ☐ ☐ ☐ Disorientation to time and place
2. ☐ ☐ ☐ Memory impairment
3. ☐ ☐ ☐ Perceptual or thinking disturbances
4. ☐ ☐ ☐ Change in personality
5. ☐ ☐ ☐ Disturbance in mood
6. ☐ ☐ ☐ Emotional lability and impairment in impulse control
7. ☐ ☐ ☐ Loss of measured intellectual ability of at least 15 I.Q. points from premorbid levels or overall impairment index clearly within the severely impaired range on neuropsychological testing, e.g., the Luria-Nebraska, Halstead-Reitan, etc.
8. ☐ ☐ ☐ Other ______________________________

B. 12.03 Schizophrenic, Paranoid and other Psychotic Disorders

☐ No evidence of a sign or symptom CLUSTER or SYNDROME which appropriately fits with this diagnostic category. (Some features appearing below may be present in the case but they are presumed to belong in another disorder and are rated in that category.)

☐ Psychotic features and deterioration that are persistent (continuous or intermittent), as evidenced by at least one of the following:

PRESENT-ABSENT-INSUFFICIENT EVIDENCE

1. ☐ ☐ ☐ Delusions or hallucinations
2. ☐ ☐ ☐ Catatonic or other grossly disorganized behavior
3. ☐ ☐ ☐ Incoherence, loosening of associations, illogical thinking, or poverty of content of speech if associated with one of the following:
   a. ☐ Blunt affect, or
   b. ☐ Flat affect, or
   c. ☐ Inappropriate affect
4. ☐ ☐ ☐ Emotional withdrawal and/or isolation
5. ☐ ☐ ☐ Other ______________________________

Form SSA-2506-BK (10-90) **(3)**

(continued)

C. 12.04 Affective Disorders

☐ No evidence of a sign or symptom CLUSTER or SYNDROME which appropriately fits with this diagnostic category. (Some features appearing below may be present in the case but they are presumed to belong in another disorder and are rated in that category.)

☐ Disturbance of mood, accompanied by a full or partial manic or depressive syndrome, as evidenced by at least one of the following:

PRESENT-ABSENT-INSUFFICIENT EVIDENCE

1. ☐ ☐ ☐ Depressive syndrome characterized by at least four of the following:

   a. ☐ Anhedonia or pervasive loss of interest in almost all activities, or

   b. ☐ Appetite disturbance with change in weight, or

   c. ☐ Sleep disturbance, or

   d. ☐ Psychomotor agitation or retardation, or

   e. ☐ Decreased energy, or

   f. ☐ Feelings of guilt or worthlessness, or

   g. ☐ Difficulty concentrating or thinking, or

   h. ☐ Thoughts of suicide, or

   i. ☐ Hallucinations, delusions or paranoid thinking

2. ☐ ☐ ☐ Manic syndrome characterized by at least three of the following:

   a. ☐ Hyperactivity, or

   b. ☐ Pressures of speech, or

   c. ☐ Flight of ideas, or

   d. ☐ Inflated self-esteem, or

   e. ☐ Decreased need for sleep, or

   f. ☐ Easy distractability, or

   g. ☐ Involvement in activities that have a high probability of painful consequences which are not recognized, or

   h. ☐ Hallucinations, delusions or paranoid thinking

3. ☐ ☐ ☐ Bipolar syndrome with a history of episodic periods manifested by the full symptomatic picture of both manic and depressive syndromes (and currently characterized by either or both syndromes)

4. ☐ ☐ ☐ Other ______________________________

Form **SSA-2506-BK** (10-90) **(4)**

D. 12.05 Mental Retardation and Autism

☐ No evidence of a sign or symptom CLUSTER or SYNDROME which appropriately fits with this diagnostic category. (Some features appearing below may be present in the case but they are presumed to belong in another disorder and are rated in that category.)

☐ Significantly subaverage general intellectual functioning with deficits in adaptive behavior initially manifested during the developmental period (before age 22), or pervasive developmental disorder characterized by social and significant communicative deficits originating in the developmental period, as evidenced by at least one of the following:

PRESENT-ABSENT-INSUFFICIENT EVIDENCE

1. ☐ ☐ ☐ Mental incapacity evidenced by dependence upon others for personal needs (e.g., toileting, eating, dressing or bathing) and inability to follow directions, such that the use of standardized measures of intellectual functioning is precluded*

2. ☐ ☐ ☐ A valid verbal, performance, or full scale I.Q. of 59 or less*

3. ☐ ☐ ☐ A valid verbal, performance, or full scale I.Q. of 60 through 70 and a physical or other mental impairment imposing additional and significant work-related limitation of function*

4. ☐ ☐ ☐ A valid verbal, performance, or full scale I.Q. of 60 through 70 or in the case of autism, gross deficits of social and communicative skills*

5. ☐ ☐ ☐ Other ______________________________

*NOTE: Items 1, 2, 3, and 4 correspond to Listings 12.05A, 12.05B, 12.05C, and 12.05D, respectively.

E. 12.06 Anxiety Related Disorders

☐ No evidence of a sign or symptom CLUSTER or SYNDROME which appropriately fits with this diagnostic category. (Some features appearing below may be present in the case but they are presumed to belong in another disorder and are rated in that category.)

☐ Anxiety as the predominant disturbance or anxiety experienced in the attempt to master symptoms, as evidenced by at least one of the following:

PRESENT-ABSENT-INSUFFICIENT EVIDENCE

1. ☐ ☐ ☐ Generalized persistent anxiety accompanied by three of the following:

   a. ☐ Motor tension, or

   b. ☐ Autonomic hyperactivity, or

   c. ☐ Apprehensive expectation, or

   d. ☐ Vigilance and scanning

2. ☐ ☐ ☐ A persistent irrational fear of a specific object, activity or situation which results in a compelling desire to avoid the dreaded object, activity, or situation

3. ☐ ☐ ☐ Recurrent severe panic attacks manifested by a sudden unpredictable onset of intense apprehension, fear, terror, and sense of impending doom occurring on the average of at least once a week

4. ☐ ☐ ☐ Recurrent obsessions or compulsions which are a source of marked distress

5. ☐ ☐ ☐ Recurrent and intrusive recollections of a traumatic experience, which are a source of marked distress

6. ☐ ☐ ☐ Other ______________________________

Form **SSA-2506-BK** (10-90) **(5)**

(continued)

F. 12.07 Somatoform Disorders

☐ No evidence of a sign or symptom CLUSTER or SYNDROME which appropriately fits with this diagnostic category. (Some features appearing below may be present in the case but they are presumed to belong in another disorder and are rated in that category.)

☐ Physical symptoms for which there are no demonstrable organic findings or known physiological mechanisms, as evidenced by at least one of the following:

PRESENT-ABSENT-INSUFFICIENT EVIDENCE

1. ☐ ☐ ☐ A history of multiple physical symptoms of several years duration beginning before age 30, that have caused the individual to take medicine frequently, see a physician often and alter life patterns significantly

2. ☐ ☐ ☐ Persistent nonorganic disturbance of one of the following:

   a. ☐ Vision, or

   b. ☐ Speech, or

   c. ☐ Hearing, or

   d. ☐ Use of a limb, or

   e. ☐ Movement and its control (e.g., coordination disturbances, psychogenic seizures, akinesia, dyskinesia), or

   f. ☐ Sensation (e.g., diminished or heightened)

3. ☐ ☐ ☐ Unrealistic interpretation of physical signs or sensations associated with the preoccupation or belief that one has a serious disease or injury

4. ☐ ☐ ☐ Other ______________________________

G. 12.08 Personality Disorders

☐ No evidence of a sign or symptom CLUSTER or SYNDROME which appropriately fits with this diagnostic category. (Some features appearing below may be present in the case but they are presumed to belong in another disorder and are rated in that category.)

☐ Inflexible and maladaptive personality traits which cause either significant impairment in social or occupational functioning or subjective distress, as evidenced by at least one of the following:

PRESENT-ABSENT-INSUFFICIENT EVIDENCE

1. ☐ ☐ ☐ Seclusiveness or autistic thinking

2. ☐ ☐ ☐ Pathologically inappropriate suspiciousness or hostility

3. ☐ ☐ ☐ Oddities of thought, perception, speech and behavior

4. ☐ ☐ ☐ Persistent disturbances of mood or affect

5. ☐ ☐ ☐ Pathological dependence, passivity, or aggressivity

6. ☐ ☐ ☐ Intense and unstable interpersonal relationships and impulsive and damaging behavior

7. ☐ ☐ ☐ Other ______________________________

Form SSA-2506-BK (10-90) (6)

H. 12.09 Substance Addiction Disorders: Behavioral changes or physical changes associated with the regular use of substances that affect the central nervous system.

Present — Absent — Insufficient Evidence

☐ ☐ ☐

If present, evaluate under one or more of the most closely applicable listings:

1. ☐ Listing 12.02—Organic mental disorders*
2. ☐ Listing 12.04—Affective disorders*
3. ☐ Listing 12.06—Anxiety disorders*
4. ☐ Listing 12.08—Personality disorders*
5. ☐ Listing 11.14—Peripheral neuropathies*
6. ☐ Listing 5.05—Liver damage*
7. ☐ Listing 5.04—Gastritis*
8. ☐ Listing 5.08—Pancreatitis*
9. ☐ Listing 11.02 or 11.03—Seizures*
10. ☐ Other ______________________________

*NOTE: Items 1, 2, 3, 4, 5, 6, 7, 8, and 9 correspond to Listings 12.09A, 12.09B, 12.09C, 12.09D, 12.09E, 12.09F, 12.09G, 12.09H, and 12.09I, respectively. If items 1, 2, 3, or 4 are checked, only the numbered items in subsections IIIA, IIIC, IIIE, or IIIG of the form need be checked. The first two blocks under the disorder heading in those subsections need not be checked.

(continued)

IV. RATING OF IMPAIRMENT SEVERITY

A. *"B" Criteria of the Listings*

Indicate to what degree the following functional limitations (which are found in paragraph B of listings 12.02–12.04 and 12.06–12.08 and paragraph D of 12.05) exist as a result of the individual's mental disorder(s).

NOTE: Items 3 and 4 below are more than measures of frequency. Describe in part II of this form (Reviewer's Notes) the duration and effects of the deficiencies (item 3) or episodes (item 4). Please read carefully the instructions for the completion of this section.

Specify the listing(s) (i.e., 12.02 through 12.09) under which the items below are being rated ________________.

FUNCTIONAL LIMITATION	DEGREE OF LIMITATION					
1. Restriction of Activities of Daily Living	None ☐	Slight ☐	Moderate ☐	Marked* ☐	Extreme ☐	Insufficient Evidence ☐
2. Difficulties in Maintaining Social Functioning	None ☐	Slight ☐	Moderate ☐	Marked* ☐	Extreme ☐	Insufficient Evidence ☐
3. Deficiencies of Concentration, Persistence or Pace Resulting in Failure to Complete Tasks in a Timely Manner (in work settings or elsewhere)	Never ☐	Seldom ☐	Often ☐	Frequent* ☐	Constant ☐	Insufficient Evidence ☐
4. Episodes of Deterioration or Decompensation in Work or Work-Like Settings Which Cause the Individual to Withdraw from that Situation or to Experience Exacerbation of Signs and Symptoms (which may Include Deterioration of Adaptive Behaviors)	Never ☐		Once or Twice ☐	Repeated* (three or more) ☐	Continual ☐	Insufficient Evidence ☐

B. *Summary of Functional Limitation Rating for "B" Criteria*

Indicate the number of the above functional limitations manifested at the degree of limitation that satisfies the listings.☐ (The number in the box must be at least 2 to satisfy the requirements of paragraph B in Listings 12.02, 12.03, 12.04, and 12.06 and paragraph D in 12.05; and at least 3 to satisfy the requirements in paragraph B in Listings 12.07 and 12.08.)

*Degree of limitation that satisfies the Listings; Extreme, Constant and Continual also satisfy that requirement.

Form SSA-2506-BK (10-90) **(8)**

C. *"C" Criteria of the Listings*

1. If 12.03 Disorder (Schizophrenic, etc.) and in Full or Partial Remission

NOTE: Item b. below is more than a measure of frequency. Describe in part II of this form (Reviewer's Notes) the duration and effects of the episodes. Please read carefully the instructions for the completion of this section.

	Present	Absent	Insufficient Evidence	
a.	☐	☐	☐	Medically documented history of one or more episodes of acute symptoms, signs and functional limitations which at the time met the requirements in A and B of 12.03, although these symptoms or signs are currently attenuated by medication or psychosocial support.
b.	☐	☐	☐	Repeated episodes of deterioration or decompensation in situations which cause the individual to withdraw from the situation or to experience exacerbation of signs or symptoms (which may include deterioration of adaptive behaviors).
c.	☐	☐	☐	Documented current history of two or more years of inability to function outside of a highly supportive living situation.

(For the requirements in paragraph C of 12.03 to be satisfied, either a. and b. or a. and c. must be checked as present.)

2. If 12.06 Disorder (Anxiety Related)

Present	Absent	Insufficient Evidence	
☐	☐	☐	Symptoms resulting in *complete* inability to function independently outside the area of one's home.

(If present is checked, the requirements in paragraph C of 12.06 are satisfied.)

(continued)

The PRTF is a multilayered document, setting forth the opinion of its author as to the claimant's mental impairment and its severity. It mirrors the requirements of the governing mental impairment regulations, outlining the part "A" and part "B" criteria for a mental impairment.

The PRTF begins with a summary, allowing readers to quickly ascertain the conclusion(s) reached by the writer, as well as the medical basis for the underlying opinion. (See Section I(A), "Medical Disposition(s).") At the outset the author is asked to define the period covered by the opinion. (See Section I(A) "Assessment.") This becomes important, given the possibility that the claim being prosecuted may extend *before* or *after* the treatment or medical data on which the author relies. The validity of the form and its conclusions depend to a large degree on the evidence underlying the author's opinion. Using the form is thus potentially time-limited, depending on the author and his or her involvement with the claimant.[28]

In Section I(B), the author is asked to express his or her opinion regarding the nature of the disposition. Whether the author considers there to be a severe impairment, and, if so, whether the impairment meets or is medically equivalent to a listed impairment, is presented at the beginning of the form. Similarly, if, in the author's opinion, the claimant's condition does not meet or medically equal a listed impairment, the question becomes whether an RFC is necessary. If so there is a box to check on the form.

Section I(C) identifies the specific listing(s) addressed. Again, if, in the author's opinion, a specific listing is implicated by the claimant's impairment, the author should so note it in this section. Remember, however, the marking of a listing does not mean that the claimant's condition meets or is medically equivalent to a listing unless it is so stated in Section III. Marking a listing in Section I(B) merely means that the claimant's impairment falls into that particular category and was considered by the author of the form.

Section III (A through I) addresses individual mental impairments, from organic mental disorders (Section III[A]) to autistic disorders and other pervasive developmental disorders (Section III[I]). Each of these descriptions coincides with the "A" criteria for the selected mental disorder. The "A" criteria are the diagnostic descriptions of the disorder, and are the symptoms required to be documented before an actual diagnosis can be made. In effect, the mental listing first requires that minimum symptomology be identified before rising to the level of diagnostic validity.

Once the part "A" criteria are satisfied, the next question is one of severity. This is where the limitations are found. How severe is the condition? Is it extreme? Marked? Moderate in severity? Mild? or, notwithstanding the diagnosis, does the condition fail to produce identifiable limitations of function (*i.e.*, none)?

The "B" criteria, found at Section IV of the PRTF, are expressed in four different categories, described as functional limitations:

- ❑ Restriction of *activities of daily living*
- ❑ Difficulties in maintaining *social functioning*
- ❑ Difficulties in maintaining *concentration, persistence, or pace*
- ❑ Repeated episodes of *decompensation*, each of extended duration

If an individual is found to suffer from *marked* or *extreme limitations* in two or more categories, this heightened level of severity is generally sufficient to meet the requirements for a listed mental impairment—such that an RFC and resulting decision at step 5 of the sequential evaluation process is not necessary. In effect, the part "B" criteria for the mental listings become self-defining limitations, descriptive of the severity of the mental impairment. However, when the impairment does not rise to the level of meeting or equaling a listed impairment, a mental RFC obtained using the more detailed Mental Medical Source Statement will describe the associated limitations.

Comparatively, the mental medical source statement is a more detailed expression of limitations arising from mental impairments. As with the physical medical source statement, several variations of the form are available. Figures 9–18 and 9–19 illustrate two types of these forms.

Figure 9–18 shows an abbreviated mental RFC form (HA-1152); it includes five areas of inquiry:

- ❑ The ability to understand, remember, and carry out instructions;
- ❑ The ability to respond to supervision, co-workers, and work pressures;
- ❑ Other capabilities;
- ❑ The effect of drug or alcohol use, if appropriate; and
- ❑ The ability to manage funds.

It is an abbreviated version of Figure 9-19.

MEDICAL SOURCE STATEMENT OF ABILITY TO DO WORK-RELATED ACTIVITIES (MENTAL)

NAME OF INDIVIDUAL **SOCIAL SECURITY NUMBER**

Please assist us in determining this individual's ability to do work-related activities on a sustained basis. "Sustained basis" means the ability to perform work-related activities eight hours a day for five days a week, or an equivalent work schedule. (SSR 96-8p). Please give us your professional opinion of what the individual can still do despite his/her impairment(s). The opinion should be based on your findings with respect to medical history, clinical and laboratory findings, diagnosis, prescribed treatment and response, and prognosis.

For each activity shown below:

(1) Respond to the questions about the individual's ability to perform the activity. When doing so, use the following definitions for the rating terms:

- None --Absent or minimal limitations. If limitations are present they are transient and/or expectable reactions to psychological stresses.
- Slight --There is some mild limitations in this area, but the individual can generally function well.
- Moderate--There is moderate limitation in this area but the individual is still able to function satisfactorily.
- Marked --There is serious limitation in this area. The ability to function is severely limited but not precluded.
- Extreme --There is major limitation in this area. There is no useful ability to function in this area.

(2) Identify the factors (e.g., the particular medical signs, laboratory findings, or other factors described above) that support your assessment.

IT IS VERY IMPORTANT TO DESCRIBE THE FACTORS THAT SUPPORT YOUR ASSESSMENT. WE ARE REQUIRED TO CONSIDER THE EXTENT TO WHICH YOUR ASSESSMENT IS SUPPORTED.

---

(1) Is ability to understand, remember, and carry out instructions affected by the impairment? ☐ No ☐ Yes
If "no," go to question #2. If "yes," please check the appropriate block to describe the individual's restriction for the following work-related mental activities.

	None	Slight	Moderate	Marked	Extreme
Understand and remember short, simple instructions.	☐	☐	☐	☐	☐
Carry out short, simple instructions.	☐	☐	☐	☐	☐
Understand and remember detailed instructions.	☐	☐	☐	☐	☐
Carry out detailed instructions.	☐	☐	☐	☐	☐
The ability to make judgements on simple work-related decisions.	☐	☐	☐	☐	☐

What medical/clinical finding(s) support this assessment?

FORM HA-1152 (4/00)

Figure 9–18 **Abbreviated Mental RFC Form**

(continued)

(0000000000)

(2) Is ability to respond appropriately to supervision, co-workers, and work pressures in a work setting affected by the impairment? ☐ No ☐ Yes

If "no," go to question #3. If "yes," please check the appropriate block to describe the individual's restriction for the following work-related mental activities.

	None	Slight	Moderate	Marked	Extreme
Interact appropriately with the public.	☐	☐	☐	☐	☐
Interact appropriately with supervisor(s).	☐	☐	☐	☐	☐
Interact appropriately with co-workers.	☐	☐	☐	☐	☐
Respond appropriately to work pressures in a usual work setting.	☐	☐	☐	☐	☐
Respond appropriately to changes in a routine work setting.	☐	☐	☐	☐	☐

What supports this assessment?

(3) Are any other capabilities affected by the impairment? ☐ No ☐ Yes

If "yes," please identify the capability and describe how it is affected.

Capability	Effect
______________________	______________________
______________________	______________________
______________________	______________________

What medical/clinical findings support this assessment?

(4) If the claimant's impairment(s) include alcohol and/or substance abuse, do these impairments contribute to any of the claimant's limitations as set forth above? If so, please list the specific limitations caused.

(5) If you have concluded that the medical record indicates that the claimant's alcohol and/or substance use/abuse contributes to any limitations as set forth above, please identify and explain what changes you would make to your answers if the claimant was totally abstinent from alcohol and/or substance use/abuse.

(6) Can the individual manage benefits in his/her own best interest? ☐ No ☐ Yes

______________________ ______________________ ______________________

Physician's/Psychologist's Signature Medical Specialty Date

FORM HA-1152 (4/00)

FORM APPROVED
OMB No. 0960-0431

MENTAL RESIDUAL FUNCTIONAL CAPACITY ASSESSMENT

NAME | SOCIAL SECURITY NUMBER

CATEGORIES *(From IB of the PRTF)*

ASSESSMENT IS FOR:

☐ Current Evaluation ☐ 12 Months After Onset: ____________ *(Date)*

☐ Date Last Insured: ____________ *(Date)*

☐ Other: ____________ *(Date)* to ____________ *(Date)*

I. SUMMARY CONCLUSIONS

This section is for recording summary conclusions derived from the evidence in file. Each mental activity is to be evaluated within the context of the individual's capacity to sustain that activity over a normal workday and workweek, on an ongoing basis. Detailed explanation of the degree of limitation for each category (A through D), as well as any other assessment information you deem appropriate, is to be recorded in Section III (Functional Capacity Assessment).

If rating category 5 is checked for any of the following items, you MUST specify in Section II the evidence that is needed to make the assessment. If you conclude that the record is so inadequately documented that no accurate functional capacity assessment can be made, indicate in Section II what development is necessary, but DO NOT COMPLETE SECTION III.

	Not Significantly Limited	Moderately Limited	Markedly Limited	No Evidence of Limitation in this Category	Not Ratable on Available Evidence
A. UNDERSTANDING AND MEMORY					
1. The ability to remember locations and work-like procedures.	1. ☐	2. ☐	3. ☐	4. ☐	5. ☐
2. The ability to understand and remember very short and simple instructions.	1. ☐	2. ☐	3. ☐	4. ☐	5. ☐
3. The ability to understand and remember detailed instructions.	1. ☐	2. ☐	3. ☐	4. ☐	5. ☐
B. SUSTAINED CONCENTRATION AND PERSISTENCE					
4. The ability to carry out very short and simple instructions.	1. ☐	2. ☐	3. ☐	4. ☐	5. ☐
5. The ability to carry out detailed instructions.	1. ☐	2. ☐	3. ☐	4. ☐	5. ☐
6. The ability to maintain attention and concentration for extended periods.	1. ☐	2. ☐	3. ☐	4. ☐	5. ☐
7. The ability to perform activities within a schedule, maintain regular attendance, and be punctual within customary tolerances.	1. ☐	2. ☐	3. ☐	4. ☐	5. ☐
8. The ability to sustain an ordinary routine without special supervision.	1. ☐	2. ☐	3. ☐	4. ☐	5. ☐
9. The ability to work in coordination with or proximity to others without being distracted by them.	1. ☐	2. ☐	3. ☐	4. ☐	5. ☐
10. The ability to make simple work-related decisions.	1. ☐	2. ☐	3. ☐	4. ☐	5. ☐

Form **SSA-4734-F4-SUP** (8-1985) ef (5-2001)
(Formerly **SSA-4734-BK-SUP** Use prior editions)

1

Figure 9–19 More Comprehensive Mental RFC Form

(continued)

	Not Significantly Limited	Moderately Limited	Markedly Limited	No Evidence of Limitation in this Category	Not Ratable on Available Evidence
Continued --SUSTAINED CONCENTRATION AND PERSISTENCE					
11. The ability to complete a normal workday and workweek without interruptions from psychologically based symptoms and to perform at a consistent pace without an unreasonable number and length of rest periods.	1. ☐	2. ☐	3. ☐	4. ☐	5. ☐
C. SOCIAL INTERACTION					
12. The ability to interact appropriately with the general public.	1. ☐	2. ☐	3. ☐	4. ☐	5. ☐
13. The ability to ask simple questions or request assistance.	1. ☐	2. ☐	3. ☐	4. ☐	5. ☐
14. The ability to accept instructions and respond appropriately to criticism from supervisors.	1. ☐	2. ☐	3. ☐	4. ☐	5. ☐
15. The ability to get along with coworkers or peers without distracting them or exhibiting behavioral extremes.	1. ☐	2. ☐	3. ☐	4. ☐	5. ☐
16. The ability to maintain socially appropriate behavior and to adhere to basic standards of neatness and cleanliness.	1. ☐	2. ☐	3. ☐	4. ☐	5. ☐
D. ADAPTATION					
17. The ability to respond appropriately to changes in the work setting.	1. ☐	2. ☐	3. ☐	4. ☐	5. ☐
18. The ability to be aware of normal hazards and take appropriate precautions.	1. ☐	2. ☐	3. ☐	4. ☐	5. ☐
19. The ability to travel in unfamiliar places or use public transportation.	1. ☐	2. ☐	3. ☐	4. ☐	5. ☐
20. The ability to set realistic goals or make plans independently of others.	1. ☐	2. ☐	3. ☐	4. ☐	5. ☐

II. REMARKS: If you checked box 5 for any of the preceding items or if any other documentation deficiencies were identified, you MUST specify what additional documentation is needed. Cite the item number(s), as well as any other specific deficiency, and indicate the development to be undertaken.

☐ Continued on Page 3

Form SSA-4734-F4-SUP (8-1985) ef (5-2001)

2

III. FUNCTIONAL CAPACITY ASSESSMENT

Record in this section the elaborations on the preceding capacities. Complete this section ONLY after the SUMMARY CONCLUSIONS section has been completed. Explain your summary conclusions in narrative form. Include any information which clarifies limitation or function. Be especially careful to explain conclusions that differ from those of treating medical sources or from the individual's allegations.

MEDICAL CONSULTANT'S SIGNATURE	DATE

Form SSA-4734-F4-SUP (8-1985) ef (5-2001) 3

(continued)

Figure 9–19 represents a far more detailed inquiry addressing:

- ❑ Understanding and memory;
- ❑ Sustained concentration and persistence;
- ❑ Social interaction; and
- ❑ Adaptation.

In all, the more detailed form asks the physician or psychologist to answer twenty different questions about the claimant's level of functioning, compared with only ten specific questions in the abbreviated form. Both forms, however, use a five-level rating scale, though the terms differ slightly.

BACK TO CHRIS

"You mean this can be a form-based practice, sort of like workers' comp?" *Maybe,* thought Chris, *this wasn't so bad.*

"No, not exactly," Steve shook his head. "You can't simply toss forms at the judge. First you have to remember the hierarchy of physicians."

"An RFC form completed by a treating doctor carries more weight than one filled out by, say, the DDS nonexamining doctor?"

"Right!"

Chris saw the look in Steve's eye. "There's more?"

Steve grinned. "Of course. Forms alone, even if they are filled out by the person's long-time attending physician. . . ."

"Her treating doctor?"

"Right. Even if you have the treating doctor, a form alone cannot be controlling as to the individual's RFC."

"Why not? I thought the treating doctor's opinion, even if put into an RFC on one of these forms, was controlling."

"Only if there is supporting medical evidence that reflects the nature and extent of the doctor's treatment."

"Like treatment or progress notes?"

"That's right. But they have to indicate a real basis for the opinion. How can you convince the judge that the doctor knows what he or she is talking about unless you also provide the supporting data that demonstrates a basis for the opinion?"

"Good point," Chris said.

"There's still something we need to talk about."

Uh-ho, thought Chris. "Something bad?"

"No, no, nothing like that. Have you thought about pain?"

"You mean with the RFC?"

"That's it. Pain is an intangible factor. It can't be measured."

"So, if it can't be measured, why include it? Can't somebody really exaggerate?"

"It's possible, but you have to understand that pain is a very real factor in a disability case. It directly affects the RFC."

"How? If you can't measure it? I thought the RFC was all about quantifying what a person could and could not do."

"Pain manifests itself in both tangible and intangible ways. First, pain is a symptom. It's what someone experiences as a result of an underlying illness, disease, or injury."

Chris nodded. "I get that. But, if you can't measure it, then how is it used in a disability case?"

"Good question. Pain affects a person's ability to do both exertional and nonexertional activities. For example, suppose someone experiences a lot of pain after sitting for an hour."

"The person would have to get up or change position."

"Because of their bad back, or the pain?" Steve asked.

"Well, I suppose," Chris thought, "both."

"Okay. Fair answer. The bad back, say from degenerative disk disease or even a herniated disk pressing on the nerves, causes the pain, then the pain causes the limitation—the inability to sit for long periods."

"I get it. The impairment causes the symptom—pain—and the symptom gives rise to the limitation—the inability to sit for a long time."

"That's an exertional limitation. Pain also has nonexertional effects."

"Such as what?"

"Suppose you're in a lot of pain. Think you can read the disability regulations and understand them?"

"Oh, I get it. Concentration."

"Exactly. Somebody in a lot of pain generally won't be able to concentrate."

"Still, it depends on how much pain. How do you know if your client is telling the truth or exaggerating?"

"Let's look at some of the regulations. That'll help you understand how pain is evaluated."

"Sounds good!"

FRONT OF YOUR MIND QUESTIONS AND CONSIDERATIONS, 9.4

Pain is perhaps one of the most difficult issues to master in a disability case, primarily because it is an intangible. Although medical science can measure pain tolerance levels, it cannot measure the pain a person actually feels. Thus, pain becomes a subjective symptom, often magnified by psychological factors, such as depression. Long-term pain, in and of itself, is potentially psychologically harmful. The disorder is commonly known as chronic pain syndrome. The *Diagnostics and Statistics Manual of Mental Disorders* (Fourth Edition, DSM-IV) calls it "pain disorder." According to the DSM-IV, a pain disorder

> **. . . is pain that is the predominant focus of the clinical presentation and is of sufficient severity as to warrant clinical attention. . . . The pain causes significant distress or impairment in social, occupational, or other important areas of functioning.**[29]

It is not sufficient, however, to simply rely on the claimant's testimony as to the nature and extent of pain. Like any other symptom, it must be documented with medical signs and laboratory findings. (See Title 20 C.F.R. § 404.1529.) The resulting pain must be reasonably expected as a result of the documented impairment. A variety of factors are considered when weighing the credibility of allegations of pain. According to the regulations

> **"[W]e consider . . . factors relevant to your symptoms . . . which . . . include:**
>
> **(i) Your daily activities;**
> **(ii) The location, duration, frequency, and intensity of your pain or other symptoms;**
> **(iii) Precipitating and aggravating factors;**
> **(iv) The type, dosage, effectiveness, and side effects of any medication you take or have taken to alleviate your pain . . . ;**
> **(v) Treatment, other than medication, you receive or have received for relief of your pain . . . ;**
> **(vi) Any measures you use or have used to relieve your pain . . . (e.g., lying flat on your back, standing for 15 to 20 minutes every hour, sleeping on a board, etc.);**
> **(vii) Other factors concerning your functional limitations and restrictions due to pain. . . ."**[30]

So, although a client may allege such disabling pain that he or she can do nothing, such a statement should not be accepted without further evaluation. When pain is a significant factor, credibility is the problem for the judge. How does the judge know whether statements about the nature, intensity, and duration of the pain are believable?

Pain, like other issues of functional inability, becomes more or less credible by the presentation of corroborative evidence. Such evidence could include medical reports, objective findings, or testimony from third persons, but the judge must still reach the conclusion that the evidence is credible—or not. In making this critical decision, the judge carefully weighs the client's testimony, listens to the descriptive words, and considers them in conjunction with other parts of the testimony. If the testimony is inconsistent, the judge is more likely to conclude that statements about pain are not credible. If the statements are consistent it is more likely, depending on the existence of corroborating evidence, that the claimant's assertions will be viewed as credible. Testimony about pain usually has to do with the nature of the pain, its frequency, duration, and intensity.

THE NATURE OF PAIN

When asked to describe the nature of "your pain," many claimants do not understand the question and fumble with the answer. Make the question simple, and do not ask too much at once. Ask direct questions that require specific answers. An example of a poor question might be

"Tell us about your pain."

A typical response might be

"It hurts all over. My neck, my back, then down. All over."

Although such a response might evoke a sympathetic response, it does little to support a claim for disability. The law requires that a claimant's RFC be expressed so that a function-by-function analysis can be undertaken. This requires specificity. Generalized allegations of pain, without specific inquiry, do not provide sufficient information for a judge to find of disability. More is needed.

Here is another poor question:

"Where does it hurt?"

This question is too general. Request the specific location of the pain, rather than a broad question. Similarly poor is the question:

"How often does it hurt?"

This question is vague and will generally yield a vague response:

"It hurts all the time."

What does "all the time" mean? Is it a literal response? Is the pain the same all the time or does it vary depending on activity? The question only raises more questions.

To effectively answer the question about the "nature of the claimant's pain," focus the claimant's response:

"Which part of your body has the most pain?"

Once that question is answered, then ask for a description.

"My neck. It's my neck that hurts the most."
"Can you describe what the pain feels like when it is at its worst?"
"Like a stabbing, burning pain."
"Where?"
"Right at the base of my neck."

Which leads you to the next inquiry: frequency and duration of pain.

FREQUENCY AND DURATION OF PAIN

Once the claimant has identified the location of the primary pain, do not ask for secondary locations. Fully develop the inquiry regarding the primary location before moving to a different area of the body. It is important to fully explore each afflicted area of the body in a methodical, easily recorded fashion.

The objective is to identify not only the location of the pain and its description but also the frequency and duration of its worst occurrence(s). This is necessary in order to quantify, to the extent possible, pain at its worst, so that an inquiry can later be framed to the vocational expert in the form of a limitation.

An inquiry might go something like this:

"You indicated that at its worst, the pain in your neck felt like a stabbing, burning pain. How often does it feel like that?"

If the response is "All the time," do not immediately accept the answer given, because pain at its worst intensity usually only occurs intermittently. For the claimant in pain, however, it may seem like all the time. If, indeed, that is the answer to the question about pain, make sure "all the time" actually means "all the time" and is not a subjective perception. Focus on the issue so that a precise picture is created. Thus, the follow-up question:

> **"Are there times the pain is worse than at other times?"**

Or

> **"Do you have good days and bad days?"**

Answer:

> **"Yes."**
> **"When is it worse?"**

If the response is "I have good days and bad days," the next part of the interview is straightforward.

> **"How many days a week would you say you have bad days because of pain?"**
> **"Three."**

The next question then becomes more descriptive:

> **"Can you tell me what a bad day is like?"**

Or,

> **"Can you tell me what the pain feels like on a bad day?"**

Either answer produces a description, from which more specific information can be requested.

> **"The pain is there when I wake up and it won't go away, so I just stay in bed all day."**

This requires clarification.

> **"When you say the pain won't go away, do you mean that it stays bad all day long, so that you are actually in bed through the entire day?"**
> **"Yes."**

The claimant should explain how the process works, and the nature of the pain.

> **"Is this the stabbing, burning pain at the base of your neck?"**
> **"Yes."**

Then draw the conclusion, which leads to an identifiable limitation.

> **"So, you're telling the judge that you have to stay in bed because of this stabbing, burning pain three days a week, on average, every week?"**
> **"It's the only way I can handle the pain. I take my medication, and that makes me drowsy, so I stay in bed, stay still, and try not to move."**

But, the questioning does not stop there. The bad day must be contrasted with a good day, so the judge can realize the difference and reach a conclusion about the claimant's credibility.

> **"Tell us what a good day is like. How is it different from a bad day?"**
> **"The pain isn't there when I wake up on a good day. I guess the medicine and rest help, so I can move around without that stabbing, burning pain."**
> **"Are you saying you don't have any pain?"**

"Oh, no, not at all. I have pain all the time. Just on the good days, it's less. I can get around some."
"So you don't stay in bed on a good day?"
"No, I don't."
"Can you describe the pain on a good day?"
"It's like a dull ache. Sore. Just not stabbing. Still there, though."

Now the judge will have a fair understanding of the nature, frequency, and duration of the pain. As a result, the following limitation may be framed and, ultimately, put to the vocational expert:

> **"Assume that the individual suffers from a fractured vertebrae of the neck that produces pain, which because of its intensity is worse three days, on average, each week, causing the claimant to stay in bed to attempt to alleviate pain."**

THE PAIN SPECTRUM

The preceding discussion illustrates a cause-and-effect spectrum that begins with a declaration of pain and ends with a well-defined limitation of function as a result of pain. All pain can generally be addressed in this manner. Figure 9–20 describes the pain spectrum.

The challenge for the representative is to take an amorphous intangible and turn it into a tangible factor on which the decision may turn. The process begins as an unrefined description and becomes a defined phenomena, resulting in an accountable limitation. The representative's task is to make that transition happen. Figure 9–21 illustrates the representative's role.

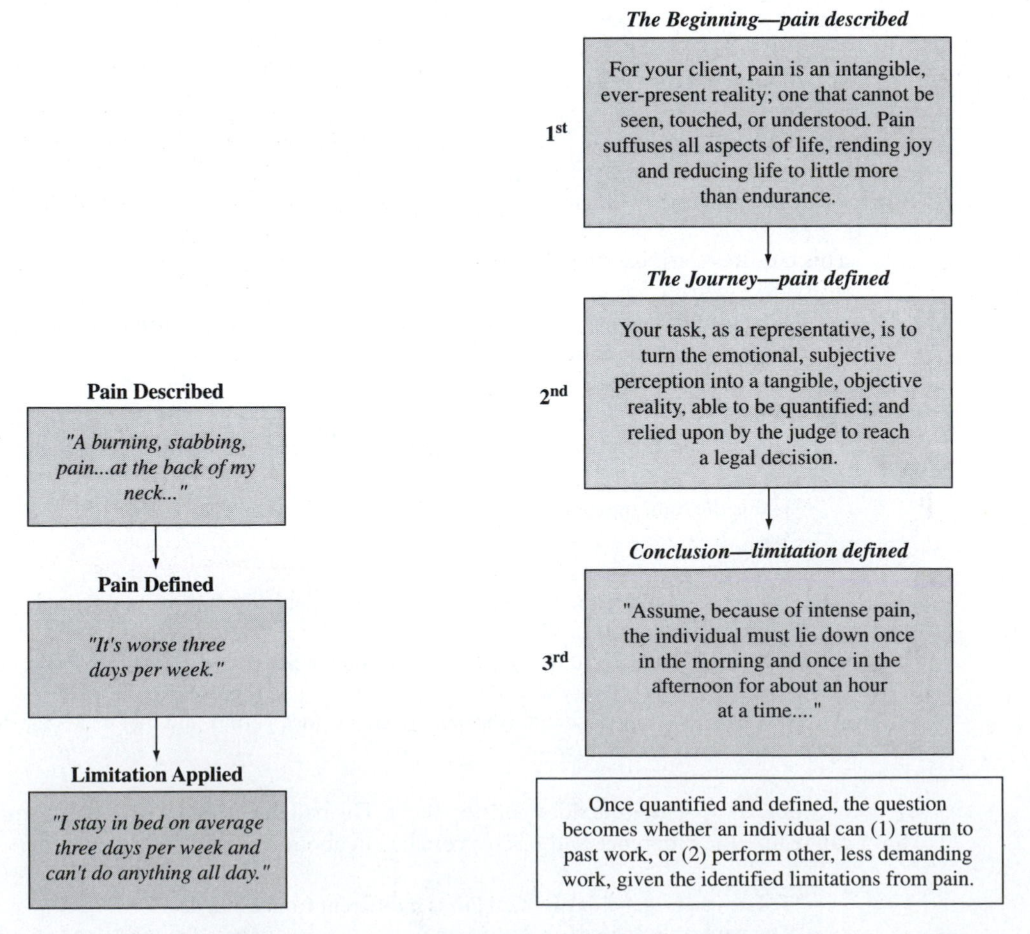

Figure 9–20 **The Pain Spectrum**

Figure 9–21 **The Representative's Role in the Pain Spectrum**

PROOF OF PAIN: DIRECT AND INFERENTIAL EVIDENCE

Before a limitation based on pain can be articulated, there must be proof of the existence of pain. Proof of pain is possible in two ways:

1. Direct testimony from the client about the nature, extent, frequency, and duration of the pain; and
2. Evidence other than the claimant's testimony of the existence, frequency, and intensity of the pain.

Direct evidence is simply that: evidence from the individual claimant as to the nature, extent, frequency, and duration of pain. The problem, of course, is that pain is a perception and, therefore, subjective in nature. Thus, evidence from a source other than the claimant is inferential. That is, the observation, opinion, or conclusion about the pain is based on interpretation of other than direct evidence (i.e., on something other than direct experience).

For example, if a claimant's brother were to testify about the claimant's pain, the testimony would be offered on (1) the brother's observation of the claimant in different settings and (2) the claimant's statements to the brother about the pain. The testimony would not be based on direct experience of the pain, because, clearly, the brother is not experiencing it.

Equally prevalent in disability hearings are doctor's notes, reports, opinions, and conclusions (either written or oral) that a claimant is or is not "in [*add adjective*] pain." These are similarly inferential, because they are statements from a third party, not from the claimant about the claimant's pain. However, unlike a brother's, friend's, or other layperson's statement, doctors' statements are professional opinions based on assessments of medical evidence. Specifically, a doctor evaluates allegations of pain by first assessing the nature and extent of the pain alleged (i.e., what is the patient actually saying about his or her pain?). Next, the doctor examines the medical history. An examining physician will look for medical signs (clinical evidence) of pain, consistent with (1) the impairment and (2) the patient complaints and allegations. If the doctor finds the medical signs and laboratory findings consistent with the claimant's diagnosed impairment and complaints, then the claimant's allegations are deemed credible. This is especially true where there are complaints of pain.

If, however, the doctor fails to find consistency, she or he will probably conclude the claimant's allegations are not believable, hence not credible. Representatives strive to present a client's testimony, such that the judge is able to conclude the client is credible. This requires thoughtful understanding of the nature of medical evidence regarding pain and of the roles of the three different doctors who offer opinions.

A nonexamining physician relies on the reports and findings of other doctors, even to the extent of adopting conclusory statements about the client's condition. How can a physician render a credible opinion about the nature, frequency, and duration of pain without an examination? Nonexamining doctors render expert opinions based on a review of medical records. They apply the specialized knowledge of their profession in analyzing the significance of reported test results, medical signs, and laboratory findings.

The problem is that many so-called nonexamining experts are not present at the hearing. This is especially true of DDS physicians who initially deny the claim, and then do so again on reconsideration. The difference between a medical expert, present at a hearing and testifying on review of the evidence, and a DDS physician is that the DDS physician is *not* present. Often there is little known about why a DDS physician reached a particular decision except what is written in very cursory DDS reports. When a present medical expert renders an opinion, it is a simple matter to explore with him or her the basis of the opinion offered.

Another essential problem is that the DDS nonexamining physician actually made a decision in the case—and more to the point, a negative decision. Thus, his or her opinion differs from that of a medical expert and a consultative examiner (CE) in that the CE, although actually examining the claimant, does not, in fact, make a decision, but simply issues a report. Similarly, a medical expert offers an opinion, not a decision.

Thus, when eliciting a client's testimony, the representative already knows what the CE's report says and what the DDS physician's conclusions are. At that point do not simply contradict the given medical evidence, but submit testimony and additional documentary evidence that *expands* the record from that which existed at the time of the initial and reconsideration decisions. Only in this way can the judge be persuaded that the prior administrative decision has been superceded by new information, reflecting a better understanding of the prior condition. As a result, an RFC reflective of the client's condition can be constructed, which takes into account the effects of pain, according to the client *and* newly submitted medical records.

Through this process the evidence offered by an examining or treating doctor is best put to use. Treating physicians have potential to offer both evidence of treatment as well as opinion evidence as to the claimant's RFC. Treatment evidence corroborates opinion evidence. Opinion evidence that addresses the effect of pain has the potential to corroborate the claimant's own testimony, thus *expanding* the record from that on which the underlying administrative denial was based.

Proof of pain, apart from the client's testimony, is, therefore, inferential. It is important to understand the necessity of expanding on the administrative record as it existed at the time of the administrative determinations by the state DDS. Failure to expand the record, particularly as to the basis for heightened allegations of pain, will result in a failure to substantiate a pain-driven RFC. The client's allegations, apart from medical evidence, regardless of whether they are consultative examinations, treatment records, or opinions of treating physicians, are a vital part of the persuasive presentation of the case. (See Figure 9–22.)

BACK TO CHRIS

"Expand the record? Do you mean have more evidence at the hearing?"

"Absolutely, Chris," Steve replied. "Think about it. The state agency already denied the case. Do you think the judge is simply going to agree with you because your client testifies? Or because the client says something like, 'the consultative doctor only spent five minutes with me'? You've got to be really prepared at the hearing. And that means up-to-date medical records as well as opinions from Mr. Carson's treating doctors."

"What if somebody can't afford to go to the doctor?"

"Then you ask for a consultative examination."

"From the judge?"

"Yes. Make the request in writing well in advance of the hearing and make sure you ask for specific tests and an RFC."

"So, I have to know what kind of tests are needed for certain kinds of impairments?" *Uh-oh, playing doctor.*

"You do. But only generally. You don't have to be a healthcare professional to do this."

"Can you give me an example?"

"Sure. Suppose you've got someone complaining of a bad low back, who hasn't been able to go to the doctor. You ask for an orthopedic examination, with X-rays of the lumbar spine, and a complete range-of-motion study of all major joints and the spine. You should also ask for blood work to see if there is a degenerative process."

"Like what?"

"Test for the rheumatoid factor—that's an "RA factor" test; and ask for an "ESR"—elevated sedimentation rate—that tests for arthritis. Also an "ANA panel"—antinuclear antibodies—which reveals if the immune system is involved."

"Wow."

"It's not that difficult. Just something you pick up pretty quickly in order to help your client."

"What if the judge won't allow the testing?"

"The law requires the Administrative Law Judge to ensure that the record before him or her is fully developed before making a decision in the case. This means the ALJ is supposed to order tests if the record reasonably suggests that there are impairments that have not yet been fully explored." Steve shrugged. "If it isn't done, it becomes a basis for an appeal to the Appeals Council."

"Reasonable? Is that like a preponderance of the evidence?"

"No. It's actually less. It doesn't have to be 'more likely than not'; just such that a reasonable person, viewing the same evidence, would think it appropriate."

"Reasonable? Gotcha," Chris said, feeling much more at ease with the process.

"Now," said Steve, "let's do some 'What if.' "

You must build your client's case by expanding the record to show the basis for complaints of pain. This requires updated treatment records, opinions, and statements of Residual Functional Capacity from consultative or treating physicians.

Client's testimony

Consultative examinations and RFCs

Treating physician records, opinions, and RFCs

Unless your client has a firm foundation on which to base his or her complaints of pain, you run the risk of the judge reaching the conclusion that the complaints are not credible. Only with this foundation can the case be securely built.

Figure 9–22 **How to Provide Proof of Pain**

WHAT IF . . . ? SAMPLE PROBLEMS

WHAT IF . . .

What if your client tells you he cannot lift more than five pounds. The DDS physician renders an opinion that your client can "frequently lift ten pounds" and "occasionally lift up to twenty pounds." What do you do?

1. Have your client testify and contradict the DDS physician.
2. Obtain a written narrative report from your client's treating physician as well as an RFC statement setting forth your client's limitation at five pounds.
3. Have your client's spouse testify as to what he or she can no longer do.
4. Ask for a consultative examination with an RFC.

Answer: The best, although not necessarily the only answer, is (2). Although your client may (and will) certainly testify, his or her testimony alone will not serve to contradict a medical opinion that effectively negates the proffered RFC. Your client's testimony must be supported by an expanded medical record, preferably from his or her treating physician—the person best able to opine, over time, what your client's capability for exertional and nonexertional activity actually is. If not, then request a consultative examination with a "physical RFC."

WHAT IF . . .

What if your client has no diagnosed physical impairment, but complains of a myriad of aches, pains, and other problems for which no medical cause is documented?

1. Give up. Tell your client he has no legal basis for disability.
2. Go forward with your client's testimony anyway. The judge could always find for her in a long-shot decision.

3. Ask for a consultative examination by a psychologist, who will administer the Minnesota Multiphasic Personality Inventory (MMPI), a mental status examination, the Wechsler Adult Intelligence Scale (Fourth Edition), an assessment of global assessment of functioning (GAF), and a MMSS.
4. Have your client see a chiropractor, and present the chiropractor's report as that of a treating physician.

Answer: The best answer is 3. Although you can (and should) allow your client to testify, symptoms without a diagnosed impairment cannot form the basis for disability, so the case will undoubtedly be denied for failure to establish a "medically determinable impairment." However, the presence of multiple symptoms without apparent physical cause may be indicative of a somataform disorder, which will be uncovered through appropriate psychological testing. Although not physical, a psychological disorder may give rise to physical limitations and so may form the basis for an award of disability. Although chiropractic care may provide relief, records from chiropractic treatment are not considered an "acceptable medical source," hence they should not be sought to document the existence of an impairment in this venue.

WHAT IF . . .

The best source for a physical RFC for the period January 1, 1999, through the present is

1. The claimant's own testimony about his life and limitations during this time.
2. A DDS nonexamining physician's opinion, obtained after review of the medical records existing at the time of the initial and reconsideration determinations.
3. The claimant's treating physician, who has been treating him since 1997.
4. An examining physician who served as a consultative examiner once at the request of the Social Security Administration.

Answer: The best source is the claimant's treating physician who has been treating him since 1997. A treating physician's assessment is given controlling weight, if supported by appropriate medical records. Thus, the doctor's complete records from 1997 to the present, when coupled with his or her opinion about the claimant's limitations, will likely be found to be controlling; provided the doctor's assessment is consistent with the diagnosis and treatment found in the doctor's records.

A claimant's rendition of his or her limitations is an allegation, which must be supported by other evidence, usually medical evidence. A DDS doctor has done nothing more than examine the medical records. The issue is whether the non-examining DDS doctor has reviewed all the records; or, only those which happened to be before him or her at the time of the initial administrative decision. Because the DDS doctor is a non-examining physician, he or she has never seen the claimant; thus, engaging in what is essentially an academic review. An examining physician can render an opinion based on a single examination, but this will not control the outcome in the face of a well-supported opinion by a treating physician who has actually treated the claimant over the period of time at issue.

WHAT IF . . .

Which of the following are true?

1. A case must always be decided on either a physical or mental RFC but never both.
2. A physical RFC must always address all exertional functions.
3. Pain is an impairment.
4. A case can be decided on pain alone.
5. Proof of the intensity or severity of pain can be provided by the claimant's own testimony, the testimony of others (including friends, family, and health care professionals), and medical records and consultative examinations.
6. The following RFC is for light work:

- ❏ Lift ten pounds frequently, twenty pounds occasionally;
- ❏ Sit six of 8 hours a day; and
- ❏ Stand four of 8 hours a day.

7. The following RFC is nonexertional in nature:

- ❑ Unable to carry out and remember detailed instructions;
- ❑ Unable to work with the general public;
- ❑ Unable to accept criticism from supervisors;
- ❑ Unable to work with co-workers without distraction; and
- ❑ Unable to engage in fine-motor manipulation with the dominant right hand.

Discussion

1. Mental or physical RFCs are appropriate, depending on the nature of the case. If only physical impairments produce physical limitations (i.e., in the absence of evidence of a mental impairment), a mental RFC is unnecessary. The statement is false.
2. Ideally, a physical RFC, whether it be in the form of a medical source statement, narrative report, or progress note, should address all physical functions. However, an RFC should only address limitations for which there is medical evidence. In the absence of medical evidence, the doctor should not speculate. Hence, it is not necessary that an RFC address all exertional functions to be valid. The statement is false.
3. Pain is not an impairment. An impairment is a medically diagnosed condition, either physical or mental, which reasonably gives rise to limitations of function, and which has lasted at least twelve months or is expected to last twelve months or result in death. Impairments give rise to symptoms, which, in turn, give rise to limitations of function. Pain is a symptom, which produces a limitation of function. The statement is false.
4. This question is somewhat tricky. Pain, as a matter of law, is a symptom, not an impairment, so pain, without any underlying cause (physical or mental) cannot be the basis for an award. If, however, there is an underlying diagnosis, pain can, in and of itself, be debilitating. For example, migraine headaches, which cause a person to lie down in quiet darkness for a certain number of hours per day or week, will effectively prevent competitive work. The best answer is true.
5. Proof may be provided in a variety of ways. Clearly, the claimant's own testimony is critical. It may then be corroborated by third parties, such as family and friends; it should then be further substantiated with medical records showing the underlying impairment likely to cause the pain; other medical reports then note the physician's observations of the pain. The statement is true.
6. Light work is a legal term defined in the regulations. The exertional requirements include the following:

   - ❑ Lifting ten pounds frequently and twenty pounds occasionally;
   - ❑ Standing and walking six hours of an eight-hour work day;
   - ❑ Sitting at least two hours of an eight-hour work day.

   In this question, however, the RFC only permits standing and walking four hours of an eight-hour work day. This is below the level actually required for light work, so this RFC is for less than light work. The correct answer is false.

7. Nonexertional limitations are limitations that do not involve the recognized exertional functions:

   - ❑ Sitting;
   - ❑ Standing;
   - ❑ Walking;
   - ❑ Lifting;
   - ❑ Carrying;
   - ❑ Pushing; and
   - ❑ Pulling.

   Here, each of the limitations is nonexertional, having (with the exception of one) to do with mental or emotional capacity. Fine-motor manipulation is regarded as nonexertional, because it does not involve strength. The correct answer is true.

[1]Title 20 C.F.R. § 404.1505 (Title II claims) and Title 20 C.F.R. § 416.905 (Title XVI claims).
[2]Ibid.
[3]See Title 20 C.F.R. § 404.1545.
[4]Title 20 C.F.R. § 404.1523.
[5]Title 20 C.F.R. § 404.1545.
[6]See Title 20 C.F.R. § 404.1513(a).
[7]Title 20 C.F.R. § 404.1528.
[8]Title 20 C.F.R. § 404.1528(a).
[9]Ibid.
[10]Title 20 C.F.R. § 404.1528(b).
[11]Ibid.
[12]Ibid.
[13]Ibid.
[14]Title 20 C.F.R. § 404.1528(c).
[15]It should be noted, however, that such evidence, whether it be the client's allegations, his or her statements to a physician, the doctor's observations and findings, or laboratory findings, may not necessarily be favorable. The representative's obligation, however, is to present a complete picture of the client. See Chapter 2 for a more detailed discussion on the ethics of representation.
[16]Title 20 C.F.R. § 404.1569(b).
[17]Title 20 C.F.R. § 404.1567(a).
[18]Title 20 C.F.R. § 404.1567(b).
[19]Title 20 C.F.R. § 404.1567(c).
[20]Title 20 C.F.R. § 404.1567(d).
[21]Title 20 C.F.R. § 404.1567(e).
[22]Title 20 C.F.R. § 404.1521(b).
[23]*Young v. Apfel,* 198 F.3d 260, 1999 Colo. J. C.A.R. 5957 (10th Cir. 1999).
[24]See Title 20 C.F.R. § 404.950(c).
[25]20 C.F.R. § 404.944.
[26]Title 20 C.F.R. § 404.949.
[27]See Title 20 C.F.R. § 404.950(d).
[28]For example, if the author is an examining physician, he or she may only address the limited time in which he or she actually saw the claimant; whereas a treating physician may define the period as extending from the date of his or her first treatment of the claimant.
[29]American Psychiatric Association. *Diagnostics and Statistical Manual of Mental Disorders* (4th ed., p. 458). (1994). Washington, D.C.: American Psychiatric Association.
[30]20 C.F.R. § 404.1529(c)(3).

CHAPTER 10

Step 4: Past Relevant Work

HIGHLIGHTS

- ❑ Step 4 in the sequential evaluation
- ❑ Using a vocational expert

CHRIS

"So, here I am, head all muddled with RFC this and RFC that, and no place to go."

"Don't you mean, all dressed up and nowhere to go?"

"Steve! I didn't see you there."

"Been talking to yourself a lot lately?"

"This Social Security case. You know."

Steve nodded sagely. "You've got somebody's life in your hands. Not an easy thing at times."

"What if I, you know. . . ."

"Mess up?"

"Well. . . ."

"I understand. Look, you can only do your best. This is a human endeavor. We're human. So's Mr. Carson. And, most importantly, so's the judge. Mistakes are bound to be made. Even the judge knows that. The judge'll be trying to make the right call. Your job is to make it easier to do."

"OK. You're right." Chris brightened. "So, what's next, now that we have the RFC?"

"What step are you at in the sequential evaluation process?"

"Step 4." Chris pointed to a diagram he'd drawn showing progress so far. (See Figure 10–1.)

FRONT OF YOUR MIND QUESTIONS AND CONSIDERATIONS, 10.1

THE IMPORT OF PAST RELEVANT WORK

Step 4 of the sequential evaluation process asks whether an individual can return to his or her "past relevant work." This is the first point in the process in which residual functional capacity for work is measured against actual work. It is the first point at which the full public policy underlying the disability program is tested: Given the client's *residual functional capacity (RFC)* for work, can she or he actually engage in competitive work?

Step 1 of the Sequential Evaluation

- ❑ Is the claimant engaged in *substantial gainful activity* (SGA) at any point during the alleged period of disability? This is a two-part test: the activity must be "substantial" *and* it must also be "gainful." Only then will it affect the individual's claim for benefits.
- ❑ Does the claimant have earnings which exceed $740.00 per month? If so, he or she may be found to have engaged in SGA.
- ❑ The general rule is, if there is SGA, then benefits cannot be awarded.

Step 2 of the Sequential Evaluation

- ❑ Does the claimant suffer from a "severe" impairment—one that has lasted, or is expected to last at least 12 months; or, result in death?
- ❑ Is the impairment medically determinable—is the impairment supported by objective medical evidence?
- ❑ Does the impairment reasonably give rise to limitations of function which, at least minimally, affect one's ability to engage in competitive work (5 days per week, 8 hours per day)?

Step 3 of the Sequential Evaluation

- ❑ Does the impairment "meet," or is it "medically equivalent in severity" to an impairment listed within the federal regulations (Subpart P of Appendix 2, "The Listings of Impairments")?
- ❑ In other words, do the medically documented signs and symptoms, as found within the medical record, match those with an impairment set forth within one or more of 14 identified bodily systems described in the Code of Federal Regulations?

Step 4 in the Sequential Evaluation

- ❑ Can the individual return to his or her past relevant work, performed within the past 15 years?
- ❑ This is a two part process, examining: (1) work performed within the past 15 years; and (2) relevant work—work performed for a sufficiently long period of time to permit the person to actually learn how to do the job. Generally, this means that the work must have been performed at SGA levels.
- ❑ This assessment requires formulation of the individual's "RFC" for the period in question.

Figure 10–1 **Where Is Chris in the Sequential Evaluation?**

At Step 4 the question specifically concerns whether work performed within the past fifteen years can now be performed, measured retrospectively from the date of the hearing. If the client can return to past work, the consequence is set forth simply in the regulations:

> **If you can do your previous work (your usual work or other applicable past work), we will determine that you are not disabled.**[1]

Thus, the question as to whether *past relevant work* can be performed holds the potential to end the case and must be treated carefully. In other words, step 4 is not a step at which a client can be paid and so is often underestimated. In this, it holds potential for premature demise. Be careful, however, not to look so forward to your case at step 5 that you fail to adequately prepare for step 4.

In order to reach step 5 (where the client *can* be paid), the Administrative Law Judge must determine

1. The client suffers from an impairment giving rise to limitations (i.e., the judge must determine the claimant's RFC); and
2. Given the client's limitations, he or she cannot return to past relevant work (i.e., work performed at a competitive level during the immediate past fifteen years).

Assessment of work performed, including "past relevant work," requires that certain vocational factors be taken into account.

SIGNIFICANCE OF THE REGULATORY VOCATIONAL FACTORS AT STEP 4

If the Administrative Law Judge determines that a client's RFC permits him or her to return to a job held within the past fifteen years, the case is over. The objective, therefore, is to fully develop the case so the full measure of the evidence is presented in two vital areas:

1. A detailed description of past work performed; and
2. Sufficient persuasive evidence of the alleged RFC such that you prove your client's limitations by a preponderance of the evidence.

Both areas of inquiry are of great magnitude. Failure to adequately inform oneself of the details of a client's past work could result in a vocational expert's, and, ultimately, the judge's assessment, that a client's past work was not as demanding as perhaps it actually was.[2] Worse yet, failure to fully explore the nature, scope, and duration of past work may result in an assessment of work performed, when, in fact, the work was not performed at the level required for relevant work.

The Importance of a Detailed Description of Past Work Performed

Past work is referred to as *work experience* in the federal regulations (see Title 20 C.F.R. § 404.1565). Generally, past work is work that has been performed for a period of sufficient duration (in terms of time—thirty days, ninety days, etc.) to allow the worker to acquire the skills (if any) needed to perform the work at competitive levels (generally at wages that rise to the level of substantial gainful activity, or eight hours a day, five days a week, or some other means of accounting for a full-time work week.) Job and professional skills, as discussed later, can also be acquired as a result of specialized training, certification, or education.

Past work, or work experience, must be clearly defined, because it becomes the yardstick that measures the case at Step 4. First, the description of past work becomes evidence on which the vocational expert bases his or her testimony. The vocational expert renders an opinion that includes the following characteristics about the client and his or her work:

- ❑ The job title, with appropriate reference to the job listing set forth in the *Dictionary of Occupational Titles* (*DOT*);[3]
- ❑ The exertional level required by the job (sedentary, light, medium, heavy, or very heavy); and
- ❑ The skills associated with performing the job.

Once the job title is known, the vocational expert may, without specific testimony from the client, derive the work's exertional and skill components by referring to the *DOT*. The *DOT* lists the exertional components required to do the job (such as reaching, handling, fingering, etc.) as well as the skill level at which the job is performed, as shown in Figure 10–2.

It is critical to understand the nature of the client's work, so specific testimony can be elicited from the client to provide the basis for accurate classification under the *DOT* by the vocational expert.

Remember, however, that the *DOT* has not been updated in many years. As a result, job descriptions have changed and many jobs now exist that are not described in the *DOT*. Nevertheless, the vocational expert will often attempt to categorize a client's past work using equivalencies to jobs that *are* listed. The danger, of course, is that without specific testimony about actual work duties, the client may be held to the standard of the "approximated" *DOT* entry, which may or may not reflect the work actually done on the job.

Thus, if you fail to become fully informed of the details of a client's past work, you could end up on the losing end of testimony from the vocational expert, to the effect of "the job that most closely approximates that performed by the claimant . . . ." This is potentially harmful, because it may assume certain capabilities—for both physical exertion and the level of skill required, which the client may not possess. It is important, then, to fully explore the details of a client's past work—both before and during the hearing.

The temptation, to which many representatives succumb, is to let a job title be self-descriptive: "My client was a janitor. Everybody knows what a janitor does. I don't need to explore it further." The problem with this is that you don't really know what the client actually did. Do not assume job duties and responsibilities from a job title. For example, suppose the client worked as a janitor. From a lay perspective, janitorial work would seem to be clearly something more than sedentary in nature. But, is it light, medium, or heavy work? Weight

523.682-014 COFFEE ROASTER (food prep., nec)

—Controls gas fired roasters to remove moisture from coffee beans: Weighs batch of coffee beans in scale-hopper, and opens chute to allow beans to flow into roasting oven. Observes thermometer and adjusts controls to maintain required temperature. Compares color of roasting beans in oven with standard to estimate roasting time. Opens discharge gate to dump roasted beans into cooling trays. Starts machine that blows air through beans to cool them. Records amounts, types, and blends of coffee beans roasted.

GOE: 06.02.15 STRENGTH: L GED: R3 M2 L2 SVP: 4 DLU: 77

Part A

		06.02			**Production Work**
		S	Physical Demands		Environmental Conditions
		V	S C B S K C C R H F	F T H T N F D A C F	W C H H N V A M E H R E T O
DOT Code	DOT Title/DOT Industry Designation(s)	P	i l a t n o w e a i	e a e S A A P c V V	e o o u o i C P S E a x C i
523.682-014	COFFEE ROASTER (food prep., nec)	5	L N N N N N N F F F	N N N N F N N N F N	N N N N 4 N N N N N N N N N

599.685-042 FILTER-PRESS TENDER (beverage: chemical)

—Tends filter press that filters liquors, such as gelatin, glue, and malt beverages: Turns valves to open lines, and pumps liquor through cotton, silk, or woodpulp filter. Inspects filtered liquors for specified degree of clarity. Recirculates cloudy liquor through filter until clear, or connects line to fresh filter press. Reads gauges that indicate pressure in lines and turns valves to maintain specified pressure. Turns valves to transfer clear liquor to specified department. May clean filter by backwashing it with water. May add *chill-proof* enzymes to filter when filtering beer.

GOE: 06.04.19 STRENGTH: L GED: R2 M1 L2 SVP: 3 DLU: 77

Part A

		06.02			**Production Work**
		S	Physical Demands		Environmental Conditions
		V	S C B S K C C R H F	F T H T N F D A C F	W C H H N V A M E H R E T O
DOT Code	DOT Title/DOT Industry Designation(s)	P	i l a t n o w e a i	e a e S A A P c V V	e o o u o i C P S E a x C i
599.685-042	FILTER PRESS TENDER (beverage, chemical)	3	L O N O N O N F F O	N N N N F N N N O N	N F N O 3 N N N N N N N N N

Figure 10–2 **Sample Page: Dictionary of Occupational Titles (DOT numbers are shown as headings)**

lifted through the course of a work shift may only provide part of the answer. Other exertional factors must be considered as well (i.e., pushing, pulling, reaching, standing, and walking).

Within the janitorial category are various levels of such work: cleaner, housekeeper, janitor, or maintenance engineer. A housekeeper generally performs at a light level, whereas a janitor who uses a buffing machine generally performs at the medium level. A cleaner or housekeeper is generally classed as an unskilled job, whereas a maintenance engineer may be semiskilled or skilled, depending on training and certifications held. Detailed questions reveal information about (1) exertional levels, (2) job duties, and (3) tasks performed and equipment operated. Do not allow the client to become the victim of assumptions.

A good example is the case of an individual who testified that he or she was "head supervisor" in a poultry plant. It is reasonable to assume that as head supervisor this person drafted work schedules, coordinated work activity, ensured quality control, and filled out appropriate reports of ongoing production activity. In some circumstances it might even be assumed that he or she had the ability to hire or fire. When asked, however, the individual revealed he or she was a "leadman"—someone who worked alongside co-workers, filled out no reports, had no hiring or firing capability, and did not actually direct the work of others. The title was "supervisor" in name only.

Had you assumed the person did all the things a supervisor might do, the client would have been accorded much higher performance attributes, and the work might have been considered semiskilled or skilled by a vocational expert.

Why does it matter? It matters because the more skill a client has, the more likely he or she will be found not disabled. This is discussed in more detail later, but the Administrative Law Judge may find that skills acquired from past work are transferrable to other, less demanding jobs, thus precluding an award of disability.

Similarly, failure to understand the true nature of a client's work may prevent the discovery that a client performed at a greater exertional level than a job is generally performed (different, for example, than the typical job described in the *DOT*). Or, an employer may have accommodated a disability by allowing performance at less than competitive levels. A typical example is an individual suffering fatigue or pain who must, as a result of the condition, lie down or take frequent rest breaks. On paper, the individual is employed full time. On inquiry, the employer may have allowed rest every hour for up to ten minutes at a time, thus effectively reducing the normal work hour to fifty minutes. Such an accommodation is not competitive work and likely eliminates the job from consideration as past work—that is, eight rest periods (one each hour of an eight-hour workday), each lasting ten minutes, resulting in eighty minutes of rest, almost an hour-and-a-half less than a full eight-hour workday.

Another example is a family member who works in a family-owned business. Oftentimes, the family member running the business will testify, "we let Uncle Bill come in and sit in an office" because either he needed to be watched or it was good for his "self-esteem," when, in fact, he did little or nothing that could be considered competitive in nature. Figure 10–3 outlines the inquiry required to fully explore past work.

Age as a Vocational Factor at Step 4

The inquiry at step 4 of the sequential evaluation process is whether the claimant can return to work that he or she has done within the past fifteen years. Age is not a direct factor in answering this question. As a matter of public policy, age is indirectly factored into the equation by limiting the inquiry to the immediate past fifteen years. Beyond that time, it is presumed that job skills will have deteriorated. Within the fifteen-year time frame, it is presumed, given work performed at the competitive level, that job skills do not deteriorate

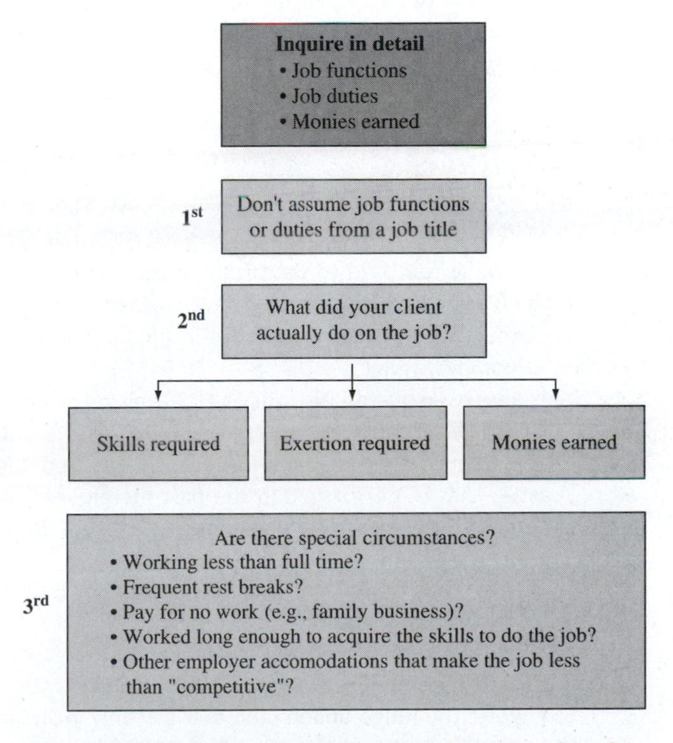

***Figure 10–3* Inquiry about Past Work Requires Careful Questioning about Job Duties, Tasks, and Exertional Levels**

with age for purposes of a step 4 inquiry. This is reflected to a certain extent in the regulations themselves. Title 20 C.F.R. § 404.1563 provides in part:

> **Age refers to how old you are . . . and the extent to which your age affects your ability to adapt to a new work situation and to do work in competition with others. However, we do not determine disability on age alone. We must also consider your residual functional capacity.**

Given a determination that work had been performed at the competitive level within the past fifteen years, the fact that the claimant may be as much as fifteen years older does not factor into a determination of whether past work may be performed. The deciding factor is the claimant's residual functional capacity, not age. Age, therefore, is not a direct factor in the step 4 analysis.

Education as a Vocational Factor at Step 4

As with age, education at step 4 of the sequential evaluation process is not a direct factor in determining whether an individual can return to past relevant work. Because the individual once did the job(s), education after the fact will not preclude a return to earlier work. Because education cannot be lost, it can only enhance an individual's capacity for work.

However, if an individual has suffered an organic brain injury, such that he or she can no longer use his or her educational skills, the functional limitations attributable to the organic loss become part of the residual functional capacity, hence, not directly related to the fact of education.

As with age, education is not, therefore, a factor to be directly considered in evaluating the question of whether an individual can return to past relevant work.

Skill as a Vocational Factor at Step 4

Skill is not a factor so much at step 4 as it is at step 5 of the sequential evaluation process. At step 4 the question is one of the definition of past work, as a foundation for the step 5 inquiry. The nature of past work, both in terms of its exertional demands and its skill level, is key to a determination at step 5.

Thus, the question is not whether the presence or absence of a skill precludes a return to past work, but whether as a result of past work, the claimant has *acquired* a skill that is transferrable to other, less demanding work at step 5, presuming the Administrative Law Judge determines that the claimant's residual functional capacity does not permit a return to past work.

BACK TO CHRIS

"At step 4, then, what I need to know is what kind of work Mr. Carson did during the past fifteen years?"

"That's right. You have to be careful to include only competitive work and then only if it was done long enough for Mr. Carson to have learned how to do it."

"That means I have to be selective in Mr. Carson's testimony? Ask only about those jobs he worked at competitively?"

Steve shook his head. "No, not at all. Don't be selective in Mr. Carson's testimony. Have him tell the judge everything!"

"Wait a minute. I thought you just said that at step 4 we were only concerned with jobs that were "past"—that is, performed in the past fifteen years; and that were "relevant"—that is, performed competitively and for a long enough period of time for Mr. Carson to have learned how to do them—to have acquired the skills to do them."

"You've got it right as far as the law goes, but you'd be making a big mistake if you tried to screen the evidence at a hearing."

Chris was puzzled. "Screen the evidence?"

"Give the judge only selected parts of the fifteen-year work history."

"But, won't the judge understand that I'm only including the competitive jobs?"

"It's more likely that the judge will think you're trying to keep something out of the record. Better to give the judge a chronological work history—in detail—and then summarize at the end."

"I don't get it? Why?"

- Always begin by asking about the most recent work
- Ask about details of job performance, including hours worked, monies earned, duties and tasks performed
- Then move backward chronologically for fifteen years, asking about each previous job

When did you last work at any job?
- What job?
- When did it begin/end?
- Job title?
- What did you do?
- How much did you lift?
- Did you hire/fire?
- And so on.

What did you do before that?
- What job?
- When did it begin/end?
- Job title?
- What did you do?
- How much did you lift?
- Did you hire/fire?
- And so on.

What did you do before that?
- What job?
- When did it begin/end?
- Job title?
- What did you do?
- How much did you lift?
- Did you hire/fire?
- And so on.

Figure 10–4 **Claimant Inquiry Regarding Past Work**

"Remember reading about a DEQY and a SEQY?"

Chris paused, then brightened. "The earnings record?"

"Correct. Those are exhibits in the file. Also, Mr. Carson completed a work history report when he filed his application for disability benefits. The judge and the vocational expert will have both records and have a pretty good idea of the various jobs Mr. Carson's had."

"Do those reports tell whether they were done competitively or not?"

"Indirectly. They show how long he worked and how much money he made. You can draw some preliminary conclusions from that information."

"So?"

"So, you can't be selective in your presentation. The judge will think you're leaving things out, and that will seem unusual. The judge might even think you're trying to hide something."

"OK. What's the best way to present Mr. Carson's testimony about his past work?"

"Chronologically. Don't ask him what work he did in the past fifteen years. Most people tend to ramble if they're asked a question that vague. Besides, they're probably nervous. You have to give them a structure they can follow—a structure that cues their memory."

Chris thought it through. "You mean start with the first job, then work forward?"

"No." Steve grabbed a sheet of paper. "Start with the most recent job—the last job your client did first, then work backward. Like this." Steve drew a quick diagram as seen in Figure 10–4.

"I get it. It's a memory tool. My client is going to be more likely to remember the recent work, and talking about that will help trigger each previous job."

"Exactly. And, you'll end up covering all the jobs, so the Administrative Law Judge will know you're being as complete as possible."

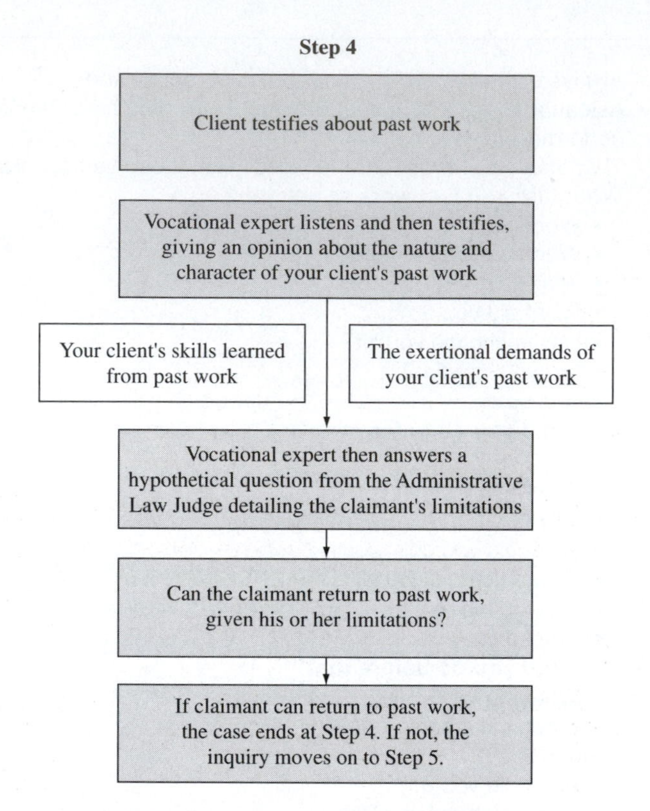

Figure 10–5 **Vocational Experts Are Used at Steps 4 and 5 of the Sequential Evaluation Process**

"And," added Chris, "as forthright."
Steve nodded, "That too."
"What about the vocational experts?"
"They participate at both the fourth and fifth steps in the sequential evaluation process."
"How?"
"Here, let me draw another diagram," Steve said. (See Figure 10–5.)
"Now we need to know about vocational experts, I guess?"
"It's fun," said Steve with a wink.
Chris glanced askance at Steve.
"Really! It is!" Steve exclaimed.

FRONT OF YOUR MIND QUESTIONS AND CONSIDERATIONS, 10.2

USING A VOCATIONAL EXPERT AT STEP 4 OF THE SEQUENTIAL EVALUATION PROCESS

In order to reach the question of whether an individual is capable of returning to work performed within the past fifteen years, the Administrative Law Judge generally calls a vocational expert to testify. This individual is usually a licensed professional counselor, a vocational rehabilitation specialist, a psychologist, or other professional whose career has involved job placement, career counseling and working with job placement for the disabled.

Although the vocational expert (VE), is called by the judge, the VE is neither a government nor a claimant's witness. Rather, having been called by the judge, the VE's task is to offer a neutral opinion based on (1) the evidence adduced at the hearing and (2) the judge's determinations as to the claimant's limitations of function. The VE receives a set fee for each case in which he or she appears. As a general rule, the fee is paid to the VE regardless of whether testimony is offered; the fee is for time appearing at the hearing. Judges may not select the VE to be used. Rather, the Hearing Office maintains a standing roster of available VEs, and they are called in rotation to appear at the next scheduled docket. If a VE is unavailable for a given docket, the case technician (Hearing Office support personnel) calls the next VE listed on the roster.

Most Administrative Law Judges inquire whether a representative has any objection to the qualifications of the proposed VE as an expert witness. Unless a serious issue arises as to the proposed expert's bias or qualifications, no objection should be voiced. A VEs resume, or CV (curriculum vitae), is made a part of the record and is available for review prior to the hearing.

When notice of a hearing is given, the presence or absence of experts, including a VE is noted. Thus, the representative and his or her client are notified in advance of the presence of the vocational or other expert. Generally, however, VEs do not make themselves available for interview prior to the hearing, and in some cases, VEs prepare for the case the day of or the day before the hearing.

MATERIALS REVIEWED BY THE VOCATIONAL EXPERT PRIOR TO THE HEARING

Prior to a hearing, the VE reviews the following documents:

1. The DEQY (detailed earnings query);
2. The SEQY (summary earnings query);
3. The Disability Report;
4. The Form 831; and
5. Any vocational reports or summaries of record prior to the hearing.

Figure 10–6, the disability report, is completed by the claimant, and it contains a summary of past work.

Figure 10–7, Form SSA-831, is a summary description of the claimant's impairment(s), age, education, and claim type. This is important because it provides a "snapshot" of the claimant, the claim, and the basis for the claim. However, no direct vocational evidence is found on Form SSA-831.

Although the DEQY contains a list of employers it actually represents payment of the amount of money actually paid—and sometimes not from the actual employer but from a holding company or parent corporation. Thus, the information available to the VE prior to the hearing is largely prepared by the claimant at the time of the initial application. A well-prepared VE attempts to correlate the objective data—the information generated by the Social Security Administration in the DEQY and SEQY—with the subjective data—the reports completed by the claimant at the time of the initial application.

If permitted by the Administrative Law Judge, the extent to which the data do not correlate forms the initial basis for any inquiry by the VE of the claimant. The representative should examine this information prior to the hearing in order to understand the information base the VE will use.

WHY USE A VOCATIONAL EXPERT?

The information assessed by the vocational expert is essential to a full, fair, and just decision. The VE testifies as an expert because his or her knowledge is beyond that of a layperson. Neither the judge nor the claimant can be expected to assess either the exertional or skill demands of work, especially as such categories are classed by the Department of Labor in the *Dictionary of Occupational Titles.* Such knowledge is beyond the ken of the ordinary person and, thus, requires an expert.

Never blandly assume that the individual appearing to testify as a vocational expert is, in fact, so qualified, but be assured to a certain extent that his or her qualifications have been examined by the Social Security Administration. Every expert (whether medical or vocational) called by the Administrative Law Judge must be certified by the Social Security Administration, Office of Hearings and Appeals. The certification process entails a review of education, experience, licensure, and specialization, if any. Once certified the expert's name is added to the experts roster maintained at the Regional Chief Judge's office as well as the local Hearing Office. Hearing Office procedure then generally requires experts to be assigned in the order in which they appear on the roster, depending, of course, on availability. An expert is not preselected by a judge or claimant, but appears in rotation. This assures fairness, because no particular expert is aligned with a particular judge in any given hearing.

SOCIAL SECURITY ADMINISTRATION

DISABILITY REPORT - FIELD OFFICE

IDENTIFYING INFORMATION

1. NAME OF PERSON ON WHOSE SOCIAL SECURITY RECORD THIS CLAIM IS BEING FILED	HIS OR HER SOCIAL SECURITY NUMBER
NAME OF CLAIMANT *(if different from above)* ☐ Male ☐ Female DOB ____________	SSN *(if different from above)*

2. CLAIMANT'S ALLEGED ONSET DATE (AOD) ____________

3. RECOMMENDED ONSET DATE *(if different from above)* *(check type of claim(s) and enter recommended onset)* ☐ SSI ____________

☐ DIB/Freeze ____________ ☐ DWB ____________ ☐ CDB ____________ ☐ OTHER ____________

4. REASON FOR RECOMMENDED ONSET DATE

☐ SSI Application Date ☐ Controlling Date

☐ SSI Alien ☐ Statutorily Blind

☐ Date Last Insured ☐ Work Before/After AOD

☐ Date First Insured ☐ UWA ☐ SGA ☐ Not SGA ☐ 820/821 In File

☐ Other (explain in item 5)

5. EXPLANATION FOR RECOMMENDED ONSET DATE, WHEN APPLICABLE:

☐ 820/821 Pending Date Requested ____________

MISCELLANEOUS INFORMATION

6. Protective filing date ____________ Date last insured (DIB/Freeze case) ____________

Beginning of Prescribed Period (DWB) ____________ End of Prescribed Period ____________

Controlling date ____________

Closed period case ☐ Yes ☐ No

PRIOR FILING INFORMATION - Use Remarks, if additional space is needed.

7. Prior filing(s) ☐ Yes ☐ No

If yes, and you are not sending the prior folder(s) to the DDS, enter the following;

Type of prior claim(s) ____________

SSN(s) of prior claim(s) ____________

Date of last decision ____________ Level of last decision ___ ☐ Allowance ☐ Denial

Date of prior termination (if applicable) ____________

Location of prior folder ____

Prior folder requested ☐ Yes ____________ (date requested) ☐ No

FORM **SSA-3367-F4** (12/1998) 7/1998 EDITION(S) MAY BE USED UNTIL EXHAUSTED EF (9-2000) PAGE 1

Disability Report - Field Office Form SSA-3367

Figure 10–6 **Disability Report (completed by the claimant)**

8. CHECK ANY OF THE FOLLOWING FO PD/PB CRITERIA THAT APPLY IN AN SSI CLAIM PER DI 11055.230ff.

☐ 1. Amputation of two limbs.

☐ 2. Amputation of a leg at the hip.

☐ 3. Allegation of total deafness.

☐ 4. Allegation of total blindness.

☐ 5. Allegation of bed confinement or immobility without a wheel chair, walker, or crutches, due to a longstanding condition -- excluding recent accident and recent surgery.

☐ 6. Allegation of a stroke (cerebral vascular accident) more than 3 months in the past and continued marked difficulty in walking or using a hand or arm.

☐ 7. Allegation of cerebral palsy, muscular dystrophy, or muscle atrophy and marked difficulty in walking (e.g., use of braces), speaking, or coordination of hands or arms.

☐ 8. Allegation of diabetes with amputation of a foot.

☐ 9. Allegation of Down Syndrome.

☐ 10. Allegation of severe mental deficiency made by another individual filing on behalf of a claimant who is at least 7 years of age. For example, a mother filing for benefits for her child states that the child attends (or attended) a special school, or special classes in school because of mental deficiency or is unable to attend any type of school (or if beyond school age, was unable to attend), and requires care and supervision of routine daily activities.

Note: "Mental deficiency" means mental retardation. This PD category pertains to individuals whose dependence upon others for meeting personal care needs (e.g., hygiene) and in doing other routine daily activities (e.g., fastening a seat belt) grossly exceeds age-appropriate dependence as a result of mental retardation.

☐ 11. A child is age 6 months or younger and the birth certificate or other evidence (e.g. hospital admission summary) shows a weight below 1200 grams (2 pounds 10 ounces) at birth.

☐ 12. Human immunodeficiency virus (HIV) infection (See DI 11055.241)

☐ 13. A child is age 6 months or younger and available evidence (e.g., the hospital admission summary) shows a gestational age at birth on the table below with the corresponding birth weight indicated:

Gestational Age (in weeks)	Weight at Birth	
37-40	Less than 2000 grams	(4 pounds, 6 ounces)
36	1875 grams or less	(4 pounds, 2 ounces)
35	1700 grams or less	(3 pounds, 12 ounces)
34	1500 grams or less	(3 pounds, 5 ounces)

☐ 14. A physician or knowledgeable hospice official confirms an individual is receiving hospice services because of terminal cancer. (See DI E11010.001ff. for terminal illness procedures.)

☐ 15. Allegation of inability to ambulate without the use of a walker or bilateral hand-held assistive device more than two weeks following a spinal cord injury with verification of such status from an appropriate medical professional.

FORM **SSA-3367-F4** (12/1998) 7/1998 EDITION(S) MAY BE USED UNTIL EXHAUSTED EF (9-2000) PAGE 2

(continued)

9. OBSERVATIONS/PERCEPTIONS

☐ Teleclaim with claimant (Complete 1-8 and 15 below) ☐ Face-to-face with claimant (Complete 1-15 below) ☐ No contact with claimant (Go to Page 4)

If the claimant had difficulty with the following, check the "yes" block and explain in "observations" or check "no" or "not observed/perceived." (Explain any "no" answers that you think would assist the DDS in making a decision.)

1. Hearing	☐ Yes	☐ No	☐ Not observed/perceived
2. Reading	☐ Yes	☐ No	☐ Not observed/perceived
3. Breathing	☐ Yes	☐ No	☐ Not observed/perceived
4. Understanding	☐ Yes	☐ No	☐ Not observed/perceived
5. Coherency	☐ Yes	☐ No	☐ Not observed/perceived
6. Concentrating	☐ Yes	☐ No	☐ Not observed/perceived
7. Talking	☐ Yes	☐ No	☐ Not observed/perceived
8. Answering	☐ Yes	☐ No	☐ Not observed/perceived
9. Sitting	☐ Yes	☐ No	☐ Not observed/perceived
10. Standing	☐ Yes	☐ No	☐ Not observed/perceived
11. Walking	☐ Yes	☐ No	☐ Not observed/perceived
12. Seeing	☐ Yes	☐ No	☐ Not observed/perceived
13. Using hand(s)	☐ Yes	☐ No	☐ Not observed/perceived
14. Writing	☐ Yes	☐ No	☐ Not observed/perceived
15. Other (specify)			

OBSERVATIONS: Describe the claimant's behavior, appearance, grooming, degree of limitations, etc.

FORM **SSA-3367-F4** (12/1998) 7/1998 EDITION(S) MAY BE USED UNTIL EXHAUSTED EF (9-2000) PAGE 3

10. Development initiated by FO

A. Medical

Source	Date Requested	Tickle/Diary Date	Evidence to be Forwarded by Source to		Capability Development Requested
			DDS	FO	

B. Other

Source	Date Requested	Tickle/Diary Date	Evidence to be Forwarded by Source to	
			DDS	FO

C. Forms to be completed by applicant and sent to the DDS.

☐ SSA-3370 ☐ SSA-3371 ☐ SSA-3369 ☐ Other ____________

11. If medical evidence was brought in to the FO by the claimant, check here ☐

12. Is DDS capability development needed? ☐ Yes ☐ No

REMARKS

NAME OF INTERVIEWER (Print)

Area Code Phone Number

NAME OF PERSON COMPLETING FORM (Print) *(if different from interviewer)*

DATE

SOCIAL SECURITY ADMINISTRATION

Form Approved
OMB No. 0960-0437

DISABILITY DETERMINATION AND TRANSMITTAL

1. DESTINATION — DDS ☐ ODO ☐ DRS ☐ DQB ☐ INTPSC ☐
2. DDS CODE
3. FILING DATE
4. SSN
BIC (if CDB or DWB CLAIM)
5. NAME AND ADDRESS OF CLAIMANT (include ZIP Code)
6. WE'S NAME *(IF CDB OR DWB CLAIM)*
7. TYPE CLAIM (Title II) — DIB ☐ FZ ☐ DWB ☐ CDB-R ☐ CDB-D ☐ RD-R ☐ RD-D ☐ RD ☐ P-R ☐ P-D ☐ MQFE ☐
8. TYPE CLAIM (Title XVI) — ☐ DI ☐ DS ☐ DC ☐ BI ☐ BS ☐ BC
9. DATE OF BIRTH
10. PRIOR ACTION — ☐ PD ☐ PT
11. REMARKS
12. DISTRICT-BRANCH OFFICE ADDRESS (include ZIP Code)
DO-BO CODE
13. DO-BO REPRESENTATIVE
14. DATE
11A. ☐ Presumptive Disability
11B. ☐ Impairment

DETERMINATION PURSUANT TO THE SOCIAL SECURITY ACT, AS AMENDED

15. CLAIMANT DISABLED
A. ☐ Disability Began
B. ☐ Disability Ceased
16A. PRIMARY DIAGNOSIS — BODY SYS. — CODE NO.
16B. SECONDARY DIAGNOSIS — CODE NO.
17. DIARY TYPE — MO./YR. — REASON
18. CASE OF BLINDNESS AS DEFINED IN SEC. 1614(a)(2)/(216)(i)
A. ☐ Not Disab. for Cash Bene. Purp.
B. ☐ Disab. for Cash Benefit Purp. Beg.
19. CLAIMANT NOT DISABLED
A. ☐ Through Date of Current Determination
B. ☐ Through ______
C. ☐ Before Age 22 (CDB only)
20. VOCATIONAL BACKGROUND — OCC YRS. — ED YRS.
21. VR ACTION — SC IN A. ☐ — SC OUT B. ☐ — Prev Ref C. ☐
22. REG-BASIS CODE
23. MED LIST NO.
24. MOB CODE
25. REVISED DET ☐
25A. Initial A. ☐ — Recon B. ☐ — Recon DHU C. ☐ — ALJ Hearing D. ☐ — Appeals Council E. ☐ — U.S. District Court F. ☐
26. LIST NO. — A. — B. — C. — D. — E. — F.
27. RATIONALE — ☐ See Attached SSA-4268-U4/C4 — ☐ Check if Vocational Rule Met. Cite Rule
28. A. ☐ Period of Disability — B. ☐ Disability Period — C. ☐ Estab Beg ______ AND D. ☐ Continues — E. ☐ Term ______
29. LTR/PAR NO.
30. DISABILITY EXAMINER-DDS
31. DATE
32. PHYSICIAN OR MEDICAL SPEC. SIGNATURE
33. DATE
32A. PHYSICIAN OR MEDICAL SPEC. NAME *(Stamp, Print or Type)*
32B. SPEC. CODE
34. REMARKS
MULTIPLE IMPAIRMENTS CONSIDERED
34A. COMBINED MULTIPLE NONSEVERE-SEVERE
34B. COMBINED MULTIPLE NONSEVERE-NONSEVERE
35. BASIS CODE
36. REV. DET. CODES
37. SSA REPRESENTATIVE
SSA CODE
38. DATE

Form **SSA-831 C3/U3** (5-1989) EF (06-2001)

State Agency/Data Copy

Electronic Input: ☐ DECISION ☐ CASE CONTROL

Figure 10–7 **Disability Determination and Transmittal (generated by SSA)**

Nevertheless, if there are questions about the qualifications of an expert, inquiry about his or her qualifications may be made. The expert may be examined on the record before he or she testifies about a claimant. How is that done? A vocational expert's qualifications involve the following:

- ❑ Education;
- ❑ Training;
- ❑ Certifications/licensure; and
- ❑ Professional experience.

Determine whether the proposed expert is, indeed, so qualified. To determine whether an expert is qualified, the inquiry should proceed something like this:

Can you please tell us your name?

What is your current occupation or training?

What degrees do you hold?

- ❑ Inquire about the date entered and graduated.
- ❑ Inquire about honors earned.
- ❑ Inquire about specific course of study (if applicable to the question of qualifications in the hearing).

What certifications or licenses do you hold?

What is your current professional position?

- ❑ Inquire about start date.
- ❑ Inquire about duties.

What positions have you held in the past?

- ❑ Inquire as to duties and responsibilities.

To what professional organizations do you belong?

- ❑ Inquire about positions held.

Have you worked with people who are handicapped or disabled?

Have you published professionally?

Are you familiar with job placement issues?

Once professional qualifications are established, the representative may then indicate agreement that the vocational expert may testify as such. If there are no outstanding issues with the proposed expert's qualifications and no further inquiry is required, the representative may simply indicate to the judge that the expert's qualifications are acceptable.

What if there is a question about the expert unrelated to his or her actual qualifications? How are questions raised that go beyond the initial qualifications? Simply put, how and when questions are asked depends on the subject. If the question concerns overt bias on the part of the vocational expert, such as his or her relationship with a client, or if it concerns other issues of fairness, the inquiry should be made before the vocational expert testifies. If the question concerns the expert's opinion, the inquiry should be made after the Administrative Law Judge has elicited the VE's testimony.

In effect, a vocational expert eliminates the guesswork as to whether the claimant can return to past relevant work. The danger, of course, is that the opinion offered by the expert may be based on incomplete or incorrect information. Or, the judge's findings with respect to the claimant's residual functional capacity or limitations may differ from the representative's. The representative must, therefore, play an active role in examining the expert. This necessarily requires the proper vocational foundation to be laid, either in writing or through testimony.

INQUIRY BY THE ADMINISTRATIVE LAW JUDGE AT STEP 4

Once the expert is qualified to testify as a vocational expert, the judge takes the lead in the initial examination. This, again, is a result of the hybrid jurisprudence underlying these administrative hearings. More to the point, the judge *must* make a determination at step 4 of the sequential evaluation process. Because the government is unrepresented in the hearing, it is the judge's responsibility to elicit the necessary testimony from the vocational expert as to

1. The nature, scope, and extent of the claimant's past work; and
2. The skill and exertional demands of the claimant's past relevant work.

The questioning by the Administrative Law Judge proceeds something like this:

Judge: Do you have an opinion as to the work performed by the claimant during the past fifteen years? And, if so, can you tell us what your opinion is as to the exertional and skill demands of each of the claimant's jobs? In answering, please provide the *DOT* number as well.

VE: I do. The claimant last worked as a ______, which, according to the *DOT* is performed at the light level and is semiskilled work with an SVP [specific vocational preparation] of 4. She next worked as a ______, which is also light work, but is unskilled, with an SVP of 2. Finally, she worked as a ______, which is medium work, also unskilled, with an SVP of 2.

Judge: Can you tell us the *DOT* numbers for each of those positions?

VE: Certainly. The first is [*DOT* No.]. The second position, as a ______, is [*DOT* No.], and the third, working as a ______, is [*DOT* No.].

Judge: Do you have an opinion as to whether the claimant possesses skills that are transferrable to other jobs?

VE: Yes, in my opinion she does. [The VE then proceeds to list various skills and the judge may ask the VE to explain the basis for the opinions given.]

Judge: Does the claimant's educational attainment or training permit her to directly enter skilled work?

VE: No. She has only a high school education, with one year of community college. She has no other training. Therefore, she cannot directly enter skilled work.

Judge: Assume with me the existence of a person who is the same age as the claimant, with the same vocational and educational background. Next assume the following limitations:

A. The individual can only sit for one to two hours at a time, before having to stand;
B. The individual can lift a maximum of ten pounds;
C. The individual can stand and walk up to thirty minutes at a time before having to sit down and rest.

Given these limitations, do you have an opinion as to whether the individual would be able to perform the claimant's past relevant work?

VE: In my opinion, the individual would not.

Judge: Why not?

VE: The claimant's past work was light and medium, requiring that she be able to frequently lift ten pounds and occasionally twenty pounds for light work; and frequently lift twenty-five pounds and occasionally fifty pounds for medium work. With the limitation here, that the individual can only lift up to ten pounds maximum, both light and medium work are precluded.

Judge: How would you classify this individual's residual functional capacity, given these limitations?

VE: In my opinion, this is an RFC for sedentary work requiring a sit–stand option.

Judge: What do you mean by a sit–stand option?

VE: The claimant would have to have the option of sitting or standing while performing a job, because of her inability to sit longer than one or two hours at a time. Some jobs are sit–stand jobs in that they require the employee to shift position as part of the job. Other jobs may be performed in either the sitting or standing position. This is the type of position I am referring to when I say a sit–stand option. What I mean is that the option to sit or stand is the employee's and not required by the job itself.

The foregoing examination illustrates vocational testimony at step 4 of the sequential evaluation process. Careful analysis of the questioning reveals discrete inquiries, requiring further explanation.

First, the judge asked the vocational expert to render an opinion, characterizing the claimant's past relevant work in accord with the *Dictionary of Occupational Titles*. In answering, the vocational expert opined that the claimant's past work was performed at a specific exertional level, and demanded a level of skill measured by his or her *specific vocational preparation* (SVP).

SVP stands for "specific vocational preparation" and refers to the amount of time it takes an individual to learn to do a given job. Job performance includes the techniques, information, and facilities necessary to do a specific job. Learning to do a job may be a result of actual job performance over time, or it may be a result of occupational or vocational training, or professional education. Vocational training includes vocational education, apprenticeship, in-plant training, or on-the-job training.

The higher the SVP number, the greater the skill required to do a job, or the skill acquired as a result of doing the work. When the vocational expert opines that past work was performed at a certain skill level (i.e., unskilled, semiskilled, or skilled), the corresponding SVP level defines more precisely the level. Figure 10–8 describes the SVP scale.

Vocational experts use SVP levels as "breakpoints" between different skill categories. Thus, whether a job is described as unskilled, semiskilled, or skilled depends on the SVP assigned by the vocational expert. Figure 10–9 illustrates commonly accepted breakpoints.

The exertional demands of a given job are defined in the *DOT* as such jobs are generally performed in the national or regional economies. A claimant's testimony describes how he or she actually performed past work, which may differ from the DOT description. Often there is no difference between how a claimant's job is generally performed in the national or regional economies and how he or she actually did it. Sometimes, however, individual performance varies from the general description in the *DOT*. It becomes the VE's—and the representative's—task to fully define the claimant's actual job performance so that it can be ascertained, whether he or she can return to past relevant work.

When answering the question of exertional demand, the implementing regulations found under both Title II and Title XVI of the Social Security Act adopt the exertional definitions originally found in the *DOT*. Thus, Social Security's definitions for sedentary, light, medium, and heavy work are those initially compiled by the Department of Labor and found in the *Dictionary of Occupational Titles*.

Will vocational experts' opinions differ based on their experience and interpretation of the claimant's testimony? Absolutely. And, therein lies part of the reason for the *DOT*. The *DOT* becomes an objective measure against which the opinions of the vocational expert are measured.

The SVP level reflects the time it actually takes to learn to do the job, and thereby acquire the skills necessary to its performance.

SVP Level	Time Required to Acquire the Level
Level 1	Only a short demonstration is required to learn the job
Level 2	Anything beyond a short demonstration, up to 30 days to learn the job
Level 3	More than 30 days, up to and including 3 months to learn the job
Level 4	More than 3 months, and up to 6 months to learn the job
Level 5	More than 6 months, and up to and including 1 year to learn the job
Level 6	More than 1 year, and up to and including 2 years to learn the job
Level 7	More than 2 years, and up to and including 4 years to learn the job
Level 8	More than 4 years, and up to and including 10 years to learn the job
Level 9	More than 10 years

***Figure 10–8* SVP Scale**

Unskilled Work	Semiskilled Work	Low-Skilled Work	Skilled Work
SVP 1 2	SVP 3 4	SVP 5 6	SVP 7 8 9

***Figure 10–9* SVP "Breakpoints" for Job Skills**

If the vocational expert's opinion about either the exertional level or the skill demands of a given job differs from the *DOT*, the expert should be required to explain the difference. If, on direct examination by the Administrative Law Judge, the expert fails to provide the *DOT* job classification number, the representative should, on cross-examination, elicit the information and then inquire about any differences between the *DOT* description and the proffered opinion.

Once the vocational expert has offered an opinion about the claimant's past work, the judge should ask whether the claimant possesses transferable skills. Transferable skills are skills the claimant acquired from past work that may be used in jobs other than those he or she has performed in the past. Having transferable skills means a wider array of jobs is available to the claimant in the national or regional economies.

Whether a claimant has acquired skills from working, schooling, or other training depends on the nature of his or her past work, education, and training. The consequences are particularly significant. If an individual possesses skills that are transferable, it is less likely that he or she will be found disabled at step 5 of the sequential evaluation process. The vocational expert's assessment of the claimant's past relevant work at step 4 thus becomes a foundation for later testimony at step 5.

Finally, during the vocational expert's testimony, many practitioners find it helpful to use a preprinted form, separating the testimony into its component parts. Figure 10–10 is an example of such a form. *S* stands for skilled; *S/S*, for semiskilled; and *U/S*, for "unskilled" work. *S, L, M, H,* and *VH* stand for sedentary, light, medium, heavy, and very heavy, respectively.

BACK TO CHRIS

"Let me see if I get this. The vocational expert tells you about your client's past work in terms of exertion and skill?"

Steve frowned slightly. "It's not that the vocational expert *tells* you. It's that he or she gives you an *opinion*. It's what the vocational expert thinks as a result of what he or she has learned, both from the administrative record and from hearing your client's testimony."

Chris remained silent for a few seconds. "That's why it's really important that I understand exactly what my client did—that is, what Mr. Carson did?"

"That's right. If you assume too much, your client may be described as having skills he really didn't have or use at all."

"Which could mean that he is not found disabled when we get to step 5?"

"It has to do with fair and zealous representation of your client. If Mr. Carson did not acquire skills that are transferrable to other types of jobs, then he should not be held to that standard."

"OK. I understand that. But, where does the RFC come into play?"

"Here," Steve said, "let me show you."

FRONT OF YOUR MIND QUESTIONS AND CONSIDERATIONS, 10.3

APPLYING THE RFC AT STEP 4

After eliciting the vocational expert's opinion as to the exertion and skill demands of the claimant's past work and having further elicited the expert's opinion regarding transferability of skills to other work, the judge may proceed in one of two ways. First, if the vocational expert opines that the claimant (your client) possesses skills that *are* transferable, the judge may specifically inquire about available jobs.

Judge: **Having determined that the claimant has skills that are transferable to other jobs, do you have an opinion as to what those jobs might be?**

VE: **Yes. The claimant has the skill of _____ which is transferable to the job of telemarketer. This is a sedentary, semiskilled position.**

Claimant: ______________________ SSN: ______________________

Past Work History:

Job Title:	S	S/S	U/S	SVP

S	L	M	H	VH

Transferability: Yes No

____

____

____

Hypothetical:

____

____

____

____

____

____

____

Other Work:

Job Title:	S	S/S	U/S	SVP

S	L	M	H	VH

R	N

Figure 10–10 Form Illustrating Vocational Expert Testimony

Judge: **Do you have an opinion as to how many such positions exist, both in the national and regional economies?**

VE: **Yes. Considering the state of Oklahoma as the region, there are 1,500 such positions in the state and 125,000 nationally.**

Second, if the client has no transferrable skills, the Administrative Law Judge will not inquire as to (1) whether there are jobs to which skills transfer and (2) the numbers of such jobs. Instead, the judge will immediately posit a hypothetical question to the vocational expert designed to determine whether the claimant can return to past work.

This type of inquiry is not, however, in sequence. Although some judges may so proceed, the literal requirement of the sequential evaluation process requires that the question of whether past work can be performed be asked first. Once past work has been defined, the only questions remaining concern the claimant's limitations, if any.

Judge: **Assume with me the existence of a person who is the same age as the claimant, with the same vocational and educational background. Next assume the following limitations:**

- ❑ **The individual can only sit for one to two hours at a time before having to stand;**
- ❑ **The individual can lift a maximum of ten pounds;**
- ❑ **The individual can stand and walk up to thirty minutes at a time before having to sit down and rest.**

Given these limitations, do you have an opinion whether the individual would be able to perform the claimant's past relevant work?

VE: **In my opinion, the individual would not.**

To ascertain whether past relevant work can be performed, there does not need to be an inquiry about transferability of skills. That issue only arises at step 5 of the sequential evaluation. At step 4, the issue is whether work performed (at SGA levels) in the past fifteen years could be undertaken considering the claimant's limitations.

If the vocational expert testifies that the claimant can return to past work, the case is over. If the judge adopts the vocational expert's testimony (and it is likely, absent any challenge, that the judge will), the only result is denial of benefits. The only choice when vocational testimony is such that a client can return to past work is to challenge the expert.

A claimant in an administrative hearing in this situation is faced with the awkward reality of the absence of government counsel. Instead, as discussed earlier, the judge asks the vocational expert about the step 4 issue(s). Thus, any challenge must be substantive in nature. Unfortunately, such a challenge rests directly on the *judge's* conclusions about the claimant's residual functional capacity (i.e., the judge has asked the vocational expert to assume certain limitations and from those assumptions the vocational expert has opined that a client can return to past relevant work.)

A challenge, in the form of cross-examination of the expert, must, therefore, be based on (1) the client's testimony and (2) medical records and reports. From this evidence it can be argued that the record supports a different conclusion. For example, the judge in the foregoing example accepted the conclusion reached by the vocational expert that the claimant could perform only sedentary work, which precluded the claimant from returning to past work, which was light and medium. If the claimant had worked at a sedentary level in the past fifteen years, the inquiry might have proceeded differently:

Judge: **Assume with me the existence of a person who is the same age as the claimant, with the same vocational and educational background. Next assume the following limitations:**

- ❑ **The individual can only sit for one to two hours at a time, before having to stand;**
- ❑ **The individual can lift a maximum of ten pounds;**
- ❑ **The individual can stand and walk up to thirty minutes at a time before having to sit down and rest.**

Given these limitations, do you have an opinion as to whether the individual would be able to perform the claimant's past relevant work?

VE: **In my opinion, the individual would be able to return to work as a surveillance monitor, which he did ten years ago.**

Judge: **Why?**

VE: **A surveillance monitor is a sedentary job, entry level, or unskilled, and may be performed either sitting or standing, as long as the employee is able to monitor the surveillance screens.**

At that point the judge might close the proceeding, assuming that no further testimony is necessary. The representative should then cross-examine the expert for other limitations, more restrictive than those voiced by the judge. Otherwise, the decision will be to deny benefits at step 4 of the sequential evaluation process because the claimant can still perform past relevant work. Cross-examination of the vocational expert creates a contrary record, relying on medical evidence and testimony to lay a foundation for a different result.

The RFC is the heart of the judge's initial examination, and it must be the heart of a cross-examination. Just like the judge, a representative must be ready to ask about the effects of certain *limitations,* which, if not suggested by the judge, form the basis of the representative's inquiry. However, do not ask the vocational expert about the effect of a given *impairment;* instead, ask about a *limitation.* Vocational experts are not medically trained. They cannot testify as to the vocational effects of impairments; they testify about the effects of limitations (which, of course, arise from impairments). The following cross-examination is illustrative:

Representative: You testified that the claimant could perform sedentary work and return to her employment as a surveillance monitor. Correct?

VE: **That's correct.**

Representative: **Now, assume with me that the claimant suffers from cerebral palsy. Would she be able to perform such work?**

VE: **I'm sorry, I can't respond to that question. Can you tell me what the limitations are as a result of the cerebral palsy?**

The representative failed to ask the vocational expert about limitations, asking instead about the effect of an impairment, without any quantifying information. To be vocationally understandable, the functional effects of an impairment must be quantified. However, the representative can easily remedy the mistake:

Representative: **You mean, what the cerebral palsy restricts the claimant from being able to do?**

VE: **Yes.**

Representative: **OK. Assume with me that because of cerebral palsy the claimant suffers from severe fatigue, a lack of stamina, such that she must lie down at least two times a day at irregular intervals for up to two hours a time. Would she be able to perform her past work as a surveillance monitor?**

VE: **I can answer that question. No, she would not be able to perform her past work or any other competitive work, because the need to lie down at irregular, and thus unpredictable, times constitutes too many and too lengthy rest breaks for competitive work.**

Representative: **How many rest breaks are allowed for competitive work?**

VE: **Normally, a fifteen-minute rest break every two hours.**

Representative: **So, a person who suffers from cerebral palsy who, because of fatigue, must lie down up to four hours in a given work day would be off work too much—would have too many rest breaks to perform competitively?**

VE: **Yes. The only way such a person could perform such a job is with employer accommodations.**

Representative: **Meaning that the employer would have to make special arrangements, above and beyond what he or she would have to do for a normal worker—thus removing this job from competitive work?**

VE: **Correct.**

The representative has effectively *quantified* the limitation, enabling the expert to consider the ramifications of the limitation in a concrete fashion. To be effective during cross-examination of the vocational expert, the representative must be specific. Following are several examples:

Representative: **Assume with me that the claimant cannot sit very long at one time before having to change position. Would she be able to return to her past work?**

VE: **I can't answer that question. I don't know how long you mean when you say very long."**

Or,

Representative: **Assume with me that the claimant cannot concentrate very long at one time. Would she be able to return to her past work?**

VE: **I can't answer that question. I don't know how long you mean when you say very long.**

Ideally, a list of impairments and limitations should be created before the hearing. When the judge asks a hypothetical question, check the list to ensure that all of the limitations identified have been addressed. If not, cross-examination of the vocational expert will center on those areas *not* covered by the judge. Figure 10–11 illustrates the process.

A checklist prepared in advance of the hearing helps you organize your thoughts in preparation for the administrative hearing. Note each of the limitations asked of the vocational expert by the judge as each limitation is asked. Note for yourself, whether the judge's limitation was one you had considered, circling "Y" or "N" on the checklist. This will help you remember what has and what has not been asked.

Use your checklist, made in advance of the hearing, to set forth limitations you believe are supported by the evidence (including that to be offered by your client.) During cross-examination of the vocational expert, refer to this list to ensure that you have made a complete record of all limitations. During closing remarks this same list will aid you in making final arguments to the judge in an attempt to persuade him or her of the efficacy of your case.

Limitations included by the judge in direct examination of vocational expert	Included by representative	Limitations included by the representative in prehearing review
1.	Y N	1.
2.	Y N	2.
3.	Y N	3.
4.	Y N	4.
5.	Y N	5.
6.	Y N	6.

Figure 10–11 **Exemplar Representative's Checklist of Limitations**

Finally, it is important that the synergistic effects of limitations be considered, that is, all credibly supported limitations should be considered in combination with one another. The following is illustrative:

Judge: **Assume with me that the claimant suffers from a seizure disorder, which is well controlled with medication, such that the only limitation is that she cannot operate a motor vehicle. How does that limitation affect her ability to perform her past work?**

VE: **It will not preclude past work. [Note: The inability to get to work via an automobile or other vehicle is not a factor to be considered in determining whether the claimant can perform past or other work.]**

Now consider the additional limitation added by the representative on cross-examination:

Representative: **Assume with me that while medication controls the claimant's seizure disorder, medication side effects cause her to become drowsy within thirty minutes after taking the medication. She must take her medication three times a day, and the drowsiness causes her to sleep or lie down for at least thirty to forty-five minutes each time.**

VE: **Let me see if I can summarize. Because of her medication, she becomes drowsy three times each day, causing her to lie down from thirty to forty-five minutes each time?**

Representative: **Yes.**

VE: **And, even with the medication, she would not be able to drive?**

Representative: **Yes, and add to that, the additional limitation that she will not be able to drive, operate, or be around dangerous or moving machinery.**

VE: **She would not be able to return to her past work. She takes the medication to avoid the effects of the seizure disorder, but she still cannot be around moving machinery; but the medication itself causes a problem because she must lie down up to three times a day. This would constitute too many breaks from the regular work schedule and would no longer be competitive.**

OTHER CONSIDERATIONS

There are other considerations as well, including the burden of proof, mental limitations, and age.

Burden of Proof

It is important to note that although this is a nonadversarial process, the courts still find that there is a "burden" to be met. In legal terms, a "burden" is an obligation. In Social Security appeals, the "burden" is said to be on the claimant in steps 1 through 4. In legal parlance, the burden is one of "proof." It is the claimant who must prove by a preponderance of the evidence each of the requirements necessary to keep advancing through the sequential evaluation process. At step 4, the burden is on the claimant to prove that he or she can no longer perform past work.

The caveat lies in the fact that the Administrative Law Judge has a continuing duty (reduced but still present even if the claimant is represented) to ensure that the administrative record is "fully developed."[4] Thus, although the burden of proof is on the claimant to show that past relevant work can no longer be performed, the judge must, to some degree, assist in gathering the necessary evidence to ensure that the issues have been fully considered.

The Effect of Mental Limitations on Skills

If the claimant's past work has been either semiskilled or skilled, the effect of mental or emotional limitations cannot be ignored. Unskilled work is defined as work "which needs little or no judgment to do simple duties that can be learned on the job in a short period of time."[5] Thus, if a claimant suffers from a mental limitation that precludes the ability to do detailed or complex work tasks, or to comprehend detailed or complex instructions (i.e., the ability to remember and carry out . . .), the claimant will be unable to return to semiskilled or skilled work.

Similarly, an inability to cooperate with others (co-workers and members of the general public) will often preclude semiskilled or skilled work that requires the claimant to interact with others, either in a supervisory or other capacity.

Age at Step 4

Finally, age is not an issue with respect to the ability to return to past relevant work. It only becomes operative as a decisional factor at step 5 of the sequential evaluation process, where it, together with skill and education, are considered along with the claimant's residual functional capacity.

WHAT IF . . . ? SAMPLE PROBLEMS

WHAT IF . . .

What if the judge asks the vocational expert if she needs to hear any testimony from your client regarding his past work, and the vocational expert says, "No, I don't. I've reviewed the record and I've got everything I need." What should you do?

1. Nothing. It's proper procedure. According to federal regulations the conduct of the hearing is the judge's responsibility.
2. Object orally to the judge's question to the vocational expert.
3. Listen carefully to the vocational expert's description of your client's past work. If it is not accurate, correct the vocational expert.
4. Proceed to elicit testimony from your client even if the judge does not.

Discussion

An accurate description of your client's past work is key to both step 4 and step 5 of the sequential evaluation process. Do not assume (1) that the vocational expert has reviewed everything you have reviewed in preparation for the hearing, (2) that the vocational expert will place the same emphasis on aspects of your client's past work as do you, or (3) that a complete history of your client's work appears within the administrative record. Too much depends on an accurate assessment by the vocational expert of your client's exertion and skill level. To ensure that your client's full work history, together with the details of past work, is made a part of the record, ask your client about her work history yourself, even if the judge does not. The best answer is (4).

WHAT IF . . .

What if the claimant's past work is light and medium and the judge asks the VE to consider an RFC that includes lifting ten pounds frequently and twenty pounds occasionally but ignores medication side effects?

1. Do not irritate the judge. Don't ask anything else.
2. Ask the VE a hypothetical question on cross-examination: "Assume with me that because of medication side effects an individual of the same age as the claimant, with the same vocational history, must lie down two times a day, for up to thirty minutes at a time. Will such a person be able to return to any of the claimant's past work?
3. Appeal.
4. Call your own expert.

Discussion

The challenge in every hearing is whether the administrative law judge will find your client to be as limited as you believe the evidence shows her to be. It is entirely possible that the judge will fail to include a critical limitation in his or her RFC to the vocational expert, notwithstanding submission of evidence and testimony to the contrary. Your task under such circumstances is to fill in the gap. You may call your own expert, but many persons cannot afford such measures. You must, therefore, use the expertise of the neutral expert called by the administration. Simply ask your own hypothetical question, containing all of the judge's limitations, adding the critical limitation(s) you believe are supported by the record. In this way, you have made a record of an alternative outcome, and laid the groundwork for an appeal if the judge rejects the revised testimony. The best answer is (2).

WHAT IF . . .

Which of the following are true?

1. Medical experts can testify whether your client can perform his or her past relevant work.
2. Transferability of skills is an issue at step 4 of the five-step sequential evaluation process.
3. No grant of benefits can be made at step 4 of the five-step sequential evaluation process.
4. The relevancy requirement in past relevant work refers to the issue of whether the claimant performed the work for a sufficient period of time to learn how to do the job.

Discussion

1. Medical experts offer opinions on the issue of whether the claimant's impairment(s) meet or medically equal a listing at step 3 of the sequential evaluation. Sometimes, they are tempted to offer opinions as to employability, but this is beyond the scope of their expertise. If a claimant's impairment does not meet or equal a listed impairment at step 3 of the sequential evaluation, a medical expert may opine, given sufficient evidence, about the claimant's limitations. This testimony may then be posed to the vocational expert in an RFC. The medical expert may not give his or her opinion about the claimant's limitations and then offer another opinion as to whether he or she will be able to return to past relevant work. The statement is false.
2. Whether your client can return to past work, performed within the past fifteen years is a question of his or her current residual functional capacity for work. Your client will be limited only to the extent that

RFC has eroded, preventing engaging in physical or mental activities necessary to perform past work. Whether, as a result of current RFC, your client cannot engage in past work is a function of the RFC, not transferability of skills—an issue that arises at step 5 of the sequential evaluation. The statement is false.

3. Step 4 of the five-step sequential evaluation process addresses a simple public policy question: Notwithstanding your client's reduced RFC, is there work that he has already performed in his life which he could still do? If there is still work that he could do, even if done many years ago, as long as the work was performed within the past fifteen years, the assumption is that he could return to that job. Admittedly, fifteen years is an arbitrary breakpoint, it too is an assumption. The assumption is that work processes, tools, and so forth, learned more than fifteen years ago are stale. Work processes, tools, and so forth learned within the immediate past fifteen years are deemed (assumed) not to be stale—that is, they are recoverable, provided the individual still retains the physical and mental capacities for the work. Whether that work also gave rise to skills that are employable in other work settings is not an issue at step 4. The statement is true.
4. Not every job performed within the past fifteen years should be counted as among those to which the claimant might conceivably return. Only those jobs that were generally performed at SGA levels—competitive levels—should be included. Relevancy refers to the simple question of whether the claimant performed the work for a sufficient period and at sufficient levels to enable him to learn the requirements for such work. Thus, work performed for a week or even for several months, may not qualify as past relevant work if not of sufficient duration to enable the claimant to learn how to do the work. Similarly, part-time work may not qualify as past relevant work if it was not performed for sufficient duration to enable the claimant to acquire the knowledge necessary to do the work full time. The statement is true.

---

[1]Title 20 C.F.R. § 404.1561.

[2]The significance of this is that the more demanding a client's past work is, the less likely it is that he or she will be able to return to that work, depending, of course, on how restrictive his or her RFC is. Equally important, of course, is the need to obtain and present persuasive evidence descriptive of the client's limitations. This often requires effort above and beyond the call of duty in persuading a treating physician to cooperate and complete a report, or participate in a teleconference with the judge. Go beyond what your client is capable of doing for himself or herself and obtain credible, supported opinions and medical evidence that document the client's limited capabilities.

[3]Usually the DOT number.

[4]See Title 20 C.F.R. § 404.944, which provides in-part

> *At the hearing, the Administrative Law Judge looks fully into the issues.*

[5]Title 20 C.F.R. § 404.1568(a).

11

Chapter Eleven

Step 5: Other Work

Highlights

- ❑ Step 5 in the sequential evaluation
- ❑ Using a vocational expert
- ❑ Using Medical–Vocational Guidelines (The Grids)

Chris

Chris tossed and turned, sleepless, knowing that there was more to know, uncomfortable in not knowing. *Vocational experts are important in the last two steps,* was the last thought echoing through Chris's mind as sleep finally overtook anticipation.

The next day dawned brightly, and Chris was in the office early.

"Progress?" called Steve, seeing the spread of books and papers across Chris's desk.

"I think so. I got through the stuff at step 4, and I'm ready to jump into step 5."

"Great!"

"There's one thing bothering me, though."

Steve stopped in midstep, pivoted and returned to Chris's doorway. "What's that?"

"What if the judge doesn't use a vocational expert? I mean don't you end up arguing with the judge? Who would want to do that? It seems like a surefire way to lose."

Steve grimaced. "It's a chance you have to take. Most circuit courts now require a vocational expert at step 5. If one isn't present, and benefits are denied, it's a sure bet that you can make an argument on appeal."

"The judge playing at being a vocational expert?"

"Exactly. Think about it. How is a judge to know what the demands of work are, or, more importantly, whether there are "significant numbers" of jobs within the regional or national economies?"

"Because a judge is a legal professional, not a rehabilitation consultant or career planner?"

"That's right. Ultimately, the judge must address the bottom-line legal standard—whether there are significant numbers of jobs remaining within the national or regional economies. If the judge guesses at the answer, without evidence to support the legal conclusion, it's reversible error."

"So, you pretty much have to have a vocational expert at step 5?"

"As a general rule, yes. Now, if the treating doctor comes back with a supportable RFC to the effect that the individual can only be up and around four hours each day, you know then as a matter of *common sense* that such a person could not work a full eight-hour day."

"So, the judge could make such a decision without a vocational expert?"

"Under those limited circumstances, yes. But, remember, in that case the judge is deciding in your client's favor. What about the case in which no vocational expert is used and the judge decides *against* your client?"

"I see your point. So, if I get the notice of hearing and a vocational expert is not listed, I better go on record as asking for one before the hearing?"

"Absolutely. Here," Steve said, stepping into Chris' office, "let's talk more about step 5."

FRONT OF YOUR MIND QUESTIONS AND CONSIDERATIONS, 11.1

THE IMPORT OF STEP 5 OF THE SEQUENTIAL EVALUATION PROCESS

Step 5 of the sequential evaluation process is one of two points in the five-step evaluation process where an individual can be paid—that is, where benefits can be awarded. As the final step in the sequential evaluation, it is also a place in the process where benefits can be denied. It is at step 5 that a client's residual functional capacity (RFC) determines whether there are other, less demanding jobs that can be performed, or, if not, whether disability benefits will be awarded.

Critically, then, once the determination has been made at step 4 that a claimant cannot return to *past work* because of limitations, the stage is set for a step 5 decision. If the judge determines that there is "other work" that a claimant can perform, the decision will be to deny benefits, unless the number of such jobs is not "significant." If the judge determines that, because of the claimant's RFC, there are no other jobs that can be performed (or, that there are not significant numbers of such jobs in the regional economy) benefits will be granted (see Figure 11–1).

Is the vocational expert the single resource for this determination? Does the determination rest solely on the VE's opinion? At step 5, inquiry is multifaceted and begins first with the Medical–Vocational Guidelines.

THE MEDICAL–VOCATIONAL GUIDELINES

The decision-making process at step 5 focuses on the Medical–Vocational Guidelines, euphemistically known as "the Grids." The Medical–Vocational Guidelines are actually a series of rules, expressed in the form of three tables, found within Appendix 2, Subpart P of Part 404, of Title 20, Code of Federal Regulations. Figures 11–2 through 11–4 are the sedentary, light, and medium tables. There is no table for heavy work.

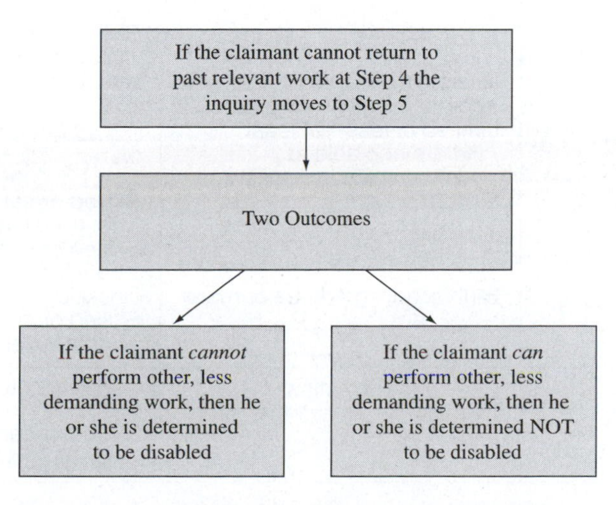

Figure 11–1 **Two Possible Outcomes at the Final Step of the Five-Step Sequential Evaluation**

Table No. 1—Residual Functional Capacity: Maximum Sustained Work Capability Limited to Sedentary Work as a Result of Severe Medically Determinable Impairment(s)

Rule	Age	Education	Previous work experience	Decision
201.01	Advanced age	Limited or less	Unskilled or none	Disable.
201.02	do	do	Skilled or semiskilled—skills not transferable[1].	Do.
201.03	do	do	Skilled or semiskilled—skills transferable[1].	Not disabled.
201.04	do	High school graduate or more—does not provide for direct entry into skilled work[2].	Unskilled or none	Disabled.
201.05	do	High school graduate or more—provides for direct entry into skilled work[2].	do	Not disabled.
201.06	do	High school graduate or more—does not provide for direct entry into skilled work[2].	Skilled or semiskilled—skills not transferable[1].	Disabled.
201.07	do	do	Skilled or semiskilled—skills transferable[1].	Not disabled.
201.08	do	High school graduate or more—provides for direct entry into skilled work[2].	Skilled or semiskilled—skills not transferable[1].	Do.
201.09	Closely approaching advanced age.	Limited or less	Unskilled or none	Disabled.
201.10	do	do	Skilled or unskilled—skills not transferable.	Do.
201.11	do	do	Skilled or semiskilled—skills transferable.	Not disabled.
201.12	do	High school graduate or more—does not provide for direct entry into skilled work[3].	Unskilled or none	Disabled.
201.13	do	High school graduate or more—provides for direct entry into skilled work[3].	do	Not disabled.
201.14	do	High school graduate or more—does not provide for direct entry into skilled work[3].	Skilled or semiskilled—skills not transferable.	Disabled.
201.15	do	do	Skilled or semiskilled—skills not transferable.	Not disabled.
201.16	do	High school graduate or more—provides for direct entry into skilled work[3].	Skilled or semiskilled—skills transferable. Skilled or semiskilled—skills not transferable.	Do.
201.17	Younger individual age 45–49.	Illiterate or unable to communicate in English.	Unskilled or none	Disabled.
201.18	do	Limited or less—at least literate and able to communicate in English.	do	Not disabled.
201.19	do	Limited or less	Skilled or semiskilled—skills not transferable.	Do.
201.20	do	do	Skilled or semiskilled—skills transferable.	Do.
201.21	do	High school graduate or more	Skilled or semiskilled—skills not transferable.	Do.
201.22	do	do	Skilled or semiskilled—skills transferable.	Do.
201.23	Younger individual age 18–44.	Illiterate or unable to communicate in English.	Unskilled or more	Do.[4]
201.24	do	Limited or less—at least literate and able to communicate in English.	do	Do.[4]
201.25	do	Limited or less	Skilled or semiskilled—skills not transferable.	Do.[4]
201.26	do	do	Skilled or semiskilled—skills transferable.	Do.[4]
201.27	do	High school graduate or more	Unskilled or none	Do.[4]
201.28	do	do	Skilled or semiskilled—skills not transferable.	Do.[4]
201.29	do	do	Skilled or semiskilled—skills transferable.	Do.[4]

[1]See 201.00(f).
[2]See 201.00(d).
[3]See 201.00(g).
[4]See 201.00(h).

Figure 11–2 **The Sedentary Table of the Medical–Vocational Guidelines Used at Step 5 of the Sequential Evaluation**

TABLE NO. 2—RESIDUAL FUNCTIONAL CAPACITY: MAXIMUM SUSTAINED WORK CAPABILITY LIMITED TO LIGHT WORK AS A RESULT OF SEVERE MEDICALLY DETERMINABLE IMPAIRMENT(S)—CONTINUED

Rule	Age	Education	Previous work experience	Decision
202.02 _____	_____ do _______	_____ do _______	Skilled or semiskilled—skills not transferable.	Do.
202.03 _____	_____ do _______	_____ do _______	Skilled or semiskilled—skills transferable[1].	Not disabled.
202.04 _____	_____ do _______	High school graduate or more—does not provide for direct entry into skilled work[2].	Unskilled or more _____	Disabled.
203.05 _____	_____ do _______	High school graduate or more—provides for direct entry into skilled work[2].	_____ do _______	Not disabled.
203.06 _____	_____ do _______	High school graduate or more—does not provide for direct entry into skilled work[2].	Skilled or semiskilled—skills not transferable.	Disabled.
202.07 _____	_____ do _______	_____ do _______	Skilled or semiskilled—skills transferable[2].	Not disabled.
202.08 _____	_____ do _______	High school graduate or more—provides for direct entry into skilled work[2].	Skilled or semiskilled—skills not transferable.	Do.
202.09 _____	Closely approaching advanced age.	Illiterate or unable to communicate in English.	Unskilled or none _____	Disabled.
202.10 _____	_____ do _______	Limited or less—at least literate and able to communicate in English.	_____ do _____	Not disabled.
202.11 _____	_____ do _______	Limited or less _____	Skilled or semiskilled—skills not transferable.	Do.
202.12 _____	_____ do _______	_____ do _______	Skilled or semiskilled—skills transferable.	Do.
202.13 _____	_____ do _______	High school graduate or more	Unskilled or none _____	Do.
202.14 _____	_____ do _______	_____ do _______	Skilled or semiskilled—skills not transferable.	Do.
202.15 _____	_____ do _______	_____ do _______	Skilled or semiskilled—skills transferable.	Do.
202.16 _____	Younger individual	Illiterate or unable to communicate in English.	Unskilled or none _____	Do.
202.17 _____	_____ do _______	Limited or less—at least literate and able to communicate in English.	_____ do _______	Do.
202.18 _____	_____ do _______	Limited or less _____	Skilled or semiskilled—skills not transferable.	Do.
202.19 _____	_____ do _______	_____ do _______	Skilled or semiskilled—skills transferable.	Do.
202.20 _____	_____ do _______	High school graduate or more	Unskilled or none _____	Do.
202.21 _____	_____ do _______	_____ do _______	Skilled or semiskilled—skills not transferable.	Do.
202.22 _____	_____ do _______	_____ do _______	Skilled or semiskilled—skills transferable.	Do.

[1]See 202.00(f).
[2]See 202.00(c).

Figure 11–3 **The Light Table of the Medical–Vocational Guidelines Used at Step 5 of the Sequential Evaluation**

Table No. 3—Residual Functional Capacity: Maximum Sustained Work Capability Limited to Medium Work as a Result of Severe Medically Determinable Impairment(s)

Rule	Age	Education	Previous work experience	Decision
203.01	Closely approaching retirement age.	Marginal or none	Unskilled or none	Disabled.
203.02	do	Limited or less	None	Do.
203.03	do	Limited	Unskilled	Not disabled.
203.04	do	Limited or less	Skilled or semiskilled—skills not transferable.	Do.
203.05	do	do	Skilled or semiskilled—skills transferable.	Do.
203.06	do	High school graduate or more	Unskilled or none	Do.
203.07	do	High school graduate or more—does not provide for direct entry into skilled work.	Skilled or semiskilled—skills not transferable.	Do.
203.08	do	do	Skilled or semiskilled—skills transferable.	Do.
203.09	do	High school graduate or more—provides for direct entry into skilled work.	Skilled or semiskilled—skills not transferable.	Do.
203.10	Advanced age	Limited or less	None	Disabled.
203.11	do	do	Unskilled	Not disabled.
203.12	do	do	Skilled or semiskilled—skills not transferable.	Do.
203.13	do	do	Skilled or semiskilled—skills transferable.	Do.
203.14	do	High school graduate or more	Unskilled or none	Do.
203.15	do	High school graduate or more—does not provide for direct entry into skilled work.	Skilled or semiskilled—skills not transferable.	Do.
203.16	do	do	Skilled or semiskilled—skills transferable.	Do.
203.17	do	High school graduate or more—provides for direct entry into skilled work.	Skilled or semiskilled—skills not transferable.	Do.
203.18	Closely approaching advanced age.	Limited or less	Unskilled or none	Do.
203.19	do	do	Skilled or semiskilled—skills not transferable.	Do.
203.20	do	do	Skilled or semiskilled—skills transferable.	Do.
203.21	do	High school graduate or more	Unskilled or none	Do.
203.22	do	High school graduate or more—does not provide for direct entry into skilled work.	Skilled or semiskilled—skills not transferable.	Do.
203.23	do	do	Skilled or semiskilled—skills transferable.	Do.
203.24	do	High school graduate or more—provides for direct entry into skilled work.	Skilled or semiskilled—skills not transferable.	Do.
203.25	Younger individual	Limited or less	Unskilled or none	Do.
203.26	do	do	Skilled or nonskilled-skills not transferable.	Do.
203.27	do	do	Skilled or semiskilled—skills transferable.	Do.
203.28	do	High school graduate or more	Unskilled or none	Do.
203.29	do	High school graduate or more—does not provide for direct entry into skilled work.	Skilled or semiskilled—skills not transferable.	Do.
203.30	do	do	Skilled or semiskilled—skills transferable.	Do.
Rule	Age	Education	Previous work experience	Decision
203.31	do	High school graduate or more—provides for direct entry into skilled work.	Skilled or semiskilled-skills not transferable.	Do.

Figure 11–4 **The Medium Table of the Medical–Vocational Guidelines Used at Step 5 of the Sequential Evaluation**

Once the VE opines that the claimant cannot perform his or her past work, the decision at step 5 is a function of the Medical–Vocational Guidelines. The three tables reflect exertional limitations and are used in conjunction with the claimant's RFC, as determined by the judge. If the evidence indicates that the claimant is capable of only performing sedentary work, the *sedentary* Grid is used. Similarly, if the evidence indicates only an ability to engage in light work, the *light* Grid is used, and if medium work is indicated, the *medium* Grid. Examine Figure 11–5.

The Grids are used in two ways. First, if there are no nonexertional limitations, the rules found within each Grid determine the result. If, however, there *are* nonexertional limitations, which are factored into the claimant's RFC, the Grid rule does *not* determine the result, but must, instead, be used as a framework—describing who the individual is in terms of education, past work, and age, but not directing the outcome.

What exactly is a Grid rule? Grid rules represent outcome-determinative assumptions. If a specific set of conditions exists, considering a variety of factors, the law presumes that the claimant is or is not disabled. Grid rules are numbered according to the specific grid in which they are found. Grid rules in the sedentary table are numbered 201; Grid rules in the light table are numbered 202; and rules in the medium table are 203. (See Figure 11–6.) Figure 11–7 illustrates the anatomy of Grid rule 201.06.

In each Grid rule are discrete factors that must be determined in order to properly apply the rules. If, for example, a claimant was found to be limited to sedentary work, was fifty-five years of age, was a high school graduate, but whose education did not otherwise provide for direct entry into skilled work, and whose skills

A ***sedentary RFC*** means that the *Sedentary Grid* must be referenced

A ***light RFC*** means that the *Light Grid* must be referenced

A ***medium RFC*** means that the *Medium Grid* must be referenced

Figure 11–5 The Grid Used Depends on RFC

Medical–Vocational Table (Grid Corresponds with RFC)	Rule or Number Series
Sedentary	201 Series
Light	202 Series
Medium	203 Series

Figure 11–6 Each Grid References a Series of Rules

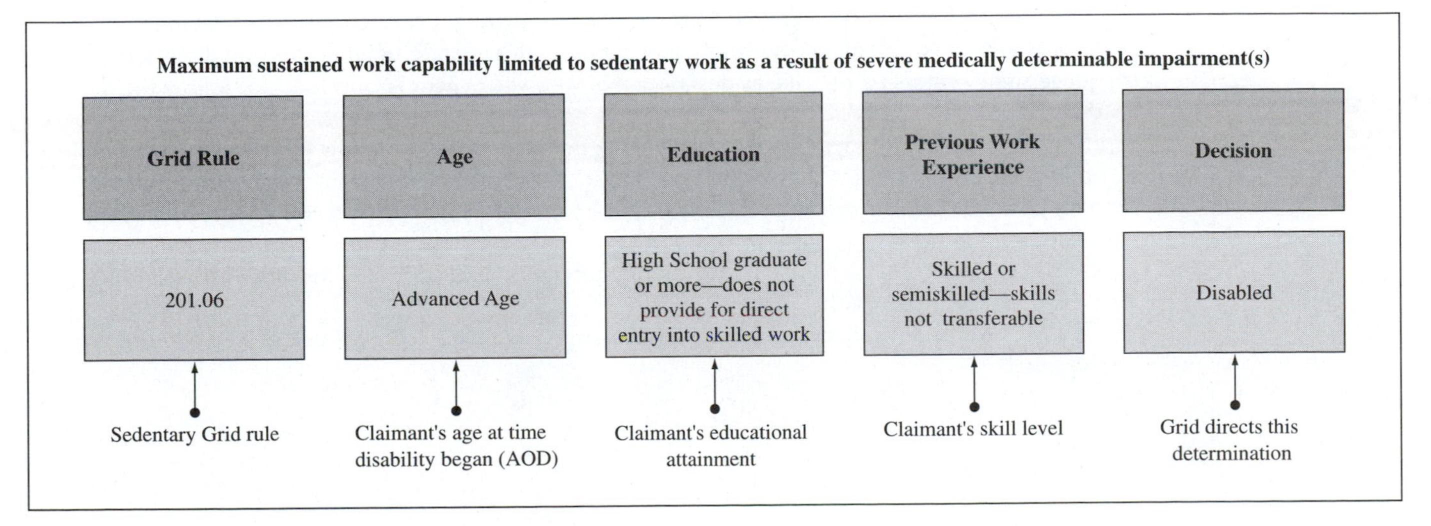

Figure 11–7 Anatomy of a Grid Rule (Rule 201.06)

were *not* transferable, Grid rule 201.06 would direct a decision of disabled. The factors to consider include the following:

- ❑ Claimant's age;
- ❑ Claimant's educational attainment;
- ❑ Claimant's skill level (previous work experience); and
- ❑ Claimant's exertional level

Each factor represents a sliding scale of possibilities, and each possibility has the potential to dramatically affect the outcome shown by the Grid rule.

AGE

Social Security law recognizes a basic aspect of human development—the older you are, the more likely you are to be found disabled. Age is "bracketed" as shown in Figure 11–8. Although age is generally treated the same across all three exertional tables, there are slight differences between young people on the sedentary Grid and older people on the medium Grid. Specifically, each category is subdivided once, creating two younger categories on the sedentary Grid and two older categories on the medium Grid.

The practical result of such divisions is to recognize the effect of age. On the sedentary Grid, this rule is evident among the subdivided younger ages with the addition of Rule 201.17, which recognizes that a younger individual may be found to be disabled if "illiterate or unable to communicate in English." Every other decision directed by the rules in the younger individual (18–44) category is "not disabled." Thus, an individual over age forty-four, but less than fifty may be found to be disabled using the rules if she or he is also illiterate, but under no other circumstances.

BACK TO CHRIS

"Wait! Hold on!" Chris looked up sheepishly, realizing no one else was in the room.

Steve had gone.

"Does this mean nobody under age fifty who is limited to sedentary work can ever be found to be disabled unless she or he is illiterate? That doesn't make sense!"

Steve popped his head into Chris' office, grinning. "Muttering to yourself again?"

"No, it's just that I don't understand how this is fair. Does it mean that people under age fifty can be found disabled only if they are illiterate?"

"The Grids?"

Chris nodded.

Steve shook his head. "Not at all. It's simply that the rules don't *direct* a disabled decision. Remember, the Grids can also be used as a framework.

"What does that mean?"

"It simply means that you follow along the rule until you get to the decisional column. If the vocational expert has testified that your client cannot work in spite of what the rule directs, then the judge simply refers to the rule as descriptive of who your client is, but does not follow the direction of the rule."

"You mean, if the VE says my client can't work because his pain is so severe that he has to lie down two times a day during the normal workday such that he cannot complete an eight-hour day, then my client is disabled, even if the rule that otherwise describes him in terms of age, education, and skill says otherwise?"

"If the judge finds that your client's testimony about pain is credible—if the judge believes what your client says—then yes, that's right."

"So, when reaching a decision about my client, the judge must follow a rule at step 5, one way or the other?"

"You got it! At step 3 the judge can find that your client meets or equals a listed impairment, which is also a reference to the regulations. At step 5, the judge must again reference the regulations—this time, a rule set out in the Medical–Vocational Guidelines—whether granting or denying benefits."

"OK. So the idea of a framework simply means that the judge is not bound by the strict reading of the rules?"

"If he or she was bound by the strict reading of the rules, there might be little reason to have a judge in the first place. The truth of the matter is that people do not fall into neat little categories. There is no way the framers of the disability program and its implementing regulations could predict every circumstance affecting people. So, they laid out a set of rules and allowed the judge discretion to deviate as justice demands."

Age	Exertional Table Where Found
Younger (18–44)	Sedentary
Younger (45–49) Younger (18–49)	Sedentary Light and medium
Closely approaching advanced age (50–54)	Light Medium
Advanced age (55–59)	Sedentary Light Medium
Closely approaching retirement age (60–64)	Medium

Figure 11–8 **Age Categories in the Grids**

FRONT OF YOUR MIND QUESTIONS AND CONSIDERATIONS, 11.2

MORE ON AGE

The governing regulations (at Title 20 C.F.R. § 404.1563) provide as follows:

- ❑ *A younger individual.* The regulations provide (and assume) "that . . . age will [not] seriously affect . . . ability to adapt to new work";
- ❑ *A person approaching advanced age.* When a person is approaching advanced age, the regulations "consider that . . . age, along with a severe impairment and limited work experience, may seriously affect . . . [the] ability to adjust to a number of jobs in the national economy";
- ❑ *A person of advanced age.* When a person is of advanced age and "cannot do medium work," the individual "may not be able to work" unless she or he possesses "skills that can be used (transferred to) less demanding jobs which exist in significant numbers in the national economy."

Figure 11–9 illustrates the critical factors in each age category when the Medical–Vocational Guidelines are used to direct a finding.

Age Category	Critical Factor(s) That Determine Disability
Younger individual	Education (literacy/inability to communicate in English)
Closely approaching advanced age	Education/lack of skills
Advanced age	Education/lack of skills

Figure 11–9 **Critical Factors for Medical–Vocational Guidelines**

Educational Category	Description
Illiteracy (404.1564[b][1])	Little or no formal schooling; inability to read or write simple instructions
Marginal (404.1564[b][2])	Formal schooling at sixth-grade level or less; ability to do simple, unskilled jobs
Limited (404.1564[b][3])	Formal schooling from seventh to eleventh grade; ability to do most semiskilled and some skilled tasks
High school and above (404.1564[b][4])	Formal schooling at twelfth-grade level and above; ability to do semiskilled and skilled work
Inability to communicate in English (404.1564[b][5])	Inability to speak, read, and understand English; difficulty doing a job regardless of education if unable to communicate in English

Figure 11–10 **Educational Categories**

MORE ON EDUCATION

The regulations also recognize *education* as affecting employability—that is, the ability to perform competitive work. Generally, the less education an individual has, the more likely he or she is to be found disabled. As with age, education is treated as a variable along a sliding scale of possible outcomes, depending on which Grid is referenced.

Education is described in stages, depending on the amount of schooling completed. Figure 11–10 describes various educational levels.

An individual who is *illiterate* is generally ill-equipped to perform work other than at the physical or manual level. Thus, if a claimant is determined to be capable only of sedentary work, illiteracy may be the deciding factor in awarding an individual benefits.

A person with a *marginal education* (less than seventh grade) may qualify for jobs in which only simple written instructions are communicated and followed.

A person with a *limited education* (more than the sixth grade but no higher than the eleventh grade) may be able to perform semiskilled and most skilled work.

A *high school education or higher* enables the individual to engage in semiskilled and skilled work.

An individual who is *unable to communicate in English,* regardless of educational attainment, is generally considered to have limited capability for competitive work, because English is the dominant language in the United States.

In assessing educational attainment, it is important to understand not only how much an individual has achieved in school but also the quality of the educational experience. If the claimant participated in special education, or another accommodated educational program indicative of a special need in educational accomplishment, such information is important. It reflects actual capability, which may differ from capabilities that may otherwise be assumed because of education.

In a younger individual, recently graduated from high school, educational (school performance) records may be helpful, particularly if they are poor. The records may reflect performance in the "worklike" environment of school. Such records are important, as is discussed later, as concerns childhood disability, because the school is the child's workplace.

If a person has completed a course of study that facilitates direct entry into skilled work (e.g., a course of professional study), the outcome on the Grid will be affected. The representative's challenge is straightforward. The representative must inquire whether, because of the individual's impairment(s) and resulting limitations, the claimant would still be capable of performing at the level to which she or he has been trained. For example, if the claimant has completed law school or medical school, direct entry into skilled work is a foregone conclusion. Unless the claimant's limitations precluded such work, it is likely, at all exertional levels, that the Grid will direct a finding of "not disabled." If, however, the claimant suffered a traumatic head injury or other organic process that led to a documented loss of mental ability, it would be argued that the claimant was unable to function at the skill level to which he or she had been trained.

The correlation between *education* and *skill* is, therefore, direct. The more education, the more likely the individual is to have worked in a job from which he or she acquired skills. And, the more education, the more likely the claimant is to have skills enabling direct entry into skilled work.

TRANSFERABILITY OF SKILLS

As discussed in Chapter 10, transferability of skills is an issue arising at step 5 of the sequential evaluation process. This is a critical issue concerning the claimant's ability to do other work, because the presence of transferrable skills indicates the claimant can probably perform in other, less demanding jobs, precluding an award of disability benefits. The Grid rules describe the skill levels as follows:

- None;
- Unskilled;
- Unskilled or none;
- Skilled or semiskilled—skills transferable; and
- Skilled or semiskilled—skills not transferable.

Each category refers to the claimant's past (or previous) work experience and describes it. Figure 11–11 describes each category.

If a person has skills or semiskills, the question for purposes of the Grid rule is whether the skill or semiskill is transferable. Transferability of skills is defined in the regulations, as follows:

> **We consider you to have skills that can be used in other jobs, when the skilled or semi-skilled work activities you did in past work can be used to meet the requirements of skilled or semi-skilled work activities of other jobs or kinds of work.[1]**

Whether a person's skills are transferable is a function of both age and limitation. The regulations specifically recognize that age affects transferability of skills. If a person is limited to sedentary work, the threshold age triggering an inquiry into transferability of skills is fifty-five. Medical–Vocational Rule 201.00(f) sets the standard:

> **In order to find transferability of skills to skilled sedentary work for individuals who are of advanced age (55 and over), there must be very little, if any, vocational adjustment required in terms of tools, work processes, work settings, or the industry.**

In effect, Rule 201.00(f) asks a simple question:

> **Assuming that the claimant would otherwise have skills he has acquired from work or school, and assuming that the claimant is now limited to sedentary work as a result of a severe impairment, can he or she apply those skills in a sedentary work environment with very little vocational adjustment?**

If the individual has never worked in a sedentary setting before, the question concerning vocational adjustment is self-evident. The answer is *yes,* more than a "little" adjustment would be required.

Claimant's Work Experience	Description in the Rules
No past relevant work	None
Experience has been in work that requires little or no judgment; simple duties can be learned and performed in a short period of time	Unskilled
Either unskilled work experience or no work experience	Unskilled or none
Work experience involves exercising judgment in determining which machine or manual operation must be performed to achieve certain results, or in dealing with personnel, or abstract ideas at a high level of complexity. More than 30 days are required to achieve average successful job performance. The skills learned can be used in other semiskilled or skilled jobs within the claimant's RFC	Skilled or semiskilled—skills transferable
Work experience as above, but the skills learned cannot be used in other work within the claimant's RFC	Skilled or semiskilled—skills not transferable

Figure 11–11 **Five Categories of Skills in the Grid Rules**

To what must the person adjust? The regulation is, again, self-evident. Transferability of skills to sedentary work, for a person age fifty-five or older, must require "very little" adjustment "in terms of tools, work processes, work settings, or the industry." The requirement addresses four discrete factors:

- Tools;
- Work processes;
- Work settings; or
- The industry.

If the Administrative Law Judge concludes that more than very little adjustment would be required in any one area, he or she must conclude that skills are not transferable. Such a finding benefits the claimant, particularly in the advanced age category, because it changes the finding from "not disabled" to "disabled."

Tools are devices, instruments, and equipment used in the everyday performance of a job. Work processes refer to the procedures used in performing the work. Work settings refer to the work environment itself. The industry refers to the nature of the work. If, for example, an individual was a supervisor of heavy equipment workers on commercial construction sites, he or she would potentially have transferable skills of hiring and firing, supervising, and completing reports—all within the context of commercial construction.

If, because of a severe impairment, the individual became limited to sedentary work, would the skills used as a heavy equipment supervisor be transferable to a sedentary setting, where the person would, perhaps, work in an office, using office equipment, far removed from the realm of commercial construction? Under such circumstances, the judge might find that more than very little adjustment would be required and that the skills used as a heavy equipment supervisor would not be transferable to the sedentary setting. The key to any such inquiry is "vocational adaptability." How adaptable is the person, given his or her past work history?

This same analysis is true at the light table. Because of the increased demand for exertional activity, the threshold age increases from sixty to sixty-four. (See Rule 202.00[f]). The older an individual is when the *sedentary* and *light* Grids are used, the more likely it is that transferability of skills will be the deciding factor in the award of disability. On the sedentary table, Rule 201.03 describes a person of advanced age and directs a finding of "not disabled" if the person is said to be "skilled or semiskilled—skills transferable." Similarly, Rule 202.03 on the light table directs a finding of "not disabled" in a person of advanced age. (See Figure 11–12.)

Table	Threshold age
Sedentary	55 years of age
Light	60 years of age

Figure 11–12 **Transferability of Skills Depends on Exertional Level (RFC) and Age**

Apart from age, the regulations provide that "transferability is most probable" where

- The same or a lesser degree of skills is required;
- The same or similar tools and machines are used; and
- The same or similar raw materials, products, processes, or services are involved (See Title 20 C.F.R. § 404.1568[d][2]).

However, "a complete similarity of all three factors is not necessary for transferability."[2] If an individual suffers from a limitation that prevents the performance of work at a particular skill level, transferability is defeated. So, although skilled work may require such activities as "reading blueprints or other specifications, or making necessary computations or mechanical adjustments to control or regulate the work,"[3] if an individual suffers from a mental or psychological disorder, such that functioning at that level is not possible, a determination may be made that the skills are *not* transferable. The same occurs with physical limitations. The issue is whether age or a person's limitations affect the final determination of transferability if past work helped develop skills that would otherwise be transferable.

Back to Chris

"We're back to vocational experts again, aren't we?"

"Chris, why ever would you say that?" Steve exclaimed, with a wink.

"I knew it."

"Hey, what's so bad about that?"

"Examining an expert makes me nervous."

"Remember, this is an administrative hearing before the Office of Hearings and Appeals. The judge asks questions first. You simply follow along."

"So, how do you get the expert to talk about transferability of skills?"

"Hopefully, the judge will make the necessary inquiry. If not, you've got to follow up."

"What do you mean, the necessary inquiry?"

"After the judge asks the vocational expert the step 4 questions, the judge should go right to the step 5 questions."

"Without any break?"

"Well, the judge asks if the person can return to past work. If the answer is negative, that's when the judge goes on."

"Does the judge simply ask another hypothetical question and see what the expert says? How does she or he get to the question of transferability of skills?"

Steve peered over his glasses at the young would-be representative. "Just brimming with questions, aren't you?"

Chris blushed. "It's just that I haven't been to a hearing, so I'm trying to anticipate everything that will happen."

"OK. Actually, it's pretty straightforward. Once the judge determines that the individual cannot return to past work, she or he will ask whether, in the vocational expert's opinion, the claimant possesses skills that are transferable."

"That's it?"

"Well, not exactly. Some judges might ask whether the skills are transferable to a specific exertional level, such as sedentary or light, if they've already decided where the claimant's limitations are. Or, if the person is at or over the threshold age, the judge might simply ask whether there would be significant vocational adjustment in terms of tools, settings, work processes, or the industry, given the claimant's age."

"What about limitations?"

"That too. The judge may ask whether a specific set of limitations will preclude the exercise of skills, or may ask the vocational expert whether an individual with a specific RFC has transferable skills."

"There's no set way to address these issues, is there?"

"No. Every case is different, and, frankly, each judge is different, bringing with him or her a different judicial philosophy about these cases. That's why you have to know the theory as well as the rule."

"I get it. Thanks!"

FRONT OF YOUR MIND QUESTIONS AND CONSIDERATIONS, 11.3

GRID "SECRETS"

Although there really is no secret to the Grids, they are, nonetheless, constructed using discrete patterns, which, when understood, tend to drive a representative's strategy and tactical approach. Because, apart from step 3, step 5 is the only other point in the five-step sequential evaluation process at which benefits can be paid, it is necessary to understand how the factors represented by the Grids operate in combination with one another. Doing so enables appropriate emphasis to be placed on the presentation of evidence and testimony, thereby maximizing the opportunity to prevail in the quest for an award of benefits.

As noted, age, education, and skill (previous work experience) are the driving factors behind the construction of the Grids. Each factor embodies a discrete public policy assumption as illustrated in Figure 11–13. These factors carry the following assumptions:

- ❑ **Age:** The older you are, the less likely you are to be able to work.
- ❑ **Education:** The less education you have, the less likely you are to be able to work.
- ❑ **Skill:** The less skill you have—or, the less experience you have working—the greater the likelihood of being found disabled.

It is important for the effective representative to understand how these factors are integrated with one another. The underlying assumptions are obvious when viewed singly. More significant, however, is the *synergistic effect* of these factors—that is, how they work in combination with one another. It is the synergistic effect, the result of each variable acting in concert with the others, that ultimately determines eligibility for disability benefits. Put differently, no single factor, whether it be *age, education,* or *skill level,* can, by itself, determine disability on the Grid. A step 5 analysis requires assessment of all three factors, and the astute practitioner understands this interdependence.

To examine the interdependence of these three factors, focus initially on one factor, then assess the effect of the other two. The cardinal factor, apart from the claimant's RFC is age. Age affects a determination

Grid Factor	Underlying Assumption
Age	The older you are, the less likely it is that you will be able to perform competitive work
Education	The less education you have, the less likely it is that you will be able to perform competitive work
Skill	The less skill, or work experience you have, the greater the likelihood that you will be found disabled

Figure 11–13 **Assumptions Underlying the Grid Factors**

more dramatically than education or skill level but, cannot determine entitlement by itself. In rank order of importance to the *determination at step 5, apart from an individual's RFC, the three factors are:*

1. Age;
2. Education; and
3. Skill level.

Figure 11–14 plainly demonstrates the operational effect of age. By and large, the overwhelming number of instances where benefits are "directed" to be awarded by the Grid rule (i.e., a directed finding of disabled)

	Sedentary	Light	Medium
Disabled	Advanced age + Limited education Advanced age + Limited education Advanced age + No skill Advanced age + No skill Closely approaching advanced age + Limited education Closely approaching advanced age + No skill Younger + Illiterate + No skill	Advanced age + Limited education Advanced age + Limited education Advanced age + No skill Advanced age + No skill Close age + Illiterate + No skill	Closely approaching retirement age + Marginal education Closely approaching retirement Advanced Age + Limited education Advanced age + Limited education + No work history
Not disabled	Advanced age + Limited education with skills Advanced age + High school education with no skills Advanced age + High school education with skills Closely approaching advanced age + Limited education with skills Closely approaching advanced age + High school education with no skills Closely approaching advanced age + High school education with skills Younger + Limited education with no skills Younger + High school education with no skills Younger + High school education with skills	Advanced age + Limited education with skills Advanced age + High school education with skills Closely approaching advanced age + Limited education with no skills Closely approaching advanced age + Limited education with skills Closely approaching advanced age + High school education with no skills Closely approaching advanced age + High school education with skills Younger + Illiterate with no skills Younger + Limited education with no skills Younger + Limited education with skills Younger + High school education with no skills Younger + High school education with skills	Closely approaching retirement age + Limited education with no skills Closely approaching retirement age + Limited education with skills Closely approaching retirement age + High school education with no skills Closely approaching retirement age + High school education with skills Advanced age + Limited education with no skills Advanced age + Limited education with skills Advanced age + High school education with no skills Advanced age + High school education with skills Closely approaching advanced age + Limited education with no skills Closely approaching advanced age + Limited education with skills Closely approaching advanced age + High school education with no skills Closely approaching advanced age + High school education with skills Younger + Limited education with no skills Younger + Limited education with skills Younger + High school education with no skills Younger + High school education with skills

Figure 11–14 **Overview of Factors Affecting Grid Determinations (How the Grid Factors Match Up)**

are in the upper age categories, regardless of RFC. Though the number of instances decreases as the individual's RFC increases, it is clear that age is the dominant factor.

Equally clear is the effect of an individual's educational attainment. Nowhere is this more apparent than in the case of a younger person limited to sedentary work. The only instance in which the Grid directs a finding of disability for a younger person is when the individual is illiterate. Education, at that point, becomes the deciding factor.

When viewed globally, apart from the younger finding on the sedentary table, the only other instances in which the Grids direct a finding of disability is where the individual is fifty years of age or older. Education is, again, the deciding factor on the light table, where the youngest person eligible for an award is between fifty and fifty-four years of age. The deciding factor is education. Only if the person is shown to be illiterate does he or she qualify for an award of disability, even though he or she is capable of light work.

Similarly, an individual closely approaching retirement or of advanced age, even though he or she may be able to engage in medium work, will be found disabled if he or she has only a marginal or limited education.

Skill level is also important; it too may tip the balance, depending on the other descriptive factors. Examining the Grids as a whole, skill level affects outcome, like education, at the upper age categories.

The Grid secret is, therefore, simple. Once you have established an "upper" aged person (i.e., someone age fifty or older), can you tip the scale by adding one other factor? A person in this age category, lacking education or skill, will generally "grid out"—be determined disabled. Figure 11–15 depicts the analysis.

BACK TO CHRIS

"Wait! Wait! You've been talking about using the Grids straight up."

Steve pursed his lips. "You mean, applying the Grid to determine the result—that is, reading across the appropriate rule to see whether the finding is disabled or not disabled?"

"That's right."

"Absolutely. You have to understand how the Grid works, as you say 'straight up,' before you can apply it as a framework."

"Uh oh. This sounds complicated."

Steve shook his head gently. "Not at all. It's really quite simple. Here," Steve thrust the CFR at Chris. "What do you see?"

Chris peered intently. "The Grids I guess."

"And?" Steve prompted.

"Well, I guess the Grids are really tables of exertional levels—broken down into three different levels of physical capability."

"Bingo!"

"Bingo?"

"What happens if you have someone who doesn't have a physical impairment?"

"Well," Chris said tentatively, "I guess that means the person is not disabled."

"No. It simply means that the impairment is not physical."

"It could be mental you mean?"

"Correct. That's one of several possible examples. So, where," continued Steve, "are the Grids for mental impairments?"

"I don't know what you mean," Chris fumbled for words. "I mean, I don't think there are any."

"Correct again. The point is, the Grids are the Grids for *all impairments,* even if they don't have a physical component."

"OK. Let me get this straight. Even if my client does not have a physical impairment, I'm supposed to use the Grids to determine entitlement to disability benefits?"

"But only as a framework—which means you don't simply read across the line and reach the result."

"Then how do you figure out what the result is?"

"Using a vocational expert."

"But, if there's no physical impairment, and, therefore, no physical limitation, how do you know what table to use?"

"You're getting ahead of yourself. You're assuming this is an all-or-nothing proposition. It isn't."

"What do you mean?"

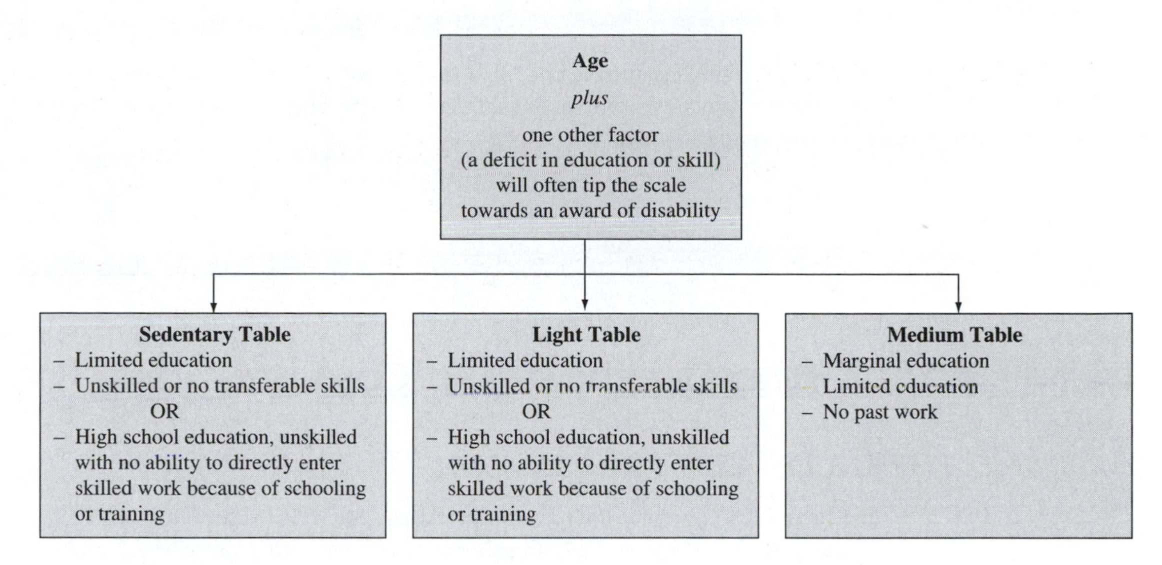

Figure 11–15 **The Real Secret to the Grids Is Age**

	Limitations Will Likely Be	Limitations May Also Be
Physical impairments	Exertional limitations	Nonexertional limitations
Mental or emotional impairments	Nonexertional limitations	Exertional limitations

Figure 11–16 **Type of Impairment Often Dictates the Nature of the Resulting Functional Limitation**

"The unfortunate reality is that injury, illness, and disease afflict people in all sorts of ways. For purposes of a disability determination, we break down the possibilities into two basic categories, with two possible outcomes in each category. Here, let me show you."

Whereupon, Steve got out his magic marker and drew a quick chart as seen in Figure 11–16.

"So, if a person suffers from an impairment, physical, mental, or both, and as a result, suffers with limitations that are exertional and nonexertional, the Grids are used as a framework?"

"That's right. Whenever you have nonexertional limitations, you can no longer use the Grids, as you say 'straight-up.' "

"Because the Grids are tables based only on exertional limitations?"

"Exactly. Do you see anything on the Grids that says something about the effects of depression, the inability to get along with others, or any other emotional or psychological issues?"

"Nowhere actually."

"That's right. The law says we can't simply ignore those things. Those kinds of limitations are as real as a bad back or a bad arm."

"But mental limitations are not the only kinds of nonexertional limitations, are they?"

"No, as we discussed earlier, when we were talking about the RFC, nonexertional limitations include such things as pain, the senses (sight, hearing, speech, touch, and feel), deleterious effects of medications (side effects), and fine motor manipulation, among other things."

"None of these are mentioned in the Grids?"

Steve shook his head. "They're not mentioned at all. But these limitations must still be considered when assessing a person's ability to do work."

"If the Grids don't direct a determination, then how do we account for these nonexertional limitations at step 5?" Chris hesitated, then answered the question before Steve could respond. "Vocational experts?"

"That's right. Essentially, the Grid is used only as a descriptor of the person. But, when considering the effect of nonexertional limitations, an expert must assess whether the person could perform competitive work—"

"Given the nonexertional limitations?"

"Correct!"

"I get it!" Chris smiled.

FRONT OF YOUR MIND QUESTIONS AND CONSIDERATIONS, 11.4

APPLYING THE GRIDS AS A FRAMEWORK

If a client's RFC does not include nonexertional limitations of function, the Grids may be applied as written. In that case, the claimant's RFC, together with age, educational attainment, and skill level, determine the outcome of the case. In all other cases, where there is a preponderance of evidence that the claimant suffers from one or more nonexertional limitations, the Grids are not used to determine the case.

Instead, the Grid rule becomes a reference point, describing a client in terms of physical capability (sedentary, light, medium, or heavy), age, education, and skill level, but it does not direct a determination. The Grid rule does not direct a determination in the case. To account for nonexertional limitations, a vocational expert is used. The vocational expert considers not only the exertional limitations but also the nonexertional limitations, rendering an opinion based on all of the existing evidence. Specifically, the vocational expert assumes the existence of various limitations and the effect, if any, of such limitations (or the combination of such limitations) on an individual's ability to perform competitive work.

In effect, the claimant's complete RFC must be considered at step 5, an assessment that includes both exertional and nonexertional limitations. This is the legal standard. The representative must ensure that the vocational expert fully considers the effects of all limitations supported by the evidence of record. (See Figure 11–17.)

Full consideration of all the claimant's limitations usually results in a combination of exertional and nonexertional limitations. This combination initially directs the decision maker to the Grid defined by the exertional limitations. For example, if an individual is limited to lifting no more than ten pounds at a time, but, because of pain and fatigue, must lie down two hours each day in the afternoon, the applicable Grid rule is on the sedentary Grid. Unless the sedentary Grid rule directs a finding of disabled without considering the effect of the nonexertional limitation, the Grid rule cannot direct the outcome because of the nonexertional limitation (lying down two hours each day). The Grid rule does not, on its face, consider the effect of nonexertional limitations, so it cannot be followed.

If an individual suffers only from nonexertional limitations, a Grid rule is still referenced (Rule 200.00[e][1]), but the decision is based on the testimony of the vocational expert, not on the rule. Figure 11–18 provides a simple illustration of using the Grids as a framework. As shown, the Grids are only used to direct a determination when nonexertional limitations are *not* present. When nonexertional limitations *are* present, the Grids are only used as a framework.

The regulations themselves provide the process. Appendix 2 to Subpart P of Part 404 (the Medical–Vocational Guidelines or Grids) provides at Rule 200.00(e)(2)

> **Where an individual has an impairment or combination of impairments resulting in *both strength limitations and nonexertional limitations,* the rules in this subpart are considered in determining first whether a finding of disabled may be possible based on the strength limitations alone and, *if not,* the rule(s) reflecting the individual's maximum residual strength capabilities, age, education and work experience provide *a framework* for consideration of how much the individual's work capability is further**

Step 5

In considering whether there are other less demanding jobs that the claimant can perform, the vocational expert considers the limitations included in a hypothetical question initially posed by the judge.

If the judge does not include all exertional and nonexertional limitations that the representative believes are supported by the evidence, the representative should pose his or her own hypothetical question(s).

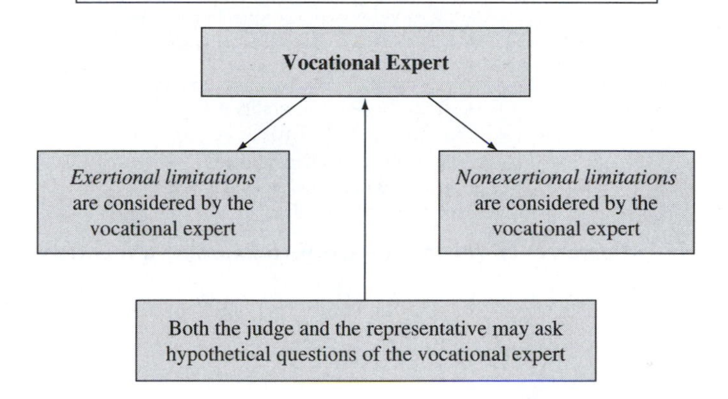

Figure 11–17 **Vocational Experts Consider Limitations Expressed by Counsel and Judge in Hypothetical Questions**

	The Grids Direct a Determination	The Grids Used as a "Framework"
Exertional limitations only	✔	
Mixed exertional and nonexertional limitations		✔
Nonexertional limitations only		✔

Figure 11–18 **When The Grids Are Used as a Framework**

diminished in terms of any types of jobs that would be contraindicated by the nonexertional limitations. (Emphasis added)

Where an individual has *only nonexertional limitations* Rule 200.00(e)(1) provides

In the evaluation of disability where the individual has solely a nonexertional type of impairment, determination as to whether disability exists shall be based on the principles in the appropriate sections of the regulation, giving consideration to the rules for specific case situations in this appendix 2. *The rules do not direct factual conclusions of disabled or not disabled for individual with solely nonexertional types of impairments.*" (Emphasis added)

As the rule implies, impairments that are solely nonexertional generally give rise to nonexertional limitations. In such cases, the nature and type of limitations that flow from nonexertional impairments must first be assessed; then the effect of such nonexertional limitations on the claimant's ability to perform competitive work within the regional economy should be considered. Apart from those cases in which common sense dictates the result (i.e., the claimant is catatonic, comatose, or otherwise clearly not able to function), a vocational expert should always assess the effect of nonexertional limitations. (See Figure 11–19.)

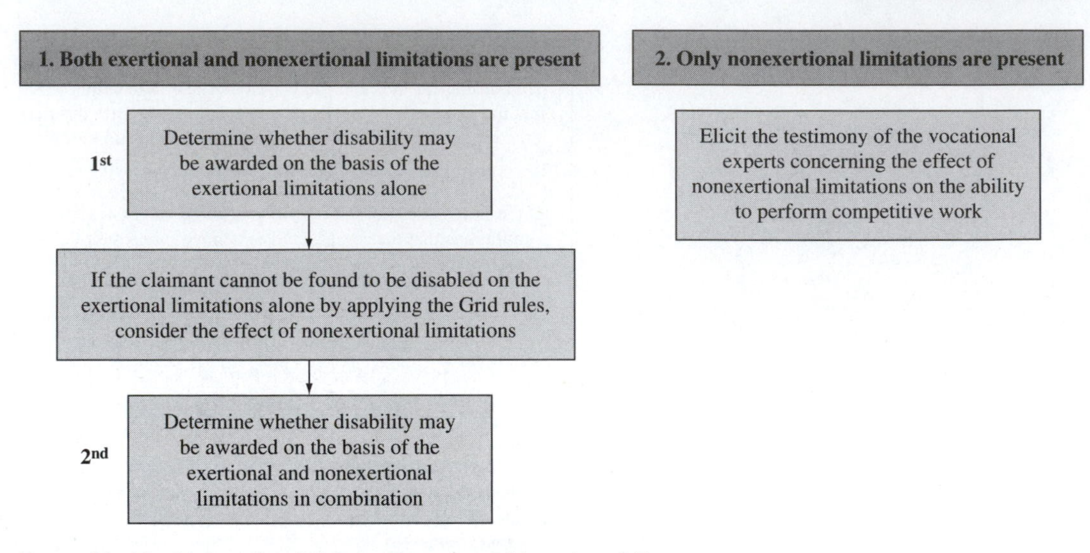

Figure 11–19 **Using the Grids to Examine a Vocational Expert**

Examining the Vocational Expert

As in step 4, the initial inquiry at step 5 is conducted by the Administrative Law Judge. Once the judge has determined that the claimant cannot return to past work, the judge inquires about other, less demanding jobs (i.e., begins the step 5 inquiry):

Judge: **Given your opinion that the claimant cannot return to past work, assume with me the existence of an individual the same age as the claimant, with the same vocational history and education. Now assume that this person can only lift fifteen pounds at a time, cannot sit longer than one hour at a time before having to stand; cannot stand for more than thirty minutes at a time before having to sit, and, because of asthma cannot be exposed to dust, gases, fumes, or odors. Are there other, less demanding jobs that this individual can perform?**

The judge's inquiry takes the form of a hypothetical question. The judge asks the vocational expert to assume certain facts, such as the existence of a hypothetical (or pretend) individual who is the same age as the claimant and has the same educational and occupational history. After laying this foundation, the judge poses a set of limitations, asking whether, given these limitations, there are other, less demanding jobs that the individual can perform. This is the step 5 inquiry.

Back to Chris

"Why does the judge ask a hypothetical question?"

"Good question," Steve replied. "A hypothetical question is used because the judge is asking an expert witness, the vocational expert, to render an opinion that will ultimately affect the claimant, even though the expert does not know anything about the claimant's actual capabilities."

"Still, why can't the judge simply ask the expert about the claimant directly?"

"The *hypothetical question* is a legal device the judge and the representative use to address the claimant's ability to do work. Because the expert has never actually examined or tested the claimant, he or she cannot testify based on actual knowledge, so it has to be phrased in the form of a hypo."

Chris's features scrunched into a puzzled look. "Hypo?"

"Legalese for hypothetical question."

"But it counts the same as if the expert were answering a direct question about the claimant?"

"Yes and no. Yes, because the limitations posed to the expert actually reflect the claimant's capabilities. No, because of that same issue—the limitations the expert is asked to consider may or may not be supported by a preponderance of the evidence. If they are not, I suppose you could say that it's not the same as having had the expert actually examine and test the person."

"I see," Chris said, the light dawning yet again.

"To cover all the bases, so to speak, the judge usually asks a series of hypothetical questions. The most common practice is for the judge to begin with the limitations that are least restrictive and then add limitations, so the RFC the vocational expert is considering gradually becomes more limiting."

"Why?"

"It has to do with the evidence. Because the RFC the judge finally settles on must be supported by a preponderance of the evidence (an analysis that often requires a judicial determination of the claimant's credibility), the judge asks a series of hypothetical questions addressing all the alleged limitations. After the hearing, the judge makes a determination as to which limitations are actually supported by the medical evidence and testimony."

Chris's face lit up. "So, the judge really is covering all the bases. If she doesn't believe the claimant about pain, or something else, she can still discover what the result of the allegation would be if it were factored in?"

"That's it exactly," Steve nodded. "By asking a series of hypothetical, or "What if," questions of the vocational expert, the judge can determine what the effect would be not only of an individual limitation but also of a combination of limitations on the claimant's ability to perform competitive work."

"You know," Chris said, "it's actually pretty slick. The judge develops a complete picture of all the possibilities, considering the VE's testimony as well as what the claimant alleges."

"That's right. And it gives the representative a chance to include anything in the mix that the judge doesn't."

"You mean, if the judge fails to include a limitation that the representative thinks ought to be part of the RFC, the representative can ask a hypothetical question of the vocational expert and see what he or she says?"

"Exactly!"

FRONT OF YOUR MIND QUESTIONS AND CONSIDERATIONS, 11.5

MORE ON VOCATIONAL EXPERT EXAMINATION

When examining the vocational expert in the step 5 inquiry, the Administrative Law Judge generally asks a series of hypothetical questions, beginning with the least restrictive RFC and adding new limitations with each additional hypothetical question. (See Figure 11–20.)

Judge: **Assume with me an individual the same age as the claimant, with the same vocational and educational history. Now assume with me an individual able to lift ten pounds frequently, and twenty pounds occasionally, with no limits on sitting, standing, and walking. Are there jobs within the national or regional economies that such an individual can perform?**

This is a simple expression of an RFC limiting the individual to light work. The ability to lift only ten pounds frequently and twenty pounds occasionally reduces the individual's capacity to light. Note, however, that this reduction must be the result of a severe impairment that produces this functional limitation. The individual would likely be able to perform a full range of light work. If this were the final RFC at step 5, the result would be denial of benefits, because the person could return to some form of light work. If, however, this is the first in a series of hypothetical questions, the next question would be more limiting:

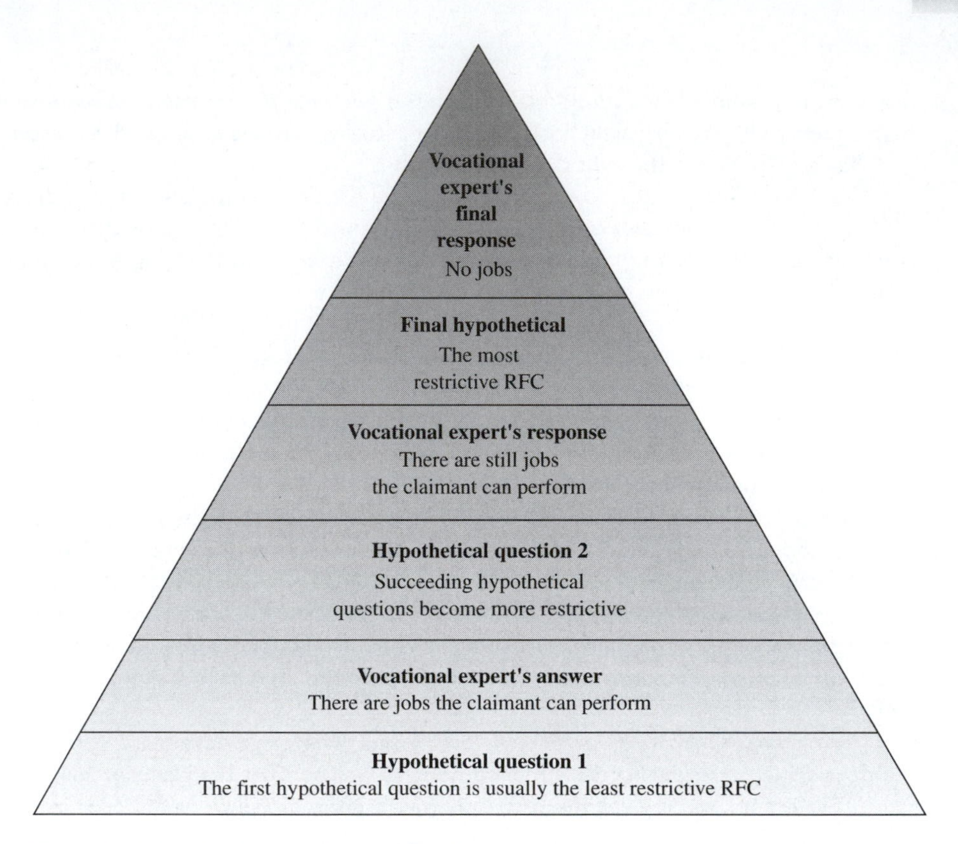

Figure 11–20 **The Layered Vocational Inquiry**

Judge: **Now assume with me the additional limitations that because of back pain this individual is unable to sit more than thirty minutes at a time, before having to stand; that she cannot stand for more than thirty minutes before having to sit; and can only occasionally bend or stoop.**

The second hypothetical question builds on the first, using the original limitations as a foundation on which new, more restrictive limitations are layered. As a result of the restriction brought on by back pain, limiting the person to sitting and standing only thirty minutes at a time, the individual requires a job that can be done sitting and standing alternatively. Vocationally, this is termed a "sit–stand option." Sit–stand options are of two types:

- ❑ Sit–stand option at the will of the employee; and
- ❑ Sit–stand option required by the demands of the job itself.

Because of the sit–stand option, the number of jobs available are reduced.[4] The question then becomes, in light of the individual's past work experience, age, and education, whether there are significant numbers of such jobs remaining in spite of the reduction. Assuming the vocational expert testifies to the continuing existence of jobs, and the judge determines the number of jobs remaining to be significant, a third hypothetical question may be asked, incorporating additional limitations supported by the evidence, further limiting individual function:

Judge: **Now assume with me yet another limitation. Assume that because of pain, the individual must take prescription pain medication that causes drowsiness. This medication must be taken once in the morning and once in the early afternoon, causing drowsiness within thirty minutes after taking it, such that the individual must lie down for up to an hour at a time, on each occasion. Given this limitation, together with the earlier-stated limitations,**

are there jobs remaining within the national or regional economies that the individual could perform?

The third hypothetical question considers a potential side effect from prescription pain medication, in this case, drowsiness. Other side effects include nausea, dizziness, inability to concentrate, and photophobia, among others. Such effects are nonexertional limitations.

The vocational expert will probably testify that the need to lie down twice during the normal workday will eliminate competitive work. The expert may also add that such a limitation will require an accommodation by an employer (i.e., the employer will have to allow the person a special exception not normally part of competitive work). This special exception is necessary in order for the claimant to complete an eight-hour day.

The hypothetical questions asked by the judge of the vocational expert are sequential, beginning with the least restrictive RFC and culminating in the most restrictive. For example, the foregoing sequence is as follows:

- ❑ A light RFC (frequently lift ten pounds, occasionally twenty pounds); then
- ❑ A light RFC with sit–stand option (sit thirty minutes; stand thirty minutes); and then
- ❑ A light RFC, with sit–stand option *and* the need to lie down two times each day (in the morning and afternoon because of drowsiness from medication side effects).

This layered effect allows both the judge and the representative to clearly delineate the claimant's restrictions, and further allows the representative to monitor the limitations the judge is considering. This is crucial, given the nature of the decision-making process, discussed in the next section.

STRATEGY AND TACTICS AT STEP 5

The heart of step 5 is the claimant's RFC, including how present information affects the ultimate RFC formulation. Critical factors in the step 5 decision-making process include assessments of the claimant's age, education, and previous work experience. The representative has several objectives with respect to these individual factors, as well as the RFC generally.

The Descriptive Factors: Age, Education, and Previous Work Experience

Various factors describe the claimant as an individual in three essential areas: age, education, and previous work experience. These factors are recognized in the regulations as affecting the ultimate disability determination.

Age

It would seem that a person's age could not logically be the subject of strategy and tactics. Not so. The Medical–Vocational Guidelines or "Grids" are not to be applied mechanically. The rules in the Grids are not rigid mechanistic barriers. They are flexible, recognizing that the human experience is as varied as individuals.

Thus, the age breakpoints, at fifty, fifty-five, sixty, and sixty-four, are not to be applied rigidly. An individual in a lower age category may be "deemed" to qualify for the next higher category if he or she is within six months of a birthday. An individual who is forty-nine years old at the alleged onset disability may argue that the more favorable rules in the fifty to fifty-four age category should apply, particularly if the individual is within six months of actually turning fifty. This strategy applies in all age categories.

A representative should assess all the evidence, looking for a significant event that might signal the onset of disability. Events might include a hospitalization, after which the individual fails to return to work; an accident causing the underlying impairment; initial diagnosis of the disease; a time when the individual's condition worsened; or the point at which the claimant was unable to continue work as a result of the impairment. This date should be compared with the claimant's age at the time of the event.

If, for example, the individual is younger (age 49), the issue is whether it would be appropriate to amend the alleged onset date of disability (AOD) to coincide with the fiftieth birthday or another event within six months of the fiftieth birthday. Rather than deal with a more difficult argument applying a Grid rule at a younger age, the alleged onset date of disability may be amended for a more favorable age category, which may facilitate the award of disability with little trade-off in terms of forfeited benefits.

If the claimant, by and through his or her representative amends the AOD to a later date than originally claimed, he or she is giving up months or even years for which benefits might have otherwise been paid or a period of disability (POD) established. This decision depends on the evidence. Simply because an individual left work, may not, in and of itself, be sufficient cause for a disability award. Later evidence, such as more complete medical documentation or evidence of a worsening of condition, may suggest a more appropriate date and may bring the individual within range of a more favorable age category. This balancing process must be addressed on a case-by-case basis. The effective representative should examine all contingencies.

Education

Like age, an individual's educational attainment would not seem to be subject to strategy and tactics. Either an individual has attained certain education or training or has not. Simple, right?

Wrong. Like age, presentation of an individual's educational attainment requires careful consideration of the actual facts. To simply label an individual as a "high school graduate" may suggest too many assumptions, which, once examined, may reveal unexpected facts altogether. One common assumption is that an individual with a high school diploma is equipped with the skills usually associated with a high school education. However, an individual enrolled in special education or other educational program that accommodates a learning or other disability may not, in fact, possess these skills. It is important to determine the exact nature of secondary schooling.

If the client participated in special education, that fact should be made known at the hearing. Actual capability in mathematics, reading, and writing should be presented. Careful attention should also be paid to the paperwork, which is part of the administrative record, necessary to initiate the claim. Who completed the documents? The claimant? Did a family member or friend complete the paperwork because, despite a high school education, the claimant cannot adequately read or write? These direct questions should be asked of the claimant. If an educational deficit exists, it should be part of the RFC.

Other training should be noted as well. If, for example, the claimant client completed a vocational-technical course of study, two questions should be asked:

1. *How long ago was the course completed?* If it was completed more than fifteen years earlier, such training is too remote to be counted in terms of transferable skills;
2. *Was work ever done in the field?* If the training was less than fifteen years ago, but the claimant never used the skills learned, it can be reasonably argued that there are no transferable skills from the training.

If a client has a college education, does this prepare him or her for direct entry into skilled work? Arguably, a liberal arts degree does not; whereas a degree in accounting should. Again, did the client ever actually do anything with the degree? If not, that fact should be brought out at the hearing.

If the client does not have a high school diploma and has tried unsuccessfully to obtain a general educational development diploma (GED), that fact should also be noted. Unsuccessful attempts to obtain a GED reinforces the lack of a high school diploma, showing not only the absence of the diploma but also the actual inability to function at that level.

Previous Work Experience

Accurate characterization of previous work is critical to a fair assessment of a claimant's capabilities. At step 5 the issue is no longer whether the individual can return to previous work. The focus shifts to transferable skills. If a claimant has a past work history of unskilled work, the issue is not relevant. However, if a claimant has previous work that may be either semiskilled or skilled, it is important to assess the details of work performance to avoid assumptions that may arise as a result of a job title.

For example, an individual might tell you (with some pride) that he or she was a "supervisor." For the client, this "title" is a source of self-esteem, an accomplishment of which to be proud. The problem, of course, is that a supervisor in the traditional sense has skills beyond the average worker. Having such skills makes it more difficult to be found disabled. Thus, it is important to look beyond titles and ask about specific job tasks and responsibilities. It must be determined whether the assumed skills are actually part of a claimant's vocational experience.

For example, if a claimant reveals he was a supervisor, several follow-up questions will determine whether he was a supervisor or a "leadman"—someone who did the same work as those whom he nominally "supervises" but with limited authority. Such questions include the following:

- ❑ Did you keep and make reports?
- ❑ Did you have the ability to hire and fire?
- ❑ Did you have the authority to grant pay increases or award promotions?
- ❑ Did you make out work schedules? How often? Did you have the authority to change schedules?
- ❑ Did you perform the same work as those whom you supervised?

An individual who did not make reports, and who did not have the ability to hire and fire, and who performed the same work as those over whom he nominally exercised supervision was not a supervisor in the traditional sense of the word. Such detail will likely reduce what would have been a skilled supervisor's position to a semiskilled or even unskilled leadman job. Additionally, the skills learned are probably not transferable to a reduced exertional level (e.g., from medium to sedentary work).

Another common example is found when the claimant is self-employed. This general descriptor requires further explanation, because the possibilities range from a small business owner, to professional, to contract laborer. Small business owner is a subcategory of self-employed. The temptation (especially for many vocational experts) is to attribute significant skills to someone who is described as the owner of a business. For the owner of a small business, it is important to have a complete description of the business operation and the owner's role in the business. Ask questions such as

- ❑ How many employees did you have?
- ❑ Did you do the company books?
- ❑ Who handled the money?
- ❑ Did you do any of the actual work of the business; or was your role limited to that of supervision? If you did not even supervise, what did you do in terms of the business operation?

Commonly, people will say, "I owned my own business. I was president of Trumble Painting Contractors." It sounds impressive. When asked more about the business, it may be discovered that the business was a one-man operation with a big name. A for-hire painter is a much different proposition than a painting contractor with office workers and on-site painters.

The need for details drives all such inquiry. Never accept a job title as descriptive of work. At step 5, the objective is to present a claimant either as possessing skills that do not transfer to lighter exertional levels or simply as unskilled. The most effective way to do this is to defeat all assumptions linked with job titles. The claimant should explain past work in detail, thus offering fuel for the argument that the work did not involve transferable skills.

THE RESIDUAL FUNCTIONAL CAPACITY

At step 5 the overall strategy is to produce an RFC that is as restrictive as the evidence allows. Again, this requires careful exposition of the facts underlying the client's condition. Here, only one by-word will suffice:

Detail! Detail! Detail!

The examination will vary, of course, dependent on the nature of the claimant's impairment, both as to type and severity. Generally, however, presentation of evidence pertaining to RFC falls into three categories:

- ❑ Direct medical evidence, consisting of medical records, narrative reports, and so on

  A. Documentation of the impairment and its severity; and

  B. Statement(s) of restrictions or limitations from an acceptable medical source (either the treating physician or other examining doctor);

- ❏ Direct testimony
  - **A.** Testimony of the claimant regarding limitations and functioning;
  - **B.** Testimony of the treating physician or psychologist about the claimant and the impairment, limitations, functioning;
  - **C.** Testimony of an examining physician or psychologist about the claimant and the impairment, limitations, and functioning (based on an examining as opposed to treating relationship);
- ❏ Indirect testimony
  - **A.** Testimony of family and friends as to the claimant's ability to function and pursue daily life activities;
  - **B.** Testimony of nonexamining medical experts as to the nature and severity of the claimant's condition and resulting limitations of function. Because these doctors have not examined the claimant, their testimony is indirect, based on medical records, and, in a few instances, on hearing the claimant's testimony as well.

At step 5, this evidence focuses on two topics:

1. The nature and severity of the claimant's impairment generally;
   - ❏ Diagnosis;
   - ❏ Prognosis;
   - ❏ Descriptions of the nature, extent, and experience of pain as a result of the impairment; and
2. The claimant's ability to function;
   - ❏ Exertional limitations;
   - ❏ Nonexertional limitations;
   - ❏ Recitation of daily activities;
   - ❏ The claimant's self-assessment of the ability to work.

Underlying all testimony, and especially the claimant's, is *credibility.* Only if the claimant is perceived as credible will the testimony be persuasive. And only if the testimony is persuasive will the assertion concerning the claimant's RFC be adopted. Strategy and tactics regarding the RFC at step 5 centers on credibility.

For example, it is often the fact of pain that renders a person disabled as a result of a given impairment. A person with a bad back is not unable to work because of a range-of-motion limitation but because of the pain associated with the spinal deficit.

How is pain measured? The simple answer is that pain cannot be measured. If pain could be measured, credibility would involve a simple matter of measuring the "actual pain" and comparing it to that asserted by the claimant. Because pain is an intangible factor and concerns individual tolerance, the claimant's assertion of pain involves subjective interpretation. Thus, judicial assessment of how pain affects an individual, and correspondingly the ability to function, depends on whether the judge believes the claimant's testimony. The representative's job is to make that happen.

The first step is to understand what the claimant says about pain (or other limitation) and compare that description with the objective medical evidence—the medical records and reports.

- ❏ Do the medical records corroborate the claimant's assertions?
- ❏ Is there a longitudinal record over the period of claimed disability to the present that corroborates those assertions?

If corroboration exists—that is, if the assertions match the objective medical data—the next step is effective presentation. One of the most significant mistakes made by lawyers, and nonlawyer representatives, is to take the case too lightly. Failure to spend a sufficient amount of time with a client before a hearing may result in a disconnected presentation, making it seem as if the objective evidence fails to corroborate the claimant's testimony.

If you neglect to go over the evidence and fail to simulate a hearing so the client is familiar with the questions that will be asked, and the manner of inquiry, it may seem as if there is a lack of corroboration generally and an evidentiary failure over the longitudinal record specifically. A client who presents himself or herself as a "poor historian"—one who is inconsistent in delivering testimony and one who cannot appropriately respond to the questions—will be perceived as unbelievable and will be unable to persuade the judge of the truth.

To be successful, meet with the client over time. Ensure that he or she is comfortable with the subject matter, your manner, and the types of questions that will be asked. Too often, representatives perceive these cases as the small claims of federal cases and spend little time on them, believing they are not worth the effort. Horror stories abound about clients meeting representatives for the first time at OHA offices thirty minutes before a scheduled hearing. Is it any wonder that unexpected things happen and cases are lost?

Because the representative's objective is to maximize the judge's finding concerning the client's RFC—that is, to ensure the judge finds the most restrictive RFC supported by the evidence—be prepared to take advantage of specific regulations and Social Security Rulings (SSRs) that promote the adoption of information by select individuals (i.e., treating physicians, examining physicians, and other health care providers).

For example, the regulations and SSRs provide that a treating physician's opinion[5] is to be given controlling weight. An opinion from a treating doctor—if supported by the evidence (the doctor's notes, findings, etc.)—trumps opinions from others—notably DDS physicians' opinions—who are not treating physicians. Given this weighted result, why would a representative *not* obtain a narrative report from a treating physician? Surprisingly, lawyers and representatives often neglect this important stratagem.

The regulations also provide that an examining physician's opinion trumps that of a nonexamining doctor. Remembering that DDS doctors are nonexamining physicians, the claimant could be seen by a doctor on an "examining basis." The client could be examined, have tests administered, and have a report written by a doctor other than the claimant's treating doctor (someone he or she has not seen over time) who has done more than read reports (i.e., actually examined the claimant).

Any report prepared by a treating or examining doctor must be accompanied by a statement of what the doctor finds the claimant's RFC to be. It is effective to have the doctor complete a medical source statement (MSS). Ideally, the MSS should be accompanied by a narrative report that explains why the doctor completed the report as such. The MSS calls for a series of specific responses; physicians often complete the form but neglect to give the *rationale* for responses. Medical records are clearly important, but they are not written for legal purposes. Thus, a separate report from a doctor, even a page in length, summarizing the claimant's condition and the doctor's involvement is critical. (See Figure 11–21.)

BACK TO CHRIS

Chris was blunt. "Why is it critical?"

Steve glanced at the young advocate. "Good question. Remember, except for a few individuals, doctors generally prepare their everyday records for other health care professionals, not lawyers or representatives in a legal setting."

"So, their records are hard to understand?"

"It's not that they're hard to understand, it's simply that they aren't directed to answering the questions we're asking. For example, a medical record might indicate 'chronic lumbar pain,' and the doctor knows and has probably verbally explained to the patient what the patient can and cannot do. The problem is that the doctor may not have documented it in the progress notes. All the doctor needs to see is 'chronic lumbar pain' to understand what the limitations are. After all, he or she told the patient, and probably many other patients, what not do when diagnosed with this condition. The limitations are inherent in the doctor's diagnosis. The doctor assumes a set of limitations with the diagnosis. To write those same limitations down would be redundant."

"I see what you mean. The doctor doesn't write it down for the record because he or she thinks its self-explanatory."

"That's right. The problem is we legal types don't have the code. So, when we see 'chronic lumbar pain' we say, 'And. . . ? What else?' We want specific black-and-white do's and don'ts. Only then can we point to the record and say to the judge, 'This is what the treating doctor said.' "

"So, we need a narrative report to support the medical source statement?"

"Yes. Often, when we compare the doctor's progress notes with the medical source statement, the two don't seem to make any sense—at least not to us. Although the progress notes speak volumes to the doctor, they sound weak to us. That's because the doctor knows his or her patient, and the progress notes are only one aspect of that knowledge of the patient. The doctor's memory and personal knowledge complete the picture."

"But we don't have access to the doctor's memory and personal knowledge."

"Precisely. So, although the doctor may be perfectly comfortable filling out a medical source statement from the progress notes, we need more. We need a report that ties the patient's course of treatment all together in a uniform, consistent story and that gives life to the RFC in the medical source statement."

"So, what goes into a doctor's narrative report?"

"Basic information. When did the treating relationship begin? When was the diagnosis made? What is the patient's history, including hospitalizations? Has this been a gradual disease process or a sudden, traumatic onset? Under what actual limitations or restrictions does the patient operate? Have these changed over time? What is the patient's prognosis for the future?"

"Wow," Chris exhaled. "That's a lot."

"Well, it seems like a lot, but it's really pretty straightforward."

"It makes sense when you think about it. We have to look at this as *evidence,* not simply medical records."

"And, the more we do that, the better it will be for our client. We can't assume anything."

"Got it," Chris declared confidently. It really did make sense.

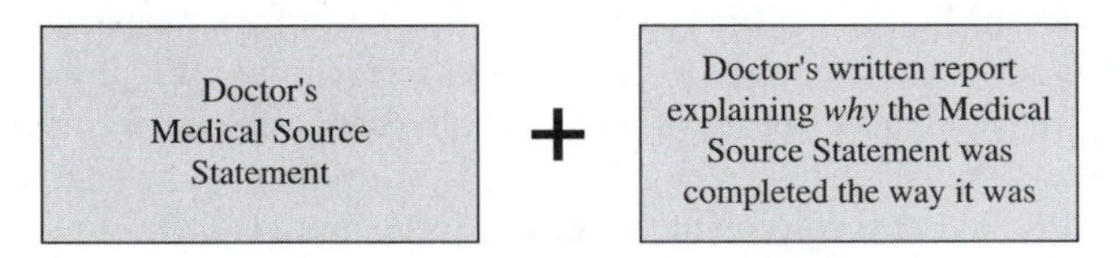

Figure 11–21 **A Medical Source Statement Must Be Supported by Underlying Treatment/Examination Records**

FRONT OF YOUR MIND QUESTIONS AND CONSIDERATIONS, 11.6

RFC STRATEGIES WITH INDIRECT TESTIMONY

Indirect testimony is particularly helpful in establishing a client's credibility. This type of testimony generally falls into three categories, establishing

- ❑ Physical capability;
- ❑ Mental capability; and
- ❑ General day-to-day functioning, which, to some extent, informs the judge about mental and physical capability.

Indirect testimony of a family member or friend is lay testimony. It is considered indirect because it does not come from the claimant, a treating physician, or an examining doctor. It is valuable because it is often a result of direct experience or observation of the claimant. Direct observation is valuable because it corroborates the claimant's own testimony. So, although the claimant may testify that she has "good days and bad days," this testimony alone may not be persuasive to a judge reviewing a medical record that does not directly reference up-and-down daily functioning. Such information is critical, because it bears directly on the ability to perform competitive work on a sustained basis. Performing at work one day and being bedridden for the next two is not consistent with competitive work. Testimony about day-to-day functioning should come from those who actually interact with the claimant on a daily basis—which the doctor generally does not do. In short, testimony from a friend or family member is important because it fills in the gaps, on a day-to-day basis that the medical records cannot address.

The reason why is simple. Generally, a claimant does not see the doctor each day. At best, visits may occur once a week or once a month. What happens in the intervening time is the gap the medical records do not fill. The testimony of a family member who lives with the claimant or nearby or a friend who regularly sees or assists the claimant becomes an invaluable resource in a case. Such testimony may not shed light on medical diagnoses, but it offers invaluable and potentially persuasive evidence of what a claimant can and cannot do on a sustained, daily basis.

Mental Capability

Corroboration of a claimant's mental capacity can take several forms. Basic information, such as the ability to read or write, easily can be corroborated by a family member or friend. Similarly, the ability to engage in simple mathematical calculations, such as making change can also be corroborated by testimony from someone who has actually been with your client under such circumstances.

Even more complex mental functioning can be the subject of such testimony. If a claimant testifies that he or she cannot *concentrate* for long periods of time, a family member or friend can testify to the inability to watch a movie or television program, or the inability to recount or understand what was viewed.

Memory is equally complex but clearly subject to comment. If a claimant testifies that his or her memory has been declining, as evidenced by an inability to "remember why I went into a room" or the constant need to "write things down," family members may be able to cite instances in which they witnessed such behavior. Similarly, family members or friends may be able to testify how they helped a claimant overcome or compensate for the deficit.

Equally important is emotional or psychological functioning. A family member or friend may talk about his or her experience with the claimant through the course of the claimant's depression. The friend could describe the condition and how it manifested itself over time. Another psychological disorder may be present, such as a personality disorder, that affects the claimant's ability to deal with people or function independently. These are all areas in which indirect testimony can help fill the gaps regarding daily activities.

Each case must stand or fall on its own facts. The representative must ask whether there are primary deficits, particularly in the area of mental functioning, and how they can be corroborated, not only through the claimant's eyes but also through the eyes of an independent observer or participant.

Physical Capability

Indirect testimony of physical capability may be essential to the case, particularly if a doctor has declined to provide a medical source statement or other summary of physical restrictions. The critical question is, What is it that your client is actually able to do on a day-to-day basis?

Testimony of a friend or family member that corroborates the inability to engage in simple or routine tasks is foundational. If a claimant cannot engage in basic personal hygiene without assistance, the testimony of someone who actually helps the claimant bathe, comb hair, or tie shoes is essential. Such testimony adds immense credibility to the claimant's testimony.

Testimony of a family member or friend concerning a claimant's physical activity is important. How much does the claimant routinely lift on a day-to-day basis? How far has the family member or friend observed the client to walk? In what kind of chair does the claimant sit? For how long? Are there particular activities that bring on pain? How so? These are the questions that are important to corroborate.

In presenting such evidence, the foundation is clearly the claimant's initial testimony. In preparing a family member or friend to testify, it is important to first understand what it is the claimant will say. The family member or friend should then be directed, by the pattern of your questions, to address the same topics, confirming the initial testimony of the claimant.

Note, however, that credibility can often be established by a family member or friend who disagrees with the claimant. For example, pride is a basic characteristic of human nature. This is particularly so for an older person who has worked steadily throughout life. When faced with the inability to function, he or she may deny the seriousness of the condition. Although it may seem incongruous, many applicants for disability are urged by family members or friends to so proceed. Personally, they may be embarrassed by the application and try desperately not to admit what they perceive to be their failings.

As a result, the claimant may hedge during his or her testimony, trying not to appear weak. For example, a man in his fifties who had worked since he was a teenager might grudgingly admit that he was injured but still maintain the position that, "while I can't do as much as I used to, I can still do a lot." Through the course of such testimony, his wife might steadily shake her head from side to side. When asked to testify, she might reveal that her husband is a proud man, unwilling to admit his own limitations. She might then describe what actually happens around the house on a day-to-day basis. Her testimony, although it diverges from that of her husband's, actually makes both their testimonies more believable because her husband's underlying pride has been exposed.

Why is this testimony credible? This testimony is credible because the message communicated by the husband is, "I want to work. I want to be a contributor like I always have been. I'm nothing without that." The message from the wife is, "he wants to work, but he really cannot." This is what the judge senses, enhancing the overall effect. In essence, the husband's and wife's testimonies become synergistic, the sum of the two being greater than each individually. The result is an effective presentation that the husband cannot really function on a sustained basis as he once could.

Daily Activities

A family member or friend becomes the eyes and ears through which the representative and the judge glimpse life from the claimant's perspective. Having heard the claimant's testimony about his or her daily life, focus on the critical points in the friend or family member's statement. In other words, do not simply allow the friend or family member to repeat the exact testimony of the claimant. Although it may seem corroborative, the net effect is cumulative, and it will only make the judge impatient.

Focus on highlights of the claimant's testimony, which, if true, will result in a finding of disability (or an inability to competitively function on a sustained basis.) Generally, the activities or daily events that affect a client's inability to engage in sustained competitive activity include the following:

- ❑ The inability to engage in personal care;
- ❑ The need to lie down through the course of the normal eight-hour workday;
- ❑ Medication side effects, such as drowsiness, dizziness, or nausea;
- ❑ The need to elevate legs;
- ❑ The need to rest after a period of sustained activity;
- ❑ The inability to use the hands or fingers for a sustained period;
- ❑ The inability to wake up at an appropriate hour of the day;
- ❑ The inability to sleep restfully each night;
- ❑ Activities to alleviate pain, such as soaking hands in an ice bath or using a heating pad during the normal workday;
- ❑ The need to frequently use the restroom (for example, once every twenty minutes, for up to ten minutes at a time);
- ❑ The need to use a nebulizer (breathing machine) through the course of the normal workday;
- ❑ Sensitivity to sunlight (photophobia);
- ❑ The inability to leave the home (agoraphobia);
- ❑ The regular onset of panic attacks with resulting behavior, including recovery period;
- ❑ The regular onset of seizures, with resulting recovery period;
- ❑ The regular use of an assistive device (wheelchair, cane, walker) through the day;
- ❑ The inability to walk on inclined surfaces; and
- ❑ Other special conditions brought on by a medical or psychological condition (such as the need to be in a darkened room).

A friend or family member testifying to these conditions as occurring daily or a certain number of times per week substantially enhances the claimant's case generally and his or her persuasiveness (credibility) specifically.

Back to Chris

"Is step 5 the most important step, then?" Chris asked.

Steve considered his answer carefully. "Yes and no. Remember this is a sequential analysis. Each step, when you reach it, is the most important at that time. But if you can't meet a listed impairment at step 3, then in terms of an award of benefits, step 5 becomes your only other chance for a disability award."

"Oh."

"It's not that daunting. Step 5 is all about RFC. It's all about persuading the judge that your client cannot perform sustained competitive activity on a day-to-day basis."

"It's just the strategy part of it. I'm not sure I can think like that."

"Sure you can. It's really a matter of common sense. You know the list we just went through?"

"Yes."

"That's a good starting point. Ask yourself, why can't this person do a regular job? Then make a list of everything that, if true, would prevent the person from doing a job five days a week, eight hours a day. Then, it is simply a matter of convincing the judge that what's on that list is actually believable."

"So, I make a list—after interviewing my client?"

"And, reading the medical record."

"And then I ask myself, 'How am I going to prove everything my client says—everything that's on this list?' "

"That's exactly right. How should you go about proving it?"

"Well, there's what my client says—"

"Right. That's what I call 'direct' testimony."

"Then, there's what the doctor says."

"Yes. But remember, there are three kinds of opinion testimony from doctors—doctor's who have actually treated your client, those who have at least examined him, and those who are simply offering an opinion from the written records."

"The treating doctor is the best?"

"Absolutely. After all, the treating doctor has seen your client over a period of time and has actually treated him."

"If I can get an RFC, a medical source statement, from the doctor that's even better."

"Right," Steve replied, grinning. Chris *was* getting it.

"Then I have to see if I can corroborate or verify what the client says with testimony from other people, such as friends or family, who know what's going on in my client's day-to-day life."

"You're doing great!"

"In asking friends or family to testify, I want to reaffirm what the claimant says are his worst problems, and then I want to focus on those things that would actually keep someone from being able to work a full eight-hour day without special accommodation, such as napping during the day."

"I'm impressed. I really am, Chris." Steve clasped the aspiring advocate on the shoulder, "you've come a long way, and you're going to do great!"

"Thanks Steve. I really mean it."

WHAT IF . . . ? SAMPLE PROBLEMS

WHAT IF . . .

What if your client claims significant pain, requiring him to lie down at least twice each day for up to an hour at a time, but the medical records make no mention of the need to lie down? How should you proceed?

1. Ignore the lack of medical records and rely on your client's testimony.
2. Have a long-lost uncle testify that the claimant tells him he must lie down each day.
3. Have the treating doctor complete a medical source statement together with a brief narrative report outlining the need to lie down.
4. Have your client's mother testify that she often finds him sleeping during the day.

Answer: *A lack of medical corroboration leaves the judge with a credibility issue. Without medical evidence the judge must decide whether to believe your client, or the judge must resort to a medical expert to weigh the medical records against your client's testimony. Either way, such a situation is beyond your control—not good for your client's case. An effective advocate anticipates potential weaknesses and attempts, through proactive measures, to plug the gap. In this case, if the treating physician can provide a medical source statement (RFC) that references the need to lie down, and can further explain why he so restricts the claimant, your case is virtually won. Having a relative relate something the claimant told him is not persuasive. Having the claimant's mother testify about intermittent observations is certainly more helpful than the long-lost uncle but still falls short of the strong evidentiary message of a medical source statement. The best answer is 3.*

WHAT IF . . .

Which of the following is true?

1. At step 5 of the sequential analysis, the purpose is to find your client unable to return to past relevant work.
2. A vocational expert is not needed at step 5 of the sequential analysis, because the determination is made simply by reading across the Grids.
3. The Grids are not to be interpreted mechanically but should be viewed flexibly.
4. Step 5 is the second-to-last step in the sequential analysis.

Answer: ***The fifth step in the sequential analysis process concerns whether there are other, less demanding jobs that the claimant can perform despite his or her limitations. To have reached step 5, the determination has already been made at step 4 that the claimant cannot return to past relevant work. In making this determination, a vocational expert is required when there are allegations of nonexertional limitations. The Grids reflect only the effect of exertional limitations; hence the presence of nonexertional restrictions requires specific vocational expertise to evaluate the effect of such limitations on the ability to perform competitive work. In this regard, the law is clear. The Grids are not to be applied mechanically, but flexibly. One example concerns age categories. A person within six months of the age breakpoint may be deemed, for purposes of the determination, to be in the next age category. And, as we have pointed out, this is a five-step sequential analysis. Step 5 is the last step in the process. Items 1, 2, and 4 are false; 3 is true.***

WHAT IF . . .

What if your client tells you he has not seen a doctor in more than a year because he cannot afford to go? His main complaint is his back, though he also complains of depression. What should you do?

1. Decline to accept the case.
2. Ask your client to schedule an appointment with his former treating physician, and to obtain a medical source statement and current (updated) medical records from that doctor after the examination.
3. Ask the judge to schedule a prehearing consultative examination with an orthopedic specialist, with X-rays of the lumbar and thoracic spine; a complete range-of-motion study of all major joints and the spine; as well as with a psychologist to evaluate depression. Only after these tests have been conducted should you have a hearing.
4. Accept the case and rely on your client's testimony as to his or her limitations.

Answer: ***You can, of course, decline any case. In this situation, however, further development of the medical evidence is required. Thus, simply accepting the case and proceeding to hearing, relying solely on your client's testimony, is not the best course of action. You know little about your client's present medical condition, because he has not seen a doctor in more than a year. The best course of action is to obtain further medical evidence. As indicated in items 2 and 3, this can be accomplished in two ways, and both avenues should be pursued. Send your client back to his former treating physician for an updated examination. The physician should complete a medical source statement and a narrative report. You probably will have to make an independent contact with the doctor to get these records. In addition, a formal request should be made for a prehearing consultative examination for both the back problem and depression. In making such a request,*** *however, never accept a general reference to a consultative physician without first specifying the nature of the examination to be undertaken. Unless specific tests are requested, the state DDS (the entity actually meeting the request) will default to the least expensive (and thus least informative) test. Request an orthopedist, X-rays of the affected areas, and a complete range-of-motion study. A psychological examination should include a mental status examination, global assessment of function (GAF) (both current and for the past year), the Minnesota Multiphasic Personality Inventory (MMPI), the Wechsler Adult Intelligence Scale (Third Edition) (WAIS-III), the Wechsler Memory Scale (Second Edition), the Beck Depression Inventory, the Beck Anxiety Inventory, and a completed mental medical source statement. The best answers are 2 and 3.*

WHAT IF . . .

The Grids are based on what four factors?

1. Age, marital status, employment status, and education.
2. Age, education, previous work experience, and exertional level.
3. Age, education, incurability, and past work experience.
4. Education, insured status under Title II, skill level, and exertional level.

Answer: The Grids consist of three tables, each representing a different exertional level (sedentary, light, and medium). Within each table three additional factors exist:

- ❑ Claimant's age;
- ❑ Claimant's education and training; and
- ❑ Claimant's previous work experience.

The correct answer is 2.

---

[1]Title 20 C.F.R. § 404.1568(d).

[2]Title 20 C.F.R. § 404.1568(d)(3).

[3]Title 20 C.F.R. § 404.1568(c).

[4]The requirement that the individual must be able to sit *or* stand (employee's option) or that the individual sit *and* stand (employer's requirement for job performance) limit the potential number of jobs because of the dual requirement of sitting and standing necessary for job performance.

[5]The reference to "physician" includes every acceptable medical source, including psychologists.

12

CHAPTER TWELVE

Childhood Disability

HIGHLIGHTS

- ❑ Childhood disability examined
- ❑ The three-step sequential analysis
- ❑ Functional equivalence

CHRIS

Chris grimaced. "Childhood disability? I don't get it. How can a child be disabled? I mean, kids can't work. You know, child labor laws and all."

"Actually, the law does provide for children to receive disability payments," said Steve.

"How? Or, better yet, why?"

"Good question. Congress has determined that the concept of disability should not only be applicable to adults. Children should be entitled to such benefits as well."

"Why? I thought that the public policy underlying disability was to provide daily sustenance and shelter for those unable to provide for themselves."

"That's right. But the same concept applies to children. Suppose a child has a severe medical problem and needs care, but the family is financially unable to care for the child. What then?"

"So childhood disability is not about work?"

"That's right. It's about children with severe medical problems whose families are financially needy."

"Then, disability for children is not about providing sustenance and daily living; it's about providing medical care?"

"Both, actually."

A puzzled look crossed Chris's face. "I don't get it."

"The public policy is this. If a child is part of a family with low income *and* suffers from an impairment that is disabling, then both medical benefits *and* a small monetary amount is provided. The money is to help with daily living and the medical is to care for the child."

"OK, that makes sense. But, what about the disability part? Is it keyed to a child's ability to work?"

Steve shook his head. "Not at all. Because work is the measure of performance for adult function, does not make it so for children. What's the measure of performance for a child?"

Chris thought. "Play?"

"Well, not exactly, but close. Development. How a child grows and develops into an adult is the measure applied to childhood disability."

"That makes sense too. So, if a child suffers from an impairment that interferes with his or her ability to grow and develop, the child is disabled?"

"Generally, yes. As you can imagine, the criteria are more specific. Let's take a closer look."

FRONT OF YOUR MIND QUESTIONS AND CONSIDERATIONS, 12.1

INTRODUCTION TO CHILDHOOD DISABILITY

The public policy underlying childhood disability is succinctly expressed in the Conference Report to Public Law 104-193, passed in 1996:

> **The conferees intend that only needy children with severe disabilities be eligible for SSI, and Listings of Impairments and other current disability determination regulations as modified by these provisions properly reflect the severity of disability contemplated by the new statutory definition.**[1]

The standard for making these determinations, like adult disability determinations, is based on a sequential evaluation process. However, unlike adult determinations, references to the ability to perform past relevant work and other less demanding work are not part of the childhood determination.

The term *child* is defined as an individual "who has not attained age 18."[2] The issue of "childhood disability" thus applies to persons under age eighteen. Like adults, initial applications for disability are made to the Social Security field office and are forwarded to the state Disability Determination Service (DDS) for actual medical review. If denied on initial determination, the child, by and through his or her parents or guardian, has sixty days to ask for reconsideration. If denied a second time, a Request for Hearing may be filed, asking for a hearing before a federal Administrative Law Judge, again, within sixty days of the reconsideration denial.

The determination at a hearing before a federal Administrative Law Judge is made in much the same way as for an adult. Evidence is presented, both in the form of medical and other records, and testimony is taken. Like adult determinations, this is the first time the child, by and through his or her parents, has the opportunity for a face-to-face presentation. Like adults, the burden of proof falls on the child to show that he or she is entitled to an award of disability by a preponderance of the evidence.

Although the procedural rules are the same, the substantive rules are not. A five-step sequential evaluation for adult determination is reduced to a three-step sequential evaluation for children. The three steps are as follows:

Step 1. **"If you are doing substantial gainful activity, we will determine that you are not disabled and not review your claim further."[3] "If you are working and the work you are doing is substantial gainful activity, we will find that you are not disabled regardless of your medical condition or age, education or work experience."[4]**

Step 2. **"If you are not doing substantial gainful activity, we will consider your physical or mental impairment(s) first to see if you have an impairment that is severe."[5]**

Step 3. **If your impairment(s) is severe, we will review your claim further to see if you have an impairment(s) that meets, medically equals or functionally equals the listings."[6]**

Figure 12–1 is illustrative.

BACK TO CHRIS

"Hey! Only three steps in the sequential evaluation. That should be easy, right?"

"Hold on there. It's a mixed bag. Depending on who you talk to, childhood disability is thought of as *harder!*"

"How come? You don't have to deal with work. It should be easier!"

"It is, to some degree, much more medically intensive. The three-part requirement, which includes functional equivalence, can be particularly thorny."

"Functional equivalence?" Chris's face scrunched up. "That's different from adults, isn't it?"

Steve nodded in agreement. "Absolutely. So, on one hand, you give up the work issues; however, on the other hand, you get a new area of potential entitlement."

"Another way to pay your client?" Chris asked, brightening.

"That's a great way to think of it. Here, let me show the difference in the law."

Chris groaned inwardly. *More law!*

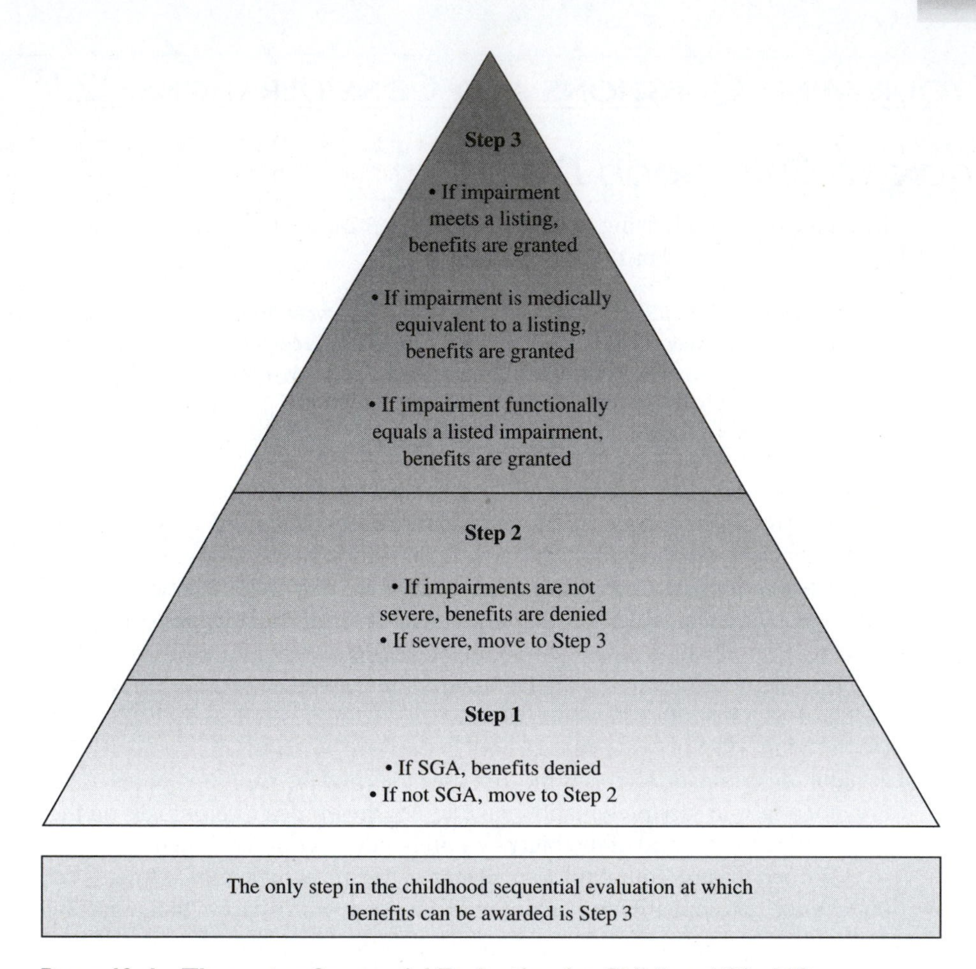

Figure 12–1 **Three-step Sequential Evaluation for Childhood Disability**

A Trip to the Hard Drive, 12.1

Regulatory Foundation for Childhood Disability

Childhood disability is found under Title XVI of the Social Security Act. Regulations are promulgated under part 416, as part of the Supplemental Security Income (SSI) regulatory scheme. Interestingly, however, like SSI, reference is made back to part 404 of Title 20, incorporating Appendix 1, the Medical Listings.

The basic definition of disability for children is found at Title 20 C.F.R. § 416.906. The regulation sets forth the three-step sequential evaluation for childhood disability determinations, referencing Title 20 C.F.R. § 416.924 and following. Section 416.902 describes general definitions and a new standard for children: "marked and severe."

Section 416.913 makes specific reference to medical and other evidence of the child's impairment, describing the significance of a medical source who compares the child's functional limitations to children of the same age "who do not have impairments." Other sources include educational personnel, public and private social welfare agency personnel, parents, care givers, siblings, and other relatives.

Section 416.924 sets forth the sequential evaluation in detail, and § 416.924(b) describes the function of age as a factor in evaluating whether the impairment meets or medically equals a listing.

Section 416.924(a) describes the types of information that may be considered in evaluating a child's disability claim. This information includes medical evidence, test scores, information from other people, records from early intervention and preschool programs, and school records.

Significantly, § 416.924(a) also describes how an alleged disabled child's functioning is to be compared to children without impairments. Special education or structured settings are considered, as are what the reg-

Childhood Regulation	Subject Matter
§ 416.90	Scope of the new childhood regulations, including reference to new definitions of "marked and severe" and "marked and severe functional limitations"
§ 416.902	General definitions and terms
§ 416.906	Basic definition of disability for children
§ 416.911	Definition of a disabling impairment
§ 416.913	Medical and other evidence of a child's impairment
§ 416.919n(c)(6)	Nature of the medical source statement for children
§ 416.924	How disability is determined for children (the sequential evaluation)
§ 416.924(a)	Things that are considered in determining childhood disability
§ 416.924(b)	How age factors into childhood disability determinations
§ 416.926(a)	The meaning of functional equivalence in childhood disability determinations
§ 416.929	How symptoms, including pain are evaluated for childhood disability
§ 416.987	Disability redeterminations for children on reaching age eighteen

Figure 12–2 **Childhood Disability Regulations Overview**

ulations describe as "unusual settings."[7] This section further describes the effects of treatment, including medications.[8] Of note is § 416.926(a), describing "functional equivalence for children."

Section 416.929 discusses how pain is to be assessed for children, and § 416.987 addresses redeterminations of childhood disability decisions once the child reaches eighteen years of age. See Figure 12–2.

BACK TO CHRIS

"That's a mouthful!" Chris declared.

"Like the adult regulations, there are no shortage of words in those dealing with children," said Steve.

"Almost too much."

"No. It only seems like a lot. Once you get into it, it's pretty straightforward. You just have to reorient your thinking from the disabled-equals-inability-to-work mindset to one that considers disability in terms of childhood growth and development."

"How?"

"Let's look at each of the listings."

"Sounds like a plan."

FRONT OF YOUR MIND QUESTIONS AND CONSIDERATIONS, 12.2

STEP 1 IN THE CHILDHOOD SEQUENTIAL EVALUATION

Step 1 in the childhood disability evaluation is no different from that for adults. If a child's earnings exceed a monthly income limit ($780 per month at this writing), then it is presumed that the child is engaged in substantial gainful activity (SGA) and benefits will be denied. Indeed, as with adult determinations, because the analysis is sequential the inquiry stops at step 1 if SGA is found.

Clearly, when considering SGA for children, the question must be examined closely. Is the child actually engaged in competitive work as measured against an adult standard, or is the work activity accommodated in some way because of the child's age? If work is accommodated, such that it is not competitive, a serious question arises, perhaps sufficient to rebut any presumption of SGA.

Furthermore, if the child is engaged in activity that is related to schooling, such as a work–study or similar program related to paying tuition, room, board, and so on, it can be argued that the activity is educational in nature, and thus exempt from SGA consideration. Similarly, a student involved in an internship, or other similar program may also not be engaged in SGA because of the educational nature of the program.

STEP 2 IN THE CHILDHOOD SEQUENTIAL EVALUATION

Step 2 in determining childhood disability asks the same question as step 2 in the adult determination: Does the child have a severe impairment?

Generally, a severe impairment is one that is medically determinable (diagnosed by a medical doctor or psychologist, has lasted for at least twelve months, is expected to last twelve months or result in death, and reasonably gives rise to "more than minimal functional limitations").[9]

In children, unlike in adults, a functional limitation is not related to whether the limitation reasonably affects the ability to engage in work or worklike activity. Instead, the regulations require that the child's functioning be compared to that of a normal child. Specifically, the regulations state that

> **[W]e will look at whether you do the things that other children your age typically do or whether you have limitations and restrictions because of your medically determinable impairment(s).[10]**

In effect, severity is determined by considering the effect of the impairment(s) on the child's functioning compared with children who are not so afflicted. The regulations further clarify this analysis by considering the child's actual behavior and performance:

> **We will also look at how well you do the activities and how much help you need from your family, teachers or others. Information about what you can and cannot do, on a day-to-day basis at home, school, and in the community, allows us to compare your activities to the activities of children your age who do not have impairments.[11]**

Normally, diagnoses from a medical doctor, such as asthma, a spinal defect, mental retardation, and so on, will not trigger a serious inquiry as to whether the child suffers from a severe impairment. If a disease process, injury, or illness has not yet lasted twelve months, or if its effects are not readily discernable, the representative should be prepared to address the issue of severity by producing information about the disease, injury, or illness itself, together with information about its day-to-day effect on the child. In garnering such information, it is important to note the venues recognized by the regulations:

- ❑ Home;
- ❑ School; and
- ❑ Community.

Each venue offers an opportunity to compare the child's functioning with that of healthy peers.

Notably, if an individual impairment does not rise to the necessary level of severity to pass muster at step 2, where there are multiple impairments, the combined effect of all impairments may be assessed to determine eligibility.[12] Thus, if a single impairment does not hinder a child's functioning other than at minimal levels, the combined effect of multiple impairments may, thus satisfying the step 2 analysis. In reaching this conclusion, the regulations require the Social Security Administration to "look comprehensively at the combined effects of [the child's] impairments on [his or her] day-to-day functioning."[13]

In considering the issue of medical severity, any inquiry must ultimately end with a discussion of the child's daily functioning. Only when the conclusion is reached that the effects of the illness, disease, or injury are minimal can a childhood claim be denied at step 2 as nonsevere.

In sum, a step 2 denial is a difficult decision to support, because it does not relate to work functioning but to a child's daily functioning, which necessarily includes growth and development—issues far broader in scope than work function. Indeed, such growth and development issues embrace the whole of the human condition, to a greater or lesser degree, depending on age.

STEP 3 IN THE CHILDHOOD SEQUENTIAL EVALUATION

Step 3 is the most significant step in the abbreviated childhood disability determination process, because it is the only step at which benefits can be awarded. Benefits can be denied at all three steps. Figure 12–3 illustrates this. There are three ways to find an award of disability at step 3 in the childhood disability analysis:

- The child's impairment *meets* a listed impairment in the Listings of Impairments (Appendix 1);
- The child's impairment(s) *medically equals* a listed impairment in the Listings of Impairments (Appendix 1); or
- The child's impairment(s) *functionally equals* a listed impairment in the Listings of Impairments (Appendix 1).

Step 3 for children differs from that for adults. Under the adult analysis, a claimant can meet a listed impairment or an impairment can be medically equivalent in severity to a listed impairment. If disability is not awarded at step 3, the adult analysis moves to step 4 and eventually step 5, where, based on the adult's residual functional capacity there is further opportunity for an award of benefits.

In effect, the step 3 analysis for children condenses the step 4/step 5 adult analysis into a single step 3 analysis. Like the adult analysis, the key inquiry centers on *function*. Unlike adults, however, the childhood functional analysis is concerned with the child's growth and development, as compared with children

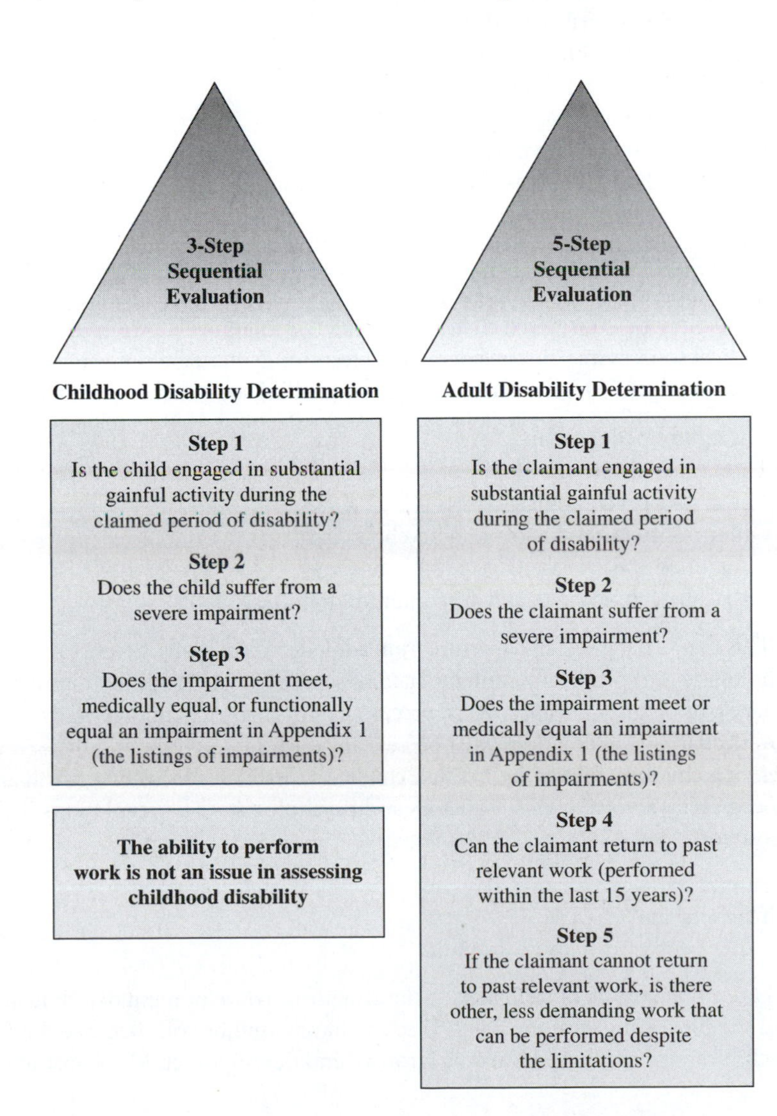

Figure 12–3 **Childhood Disability versus Adult Disability**

not afflicted by an impairment(s). For adults, the issue concerns exertional and nonexertional limitations, all directed at the ability to perform work or worklike activity.

For children, the focus of "functionality" is on daily activities in the home, the school, and the community. Function is divided into six major domains (discussed later in the chapter) describing a child's growth and development.

Meets a Listing

Part B of Appendix 1 to subpart P of part 404 presents "Medical criteria for the evaluation of impairments for children under age 18." These are the listings for children. Like the adult listings, they include thirteen categories (Category 108.00 is reserved):

- ❑ Section 100.00 Growth impairment
- ❑ Section 101.00 Musculoskeletal system
- ❑ Section 102.00 Special senses and speech
- ❑ Section 103.00 Respiratory system
- ❑ Section 104.00 Cardiovascular system
- ❑ Section 105.00 Digestive system
- ❑ Section 106.00 Genito-urinary system
- ❑ Section 107.00 Hemic and lymphatic system
- ❑ Section 108.00 [Reserved]
- ❑ Section 109.00 Endocrine system
- ❑ Section 110.00 Multiple body systems
- ❑ Section 111.00 Neurological
- ❑ Section 112.00 Mental disorders
- ❑ Section 113.00 Neoplastic diseases, malignant
- ❑ Section 114.00 Immune system

As with the adult procedure, the child's impairment must meet or match the required symptoms, medical signs, and laboratory findings specified within the given listing. However, for children, a broader range of sources may be considered than are considered in adult determinations. Specifically, both medical and nonmedical sources may be considered in determining that a child meets a listing. For the representative, this means throwing a wider net out for evidence. Medical sources include the following:

- ❑ The child's pediatrician;
- ❑ The child's physician;
- ❑ The child's psychologist;
- ❑ Other nontreating doctors and psychologists;
- ❑ A qualified speech-language pathologist; and
- ❑ Physical, occupational, and rehabilitation therapists.

This marks a significant departure from adult determinations, because nonphysicians and non–Ph.D.-level psychologists are specifically contemplated as sources for determining disability in children. Thus, a speech-language pathologist is an approved source, as are physical, occupational, and rehabilitation therapists—none of whom need to be medical doctors or possess any doctoral-level training. This is consistent with the philosophy underlying childhood disability, because children's disabilities focus on growth and development, which does not necessarily involve medical doctors and psychologists. The regulations include the following nonmedical sources:

- ❑ Parents;
- ❑ Teachers; and
- ❑ Other people who know the child.[14]

Parents and teachers are critical in the growth and development of a child and are usually the people who spend the most time with the child. Teachers have a unique role, because they are specially trained to work with children for continued learning, growth, and development. Most startling about the childhood listings is the absolutely wide-open venue for all other people who know the child. The rationale for this wide-open approach is set forth plainly in the regulations:

> **Every child is unique, so the effects of your impairment(s) on your functioning may be very different from the effects the same impairment(s) may have on another child. Therefore, whenever possible and appropriate, we will try to get information from people who can tell us about the effects of your impairment(s) on your activities and how you function on a day-to-day basis.[15]**

This allows for any and all evidence to be offered, provided the people know the child. In presenting evidence, balance an overabundance of similar information against the judge's need to be informed about the child's day-to-day functioning. If the record is burdened with too much material, the critical evidence may get lost in a flurry of less important material.

As with all things in the realm of advocacy, persuasion is the goal. The amount of information provided must be tempered by the value of the data. Submitting a myriad of reports from people who know the child may simply distract the judge or the medical expert from the central focus of the case. Do not be tempted to load up the record. Persuasive presentation of evidence requires that witnesses be presented, documents offered, and experts brought forth, all with a specific goal.

If the child's impairment meets the criteria for a specified listing, the evidentiary presentation should be directed to that goal. Evidence should focus on the listing. A proof matrix helps focus efforts, identifying elements to be proved and the means of accomplishment. Essentially, this is a simple device that asks, "What do I need to show under the law, and how am I going to prove it?" (See Figure 12–4.)

Equals a Listing

As with determinations in the adult listings, medical equivalency is a function of medical findings subject to a medical opinion. The governing regulation is found at Title 20 C.F.R. § 416.926. As with adults, a determination of medical equivalency may not be made by the judge without a physician's input. However, a physician's considerations in reaching a conclusion are broader for children than for adults.

> **In addition to evidence from acceptable medical sources . . . we may also use evidence from other sources to show the severity of your impairment(s) and how it affects your ability to work, or, if you are a child, how you typically function compared to children your age who do not have impairments.**

Medical equivalence may be found under one of two circumstances:

1. If the claimant's impairment is listed in Appendix 1 but not attended with all the required symptoms, medical signs, and laboratory findings; or
2. If the claimant's impairment is not listed in Appendix 1.

Sample Proof Matrix 101.13
(deficit in musculoskeletal function)

	Dr. Smith (pediatrician)	Mrs. Jones (mother)	Ms. Temple (teacher)	General Hospital
Deformity of Right Arm	Treatment records	Testimony	Affidavit	Surgical records
Inability to perform age-related personal care		Testimony	Affidavit	

Figure 12–4 **Sample Proof Matrix for Musculoskeletal Impairment**

In the first instance, the exacerbation of one or more previously documented medical signs, laboratory findings, or symptoms, or the addition of other symptoms, medical signs, and laboratory findings from additional impairments may give rise to a determination of medical equivalence. In the second case, an impairment, though not actually listed, may be analogous to a listed impairment in terms of medical severity. The determination of medical equivalence is essentially the same for children as for adults, except that severity may take on different forms in children than adults.

Functional Equivalence

Functional equivalence for children has been a high profile, dynamic area of legislative action. Following the Supreme Court's decision in *Sullivan v. Zebley* (493 U.S. 521 [1990]), the Social Security Administration adopted a standard for determining childhood disability that examined the comparable severity of a child's medical condition with that of an adult. Put simply, if the child's condition was comparable in severity to a medical condition that would disable an adult, benefits were awarded to the child.

The Personal Responsibility and Work Opportunity Reconciliation Act of 1996 eliminated the comparable severity standard, adopting instead a functional equivalence standard. Under this new standard a child

> **[S]hall be considered disabled . . . if that individual has a medically determinable physical or mental impairment, which results in marked and severe functional limitations, and which can be expected to result in death or which has lasted or can be expected to last for a continuous period of not less than 12 months.[16]**

Governing regulations now require that an individual under age eighteen "must have marked and severe functional limitations." This is the standard of disability for children claiming SSI benefits.[17] In plain language, to be found disabled, a child must meet, medically equal, or functionally equal a listing. Apart from this standard, disability may not be awarded to children.

The new rules embody what the Social Security Administration describes as "a higher level of severity than under the former IFA [Individual Functional Assessment]."[18] The new standard is specifically implemented at Title 20 C.F.R. § 416.926(a). According to the regulation the order in applying the three methods of childhood disability is as follows: Before considering whether a child's impairment is functionally equivalent to a listed impairment, the judge must consider whether the child's impairment meets a listing. If not, the judge must then consider whether the child's impairment is medically equivalent to a listed impairment; and only if the judge concludes that the child's impairment does not meet or equal a listed impairment may he or she consider whether the child's impairment is functionally equivalent to a listed impairment. Figure 12–5 depicts functional equivalence.

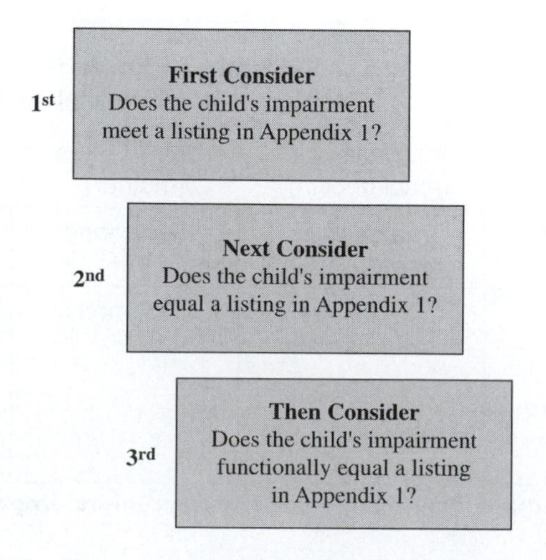

***Figure 12–5* Three Step Childhood Disability Evaluation**

BACK TO CHRIS

"This is getting a little confusing," Chris said in a long, drawn-out voice.

"What do you mean?"

"Well, what does 'functional equivalence' really mean? There's a lot of stuff here! Let's get down to brass tacks!"

"OK." Steve reached for the new regulations. "Functional equivalence for children is a really simple concept but complex in its execution."

"I was afraid you were going to say that."

"Well, look at this." Steve drew out a page of fine-print regulations.

"Great," Chris muttered.

"What?"

"Huh? Oh, nothing. Let's see."

FRONT OF YOUR MIND QUESTIONS AND CONSIDERATIONS, 12.3

THE SIX DOMAINS OF CHILDHOOD FUNCTIONING

To determine whether a child is disabled, the Social Security Administration recognizes "broad areas of functioning intended to capture all of what a child can or cannot do."[19] The six domains of childhood functioning include the following:

- ❑ Acquiring and using information;
- ❑ Attending and completing tasks;
- ❑ Interacting and relating with others;
- ❑ Moving about and manipulating objects;
- ❑ Caring for yourself; and
- ❑ Health and physical well-being.

To determine disability, a child's ability to function in each domain is evaluated. The regulations postulate six discrete questions designed to determine "whether [the child's] activities are typical of other children [the child's] age who do not have impairments."[20] The questions include the following:

- ❑ What activities are you able to perform?
- ❑ What activities are you not able to perform?
- ❑ Which of your activities are limited or restricted compared to other children your age who do not have impairments?
- ❑ Where do you have difficulty with your activities—at home, in child care, at school, or in the community?
- ❑ Do you have difficulty independently initiating, sustaining, or completing activities?
- ❑ What kind of help do you need to do your activities, how much help do you need, and how often do you need it?

On close examination of the questions posed by the regulation, it is quite plain that the central focus of the functional evaluation is on what a child can and cannot do on a day-to-day basis. Consider the old saying, "For a child play is work." With adults, we ask how a person is limited in the ability to perform basic activities, on which the ability to perform work is predicated; whereas, for children we consider the ability to function or operate in daily life. For adults, the focus is on work; for children, who are yet growing and developing, it is on the processes of life itself. How well do you navigate through the world? (See Figure 12–6.)

A child's impairment is functionally equivalent to a listing when the child has *marked limitations* in two of the six childhood domains. Additionally, a child's impairment is functionally equivalent to a listing when the child has an *extreme limitation* in one of the six childhood domains. *Note:* When determining functional equivalence, no particular listing is identified, nor are the individual requisites (symptoms, medical

- ❑ Acquiring and using information
- ❑ Attending and completing tasks
- ❑ Interacting and relating with others
- ❑ Moving about and manipulating objects
- ❑ Caring for yourself
- ❑ Health and physical well-being

Figure 12–6 **The Six Functional Domains**

signs, or laboratory findings) identified. It is presumed as a matter of law that a child who suffers from a marked limitation in two domains or an extreme limitation in one domain has an impairment that is of listing-level severity without the need to identify the actual listing.

In the first domain, acquiring and using information, the issue is how well the child learns and uses new information. In the second domain, attending and completing tasks, the issue is how well the child focuses and maintains attention, and keeps pace carrying out and completing tasks.

The third domain, interacting and relating to others, examines how well the child initiates and sustains emotional connections with others, including cooperating with others, complying with rules, responding to criticism, and taking care of possessions.

The fourth domain, moving about and manipulating objects, examines how the child ambulates, moves about, and manipulates objects considering the development of gross- and fine-motor skills.

The fifth domain, caring for yourself, considers personal care, including both physical and emotional health; how the child copes with stress and a changing environment.

The sixth and final domain, health and physical well-being, considers the cumulative physical effects of physical or mental impairments and their associated treatments or therapies on the child's functioning. See Appendix A-3 for an overview of the domains.

In examining each domain, the issue is what limitation, if any, does the child suffer? To reach a determination, the judge must rely not only on medical records but also on the testimony of medical personnel, parents, teachers, family members, and others who know the child. This is a potentially massive undertaking and requires careful coordination by the representative to ensure a cogent, cohesive, goal-directed presentation. (See Figure 12–7.)

THE MEANING OF "MARKED"

In determining whether a marked limitation is present, all functional limitations from all impairments should be considered. Importantly, all interactive and cumulative effects should also be considered. A *marked limitation* is found "when [the] impairment interferes seriously with [the child's] ability to independently initiate, sustain, or complete activities."[21] A marked limitation is also defined as "more than moderate" but "less than extreme."[22]

When compared with performance on standardized testing, marked is the equivalent of performance with "scores that are at least two, but less than three, standard deviations below the mean."[23] Note, however, that where there is a standardized score within this range, the regulations also require the child's day-to-day functioning be consistent with the lowered level.

In terms of growth and development before age three, the regulations chart an age-based curve, defining marked limitations as being present when age-related behavior reaches specific deficits. Specifically, for a child age three or younger, developmental functioning at a level equivalent to that between one-half and two-thirds of the child's chronological age is marked.

Finally, a child who is frequently ill, or who suffers frequent exacerbations of impairment(s), may be considered to have marked limitations in the health domain, where such illness or exacerbation results in "significant, documented symptoms or signs."[24] "Frequent" is defined as occurring, on average, three times per year, with each episode lasting two weeks or more. If episodes occur more frequently, but last for a shorter time, such occurrences may also be considered marked if the overall effect is equivalent in severity. (See Figure 12–8.)

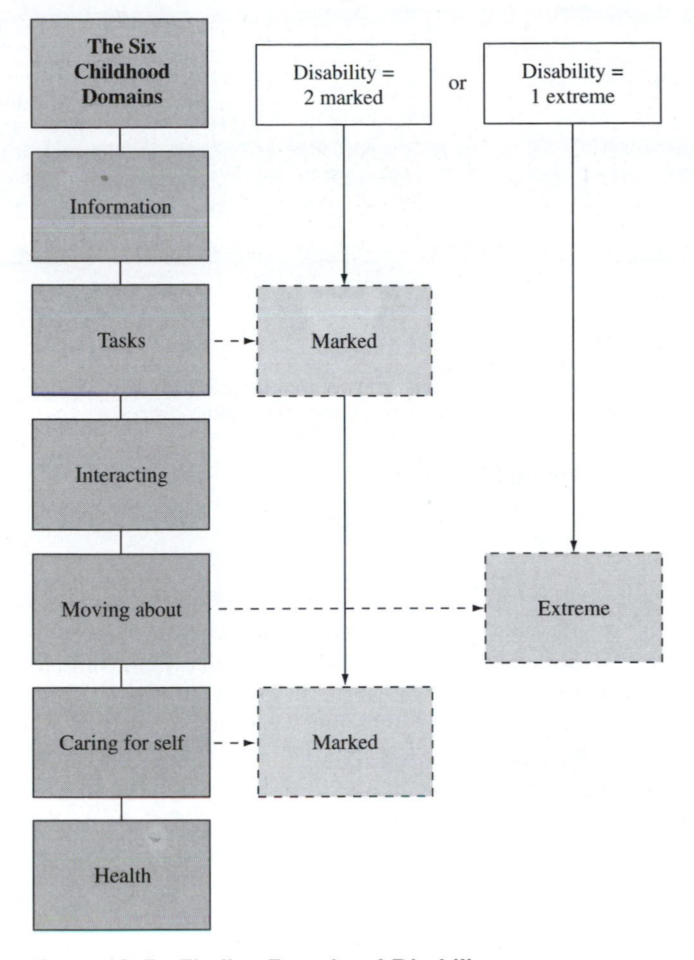

Figure 12–7 **Finding Functional Disability**

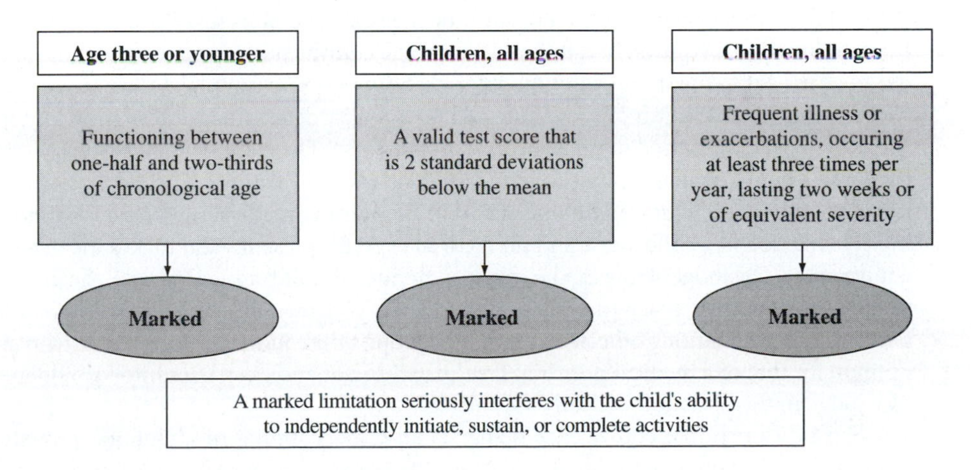

Figure 12–8 **A Marked Limitation**

THE MEANING OF "EXTREME"

An *extreme limitation* is one that "interferes very seriously with [the child's] ability to independently initiate, sustain or complete activities."[25] An extreme limitation is more than marked and is described in the regulations as "the worst rating we give to the worst limitations."[26] Notably, however, though worse than marked,

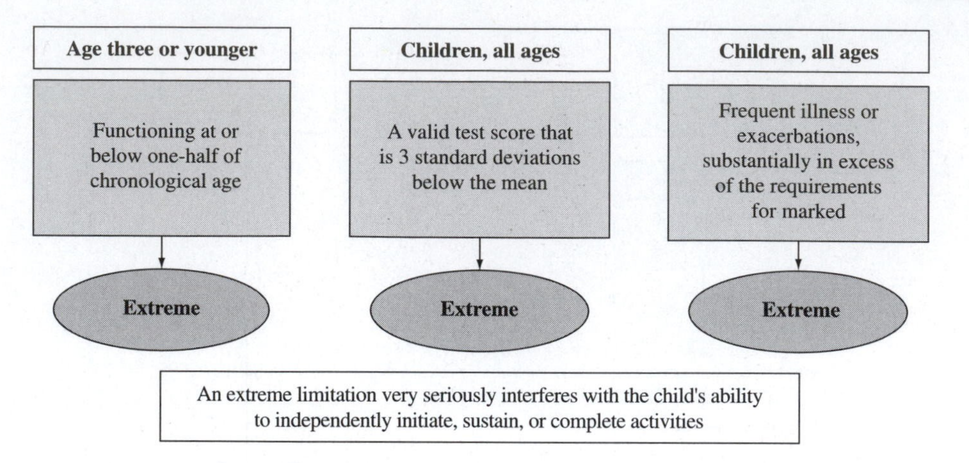

Figure 12–9 **An Extreme Limitation**

the ability to function is still considered limited and not eliminated. To reach the extreme level, there need not be a complete inability to function. Instead, it is equivalent to test scores that are at least three standard deviations below the mean. If a child is under three, an extreme limitation will be found where functioning is at one-half or below chronological age. In the health domain, a child will be found to have an extreme limitation if frequency of illness or exacerbation results in symptoms or medical signs "substantially in excess of the requirements for showing a marked limitation."[27] (See Figure 12–9.)

In assessing an extreme limitation, all factors should be considered, and even if test scores do not fall three standard deviations from the mean, scores that are two standard deviations, coupled with actual functioning far below expected levels of functioning, may warrant a finding of extreme limitation. Clearly, the opinion of a medical expert or treating source is of value in reaching such a conclusion.

Assessing a Child's Limitations

If the child's impariment(s) does not meet or medically equal in severity a listed impairment, the analysis turns to functional equivalence. Because functional equivalence considers the whole of the child's life in order to assess entitlement, the question naturally becomes, *who* can make such an assessment?

Careful consideration of the nature of the disability determination can only lead to one conclusion: A Medical Expert is required in each and every child's case. There are several reasons for this conclusion. First, the three-step sequential analysis for children focuses on the listings. The Listings of Impairments are medical descriptions and require a finding of specific symptoms, medical signs, and laboratory findings. If a hearing is scheduled in a child's case and no medical expert is present, who makes the determination of medical equivalence? The judge? How can he or she so decide? To fulfill a medical role, the judge must make medical judgments—in effect, reach medical opinions. These judgments are distinctly different from the evidentiary and legal determinations otherwise within the scope of the judge's role. A judge who substitutes his or her opinion for that of a medical doctor in fact "plays" doctor and trespasses into forbidden territory. A decision by a judge in this situation is clearly appealable.

Second, functional equivalence demands an understanding of childhood growth, development, and function. Such an understanding demands specific expertise. Does a judge know what behavior is normal for a two year old? Should a judge understand appropriate functioning in any of the six domains? As a general proposition, without specific reports and written findings of record, the judge may not so act. Thus, a medical expert, either a pediatrician (if the child's impairments are medical) or a psychologist (if the child's impairments are cognitive, emotional, or school based), is always appropriate. Pediatric psychiatrists should also be sought if available.

The regulations present specific examples of functioning in each domain. (See Appendix A-3 for a complete listing of the childhood regulation on functional equivalence.) Because expected and normal behavior change as children grow and develop, the examples are, as might be expected, linked to age. The age categories listed in the regulations are as follows:

- Newborns and infants;
- Older infants and toddlers;
- Preschool children;
- School-age children, ages six to twelve; and
- Adolescents, ages twelve to eighteen.

Expected behavior in each domain is established by age category. This information potentially provides a wealth of cross-examination material for experts who conclude that there is no showing of functional equivalence. It also provides an excellent reference for guiding a representative in prioritizing the strategic importance of selected information.

For example, if a medical expert testifies that there is only a moderate deficit or limitation in acquiring and using information (the first domain), inquiry can be made about select activities, relying on the exemplar activities in the regulations themselves. As examples of deficits in school-age children, the regulation indicates limited performance in acquiring and using information in the following activities:

- Inability to rhyme words or sounds in words;
- Inability to recall things learned yesterday in school;
- Inability to solve mathematics questions; and
- Capability to speak only in short, simple sentences.

The expert can be asked how each of these activities was assessed. In so proceeding, corollary questions might include the following:

- On what did you rely to reach your conclusion?
- Why do you conclude there is only a moderate limitation given the child's inability to [fill in the blank]?
- How does the combination of the child's deficits affect overall functioning in his or her ability to acquire and use information?
- Do you find the mother/parent/guardian credible in his/her description of the child's behavior/ability to acquire and use information? Why or why not? Please explain.

In assessing the available evidence, the exemplar activities outlined in the regulations (what the child should be able to do, as well as what the child cannot do) aid in an understanding of what is available and what must yet be obtained. In the foregoing example, school records, including information from teachers or others involved in a child's instruction, are important, not simply as a general matter but in response to the specific functions described. School records help frame the theory of a child's ability to acquire and use information.

If a case can be made that a child is markedly limited in the ability to acquire and use information, obtain school records that specifically address the activities listed in the regulation. Similar activities are identified for each of the other domains, with the exception of health and physical well-being, which, clearly, is not age dependent. (See Figure 12–10.)

For school-age children, teachers, tutors, and other special education assistants or instructors should be asked to assess the child's actual performance. Information should be obtained rating the child as compared to children not so impaired.

Medical experts, particularly in children's cases, should be asked what additional tests should be performed to gain a better picture of the child's functioning. Ask the expert to be specific in naming tests, and ask why such tests are of value. Remember, it is the Administrative Law Judge's responsibility to ensure that the record is fully developed. If further testing would shed more light on a child's condition and enhance the medical expert's view of the case, ask for such tests to be done.

	General	Newborn	Toddler	Preschool	Ages 6–12	Ages 12–18
Acquiring information	Learning concepts and symbols through play	Exploring environment; recognition of familiar sights and sounds	Learning how objects go together in different ways; forming concepts, solving simple problems	Learning to use skills leading to reading and writing; listening, coloring, using words to ask questions; giving answers	Learning to read, write, do math, discuss history and science; doing group work; entering into class discussions; using complex language	Using what has been learned in daily living; understanding and knowing simple and complex ideas; applying skills in practical ways
Attending and completing tasks	Regulating, initiating, and maintaining levels of alertness and concentration; looking ahead and predicting possible outcomes of actions	Responding to various external stimuli—light, sound, touch, and temperature	Showing sustained attention (looking at picture books, building with blocks)	Paying attention when spoken to directly; sustaining play; performing self-care activities, such as dressing and feeding	Focusing attention on a variety of situations; following directions; remembering and organizing school materials; changing activities or routines without distraction	Independent planning; preparing and completing long-range projects; organizing time and tasks; maintaining attention for extended periods of time
Interacting and relating to others	Initiating and responding to exchanges with other people; forming relationships with others	Responding visually and vocally to care giver(s) responding to a variety of emotions	Expressing emotions and responding to feelings of others; beginning to initiate and maintaining relationships with adults	Socializing with children as well as adults; using words instead of actions to express yourself	Developing lasting friendships; working in groups to create projects and solve problems	Initiating and developing friendships with peers and relating to children and adults; intelligently expressing feelings and asking for assistance to meet needs in all types of settings

Figure 12–10 **Overview of Activities Associated with Each Functional Domain Shown by Age.**

BACK TO CHRIS

"Wow! That's a ton of detail!"

Steve nodded, with a twinkle in his eye. "Do you think you need to know all that? I mean, memorize it?"

"Well, I, that is," Chris stumbled, unsure of the correct answer.

"Relax. You only need to know that this information is available—in the regulations. You can't be expected to memorize all of it. What you do need to know is that it's available. This is the gist of 'functional equivalence.' "

"So, I can always pull out the C.F.R.?"

"Yes. No lawyer knows all the law. What they do know is the general principle and where to look for the details."

"I need to know about the domains, what each one of them covers generally, and then where to look specifically?"

"Right. But remember, each child is unique. Your job is to persuade the judge that your client is entitled to disability benefits. The best way you can do that in the case of children is with a medical professional. You should be able to produce narrative reports or at least a childhood functional evaluation."

Figure 12–10 (continued)

	General	Newborn	Toddler	Preschool	Ages 6–12	Ages 12–18
Moving about and manipulating objects	Multiple bodily actions, including rolling, rising to stand, raising head, arms, legs, transferring self from one surface to another; moving through space; carrying, handling, and working with a variety of objects	Moving body and limbs; holding head up, learning to sit, stand, crawl; beginning eye–hand control	Beginning to actively explore wide area of immediate space; beginning to walk and run; trying to handle small objects	Walking and running with ease; using gross-motor skills (climbing, etc.) with little supervision; completing puzzles, stringing beads, building with blocks; increasing control of crayons	Increasing strength and coordination; enjoying physical activities; running, jumping, throwing, kicking, and catching; using kitchen and other small tools independently	Participating in a full range of individual and group physical fitness activities; mature eye–hand coordination skills; fine-motor skills to write legibly or use keyboard
Caring for yourself	Responding to changes in emotions and daily demands; taking care of personal needs; relying on personal abilities	Recognizing bodily signals (hunger, pain, discomfort); consoling with thumb or hand sucking	Increased ability to console self (carrying blanket); learning to cooperate with care giver(s); showing what is wanted (point to bathroom etc.)	Desiring personal care; attempting new things (tying shoes, climbing chair, etc.)	Independence in most day-to-day self-care activities (dressing, etc.); developing sense of right and wrong; showing consistent control of self	Feeling increasingly independent from others in all activities; noticing significant changes in bodily growth; discovering appropriate ways to express feelings, both good and bad; thinking seriously about future plans
Health and physical well-being	**Not age dependent**	**Not age dependent**	**Not age Dependent**	**Not age dependent**	**Not age dependent**	**Not age dependent**

"Like this?" Chris held out a form for Steve to see.

"That's the one. It's Form 538, otherwise known as a Childhood Disability Evaluation Form." (See Figure 12–11.)

Chris turned the pages of the form. "Hey, this form has all the domains right in it."

"Now you're catching on."

"Who fills this out?"

"The best person is the child's treating physician—as long as he or she explains why the assessment is being made as it is."

"You mean on the domain part, where it asks the doctor to give the severity of the limitation?"

"That's right. If the doctor simply checks the degree of limitation, but doesn't explain why he or she checked it that way, the judge won't be able to give the doctor much credence. So, it's critical, even with the doctor's notes and records in the file, to have the doctor share his or her thinking by writing the underlying opinion on the Childhood Disability Evaluation Form."

"I get it. Functional evaluation considers the child's actual ability to function, depending on his or her age, in comparison to the functioning of a child of the same age who doesn't have an impairment."

"Bingo!" Steve grinned. "We're going to make a disability advocate out of you yet!"

"Thanks Steve!"

Figure 12–11 **Childhood Disability Evaluation Form**

CHILDHOOD DISABILITY EVALUATION FORM

Name: SNN: Date of birth:	Level of Determination: ☐ Initial ☐ CDR ☐ Reconsideration ☐ CDR Reconsideration ☐ Other Is this child engaging in SGA? ☐ Yes ☐ No Filing Date: ________________

I. SUMMARY

A. IMPAIRMENTS:

B. DISPOSITION: Check one entry that best describes your findings in this case. **Complete this section last.**

1. ☐ NOT SEVERE—No medically determinable impairment OR Impairment or combination of impairments is a slight abnormality or a combination of slight abnormalities that results in no more than minimal functional limitations. (Explain below.)

Explanation:

☐ Continued in section III

2. ☐ MEETS LISTING ______________________________ . (Cite **complete** Listing and subsection(s), including any applicable B criteria for 112.00.)

3. ☐ MEDICALLY EQUALS LISTING ___________________. (Cite **complete** Listing and subsection(s), including any applicable B criteria for 112.00 and explain below.)

Explanation:

☐ Continued in section III

4. ☐ FUNCTIONALLY EQUALS THE LISTING - The child's medically determinable impairment or combination of impairments results in marked limitations in two domains or an extreme limitation in one domain (Explained in Section IIA&B), OR the impairment or combination of impairments is one of the examples cited in POMS DI 25225.060 (20 CFR 416.926a(m)), example #______________ (Explained in Section III.)

5. ☐ IMPAIRMENT OR COMBINATION OF IMPAIRMENTS IS SEVERE, BUT DOES NOT MEET, MEDICALLY EQUAL, OR FUNCTIONALLY EQUAL THE LISTINGS. (Explained in Section(s) IIA&B and, if applicable, III.)

6. ☐ DOES NOT MEET THE DURATION REQUIREMENT-The child's medically determinable impairment(s) is or was of listing-level severity, but is not expected to be, or was not, of listing-level severity for 12 continuous months, and is not expected to result in death. (Explained in Section(s) IIA&B and, if applicable, III.)

7. ☐ OTHER (Specify) ____ (Explained in Section III.)

C. ASSESSMENT OF FUNCTIONING THROUGHOUT SEQUENTIAL EVALUATION

☐ **I affirm, by signing below, that when I evaluated the child's functioning in deciding:**

- If there is a *severe impairment(s);*
- If the impairment(s) *meets or medically equals a listing* (if the listing includes functioning in its criteria); and
- If the impairment(s) *functionally equals the listings;*

I considered the following factors and evidence.

FACTORS

1. How the child's functioning compares to that of children the same age who do not have impairments; i.e., what the child is able to do, not able to do, or is limited or restricted in doing.
2. Combined effects of multiple impairments and the interactive and cumulative effects of an impairment(s) on the child's activities, considering that any activity may involve the integrated use of many abilities. So,
   - A single limitation may be the result of one or more impairments, and
   - A single impairment may have effects in more than one domain.
3. How well the child performs activities with respect to:
   - Initiating, sustaining, and completing activities independently (range of activities, prompting needed, pace of performance, effort needed, and how long the child is able to sustain activities);
   - Extra help needed (e.g., personal, equipment, medications);
   - Adaptations (e.g., assistive devices, appliances);
   - Structured or supportive settings (e.g., home, regular or special classroom), including comparison of functioning in and outside of setting, ongoing signs or symptoms despite setting, amount of support needed to function within regular setting.
4. Child's functioning in unusual settings (e.g., one-to-one, a CE) vs. routine settings (e.g., home, childcare, school).
5. Early intervention and school programs (e.g., school records, comprehensive testing, IEPs, class placement, special education services, accommodations, attendance, participation).
6. Impact of chronic illness, characterized by episodes of exacerbation and remission, and how it interferes with the child's activities over time.
7. Effects of treatment, including adverse and beneficial effects of medications and other treatments, and if they interfere with the child's day-to-day functioning.

EVIDENCE:

For all dispositions, wherever appropriate, I have explained how I considered the medical, early intervention, school/preschool, parent/caregiver, and other relevant evidence that supports my findings, how I weighed medical opinion evidence, evaluated physical and mental symptoms, resolved any material inconsistencies, and weighed evidence when material inconsistencies in the file could not be resolved. I have considered and explained test results in the context of all the other evidence.

The consultant with overall responsibility for the findings in the SSA-538 must complete the first signature line (See DI 25230.001B4). If any additional consultants provided input to these findings, they must also sign in the boxes following.

☐ **THESE FINDINGS COMPLETE THE MEDICAL PORTION OF THE DISABILITY DETERMINATION.**

Consultant with overall responsibility (Sign, print name and specialty)	Date

Additional consultant signature (Sign, print name and specialty)	Date
Additional consultant signature (Sign, print name and specialty)	Date

(continued)

Figure 12–11 **Childhood Disability Evaluation Form (continued)**

II. FUNCTIONAL EQUIVALENCE

Consider functional equivalence when the child's medically determinable impairment(s) is "severe" but does not meet or medically equal a listing. An impairment(s) functionally equals the listings if it results in "marked and severe functional limitations," i.e., the impairment(s) causes "marked" limitations in two domains or an "extreme" limitation in one domain. FOR DEFINITIONS OF "MARKED" AND "EXTREME" see page 5.

Describe and evaluate the child's functioning in all domains; see POMS DI 25225.025-.055 (20 CFR) 416.926a(f)-(l). Then discuss the factors that apply in the child's case and how you evaluated the evidence as described in Section IC above and in POMS DI 25210.001ff. (20 CFR 416.924a). Rate the limitations that result from the child's medically determinable impairment(s).

Check **one** box for **each** domain to indicate the degree of limitation assessed.

A. DOMAIN EVALUATIONS

1. Acquiring and Using Information	no limitation	less than marked	marked	extreme
	☐	☐	☐	☐

☐ Continued in section III

2. Attending and Completing Tasks	no limitation	less than marked	marked	extreme
	☐	☐	☐	☐

☐ Continued in section III

3. Interacting and Relating With Others	no limitation	less than marked	marked	extreme
	☐	☐	☐	☐

☐ Continued in section III

A. DOMAIN EVALUATIONS (continued)

4. Moving About and Manipulating Objects	**no limitation**	**less than marked**	**marked**	**extreme**
	☐	☐	☐	☐

☐ Continued in section III

5. Caring For Yourself	**no limitation**	**less than marked**	**marked**	**extreme**
	☐	☐	☐	☐

☐ Continued in section III

6. Health and Physical Well-Being (Reminder—see additional definitions of marked and/extreme for this domain on page 5)

	no limitation	**less than marked**	**marked**	**extreme**
	☐	☐	☐	☐

☐ Continued in section III

(continued)

Figure 12–11 **Childhood Disability Evaluation Form (continued)**

B. CONCLUSION

Does the impairment or combination of impairments functionally equal the listings?

☐ **Yes — Marked limitation in two domains; findings explained in Section IIA.**

Marked limitation *See* POMS DI 25225.020B (20 CFR 416.296a(e)(2)).

The impairment(s) **interferes seriously** with the child's ability to independently initiate, sustain, or complete domain-related activities. Day-to-day functioning may be seriously limited when the child's impairment(s) limits only one activity or when the interactive and cumulative effects of the child's impairment(s) limit several activities.

- "More than moderate" but "less than extreme" limitation (i.e., the equivalent of functioning we would expect to find on standardized testing with scores that are at least two, but less than three, standard deviations below the mean), or
- Up to attainment of age 3, functioning at a level that is more than one-half but not more than two-thirds of the child's chronological age when there are no standard scores from standardized tests in the case record, or
- At any age, a valid score that is two standard deviations or more below the mean, but less than three standard deviations, on a comprehensive standardized test designed to measure ability or functioning in that domain, and the child's day-to-day functioning in domain-related activities is consistent with that score.

For the **"Health and Physical Well-Being"** domain, we may also find a "marked" limitation if the child is frequently ill or has frequent exacerbations that result in significant, documented symptoms or signs. For purposes of this domain, "frequent" means episodes of illness or exacerbations that occur on an average of 3 times a year, or once every 4 months, each lasting 2 weeks or more. We may also find a "marked" limitation if the child has episodes that:

- occur more often than 3 times in a year or once every 4 months but do not last for 2 weeks, or
- occur less often than an average of 3 times a year or once every 4 months but last longer than 2 weeks, if the overall effect (based on the length of the episode(s) or its frequency) is equivalent in severity.

☐ **Yes — Extreme limitation in one domain; findings explained in Section IIA.**

Extreme limitation *See* POMS DI 25225.020C (20 CFR 416.926a(e)(3)).

The impairment(s) **interferes very seriously** with the child's ability to independently initiate, sustain, or complete domain-related activities. Day-to-day functioning may be very seriously limited when the child's impairment(s) limits only one activity or when the interactive and cumulative effects of the child's impairment(s) limit several activities. "Extreme" describes the worst limitations, but does not necessarily mean a total lack or loss of ability to function.

- "More than marked" limitation (i.e., the equivalent of the functioning we would expect to find on standardized testing with scores that are at least three standard deviations below the mean), or
- Up to attainment of age 3, functioning at a level that is one-half of the child's chronological age or less when there are no standard scores from standardized tests in the case record, or
- At any age, a valid score that is three standard deviations or more below the mean on a comprehensive standardized test designed to measure ability or functioning in that domain, and the child's day-to-day functioning in domain-related activities is consistent with that score.

For the **"Health and Physical Well-Being"** domain we may also find an "extreme" limitation if the child is ill or has frequent exacerbations that result in significant, documented symptoms or signs substantially in excess of the requirements for showing a "marked" limitation. However, if the child has episodes of illness or exacerbations of the impairment(s) that we would rate as "extreme" under this definition, the impairment(s) should meet or medically equal the requirements of a listing in most cases.

☐ **No — Findings explained in Section IIA.**

III. EXPLANATION OF FINDINGS

Use this section:

- To explain any functional equivalence "example" cited in disposition 4;
- To explain disposition 7;
- For any continued explanation of dispositions 1, 3, 5, and 6, or functional equivalence findings that do not fit into Section II;
- To discuss any relevant factors and evidence not explained elsewhere; e.g., how you weighed evidence when material inconsistencies in the file could not be resolved;
- At the discretion of the adjudicative team, to explain disposition 2; to make clear other issues particular to individual cases; to record **all** of the required elements of a rationale rather than on an SSA-4268-U4/C4 per POMS DI 25235.001.

The Privacy and Paperwork Reduction Acts

The Social Security Administration is authorized to collect the information on this form under sections 1614 and 1633 of the Social Security Act. The information on this form is needed to make a decision on a claim for benefits. Completion of this form is required under 20 CFR section 416.924(g). If you do not provide the requested information, we may not be able to make a decision on the child's claim for benefits. Although this information is almost never used for any purposes other than making a determination about the child's claim, the information may be disclosed to another person or governmental agency as follows: (1) to enable a third party or agency to assist Social Security in establishing rights to benefits and/or coverage; (2) to comply with Federal laws requiring the release of information from Social Security Administration records (e.g., to the General Accounting Office and the Department of Veterans Affairs); and (3) to facilitate statistical research and such activities necessary to assure the integrity and improvement of the Social Security Programs (e.g., to the Bureau of the Census and private concerns under the contract to Social Security).

We may also use this information when we match records by computer agencies. Many agencies may use matching programs to find or prove that a person qualifies for benefits paid by the Federal government. The law allows us to do this even if you do not agree to it.

Explanations about these and other reasons why this information you provide may be used or given out are available in Social Security offices. If you want to learn more about this, contact any Social Security office.

This information collection meets the clearance requirements of 44 U.S.C. § 3507, as amended by section 2 of the Paperwork Reduction Act of 1995. You are not required to answer these questions unless we display a valid Office of Management and Budget control number. We estimate that it will take about 25 minutes, on average, to complete this form. This includes the time it will take to read the instructions and complete the appropriate sections.

WHAT IF . . . ? SAMPLE PROBLEMS

WHAT IF . . .

What if the child's treating doctor's report indicated the child's medical condition met the requirements of a listed impairment and identified the listing. Is a Childhood Disability Evaluation Form still needed?

1. No. The form is used only for functional equivalence determinations.
2. Yes. The Childhood Disability Evaluation Form addresses all three ways in which a child could be found disabled.
3. Yes, but only if there are no narrative reports.
4. No. A treating physician never has to fill out a form. We're lucky if we can get a response to anything.

Answer: ***The Childhood Disability Evaluation Form (538) addresses childhood disability generally. It contains a section entitled, Disposition, which specifically asks for the basis of the opinion. It may be completed by a medical expert at the hearing, the state DDS nonexamining physician, a consultative examining physician, or the child's treating physician. Ideally, if it is completed by the treating physician, or other examining doctor, the physician's notes should be attached or made part of the administrative record. Treating physicians often cooperate in their patient's desire for benefits, and it is no less so in the case of children. The correct answer is 2.***

WHAT IF . . .

Which of the following is true?

1. The childhood disability determination is a five-step process, just like that for adults.
2. To be found disabled, the child's disability must meet or medically equal a listed impairment.
3. Functional equivalence concerns whether a child suffers from an impairment that is functionally equivalent to a disabling impairment in an adult.
4. Childhood disability is a means-tested program under Title XVI of the Social Security Act.

Discussion

1. The childhood disability determination is a three-step sequential evaluation process. The first step is identical to step 1 in the adult listings. The second step is similar, asking whether a child suffers from a severe impairment (but measured against the child's ability to function day-to-day, as opposed to engaging in work); the third step is also similar to the adult step, but adds the concept of functional equivalence. The statement is false.
2. In addition to disability predicated on meeting a listing and medically equaling a listing, the childhood disability determination includes the concept of functional equivalence by which a child may be entitled to disability by functionally equalling the listing. Functional equivalence assumes childhood functioning in six domains. If a child is markedly limited in two domains or extremely limited in one domain, the law presumes that such limitation is functionally equivalent to meeting a listed impairment. The statement is false.
3. Functional equivalence considers a child's functioning in six domains and compares the child with the functioning of a child of the same age who does not have impairments. The statement is false.
4. To qualify for childhood disability, the family must meet the means test found under Title XVI of the Social Security Act for those making application for SSI benefits. Even though a child may be disabled, benefits cannot be obtained unless the family meets the means test. The statement is true.

[1]H.R. Conf. Rep. No. 725, 104th Cong., 2d Sess. 328 (1996), reprinted in 1996 U.S. Code Cong. and Ad. News 2649, 2716.
[2]Title 20 C.F.R. § 416.902 (2000).
[3]Title 20 C.F.R. § 404.924(a).
[4]Ibid.
[5]Ibid.
[6]Title 20 C.F.R. § 404.924(a) (2001).
[7]Title 20 C.F.R. § 416.924a(b)(6) (2001).
[8]Title 20 C.F.R. § 416.924a(b)(9) (2001).
[9]Title 20 C.F. R. § 416.924e (2000).
[10]Title 20 C.F.R. § 416.924a(b)(3) (2001).
[11]Ibid.
[12]Title 20 C.F.R. § 416.923 (2000).
[13]Title 20 C.F.R. § 416.924a(b)(4))2001).
[14]Title 20 C.F.R. § 416.924(a) (2001).
[15]Ibid.
[16]Section 1614(a)(3)(C) of The Personal Responsibility and Work Opportunity Reconciliation Act of 1996, 110 Stat. 2105 (1996).
[17]See Title 20 C.F.R. § 906 (2001).
[18]65 *Federal Register*, No. 176, p. 54748 (September 11, 2000).
[19]Title 20 C.F.R. § 416.926a(b)(1) (2001).
[20]at § 416.926a(b)(2) (2001).
[21]Title 20 C.F.R. § 416.926a(d)(2) (2001).
[22]Ibid.
[23]Ibid.
[24]Ibid.
[25]Title 20 C.F.R. § 416.926a(e)(3) (2001).
[26]Ibid.
[27]Ibid.

Chapter Thirteen

Conducting the First Interview in Social Security Disability Appeals

Highlights

- ❑ The first interview with the client

Chris

Chris shuffled the file one more time. Mr. Carson was finally due. Looking at the file the night before, Chris realized the initial interview with Mr. Carson had to track the five-step sequential evaluation process. But there was more to the interview than that. It set the tone for the entire relationship. What Chris told Mr. Carson, and what Mr. Carson told Chris, would be important touchstones. The first interview marks the beginning of a professional relationship—one that could continue over the course of many months, perhaps even a year or more.

And it was up to Chris to get the relationship off on the right foot.

What are the hallmarks of an ongoing professional relationship? Chris knew that above everything else, it was important to establish a good relationship with Mr. Carson, not only for the future of Mr. Carson's case but also for the future of Chris's own practice. If Mr. Carson liked the way he was treated, he would likely recommend Chris to others. Word of mouth is the most common way for professional recommendations to be made. Because of this, Chris knew that the relationship must be carefully nurtured.

But, Chris thought, *first things first.* Turning to a sheaf of forms, Chris plucked the top one, trying to remember what was important.

Front of Your Mind Questions and Considerations, 13.1

Structuring the Initial Interview

Structuring the initial interview with the client requires careful consideration on several levels, both substantive and relational. Substantively, the five-step sequential evaluation process is the foundation for the initial inquiry. Relationally, Chris must establish a rapport with Mr. Carson, laying the groundwork for future communication and trust. Initially, however, a representative must consider the following:

1. Does the individual have a "case?" and
2. Will it be worthwhile to "take the case?"

Both are important legal and professional decisions requiring an initial abbreviated inquiry. The task at this stage is seemingly straightforward, but it requires careful pacing. Enough information must be garnered to make an informed decision, but at the same time limiting the inquiry until the actual decision to represent the claimant is made. Why? Two reasons. First, time is valuable. A key element in any successful practice is time management. As a practice builds, new clients will require time throughout the various stages of case development and presentation. Balancing a variety of activities becomes an integral aspect of daily professional life. Second, the individual's expectations may be raised prematurely. Thus, any initial interview must be prefaced with a simple advisory:

> **Before I decide to take your case and represent you, we've got to go over certain basic information about you and your claim. Until I actually decide to take your case, I am not your representative. We must first explore your claim so that I can make a decision as to whether I can help you.**

Or words to that effect.

It is important, however, that any would-be client understand that the decision to take a case is as important a part of the process as was the initial decision to contact a disability representative. With a potentially new client, the representative's role at the outset is *not* counselor, confessor, or therapist. Many claimants will have many difficulties. The representative may be one of the first, or possibly the *only,* person to spend time with a claimant. The temptation to do more than an initial intake interview is great. And once the critical decision to take a case has been made, it must be determined whether, indeed, there is more that can be done to meet immediate needs. For example, consider whether a client falls into the "dire need" category, that is, someone about to lose his or her home, in need of immediate medical intervention, or faced with another immediate and dire circumstance. If so, contact the Office of Hearings and Appeals and so advise them.[1] This will cause the case to be moved up in priority. Ultimately, the lesson is plain. To be effective, representatives must engage in comprehensive triage. This means obtaining critical identifying and personal information about the client.

Identifying Information

Who is this person seeking help? Information must be gathered. Several obvious questions come to mind, including the following:

1. What is this person's name?
2. What is this person's age?
3. What is this person's address and telephone number?
4. Does this person have education and training?
5. Are there family relationships? and
6. What is this person's Social Security number?

See Figure 13–1.

Obtain at the Minimum

- Identifying information
- Contact information
- Educational background and training, including all certifications, licenses, and so on
- Family information
- Living circumstances
- Employment history

Figure 13–1 **Meeting the Claimant for the Initial Interview**

Name

Simply asking for a person's name is not sufficient. Ask for the name as it originally appeared on the birth certificate. Verify the name with a copy of the birth certificate. Photocopy the driver's license or other state identification, including the Social Security card.

Has the client ever changed names, either by formal court proceeding or marriage? If by court proceeding or marriage, obtain copies of the final court order, or the marriage certificate. Has the client's name changed as a result of divorce or marriage dissolution proceeding? Again, obtain copies of the final divorce decree or dissolution of marriage. Finally, has the client ever been known by or used other names? Include nicknames, pseudonyms, or other, informal designations. Inquire carefully, because later development of evidentiary materials may hinge on asking medical providers for the correct name.

Why go to all this trouble? Too often individuals are known, either formally or informally, by other than their given names. Frequently, medical records are coded by a nickname, pet name, or married name simply because that is how they have been known for many years by a familiar medical office staff. Avoid the dilemma of not having medical records simply because a client uses a pet name.

Age

Verification of a client's age is very important, because the legal determination of disability is keyed, in significant measure, to age. Verify age with a birth certificate and corroborate the apparent age with the Social Security Administration. Ensure that SSA's records are accurate as corroborated by an official birth certificate. This becomes particularly significant with clients who cannot immediately produce records, or who, because of a medical or psychological condition, are not able to be of effective assistance in the prosecution of the claim.

Address and Telephone Number

Although the address and telephone information may seem innocuous, it is important that accurate contact information be obtained and cross-checked with Social Security records. The Social Security Administration currently does not maintain information or initiate contact through e-mail. But nothing prevents a representative from using this form of communication with a client, as appropriate in individual cases.

It is the representative's responsibility to ensure that essential data is accurately maintained, both for office and SSA records. If SSA's records are inaccurate, a client may miss notices, potentially losing the case in the process. Equally important, if office records are inaccurate, the opportunity to be an effective advocate may be lost. Inability to contact a client will result in an ineffectively prepared case and miscommunication with a client. Without a reliable address and telephone number, communication with a client depends entirely on client-initiated contact, which often proves problematic.

Frequent problems arise when an individual lives with a third party—a relative or a friend. How often has the client moved? How long will the client continue to live at the given address? These and similar questions are necessary in order to verify information and impress on the client the importance of maintaining contact. Because disability appeals often extend over long periods of time, an effective plan for ongoing contact should include a strategy for checking the status of a client. For example, send the client a letter every two to four months with a self-addressed, stamped postcard that he or she can return, verifying contact information.

Education and Training

Although a client's educational status may not seem immediately significant (except to interact and communicate), several issues require careful attention. Educational status may reflect the claimant's ability to read, write, engage in simple day-to-day mathematics, or make simple work-related decisions. A claimant who was enrolled in special education classes; or who was designated as having a learning disability; or as being in SED, ED, or MR (severely emotionally disturbed, emotionally disturbed, or mentally retarded) classes will likely present similar, vocationally related issues in his or her past attempts to engage in competitive work. Alternately, these same characteristics may describe the very issues that prevent competitive work at any time.

Thus, it behooves the representative to carefully assess a client's educational background, including all postsecondary vocational training, college, or other vocationally significant activity. This becomes important in terms of discovery, as addressed more fully later.

Family Relationships

Award of benefits to a claimant often implicates the award of auxiliary benefits to family and dependents. It is, therefore, important that family information be complete. *Family* should be widely interpreted to include spouse, whether formal or common law; children, natural or adopted; and all others living under the same roof.

The full names, Social Security numbers, and ages of all family members should be part of the file, together with a brief statement of their relationships to the claimant. Equally important, individuals, friends, or family who assist the claimant in daily activities, personal care, or social functioning should also be noted. Should a hearing be necessary, these persons may be important witnesses. Contact information for friends and family should also be noted.

USING THE FIVE-STEP SEQUENTIAL EVALUATION AS A SUBSTANTIVE BASIS FOR THE INITIAL INTERVIEW

The five-step sequential evaluation should be the starting point for any formulation of initial interview questions. Typically, questions can be grouped into categories mirroring each step of the five-step sequential evaluation (see Figure 13–2).

Step 1

Step 1 in the five-step sequential evaluation process asks if the claimant is engaged in substantial gainful activity, or work. If so, then, from a broad perspective, the public purposes of the Social Security Act are not served by providing benefits. In other words, the purpose of the Social Security Act is to replace lost income required for maintenance and support (daily living needs) if an individual can no longer work. Generally, if an individual *is* working at competitive levels, the public purpose of the Act is moot.

As in all things, however, there are exceptions. The level of activity required for work is characterized by two words: *substantial* and *gainful.* Each of these descriptors provides grist for the initial interview.

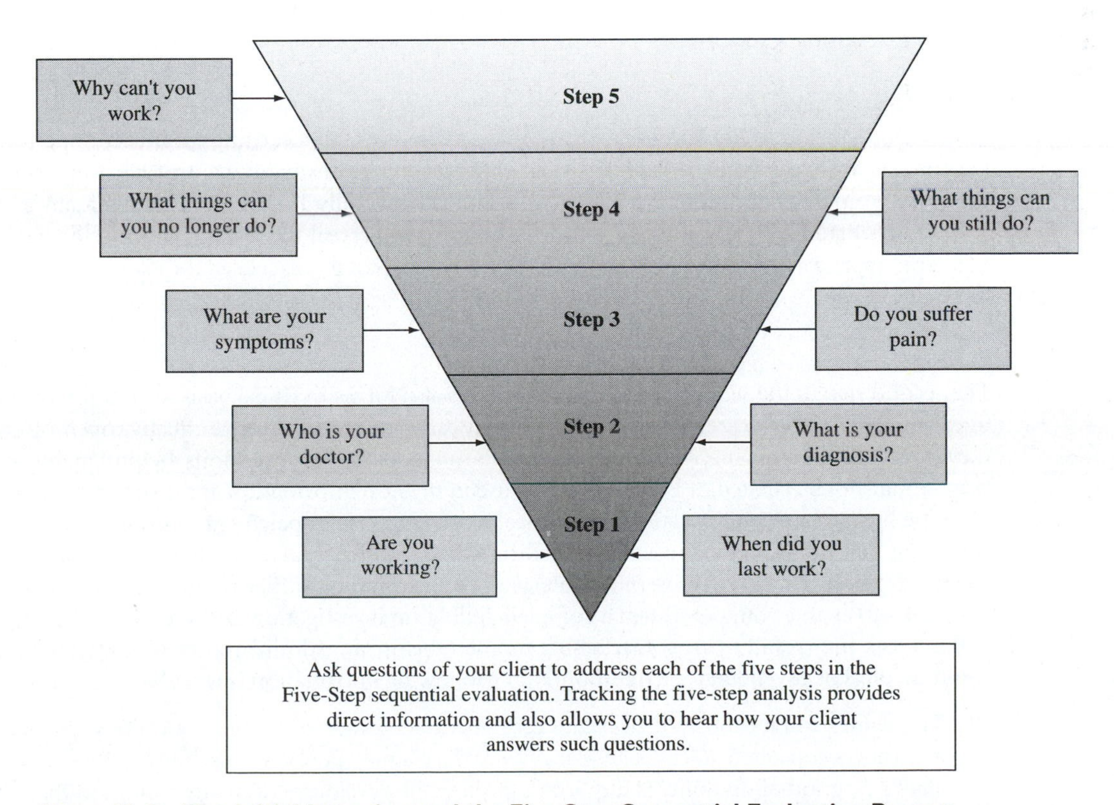

Figure 13–2 **The Initial Interview and the Five-Step Sequential Evaluation Process**

Substantial Activity

Once the client's identifying information is obtained, the first question in any interview must be whether the individual has worked at any point during the period of claimed disability. One might be tempted to simply ask that exact question:

> **"Have you worked since [date]?"**

Many people assume that the word *work* means "full time work" and answer "no," when, in reality, they may have been engaged in part-time work. To make the question meaningful, the term *work* must be explained:

> **"Work means any job you have done, full or part time, regardless of how long you performed the job, or how little or how much money you earned."**

The forthcoming response should address any work, regardless of duration or pay, even though "competitive work" is generally defined by the regulations as work occurring forty hours, five days a week.

Such information is important not only to an analysis of the individual's entitlement to disability at step 1 of the five-step sequential evaluation but also to the case as a whole. Representatives who fail to be so thorough often find themselves in the midst of an administrative proceeding, advocating their client's disability, only to have the client recite for the first time recent part-time work not previously disclosed in prehearing conferences. However, if a client has an issue of "insured status," such that there is a question as to whether he or she is insured under Title II of the Social Security Act, it is vital to have an accurate assessment of past work so that it may be compared with the earnings record maintained by the Social Security Administration.

Although the presence of work itself may not affect entitlement (because it is of insufficient duration or for too little money to constitute substantial gainful activity), the subtle damage to the case as a whole may be significant. Sudden injection of work evidence during the claimed period of disability will, if "discovered" by the Administrative Law Judge, magnify the consequence of such effort. The judge may believe that the claimant deliberately concealed the information and only through artful inquiry disclosed the same.

Voluntary disclosure of work or worklike activity during the claimed period of disability will deprive the disclosure of much of its sting. If the claimant's representative discloses the information, the nature of the work can be described in advance, in effect, "stealing" the judge's thunder and defusing what might have become a case-losing revelation.

Gainful Activity

Part of any description of work must include a discussion of actual earnings. If the work performed was for less than what is deemed to be gainful, the activity may not be disqualifying. In 1999, the earnings limit was increased from $500 per month to $700 per month effective July 1, 1999. If an individual was working but earning less than $700 per month, appropriate inquiry will reveal the level of pay and the periods of work. Similarly, appropriate inquiry must be made even if the level of pay exceeded the allowable monthly earnings limit; now, $780.

Step 2

The second step in the sequential evaluation process also forms a critical basis for inquiry during the initial interview. Asking, "Why are you disabled?" or "Why can't you work?" may be effective opening questions, but they cannot be the only inquiry. Depending on the answers to these questions, helpful medical information may or may not be elicited. It is vital to secure useful medical information at the outset.

The heart of a disability claim is a "medically determinable impairment," meaning a mental or physical condition that has been diagnosed by a medical doctor (a physician), a podiatrist, psychiatrist, or licensed clinical psychologist. An effective initial interview requires getting sufficient information about a client's impairments to enable you to perform a complete follow-up investigation afterward. Incomplete information at the outset may result in an embarrassing moment before an Administrative Law Judge. When inquiring about medical or psychological condition(s), the following information is essential:

1. The names and locations of all health care providers consulted within the claimed period of disability and others consulted at least one year *prior to* the claimed period of disability. Information prior to the claimed period of disability is important to show the development of any condition that ultimately led to an inability to work.

2. Any and all hospital or clinic admissions for same time period;
3. Any and all hospital or clinic treatments, regardless of admission for the same period;
4. Any and all emergency room (ER) treatments; and
5. The names and locations of any and all mental health providers (including counselors, ministers, or groups, such as AA, Narc-Anon, etc.).

In obtaining such information it is important not to assume anything. Ask for medical information on several different occasions. Often, clients assume you want only information about doctors who have treated them for conditions that they (the clients) think are disabling. As a result, the client may only reveal the doctors' names that the client believes relate to his or her "disabling" condition, not all the doctors he or she has actually seen. In so doing, the client interposes an unconscious filter—one the representative must bypass.

Defeating the client's filter is relatively straightforward. Although asking several times about the names of doctors may ferret out some or even all doctors, it does not tap into the client's memory as effectively as simply walking the client back through his or her life step by step. Starting with the most recent treatment, ask the client about each of his or her doctors to a point at least one year before the alleged onset of disability. This technique often jars a client's memory, bringing to the surface information about all treatments, regardless of the client's unintended filter.

Step 3

The third step in the sequential evaluation process also provides a basis for inquiry during the initial interview. Although obtaining a complete record of medical treatment is important, not all ailments are equal. For many, a singular condition overarches all others. If, on initial assessment, a client's condition appears to meet or closely approximate the requisite criteria for a listed medical impairment, it is important to obtain sufficient information to document the history and severity of the condition. Thus, it is important to clearly understand the nature and scope of each of the client's impairments, his or her symptoms, and the resulting limitations of function. This information becomes a template by which to focus direct or expert testimony during a hearing.

Step 4

The fourth step in the sequential evaluation process requires an assessment of functional capability. Inquiry must be tailored to an understanding of the limitations of function suffered by the client as a result of his or her medical or psychological condition(s). Functional limitations fall into two basic categories:

1. Exertional limitations of function; and
2. Nonexertional limitations of function.

Obviously, a client cannot simply be asked to list his or her exertional or nonexertional limitations. He or she probably will have no idea what this means. Instead, the representative should keep in mind an independent conception of the nature and scope of exertional and nonexertional limitations of function, such that the representative, and not the client, categorizes the elicited information.

This requires that the representative understand (1) the nature of a limitation of function generally; (2) the type of limitations commonly associated with a variety of disease processes, both physical and mental; and (3) the effect, generally, of differing types of limitations on the ability to engage in competitive activities.

Each bodily system has potential, in its impairment, to affect an individual's ability to perform competitive activity. It becomes incumbent on the representative to understand the individual as well as the synergistic effect of all such impairments.

Exertional limitations restrict an individual's ability to

- ❑ Sit;
- ❑ Stand;
- ❑ Walk;
- ❑ Lift;
- ❑ Carry;
- ❑ Reach;
- ❑ Push; and
- ❑ Pull.

Nonexertional limitations are restrictions that do not involve direct gross-motor function. They include the following:

- ❑ Limitations as a result of mental or emotional disorders;
- ❑ The effect of pain;
- ❑ The effect of medication (side effects);
- ❑ Limited fine-motor manipulation (use of the fingers);
- ❑ Limited use of the senses (sight, sound, touch, and feel);
- ❑ General fatigue;
- ❑ Reduced concentration; and
- ❑ Other, similar effects.

Initial and follow-up interview and counseling sessions should, therefore, necessarily focus on the individual's capability as expressed in terms of exertional and nonexertional limitations of function.

Step 5

The fifth step in the sequential evaluation process asks simply whether there are other, less demanding jobs the individual could perform, given the inability to perform past relevant work. Thus, if the administrative law judge determines that a client cannot return to past relevant work, the only remaining question is whether there are other, less demanding competitive jobs that can be performed.

For a case to succeed, the Administrative Law Judge must conclude that there are not significant numbers of jobs within the national or regional economies that the individual can perform. This requires an exploration not only of those limitations affecting a client's ability to perform past work but also other limitations. The goal is to exclude all competitive work. This requires a comprehensive examination of each impairment, and extrapolating, exploring, and ultimately documenting the resulting limitations of function.

SUMMARY

The initial interview is a multifaceted endeavor, challenging in its breadth. It is here that the foundation for the case is laid. To be effective, lead the client through a medical–legal dialogue designed to elicit information tailored to the five-step sequential evaluation process. The initial interview is the foundation on which the balance of the case is built. Evidence developed as a result of the initial interview will accumulate and broaden the case as time goes by.

Once the foundation is built, construct the case. Devise a legal theory for recovery. Specifically, at what point in the sequential evaluation process does the client become entitled to benefits? Is there an alternate theory?

Once it is determined at which point the client should win, set out to *persuade* the Administrative Law Judge that this theory is correct. A successful presentation demands a comprehensive understanding of the client's medical condition, daily activities, family relationships, and social life. The representative's job is to reduce the myriad facts into a cohesive legal theory, incorporating relevant medical, social, and life activity facts into a uniform theory of disability.

BACK TO CHRIS

Regulations, thought Chris. *I need to review the regulations. In order to really understand this process and conduct an effective interview, that's where I need to start. But,* Chris admitted, *I'm really nervous. What if I come across like a know-it-all? Or, worse, an incompetent?*

Standing, Chris strode to the window.

"Something up?"

Chris turned. It was Steve. "Just worried about the interview with Mr. Carson."

"What's to worry?"

"You know. Going over all this stuff. I'm afraid I'll sound like a stuffed shirt."

"Look, Chris. There's no magic to this process. You have to give it some thought, be prepared, and most importantly, be yourself. Don't try to be someone you're not."

"Aren't there special classes or techniques for interviewing?"

"Well, sure. And you can take courses. But most importantly, you have to be prepared. And only you can do that."

"I understand," Chris said thoughtfully. "But, could you give me a little insight into interviewing techniques?"

"Sure," Steve said. "Let's go to the library."

A TRIP TO THE HARD DRIVE, 13.1

Preparation is the keyword for any interview. If you don't know the course, it's difficult to plan the journey. The first step in preparing for a client interview in a Social Security disability appeals case is understanding the applicable regulations in the Code of Federal Regulations (CFR). Clearly, all the regulations are important. Different sections become more important depending on the nature of a case and the issues addressed. Certain regulations, however, are fundamental to any case. These regulations form the substantive foundation for any disability claim. They include the following:

- Title 20 C.F.R. § 404.1520. This regulation sets forth the "steps in evaluating disability." In assessing the legal question of disability, the law requires that "all evidence" be considered.[2] Section 404.1520(b) addresses *step 1;* Section 404.1520(c) sets forth *step 2;* Section 404.1520(d) describes *step 3;* Section 404.1520(e) outlines *step 4;* and Section 404.1520(f) sets forth *step 5.*
- Title 20 C.F.R. § 1520a describes the evaluation process for *mental impairments.* This assessment not only requires proof of the existence of the impairment but also of its severity. Thus, as we shall see later, mental impairments require diagnosis (applying the "A criteria") as well as an assessment of how the impairment actually affects the individual. This analysis embraces the "B criteria." The B criteria requires an evaluation of the effect of the impairment on *activities of daily living; social functioning; concentration, persistence, and pace;* as well as *notation of the number of instances the individual may have decompensated on the job as a result of the impairment.* Thus, these areas also form instances of specific inquiry during the initial interview.
- Title 20 C.F.R. § 1529 discusses evaluation of symptoms, including pain. Pain is evaluated in terms of *intensity* and *persistence,* assessing both issues in light of how these symptoms "limit your capacity for work."[3]

It is not enough to simply have a list of regulations on hand. A representative must become familiar with the regulations prior to conducting client interviews. Failure to do so may impact a representative's conception of a client's difficulty. After reviewing the regulations and gaining a basic understanding of the issues central to the five-step sequential evaluation process, construct a set of basic questions designed as prompts for the interview. A sample questionnaire might look something like the sample interview worksheet in Figure 13–3.

Once the interview is completed, the representative decides whether to accept the case. With experience, this decision will be made as the initial meeting with the prospective client concludes. To begin, however, it is important to thoughtfully consider the issues and the nature of the claim. Only when the facts are certain and the applicable legal theory on which an appeal will be based is established, should the case be accepted. If the facts are uncertain and there is no reasonable assurance that they can be developed sufficiently, the case should not be accepted.

Similarly, if, given the facts, it is unlikely that the claimant will prevail, because the initial decision denying disability was correct, the case should be turned down. Conversely, if philosophically you believe the individual is entitled to a hearing with representation, proceed with a case, provided it is done so competently and with full regard for the obligation to deal fairly with the Administrative Law Judge through the course of the proceeding.

Interview Worksheet

Part 1 Essential Information

Name of claimant: ______________________

Date of interview: ______________________

Claimant's SSN: ______________________

Claimant's address: ______________________

Claimant's telephone: ______________________

1. *Message:* ______________________

Other contact information: ______________________

Claimant's marital status: ______________________

- ❑ *Spouse:* ______________________
- ❑ *Children:* ______________________

Part II Information about the Claim

Type of claim: ______________________

Diagnosis (related by claimant): ______________________

Claimant's doctor(s): ______________________

Last full-time work: ______________________

Company: ______________________

Last part-time work: ______________________

- ❑ *Company:* ______________________

Claimant says he/she cannot work because: ______________________

Figure 13–3 **Sample Interview Worksheet**

Part III Information Keyed to the Five-Step Sequential Analysis

Step 1: Current work? ______________________________

Work during the alleged period of disability?

____

____

Step 2: Diagnosis: ______________________________

❑ Date of diagnosis ______________________________

❑ Prognosis ______________________________

Doctor(s): ______________________________

Hospital(s): ______________________________

Other information: ______________________________

____

Step 3: Medical listings: ______________________________

Listing considered: ______________________________

Documented symptoms: ______________________________

Step 3 1/2: Residual functional capacity
Claimant's allegations (physical):

❑ Sit: ______________________________

❑ Stand: ______________________________

❑ Walk: ______________________________

❑ Lift: ______________________________

❑ Carry: ______________________________

❑ Reach: ______________________________

❑ Handle: ______________________________

❑ Finger/feel: ______________________________

❑ See: ______________________________

❑ Hear: ______________________________

(continued)

Figure 13–3 Sample Interview Worksheet (continued)

Step 3 1/2: Residual functional capacity
Claimant's allegations (physical): (continued)

Claimant's allegations (mental/emotional):

- ❑ Depression? ______________________
- ❑ Anxiety? ______________________
- ❑ Cognition/memory? ______________________
- ❑ Other (describe): ______________________

Claimant's allegations of nonexertional limitations:

- ❑ Medication side effects: ______________________
- ❑ Fatigue/lie down: ______________________
- ❑ Elevate feet/legs: ______________________
- ❑ Other effects: ______________________

Objective evidence of physical restrictions/limitations:

- ❑ Doctor(s): ______________________
- ❑ Hospital(s): ______________________
- ❑ Other: ______________________

Objective evidence of mental/emotional restrictions/limitations:

- ❑ Doctors(s): ______________________
- ❑ Hospital(s): ______________________
- ❑ Other: ______________________

Objective evidence of nonexertional limitations:

- ❑ Doctor(s): ______________________
- ❑ Hospital(s): ______________________
- ❑ Other: ______________________

Step 4: Past relevant work

List all claimant's past work ______________________
(past 15 years) ______________________
____
____

Figure 13–3 (continued)

Job/Position	Description/exertional/skill level (Circle one of each)
	Sedentary/light/medium/heavy; skilled/semiskilled/unskilled
	Sedentary/light/medium/heavy; skilled/semiskilled/unskilled
	Sedentary/light/medium/heavy; skilled/semiskilled/unskilled
	Sedentary/light/medium/heavy; skilled/semiskilled/unskilled
	Sedentary/light/medium/heavy; skilled/semiskilled/unskilled
	Sedentary/light/medium/heavy; skilled/semiskilled/unskilled
	Sedentary/light/medium/heavy; skilled/semiskilled/unskilled
	Sedentary/light/medium/heavy; skilled/semiskilled/unskilled
	Sedentary/light/medium/heavy; skilled/semiskilled/unskilled
	Sedentary/light/medium/heavy; skilled/semiskilled/unskilled

Objective evidence that claimant cannot return to past work:

____

____

Step 5: Other less demanding work.

Why can't claimant do other, less demanding work?

____

____

____

____

Other considerations (including representative payee; children, etc.)

____

____

BACK TO CHRIS

"Time out!" Chris yelled, standing away from the desk. "How do I know when to take a case and when not to?"

A TRIP TO THE HARD DRIVE, 13.2

Choosing to accept a claimant's case is a matter of professional judgment. Proper exercise of that judgment depends in large measure on the information that develops about the claimant and his or her impairment(s) and limitation(s) of function. Failing to conduct a thorough initial interview will result in a corresponding impairment in subsequent information gathering.

Proper exercise of professional judgment requires engaging in weighing of the evidence at each step of the sequential analysis. The goal is to make an informed decision whether to accept the case. (See Figure 13–4). For example, if the claimant is working full time, and has never stopped working, even though he or she is claiming disability, it may be properly concluded that he or she is not a candidate for an award of benefits. However, should the facts indicate that he or she is working, but only on a part-time basis, or is employed by a family member who makes no real vocational demands, the facts may indicate proceeding with the case. In the end, each case stands on its own merits. In exercising professional judgment, evaluate the likelihood of a favorable decision in light of the following:

1. The claimant's work or worklike activity during the claimed period of disability;
2. The claimant's diagnosis;
3. The claimant's prognosis;
4. The claimant's daily activities, as indicative of a lowered capability to perform competitive work;
5. The cooperative nature of the claimant's physician(s) in providing information; and
6. The claimant's ability to cooperate and participate in the development of the case.

Lacking information in one or more of the foregoing categories may require an alternative plan for representation or may ultimately require declining representation. Each case must be assessed on its own merits. No special formula for success exists, yet the key, as in other areas of the law, is preparation. Still, questions may yet arise.

- ❑ The claimant's work or worklike activity during the claimed period of disability
- ❑ Claimant's diagnosis
- ❑ Claimant's prognosis
- ❑ Claimant's daily activities
- ❑ Claimant's cooperation and participation in prosecution of the claim
- ❑ The medical evidence, including whether the claimant's doctors are cooperative

Figure 13–4 **Issues to Consider When Deciding to Accept a Case**

WHAT IF . . . ? SAMPLE PROBLEMS

WHAT IF . . .

What if your client is unable to effectively communicate, such that you cannot clearly understand what medical or psychological treatment he or she has actually received? What is the best solution?

1. Give up, drop the case.
2. Hire a private investigator.
3. Find and speak with a family member or friend to obtain the information.
4. Log onto the Internet and do your own investigation.

Discussion

Doing your own investigation, whether by "private eye" or "Internet" is not the most effective (or cost efficient) method for discovering this information. Instead, connect with close family members or friends who know your client. Ask them to tell you about:

1. Their interaction with your client's life; and
2. Their perception of your client's medical problems. Sometimes this person will also be the one taking your client to his or her medical appointments.

Answer: 3

WHAT IF . . .

What if your client has no recent medical treatment (within the alleged period of disability) but complains of seemingly serious medical problems? What is the best solution?

1. Engage in an ad hoc medical examination yourself (taking vital signs, height, weight, etc.) and prepare your own report.
2. Request medical examinations be conducted by the Social Security Administration, identifying specific testing to be conducted, such as consultative examinations.
3. Pay for medical examinations yourself.
4. Decline to accept the case.

Discussion

Understanding the nature, extent, and severity of your client's medical condition is critical to successful representation. If your client has not received treatment, it may be because he or she has insufficient financial resources.

If there is a "reasonable basis" in the record to support further medical investigation or testing, you may request a consultative examination from the Office of Hearings and Appeals (if your client's case is at that level).

Examinations conducted prior to a hearing are termed *prehearing CEs;* examinations conducted after a hearing are referred to as *posthearing CEs.* Some judges readily order consultative examinations on request, whereas others require a definitive showing of their necessity and are unwilling to simply test without substantial evidence of an impairment.

When making a request, always do so in writing, and verify that your request is "of record." Doing so, creates a record and protects the issue in the event of a subsequent appeal.

Answer: 2

WHAT IF . . .

What if you cannot verify your client's work history, or your client is not a good historian and cannot credibly recount his or her employment? What is the best solution?

1. Hire a hypnotist to jog your client's memory.
2. Fake it.
3. Disregard any past work.
4. Contact the Office of Hearings and Appeals or the SSA field office and request an earnings record.

Discussion

Whether your case is before the state agency or the Office of Hearings and Appeals, you may request that an earnings record be provided. Generally, earnings records come in two forms:

1. A SEQY is a summary record that provides earnings on a year-by-year basis.
2. A DEQY is a detailed earnings record, which also provides the name of individual employers during each year of employment.

This information is far more desirable than anything else you may develop because it represents the agency's own records.

Answer: 4

---

[1]The contact should be in writing to the assigned judge, or, if no judge has yet been assigned, to the Hearing Office director.
[2]Title 20 C.F.R. § 404.1520.
[3]Title 20 C.F.R. § 404.1529(c)(1).

14

Chapter Fourteen

The Hearing Process

Highlights

- ❑ The hearing process
- ❑ Presenting your case

Chris

"That's it? We're done! I'm now ready?" Chris was almost jumping with excitement.

"Not quite," Steve cautioned. "Going through a hearing involves more than simply knowing the law. You have to know the procedure, as well."

"I know. But, in talking about the law, you gave me a lot of good tips and insights into the hearings process as well."

"Thanks, Chris. It's all tied up together in some ways, but, it's still important to touch on the highlights."

"OK, Steve, I'm ready!"

Front of Your Mind Questions and Considerations, 14.1

Introduction

The administrative hearing before an Administrative Law Judge is the most significant step throughout the entire process. Although there has been some experimentation with face-to-face encounters between claimants and disability examiners (DEs) at the state level, such programs are not the norm. Generally, most disability claims are reviewed at the state level without face-to-face interaction, and, often, without any contact at all. It is a paper review—the DE, functioning under the medical supervision of a doctor or psychologist, makes a five-step analysis on the paper record alone. Issues, such as pain, credibility, and so forth, are measured against the claimant's medical condition as gleaned from the written record. Sometimes, the Disability Determination Service (DDS) will decide a consultative examination is needed and send the claimant for a medical examination but will not speak with the claimant afterward. Instead, the CE's report becomes another report for consideration in the paper record.

When an appeal is taken to a Federal Administrative Law Judge by filing a Request for Hearing, a face-to-face proceeding is the norm. Note, however, that a hearing, once requested, can be waived. If it is waived, the claimant is not waiving an appeal but simply the face-to-face oral proceeding.[1] An Administrative Law Judge still reviews the file, evidentiary materials can be submitted, and arguments can be made in writing. To waive the hearing, simply check the appropriate box on the Request for Hearing form, as shown in Figure 14–1.

Hearings before federal Administrative Law Judges are generally governed by the Administrative Procedure Act (APA), which governs all on-the-record adjudications. A hearing that is on the record is recorded verbatim. A hearing file is maintained containing enumerated exhibits, all of which constitute the record on which the decision is made. However, the term *on the record* is sometimes bandied about among insiders when referring to a decision made *without* an oral hearing. In this usage, the term *on the record* means "on the written record alone." The use is shorthand reference for a decision made without need of a hearing.

Proceedings before courts are attended by formal rules of evidence and procedure. This is not the case for proceedings before Administrative Law Judges in Social Security appeals. Although the courts constitute the judicial branch of government, administrative hearings before Federal Administrative Law Judges take place within the executive branch. Unless promulgated by regulation, the executive branch agency may elect to dispense with rules that are otherwise the norm in a court proceeding. In an effort to maintain a user-friendly atmosphere, the Social Security Administration has not promulgated formal rules of proceeding in such hearings.

The original concept underlying these proceedings was that few people would be represented. It was thought that the judge would undertake the role of neutral decision maker, assist the claimant in ensuring that all materials were obtained necessary for a fair decision, and proceed in an informal fashion. Indeed, many still describe present-day proceedings as "informal" and, in doing so, mistake the meaning of the word. In jurisprudential terms, "informal" properly refers to the fact that no formal rules of evidence and procedure govern these administrative proceedings. Many claimants and their representatives operate on the incorrect assumption that "informal" means

- Shoot from the hip;
- Defer the gathering of evidence to the judge after the hearing;
- Dress casually;
- Treat hearing office staff with disdain;
- Come ill prepared;
- Come unorganized; and
- Defer actual representation to the judge.

Each of these assumptions or actions is incorrect. The fact that these proceedings are closed proceedings—closed to the public—and are not attended with formal rules of evidence and procedure is no reason to be casual, or take the hearing process less seriously.

RULES

Administrative hearings in which an Administrative Law Judge presides before the Social Security Administration are governed by federal regulations. A few key principles apply:

- The Administrative Law Judge decides when the evidence is presented and when the issues will be discussed (Title 20 C.F.R. § 404.944);
- The hearing is open to the parties and others the Administrative Law Judge considers necessary and proper (Title 20 C.F.R. § 404.944);
- The Administrative Law Judge accepts as evidence any documents that are material to the issues (Title 20 C.F.R. § 404.944);
- The Administrative Law Judge may reopen the hearing at any time before making a decision to accept new and material evidence (Title 20 C.F.R. § 404.944);
- The claimant and/or representative may appear to state the case before the Administrative Law Judge or present written argument (Title 20 C.F.R. § 404.949);
- The claimant and/or representative may appear to present evidence before the Administrative Law Judge and present witnesses in support of the claimant's position; or, may wave personal appearance before the judge (Title 20 C.F.R. § 404.950);
- The rules of evidence normally applicable in a court are not applicable (Title 20 C.F.R. § 404.950);
- A subpoena may be issued by the Administrative Law Judge, either on his or her own motion (*sua sponte*) or at the request of a party, with at least five days written notice before the noticed hearing (Title 20 C.F.R. § 404.950[d]);

SOCIAL SECURITY ADMINISTRATION
OFFICE OF HEARINGS AND APPEALS

Form Approved
OMB No. 0960-0269

REQUEST FOR HEARING BY ADMINISTRATIVE LAW JUDGE
[Take or mail original and all copies to your local Social Security Office]

PRIVACY ACT NOTICE ON REVERSE SIDE OF FORM.

1. CLAIMANT	2. WAGE EARNER, IF DIFFERENT	3. SOC. SEC. CLAIM NUMBER	4. SPOUSE's CLAIM NUMBER

5. I REQUEST A HEARING BEFORE AN ADMINISTRATIVE LAW JUDGE. I disagree with the determination made on my claim because:

An Administrative Law Judge of the Office of Hearings and Appeals will be appointed to conduct the hearing or other proceedings in your case. You will receive notice of the time and place of a hearing at least 20 days before the date set for a hearing.

6. If you have additional evidence to submit check the following block and complete the statement: ☐

I have additional evidence to submit from (name and address of source): ______________________

(Please submit it to the Social Security Office within 10 days. Attach an additional sheet if you need more space.)

7. Check one of the blocks:

☐ I wish to appear at a hearing.

☐ I do not wish to appear and I request that a decision be made based on the evidence in my case. (Complete Waiver Form HA-4608)

You have a right to be represented at the hearing. If you are not represented but would like to be, your Social Security Office will give you a list of legal referral and service organizations. (If you are represented and have not done so previously, complete and submit form SSA-1696 (Appointment of Representative).)

[You should complete No. 8 and your representative (if any) should complete No. 9. If you are represented and your representative is not available to complete this form, you should also print his or her name, address, etc. in No. 9.]

8. (CLAIMANT'S SIGNATURE)			9. (REPRESENTATIVE'S SIGNATURE/NAME)		
ADDRESS			(ADDRESS) ☐ ATTORNEY; ☐ NON ATTORNEY;		
CITY	STATE	ZIP CODE	CITY	STATE	ZIP CODE
DATE	AREA CODE AND TELEPHONE NUMBER		DATE	AREA CODE AND TELEPHONE NUMBER	

TO BE COMPLETED BY SOCIAL SECURITY ADMINISTRATION-ACKNOWLEDGMENT OF REQUEST FOR HEARING

10.
Request for Hearing RECEIVED for the Social Security Administration on ______________ by: ______________

(TITLE) ADDRESS

11. Was the request for hearing received within 65 days of the reconsidered determination?
☐ YES ☐ NO

If no is checked, attach claimant's explanation for delay; and attach copy of appointment notice, letter, or other pertinent material or information in the Social Security Office.

12. Claimant not represented -
☐ list of legal referral and service organizations provided

13. Interpreter needed -
☐ enter language (including sign language): ______________

14.
Check one: ☐ Initial Entitlement Case
☐ Disability Cessation Case
☐ Other Postentitlement Case

16.
HO COPY SENT TO: ______________ HO on ______________
☐ CF Attached: ☐ Title II; ☐ Title XVI; or
☐ Title II CF held in FO to establish CAPS ORBIT; or
☐ CF requested ☐ Title II; ☐ Title XVI
(Copy of teletype or phone report attached)

17.
CF COPY SENT TO: ______________ HO on ______________
☐ CF Attached: ☐ Title II; ☐ Title XVI
☐ Other Attached: ______________

15.
Check claim type(s):
☐ RSI only ----------(RSI)
☐ Title II Disability-worker or child----------(DIWC)
☐ Title II Disability-widow(er) only----------(DIWW)
☐ SSI Aged only----------(SSIA)
☐ SSI Blind only----------(SSIB)
☐ SSI Disability only ----------(SSID)
☐ SSI Aged/Title II ----------(SSAC)
☐ SSI Blind/Title II ----------(SSBC)
☐ SSI Disability/Title II ----------(SSDC)
☐ HI Entitlement ----------(HIE)
☐ Other-Specify: (______________)

FORM **HA-501-U5** (5-1996) EF (7-2000)
Issue old stock

CLAIMS FOLDER

Figure 14–1 **Request for Hearing before an Administrative Law Judge**

- Subpoenaed witnesses receive the same fees and mileage as witnesses before the federal courts (Title 20 C.F.R. § 404.950);
- A written record of the proceeding is retained by the Administrative Law Judge (Title 20 C.F.R. § 404.951);
- The Administrative Law Judge may consolidate (combine) multiple claims in one proceeding (Title 20 C.F.R. § 404.952);
- The decision of the Administrative Law Judge shall be in writing (Title 20 C.F.R. § 404.953);
- A Request for Hearing may be dismissed by the claimant at any time before a hearing decision is mailed (Title 20 C.F.R. § 404.957);
- Failure to appear at a hearing may result in dismissal (though usually after an order to show cause why the hearing was missed) (Title 20 C.F.R. § 404.957);
- Prehearing and posthearing conferences may be held with seven days written notice (Title 20 C.F.R. § 404.961);
- Twenty days written notice of a hearing is required (Title 20 C.F.R. § 404.938); and
- A motion may be made to disqualify the Administrative Law Judge "if he or she is prejudiced or partial with respect to any party, or has an interest in the matter pending for decision" (Title 20 C.F.R. § 404.940).

These rules embody time-honored principles of fair play and justice. In many respects, the absence of formal rules of proceeding is designed to assist the claimant by preventing what is perceived to be unnecessary entanglement in procedural matters and encouraging an equitable process not bound by formal requirements. Above all else, however, these proceedings are governed by essential standards of fundamental fairness and due process.

POSSIBLE OUTCOMES

The outcome of a Request for Hearing does not necessarily depend on whether an oral hearing is held. Essentially, the outcomes are as follows:

- "Fully favorable" decision. A fully favorable decision is one in which the claimant is entirely successful on appeal and is found entitled to everything originally requested.
- "Partially favorable" decision. A partially favorable decision is one in which the claimant receives part of what he or she originally claimed. Usually this is as a result of an "amended" onset date (where the claimant agrees to amend the original claimed date of disability) or a "later onset date" (where the judge finds that the claimant is entitled to disability but at a later onset date).
- "Partial denial." In a partial denial decision, the judge determines that the claimant is not entitled to everything originally claimed, and the claimant has not voluntarily amended his or her onset date.
- "Denial." In a denial decision, the judge determines that the claim should be denied.

See Figure 14–2.

On appeal from the Administrative Law Judge, a case may be remanded by the Appeals Council, to be reheard by the same Administrative Law Judge or another Administrative Law Judge. The earlier decision may be fully or partially vacated and a new hearing held.

If a claimant has filed an earlier claim, which may have been denied, it is possible, within certain time constraints, to revisit that earlier claim in the context of a new claim. Note that nothing prevents successive filing of claims, except that once a period of time has been "adjudicated" the doctrine of "administrative finality" prevents repeated examination of a claim already once denied. The exception to this is, of course, appeal through the normal course or a motion to reopen the earlier determination or decision.

A motion to reopen an earlier decision or determination may be brought under limited circumstances as set forth at Title 20 C.F.R. § 404.988. "Good cause" for reopening is defined at Title 20 C.F.R. § 404.989. Under § 404.988 a prior determination or decision may be reopened:

- Within twelve months of the date of the initial DDS notice *for any reason;*
- Within four years of the date of the initial DDS notice for *good cause;*
- At any time if the decision was obtained by fraud or similar fault;
- At any time if another person files a claim that adversely affects the original claim;
- At any time if a person once thought deceased is found alive; or
- At any time if a person was supposed deceased but that fact could not be proved, and proof later arises.

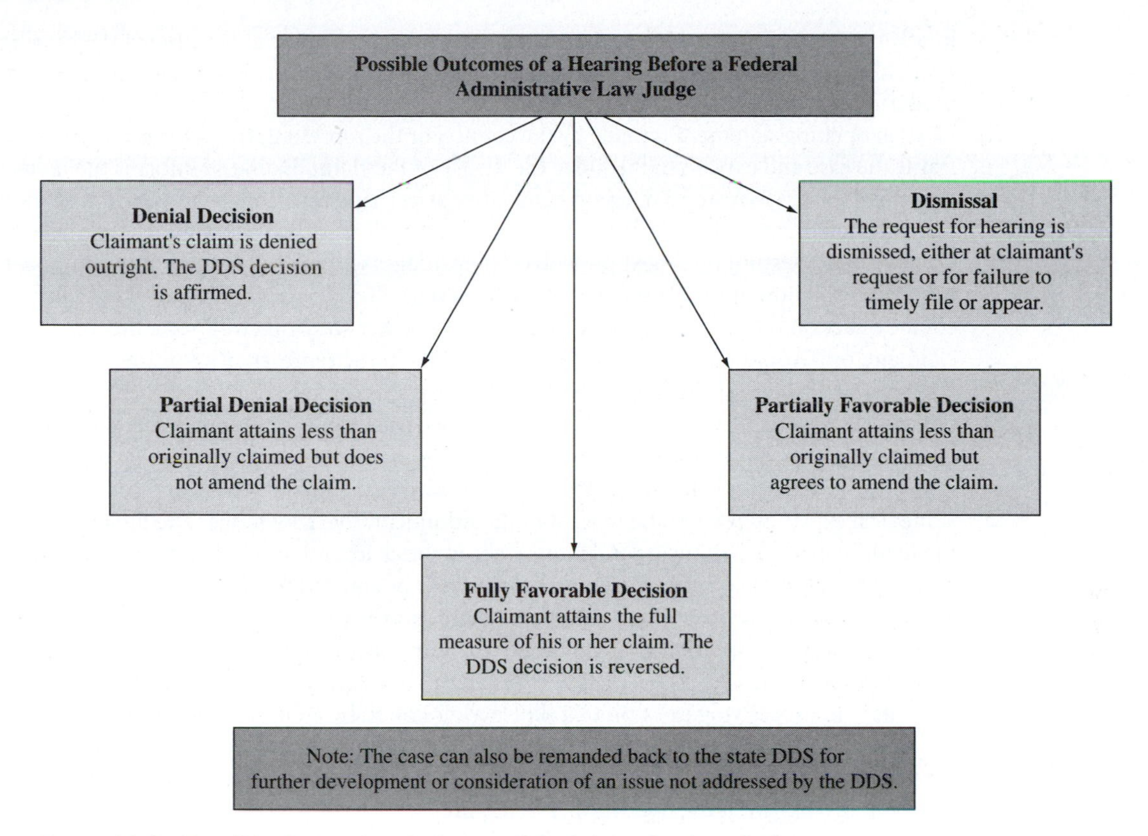

Figure 14–2 **Possible Outcomes before an Administrative Law Judge**

Good cause is generally found where "new and material evidence is provided; where a clerical error in computation has occurred; or where the evidence clearly shows on its face that an error was made."[2]

A typical scenario in which the issue of reopening might arise occurs when a claim is made by a claimant without representation. On denial by the state agency (DDS), no appeal is taken to the Federal Administrative Law Judge. Two years later, a representative is retained and, on filing, learns of the earlier claim. New evidence is obtained that offers insight into the claimant's condition during the earlier period. At the hearing, the representative might properly ask not only for a favorable decision on the current claim but for reopening of the earlier case as well. If it is successful, the application date is taken to be the *earlier,* not the later, date.

The significance of this is that the claimant is able to claim Title II benefits no more than one year retroactive from the date of the filing. If that date is moved back in time, there is an increase in back-due benefits (and, correspondingly, attorney's and representative's fees). In a Title XVI claim, benefits flow from the date of the application. If it is reopened, the application date of the earlier claim is deemed to be the operative date, also resulting in an increase in back-due benefits.

THE COURSE OF A "NORMAL" HEARING

A typical hearing unfolds in the following order:

- The introduction of the hearing typically begins with an introductory or explanatory statement from the judge directed to the claimant explaining the nature of the proceeding and outlining the issues to be addressed;
- The exhibits are then admitted into the administrative record. Unlike court proceedings, all new documents are submitted at the beginning of the hearing, marked, made a part of the administrative record, and need not be "sponsored," because there are no formal rules of evidence. (Many judges request new exhibits be submitted well before the hearing—usually ten days—and may not look

kindly on significant numbers of new documents being submitted at the time of the hearing itself—particularly if there is a medical expert present who must then review the new documents prior to rendering any opinion.)

- Next an opening statement is made by the counsel or the representative. This is the opportunity to frame the case and explain to the judge the theory of the claim. Doing so informs the judge of the claim (e.g., a step 3 or step 5 decision in an adult or perhaps functional equivalency in a child). The opening statement also serves to inform the judge that the case has been prepared thoroughly.
- The claimant's testimony is next presented. Many judges will ask the representative to undertake the initial examination of the claimant. Others, however, will chart that course for themselves. The proper course of action is to politely inquire of the judge whether she or he will make the initial inquiry of the claimant, or, "Would Her Honor prefer I do so?" Even if the representative makes the initial inquiry, the usual practice is for the judge to follow up with clarifying questions.
- Other witnesses are then presented. Usually the judge will defer to the representative who brings additional witnesses, allowing the representative to begin the inquiry, because the judge may have little idea why the witness is being presented. Nothing prevents the judge from asking clarifying questions.
- A medical expert appears at the request of the Administrative Law Judge. The judge usually examines the medical expert, making general inquiry about the claimant's documented impairment(s) and eliciting the expert's opinion whether a listing is met or equaled. Due process (fairness) demands the representative be given an opportunity for examination as well.
- A vocational expert appears at the request of the Administrative Law Judge. The judge usually examines the vocational expert, eliciting the expert's opinion about the nature of the claimant's past relevant work, specifying exertion and skill level; followed by an inquiry about transferable skills; and ending in a series of hypothetical questions in which various limitations are expressed as part of the claimant's (hypothetical) residual functional capacity. Again, due process demands that the representative be given the opportunity to inquire.
- Closing arguments are presented. At the conclusion of the hearing, the judge will likely give the representative the opportunity to make any final remarks. Neither the closing arguments nor the opening statements should be lengthy—after all, there is no jury to impress. The remarks should cogently express the theory of your case (opening) and summarize the evidence that supports that theory (closing).

See Figure 14–3.

On Opening Statement

An opening statement is the opportunity to inform the decision maker—in this case, the Administrative Law Judge—of the nature of the case, with specific reference to the evidence that will be presented during the case-in-chief; that is, during the time the claimant's case is presented. More importantly, it is the opportunity to articulate and promote the theme of the case. It is not an opportunity to argue against opposing evidence but rather a chance to succinctly state the basis for the claim. It is a *statement,* not an argument.

Theme

Why does the evidence support the claim for disability? This is the basic question. Answering it brings you close to framing the theory of the case. In Social Security appeals there are limited opportunities to win. For adults, winning takes place at the following steps:

- Step 3: meets or medically equals a medical listing;
- Step 5: satisfies the requisite criteria for an award of disability based on the Medical–Vocational Guidelines (the Grids); or
- Step 5: disability awarded using the Grids as a framework, given that the claimant suffers from nonexertional limitations.

For children, the opportunities to win are equally limited:

- Step 3: meets a medical listing;
- Step 3: medically equals a medical listing; or
- Step 3: functionally equals a medical listing.

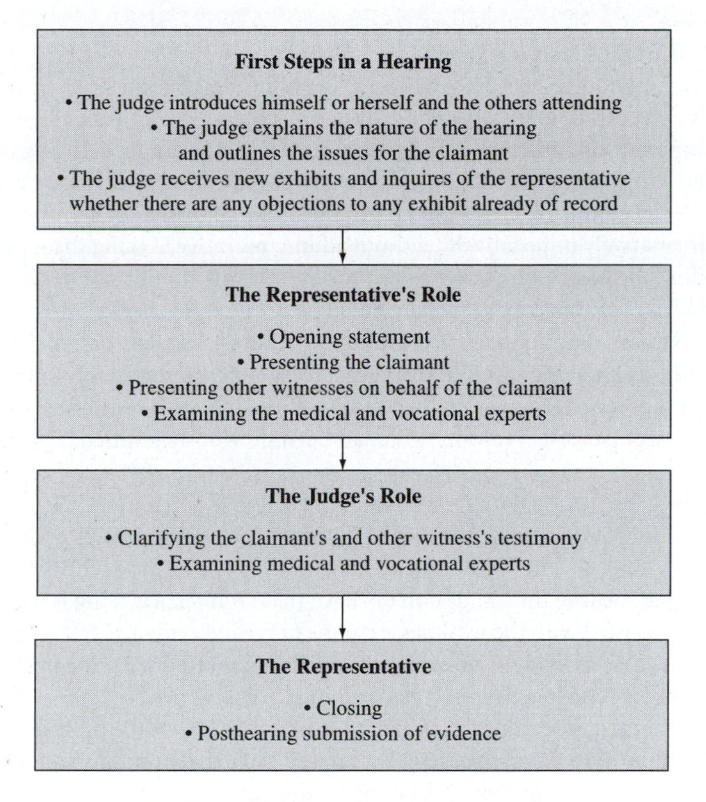

Figure 14–3 **Orderly Course of a Hearing**

The theme should clearly inform the judge of the theory of the case. What rule can be used to win? What step in the sequential evaluation will help the judge decide the case? Tell the judge briefly how it will be proved (provide witnesses' names and tell why they are being presented.) Opening statements should be short and to the point. Don't linger. The judge likely has a busy schedule. To be perceived as prepared, get to the point quickly, but comprehensively.

Examination of Witnesses

A client's story is revealed using both medical records and oral testimony. Direct examination of a client is a critical element in persuading the judge of the efficacy of a case.

Direct Examination

Direct examination includes the questioning of witnesses during the case-in-chief. The questions are open ended and do not suggest answers. If leading questions are asked, the judge will likely interrupt, suggesting that the case is ill-served by them, because the questioner, and not the claimant seems to be supplying the substantive information. Of course, there will be times when the claimant will not understand, become confused, or be nervous, and the representative must assist. The best advice is to use leading questions sparingly, but do not hesitate to assist a claimant if he or she becomes flustered or nervous.

The purpose of direct examination is to give a witness (and especially the claimant) the opportunity to tell his or her story. Effective direct examination allows the witness to bolster his or her credibility, both in demeanor, while testifying, and in the substance of the testimony itself. Thus, it is important to assist the witness throughout the examination in organizing testimony so it is consistent and understandable. It is also important to assist the witness in presentation and appearance. Appropriate suggestions for dress and other aspects of nonverbal communication are important (eye contact, voice volume, rate of speech, using plain English, etc.). Remember, questions should be simple and direct.

Cross-Examination

Cross-examination has several purposes, including impugning the witness's credibility (focusing on the witness's perception, memory, and the inherent consistency of his or her story during direct examination, or as compared with other evidence or testimony already adduced during the proceedings), discrediting his or her testimony, and using the witness to corroborate facts or evidence adduced during the case-in-chief. Questions posed during cross-examination should be closed ended; the witness generally has to respond either affirmatively or negatively, without adding narrative. Asking the witness "why" may be helpful in understanding the basis of an expert's testimony, but this should not be done routinely. The general rule is, *Never ask the "why" question if you do not already know the answer.*

The witness should not be given an opportunity to explain himself or his testimony. The key in cross-examination is knowing when to stop. An effective cross-examination need not be lengthy, but it must not leave the judge wondering about the veracity of the witness's testimony, the witness's credibility, and his or her ability to persuasively recount what has been previously testified.

Closing

Unlike opening statements, a closing argument is an opportunity to compare and contrast evidence presented in the case-in-chief with evidence that appears to contradict the theory of the case. It is, however, more than a simple "believe this" and "don't believe that." Rather, a closing is a cohesive synthesis of the strengths of a case contrasted with the weaknesses of the opposing evidence. It is a unique opportunity to explicate the theme of the case in light of the evidence actually adduced during the proceeding just concluded. In this respect, closing is retrospective, whereas opening is prospective.

Having heard the evidence, closing is the opportunity for the representative to interpret the significance of the testimony relevant to the theme of the case. Note that opinions about the claimant's medical status may not be interjected during closing. In drawing the judge's attention to key evidence, comments are limited to the evidence; matters not part of the proceeding may not be commented on or referenced.

Keep it simple. Reinforce the theme. Explain how all the evidence fits together to meet the listing or equal the listing, or why a particular limitation should be adopted. Be succinct.

Back to Chris

"It's exciting to think about!"

"A hearing?"

"Yes."

Steve suppressed a smile. "I thought you were nervous, and maybe a little put off? Like having second thoughts?"

"Wellllll. . . ."

"Truth," Steve chided.

"OK," Chris admitted. "I was. Now I'm excited."

"Still a couple of things to talk about."

"Like?"

"What if the claimant doesn't want to appear but still wants to appeal the DDS decision; and what happens after a hearing?"

"Oh. You mean you can appeal, but choose to, in effect, stand on the written record and not offer any oral testimony?"

"Yes, much like a traditional appeal, except the written record is evidence the judge must consider, and if necessary, ensure that the full record is properly developed before making a decision."

"Even if the claimant chooses not to appear?"

"Even then. Here, look at this 'Waiver of Your Right to Appear.'" (See Figure 14–4.)

Chris thought for a long moment. "What else?" There *had* to be more.

"And, I want to show you a sample case file."

"Cool!"

"One more thing."

Social Security Administration/Office of Hearings and Appeals

WAIVER OF YOUR RIGHT TO PERSONAL APPEARANCE BEFORE AN ADMINISTRATIVE LAW JUDGE

Claimant	Wage Earner (Leave blank if same as claimant)	Social Security Claim Number

NOTE: Please read the PRIVACY ACT statement on reverse and the statements below. Then, print, write, or type your response to the statements in the space provided below. If you need more space, attach a separate page to this form.

- I have been advised of my right to appear in person before an Administrative Law Judge. I understand that my personal appearance before an Administrative Law Judge would provide me with the opportunity to present written evidence, my testimony, and the testimony of other witnesses. I understand that this opportunity to be seen and heard could be helpful to the Administrative Law Judge in making a decision.

- Although my right to a personal appearance before an Administrative Law Judge has been explained to me, I do not want to appear in person. I want to have my case decided on the written evidence. The reason I do not want to appear in person at a hearing is:

- I understand that if I do not appear before an Administrative Law Judge, I still have the right to present a written summary of my case, or to enter written statements about the facts and law material to my case in the record.

- If I change my mind and decide to request a personal appearance before the Administrative Law Judge, I understand that I should make this request to the Hearing Office **before** the decision of the Administrative Law Judge is mailed to me.

- I understand that I have a right to be represented and that if I need representation, the Social Security office or hearing office can give me a list of legal referral and service organizations to assist me in locating a representative.

SIGNATURE OF CLAIMANT (OR AUTHORIZED REPRESENTATIVE)	DATE

Form **HA-4608** (8-95)
Issue old stock

Printed on recycled paper

Figure 14–4 **Waiver of Right to a Personal Appearance at an Administrative Hearing**

(continued)

Figure 14–4 **Waiver of Right to a Personal Appearance at an Administrative Hearing** *(continued)*

PRIVACY ACT/PAPERWORK ACT NOTICE

The Social Security Act (sections 205(a), 702, 1631(e)(1)(A) and (B),and 1869(b)(1) and (c), as appropriate) authorizes the collection of information on this form. We will use the information you provide to determine if your claim may be decided without an oral hearing. You **do** not have to give it, but if you do not you may not receive benefits under the Social Security Act. We need to get more information to decide if you are eligible for benefits or if a Federal law requires us to do so. Specifically, we may provide information to another Federal, State, or local government agency which is deciding your eligibility for a government benefit or program: or to the Department of Justice to represent the Federal Government in a court suit related to a program administered by the Social Security Administration. We explain, in the Federal Register, these and other reasons why we may use or give out information about you. If you would like more information, get in touch with any Social Security office. We may also use the information you give us when we match records by computer. Matching programs compare our records with those of other Federal, State, or local government agencies. Many agencies may use matching programs to find or prove that a person qualifies for benefits paid by the Federal government. The law allows us to do this even if you do not agree to it.

Explanations about these and other reasons why information you provide us may be used or given out are available in Social Security offices. If you want to learn more about this, contact any Social Security office.

Form **HA-4608 (8-95)**

Chris looked up. "What's that?"

"Have you ever seen a hearing room where these hearings are conducted?"

The thought hit Chris like a lightening bolt. "No, I thought it would be like a courtroom, you know."

"No. These are closed proceedings. Only the claimant, the experts, and those approved by the claimant are allowed. These aren't open to the public, so the hearing rooms don't have to accommodate public viewing."

"So, the hearing rooms are like conference rooms?"

"No, not really. Here, let me show you." Steve passed across a sheet of paper on which he'd drawn a typical hearing room. (See Figure 14–5.)

"So, the judge has a bench, but the representative, the court reporter, the claimant, and the experts all sit at the same table?"

"Pretty much. Because the government is not represented, there is no need for a second table."

"This is really interesting. Does the representative stand up when asking the witness questions?"

"Generally not. Everyone remains seated, but don't make the mistake of thinking that that means the proceeding is laid back. For these judges, this is a full-blown hearing in which the full measure of an individual's due process rights apply. You have to regard the setting with respect and dignity."

"Oh." Chris was suddenly somber. The picture of the hearing room suddenly made it seem real.

"Take heart," said Steve. "You'll do great!"

Chris grinned, suddenly excited to be there.

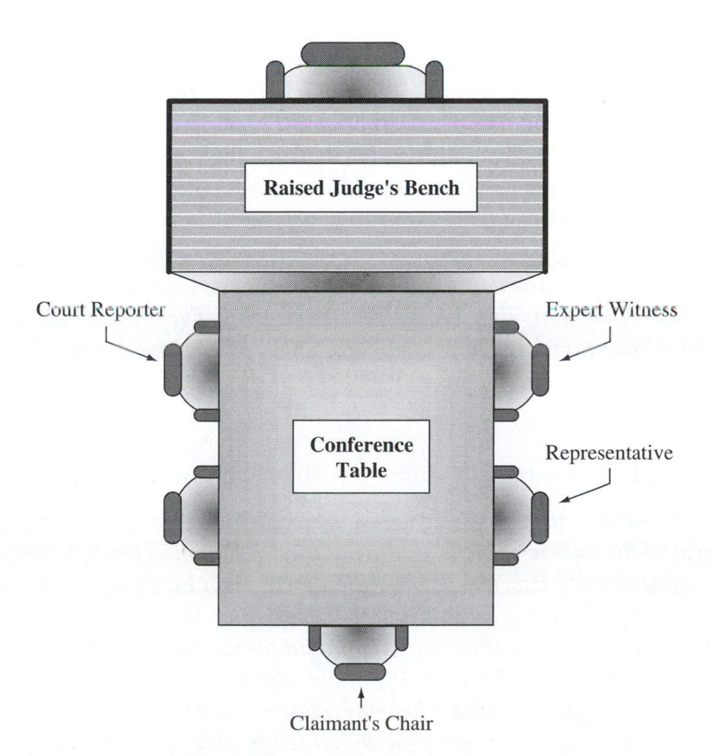

Figure 14–5 **Typical Hearing Room Configuration (top view)**

WHAT IF . . . ? SAMPLE PROBLEMS

WHAT IF . . .

What if you appear on time for a hearing but your client fails to appear?

Answer: ***Rather than panic, deal with the situation. One unfortunate consequence of disability is the sometimes inability to make a timely appearance. If your client fails to appear and phoning yields no answer, see if the case can be handled without taking your client's testimony. Without waiving your client's right to appear and testify, ask the judge if he or she would consider reviewing the written evidence of record to determine whether a favorable, or partially favorable, result can be achieved without your client's testimony (with the understanding that, if such a result cannot be reached, the case should be postponed so your client may appear and testify). Proceeding conditionally, without your client, is a particularly inviting possibility where a medical expert is present, because he or she can render an opinion, both retrospectively and prospectively on the written record, depending on the nature of the impairment(s) and the then-existing documentation. If the judge will not consider the case without your client, ask for a postponement, and indicate to the judge your willingness to waive your right to twenty days written notice of the new setting. This will speed the setting of the new hearing, and you might even be able to add your case to an already scheduled docket. In any event, make sure that your discussion with the judge is on the record.***

WHAT IF . . .

What if your client becomes surly or otherwise demonstrates dissatisfaction with the judge or the process? What do you do then—in the middle of the hearing?

Answer: ***Don't panic. But do something. If your client's voice tone, body language, or facial expressions indicate that he or she is unhappy, dissatisfied, angry, or upset, take immediate but discrete action. Ask the judge for a brief recess. This will give your client a break and give you time to mend the trouble. When you are alone with your client, find out what caused the reaction. Address it as quickly as possible. Remind your client that even nonverbal communication can affect the outcome of a hearing.***

One of the critical areas a judge must address is the claimant's credibility. This is especially so where pain is alleged. A disgruntled client runs the risk of negatively influencing the judge, possibly causing the judge—either rightly or wrongly—to conclude that your client is lacking credibility. These issues must be addressed with your client before the hearing, so if a break becomes necessary, you can simply remind your client of your previous discussion, not educate him or her anew. The most important thing is to return to the hearing having dropped the body language, voice tone, or facial expression(s).

WHAT IF . . .

What if crucial medical records cannot be obtained by the time of the hearing?

Answer: ***Proceed with the hearing unless the record is so sparse that the judge will not even be able to make a finding as to the nature of the impairment, the onset, and so forth. If this is the case, call the judge's paralegal specialist or staff attorney no later than forty-eight hours before the scheduled hearing and request a postponement. If obtaining records is problematic, such that a subpoena may be necessary, couple your request for a postponement with a request for a subpoena. Note, however, that a request for a subpoena must be made in writing, and be made a part of the administrative record.***

If you choose to proceed with a hearing, do so having made a request on the record for leave to submit the additional documents or records within a reasonable time after conclusion of the hearing. It is best to secure this request before the start of the hearing, being as straightforward with the judge as possible. Remember, however, that a formal request for a subpoena must be made in writing, five days before the actual scheduled hearing. See Title 20 C.F.R. § 404.950(d).

WHAT IF . . .

What if the judge does or says something that you believe to be inappropriate, demonstrating bias or prejudice?

Answer: *Make sure the comment or action is "of record." If the comment or action you are concerned about is not "of record," very little can be done to alleviate the situation. So, if on entering the hearing room, the judge looks at you and says, "So, your client is a drunk and wants benefits?" the first thing you should do is ask the judge whether "we are on the record?"—whether the tape recorder is running. If so, good. With the tape running, formally request the judge to recuse—or disqualify himself or herself—based on the obvious conclusion implied by the remark. If the judge refuses, conduct your hearing, and if denied, appeal not only on any substantive ground that may present itself but on bias as well.*

If the tape is not running, ask that it be turned on. If the judge refuses, wait until the start of the hearing and, with the tape running, make an opening statement documenting the judge's comment. You will, no doubt, irk the wayward jurist, but, given the nature of the remark, you (and your client) likely have little to lose. If the judge does turn the tape on when first asked, document the remark ("Let the record reflect the following remark made by the Administrative Law Judge . . ."), then ask the judge to recuse (withdraw) from the case. Your tone should at all times be respectful and calm. Do not get into a "he said–she said" debate with the judge; simply note the remark made for the record.

If the judge does something in the hearing, such as falling asleep (it actually has happened in court as well as in administrative proceedings), document the record; "Let the record reflect that the judge is asleep." Again, this will provide a basis for appeal in the event benefits are denied. This same procedure applies for any other conduct that you believe adversely affects your client. Document the record, preserving the conduct or action you believe to be untoward, so that it can be raised, if necessary, on appeal. See Title 20 C.F.R. § 404.940 for disqualification of the judge.

WHAT IF . . .

What if you believe further medical testing should be done?

Answer: *If you believe that the medical evidence reasonably supports the need for one or more consultative examinations, make your request in writing well in advance of a scheduled hearing. Be specific. Ask not only for the type of examination (e.g., a psychological examination) but also specify the actual testing you want done (e.g., the Minnesota Multiphasic Personality Inventory [MMPI]; the Wide Range Achievement Test [WRAT]; the Wechsler Adult Intelligence Scale, Third Edition [WAIS-III]; etc.).*

When making a written request, make sure a copy of the request is sent not only to the judge, in which case it will probably go directly to the file and not be seen by the judge, but also to a senior case technician or paralegal specialist working with the judge. That way, it is more likely your request will actually be acted on in advance of the hearing. Requests should be documented, indicating the medical basis in the record giving rise for the need for further examination.

When making a request at the hearing, do so on the record (while the tape is running) and, if at all possible, secure an answer from the judge (also, on the record). If denied, your request may form the basis for an appeal, because the judge has a continuing and affirmative duty to develop the record. See Title 20 C.F.R. § 404.944, wherein the regulations require that the Administrative Law Judge "look fully into the issues," which is the basis for the affirmative duty placed on the judge to develop the record.

---

[1]Title 20 C.F.R. § 404.948(b) (2000).

[2]Title 20 C.F.R. § 404.989. (2000.)

15

Chapter Fifteen

The Posthearing Process

Highlights

- ❑ The posthearing process
- ❑ Posthearing CEs
- ❑ Filing an appeal
- ❑ Getting paid

Chris

"Posthearing, huh?"

"There's still a lot of stuff that goes on."

Chris nodded thoughtfully. "This is a detailed process. It requires follow through, doesn't it?"

"You're right. So what do you think comes after the hearing?"

"Well, you talked about 'posthearing consultative examinations'—I suppose that has to be kept up with?"

"Correct. What else do you think?"

"What if we lose?"

"Then you appeal."

"OK. What if we win?"

"Then you've got to get paid."

"Good point. Let's see what it's all about!"

Front of Your Mind Questions and Considerations, 15.1

Posthearing Consultative Examinations

At the conclusion of the hearing, the judge, having the responsibility to fully develop the administrative record, may call for one or more consultative examinations (CEs). The CE is paid for by the Social Security Administration and generally made with a physician or psychologist under contract with the state agency (DDS). Once a CE is ordered, a formal request is made by the Office of Hearings and Appeals to the state DDS, requesting the appointment be made for the claimant. The consultative examination will be ordered when

- ❑ The evidence as a whole, both medical and nonmedical, is not sufficient to support a decision on a claim;
- ❑ The additional evidence needed is not contained in the claimant's treating physician's records;

- Evidence from the treating physician is not readily available;
- Highly technical or specialized medical evidence is not available from the treating or other medical sources; or
- A conflict, inconsistency, ambiguity, or insufficiency in the evidence must be resolved.

If a CE is ordered, and if the judge does not detail specific testing (i.e., the judge only orders an orthopedic examination or a psychological examination), ask for specific testing. Otherwise, the DDS will order a minimal examination. Of particular import is completion of a medical source statement. This provides concrete evidence of the claimant's limitations.

For example, a psychological examination ordered by the DDS consists of a simple mental status examination with no objective testing. A comprehensive psychological examination includes the following:

- Minnesota Multiphasic Personality Inventory (MMPI-II);
- Wechsler Adult Intelligence Scale, Third Edition (WAIS-III);
- Wechsler Memory Scale, Third Edition;
- Mental status examination, with Global Assessment of Function (GAF);
- Beck Depression Inventory (BDI-II);
- Beck Anxiety Inventory; and
- Mental medical source statement (Mental RFC).

The more information available the more likely it is that a client will benefit. If a CE is deemed necessary, it should be comprehensive.

A CE takes from forty-five to sixty days to complete. Once complete, a copy of the CE report is sent to the representative. If, on review, a further hearing is not necessary, make a written motion to that effect. The motion may take the form of a letter to the judge, outlining why, in light of the CE, benefits should be awarded. Alternately, a brief, made part of the record, to be reviewed at a supplemental hearing, should be prepared. Such a brief should identify the basis for an award, citing specific evidence, referring to the CE and applicable regulation, as well as other medical evidence already of record.

LOSING

If benefits are denied by the Administrative Law Judge, the question is what to do next. In answering that question, the administrative appeals structure should be the central focus. Within sixty days after receiving notice of the hearing decision or dismissal, a written request for review may be made of the Appeals Council (AC). Title 20 C.F.R. § 404.968 provides that "any documents or other evidence you wish to have considered by the Appeals Council should be submitted with your request for review."

The Appeals Council review is a paper review. The Appeals Council, located in Falls Church, Virginia, rarely undertakes oral argument. Instead, Appeals Analysts, working under the direction of Administrative Appeals Judges, review the entire record, including a transcript of the hearing before the Administrative Law Judge, and determine, as a matter of law, whether

- There was an abuse of discretion by the Administrative Law Judge;
- There was an error of law;
- The action, findings, or conclusions of the Administrative Law Judge are not supported by substantial evidence; or
- There is broad policy or procedural issue(s) that may affect the general public interest.[1]

See Figure 15–1, a Request for Review form. Interestingly, although appellate courts in the judicial branch are *not* empowered to consider new evidence, but must, with "new and material evidence," remand the case back to the trial court, the Appeals Council will entertain "new and material evidence" as long as it pertains to the period on or before the Administrative Law Judge's decision.[2] The Appeals Council may

- Review the case, *reverse* the Administrative Law Judge's decision, and award benefits;
- Review the case and *modify* the decision of the Administrative Law Judge;
- Review the case and *remand* the case back to the Administrative Law Judge for further proceedings, should additional evidence be required;

SOCIAL SECURITY ADMINISTRATION/OFFICE OF HEARINGS AND APPEALS

Form Approved
OMB No. 0960-0277

REQUEST FOR REVIEW OF HEARING DECISION/ORDER

(Take or mail original and all copies to your local Social Security Office)

See Privacy Act Notice on Reverse

1. CLAIMANT	2. WAGE EARNER, IF DIFFERENT
3. SOCIAL SECURITY CLAIM NUMBER	4. SPOUSE'S NAME AND SOCIAL SECURITY NUMBER *(Complete ONLY in Supplemental Security Income Case)*

5. I request that the Appeals Council review the Administrative Law Judge's action on the above claim because:

ADDITIONAL EVIDENCE

If you have additional evidence submit it with this request for review. If you need additional time to submit evidence or legal argument, you must request an extension of time in writing now. If you request an extension of time, you should explain the reason(s) you are unable to submit the evidence or legal argument now. If you neither submit evidence or legal argument now nor within any extension of time the Appeals Council grants, the Appeals Council will take its action based on the evidence of record.

IMPORTANT: Write your Social Security Claim Number on any letter or material you send us.

SIGNATURE BLOCKS: You should complete No. 6 and your representative (if any) should complete No. 7. If you are represented and your representative is not available to complete this form, you should also print his or her name, address, etc. in No. 7.

DATE	☐ ATTORNEY ☐ NON-ATTORNEY	
6. CLAIMANT'S SIGNATURE	7. REPRESENTATIVE'S SIGNATURE	
PRINT NAME	PRINT NAME	
ADDRESS	ADDRESS	
(CITY, STATE, ZIP CODE)	(CITY, STATE, ZIP CODE)	
TELEPHONE NUMBER (INCLUDE AREA CODE)	TELEPHONE NUMBER	FAX NUMBER(INCLUDE AREA CODE)

THE SOCIAL SECURITY ADMINISTRATION STAFF WILL COMPLETE THIS PART

8. Request received for the Social Security Administration on ______________ by: ______________________________

(Title) (Address) Servicing FO Code PC Code

9. Is the request for review received within 65 days of the ALJ's Decision/Dismissal? ☐ Yes ☐ No

10. If no checked: (1) attach claimant's explanation for delay; and
(2) attach copy of appointment notice, letter or other pertinent material or information in the Social Security Office.

11. Check one: ☐ Initial Entitlement
☐ Termination or other

12. Check all claim types that apply:

- ☐ Retirement or survivors (RSI)
- ☐ Disability-Worker (DIWC)
- ☐ Disability-Widow(er) (DIWW)
- ☐ Disability-Child (DIWC)
- ☐ SSI Aged (SSIA)
- ☐ SSI Blind (SSIB)
- ☐ SSI Disability (SSID)
- ☐ Health Insurance-Part A (HIA)
- ☐ Health Insurance-Part B (HIB)
- ☐ Other - Specify: ______________

APPEALS COUNCIL
OFFICE OF HEARINGS AND APPEALS, SSA
5107 Leesburg Pike
FALLS CHURCH, VA 22041 - 3255

Form **HA-520-U5** (12-95) EF (3-99)
Issue Old Stock

CLAIMS FOLDER

Figure 15–1 **Request for Review by the Appeals Council of the Social Security Administration**

Figure 15–1 (continued)

PAPERWORK/PRIVACY ACT NOTICE

The Social Security Act (sections 205(a), 702, 1631(e)(1)(A) and (B), and 1869(b)(1) and (c), as appropriate) authorizes the collection of information on this form. We need the information to continue processing your claim. You do not have to give it, but if you do not you may not receive benefits under the Social Security Act. We may give out the information on this form without your written consent if we need to get more information to decide if you are eligible for benefits or if a Federal law requires us to do so. Specifically, we may provide information to another Federal, State, or local government agency which is deciding your eligibility for a government benefit or program; to the President or a Congressman inquiring on your behalf; to an independent party who needs statistical information for a research paper or audit report on a Social Security program; or to the Department of Justice to represent the Federal Government in a court suit related to a program administered by the Social Security Administration. We explain, in the Federal Register, these and other reasons why we may use or give out information about you. If you would like more information, get in touch with any Social Security office.

We may also use the information you give us when we match records by computer. Matching programs compare our records with those of other Federal, State, or local government agencies. Many agencies may use matching programs to find or prove that a person qualifies for benefits paid by the Federal government. The law allows us to do this even if you do not agree to it.

Explanations about these and other reasons why information you provide us may be used or given out are available in Social Security offices. If you want to learn more about this, contact any Social Security office.

The **Paperwork Reduction Act of 1995** requires us to notify you that this information collection is in accordance with the clearance requirements of section 3507 of the Paperwork Reduction Act of 1995. We may not conduct or sponsor, and you are not required to respond to, a collection of information unless it displays a valid OMB control number. We estimate that it will take you about 10 minutes to complete this form. This includes the time it will take to read the instructions, gather the necessary facts and fill out the form.

- ❑ Decline to review the case and *dismiss* the appeal; or
- ❑ Review the case and *affirm* the decision of the Administrative Law Judge.

If the case is affirmed, or the appeal dismissed, the decision of the Administrative Law Judge becomes the final decision of the Commissioner of Social Security.

The submission to the Appeals Council should focus on the specific issue(s) that warrant review. To seek review based on broad-sweeping assertions such as

- ❑ "The judge erred";
- ❑ "The record as a whole does not support the judge's decision";
- ❑ "The Administrative Law Judge was biased";
- ❑ "Due process was not followed"; or
- ❑ "The judge disregarded applicable Social Security rulings."

is an invitation for failure. To be successful, direct the Appeals' Council to the *specific errors of law or evidentiary omission(s).*

Why? The Appeals Council has suffered from an increasing decisional backlog. As the number of hearings increase, the number of appeals increases. Staffing levels, both at the hearing and at the appeals level, however, have not increased. The result is a growing backlog of cases. Failure to be specific invites a general response—most likely, an affirmation. To be specific, return to the *original theme* of the case. Articulate the theme for the Appeals Council.

- ❑ Why the client is entitled to benefits; and
- ❑ At what step of the sequential analysis for adults or for children the decision should have been made.

In addressing these fundamental issues, the Appeals Council can focus on specific issues, which, if verified, aid review. Remember, just as the hearing is a "unilateral" affair—the government is not represented—so too is the appeal. No opposing brief will be filed to oppose the appeal. Therefore, because the representative's voice is the only one that will be heard on appeal, it must be precise. Cogent analysis best serves the client's interests. In articulating the theme of the case, ground the appeal on legal principles. These include references to

- ❑ Pertinent regulation(s);
- ❑ Circuit case law;
- ❑ Social Security Rulings; and
- ❑ HALLEX.

Finally, once an appeal has been perfected (made), consider carefully whether the client should be advised to file a further claim. Although a succeeding claim cannot supercede a previously filed appeal (though many such filings overlap anyway), nothing prevents a separate and new claim beginning the day *after* the Administrative Law Judge's original decision. Thus, it is entirely possible to have a decision on appeal at the Appeals Council while a new claim wends its way through the state agency (DDS). Sometimes a remand from the Appeals Council coincides with a Request for Hearing on a new claim from the state agency. In those rare circumstances, the claims will be consolidated. The judge should, of course, be made aware of pending appeals or claims. This will aid the client, because two unconnected pending claims may cause conflicting results. The appeals process is illustrated in Figure 15–2.

BACK TO CHRIS

"Cover all your bases, right?"

"That's the theory. If the judge decides against you, appeal. Also think about filing a new claim."

"Got it!"

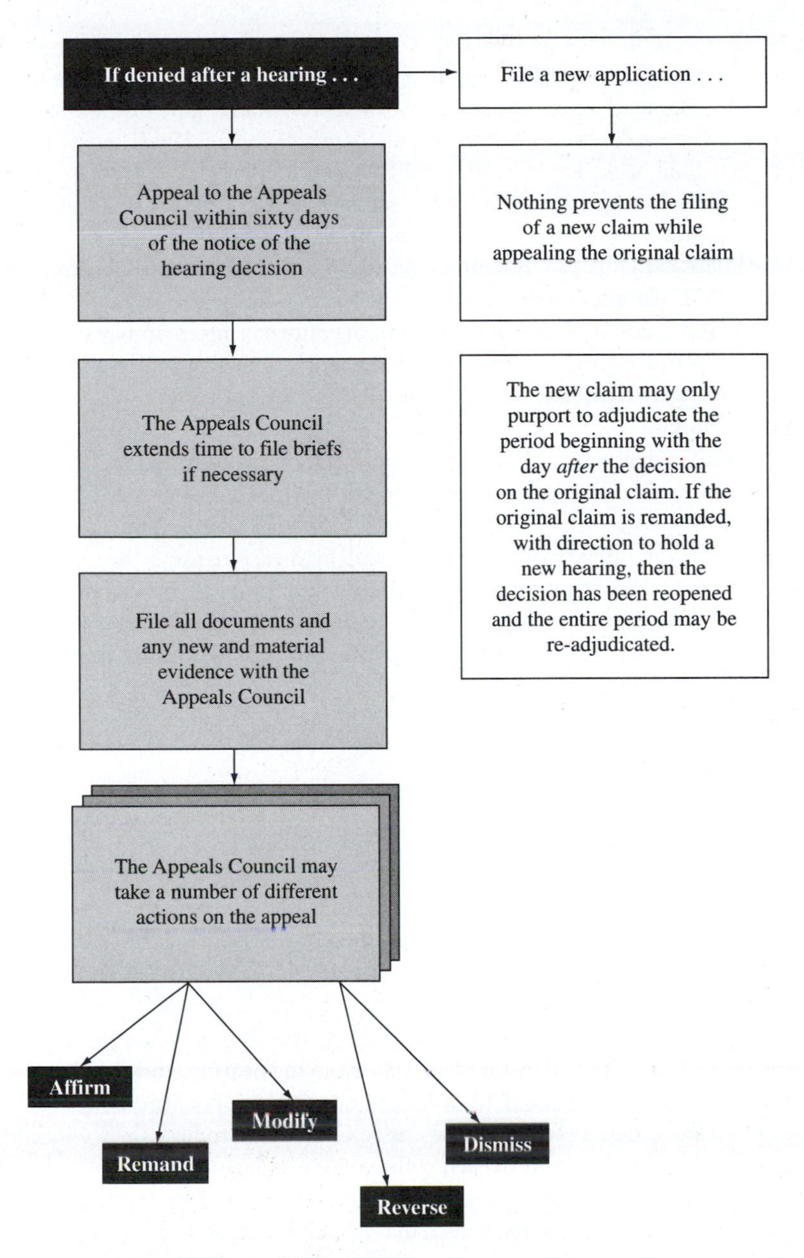

Figure 15–2 **The Appeals Process**

FRONT OF YOUR MIND QUESTIONS AND CONSIDERATIONS, 15.2

WINNING

Winning entitles the representative to a fee. Because these are "contingent" cases, winning is the only way to be paid. There are two payment methods:

❑ A fee petition; or
❑ A fee agreement.

Figure 15–3 describes the two ways of getting paid. The best tactic is to submit a fee agreement. A fee agreement is simply what it implies: It is an agreement, in writing, between the representative and the claimant, whereby the claimant agrees to pay a fee to the representative if he or she is successful; provided, however, that the fee agreement complies with the requirements of federal law. The law requires that a fee cannot exceed 25 percent of all back-due benefits, or $5,300, whichever is less. "Back-due benefits" are those monies paid from the date disability is found (the onset date) to the date of the decision. The fee is calculated on this amount, not monies accruing after the date of the decision. (See Figure 15–4.) As long as the language of the fee agreement contains this limitation, the agreement will be approved. An exemplar fee agreement is found in Figure 15–5. Another form of such an agreement is illustrated in Figure 15–6.

If the representative is an attorney, and the attorney agrees to pay the Social Security Administration a surcharge for processing, the fee will be deducted directly from the claimant's back-due award. If the attorney does not agree to the surcharge, the fee, like that for a nonlawyer representative, must be collected directly from the claimant.

An Administrative Law Judge must approve the fee agreement to be paid. If the fee agreement does not contain the limiting language previously noted, it will be disapproved. The representative must then file a fee petition.

A fee petition differs from a fee agreement, because it requires the representative to prove entitlement to the fee. Proof includes time records and documentation of activities undertaken on behalf of the claimant. As such, a fee petition is far more time consuming, but it enables the representative, if approved by the judge, to collect a larger fee, provided the time records and activities undertaken are justified. When considering a fee petition, the following factors are weighed by the Administrative Law Judge:

- ❑ Dates services began and ended;
- ❑ Amount of the fee to be charged;
- ❑ Amount of expenses incurred;
- ❑ Description of the representative's "special qualifications" that enabled him or her to give valuable help to the claimant;
- ❑ Complexity of the case;
- ❑ Level of skill and competence required;
- ❑ Amount of time actually spent; and
- ❑ Results obtained.[3]

If more than one lawyer or representative claims a fee in a case (for example, if representative 1 began the case but was discharged by the claimant before the hearing, and representative 2 actually appeared at the hearing), a fee petition is required in order to properly apportion the fee between the two representatives. Without an agreement between the two representatives as to how the fee should be split, the judge will have to consider the relative merits of each petition and render a final decision as to the fee to which each is entitled. In any case, the total fee should not exceed 25 percent of back-due benefits.

If a case is unusually complex, such that it has been on appeal several times, perhaps to the federal courts and back, a fee petition may more properly reflect the complexity of the case, and the increased entitlement

Fee agreement

- ❑ Signed contract between the representative and the claimant for services rendered before the Social Security Administration
- ❑ Limited to 25% of past-due benefits or $5,300, whichever is less

Fee petition

- ❑ A formal written request for approval of the fee to be charged
- ❑ Eight essential criteria, including time, approved fee, expenses, and any special qualifications that enabled the representative, if not an attorney, to provide valuable help

Figure 15–3 **Two Ways of Getting Paid**

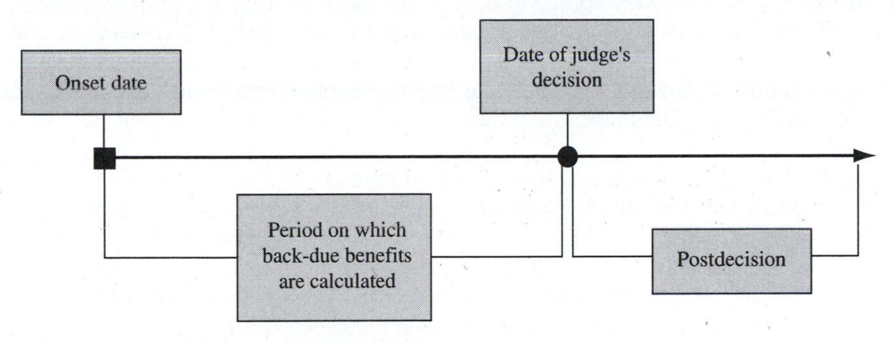

Figure 15–4 **Fee Can Be Based on Back-Due Benefits**

ATTORNEY FEE AGREEMENT

I, _________________________, hereby retain the LAW OFFICES OF ____ to represent me in the cessation of my Social Security benefits.

My representative and I agree that if SSA favorably decides my claim, the attorney's fee will be 25% of my disability benefits and 25% of my children's benefits accruing during the pending of this appeal, beginning with my benefits for March ________ and ending the month that SSA effectuates a favorable determination or decision in my claim, but in no event will more than $5,300 be collected. We understand that the fee may not exceed the lesser of $5,300 or 25%. I will bring to my attorney the amount of $______ which represents 25% of my disability benefits every month beginning May _____.

If a favorable decision is not issued at the hearing level, my attorney will refund all monies collected at that time.

In addition to the fee, I agree to pay my attorney's reasonable expenses, which are incurred in representing me, subject to SSA approval. Such expenses may include long distance telephone calls, medical reports, doctor examinations, postage, and photocopying charges.

We agree that I am not obligated to use THE LAW OFFICES OF _______________________________________ for any appeal in the event that Social Security terminates my benefits nor is THE LAW OFFICES OF _______________ ___________________________ obligated to represent me in appealing the cessation of my Social Security benefits unless we make another agreement for that purpose.

_______________________________ DATED

_______________________________ CLIENT

LAW OFFICES OF ____

Figure 15–5 **Exemplar Fee Agreement**

SECURITY ATTORNEY RETAINER AGREEMENT

Scope—The Client retains ____

for the sole purpose of pursuing a claim for disability benefits under the Social Security Act, together with any auxiliary benefits under the Social Security Act. Attorney agrees to pursue this claim through any and all administrative appeals within the Social Security Administration and any and all appeals in the United States Court System. Said appeals are subject to the _____ professional judgment to determine if further appeals are meritorious and necessary. Attorney does not agree by this agreement, to pursue any other remedies or claims that client may have except for Social Security and/or Supplemental Security Income Disability Benefits.

Attorney fee—Attorney may charge for actual services performed *only if the Client receives a favorable decision.* This is called a contingent attorney fee. The attorney fee does not include "out-of-pocket" expenses (see below). Client agrees to pay Attorney as a fee the ***lesser of*** (a) 25% of all past-due benefits payable to client and family or (b) $5,300.00. Said fee only relates to services rendered before the Social Security Administration. In the event that the case is appealed to the Appeals Council of the Social Security Administration and/or to the United States District Court, the attorney reserves the right to charge a fee in excess of $5,300, but in no event in excess of 25% of the past-due benefits. If Client does not receive a favorable decision, Client will not be obligated to pay any fee to Attorney as a fee for actual services performed. Client understands that all time records in this case will be kept on a 1/4 hour convention and charged at the rate of $150.00 per hour.

Client has been advised of the right to object to any fee requested by Attorney, regardless of the amount. Client agrees that the lesser of (a) 25% of the past-due benefits to client and family or (b) $5,300 is a fair and reasonable fee for the Administrative portion of this case in light of the contingent nature of this agreement, the lack of available qualified counsel in this State, the complexity of the case, and other factors.

Expenses—An expense is money which must be paid out-of-pocket in order to proceed with a case. Client agrees to reimburse Attorney for any out-of-pocket expenses which are incurred in representing the Client *whether or not Client receives a favorable decision.* Examples of expenses include but are not limited to copy expenses for briefs; court filing fees; travel expenses to the Circuit Court of Appeals; and charges by doctors or hospital for copies of medical records or reports.

Client acknowledges that a copy of this agreement has been received.

Agreed this __________ day of ______________________________

____
Client

SSN: ______________________________

____
Attorney

Figure 15–6 **Fee Agreement Providing for a Retainer**

to fees. The fee petition process is not capped at $5,300 as is the fee agreement. Instead, the limit is simply 25 percent of back-due benefits, which may exceed $5,300 if the back-due benefits exceed $21,000.

Note: The fee agreement should be "of record" (part of the administrative record) no later than the actual date of the hearing. A fee petition should be filed no later than sixty days following the notice of a favorable decision.[4] If the Administrative Law Judge's decision on the fee is unacceptable, file a request for review of the fee, in the form of a letter to the regional chief Administrative Law Judge who presides over the region in which the hearing takes place. Such a request should be made no later than thirty days following receipt of the Administrative Law Judge's decision.[5]

Figure 15–7 shows the required Petition to obtain Approval of a Fee for Representing a Claimant Before the Social Security Administration. This form is filed only when the fee petition process is followed. There is no form, apart from the fee agreement itself, when a fee agreement is submitted. Because the fee petition form is submitted after the hearing, the dollar amounts claimed are specifically set forth, as is the claimant's approval in the form of his or her signature. An explanatory cover sheet is illustrated in Figure 15–8. This is the Social Security Administration's explanation of the fee process.

Figure 15–9 illustrates a completed Petition to Obtain Approval of a Fee for Representing a Claimant Before the Social Security Administration. Note the response to question 2, which asks whether a fee agreement has been entered into—and setting the agreed-on fee at $150 per hour. This means that an agreement was reached as to an hourly amount. It does not mean, however, that the representative can, in fact, collect such a fee. Instead, it signifies that the client has agreed to pay an hourly amount, which cannot, by law, exceed 25 percent of back-due benefits. Indeed, without approval from the Administrative Law Judge, no fee can be collected in any amount.

Figure 15–10 is the attachment to the official fee petition and sets forth an itemization of expected hours and activities. Hours are billed in increments (here, in tenths). Other divisions work equally well. The total fee billed is a computation of hours spent multiplied by the agreed-on hourly rate. The total (here, $675) must fall within 25 percent of the total back-due benefits in order for the judge to approve the requested fee. Note, however, the billing for .5 hours for preparation of the fee petition on November 12, 1998. This time (and dollar amount) must be *excluded* from the fee actually approved, because preparation of the fee petition may not be included.

BACK TO CHRIS

"What does that mean—that you have to get your fees directly from your client?"

"It's like any other professional. You receive a fee for services rendered. The important thing is to take your fee as a lump sum. Your client will be paid back-due benefits as a lump sum, and you should have some arrangement whereby you are notified by the client when he or she is paid."

"Can't the back-due check from the government be made out to both me and my client?"

"Good idea, but the government won't do it. You simply have to make sure that there's a level of trust between you and your clients so that you will be paid once they are."

"OK, sounds good!"

SOCIAL SECURITY ADMINISTRATION | TOE 850 | Form Approved OMB No. 0960-0104

PETITION TO OBTAIN APPROVAL OF A FEE FOR REPRESENTING A CLAIMANT BEFORE THE SOCIAL SECURITY ADMINISTRATION

IMPORTANT INFORMATION ON REVERSE SIDE

PAPERWORK/PRIVACY ACT NOTICE: Your response to this request is voluntary, but the Social Security Administration may not approve any fee unless it receives the information this form requests. The Administration will use the information to determine a fair value for services you rendered to the claimant named below, as provided in section 206 of the Social Security Act (42 U.S.C. 406).

I request approval to charge a fee of ⟶ Fee $ ______ (Show the dollar amount)

for services performed as the representative of ⟶ Mr. Mrs. Ms.

My Services Began: ____ / ____ / ______ (Month / Day / Year)

My Services Ended: ____ / ____ / ______

Type(s) of claim(s)

Enter the name and the Social Security number of the person on whose Social Security record the claim is based
___ ___ ___ / ___ ___ / ___ ___ ___ ___

1. Itemize on a separate page or pages the services you rendered before the Social Security Administration (SSA). List each meeting, conference, item of correspondence, telephone call, and other activity in which you engaged, such as research, preparation of a brief, attendance at a hearing, travel, etc., related to your services as representative in this case.
Attach to this petition the list showing the dates, the descriptions of each service, the actual time spent in each, and the total hours.

2. Have you and your client entered into a fee agreement for services before SSA? ☐ YES ☐ NO
If "yes," please specify the amount on which you agreed, and attach a copy of the agreement to this petition. $ ______ and ☐ See attached

3. (a) Have you received, or do you expect to receive, any payment toward your fee from any source other than from funds which SSA may be withholding for fee payment? ☐ YES ☐ NO
(b) Do you currently hold in a trust or escrow account any amount of money you received toward payment of your fee? ☐ YES ☐ NO
If "yes" to either or both of the above, please specify the source(s) and the amount(s).
Source: ______________________ $ ______
Source: ______________________ $ ______
Note: If you receive payment(s) after submitting this petition, but before the SSA approves a fee, you have an affirmative duty to notify the SSA office to which you are sending this petition.

4. Have you received, or do you expect to receive, reimbursement for expenses you incurred? If "yes," please itemize your expenses and the amounts on a separate page. ☐ YES ☐ NO

5. Did you render any services relating to this matter before any State or Federal court? If "yes," what fee did you or will you charge for services in connection with the court proceedings? ☐ YES ☐ NO $ ______
Please attach a copy of the court order if the court has approved a fee.

I certify that the information above, and on the attachment(s), is true and correct to the best of my knowledge and belief. I also certify that I have furnished a copy of this petition and the attachment(s) to the person(s) for whom I performed the services. I understand that failure to comply with Social Security laws and regulations pertaining to representation may result in suspension or disqualification from practice before SSA, the imposition of criminal penalties, or both.

Signature of Representative	Date	Address (include Zip Code)

Firm with which associated, if any	Telephone No. and Area Code

[Note: The following is optional. However, SSA can consider your fee petition more promptly if your client knows and already agrees with the amount you are requesting.]

I understand that I do not have to sign this petition or request. It is my right to disagree with the amount of the fee requested or any information given, and to ask more questions about the information given in this request (as explained on the reverse side of this form). I have marked my choice below.

☐ I agree with the $ ______ fee which my representative is asking to charge and collect. By signing this request, I am not giving up my right to disagree later with the total fee amount the Social Security Administration authorizes my representative to charge and collect.

OR

☐ I do not agree with the requested fee or other information given here, or I need more time. I understand I must call, visit, or write to SSA within 20 days if I have questions or if I disagree with the fee requested or any information shown (as explained on the reverse sides of this form).

Signature of Claimant	Date

Address (include Zip Code)	Telephone No. and Area Code

Form **SSA-1560-U4** (7-2000) EF (7-2000)
Destroy Prior Editions

FILE COPY

Figure 15–7 **Petition for Approval of a Fee for Representing a Claimant**

Figure 15–7 (continued)

INSTRUCTIONS FOR USING THIS PETITION

Any attorney or other representative who wants to charge or collect a fee for services, rendered in connection with a claim before the Social Security Administration (SSA), is required by law to first obtain SSA's approval of the fee [sections 206(a) and 1631(d)(2) of the Social Security Act (42 U.S.C. 406(a) and 1383(d)(2)); section 413(b) of the Black Lung Benefits Act (30 U.S.C. 923(b)); and sections 404.1720, 410.686b, and 416.1520 of Social Security Administration Regulations Numbers 4, 10, and 16, respectively].

The only exceptions are if the fee is for services rendered (1) when a nonprofit organization or government agency pays the fee and any expenses out of funds which a government entity provided or administered and the claimant incurs no liability, directly or indirectly, for the cost of such services and expenses; (2) in an official capacity such as that of legal guardian, committee, or similar court-appointed office and the court has approved the fee in question; or (3) in representing the claimant before a court of law. A representative who has rendered services in a claim before both SSA and a court of law may seek a fee from either or both, but generally neither tribunal has the authority to set a fee for services rendered before the other [42 U.S.C. 406(a) and (b)].

When to File a Fee Petition

The representative should request fee approval only after completing all services (for the claimant and any auxiliaries). The representative has the option to petition either before or after SSA effectuates the determination(s).

In order to receive direct payment of all or any part of an authorized fee from past-due benefits, the attorney representative should file a request for fee approval, or written notice of intent to file a request, **within 60 days** of the date of the notice of the favorable determination is mailed. When there are multiple claims on one account and the attorney will not file the petition within 60 days after the mailing date of the first notice of favorable determination, he or she should file a written notice of intent to file a request for fee approval within the 60-day period.

Where to File the Petition

The representative must first give the "Claimant's Copy" of the SSA-1560-U4 petition to the claimant for whom he or she rendered services, with a copy of each attachment. The representative may then file the original and third carbon copy, the "OHA Copy," of the SSA-1560-U4, and the attachment(s), with the appropriate SSA office:

- If a court or the Appeals Council issued the decision, send the petition to the Office of Hearings and Appeals. Attention: Attorney Fee Branch, 5107 Leesburg Pike, Falls Church, VA 22041-3255.
- If an Administrative Law Judge issued the decision, send the petition to him or her using the hearing office address.
- In all other cases, send the petition to the reviewing office address which appears at the top right of the notice of award or notice of disapproved claim.

Evaluation of a Petition for a Fee

If the claimant has not agreed to and signed the fee petition, SSA does not begin evaluating the request for 30 days. SSA must decide what is a reasonable fee for the services rendered to the claimant, keeping in mind the purpose of the social security, black lung, or supplemental security income program. When evaluating a request for fee approval, SSA will consider the (1) extent and type of services the representative performed; (2) complexity of the case; (3) level of skill and competence required of the representative in giving the services; (4) amount of time he or she spent on the case; (5) results achieved; (6) levels of review to which the representative took the claim and at which he or she became the representative; and (7) amount of fee requested for services rendered, including any amount authorized or requested before but excluding any amount of expenses incurred.

SSA also considers the amount of benefits payable, if any, but authorizes the fee amount based on consideration of all the factors given here. The amount of benefits payable in a claim is determined by specific provisions of law unrelated to the representative's efforts. Also, the amount of past-due benefits may depend on the length of time that has elapsed since the claimant's effective date of entitlement.

Disagreement

SSA notifies both the representative and the claimant of the amount which it authorizes the representative to charge. If either or both disagree, SSA will further review the fee authorization when the claimant or representative sends a letter, explaining the reason(s) for disagreement, to the appropriate office **within 30 days** after the date of the notice of authorization to charge and receive a fee.

Collection of the Fee

Basic liability for payment of a representative's approved fee rests with the client. However, SSA will assist in fee collection when the representative is an attorney and SSA awards the claimant benefits under Title II of the Social Security Act or Title IV of the Federal Coal Mine Health and Safety Act of 1969, as amended. In these cases, SSA generally withholds 25 per cent of the claimant's past-due benefits. Once the fee is approved, SSA pays the attorney from the claimant's withheld funds. **This does not mean that SSA will approve as a reasonable fee 25 per cent of the past-due benefits.** The amount that is payable to the attorney from the withheld benefits is subject to the assessment required by section 206(d) of the Social Security Act, and it is also subject to offset by any fee payment(s) the attorney has received or expects to receive from an escrow or trust account. If the approved fee is more than the amount of the withheld benefits, collection of the difference is a matter between the attorney and the client.

Penalty for Charging or Collecting an Unauthorized Fee

Any individual who charges or collects an unauthorized fee for services provided in any claim, including services before a court which has rendered a favorable determination, may be subject to prosecution under 42 U.S.C. 406 and 1383 which provide that such individual, upon conviction thereof, shall for each offense be punished by a fine not exceeding $500, by imprisonment not exceeding one year, or both. These penalties do not apply to fees for services performed before a court in supplemental security income claims because section 1383 provides no controls over such fees.

Computer Matching

We may also use the information you give us when we match records by computer. Matching programs compare our records with those of other Federal, State, or local government agencies. Many agencies may use matching programs to find or prove that a person qualifies for benefits paid by the Federal government. The law allows us to do this even if you do not agree to it.

Explanations about these and other reasons why information you provide us may be used or given out are available in Social Security Offices. If you want to learn more about this, contact any Social Security Office.

The Paperwork Reduction Act of 1995 requires us to notify you that this information collection is in accordance with the clearance requirements of section 3507 of the Paperwork Reduction Act of 1995. We may not conduct or sponsor, and you are not required to respond to, a collection of information unless it displays a valid OMB control number. We estimate that it will take you about 30 minutes to complete this form. This includes the time it will take to read the instructions, gather the necessary facts and fill out the form.

Form **SSA-1560-U4** (7-2000) EF (7-2000)
Destroy Prior Editions

NOTICE TO REPRESENTATIVE AT THE ALJ HEARING LEVEL REGARDING A FEE FOR SERVICES PROVIDED IN A TITLE II OR TITLE XVIII CASE

An attorney or other person who wants to charge or collect a fee for providing services in connection with a claim before the Social Security Administration (SSA) must first obtain our approval of the fee for representation.

To charge a fee for services, you must use one of two, mutually exclusive fee approval processes. You must file either a fee agreement or a fee petition with us. Because you did not file a fee agreement with the Administrative Law Judge (ALJ) prior to the ALJ's decision, you must file a written fee petition with the ALJ who issued the decision when you have completed your services to the claimant (and any auxiliaries) if you want to charge a fee.

Your fee petition must contain the information described in 20 CFR § 404.1725 (a); for example, the dates your services began and ended; a list of the services you gave and the amount of time you spent on each type of service; and the amount of the fee you are requesting. If you did not keep time records, estimate the time you spent and maintain records in any future Social Security cases you handle.

We are attaching a snapout petition Form SSA-1560-U4 (Petition to Obtain Approval of a Fee for Representing a Claimant Before the Social Security Administration) which you can use to provide the required information. It also provides enough copies to process your petition. Information and instructions for completing the form appear on its reverse side.

In completing the fee petition, please make sure that all copies are legible. In the event of a favorable decision resulting in an award of benefits, you may wish to submit the fee petition after you have received a copy of the award notice. If you are an attorney, you should file a fee petition or a written notice of the intent to file a fee petition within 60 days of the date SSA mails the award notice in order to receive direct payment of a fee from the claimant's past-due benefits.

You must give the claimant a copy of the fee petition and each attachment. Retain the REPRESENTATIVE'S COPY for your records. If your services end at the hearing level, send the remaining copies to the hearing office. If you appeal the case further and your services end at the Appeals Council review level, send the remaining copies to the Office of Hearings and Appeals, ATTN: Attorney Fee Branch, 5107 Leesburg Pike, Falls Church, VA 22041-3255.

REFERENCES
42 U.S.C. 406 (a)
20 CFR §§ 404.1720 through 404.1735

Form HA-533 (5–94)
Destroy old stock

Printed on recycled paper

Figure 15–8 **Social Security Administration Explanation of Fee Entitlement**

SOCIAL SECURITY ADMINISTRATION — TOE 850 — Form Approved OMB No. 0960-0104

PETITION TO OBTAIN APPROVAL OF A FEE FOR REPRESENTING A CLAIMANT BEFORE THE SOCIAL SECURITY ADMINISTRATION

IMPORTANT INFORMATION ON REVERSE SIDE

PAPERWORK/PRIVACY ACT NOTICE: Your response to this request is voluntary, but the Social Security Administration may not approve any fee unless it receives the information this form requests. The Administration will use the information to determine a fair value for services you rendered to the claimant named below, as provided in section 206 of the Social Security Act (42 U.S.C. 406).

I request approval to charge a fee of → Fee $ 675.00 (Show the dollar amount)

for services performed as the representative of → (Mr.) Mrs. Ms.

My Services Began: 06 / 24 / 98 (Month / Day / Year)

My Services Ended: 11 / 12 / 98

Type(s) of claim(s): DISABILITY INS.

Enter the name and the Social Security number of the person on whose Social Security record the claim is based ___ / ___ / ____

1. Itemize on a separate page or pages the services you rendered before the Social Security Administration (SSA). List each meeting, conference, item of correspondence, telephone call, and other activity in which you engaged, such as research, preparation of a brief, attendance at a hearing, travel, etc., related to your services as representative in this case.
Attach to this petition the list showing the dates, the descriptions of each service, the actual time spent in each, and the total hours.

2. Have you and your client entered into a fee agreement for services before SSA? ☒ YES ☐ NO
If "yes," please specify the amount on which you agreed, and attach a copy of the agreement to this petition. $150.00 Per Hour and ☐ See attached

3. (a) Have you received, or do you expect to receive, any payment toward your fee from any source other than from funds which SSA may be withholding for fee payment? ☐ YES ☒ NO
(b) Do you currently hold in a trust or escrow account any amount of money you received toward payment of your fee? ☐ YES ☒ NO
If "yes" to either or both of the above, please specify the source(s) and the amount(s).
Source: ____________ $ ______
Source: ____________ $ ______
Note: If you receive payment(s) after submitting this petition, but before the SSA approves a fee, you have an affirmative duty to notify the SSA office to which you are sending this petition.

4. Have you received, or do you expect to receive, reimbursement for expenses you incurred? If "yes," please itemize your expenses and the amounts on a separate page. N/A ☐ YES ☐ NO

5. Did you render any services relating to this matter before any State or Federal court? If "yes," what fee did you or will you charge for services in connection with the court proceedings? ☐ YES ☒ NO
Please attach a copy of the court order if the court has approved a fee. $ ______

I certify that the information above, and on the attachment(s), is true and correct to the best of my knowledge and belief. I also certify that I have furnished a copy of this petition and the attachment(s) to the person(s) for whom I performed the services. I understand that failure to comply with Social Security laws and regulations pertaining to representation may result in suspension or disqualification from practice before SSA, the imposition of criminal penalties, or both.

Signature of Representative	Date	Address (include Zip Code) TULSA, OK
Firm with which associated, if any		Telephone No. and Area Code

[Note: The following is optional. However, SSA can consider your fee petition more promptly if your client knows and already agrees with the amount you are requesting.]

I understand that I do not have to sign this petition or request. It is my right to disagree with the amount of the fee requested or any information given, and to ask more questions about the information given in this request (as explained on the reverse side of this form). I have marked my choice below.

☐ I agree with the $ ______ fee which my representative is asking to charge and collect. By signing this request, I am not giving up my right to disagree later with the total fee amount the Social Security Administration authorizes my representative to charge and collect.

OR

☐ I do not agree with the requested fee or other information given here, or I need more time. I understand I must call, visit, or write to SSA within 20 days if I have questions or if I disagree with the fee requested or any information shown (as explained on the reverse sides of this form).

Signature of Claimant	Date
Address (include Zip Code)	Telephone No. and Area Code

Form **SSA-1560-U4** (7-2000) EF (7-2000)
Destroy Prior Editions

FILE COPY

Figure 15–9 **Completed Petition for Approval of a Fee**

ATTACHMENT TO FEE PETITION

A—Court Appearance	P—Preparation
C—Conference	R—Research
F—Facts Investigation	RF—Review file
FG—Filing	TC—Telephone call
L—Letter	M—Miscellaneous
	N/C—No charge

Date	*Description*	*Hours*
6/24/98	C, init. conf. w/client	1.0
	P, req. for hrg.	.2
	M, cert. mlg.	.3
7/20/98	RF, letter from SSA re forms 827, 1696, 501, and 4486	.2
8/7/98	C, client	.9
	TC, client re hrg. test	.1
8/17/98	RF, review of additional evidence and documents	.3
	L, ltrs. to SSA re additional evidence and documents	.5
8/31/98	RF, ltr. from SSA re hrg.	.1
9/24/98	TC, re favorable decision	.1
9/28/98	RF, decision	.2
11/5/98	RF, ltr. from SSA re dismissal of req. for hrg.	.1
11/12/98	P, fee petition	.5
Total hours to 11/12/98		4.5
4.5 hours at $150.00 per hour		$ 675.00
Total fee		$675.00

Figure 15–10 Fee Petition Attachment

WHAT IF . . . ? SAMPLE PROBLEMS

WHAT IF . . .

What should the representative do if the evidence at the hearing shows an ongoing mental illness, such that the claimant testifies to depression and anxiety, but there is no medical documentation to that effect in the administrative record?

1. Nothing. The record is complete with the testimony given.
2. Suggest to the claimant that he or she pay for a psychological examination and then ask leave to submit the results later.
3. Request the judge order a consultative examination with a psychologist or psychiatrist in which a full battery of psychological tests is administered.
4. Request the judge order a consultative examination with a psychologist or psychiatrist in which only a mental status examination is administered.

Answer: ***When there is a "reasonable" basis in the record, either by reason of documentary evidence, testimony, or both to suggest a need for further development in the case, the judge should order a consultative examination to document the indicated impairment. The need for such documentation arises as a result of the requirement that an impairment must be medically documented, and must give rise to limitations of function affecting the individual's ability to perform competitive work. Where, as here, an individual testifies to depression, but no other record appears; or, the medical records are sketchy, reasonable cause arguably exists for further psychological testing. However, a simple mental status examination will not yield*** *sufficient information to assess the claimant's alleged affliction with depression and anxiety. Therefore, a full battery of tests should be ordered. The correct answer is 3.*

WHAT IF . . .

What if a fee agreement is not signed between the representative and the claimant?

1. The representative forfeits all fees for a successful representation.
2. The representative may charge whatever he or she wishes for representation.
3. The representative is limited to a fee not to exceed 10 percent of awarded benefits.
4. The representative must file a fee petition after the hearing.

Answer: ***If a fee agreement is not of record at the conclusion of the hearing, a fee petition must be filed. At no point is a representative free to charge what he or she wants. All fees must be approved by the Administrative Law Judge. If a fee agreement is signed, a fee is limited to 25 percent of back due benefits or $5,300, whichever is less. If a fee petition is submitted, fees are limited to that which is reasonable, but not otherwise limited to a specific dollar amount or percentage. The correct answer is 4.***

---

[1]Title 20 C.F.R. § 404.970 (2000).
[2]Title 20 C.F.R. § 404.970(b) (2000).
[3]Title 20 C.F.R. § 404.1725(b) (2000).
[4]Title 20 C.F.R. § 404.1730(c) (2000).
[5] Title 20 C.F.R. § 404.1720(d) (2000).

16

CHAPTER SIXTEEN

An Exemplar Case File[1]

HIGHLIGHTS

- ❑ Jurisdictional documents
- ❑ Medical records

CHRIS

"We're going to take the plunge and jump into a case file?"

"No better way to actually put the rubber to the road," Steve said. "It really helps to see how things actually appear—to put them in context."

"I agree. Let's take a look."

"The first thing you see is the "**exhibit list.**" In newer files the folder is divided into modular subparts, each with a different alphabetic designation—Part A, Part B, Part D, Part E, and Part F."

"Why?"

"The newer files make it easier to collate different types of documents. So, if you're looking for a medical record, you know just what section to find it in."

"So different types of documents are found in different sections?"

"Exactly."

"What does a file look like?"

"The so-called modular files are yellow, with interleaved dividers separating each section."

"Is an exhibit list still at the front of the file?"

"Like the old ones?"

"Is it the same?"

"Pretty much. The exhibit list is found on the left side of the inside cover, and it lists exhibits according to their subdivisions."

"Like Part A, Part B, and so forth?"

"That's right."

"Then the exhibit list is found at the beginning, in Part A?"

"Yes. Let me show you a sample exhibit list, and I'll also show you what a six-part modular file looks like." [See Figure 16–1.]

"Sounds good!"

"It looks like they have the exhibits in order by date. Is that right?"

"That's right, at least initially. When a 'raw file' is received by OHA from the state agency, there are no exhibit numbers on the various documents. Before a case can be heard, the file must be worked up. This means the exhibits must be properly noted and recorded, and an exhibit list prepared and sent to the representative."

"Is that when it's put in order by date?"

"Generally, yes. But that only applies to the records in the file at the time it is initially "worked up." New exhibits received from the representative, or directly from health care providers or others, are then listed in sequence, depending on when they were received. Documents received at the hearing are added as exhibits and noted on a revised exhibit list. Documents received after the hearing are also listed in sequence and specifically noted as being 'received after hearing.' "

"Sounds a little complicated," Chris said, self-doubt creeping into his voice.

"Relax. It's really second nature once you've done a few hearings. You don't even think about it after that. Here," Steve set a yellow folder on the desk, "let me show you the six-part modular file. The modular folder or 'modular disability folder,' otherwise known as the 'MDF,' is self-explanatory, that is, if you speak government-ese."

"What do you mean?"

"Each of the color-coded sections contains a preprinted list of what should be found in that particular section. Let me demonstrate."

SAMPLE EXHIBIT LIST

LIST OF EXHIBITS

Claimant: John Doe **SSN:**

Exh. No.	Part No.	Description	No. of Pages
		PAYMENT DOCUMENTS/DECISIONS	
1	A	Initial Disability Determination by State Agency, Title II, dated August 29, 1995, (with attachments)	2
2	A	Reconsideration Disability Determination by State Agency, Title II, dated January 30, 1996	1
		JURISDICTIONAL DOCUMENTS/NOTICES	
1	B	Social Security Notice dated August 29, 1995	5
2	B	Request for Reconsideration filed September 20, 1995	2
3	B	Social Security Notice of Reconsideration dated January 31, 1996	3
4	B	Request for Hearing filed February 23, 1996	2
5	B	Letter of Acknowledgment of Request for Hearing dated March 27, 1996 (with attachments)	2
		NON-DISABILITY DEVELOPMENT	
1	D	Leads/Protective Filing Worksheet dated November 16, 1994	1
2	D	Application for Disability Insurance Benefits filed December 7, 1994	4
3	D	Earnings record (dated/certified) May 3, 1996, Informational Copy Only	6
4	D	Worker's Compensation Information	1

	ADDITIONAL CLAIM FILE, IF APPLICABLE:
Part A (Yellow) - Payment Documents/Decisions	
Part B (Red) - Jurisdictional Documents/Notices	Part (SSI) - Supplemental Security Income
Part D (Orange) - Non-Disability Development	Part (DWB) - Disabled Widow/Widower
Part E (Blue) - Disability Related Development and Documentation	Part (CDB) - Child's Disability Benefits
Part F (Yellow) - Medical Records	

Figure 16–1 **Sample Exhibit List**

(continued)

Figure 16–1 **Sample Exhibit List *(continued)***

SAMPLE EXHIBIT LIST

LIST OF EXHIBITS

Claimant: John Doe **SSN:**

Exh. No.	Part No.	Description	No. of Pages
		DISABILITY RELATED DEVELOPMENT AND DOCUMENTATION	
	E	Disability Report dated December 7, 1994	8
2	E	Supplemental Questionnaire dated May 30, 1995	6
3	E	Report of Contact dated August 14, 1995	1
4	E	Vocational Report dated August 23, 1995	6
5	E	Reconsideration Disability Report dated September 8, 1995	6
6	E	Supplemental Questionnaire dated October 19, 1995	6
7	E	Psychiatric Review Technique (PRT) form dated January 30, 1996 (completed by DDS physician)	9
8	E	Residual Functional Capacity (RFC) assessment form dated January 30, 1996 (completed by DDS physician)	8
9	E	Claimant's Statement When Request for Hearing is Filed and the Issue is Disability undated	2
		MEDICAL RECORDS	
1	F	Hospital Records for admission on January 30, 1994, through discharge on February 6, 1994, from Charity Hospital	4
2	F	Medical records covering period from January 30, 1994, to August 15, 1994, from Orthopedic Associates of Mobile Army Surgical Hospital #3077	52
3	F	Medical records covering period from December 14, 1994, to June 21, 1995, from "Hawkeye" Pierce, M.D.	7
4	F	Psychiatric Evaluation dated July 18, 1995, by Max "Klinger," Ed.D.	2
5	F	Medical Report dated August 24, 1995, by Frank Burns, M.D.	1
6	F	Psychological Evaluation dated November 15, 1995, by "Hot Lips" Houlihan, Ph.D.	9
		SUPPLEMENTAL SECURITY INCOME (SSI)	
1	SSI	Application for Supplemental Security Income Benefits filed December 7, 1994	3
2	SSI	Initial Disability Determination by State Agency, Title XVI, dated August 29, 1995 (with attachments)	2
3	SSI	Supplemental Security Income Notice dated August 29, 1995	6
4	SSI	Reconsideration Disability Determination by State Agency, Title XVI, dated January 30, 1996	1
5	SSI	Supplemental Security Income Notice of Reconsideration-Disability dated January 31, 1996	3

Part A (Yellow) - Payment Documents/Decisions Part B (Red) - Jurisdictional Documents/Notices Part D (Orange) - Non-Disability Development Part E (Blue) - Disability Related Development and Documentation Part F (Yellow) - Medical Records	ADDITIONAL CLAIM FILE, IF APPLICABLE: Part (SSI) - Supplemental Security Income Part (DWB) - Disabled Widow/Widower Part (CDB) - Child's Disability Benefits

FRONT OF YOUR MIND QUESTIONS AND CONSIDERATIONS, 16.1

PART A OF THE SIX-PART MODULAR FOLDER

Though not noted in the preprinted section, Part A, which contains payment documents and decisions, also contains the exhibit list. It also holds

1. Disability Determination and Transmittal (SSA-831);
2. Cessation of Continuance of Disability/Blindness Determination (SSA-833);
3. Determination of Award (SSA-101);
4. Determination of Benefits Payable after Offset (SSA-1203);
5. Waiver Decision (pertaining to waiver of an overpayment determined to be due and owing);
6. The ALJ Decision/Appeals Council Decision/Court Order;
7. Attorney Fee Decision or Fee Authorization (the decision by the Administrative Law Judge approving the requested fee).

Part A of the six-part modular folder is seen in Figure 16–2. In this section are the exhibit list, the underlying state agency determination, and, in a case remanded by the Appeals Council or the district court, those decisions. In the case of an overpayment—where the government determines that a claimant was overpaid, the waiver decision, which sets out the agency determination following the claimant's application for a waiver of the overpayment, is also important. Figure 16–3 lists all possible documents that can be placed in the Part A folder of the MDF. Notably, not each file contains all these documents. The content of this section varies depending on the nature of the claim and its procedural status.

BACK TO CHRIS

"Hold up!"

"Yes?"

"That's it? I mean, that's Part A?"

"Uh-uh."

"That wasn't so bad."

"Told you. Now look at Part B."

PAYMENT DOCUMENTS/DECISIONS

FILE IN CHRONOLOGICAL ORDER

For Example:

SSA-831 (Disability Determination & Transmittal)
SSA-833 (Cessation or Continuance of Disability/Blindness Determination)
SSA-101 (Determination of Award)
SSA-1203 (Determination of Benefits Payable After Offset)
Payment Output
Waiver Decision
ALJ Decision/Appeals Council/Court Order
Attorney Fee Decision/Fee Authorization
Representative Payee Output

Figure 16–2 **Part A of the Modular Disability Folder (a yellow divider in the folder)**

PART A

PAYMENT DOCUMENTS DECISIONS

A. Initial Disability Determination by State Agency, Title II, dated _______, (with attachments)
B. Initial Disability Determination by State Agency, Title XVI, dated _______, (with attachments)
C. Reconsideration Disability Determination by State Agency, Title II, dated _______, (with attachments)
D. Reconsideration Disability Determination by State Agency, Title XVI, dated _______, (with attachments)
E. Cessation or Continuance of Disability Determination by State Agency, Title II, dated _______, (with attachments)
F. Cessation or Continuance of Disability Determination by State Agency, Title XVI, dated _______, (with attachments)
G. Reconsideration Cessation or Continuance of Disability Determination by State Agency, Title II, dated _______, (with attachments)
H. Reconsideration Cessation or Continuance of Disability Determination by State Agency, Title XVI, dated _______, (with attachments)
I. Professional Qualifications, _______
J. ALJ's decision dated _______, (with attachments)
K. Decision of the U.S. District Court for the _______ dated _______

Figure 16–3 **Documents Potentially Found in Part A of the Modular Disability Folder**

FRONT OF YOUR MIND QUESTIONS AND CONSIDERATIONS, 16.2

PART B OF THE SIX-PART MODULAR FOLDER

Part B of the MDF contains jurisdictional documents and notices, including

1. Notice of Disability/Blindness Denial;
2. Request for Reconsideration (SSA-561);
3. Notices of Reconsideration;
4. Request for Hearing by Administrative Law Judge (HA-501);
5. Acknowledgment of Request for Hearing;
6. Notice of Hearing;
7. Request for Review of Hearing Decision (HA-520);
8. Appeals Council and/or Court Remand;
9. Appointment of Representative (SSA-1696); and
10. Attorney Fee Petitions or Fee Agreement Contracts.

Part B of the MDF is shown in Figure 16-4. Most notable among these documents are the Appointment of Representative and Attorney Fee Petitions or Fee Agreement Contracts. The representative should check to be sure the administrative record properly contains these documents. If there is no record of the appointment of representative, complete one before the hearing in order to proceed. Next most important is a completed fee agreement. This must be a part of the administrative record before the conclusion of the hearing or the agreement cannot be approved. In other words, as noted earlier, the fee agreement must be submitted no later than the date of the hearing to be effective.

Figure 16–5 contains a list of all possible documents that may be found in Part B. As with all such parts of the MDF, not every file will contain all possible documents. Next, take a look at Part D of the MDF.

JURISDICTIONAL DOCUMENTS/NOTICES

FILE IN CHRONOLOGICAL ORDER

For Example:

SSA/SSI Notice(s) of Disability/Blindness (Denial/Award)
SSA-561 (Request for Reconsideration)
Notice(s) of Reconsideration (Denial/Award)
HA-501 (Request for Hearing by Administrative Law Judge)
Acknowledgement of Request for Hearing
Notice of Hearing (Claimant, Representative & Expert Witnesses)
HA-520 (Request for Review of Hearing Decision)
Appeals Council/Court Remand
SSA-1696 (Appointment of Representative)
Attorney Fee Petitions & Fee Agreement Contracts

Figure 16–4 **Part B of the Modular Disability Folder (a red divider in the folder)**

PART B

JURISDICTIONAL DOCUMENTS/NOTICES

A. Social Security Notice dated _______
B. Supplemental Security Income Notice dated ________
C. Request for Reconsideration filed ________
D. Request for Reconsideration—Disability Cessation, filed ________
E. Social Security Notice of Reconsideration dated ________
F. Social Security Notice of Reconsideration dated ________, with attached Disability Hearing Officer's decision
G. Supplemental Security Income Notice of Reconsideration-Disability dated ________
H. Supplemental Security Income Notice of Reconsideration-Disability dated ________ with attached Disability Hearing Officer's decision
I. Notice of Disability Cessation dated ________
J. Notice of Continuing Disability Review dated ________
K. Social Security Award Letter dated ________
L. Supplemental Security Income Award Letter dated ________
M. Request for Hearing filed ________
N. Letter of Acknowledgment of Request for Hearing dated ________ (with attachments)
O. Waiver of Your Right to Personal Appearance Before an Administrative Law Judge dated ________
P. Notice Regarding Substitution of Party upon Death of Claimant dated ________
Q. Statement of Claimant dated ________
R. Notice of Hearing dated ________
S. Copy of Letter dated ________, to ________, Vocational Expert, requesting attendance at hearing
T. Resume for Vocational Expert
U. Copy of Letter dated ________, to ________, Medical Expert, requesting attendance at hearing, with professional qualifications
V. Request for Review of Hearing Decision/Order filed ________
W. Order of Appeals Council dated ________
X. Action of Appeals Council on Request for Review dated ________
Y. Summons and Complaint dated ________

Figure 16–5 **Documents Potentially Found in Part B of the Modular Disability Folder**

BACK TO CHRIS

"Hey! What happened to Part C?"

Steve shook his head, grinning. "There is no Part C."

"How come?"

"What can I say? This is government efficiency at its best! You know—A, B, D, E, F—alphabet soup courtesy of the bureaucrats."

"Weird."

"Definitely."

FRONT OF YOUR MIND QUESTIONS AND CONSIDERATIONS, 16.3

PART D OF THE SIX-PART MODULAR FOLDER

Part D is an obscure part of the six-part modular folder that contains requests for evidence, requests for assistance, and similar documents of little direct bearing on the disability determination process. Two areas, however, are potentially significant: systems screen printouts and queries. Queries usually take the form of SEQYs—summaries of quarterly earnings—but can take the form of a DEQY—a detailed report of quarterly earnings. See Figure 16-6 for an illustration of the Part D divider page.

Such reports are of immediate significance because they constitute Social Security's record of a client's earnings. These reports are valuable primary resources against which the client's memory can be compared. Most importantly, they constitute objective evidence that can be used against a client, should the judge determine that the client has engaged in substantial gainful activity and, therefore, should be denied at step 1 of the five-step sequential analysis.

Because the administrative record is available prior to the hearing, these specific records can be used to obtain a report of a client's earnings beforehand. Thus, if the client disagrees with the numbers or if there is an explanation for the earnings other than work (e.g., paid sick leave) the information will be available in advance. Figure 16-7 shows a complete list of all possible documents that might find their way into Part D of the file.

PART E OF THE SIX-PART MODULAR FOLDER

Part E (see Figure 16–8) is the Disability Related Development section of the six-part modular folder. It specifically contemplates exhibits that are directly related to the issue of disability but that are nonmedical in nature. Such exhibits include the claimant's medication list and for children, school records. For all adult claimants, Part E also includes

1. The Disability Report (SSA-3368);
2. The Vocational Report (SSA-3369);
3. Authorizations for Source to Release Medical Information to the Social Security Administration (medical release forms) (SSA-827);
4. Reconsideration Disability Report (SSA-3441);
5. Claimant's Statement When Request for Hearing Is Filed and the Issue Is Disability (HA-4486);
6. Report of Continuing Disability (SSA-454);
7. Disability Update Report (SSA-455);
8. School Records; and
9. Activities of Daily Living Forms and Reports.

Part E is second in importance only to Part F—the medical records. Part E contains documents directly relevant to the question of disability. The most important are

1. The claimant's medication list;
2. The Disability Report;

NON-DISABILITY DEVELOPMENT

FILE ACCORDING TO POMS GUIDELINES

For Example:

Applications and Supplements

All Non-Disability Related Documents (Age, Relationship, Earnings, Workers' Compensation, etc.)

WC/PDB Development

Requests for Waiver and Related Development

Payee Application and Development (Capability, Choice of Representative Payee, etc.)

Other Non-Disability Post-entitlement Documentation

Figure 16–6 **Part D of the Modular Disability Folder (an orange divider in the folder)**

PART D

NON-DISABILITY DEVELOPMENT

A. Record of Intent to File dated _______
B. Record of SSI Inquiry dated _______
C. TSC Claims Referral dated _______
D. Leads/Protective Filing Worksheet dated _______
E. Application for Disability Insurance Benefits filed _______
F. Application for Supplemental Security Income Benefits filed _______
G. Application for Widow's/Widower's Insurance Benefits filed _______
H. Application for Child's Insurance Benefits filed _______
I. Medical History and Disability Report—Widow/Widower, Surviving Divorced Wife, or Disabled Child (in lieu of application) dated _______
J. Overpayment Notice dated _______
K. Special Determination dated _______
L. Waiver Determination dated _______
M. Letter Explaining Claimant's Rights
N. Earnings record (dated/certified) _______
O. W-2 Form for _______
P. Income Tax Return for _______
Q. Statement of Employer _______
R. Verification of dates of military service from _______ to _______
S. Verification of claimant's date of birth as _______
T. Birth Certificate for _______
U. Copy of Marriage Certificate for _______ and _______ (Date of Marriage: _______)
V. Divorce Decree for _______ and _______ showing date of divorce as _______
W. Death Certificate for _______
AA. Verification of Death for _______ showing date of death as _______
BB. Resident Alien Documentation
CC. Worker's Compensation Information
DD. Statement of Claimant dated _______
EE. Statement of _______ dated _______

Figure 16–7 **Documents Potentially Found in Part D of the Modular Disability Folder**

(continued)

Figure 16–7 **Documents Potentially Found in Part D of the Modular Disability Folder *(continued)***

PART D

NON-DISABILITY DEVELOPMENT

FF. Report of Contact dated _______
GG. Report of Lay Information dated _______
HH. Letter dated _______ to _______ from _______
II. Request for Waiver of Overpayment and Recovery Questionnaire dated _______
JJ. Overpayment Recovery Questionnaire dated _______
KK. Copy of letter of proffer to _______ dated _______
LL. Reply to letter of proffer from _______ dated _______
MM. Copy of letter dated _______, with additional evidence to _______ for comments
NN. Comments from _______, dated _______

DISABILITY RELATED DEVELOPMENT AND DOCUMENTATION

FILE IN CHRONOLOGICAL ORDER

For Example:

IFAs, RFCs, and PRTF
SSA-3368 (Disability Report)
SSA-3369 (Vocational Report)
SSA-827s (Authorization for Source to Release Medical Information to the Social Security Administration)
SSA-3441 (Reconsideration Disability Report)
HA-4486 (Claimant's Statement When Request for Hearing Is Filed & the Issue Is Disability)
SSA-454 (Report of Continuing Disability)
SSA-455 (Disability Update Report)
School Records (Regarding Disabling Impairment)
Activities of Daily Living Forms
Unsuccessful Attempts to Obtain Necessary Disability Documentation
DDS Development Worksheets
Any Other Documentation Relating to Development of Disability

STATE VOCATIONAL REPORTS
SSA-821, 820, and CDR Documentation

Figure 16–8 **Part E of the Modular Disability Folder (a blue divider in the folder)**

3. The Vocational Report; and
4. School Records (for children).

The medication list is a report of the claimant's medications and provides important corroborative testimony. The Disability Report and Vocational Report are completed by the claimant or by someone at his or her direction. As such they must be carefully scrutinized to ensure consistency, both between the two documents, and with the client's current recollection. What the client currently recalls may be different from what he or she said one or two years earlier. If they are inconsistent, the judge may draw an adverse conclusion regarding a client's credibility.

School records are vital, because they reflect daily conduct, behavior, and performance, both individually and socially. They include academic records, psychometric testing, health records, and disciplinary records. A complete list of all possible documents that *may* (though not necessarily will) be found within Part E is found in Figure 16–9.

PART F OF THE SIX-PART MODULAR FOLDER

The heart of the administrative record is the medical evidence that undergirds the claimant's case. This evidence is found in Part F of the six-part modular folder, which contains the following as examples of medical records:

1. Treatment records;
2. Hospital records;
3. Laboratory reports;
4. Outpatient notes;
5. Clinic notes;
6. Physician's records and reports; and
7. Cover letters from treatment sources.

PART E

DISABILITY RELATED DEVELOPMENT AND DOCUMENTATION

A. Medical History and Disability Report—Widow/Widower, Surviving Divorced Wife, or Disabled Child—dated _______
B. Request for Field Investigation of Continuing Disability dated _______
C. Disability Hearing Officer's Report of Disability Hearing dated _______
D. Worker's Compensation Information
E. Work Activity Report dated _______
F. Vocational Report dated _______
G. Disability Report dated _______
H. Reconsideration Disability Report dated _______
I. Reconsideration Report for Disability Cessation dated _______
J. Social Security Disabled Person Report dated _______
K. Disability Supplemental Interview Outline dated _______
L. Report of Continuing Disability Interview dated _______
M. Supplemental Questionnaire dated _______
N. Daily Activities Questionnaire dated _______
O. Report of Contact Regarding Daily Activities dated _______
P. Seizure Description Form dated _______
Q. Pain Questionnaire dated _______
R. Chest Pain Description dated _______ by _______
S. Statement of Claimant dated _______
T. Questionnaire for Children Claiming SSI Benefits dated _______
U. Disabled Child Supplemental Questionnaire dated _______
V. Child Activities of Daily Living dated _______
W. Claimant's Statement When Request for Hearing Is Filed and the Issue Is Disability dated _______
X. Statement of _______ dated _______
AA. Report of Contact dated _______
BB. Report of Lay Information dated _______
CC. Letter dated _______ to _______ from _______

***Figure 16–9* Documents Potentially Found in Part E of the Modular Disability Folder**

(continued)

Figure 16–9 **Documents Potentially Found in Part E of the Modular Disability Folder *(continued)***

PART E

DISABILITY RELATED DEVELOPMENT AND DOCUMENTATION

DD. School Activity Report dated _______
EE. School Function Report dated _______
FF. School Records (completed by teacher and/or other nonmedical personnel) from _______
GG. Nonmedical Report received _______ from _______
HH. List of Claimant's Medications dated _______
II. Copy of letter of proffer to _______ dated _______
JJ. Reply to letter of proffer from _______ dated _______
KK. Copy of Interrogatory to _______ dated _______
LL. Reply to Interrogatory from _______ dated _______
MM. Copy of letter dated _______ with additional evidence to _______ for comments
NN. Comments from _______ dated _______
OO. Psychiatric Review Technique (PRT) form dated _______ (completed by DDS physician)
PP. Residual Functional Capacity (RFC) assessment form dated _______ (completed by DDS physician)
QQ. Individualized Functional Assessment (IFA) form dated _______ (completed by DDS physician)

MEDICAL RECORDS

FILE ACCORDING TO POMS GUIDELINES

For Example:

Treatment Records
Hospital Records
Laboratory Records
Outpatient Notes
Clinic Notes
Physician's Records & Reports
Cover Letters from Treatment Source

SSA Pub. No. 64-061
ICN 440200

Figure 16–10 **Part F of the Modular Disability Folder (a yellow divider in the folder)**

Figure 16–10 shows the divider page for Part F of the MDF. Generally, these records are in chronological sequence, with the most recent records in the front and the oldest at the back. These records establish the basic elements for a disability claim, which include

1. Evidence of a severe impairment as required at step 2 of the five-step sequential analysis;
2. Evidence establishing the components of a severe impairment, including diagnosis, functional limitations, and duration of the illness, disease, or injury;
3. Evidence as to whether the claimant's condition meets or is medically equivalent in severity to a listed impairment in the medical listings, as set forth in step 3 of the five-step sequential evaluation;
4. Evidence of medically based restrictions of activities of daily living or function, as noted at step 4 and step 5 of the five-step sequential evaluation; and
5. Evidence bearing on the question of the claimant's credibility.

Figure 16–11 shows a complete list of documents that may (though not necessarily will) be included in this part.

PART F

MEDICAL RECORDS

A. Medical Report ENTER "s" IF PLURAL dated _______, by _______
B. Medical Records dated _______, by _______
C. Medical records covering period from _______ to _______, from _______
D. Treatment Notes covering the period from _______ to _______, by _______
E. Progress Notes covering the period from _______ to _______, by _______
F. Physical Therapy Records covering period from _______ to _______, from _______
G. Consultative Examination dated _______, by _______
H. Internal Medicine Consultative Examination dated _______, by _______
I. Orthopedic Consultative Examination dated _______, by _______
J. Neurological Consultative Examination dated _______, by _______
K. Psychiatric Evaluation dated _______, by _______
L. Psychological Evaluation dated _______, by _______
M. Hospital Records for admission on _______ through discharge on _______, from _______
N. Outpatient Medical Records covering period from _______ to _______, from _______
O. Emergency/Outpatient Record dated _______, from _______
P. Emergency Room Records dated _______, from _______
Q. Medical Evidence Obtained by Telephone for period _______, from _______
R. Professional Qualifications, _______
S. Reply to Interrogatory from _______ dated _______
T. Appeals Council Exhibit Number(s) _______—Medical Report(s) dated _______, from _______

Figure 16–11 **Documents Potentially Found in Part F of the Modular Disability Folder**

BACK TO CHRIS

"This doesn't make sense," Chris declared, leafing through the folder for Part F a third time. "I thought you said it was a six-part folder?"

"I did. It is."

"We talked about Parts A, B, D, E, and F, right?"

"That's the folder."

"Steve, that's only five parts. I count six sections in this folder."

"Oh, you're right. I'm sorry. There are six sections, but only five contain exhibits that are part of the administrative record."

"Now I'm confused. How can part of the official file folder not be part of the administrative record?"

"You're talking about the green section?"

"Right. The one labeled 'Current Development/Temporary.' " [See Figure 16–12.] "Read on. See where it indicates that each component is responsible for purging this section when it is completed?"

"Yes."

"It's a temporary holding section, not intended to contain any documents. Of course, if there are documents there, it's a good idea to look at them and see what they are. They could be misplaced and need to go in a different section."

"So, this is simply a staging area for pending document requests and things like that?"

"You got it, Chris."

Chris nodded slowly. "Just like the government to include a section in an official record that's not official."

Steve grinned. "Let's take a look at a sample file, shall we?" Gesturing to a stack of papers, Steve rested his hand lightly on the topmost file.

CURRENT DEVELOPMENT/TEMPORARY

For Example:

Requests for Evidence
Requests for Assistance
Instructions to Support Personnel
Systems Screen Printouts (MCS or MSSICS Screens)
Queries
Pre-printed Forms Not Yet Used
Requests for Assistance from Other Component
After Adjudication, Nonactionable Mail Received in the FRC

EACH SSA COMPONENT IS RESPONSIBLE FOR PURGING THIS SECTION WHEN ACTION IS COMPLETED. ESSENTIAL MATERIALS WILL BE FILED IN THE APPROPRIATE MODULE AND NON-ESSENTIAL MATERIALS WILL BE DISCARDED.

Example 1.

DDS requests a medical report. If received, request is discarded. If not received, request is moved to section labeled Disability Related Development & Documentation.

Example 2.

The Field Office requests an SEQY at initial interview. If claimant verifies correctness of earnings on application, the SEQY is discarded. If SEQY is pertinent to documentation of a decision, it is filed in the section labeled Non-Disability Development.

Figure 16–12 **Unnamed Temporary Holding Section of the MDF (a green divider in the folder)**

Chris looked at the thick file. "Are we going to go from Part A to Part F?"

"Sort of," Steve replied. "I want to start with the application, because that's the first thing your client will complete. It's found in Part D."

"Sounds good."

FRONT OF YOUR MIND QUESTIONS AND CONSIDERATIONS, 16.4

SAMPLE FILE

The sample file in this chapter consists of selected excerpts and explanations of documents typically found in a disability appeals file at the Social Security Office of Hearings and Appeals. The application for disability benefits is the first document that will be encountered when assisting an individual in the initial stages, or when being consulted after the application has been denied by the state DDS. It is important to know for what the claimant actually applied.

The Disability Application

The actual written application may be initiated by telephone contact or in person at the local Social Security field office. One type of application is made for Supplemental Security Income benefits (SSI under Title XVI), while a separate application is made for Disability Insurance Benefits (DIB under Title II).

If the application is initiated by telephone (the claimant calls to make inquiry) the date of that contact is the protective filing date and it is important in SSI claims. In an SSI claim, the claimant can only receive benefits from the date of the actual application. A telephone contact causes the Social Security Administration to prepare a Leads/Protective Filing Worksheet, which is a record of the actual telephone contact. This contact date becomes the official application date, even though no written application is yet on file, if the written application is received within thirty days of the telephone contact. Figure 16–13 depicts a typical Leads/Protective Filing Worksheet. Basic information is required over the telephone, including

1. Claimant's full name;
2. Claimant's Social Security number;
3. Contact information, including address and telephone;
4. Name of claimant's spouse (if applicable), including spousal earnings (if applicable);
5. Date last worked;
6. Any resources (in the case of a Title XVI application);
7. Name(s) of children, including residences; and
8. Nature of the place of residence (e.g., house, apartment, mobile home, houseboat).

Each application, when completed in writing, requires the following information:

1. Claimant's full name;
2. Claimant's Social Security number;
3. Claimant's date of birth;
4. Claimant's spouse, his or her birthdate, and Social Security number;
5. Date of marriage and, if applicable, date of divorce;
6. Name(s) of all children, natural or adopted, their respective birthdate(s), and Social Security number(s); and
7. Alleged date disability began ("alleged onset date").

Typical Title II disability insurance applications are shown in Figure 16–14 (one an agency printout, the other an on-line version).

A Title XVI Supplemental Security Income application requires more information than a Title II application, because it considers benefits that are need based. As such, a Title XVI claim is resource dependent, meaning an individual who has too many resources, despite any disability, will not be entitled to disability benefits. The application, therefore, requires additional information specifically related to resources and expenditures:

1. Whether the claimant resides with his or her spouse and/or children;
2. Assets, including vehicles (and their value), life insurance (including face value and date of purchase), checking and savings account(s) (including the name of the financial institution and value), and any other resources (including inheritance, real estate, stock, or interests, even if not matured);
3. All income, from any sources, including spousal earnings;
4. Work expenses because of the alleged disability; and
5. Other benefits received, such as food stamps, and so on.

Figure 16–15 shows a typical Title XVI, or SSI, application.

BACK TO CHRIS

"Okay, that's the application. But what about all of this other stuff?"

"You mean the medical records?" Steve asked.

"No," Chris pointed, "these. They don't look medical; they look like administrative forms."

"You're right. Let's take a look."

NH SSN: **PAGE 1**

LEADS/PROTECTIVE FILING WORKSHEET

NH NAME: SSN:
BIRTHDATE: PROOF CODE: SEX: DEATH:
UNIT: SHR FO: PRIOR FO:

CLAIM TYPE(S) : DIB SSIDI LEAD ESTABLISHED:
T2 CLAIM TAKEN: T16 CLAIM TAKEN:

CL NAME: SSN:
BIRTHDATE: PROOF CODE: SEX: ONSET DATE:

ADDRESS:

CITY: STATE: OK ZIP:
COUNTRY: POSTAL ZONE:
PHONE: INFO: HM PHONE: INFO:
FOREIGN PHONE:

CALLER (IF DIFFERENT):
RELATIONSHIP TO CLAIMANT:
RECONTACT BY CALLER: DATE:

CY EARNINGS: PY EARNINGS: INFORMAL DENIAL:
PROOFS REQ AGE: X MAR/DIV: DEATH: MILITARY:
MEDICAL EVIDENCE:
W-2/EARNINGS FOR SSI INC/RESR:

APPT DATE: TIME: APPT TYPE: PHONE CAL. USED:
PRIOR DATE: TIME: REASON FOR CHANGE:

DISABILITY FORMS SENT: SUPPRESS NOTICE:

SUE REQ F/UP F/UP TICKLE REC REMARKS

PROTFL
T2CO
T16CO

REMARKS

Figure 16–13 **Leads/Protective Filing Worksheet**

(A) Agency Printout

NH **SG-SSA-16, PAGE 001***

UNIT:

APPLICATION FOR DISABILITY INSURANCE BENEFITS

I APPLY FOR A PERIOD OF DISABILITY AND/OR ALL INSURANCE BENEFITS FOR WHICH I AM ELIGIBLE UNDER TITLE II AND PART A OF TITLE XVIII OF THE SOCIAL SECURITY ACT, AS PRESENTLY AMENDED.

MY NAME IS

MY SOCIAL SECURITY NUMBER IS

MY DATE OF BIRTH IS

I BECAME UNABLE TO WORK BECAUSE OF MY DISABLING CONDITION ON

I AM STILL DISABLED.

NO PREVIOUS APPLICATION HAS BEEN FILED WITH THE SOCIAL SECURITY ADMINISTRATION BY OR FOR ME.

I HAVE NOT FILED NOR DO I INTEND TO FILE FOR ANY WORKERS' COMPENSATION, PUBLIC DISABILITY OR BLACK LUNG BENEFITS.

I AM NOT ENTITLED TO NOR DO I EXPECT TO BECOME ENTITLED TO A PENSION OR ANNUITY BASED IN WHOLE OR IN PART ON WORK AFTER 1956 NOT COVERED BY SOCIAL SECURITY.

THE SOCIAL SECURITY ADMINISTRATION AND THE STATE AGENCY REVIEWING MY CLAIM DOES HAVE MY PERMISSION TO CONTACT MY EMPLOYER(S).

I AM MARRIED TO: . WE WERE MARRIED ON . * IN *

SG-SSA-16, PAGE 002*

BY A CLERGYMAN OR PUBLIC OFFICIAL. MY SPOUSE'S AGE OR BIRTHDATE IS MARCH 23, 1941, AND SOCIAL SECURITY NUMBER IS .

I DO NOT HAVE ANY CHILDREN WHO MAY BE ELIGIBLE FOR SOCIAL SECURITY BENEFITS ON THIS RECORD.

I UNDERSTAND THAT I MUST PROVIDE MEDICAL EVIDENCE ABOUT MY DISABILITY, OR ASSIST THE SOCIAL SECURITY ADMINISTRATION IN OBTAINING THE EVIDENCE.

I UNDERSTAND THAT I MAY BE REQUESTED BY THE STATE DISABILITY DETERMINATION SERVICES TO HAVE A CONSULTATIVE EXAMINATION AT THE EXPENSE OF THE SOCIAL SECURITY ADMINISTRATION AND THAT IF I DO NOT GO MY CLAIM MAY BE DENIED.

I AUTHORIZE ANY PHYSICIAN, HOSPITAL, AGENCY, OR OTHER ORGANIZATION TO DISCLOSE ANY MEDICAL RECORD OR INFORMATION ABOUT MY DISABILITY TO THE SOCIAL SECURITY ADMINISTRATION OR TO THE STATE DISABILITY DETERMINATION SERVICES THAT MAY REVIEW MY CLAIM OR CONTINUING DISABILITY.

Figure 16–14 **Title II Applications for Disability Insurance Benefits: (A) Printed from Agency and (B) On-Line Version**

(continued)

Figure 16–14 **Title II Applications for Disability Insurance Benefits: (A) Printed from Agency and (B) On-Line Version** ***(continued)***

I AUTHORIZE THE SOCIAL SECURITY ADMINISTRATION TO RELEASE ANY INFORMATION ABOUT ME TO A PHYSICIAN OR MEDICAL FACILITY PREPARATORY TO AN EXAMINATION OR TEST. RESULTS OF SUCH EXAMINATION OR TEST MAY BE RELEASED TO MY PHYSICIAN OR OTHER TREATING SOURCE.

I AUTHORIZE THAT INFORMATION ABOUT MY DISABILITY MAY BE FURNISHED TO ANY CONTRACTOR FOR CLERICAL SERVICES BY THE STATE DISABILITY DETERMINATION SERVICES.

I AGREE TO NOTIFY THE SOCIAL SECURITY ADMINISTRATION OF ALL EVENTS AS EXPLAINED TO ME.

I AGREE TO NOTIFY THE SOCIAL SECURITY ADMINISTRATION IF:

— MY MEDICAL CONDITION IMPROVES SO THAT I WOULD BE ABLE TO WORK, EVEN THOUGH I HAVE NOT YET RETURNED TO WORK.

— I GO TO WORK WHETHER AS AN EMPLOYEE OR A SELF-EMPLOYED PERSON.

— I APPLY FOR OR RECEIVE A DECISION ON BENEFITS UNDER ANY WORKERS' COMPENSATION LAW OR PLAN (INCLUDING BLACK LUNG BENEFITS FROM THE DEPARTMENT OF LABOR), OR OTHER PUBLIC BENEFIT BASED ON DISABILITY.

SG-SSA-16, PAGE 003*

— I AM IMPRISONED FOR CONVICTION OF A FELONY.

THE ABOVE EVENTS MAY AFFECT MY ELIGIBILITY TO DISABILITY BENEFITS AS PROVIDED IN THE SOCIAL SECURITY ACT, AS AMENDED.

I AGREE TO NOTIFY THE SOCIAL SECURITY ADMINISTRATION IF I BECOME ENTITLED TO A PENSION OR ANNUITY BASED ON EMPLOYMENT AFTER 1956 NOT COVERED BY SOCIAL SECURITY, OR IF SUCH PENSION OR ANNUITY STOPS.

MY REPORTING RESPONSIBILITIES HAVE BEEN EXPLAINED TO ME.

I KNOW THAT ANYONE WHO MAKES OR CAUSES TO BE MADE A FALSE STATEMENT OR REPRESENTATION OF MATERIAL FACT IN AN APPLICATION OR FOR USE IN DETERMINING A RIGHT TO PAYMENT UNDER THE SOCIAL SECURITY ACT COMMITS A CRIME PUNISHABLE UNDER FEDERAL LAW BY FINE, IMPRISONMENT OR BOTH. I AFFIRM THAT ALL INFORMATION I HAVE GIVEN IN CONNECTION WITH THIS CLAIM IS TRUE.

MY MAILING ADDRESS IS ______________________________

____

____

MY TELEPHONE NUMBER IS ______________________________

SIGNATURE ______________________________ DATE ______________

WITNESSES ARE REQUIRED ONLY IF THIS APPLICATION HAS BEEN SIGNED BY MARK (X) ABOVE. IF SIGNED BY (X), TWO WITNESSES TO THE SIGNING WHO KNOW THE APPLICANT MUST SIGN BELOW, GIVING THEIR FULL ADDRESSES.

______________________________	______________________________
SIGNATURE OF WITNESS	SIGNATURE OF WITNESS
NUMBER AND STREET ADDRESS	NUMBER AND STREET ADDRESS
CITY, STATE, AND ZIP CODE	CITY, STATE, AND ZIP CODE

SOCIAL SECURITY ADMINISTRATION ☐ TEL Form Approved OMB No. 0960-0060 TOE 120/145

(Do not write in this space)

APPLICATION FOR DISABILITY INSURANCE BENEFITS

I apply for a period of disability and/or all insurance benefits for which I am eligible under title II and part A of title XVIII of the Social Security Act, as presently amended.

PART I - INFORMATION ABOUT THE DISABLED WORKER

1.	(a) PRINT your name →	FIRST NAME, MIDDLE INITIAL, LAST NAME
	(b) Enter your name at birth if different from item (a) →	
	(c) Check (X) whether you are →	☐ Male ☐ Female
2.	Enter your Social Security Number →	___ / __ / ____
3.	(a) Enter your date of birth →	MONTH, DAY, YEAR
	(b) Enter name of State or foreign country where you were born. →	
	If you have already presented, or if you are now presenting, a public or religious record of your birth established before you were age 5, go on to item 4.	
	(c) Was a public record of your birth made before you were age 5?	☐ Yes ☐ No ☐ Unknown
	(d) Was a religious record of your birth made before you were age 5?	☐ Yes ☐ No ☐ Unknown
4.	(a) What are the illnesses, injuries, or conditions that limit your ability to work? (Give a brief description.)	
	(b) Are your illnesses, injuries, or conditions related to your work in any way? →	☐ Yes ☐ No
5.	(a) When did you become unable to work because of your illnesses, injuries or conditions? →	MONTH, DAY, YEAR
	(b) Are you still unable to work? →	☐ Yes ☐ No
	(c) If you are no longer unable to work because of your illnesses, injuries or conditions, enter the date you became able to work. →	MONTH, DAY, YEAR
6.	(a) Have you (or has someone on your behalf) ever filed an application for Social Security benefits, a period of disability under Social Security, supplemental security income, or hospital or medical insurance under Medicare? →	☐ Yes (If "Yes," answer (b) and (c).) ☐ No ☐ Unknown (If "No," or "Unknown," go on to item 7.)
	(b) Enter name of person on whose Social Security record you filed other application. →	
	(c) Enter Social Security Number of person named in (b). *If unknown, check this block.* ☐ →	___ / __ / ____
7.	(a) Were you in the active military or naval service (including Reserve or National Guard active duty or active duty for training) after September 7, 1939 and before 1968? →	☐ Yes (If "Yes," answer (b) and (c).) ☐ No (If "No," go on to item 8.)
	(b) Enter dates of service →	FROM: (Month, year) TO: (Month, year)
	(c) Have you *ever* been (or will you be) eligible for a monthly benefit from a military or civilian Federal agency? (include Veterans Administration benefits *only* if you waived military retirement pay) →	☐ Yes ☐ No

Form **SSA-16-F6** (9-1999) EF (4-2000) Page 1
Destroy prior editions

(continued)

Figure 16–14 **Title II Applications for Disability Insurance Benefits: (A) Printed from Agency and (B) On-Line Version** ***(continued)***

8.	(a) Have you filed (or do you intend to file) for any other public disability benefits? (Include workers' compensation and Black Lung benefits) →	☐ Yes (If "Yes," answer (b).)	☐ No (If "No," go on to item 9.)
	(b) The other public disability benefit(s) you have filed (or intend to file) for is (Check as many as apply): ☐ Veterans Administration Benefits ☐ Welfare ☐ Supplemental Security Income ☐ Other (If "Other," complete a Workers' Compensation/Public Disability Benefit Questionnaire)		
9.	(a) Do you have social security credits (for example, based on work or residence) under another country's Social Security System? (If "Yes," answer (b).) (If "No," go on to item 10.) →	☐ Yes	☐ No
	(b) List the country(ies): →		
10.	(a) Are you entitled to, or do you expect to become entitled to, a pension or annuity based on your work after 1956 not covered by Social Security?	☐ Yes (If "Yes," answer (b) and (c).)	☐ No (If "No," go on to item 11.)
	(b) ☐ I became entitled, or expect to become entitled, beginning	MONTH	YEAR
	(c) ☐ I became eligible, or expect to become eligible, beginning	MONTH	YEAR

I agree to notify the Social Security Administration if I become entitled to a pension or annuity based on my employment after 1956 not covered by Social Security, or if such pension of annuity stops.

11.	(a) Did you have wages or self-employment income covered under Social Security in all years from 1978 through last year?	☐ Yes (If "Yes," skip to item 12.)	☐ No (If "No," answer (b).)
	(b) List the years from 1978 through last year in which you did not have wages or self-employment income covered under Social Security.		

12. Enter below the names and addresses of all the persons, companies, or Government agencies for whom you have worked this year and last year. IF NONE, WRITE "NONE" BELOW AND GO ON TO ITEM 14.

NAME AND ADDRESS OF EMPLOYER (If you had more than one employer, please list them in order beginning with your last (most recent) employer)	Work Began		Work Ended (If still working show "Not Ended")	
	MONTH	YEAR	MONTH	YEAR
(If you need more space, use ''Remarks'' space on page 4.)				

13.	May the Social Security Administration or the State agency reviewing your case ask your employers for information needed to process your claim? →	☐ Yes	☐ No
14.	THIS ITEM MUST BE COMPLETED, EVEN IF YOU WERE AN EMPLOYEE.		
	(a) Were you self-employed this year and last year? (If "Yes," answer (b).) (If "No," go on to item 15.) →	☐ Yes	☐ No

(b) Check the year or years in which you were self-employed	In what kind of trade or business were you self-employed? (For example, storekeeper, farmer, physician)	Were your net earnings from your trade or business $400 or more? (Check "Yes" or "No")	
☐ This year			
☐ Last year		☐ Yes	☐ No
☐ Year before last		☐ Yes	☐ No

15.	(a) How much were your total earnings last year? (Count both wages and self-employment income. If none, write "None.") →	Amount $ ________
	(b) How much have you earned so far this year? (If none, write "None.") →	Amount $ ________

Form **SSA-16-F6** (9-1999) EF (4-2000) Page 2

(c) Did you receive any money from an employer(s) on or after the date in item 5(a) when you became unable to work because of your illnesses, injuries, or conditions? (If "Yes", give the amounts and explain in "Remarks" on page 4.) →	☐ Yes ☐ No Amount $ ________
(d) Do you expect to receive any additional money from an employer such as sick pay, vacation pay, other special pay? (If "Yes," please give amounts and explain in "Remarks" on page 4.)→	☐ Yes ☐ No Amount $ ________

PART II — INFORMATION ABOUT THE DISABLED WORKER AND SPOUSE

16.	Have you ever been married? → (If "Yes," answer item 17.) (If "No," go on to item 18.)	☐ Yes ☐ No

17. (a) Give the following information about your current marriage. If not currently married, show your last marriage below.

To whom married		When (Month, day, year)	Where (Name of City and State)
Your current or last marriage	How marriage ended (If still in effect, write "Not Ended.")	When (Month, day, year)	Where (Name of City and State)
	Marriage performed by: ☐ Clergyman or public official ☐ Other (Explain in Remarks)	Spouse's date of birth (or age)	If spouse deceased, give date of death
	Spouse's Social Security Number (If none or unknown, so indicate)		___ / __ /____

(b) Give the following information about each of your previous marriages. **(If none, write "NONE.")**

To whom married		When (Month, day, year)	Where (Name of City and State)
Your previous marriage	How marriage ended	When (Month, day, year)	Where (Name of City and State)
	Marriage performed by: ☐ Clergyman or public official ☐ Other (Explain in Remarks)	Spouse's date of birth (or age)	If spouse deceased, give date of death
	Spouse's Social Security Number (If none or unknown, so indicate)		___ / __ /____

(Use a separate statement for information about any other marriages.)

18.	Have you or your spouse worked in the railroad industry for 7 years or more? →	☐ Yes ☐ No

PART III — INFORMATION ABOUT THE DEPENDENTS OF THE DISABLED WORKER

19. If your claim for disability benefits is approved, your children (including natural children, adopted children, and stepchildren) or dependent grandchildren (including stepgrandchildren) may be eligible for benefits based on your earnings record.

List below: FULL NAME OF ALL such children who are now or were in the past 12 months UNMARRIED and:
- UNDER AGE 18
- AGE 18 TO 19 AND ATTENDING SECONDARY SCHOOL
- DISABLED OR HANDICAPPED (age 18 or over and disability began before age 22)

(IF THERE ARE NO SUCH CHILDREN, WRITE "NONE" BELOW AND GO ON TO ITEM 20.)

20.	Do you have a dependent parent who was receiving at least one-half support from you when you became unable to work because of your disability? (If "Yes," enter name and address in "Remarks" on page 4.)	☐ Yes ☐ No

Form **SSA-16-F6** (9-1999) EF (4-2000) Page 3

(continued)

Figure 16–14 **Title II Applications for Disability Insurance Benefits: (A) Printed from Agency and (B) On-Line Version** ***(continued)***

IMPORTANT INFORMATION ABOUT DISABILITY INSURANCE BENEFITS — PLEASE READ CAREFULLY

I. SUBMITTING MEDICAL EVIDENCE: I understand that as a claimant for disability benefits, I am responsible for providing medical evidence showing the nature and extent of my disability. I may be asked either to submit the evidence myself or to assist the Social Security Administration in obtaining the evidence. If such evidence is not sufficient to arrive at a determination, I may be requested by the State Disability Determination Service to have an independent examination at the expense of the Social Security Administration.

II. RELEASE OF INFORMATION: I authorize any physician, hospital, agency or other organization to disclose to the Social Security Administration, or to the State Agency that may review my claim or continuing disability, any medical record or other information about my disability.
I also authorize the Social Security Administration to release medical information from my records, only as necessary to process my claim, as follows:

- Copies of medical information may be provided to a physician or medical institution prior to my appearance for an independent medical examination if an examination is necessary.
- Results of any such independent examination may be provided to my personal physician.
- Information may be furnished to any contractor for transcription, typing, record copying, or other related clerical or administrative service performed for the State Disability Determination Service.
- The State Vocational Rehabilitation Agency may review any evidence necessary for determining my eligibility for rehabilitative services.

THIS MUST BE ANSWERED ➔ 21. DO YOU UNDERSTAND AND AGREE WITH THE AUTHORIZATIONS GIVEN ABOVE?
☐ Yes ☐ No (If "No," explain why in "Remarks.")

22. Check if applicable:
☐ I am not submitting evidence of ☐ my ☐ the deceased's earnings that are not yet on ☐ my ☐ his/her earnings record. I understand that these earnings will be included automatically within 24 months, and any increase in benefits will be paid with full retroactivity.

REMARKS (You may use this space for any explanation. If you need more space, attach a separate sheet.)

III. REPORTING RESPONSIBILITIES: I agree to promptly notify Social Security if:

- My MEDICAL CONDITION IMPROVES so that I would be able to work, even though I have not yet returned to work.
- I GO TO WORK whether as an employee or a self-employed person.
- I apply for or begin to receive a workers' compensation (including black lung benefits) or another public disability benefit, or the amount that I am receiving changes or stops, or I receive a lump-sum settlement.
- I am confined to jail, prison, a penal institution or correctional facility for conviction or a crime or I am confined to a public institution by court order in connection with a crime.

The above events may affect my eligibility or disability benefits as provided in the Social Security Act, as amended.

I know that anyone who makes or causes to be made a false statement or representation of material fact in an application or for use in determining a right to payment under the Social Security Act commits a crime punishable under Federal law by fine, imprisonment or both. I affirm that all information I have given in this document is true.

SIGNATURE OF APPLICANT	Date (Month, day, year)
Signature (First name, middle initial, last name) (Write in ink) **SIGN HERE** ▶	Telephone Number(s) at which you may be contacted during the day. (Include the area code)

FOR OFFICIAL USE ONLY	Direct Deposit Payment Address *(Financial Institution)*			
	Routing Transit Number	C/S	Depositor Account Number	☐ No Account ☐ Direct Deposit Refused

Applicant's Mailing Address *(Number and street, Apt No., P.O. Box, or Rural Route) (Enter Residence Address in "Remarks," if different.)*

City and State	ZIP Code	County *(if any)* in which you now live

Witnesses are required ONLY if this application has been signed by mark (X) above. If signed by mark (X), two witnesses to the signing who know the applicant must sign below, giving their full addresses. Also, print the applicant's name in Signature block.

1. Signature of Witness	2. Signature of Witness
Address *(Number and street, City, State and ZIP Code)*	Address *(Number and street, City, State and ZIP Code)*

Form **SSA-16-F6** (9-1999) EF (4-2000) Page 4

FOR YOUR INFORMATION

An agency in your State that works with us in administering the Social Security disability program is responsible for making the disability decision on your claim. In some cases, it is necessary for them to get additional information about your condition or to arrange for you to have a medical examination at Government expense.

Collection and Use of Information From Your Application — Privacy Act Notice/Paperwork Act Notice

The Social Security Administration is authorized to collect the information on this form under sections 202(b), 202(c), 205(a), and 1872 of the Social Security Act, as amended (42 U.S.C. 402(b), 402(c), 405(a), and 1395(ii). While it is VOLUNTARY, except in the circumstances explained below, for you to furnish the information on this form to Social Security, no benefits may be paid unless an application has been received by a Social Security office. Your response is mandatory where the refusal to disclose certain information affecting your right to payment would reflect a fraudulent intent to secure benefits not authorized by the Social Security Act. The information on this form is needed to enable Social Security to determine if you and your dependents are entitled to insurance coverage and/or monthly benefits. Failure to provide all or part of this information could prevent an accurate and timely decision on your claim or your dependent's claim, and could result in the loss of some benefits or insurance coverage.

Although the information you furnish on this form is almost never used for any other purpose than stated in the foregoing, there is a possibility that for the administration of the Social Security programs or for the administration of programs requiring coordination with the Social Security Administration, information may be disclosed to another person or to another governmental agency as follows: 1. to enable a third party or an agency to assist Social Security in establishing rights to Social Security benefits and/or coverage; 2. to comply with Federal laws requiring the release of information from Social Security records (e.g., to the General Accounting Office and the Veterans Administration); and 3. to facilitate statistical research and audit activities necessary to assure the integrity and improvement of the Social Security programs (e.g., to the Bureau of the Census and private concerns under contract to Social Security).

We may also use the information you give us when we match records by computer. Matching programs compare our records with those of other Federal, State, or local government agencies. Many agencies may use matching programs to find or prove that a person qualifies for benefits paid by the Federal government. The law allows us to do this even if you do not agree to it.

Explanations about these and other reasons why information you provide us may be used or given out are available in Social Security offices. If you want to learn more about this, contact any Social Security office.

PAPERWORK REDUCTION ACT NOTICE AND TIME IT TAKES STATEMENT:

The **Paperwork Reduction Act of 1995** requires us to notify you that this information collection is in accordance with the clearance requirements of section 3507 of the Paperwork Reduction Act of 1995. We may not conduct or sponsor, and you are not required to respond to, a collection of information unless it displays a valid OMB control number. We estimate that it will take you about 20 minutes to complete this form. This includes the time it will take to read the instructions, gather the necessary facts and fill out the form.

Form **SSA-16-F6** (9-1999) EF (4-2000) Page 5

(continued)

Figure 16–14 **Title II Applications for Disability Insurance Benefits: (A) Printed from Agency and (B) On-Line Version** ***(continued)***

RECEIPT FOR YOUR CLAIM FOR SOCIAL SECURITY DISABILITY INSURANCE BENEFITS

PERSON TO CONTACT ABOUT YOUR CLAIM	SSA OFFICE	DATE CLAIM RECEIVED
TELEPHONE NUMBER (INCLUDE AREA CODE)		

Your application for Social Security disability benefits has been received and will be processed as quickly as possible.

You should hear from us within days after you have given us all the information we requested. Some claims may take longer if additional information is needed.

In the meantime, if you change your address, or if there is some other change that may affect your claim, you — or someone for you — should report the change. The changes to be reported are listed below.

Always give us your claim number when writing or telephoning about your claim.

If you have any questions about your claim, we will be glad to help you.

CLAIMANT	SOCIAL SECURITY CLAIM NUMBER

CHANGES TO BE REPORTED AND HOW TO REPORT

FAILURE TO REPORT MAY RESULT IN OVERPAYMENTS THAT MUST BE REPAID

- You change your mailing address for checks or residence. To avoid delay in receipt of checks you should ALSO file a regular change of address notice with your post office.
- You go outside the U.S.A. for 30 consecutive days or longer.
- Any beneficiary dies or becomes unable to handle benefits.
- Custody Change—Report if a person for whom you are filing or who is in your care dies, leaves your care or custody, or changes address.
- You are confined to jail, prison, penal institution or correctional facility for conviction of a crime or you are confined to a public institution by court order in connection with a crime.
- You become entitled to a pension or annuity based on your employment after 1956 not covered by Social Security, or if such pension or annuity stops.
- Your stepchild is entitled to benefits on your record and you and the stepchild's parent divorce. Stepchild benefits are not payable beginning with the month after the month the divorce becomes final.
- Change of Marital Status—Marriage, divorce, annulment of marriage.
- You return to work (as an employee or self-employed) regardless of amount of earnings.
- Your condition improves.
- If you apply for or begin to receive workers' compensation (including black lung benefits) or another public disability benefit, or the amount of your present workers' compensation or public disability benefit changes or stops, or you receive a lump-sum settlement.

HOW TO REPORT

You can make your reports by telephone, mail, or in person, whichever you prefer.

If you are awarded benefits, and one or more of the above changes occur, the change(s) should be reported by calling:

(Telephone Number—Include Area Code)

Form **SSA-16-F6** (9-1999) EF (4-2000) Page 6

CLAIMANT: **PAGE 1**

APPLICATION FOR SUPPLEMENTAL SECURITY INCOME

I am applying for Supplemental Security Income and any federally administered State supplementation under Title XVI of the Social Security Act for benefits under the other programs administered by the Social Security Administration, and where applicable, for medical assistance under Title XIX of the Social Security Act.

❑ IDENTIFICATION

My name is ______________________ My social security number is ____________

My date of birth is ______________

I have not used any other name or social security number(s).
I am not blind.
I am disabled. The disability began on
I am a United States citizen by birth.
I never lived outside the United States.
I am married to ______________________
Her birthdate is ______________________ Her social security number is ____________

She has not used any other social security number(s).
She has used the following name(s):

❑ LIVING ARRANGEMENTS

The following statements describe my living arrangements as of February 1,

I began living at ______________________________ on April 1, ____

I live in a house/apartment/mobile home/houseboat.
I live with my spouse, parents, and/or children.
I do not expect these arrangements to change.

CLAIMANT: **PAGE 2**

❑ RESOURCES

I own the following as of ______________________________

Truck:

Vehicle:
This vehicle is used for medical treatment.
Value: From: To:

Automobile:

Vehicle:
This vehicle is used for employment.
Value: From: To:

Life insurance:

Company name:
Policy number:
Date purchased:
Face value:

Figure 16–15 **Title XVI Application for Supplemental Security Income Benefits**

Figure 16–15 **Title XVI Application for Supplemental Security Income Benefits** ***(continued)***

I do not own any other type of resource.
My spouse owns the following as of
Checking account:
Financial institution name:
Value: From: To:
My spouse does not own any other type of resource.

❑ INCOME

Since , I have received or expect to receive the following income:
Social Security
Wages:
Amount
From:
Employer name:

CLAIMANT: **PAGE 3**

Contact:
Phone:
I do not receive any other type of income.
I do not have work expenses due to a disability.
Since , my spouse has received or expects to receive the following income:
Wages:
Amount
From: To:
Employer name:
Contact:
Phone:
My spouse does not receive any other type of income.

❑ ELIGIBILITY FOR OTHER BENEFITS

I do not currently get food stamps.
I want to apply for food stamps.

IMPORTANT INFORMATION—PLEASE READ CAREFULLY

We will check your statements and compare our records with records from other State and Federal agencies, including the Internal Revenue Service to make sure you are paid the correct amount.

I understand that anyone who knowingly lies or misrepresents the truth or arranges for someone to knowingly lie or misrepresent the truth is committing a crime which can be punished under Federal law, State law, or both. Everything on this application is the truth as best I know it.

SIGNATURE______________________________ DATE____________

Telephone Number:

Mailing Address:

DISABILITY APPLICATION SUPPLEMENTARY DOCUMENTS

Various documents supplement the application for disability benefits. The representative should be familiar with these filings. Some are completed by the claimant; others, by the Social Security Administration.

The Disability Report

Supplemental documents are prepared contemporaneously by the claimant when completing the initial application for disability benefits. The Disability Report is one such document completed by the claimant when he or she makes an initial application for disability benefits. It is a statement by the claimant, of record, and will be scrutinized by both the vocational expert and the Administrative Law Judge. It generally contains the following information:

- ❑ The claimant's statement of his or her disabling condition;
- ❑ The alleged onset date (when the condition first bothered the claimant);
- ❑ The date the claimant stopped working;
- ❑ A list of doctors and medical intervention;
- ❑ The claimant's statement of daily activities including
    1. Household maintenance,
    2. Recreational activities and hobbies,
    3. Social contacts, and
    4. Other activities;
- ❑ The claimant's educational attainment; and
- ❑ The claimant's past work, including the weight lifted.

What's Important?

The Disability Report is extremely important because it is

1. In the client's own words (i.e., completed by him or her); and
2. A comprehensive overview of the major issues relating to the claimant's ability to perform competitive work.

Unfortunately, in many cases, the Disability Report is completed by a client before a representative is involved in the case. The report calls for summary responses by the claimant, not designed, by virtue of the form, to give significant insight into any given area. A summary statement of the claimant's daily activities, and even the nature of past work, can be misleading, not so much for what it says as what it does not say. The format of the form calls for short answers. For many, even completion of the form is a challenge. Yet, the completed form is a permanent part of the administrative record and thus holds potential to harm a client's case once before an Administrative Law Judge.

The harm, of course, lies in the testimony and evidence that may later be revealed in a hearing. If what the claimant wrote when he or she first applied for benefits and what later is revealed in a hearing differ, the claimant's credibility is at risk. It is, therefore, incumbent on the representative to be fully aware of the contents of the Disability Report before conducting a final interview with the claimant. Failure to consider the contents of the Disability Report before the administrative hearing may severely damage the claimant's presentation and may ultimately negatively influence the judge's decision.

The important focus of the Disability Report is the claimant's statements of daily activities. Apart from an attempt to conceal work, the nature of work, and ongoing or past medical care, are issues that are essentially objective in nature. Past work is as it is, and the medical records stand for themselves. What is often not so clear is the claimant's descriptions of personal capabilities. A claimant's expression of his or her capability is subjective; it is his or her description of the ability to engage in work or worklike activity. A person's presentation of capability is often distorted by pain. Even more telling: A person's pain often distorts perception itself. Pain, however, is neither readily measured nor experienced in a similar fashion among different individuals. Thus, one's daily activities reflect in large measure one's functional capability through the course of a "normal" eight-hour workday.

The capable representative must be familiar with the Disability Report and use it as a basis to further explore, in one or more interviews with the claimant, what his or her true capabilities are. Importantly, the claimant's capabilities may change over time, particularly when the time to disposition extends beyond one year. Thus, if the claimant indicates in the Disability Report that he or she "visits mother daily" but also indicates that he or she "quit driving in 1990 because of my ankle," immediate questions are raised: How does the claimant get around? If the claimant visits his or her mother daily but doesn't drive, is someone else driving? Does the claimant walk? What is the full story?

Similarly, if the claimant indicates in the Disability Report that he or she cannot stand for long periods of time and must use crutches because his or her right leg hurts but also indicates, "I cook my own meals, clean my own room, and do my own laundry," the representative must inquire, "If you can't stand for long periods of time, how is it that you are able to do all these things for yourself?" The representative must ask these questions, and the claimant must be prepared to answer them. They *will* be asked by the judge.

Failure to address these issues will only leave the judge wondering about the claimant's credibility, which ultimately impacts on the judge's assessment of the claimant's subjective perception of pain. A copy of the Disability Report is shown in Figure 16–16.

Claimant's Statement

When a request for hearing is made and the basis for the request is to contest the denial of a claim for disability benefits, another form is completed, the Claimant's Statement When Request for Hearing Is Filed and the Issue Is Disability (see Figure 16–17). Like the Disability Report, it requires summary information concerning the underlying claim. This information includes the following:

- ❑ Date last worked;
- ❑ Change in condition since date last worked;
- ❑ Daily activities;
- ❑ Medical treatment; and
- ❑ Medications.

What's Important?

This form, although more cursory than the Disability Report, is, nonetheless, significant, both in what it reveals and what it does not. As in the more lengthy Disability Report, in the claimant's statement, the claimant must relate, in his or her own words, a summary of daily activity. The problem is that it offers little room for comprehensiveness. Nevertheless, it is important that the representative review these statements to ensure consistency between both the reports and the claimant's later testimony. If a discrepancy arises, the representative must be aware of it well in advance of a hearing and be able to address these issues in a considered and thoughtful fashion.

Employee's Work History Report

The Work History Report (see Figure 16–18) is filled out by the claimant. It includes detailed past work activity provided by the claimant. The form states: "The information provided will be used in making a decision on your claim." Completion of the form is voluntary but, as noted on the form, "failure to provide all or part of the requested information could prevent an accurate and timely decision on your claim and could result in the loss of benefits." Thus, as with any other form completed by the claimant, the information on this form must be carefully reviewed. If a representative is fortunate enough to be involved at the beginning of the disability applications process, this form, and all others, should be completed by the claimant with the representative's supervision.

What's Important?

The vocational expert relies on the work history report in assessing the claimant's previous work. The vocational expert also examines the Disability Report and uses these documents, along with the DEQY, to formulate his or her testimony regarding the claimant's work history. It is, therefore, necessary to examine these documents and correlate the information in them with that obtained from interviewing the claimant. This helps prepare for the examination of the vocational expert.

Reconsideration Disability Report

The Reconsideration Disability Report (see Figure 16–19) begins where the Disability Report ends. It is completed, again, "voluntarily," when requesting reconsideration when the initial determination is unfavorable. The decision maker in this process is the state DDS.

SOCIAL SECURITY ADMINISTRATION

Form Approved
OMB No. 0960-0579

DISABILITY REPORT ADULT

For SSA Use Only
Do not write in this box.

Related SSN ______

Number Holder ______

SECTION 1- INFORMATION ABOUT THE DISABLED PERSON

A. **NAME** *(First, Middle Initial, Last)*

B. **SOCIAL SECURITY NUMBER**

C. **DAYTIME TELEPHONE NUMBER** *(If you have no number where you can be reached, give us a daytime number where we can leave a message for you.)*

____ *Area Code* ______ *Number* ☐ Your Number ☐ Message Number ☐ None

D. Give the name of a **friend or relative** that we can contact (other than your doctors) **who knows about your illnesses, injuries or conditions** and can help you with your claim.

NAME ______ RELATIONSHIP ______

ADDRESS ______
(Number, Street, Apt. No.(If any), P.O. Box, or Rural Route)

______ *City* *State* *ZIP* DAYTIME PHONE ____ *Area Code* ______ *Number*

E. What is your **height** without shoes? ____ *feet* ____ *inches*

F. What is your **weight** without shoes? ____ *pounds*

G. Do you have a **medical assistance card**? (For Example, Medicaid or Medi-Cal) If "YES," show the **number** here: ______ ☐ YES ☐ NO

H. Can you **speak English**? ☐ YES ☐ NO If "NO," what languages can you speak? ______

If you **cannot speak English**, is there someone we may contact who speaks English and will give you messages? *(If this is the same person as in "D" above show "SAME" here.)*

NAME ______ RELATIONSHIP ______

ADDRESS ______
(Number, Street, Apt. No.(If any), P.O. Box, or Rural Route)

______ *City* *State* *ZIP* DAYTIME PHONE ____ *Area Code* ______ *Number*

I. Can you **read English**? ☐ YES ☐ NO

J. Can you **write more than your name in English**? ☐ YES ☐ NO

FORM SSA-3368-BK (12-1998) EF (1-2001) The 7-1998 edition may be used until exhausted

PAGE 1

Disability Report-Adult-Form SSA-3368-BK

***Figure 16–16* The Disability Report**

(continued)

Figure 16–16 **The Disability Report *(continued)***

SECTION 2
YOUR ILLNESSES, INJURIES OR CONDITIONS AND HOW THEY AFFECT YOU

A. What are the **illnesses, injuries or conditions** that limit your ability to work? ____________

B. How do your illnesses, injuries or conditions limit your ability to work? ____________

C. Do your illnesses, injuries or conditions cause you **pain**? ☐ YES ☐ NO

D. When did your illnesses, injuries or conditions **first bother you**?

Month	*Day*	*Year*

E. When did you become **unable to work** because of your illnesses, injuries or conditions?

Month	*Day*	*Year*

F. Have you **ever worked**? ☐ YES ☐ NO *(If "NO," go to Section 4.)*

G. Did you **work at any time** after the date your illnesses, injuries or conditions first bothered you? ☐ YES ☐ NO

H. If "YES," did your illnesses, injuries or conditions cause you to: *(check all that apply)*

☐ **work fewer hours?** *(Explain below)*

☐ **change your job duties?** *(Explain below)*

☐ **make any job-related changes such as your attendance, help needed, or employers?** *(Explain below)*

I. Are you **working now**? ☐ YES ☐ NO

If "NO," when did **you stop working**?

Month	*Day*	*Year*

J. Why did you **stop working**?

FORM SSA-3368-BK (12-1998) EF (1-2001) The 7-1998 edition may be used until exhausted PAGE 2

SECTION 3 - INFORMATION ABOUT YOUR WORK

A. List the **jobs** that you have had in the **last 15 years that you worked.**

JOB TITLE *(Example, Cook)*	TYPE OF BUSINESS *(Example, Restaurant)*	DATES WORKED *(month & year)*		HOURS PER DAY	DAYS PER WEEK	RATE OF PAY *(Per hour, day, week,month or year)*	
		From	To				
						$	
						$	
						$	
						$	
						$	
						$	
						$	

B. Describe the **job above** that you did the **longest**. (What did you do all day in this job?)

____

____

C. In **this job**, did you: Use machines, tools or equipment? ☐ YES ☐ NO

Use technical knowledge or skills? ☐ YES ☐ NO

Do any writing, complete reports, or perform any duties like this? ☐ YES ☐ NO

Did you supervise other people? ☐ YES ☐ NO

If "YES," was this your main duty? ☐ YES ☐ NO

D. In **this job**, how many total hours each day did you:

Walk? ______

Stand? ______

Sit? ______

Climb? ______

Stoop? *(Bend down and forward at waist.)* ______

Kneel? *(Bend legs to rest on knees.)* ______

Crouch? *(Bend legs & back down & forward.)* ______

Crawl? *(Move on hands & knees.)* ______

Handle, grab or grasp big objects? ______

Write, type or handle small objects? ______

E. Lifting and Carrying *(Explain what you lifted, how far you carried it, and how often you did this.)*

____

F. Check **heaviest** weight lifted:

☐ Less than 10 lbs ☐ 10 lbs ☐ 20 lbs ☐ 50 lbs ☐ 100 lbs. or more ☐ Other ______

G. Check weight **frequently** lifted: *(By frequently, we mean from 1/3 to 2/3 of the workday.)*

☐ Less than 10 lbs ☐ 10 lbs ☐ 25 lbs ☐ 50 lbs. or more ☐ Other ______

FORM SSA-3368-BK (12-1998) EF (1-2001) The 7-1998 edition may be used until exhausted PAGE 3

(continued)

Figure 16–16 **The Disability Report** ***(continued)***

SECTION 4 - INFORMATION ABOUT YOUR MEDICAL RECORDS

A. Have you been seen by a **doctor/hospital/clinic** or anyone else for the illnesses, injuries or conditions that limit your ability to work? ☐ YES ☐ NO

B. Have you been seen by a **doctor/hospital/clinic** or anyone else for emotional or mental problems that limit your ability to work? ☐ YES ☐ NO

If you answered "NO" to both of these questions, go to Section 5.

C. List **other names** you have used on your medical records. ______________________

____

Tell us who may have medical records or other information about your illnesses, injuries or conditions.

D. **List each DOCTOR/HMO/THERAPIST.** Include your **next appointment.**

1.

			DATES
NAME			
STREET ADRESS			**FIRST** VISIT
CITY	**STATE**	**ZIP**	**LAST** SEEN
PHONE *Area Code* *Phone Number*	**CHART/HMO #**		NEXT **APPOINTMENT**
REASONS FOR VISITS			
WHAT **TREATMENT** WAS RECEIVED?			

2.

			DATES
NAME			
STREET ADRESS			**FIRST** VISIT
CITY	**STATE**	**ZIP**	**LAST** SEEN
PHONE *Area Code* *Phone Number*	**CHART/HMO #**		NEXT **APPOINTMENT**
REASONS FOR VISITS			
WHAT **TREATMENT** WAS RECEIVED?			

FORM SSA-3368-BK (12-1998) EF (1-2001) The 7-1998 edition may be used until exhausted PAGE 4

SECTION 4-INFORMATION ABOUT YOUR MEDICAL RECORDS

DOCTOR/HMO/THERAPIST

3.

NAME				DATES
STREET ADRESS				**FIRST** VISIT
CITY	**STATE**	**ZIP**		**LAST** SEEN
PHONE ______ Area Code ______ Phone Number		**CHART/HMO #**		NEXT **APPOINTMENT**

REASONS FOR VISITS ______________________________

WHAT **TREATMENT** WAS RECEIVED? ______________________________

If you need more space, use Remarks, Section 9.

E. **List each HOSPITAL/CLINIC.** Include your **next appointment.**

1.

HOSPITAL/CLINIC			TYPE OF VISIT	DATES	
NAME			☐ **INPATIENT** STAYS *(Stayed at least overnight)*	DATE IN	DATE OUT
STREET ADDRESS					
CITY	STATE	ZIP	☐ **OUTPATIENT** VISITS *(Sent home same day)*	DATE FIRST VISIT	DATE LAST VISIT
PHONE ______ Area Code ______ Phone Number			☐ **EMERGENCY ROOM** VISITS	DATE OF VISITS	

Next **appointment** ______________ Your hospital/clinic **number** ______________

Reasons for visits ______________________________

What **treatment** did you receive? ______________________________

What **doctors** do you see at this hospital/clinic on a regular basis? ______________

FORM SSA-3368-BK (12-1998) EF (1-2001) The 7-1998 edition may be used until exhausted PAGE 5

(continued)

Figure 16–16 **The Disability Report** ***(continued)***

SECTION 4-INFORMATION ABOUT YOUR MEDICAL RECORDS

HOSPITAL/CLINIC

2.

HOSPITAL/CLINIC			TYPE OF VISIT	DATES	
NAME			☐ **INPATIENT** STAYS *(Stayed at least overnight)*	DATE IN	DATE OUT
STREET ADDRESS					
CITY	STATE	ZIP	☐ **OUTPATIENT** VISITS *(Sent home same day)*	DATE FIRST VISIT	DATE LAST VISIT
PHONE *Area Code* *Phone Number*			☐ **EMERGENCY ROOM** VISITS	DATE OF VISITS	

Next **appointment** ______________ Your hospital/clinic **number** ______________

Reasons for visits ______________

What **treatment** did you receive? ______________

What **doctors** do you see at this hospital/clinic on a regular basis? ______________

If you need more space, use Remarks, Section 9.

F. Does **anyone else have medical records or information** about your illnesses, injuries or conditions (Workers' Compensation, insurance companies, prisons, attorneys, welfare), or are you scheduled to see anyone else?

☐ YES *(If "YES," complete information below.)* ☐ NO

NAME			**DATES**
STREET ADRESS			**FIRST** VISIT
CITY	**STATE**	**ZIP**	**LAST** SEEN
PHONE *Area Code* *Phone Number*			NEXT APPOINTMENT
CLAIM NUMBER (If any)			
REASONS FOR VISITS			

If you need more space, use Remarks, Section 9.

FORM SSA-3368-BK (12-1998) EF (1-2001) The 7-1998 edition may be used until exhausted PAGE 6

SECTION 5 - MEDICATIONS

Do you currently take any **medications** for your illnesses, injuries or conditions? ☐ YES ☐ NO
If "YES," please tell us the following: *(Look at your medicine bottles, if necessary.)*

NAME OF MEDICINE	IF PRESCRIBED, GIVE NAME OF DOCTOR	REASON FOR MEDICINE	SIDE EFFECTS YOU HAVE

If you need more space, use Remarks, Section 9.

SECTION 6 - TESTS

Have you had, or will you have, any **medical tests** for illnesses, injuries or conditions?
☐ YES ☐ NO If "YES," please tell us the following: *(Give approximate dates, if necessary.)*

KIND OF TEST	WHEN DONE, OR WHEN WILL IT BE DONE? (Month, day, year)	WHERE DONE? (Name of Facility)	WHO SENT YOU FOR THIS TEST?
EKG (HEART TEST)			
TREADMILL (EXERCISE TEST)			
CARDIAC CATHETERIZATION			
BIOPSY--Name of body part ______			
HEARING TEST			
VISION TEST			
IQ TESTING			
EEG (BRAIN WAVE TEST)			
HIV TEST			
BLOOD TEST (NOT HIV)			
BREATHING TEST			
X-RAY--Name of body part ______			
MRI/CT SCAN Name of body part ______			

If you have had other tests, list them in Remarks, Section 9.

FORM SSA-3368-BK (12-1998) EF (1-2001) The 7-1998 edition may be used until exhausted

PAGE 7

(continued)

Figure 16–16 **The Disability Report** ***(continued)***

SECTION 7-EDUCATION/TRAINING INFORMATION

A. Check the highest grade of **school** completed.

Grade school: 0 ☐ 1 ☐ 2 ☐ 3 ☐ 4 ☐ 5 ☐ 6 ☐ 7 ☐ 8 ☐ 9 ☐ 10 ☐ 11 ☐ 12 ☐ GED ☐

College: 1 ☐ 2 ☐ 3 ☐ 4 or more ☐

Approximate **date** completed: ____________________

B. Did you attend **special education** classes? ☐ YES ☐ NO *(If "NO," go to part C)*

NAME OF SCHOOL ____________________

ADDRESS ____________________

(Number, Street, Apt. No.(if any), P.O. Box or Rural Route)

____

City *State* *Zip*

DATES ATTENDED __________ TO __________

TYPE OF PROGRAM ____________________

C. Have you completed any type of **special job training, trade or vocational school?**

☐ YES ☐ NO If "YES," what type? ____________________

Approximate date completed: ____________________

SECTION 8 - VOCATIONAL REHABILITATION INFORMATION

A. Have you received services from **Vocational Rehabilitation** or any other organization to help you get back to work? ☐ YES ☐ NO *(If "NO," go to part B)*

NAME OF ORGANIZATION ____________________

NAME OF COUNSELOR ____________________

ADDRESS ____________________

(Number, Street, Apt. No.(if any), P.O. Box or Rural Route)

____

City *State* *Zip*

DAYTIME PHONE NUMBER __________ __________

Area Code *Number*

DATES SEEN __________ TO __________

TYPE OF SERVICES OR TESTS PERFORMED

(IQ, vision, physicals, hearing, workshops, etc.)

B. Would you like to receive rehabilitation services that could help you get back to work?

☐ YES ☐ NO

FORM SSA-3368-BK (12-1998) EF (1-2001) The 7-1998 edition may be used until exhausted PAGE 8

SECTION 9 - REMARKS

Use this section for any added information you did not show in earlier parts of the form. When you are done with this section (or if you don't have anything to add), be sure to go to the next page and complete the signature block.

FORM SSA-3368-BK (12-1998) EF (1-2001) The 7-1998 edition may be used until exhausted

PAGE 9

(continued)

Figure 16–16 **The Disability Report *(continued)***

SECTION 9 - REMARKS

ANYONE MAKING A FALSE STATEMENT OR REPRESENTATION OF A MATERIAL FACT FOR USE IN DETERMINING A RIGHT TO PAYMENT UNDER THE SOCIAL SECURITY ACT COMMITS A CRIME PUNISHABLE UNDER FEDERAL LAW.

Signature of **claimant** or person filing on claimant's behalf ***(parent, guardian)***	**Date** *(Month, day, year)*

Witnesses are required **ONLY** if this statement has been signed by mark (X) above. If signed by mark (X), two witnesses to the signing who know the person making the statement must sign below, giving their full addresses.

1. Signature of **Witness**	2. Signature of **Witness**
Address *(Number and street, city, state, and ZIP code)*	**Address** *(Number and street, city, state, and ZIP code)*

FORM SSA-3368-BK (12-1998) EF (1-2001) The 7-1998 edition may be used until exhausted PAGE 10

Form Approved
OMB No. 0960-0316

CLAIMANT'S STATEMENT WHEN REQUEST FOR HEARING IS FILED AND THE ISSUE IS DISABILITY

Print, type or write clearly and answer all questions to the best of your ability. Complete answers will aid in processing the claim. IF ADDITIONAL SPACE IS NEEDED, ATTACH A SEPARATE STATEMENT TO THIS FORM.

CLAIMANT'S NAME	SOCIAL SECURITY NUMBER
WAGE EARNER (Leave blank if name is the same as the claimant's)	SOCIAL SECURITY NUMBER

PRIVACY ACT AND PAPERWORK ACT NOTICE: The Social Security Act (section 205(a), 702, 1631(e)(1)(A) and (B), and 1869(b)(1) and (c), as appropriate authorized the collection of information on this form. We will use the information on your recent activities, condition, medical treatment, and medications to help us decide if we need to obtain more information. You do not have to give it, but if you do not you may not receive benefits under the Social Security Act. We may give out the information on this form without your written consent if we need to get more information to decide if you are eligible for benefits or if a Federal law requires us to do so. Specifically, we may provide information to another Federal, State, or local government agency which is deciding your eligibility for a government benefit or program; to the President or a Congressman inquiring on your behalf; to an independent party who needs statistical information for a research paper or audit report on a Social Security program; or to the Department of Justice to represent the Federal Government in a court suit related to a program administered by the Social Security Administration.

We may also use the information you give us when we match records by computer. Matching programs compare our records with those of other Federal, State, or local government agencies. Many agencies may use matching programs to find or prove that a person qualifies for benefits paid by the Federal government. The law allows us to do this even if you do not agree to it.

Explanations about these and other reasons why information you provide us may be used or given out are available in Social Security offices. If you want to learn more about this, contact any Social Security office.

TIME IT TAKES TO COMPLETE THIS FORM

We estimate that it will take you about 15 minutes to complete this form. This includes the time it will take to read the instructions, gather the necessary facts and fill out the form. If you have comments or suggestions on this estimate, or on any other aspect of this form, write to the Social Security Administration, ATTN: Reports Clearance Officer, 1-A-21 Operations Bldg., Baltimore, MD 21235-0001, and to the Office of Management and Budget, Paperwork Reduction Project (0960-0316), Washington, D.C. 20503. Send only comments relating to our estimate or other aspects of this form to the offices listed above. **All requests for Social Security cards and other claims-related information should be sent to your local Social Security office whose address is listed in your telephone directory under the Department of Health and Human Services.**

1. Have you worked since ____________, the date your request for reconsideration was filed? *(If yes, describe the nature and extent of work.)* — ☐ Yes ☐ No

2. Has there been any change in your condition since the above date? *(If yes, describe the change.)* — ☐ Yes ☐ No

3. Have your daily activities and/or social functioning changed since the above date? *(If yes, describe the changes.)* — ☐ Yes ☐ No

4a. Have you been treated or examined by a physician (other than as a patient in a hospital) since the above date? *(If yes, complete the following.)* — ☐ Yes ☐ No

NAME OF PHYSICIAN	ADDRESS *(Include ZIP code)*
AREA CODE AND TELEPHONE NUMBER	
HOW OFTEN DO YOU SEE THIS PHYSICIAN	DATES YOU SAW THIS PHYSICIAN
REASON FOR VISIT	
TYPE OF TREATMENT RECEIVED *(Include drugs, surgery, tests)*	

Form **HA-4486** (4-94) EF-PPP-INTERNET (6-95) (Over)

***Figure 16–17* Claimant's Statement**

(continued)

Figure 16–17 Claimant's Statement *(continued)*

4b. Have you seen any other physician since the above date? *(If yes, show the following:)* ☐ Yes ☐ No

NAME OF PHYSICIAN

ADDRESS *(Include ZIP code)*

AREA CODE AND TELEPHONE NUMBER

HOW OFTEN DO YOU SEE THIS PHYSICIAN

DATES YOU SAW THIS PHYSICIAN

REASON FOR VISIT

TYPE OF TREATMENT RECEIVED *(Include drugs, surgery, tests)*

If you have seen other physicians since you filed your claim, attach a list of their names, addresses, dates and reasons for visits.

5. Have you been hospitalized, or treated at a clinic or confined in a nursing home or extended care facility for your illness or injury since the above date? *(If yes, show the following:)* ☐ Yes ☐ No

NAME OF FACILITY

ADDRESS *(Include ZIP code)*

PATIENT OR CLINIC NUMBER

WERE YOU AN INPATIENT? (Stayed at least overnight) ☐ Yes ☐ No *If yes, show*

DATES OF ADMISSIONS AND DISCHARGES

WERE YOU AN OUTPATIENT ☐ Yes ☐ No *If yes, show*

DATES OF VISITS

REASON FOR HOSPITALIZATION, CLINIC VISITS, OR CONFINEMENT

TYPE OF TREATMENT RECEIVED *(Include drugs, surgery, tests)*

If you have been in other hospitals, clinics, nursing homes, or extended care facilities for your illness or injury, attach a list of the names, addresses, patient or clinic numbers, dates and reasons for hospitalization, clinic visits, or confinement.

6. Have you received medical or vocational services from a community agency since the above date? (If yes, indicate below the name, address and telephone number of the agency.) ☐ Yes ☐ No

7. Are you now taking any prescription drugs or medications? *(If yes, list them below.)* ☐ Yes ☐ No

NAME OF MEDICATION(S)	DOSAGE BEING TAKEN	NAME OF PHYSICIAN(S)

8. Are you now taking any nonprescription drugs or medications? *(If yes, list them below.)* ☐ Yes ☐ No

NAME OF MEDICATION(S)	DOSAGE BEING TAKEN

9. Have you filed (or do you intend to file) for workers' compensation? ☐ Yes ☐ No

(If you have filed for workers' compensation and have received an award, please bring a copy of the award notice, redemption order, or settlement to your hearing.)

Form **HA-4486** (4-94) EF-PPP-INTERNET (6-95)

SOCIAL SECURITY ADMINISTRATION

Form Approved
OMB No. 0960-0578

WORK HISTORY REPORT

SECTION 1 - INFORMATION ABOUT THE DISABLED PERSON

A. Name *(First, Middle Initial, Last)*	**B. SOCIAL SECURITY NUMBER**

C. DAYTIME TELEPHONE NUMBER *(If you have no number where you can be reached, give us a daytime number where we can leave a message for you.*

______ *Area Code* ______ *Phone Number* Your Number Message Number None

SECTION 2 - INFORMATION ABOUT YOUR WORK

List the kinds of jobs that you have had in the last 15 years that you worked.

Job Title *(Example: Cook)*	Type of Business *(Example: Restaurant)*	Dates Worked *(Month & Year)* From	To
1.			
2.			
3.			
4.			
5.			
6.			
7.			
8.			
9.			
10.			

FORM **SSA-3369-BK** (7/1998) EF (8-2000) DESTROY ALL PRIOR EDITIONS PAGE 1

Work History Report - Form SSA-3369-BK

Figure 16–18 **Work History Report**

Figure 16–18 **Work History Report *(continued)***

Give us more information about Job No. 1 listed on Page 1. Estimate hours and pay, if you need to.

JOB TITLE NO. 1

Rate of Pay $ ________	Per *(Check One)* ☐ Hour ☐ Week ☐ Month ☐ Year	Hours per day ____	Days per week ____

In this job, did you:

- Use machines, tools or equipment? ☐ YES *(explain below)* ☐ NO
- Use technical knowledge or skills? ☐ YES *(explain below)* ☐ NO
- Write reports or complete forms? ☐ YES *(explain below)* ☐ NO

Describe this job. What did you do all day? *(If you need more space, write in the "Remarks" section.)*

____

____

____

In **this job**, how many total hours each day did you:

Walk? ________

Stand? ________

Sit? ________

Climb? ________

Stoop? *(Bend down and forward at waist.)* ________

Kneel? *(Bend legs to rest on knees.)* ________

Crouch? *(Bend legs & back down & forward.)* ________

Crawl? *(Move on hands & knees.)*

Handle, grab or grasp big objects? ________

Write, type or handle small objects? ________

Lifting and Carrying *(Explain what you lifted, how far you carried it, and how often you did this.)*

____

____

____

Check the **heaviest** weight lifted:

☐ Less than 10 lbs ☐ 10 lbs ☐ 20 lbs ☐ 50 lbs ☐ 100 lbs. or more ☐ Other ______

Check weight you **frequently** lifted: *(By frequently, we mean from 1/3 to 2/3 of workday.)*

☐ Less than 10 lbs ☐ 10 lbs ☐ 25 lbs ☐ 50 lbs. or more ☐ Other ________

Did you supervise other people in this job? ☐ YES *(Complete items below.)* ☐ NO *(Skip to next page.)*

How many people did you supervise? ________

What part of your time was spent supervising people? ________

Did you hire and fire employees? ☐ YES ☐ NO

Were you a lead worker? ☐ YES ☐ NO

FORM **SSA-3369-BK** (7/1998) EF (8-2000) DESTROY ALL PRIOR EDITIONS

PAGE 2

Give us more information about Job No. 2 listed on Page 1. Estimate hours and pay, if you need to.

JOB TITLE NO. 2

Rate of Pay $ ______	Per *(Check One)* ☐ Hour ☐ Week ☐ Month ☐ Year	Hours per day	Days per week ______

In this job, did you:

Use machines, tools or equipment? ☐ YES *(explain below)* ☐ NO

Use technical knowledge or skills? ☐ YES *(explain below)* ☐ NO

Write reports or complete forms? ☐ YES *(explain below)* ☐ NO

Describe this job. What did you do all day? *(If you need more space, write in the "Remarks" section.)*

____

____

____

In **this job**, how many total hours each day did you:

Walk? ______

Stand? ______

Sit? ______

Climb? ______

Stoop? *(Bend down and forward at waist.)* ______

Kneel? *(Bend legs to rest on knees.)* ______

Crouch? *(Bend legs & back down & forward.)* ______

Crawl? *(Move on hands & knees.)* ______

Handle, grab or grasp big objects? ______

Write, type or handle small objects? ______

Lifting and Carrying *(Explain what you lifted, how far you carried it, and how often you did this.)*

____

____

____

Check the **heaviest** weight lifted:

☐ Less than 10 lbs ☐ 10 lbs ☐ 20 lbs ☐ 50 lbs ☐ 100 lbs. or more ☐ Other ______

Check weight you **frequently** lifted: *(By frequently, we mean from 1/3 to 2/3 of workday.)*

☐ Less than 10 lbs ☐ 10 lbs ☐ 25 lbs ☐ 50 lbs. or more ☐ Other ______

Did you supervise other people in this job? ☐ YES *(Complete items below.)* ☐ NO *(Skip to next page.)*

How many people did you supervise? ______

What part of your time was spent supervising people?

Did you hire and fire employees? ☐ YES ☐ NO

Were you a lead worker? ☐ YES ☐ NO

(continued)

Figure 16–18 **Work History Report *(continued)***

Give us more information about Job No. 3 listed on Page 1. Estimate hours and pay, if you need to.

JOB TITLE NO. 3

Rate of Pay $ ______	Per *(Check One)* ☐ Hour ☐ Week ☐ Month ☐ Year	Hours per day ______	Days per week ______

In this job, did you:

- Use machines, tools or equipment? ☐ YES *(explain below)* ☐ NO
- Use technical knowledge or skills? ☐ YES *(explain below)* ☐ NO
- Write reports or complete forms? ☐ YES *(explain below)* ☐ NO

Describe this job. What did you do all day? *(If you need more space, write in the "Remarks" section.)*

____

____

____

In **this job**, how many total hours each day did you:

Walk? ______
Stand? ______
Sit? ______
Climb? ______
Stoop? *(Bend down and forward at waist.)* ______
Kneel? *(Bend legs to rest on knees.)* ______
Crouch? *(Bend legs & back down & forward.)* ______
Crawl? *(Move on hands & knees.)* ______
Handle, grab or grasp big objects? ______
Write, type or handle small objects? ______

Lifting and Carrying *(Explain what you lifted, how far you carried it, and how often you did this.)*

____

____

____

Check the **heaviest** weight lifted:

☐ Less than 10 lbs ☐ 10 lbs ☐ 20 lbs ☐ 50 lbs ☐ 100 lbs. or more ☐ Other ______

Check weight you **frequently** lifted: *(By frequently, we mean from 1/3 to 2/3 of workday.)*

☐ Less than 10 lbs ☐ 10 lbs ☐ 25 lbs ☐ 50 lbs. or more ☐ Other ______

Did you supervise other people in this job? ☐ YES *(Complete items below.)* ☐ NO *(Skip to next page.)*

How many people did you supervise? ______

What part of your time was spent supervising people? ______

Did you hire and fire employees? ☐ YES ☐ NO

Were you a lead worker? ☐ YES ☐ NO

FORM **SSA-3369-BK** (7/1998) EF (8-2000) DESTROY ALL PRIOR EDITIONS PAGE 4

Give us more information about Job No. 4 listed on Page 1. Estimate hours and pay, if you need to.

JOB TITLE NO. 4

Rate of Pay $ ______	Per *(Check One)* ☐ Hour ☐ Week ☐ Month ☐ Year	Hours per day ______	Days per week ______

In this job, did you: Use machines, tools or equipment? ☐ YES *(explain below)* ☐ NO

Use technical knowledge or skills? ☐ YES *(explain below)* ☐ NO

Write reports or complete forms? ☐ YES *(explain below)* ☐ NO

Describe this job. What did you do all day? *(If you need more space, write in the "Remarks" section.)*

____

____

____

In **this job**, how many total hours each day did you:

Walk? ______
Stand? ______
Sit? ______
Climb? ______
Stoop? *(Bend down and forward at waist.)* ______

Kneel? *(Bend legs to rest on knees.)* ______
Crouch? *(Bend legs & back down & forward.)* ______
Crawl? *(Move on hands & knees.)* ______
Handle, grab or grasp big objects? ______
Write, type or handle small objects? ______

Lifting and Carrying *(Explain what you lifted, how far you carried it, and how often you did this.)*

____

____

____

Check the **heaviest** weight lifted:

☐ Less than 10 lbs ☐ 10 lbs ☐ 20 lbs ☐ 50 lbs ☐ 100 lbs. or more ☐ Other ______

Check weight you **frequently** lifted: *(By frequently, we mean from 1/3 to 2/3 of workday.)*

☐ Less than 10 lbs ☐ 10 lbs ☐ 25 lbs ☐ 50 lbs. or more ☐ Other ______

Did you supervise other people in this job? ☐ YES *(Complete items below.)* ☐ NO *(Skip to next page.)*

How many people did you supervise? ______

What part of your time was spent supervising people? ______

Did you hire and fire employees? ☐ YES ☐ NO

Were you a lead worker? ☐ YES ☐ NO

FORM **SSA-3369-BK** (7/1998) EF (8-2000) DESTROY ALL PRIOR EDITIONS PAGE 5

(continued)

Figure 16–18 **Work History Report *(continued)***

Give us more information about Job No. 5 listed on Page 1. Estimate hours and pay, if you need to.

JOB TITLE NO. 5

Rate of Pay $ ________	Per *(Check One)* ☐ Hour ☐ Week ☐ Month ☐ Year	Hours per day ____	Days per week ____

In this job, did you:

- Use machines, tools or equipment? ☐ YES *(explain below)* ☐ NO
- Use technical knowledge or skills? ☐ YES *(explain below)* ☐ NO
- Write reports or complete forms? ☐ YES *(explain below)* ☐ NO

Describe this job. What did you do all day? *(If you need more space, write in the "Remarks" section.)*

____

____

____

In **this job**, how many total hours each day did you:

Walk?	______	Kneel? *(Bend legs to rest on knees.)*	______
Stand?	______	Crouch? *(Bend legs & back down & forward.)*	______
Sit?	______	Crawl? *(Move on hands & knees.)*	______
Climb?	______	Handle, grab or grasp big objects?	______
Stoop? *(Bend down and forward at waist.)*	______	Write, type or handle small objects?	______

Lifting and Carrying *(Explain what you lifted, how far you carried it, and how often you did this.)*

____

____

____

Check the **heaviest** weight lifted:

☐ Less than 10 lbs ☐ 10 lbs ☐ 20 lbs ☐ 50 lbs ☐ 100 lbs. or more ☐ Other ______

Check weight you **frequently** lifted: *(By frequently, we mean from 1/3 to 2/3 of workday.)*

☐ Less than 10 lbs ☐ 10 lbs ☐ 25 lbs ☐ 50 lbs. or more ☐ Other ______

Did you supervise other people in this job? ☐ YES *(Complete items below.)* ☐ NO *(Skip to next page.)*

How many people did you supervise? ______

What part of your time was spent supervising people? ______

Did you hire and fire employees? ☐ YES ☐ NO

Were you a lead worker? ☐ YES ☐ NO

FORM SSA-3369-BK (7/1998) EF (8-2000) DESTROY ALL PRIOR EDITIONS PAGE 6

Give us more information about Job No. 6 listed on Page 1. Estimate hours and pay, if you need to.

JOB TITLE NO. 6			
Rate of Pay $ ______	Per *(Check One)* ☐ Hour ☐ Week ☐ Month ☐ Year	Hours per day ____	Days per week ____

In this job, did you:

- Use machines, tools or equipment? ☐ YES *(explain below)* ☐ NO
- Use technical knowledge or skills? ☐ YES *(explain below)* ☐ NO
- Write reports or complete forms? ☐ YES *(explain below)* ☐ NO

Describe this job. What did you do all day? *(If you need more space, write in the "Remarks" section.)*

____

____

____

In **this job**, how many total hours each day did you:

Walk?	______	Kneel? *(Bend legs to rest on knees.)*	______
Stand?	______	Crouch? *(Bend legs & back down & forward.)*	______
Sit?	______	Crawl? *(Move on hands & knees.)*	______
Climb?	______	Handle, grab or grasp big objects?	______
Stoop? *(Bend down and forward at waist.)*	______	Write, type or handle small objects?	______

Lifting and Carrying *(Explain what you lifted, how far you carried it, and how often you did this.)*

____

____

____

Check the **heaviest** weight lifted:

☐ Less than 10 lbs ☐ 10 lbs ☐ 20 lbs ☐ 50 lbs ☐ 100 lbs. or more ☐ Other ______

Check weight you **frequently** lifted: *(By frequently, we mean from 1/3 to 2/3 of workday.)*

☐ Less than 10 lbs ☐ 10 lbs ☐ 25 lbs ☐ 50 lbs. or more ☐ Other ______

Did you supervise other people in this job? ☐ YES *(Complete items below.)* ☐ NO *(Skip to next page.)*

How many people did you supervise?

What part of your time was spent supervising people? ______

Did you hire and fire employees? ☐ YES ☐ NO

Were you a lead worker? ☐ YES ☐ NO

FORM SSA-3369-BK (7/1998) EF (8-2000) DESTROY ALL PRIOR EDITIONS

(continued)

Figure 16–18 **Work History Report (continued)**

SECTION 3 - REMARKS

ANYONE MAKING A FALSE STATEMENT OR REPRESENTATION OF A MATERIAL FACT FOR USE IN DETERMINING A RIGHT TO PAYMENT UNDER THE SOCIAL SECURITY ACT COMMITS A CRIME PUNISHABLE UNDER FEDERAL LAW.

Signature of **claimant** or person filing on claimant's behalf *(parent, guardian)*	**Date** *(Month, day, year)*

Witnesses are required **ONLY** if this statement has been signed by mark (X) above. If signed by mark (X), two witnesses to the signing who know the person making the statement must sign below, giving their full addresses.

1. Signature of **Witness**	2. Signature of **Witness**
Address *(Number and street, city, state, and ZIP code)*	**Address** *(Number and street, city, state, and ZIP code)*

FORM **SSA-3369-BK** (7/1998) EF (8-2000) DESTROY ALL PRIOR EDITIONS PAGE 8

WORK HISTORY REPORT-Form SSA-3369-BK

READ ALL OF THIS INFORMATION BEFORE YOU BEGIN COMPLETING THIS FORM

IF YOU NEED HELP

If you need help with this form, complete as much of it as you can, and your interviewer will help you finish it.

HOW TO COMPLETE THIS FORM

The information that you give us on this form will be used by the office that makes the disability decision on your disability claim. You can help them by completing as much of the form as you can.

- Print or type.
- When a question refers to "you," "your," or "the Disabled Person," it refers to the person who is applying for disability benefits. If you are filling out the form for someone else, provide information about him or her.
- Be sure to explain an answer if the question asks for an explanation, or if you think you need to explain an answer.
- If more space is needed to answer any questions, use the "REMARKS" section on Page 8, and show the number of the question being answered.

WHY THIS INFORMATION IS IMPORTANT

The information we ask for on this form will help us understand how your illnesses or injuries or conditions might affect any work you are qualified to do. The information tells us about the kinds of work you did, including the types of skills you need and the physical and mental requirements of each job. In Section 2, be sure to give us all of the different kinds of work you have done in the last 15 years before you stopped working. There is a separate page to describe each different job.

REMEMBER TO SIGN THE FORM IN THE SIGNATURE SPACES ON PAGE 8

(continued)

Figure 16–18 **Work History Report *(continued)***

SOCIAL SECURITY ADMINISTRATION

Form Approved
OMB No. 0960-0059

WORK ACTIVITY REPORT (Self-Employed Person)

Name of disabled person	☐ Blind ☐ Not Blind	Social Security Number
Name of W/E *(If other than disabled person)*		Social Security Number

PAPERWORK/PRIVACY ACT NOTICE

The information requested on this form is authorized by Section 223 and Section 1632 of the Social Security Act. The informaiton provided will be used in making a decision on your claim. While completion of this form is voluntary, failure to provide all or part of the requested information could prevent an accurate and timely decision on your claim and could result in the loss of benefits. Information you furnish on this form may be disclosed by the Social Security Administration to another person or governmental agency only with respect to Social Security programs and to comply with Federal law requiring the exchange of information between Social Security and another agency.
We may also use the information you give us when we match records by computer. Matching programs compare our records with those of other Federal, State or local government agencies. Many agencies may use matching programs to find or prove that a person qualifies for benefits paid by the Federal government. The law allows us to do this even if you do not agree to it.
Explanations about these and other reasons why information you provide us may be used or given out are available in Social Security Offices. If you want to learn more about this, contact any Social Security Office.

The **Paperwork Reduction Act of 1995** requires us to notify you that this information collection is in accordance with the clearance requirements of section 3507 of the Paperwork Reduction Act of 1995. We may not conduct or sponsor, and you are not required to respond to, a collection of information unless it displays a valid OMB control number. We estimate that it will take you about 30 minutes to complete this form. This includes the time it will take to read the instructions, gather the necessary facts and fill out the form.

Please use this form to describe your work activity since (Date disability began or, if later, date of prior investigation) → **1.** Date *(to be entered by SSA)*

ANSWER EACH QUESTION AS FULLY AS POSSIBLE

2. A. List name and address of business (include zip code)

B. Please Check if ☐ Farm ☐ Non-Farm

C. Briefly indicate the primary product or service

3. A. Describe the business in terms of arrangement and /or ownership (Check one)

☐ Sole Owner ☐ Partnership ☐ Farm Tenant ☐ Farm Landlord

B. Give your monthly self-employment income since the above date (average if not sure)

Month	Year	Gross	Net	Month	Year	Gross	Net	Month	Year	Gross	Net
Month	Year	Gross	Net	Month	Year	Gross	Net	Month	Year	Gross	Net

C. List any months in which you earned more than $200.00 or worked more than 40 hours in your business since the date shown in item 1. ▶

4. A. Describe *(briefly)* what you did in the business in terms of management decisions, responsibilities, hours, production and services before your illness or injury.

B. Was this business your sole livelihood prior to your illness or injury? ☐ YES ☐ NO

5. Please describe your present work activities and any changes in your business because of your illness or injury. Explain such things as reduced hours of business, lower volume, fewer acres under cultivation or other. (If you use extra help, write "extra help" here and provide the details when you get to item 9).

Form **SSA-820-F4** (2-1991) EF (7-2000) **1**

If you need more space for any answer, use Page 3.

6. Do (did) you make management decisions after your illness or injury? ☐ YES ☐ NO
(If "yes," describe the kinds of decisions made, the time spent making them and any changes that have taken place).

7. A. If you began your business after you were injured or became ill, did you receive any special assistance from an agency or other source in setting up your business? ☐ YES ☐ NO

B. Does this assistance continue or have additional special services been supplied? ☐ YES ☐ NO
(If "yes," please describe)

8. A. What is the value of any normal business expense which you do (did) not pay including that which is furnished or paid for by another person or organization (such as free space or utilities)? Why were such items supplied to you for free and by whom were they furnished?

B. Describe any special expenses related to your illness or injury that you paid which are necessary for you to work (for example, attendant care, medical devices, equipment, prostheses, or similar items or services).

9. DESCRIBE ANY ADDITIONAL HELP YOU NEED (NEEDED) IN PERFORMING YOUR USUAL DUTIES BECAUSE OF YOUR ILLNESS OR INJURY.

A. Number of assistants	B. Time they devoted to helping you	C. What do (did) they do?
D. Are/were assistants (check one) ☐ PAID ☐ UNPAID	E. If paid, how much?	
F. Is (are) assistant(s) related to you?(checkone) ☐ YES ☐ NO	G. If yes, what is the relationship?	

H. Why was the additional help needed?

Form **SSA-820-F4** (2-1991) EF (7-2000)

If you need more space for any answer, use Page 3.

(continued)

Figure 16–18 **Work History Report** ***(continued)***

10. Use this section for additional space to answer any previous questions and to give any additional information you think will be helpful. Please refer to the previous questions by number, such as 4A or 4B or 5.

If more space is needed, use an extra sheet.

11. A. Check the appropriate block below:

☐ I am **not** receiving Social Security disability benefits and/or supplemental security income (SSI)

☐ I **am** receiving Social Security disability benefits and/or supplemental security income (SSI), and I understand that the information provided above may result in my benefits being stopped. I have been given the opportunity to submit any evidence I wanted and to make any statements concerning my claim.

PLEASE READ THE FOLLOWING STATEMENT, THEN SIGN, DATE AND PROVIDE ADDRESS AND TELEPHONE NUMBER.

Knowing that anyone who makes a false statement or misrepresentation of a material fact for use in determining a right to payment under the Social Security Act commits a crime punishable under Federal law, I affirm that the answers to questions on this form are true.

Signature of claimant/beneficiary or representative			Date
Mailing address (Number and Street, Apt. no., P.O. Box, or Rural Route.)			TELEPHONE (Include area code)
City	State	County	Zip Code

Form **SSA-820-F4** (2-1991) EF (7-2000) **3**

SSA USE ONLY

12.

A. Contact made: (check one)	☐ IN PERSON	☐ BY MAIL	☐ BY TELEPHONE
B. Completed by: (check one)	☐ CLAIMANT	☐ SSA REPRESENTATIVE	☐ OTHER

C. If "other" show Name:	Address (include zip code)
Phone Number (include area code) ( )	Relationship

13. Interviewer/reviewer check list ("Yes" answers should be developed in accordance with DI 13010ff. Rationalize "Yes" or "No" answers below except when it is necessary to complete the SSA-831-U3 and SSA-833-U3). Check all that apply:

A. Unpaid business expenses (Rent, utilities, etc.)	☐ Yes	☐ No
B. Impairment-related work expenses	☐ Yes	☐ No
C. Unpaid help, or business sponsored by an agency	☐ Yes	☐ No
D. Unsuccessful work attempt (CDI - no medical issue - DO jurisdiction for a final determination)	☐ Yes	☐ No
E. Unsuccessful work attempt (DO recommendation only - DDS jurisdiction for a final determination.)	☐ Yes	☐ No
F. Substantial gainful activity	☐ Yes	☐ No

Note: If work continues and is determined to be substantial gainful activity and no medical issue exists, prepare the appropriate final determination (SSA-831-U3 or SSA-833-U3) rationalizing the work issue. Keep in mind that preparation of the SSA-831-U3 or the SSA-833-U3 would not be appropriate if there is a possibility of a closed period of disability, a trial work period or an unsuccessful work attempt.

Rationale:

14. Remarks

15. Signature of SSA interviewer or reviewer	Title	DO code	Date

Form **SSA-820-F4** (2-1991) EF (7-2000)

SOCIAL SECURITY ADMINISTRATION

Form Approved
OMB No. 0960-0144

For SSA Use Only - Do NOT Complete This Item.	
Name of Wage Earner	Social Security Number
Name of Claimant	Social Security Number
Type of Claim:	
Title II - ☐ Freeze ☐ DIB ☐ DWB ☐ CDB ☐ Title XVI - ☐ Disability ☐ Blind ☐ Child	

RECONSIDERATION DISABILITY REPORT

PLEASE PRINT, TYPE OR WRITE CLEARLY AND ANSWER ALL ITEMS TO THE BEST OF YOUR ABILITY. If you are filing on behalf of someone else, answer all questions. COMPLETE ANSWERS WILL AID IN PROCESSING THE CLAIM.

PRIVACY ACT: The Social Security Administration is authorized to collect the information on this form under sections 205(a), 223(d) and 1633(a) of the Social Security Act. The information on this form is needed by Social Security to make a decision on your claim. While giving us the information on this form is voluntary, failure to provide all or part of the requested information could prevent an accurate or timely decision on your claim and could result in the loss of benefits. Although the information you furnish on this form is almost never used for any purpose other than making a determination on your disability claim, such information may be disclosed by the Social Security Administration as follows: (1) To enable a third party or agency to assist Social Security in establishing rights to Social Security benefits and/or coverage; (2) to comply with Federal laws requiring the release of information from Social Security records (e.g., the General Accounting Office and the Veterans Administration); (3) to facilitate statistical research and audit activities necessary to assure the integrity and improvement of the Social Security programs (e.g., to the Bureau of the Census and private concerns under contract to Social Security). These and other reasons why information about you may be used or given out are explained in the **Federal Register.** If you would like more information about this, any Social Security office can assist you.

Date Claim Filed ____________

PART I - INFORMATION ABOUT YOUR CONDITION

1. Has there been any change (for better or worse) in your illness or injury since you filed your claim? .... ☐ Yes ☐ No
   If "Yes," describe any changes in your symptoms.

2. Describe any physical or mental limitations you have as a result of your condition since you filed your claim.

3. Have any restrictions been placed on you by a physician since you filed your claim?......... ☐ Yes ☐ No
   If "Yes," give name, address, and telephone number of the physician and show what kinds of restrictions have been imposed.

4. Do you have any additional illness or injury that you feel we should know about? ☐ Yes ☐ No
   If "Yes," describe the kind of illness or injury and the date that it occurred.

Form **SSA-3441-F6** (2-88) EF (3-99) 1

Figure 16–19 **Reconsideration Disability Report**

PART II - INFORMATION ABOUT YOUR MEDICAL RECORDS

5. Have you seen any physician since you filed your claim? .... ☐ Yes ☐ No
   If "Yes," provide the following about the physician you last visited:

NAME

ADDRESS *(Include ZIP Code)*

AREA CODE AND TELEPHONE NUMBER

HOW OFTEN DO YOU SEE THIS PHYSICIAN?

DATE YOU SAW THIS PHYSICIAN

REASONS FOR VISITS

TYPE OF TREATMENT RECEIVED *(Include drugs, surgery, tests)*

6. Have you seen any other physician since you filed your claim?.. ☐ Yes ☐ No
   If "Yes," show the following:

NAME

ADDRESS *(Include ZIP Code)*

AREA CODE AND TELEPHONE NUMBER

HOW OFTEN DO YOU SEE THIS PHYSICIAN?

DATE YOU SAW THIS PHYSICIAN

REASONS FOR VISITS

TYPE OF TREATMENT RECEIVED *(Include drugs, surgery, tests)*

If you have seen other physicians since you filed your claim, list their names, addresses, dates and reasons for visits in Part V.

7. Have you been hospitalized, or treated at a clinic or confined in a nursing home or extended care facility for your illness or injury since you filed your claim?...................................... ☐ Yes ☐ No
   If "Yes," show the following:

NAME OF FACILITY

ADDRESS OF AGENCY *(Include ZIP Code)*

PATIENT OR CLINIC NUMBER

WERE YOU AN INPATIENT? *(Stayed at least overnight)*
☐ Yes ☐ No IF "YES," SHOW →

DATES OF ADMISSIONS AND DISCHARGES

WERE YOU AN OUTPATIENT?
☐ Yes ☐ No IF "YES," SHOW →

DATES OF VISITS

REASON FOR HOSPITALIZATION, CLINIC VISITS, OR CONFINEMENT

TYPE OF TREATMENT RECEIVED *(Include drugs, surgery, tests)*

If you have been in other hospitals, clinics, nursing homes, or extended care facilities for your illness or injury, list the names, addresss, patient or clinic number, dates and reasons for hospitalization, clinic visits, or confinement in Part V.

8. Have you been seen by other agencies for your injury or illness? .... ☐ Yes ☐ No
   (VA, Workmen's Compensation, Vocational Rehabilitation, Welfare, Special Schools, Unions, etc.)
   If "Yes," show the following:

NAME OF AGENCY

ADDRESS OF AGENCY (Include ZIP Code)

YOUR CLAIM NUMBER

DATES OF VISITS

NAME OF COUNSELOR, SOCIAL WORKER, ETC.

TYPE OF TREATMENT OR EXAMINATION RECEIVED (Include drugs, surgery, tests)

If more space is needed, list the other agencies, their addresses, your claim numbers, dates, and treatment received in Part V.

(continued)

Figure 16–19 **Reconsideration Disability Report *(continued)***

PART III - INFORMATION ABOUT WORK

9. Have you worked since you filed your claim?.. ☐ Yes ☐ No

If "Yes," you will be asked to give details on a separate form.

PART IV - INFORMATION ABOUT YOUR ACTIVITIES

10. How does your illness or injury affect your ability to care for your personal needs?

11. What changes have occurred in your daily activities since you filed your claim?
(If none, show, "None")

PART V - REMARKS AND AUTHORIZATIONS

12.(a) READ CAREFULLY: I authorize the Social Security Administration to release information from my records, as necessary to process my claim, as follows:

Copies of my medical records may be furnished to a physician or a medical institution for background information if it is necessary for me to have a medical examination by that physician or medical institution. The results of any such examination may be given to my personal physician.

Information from my records may also be furnished, if necessary, to any company providing clerical and administrative services for the purposes of transcribing, typing, copying or otherwise clerically servicing such information. The State Vocational Rehabilitation Agency may also have access to information in my records to determine my eligibility for rehabilitative services.

I understand and concur with the statement and authorizations given above, except as follows (If there are no exceptions, write "None" in the space below. If you do not concur with any part of the above statement, state your objections clearly):

12.(b)	Telephone number where you can be reached:	Best time to reach you:

Form **SSA-3441-F6** (2-88) EF (11-99) 3

12.(b) Use this section to continue information required by prior sections. Identify the section for which the information is provided. Note: This section may also be used for any special or additional information which you wish to be recorded.

We may also use the information you give us when we match records by computer. Matching programs compare our records with those of other Federal, State, or local government agencies. Many agencies may use matching programs to find or prove that a person qualifies for benefits paid by the Federal government. The law allows us to do this even if you do not agree to it.

Explanations about these and other reasons why information you provide us may be used or given out are available in Social Security offices. If you want to learn more about this, contact any Social Security office.

The Paperwork Reduction Act of 1995 requires us to notify you that this information collection is in accordance with the clearance requirements of section 3507 of the Paper Reduction Act of 1995. We may not conduct or sponsor, and you are not required to respond to, a collection of information unless it displays a valid OMB control number. We estimate that it will take you about 30 minutes to complete this form. This includes the time it will take to read the instructions, gather the necessary facts and fill out the form.

Knowing that anyone making a false statement or representation of a material fact for use in determining a right to payment under the Social Security Act commits a crime punishable under Federal Law, I certify that the above statements are true.

NAME (SIGNATURE OF CLAIMANT OR PERSON FILING ON THE CLAIMANT'S BEHALF)

SIGN HERE ▶	DATE

Witnesses are required ONLY if this statement has been signed by mark (X) above. If signed by mark (X), two witnesses to the signing who know the person making the statement must sign below, giving their full addresses.

1. Signature of Witness	2. Signature of Witness
Address *(Number and street, city, state, and ZIP code)*	Address *(Number and street, city, state, and ZIP code)*

Form **SSA-3441-F6** (2-88) EF (3-99) 4

(continued)

Figure 16–19 **Reconsideration Disability Report *(continued)***

PART VI - FOR SSA USE ONLY - DO NOT WRITE BELOW THIS LINE

Name of Wage Earner	Social Security Number
Name of Claimant	Social Security Number

13. Check each item to indicate whether or not any difficulty was observed:
(Explain all items checked "Yes," in Item 14 below)

Reading:	☐ Yes	☐ No	Using Hands:	☐ Yes	☐ No
Writing:	☐ Yes	☐ No	Breathing:	☐ Yes	☐ No
Answering:	☐ Yes	☐ No	Seeing:	☐ Yes	☐ No
Hearing:	☐ Yes	☐ No	Walking:	☐ Yes	☐ No
Speaking:	☐ Yes	☐ No	Sitting:	☐ Yes	☐ No
Understanding:	☐ Yes	☐ No	Assistive Devices:	☐ Yes	☐ No

Other *(Specify)*: ______________________

14. If any of the above items were checked "Yes," describe the observed difficulty:

15. Describe fully: General appearance, behavior, any unusual observed difficulties not noted elsewhere, any unusual circumstances surrounding the interviews.

Form **SSA-3441-F6** (2-88) EF (3-99) 5

16. Claimant requires assistance .... ☐ Yes ☐ No

If "Yes," show name, address, phone number, and relationship of interested person.
Also show why claimant requires assistance (foreign-speaking, unable to ambulate, etc.)

17. Capability development appears needed .... ☐ Yes ☐ No

If "Yes," indicate whether DO will undertake development because it is also developing medical evidence from a special arrangement source. (Show name and address of source.)

18. Is development of work activity necessary?.. ☐ Yes ☐ No

If "Yes," is an SSA-821 or SSA-820-F4 ☐ Pending ☐ In File

19. SSA-3441 Taken By:

☐ Personal Interview

☐ DO/BO ☐ Home ☐ Other ____________

☐ Telephone

☐ Mail

Signature of Interviewer or Reviewer	Title	DO, BO, or TSC	Date

Form **SSA-3441-F6** (2-88) EF (3-99) 6

(continued)

The Reconsideration Disability Report should be carefully compared with the Disability Report to ensure consistency in reporting. Note, however, that the Reconsideration Disability Report asks for "any change" in the claimant's condition. If there has been no change and the initial determination was unfavorable, the same conclusion probably will be reached on reconsideration. Thus, if the representative is fortunate enough to be involved at this level, the appropriate response should be, yes, there has been a change. Why? If the claimant still suffers from the alleged disabling condition, it has either gotten worse over time, or better. Thus, "yes" is almost always a proper response.

What's Important?

In completing Reconsideration Disability Report the claimant has a second chance to articulate the basis for his or her claim. As with the Disability Report this form asks for critical information bearing directly on the claim, as such information has developed since the claim was filed. This includes

- ❑ Any change in illness or injury;
- ❑ Mental or physical limitations since filing the claim;
- ❑ Restrictions placed "on you by a physician" since filing the claim;
- ❑ Additional illness or injury since filing the claim; and
- ❑ Changes in daily activities since filing the claim.

Interestingly, the Reconsideration Disability Report is the first opportunity for the claimant to indicate in writing what the claimed limitations are. It is also the first point at which the claimant can articulate, beyond what is actually in the medical records, what he or she believes are the restrictions imposed by his or her physician(s). A representative who is involved early in the process should assist the claimant in accurately reporting limitations and restrictions, being as specific as possible.

Also notable, is the further opportunity to present daily activities. For example, if the claimant relates not driving much but otherwise fails to address a wide range of other activities, the focus of the case shifts. In this brief admission, the claimant unwittingly hamstrings the case, focusing only on driving, when a number of other daily activities are potentially also involved.

The Reconsideration Disability Report offers a catchall at paragraph 12(b). The claimant can reveal educational limitations or limited work experience, touching on three areas of basic inquiry:

- ❑ Daily activities;
- ❑ Education; and
- ❑ Previous work experience.

A claimant could also note the inability to afford a doctor's visit, perhaps setting the stage for a later request for consultative examinations, ordered either by the DDS or, later, the Administrative Law Judge.

Finally, the Reconsideration Disability Report offers the Social Security Administration, through its intake personnel, the opportunity to comment. SSA remarks should be carefully scrutinized; they are supposed to be neutral observations of the claimant's demeanor and behavior. For example, the Social Security Administration employee might comment

> **He wore a brace on his right leg. He walked with a severe limp. Eyes were extremely red (said he couldn't read or write.)**

The comment is revealing. It is an observation from a Social Security employee of the simple fact that the claimant is limping, effectively corroborating the claimant's allegation of disabling leg pain. These comments should be brought to the attention of the Administrative Law Judge as part of the representative's opening statement, drawing the judge's attention to seemingly objective evidence supportive of the claimant's allegations.

DENIAL NOTICES FROM THE SOCIAL SECURITY ADMINISTRATION

The initial determination notice from the Social Security Administration to a client is a form letter (a Social Security notice, SSI notice, or both if the claim filed is a Title II or Title XVI claim, or both) with appropriate annotations that reflect the particular circumstances of a case. The form letter may incorporate the particular circumstances of a case into the body of the first few paragraphs or, as shown in Figure 16–20, as a separate page referenced in the first paragraph. See also the sample notice shown in Figure 16–21.

What's Important?

❑ The notice explains the right to appeal, informing the claimant that he or she has sixty days from the date of receiving the notice to ask for reconsideration. This is a critical deadline. If it is missed, the claimant must begin the process all over again, filing a new application for benefits.

❑ The notice sometimes also provides information as to what documents were considered by the DDS in making the denial. Within the first several paragraphs of the form letter; or, on an attached separate sheet, will be a listing of the documents actually reviewed. These are important. They reveal what is already in the record and on what the decision was actually based. Often, the records reviewed are limited, either in time (not all an individual doctor's records were obtained) or in substance (not all the records of doctors who have treated the claimant were submitted, or not every illness, disease, or injury was fully developed). For example, if a client reveals that she or he consulted a psychologist but the records do not appear, the representative knows that he or she must (1) obtain the records, and (2) then argue to the Administrative Law Judge that the DDS decision was incorrect because it did not consider the psychological issues.

❑ The notice also provides the basis of the DDS decision. For example, the notice may advise the claimant that, in DDS's opinion, he or she can perform light work, such that he or she can lift twenty pounds occasionally and ten pounds frequently. This then becomes the focal point of the appeal to the Administrative Law Judge. This facilitates the production of new records showing the DDS to be in error, such as an RFC from the claimant's treating physician that directly contradicts the DDS determination.

Personalized Determination Explanation

The following evidence along with reports listed in your previous notice were used to decide this claim:

❑ Dr. M, M.D. - report dated June 1, and covering treatment through May 15.
❑ Prison Medical Reports of treatment dated July 1 through September 1.

You said that you are unable to work because of injuries to your right leg due to a bullet wound. You said that your condition limits your ability to sit for long, lift, or be on your feet for long. You also said that your leg gives out and that you fall from time to time.

The medical records show that you suffered a gunshot wound to the right leg and that you now have poor circulation in that leg. Dr. M. said that you should lift and carry no more than 10 pounds at a time, that your standing and walking was limited to about 2 hours in an 8-hour day and that you should use a cane for long distances or over uneven surfaces. We agree with Dr. M.

We have determined that you are able to occasionally lift and carry up to 10 pounds and frequently lift and carry less than 10 pounds, and can stand and walk up to 2 hours in a normal 8-hour workday. We have also determined that you should avoid climbing ropes and ladders, although you are able to occasionally climb ramps and stairs. We realize that your condition keeps you from doing your past jobs, but we find that it does not prevent you from doing other jobs which require less physical effort. Based on your age of 43 years, a seventh-grade education, and past work experience, we have determined that you can do other work which is less demanding than your past work.

The determination on your claim was made by an agency of the State. It was not made by your own doctor or by other people or agencies writing reports about you. Doctors and other people in the State agency who are trained in disability evaluation reviewed the evidence and made the determination according to Social Security law and regulations.

If your condition gets worse and keeps you from working, write, call or visit any Social Security office about filing another application.

Figure 16–20 **Notice of Application Denial for Title II Disability Insurance Benefits**

Supplemental Security Income Notice

From: Social Security Administration

Date:
Social Security Number:

We have determined that you cannot get Supplemental Security Income payments based on the claim that you filed. The attached page explains why we decided that you are not disabled or blind. However, you may appeal this determination if you still think you are disabled or blind.

The determination on your claim was made by an agency of the State. It was not made by your own doctor or by people or agencies writing reports about you. However, any evidence they gave us was used in making this determination. Doctors and other people in the State agency who are trained in disability evaluation reviewed the evidence and made the determination based on Social Security law and regulations.

YOUR RIGHT TO APPEAL

If you think we are wrong, you can ask that the determination be looked at by a different person. This is called a reconsideration. IF YOU WANT A RECONSIDERATION, YOU MUST ASK FOR IT WITHIN 60 DAYS FROM THE DATE YOU RECEIVE THIS NOTICE. IF YOU WAIT MORE THAN 60 DAYS, YOU MUST GIVE US A GOOD REASON FOR THE DELAY. Your request must be made in writing through any Social Security office. Be sure to tell us your name, Social Security number and why you think we are wrong. If you cannot write to us, call a Social Security office or come in and someone will help you. You can give us more facts to add to your file. However, if you do not have the evidence yet, you should not wait for it before asking for a reconsideration. You may send the evidence in later. We will then decide your case again. You will not meet with the person who will decide your case. Please read the enclosed leaflet for a full explanation of your right to appeal. There are groups that can help with your appeal. Some of these groups may be able to give you the name of a lawyer who will help you for free. Contact any Social Security office if you want the names of these groups.

NEW APPLICATION

You have the right to file a new application at any time, but filing a new application is not the same as appealing this decision. You might lose benefits if you file a new application instead of filing an appeal. Therefore, if you think this decision is wrong, you should ask for an appeal within 60 days.

Enclosure:
SSA Publication No. 05-11008

EXHIBIT NO. __________
PAGE ______ OF ______

Form SSA-L444_U2 (2-90)

Figure 16–21 **Notice of Application Denial for Title XVI, Supplemental Security Income Benefits**

Contact between a Client and the Social Security Administration

The Social Security Administration may, from time to time, have voice (telephone) contact with a claimant, or the claimant may actually visit the Social Security field office, notwithstanding the presence of an attorney or representative in a case. Sometimes the contact is initiated by the claimant; sometimes by the Administration. In all such cases, a Report of Contact (ROC) is completed by the Social Security Administration employee and made part of the administrative record.

What's Important?

Four examples (ROC1, ROC2, ROC3, and ROC4) are provided for discussion, each considering its importance in the case.

ROC 1

Report of Contact 1 (see Figure 16–22) is a general contact in which the claimant is interviewed by telephone. The SSA interviewer may obtain the following information:

- ❑ Claimant's age;
- ❑ Claimant's education; and
- ❑ Claimant's previous work.

A conclusion as to benefits approval or denial is reached by applying Medical–Vocational Guideline 202.18. This is the basis of the DDS decision denying the claimant benefits. The information, because it reveals the inner thoughts behind the DDS denial, provides the foundation for argument to the judge that

- ❑ The rule cited by the DDS is inapplicable; and
- ❑ The jobs cited (router machine operator, sander, and production line solderer) cannot be performed by the claimant.

The basis for such arguments lies in a challenge to the underlying conclusion that the claimant is capable of light work. This, evidently, is the conclusion reached by the DDS following the personal contact with the claimant.

Notably, the ROC actually works against the DDS determination. Reference (in Figure 16–20) is made to the claimant's statements that his "right leg gives out"—a fact seemingly corroborated by the observations of the Social Security employee in the reconsideration Disability Report yet ignored in the final DDS determination. This information can be used to impugn the DDS determination. At the very least the ROC provides insight into the legal basis for DDS's negative conclusion.

ROC 2

The second Report of Contact (see Figure 16-23) is the "Joe Friday" DDS conclusion—laying out "just the facts and nothing but the facts." The outline includes

- ❑ An assessment of the claimant's past relevant work (PRW) categorized as heavy, skilled;
- ❑ Application of Medical–Vocational Guideline 201.25, to preclude past work; and
- ❑ Notation of other work claimant could perform, including a list of such jobs.

Comparison of ROC 1 to ROC 2 leads to an interesting fact. In ROC 1, the claimant is said to be limited to light work with application of a Medical–Vocational rule from the light table, whereas ROC 2 places the claimant at sedentary work, referencing a Medical–Vocational rule from the sedentary table. This latter conclusion certainly can be argued to the judge as indicative of the fact that a reasonable conclusion can be reached, even examining the limited medical record available to the DDS, that the claimant is at least limited to sedentary exertion.

ROC 3

The import of Report of Contact 3 is that the claimant was, at that time, incarcerated. This is significant because an individual may not receive benefits while in prison. Nothing precludes the application for benefits per se, but even if found disabled, the claimant cannot receive benefits. If, however, the claimant were married with children, the children would be so entitled. Figure 16–24 provides additional information about the claimant's status.

REPORT OF CONTACT
(use ink or typewriter)

<table>
<tr><td colspan="3">ACCOUNT NUMBER AND SYMBOL
Account Number</td></tr>
<tr><td>TO:</td><td>NE MAT SE GL WN MAM
ODO DIO DDS</td><td>NAME OF WAGE EARNER OR SE PERSON
WE Or SE</td></tr>
<tr><td colspan="3">PERSON(S) CONTACTED AND ADDRESSES
☐ WE OR SE PERSON ☐ OTHER (Specify)</td></tr>
<tr><td colspan="2">CONTACT MADE:
☐ DO ☐ BO ☐ CS ☐ HOME ☐ PHONE: ☐ OTHER</td><td>DATE OF CONTACT
2/21/</td></tr>
</table>

Subject Interview location

The claimant is 42 years old with 4 years of education and past heavy work. Current RFC is for light work with postural limitations. Using the vocational rules as a guide only, the claimant matches the intent of vocational rule 202.18 which directs a decision of NOT DISABLED.

Job Cites:

1) Router machine operator (plastic products)
   7,300 jobs in this region in the industry

2) Sander (woodworking)
   2,600 jobs regionally

3) Production Line solderer (manufacturing)
   2,300 jobs regionally

<table>
<tr><td colspan="3">SIGNATURE</td></tr>
<tr><td>DISTRICT OFFICE (Name, Address, & Code)
SSA DO</td><td>☐ CR ☐ FR ☐ SR ☐ CLAIMS CLERICAL
☐ OTHER (Specify)</td><td>DATE OF REPORT
03/20/02
PAGE 1 of 1</td></tr>
</table>

Figure 16–22 **Report of Contact 1: Vocational Information Compiled by the State DDS**

REPORT OF CONTACT
(use ink or typewriter)

ACCOUNT NUMBER AND SYMBOL
Account Number

TO:	NE MAT SE GL WN MAM ODO DIO DDS	NAME OF WAGE EARNER OR SE PERSON WE Or SE

PERSON(S) CONTACTED AND ADDRESSES
☐ WE OR SE PERSON ☐ OTHER *(Specify)*

CONTACT MADE:
☐ DO ☐ BO ☐ CS ☐ HOME ☐ PHONE: ☐ OTHER

DATE OF CONTACT

42 years old 3rd grade education

PRW = Heavy, Skilled

RFC = Sedentary, w/postural restrictions
(still full range of sedentary work)

PRW is precluded. Rule 201.25 applies.

Other work: claimant could perform:

Notch grinder, glass products (6,000 employed in industry in the region)

Suture winder, protective devices (1,500 employed regionally)

Stem mounter, light fixtures (825 employed in the region)

SIGNATURE

DISTRICT OFFICE *(Name, Address, & Code)*		DATE OF REPORT
SSA DO	☑ CR ☐ FR ☐ SR ☐ CLAIMS CLERICAL ☐ OTHER *(Specify)*	5/12 PAGE 1 of 1

Form SSA-5002 (8-81)

GPO : 1994 0 - 160 - 545

Figure 16–23 **Report of Contact 2: Further Vocational Information**

REPORT OF CONTACT
(use ink or typewriter)

ACCOUNT NUMBER AND SYMBOL
Account Number

TO:	NE MAT SE GL WN MAM ODO DIO DDS	NAME OF WAGE EARNER OR SE PERSON WE Or SE

PERSON(S) CONTACTED AND ADDRESSES ☐ WE OR SE PERSON ☐ OTHER *(Specify)*

CONTACT MADE:	DATE OF CONTACT
☐ DO ☐ BO ☐ CS ☐ HOME ☐ PHONE: ☐ OTHER	4/1

Interview Location

Claimant was interviewed in jail --- back in jail as of March 20

Description of activities based on what he did while NOT in jail.

Contact claimant through his mother's telephone

SIGNATURE		
DISTRICT OFFICE *(Name, Address, & Code)* SSA DO	☑ CR ☐ FR ☐ SR ☐ CLAIMS CLERICAL ☐ OTHER *(Specify)*	DATE OF REPORT 4/1 PAGE 1 of 1

Form **SSA-5002** (8-81) GPO : 1994 0 - 160 - 545

Figure 16–24 **Report of Contact 3: Revealing Claimant's Jailed Status**

ROC 4

Report of Contact 4 is a contact initiated by the claimant, at the Administration's request (see Figure 16–25). It is a brief interview in which basic facts are discovered:

- Prior to incarceration, the claimant visited his mother one to two times each week;
- Prior to incarceration, the claimant received food stamps, shopped for food (without assistance), had "no problem counting money," and could "recognize street signs;" and
- While in jail, he takes medicine for HBP (high blood pressure).

In obtaining these basic facts the Administration is reaching certain conclusions corroborative of the denial decision. First, although the claimant suffers from a severe impairment, it does not prevent him from engaging in normal activities of daily living (visiting his mother and shopping without assistance). Second, although he has only four years of education, the claimant can make change and recognize street signs, again, without impairment to normal activities of daily living. These facts give the representative insight into the DDS decision-making process and provide a point at which a challenge to the denial can be made. The argument might be made as follows:

> **Although the DDS concludes that he can do his own shopping, the facts are that he can only stand for thirty minutes at a time and must rest frequently, even in the grocery store. And, although it is true he can recognize street signs, he can only do so in his neighborhood; he cannot find his way in a strange place; he cannot read maps, or for that matter anything else. At best, he has developed an accommodation to his immediate neighborhood and cannot readily find his way in other places.**

The lesson is straightforward. The effective representative must be aware of the potential for contact between the Social Security Administration and the state DDS, and must counsel his or her client about comporting him- or herself if so contacted. Each case will, of course, be different. At the very least, the claimant should be advised not to initiate contact without first discussing it with the representative.

THE MEDICAL RECORDS

The heart and soul of a claimant's case is in the medical records. Here, information can be found bearing on each of the five steps in the sequential evaluation. Examined carefully, the medical record consists of discrete types of medical documents:

1. *DDS opinions.* Opinions of nonexamining DDS physicians, expressed as of RFC assessments, physical or mental;
2. *DDS-ordered consultative examinations.* Reports from examining physicians or psychologists who undertake examinations at the request of the DDS before a case proceeds to a hearing before an Administrative Law Judge;
3. *Hospital records.* Records from the hospitals administering treatment to the claimant;
4. *Institutional records.* Nonhospital records of a claimant's medical condition, including nursing homes, mental health clinics, and prisons, among others;
5. *Treating physician records.* Including progress notes, laboratory findings, and narrative reports; and
6. *Laboratory records.* Records of medical testing, including blood work, radiology, pulmonary function studies, EMGs, EEGs, EKGs, and similar testing.

REPORT OF CONTACT
(use ink or typewriter)

TO:	NE MAT SE GL WN MAM ODO DIO DDS	ACCOUNT NUMBER AND SYMBOL Account Number NAME OF WAGE EARNER OR SE PERSON WE Or SE

PERSON(S) CONTACTED AND ADDRESSES ☐ WE OR SE PERSON ☐ OTHER *(Specify)*

CONTACT MADE: ☐ DO ☐ BO ☐ CS ☐ HOME ☐ PHONE: ☐ OTHER — DATE OF CONTACT

Called claimant's mother to ask her to have claimant call me ASAP. She said that prior to his going back to jail on 3/20, he would visit her 1 – 2 x's per week.

4/15 Claimant called back. He had a driver's license but not currently --- he passed the test orally.

He got food stamps when not in jail and shopped for his own food without assistance. He has no problem counting money and can recognize street signs.

While in jail he takes medicine for HBP. Did not have $$$ for prescription when out on bail.

SIGNATURE		
DISTRICT OFFICE *(Name, Address, & Code)* SSA DO	☐ CR ☐ FR ☐ SR ☐ CLAIMS CLERICAL ☐ OTHER *(Specify)*	DATE OF REPORT PAGE 1 of 1

Form **SSA-5002** (8-81) GPO : 1994 0 - 160 - 545

Figure 16–25 **Report of Contact 4: Revealing Claimant's Daily Activities**

BACK TO CHRIS

"That's a lot of records. How do we deal with all of that?"

"Remember, your job is to prove that your client is disabled. First, familiarize yourself with the records themselves. Then plot the time line over which your client's condition is documented."

Chris looked at Steve, puzzled. "You mean, it's not enough to simply prove a disability, you've got to prove it during the entire period of the claim?"

"That's right. Suppose your client claimed disability since 1997 but only first saw a doctor in 2000. Even though she may have been suffering from the same condition in 1997, without actual medical records showing the diagnosis at the earlier time, there's no way she will get benefits."

"Because there isn't a medically determinable impairment?"

"Exactly." Steve was confident that Chris was getting it. Mr. Carson was going to be in good hands.

"So, I've got to screen these records on at least two levels—first, to see *what* the diagnosis is, and second *when* it is?" [See Figure 16–26.]

"Yes, at least initially. But, there's more to it as well."

"Like what?" Chris asked, trying not to think too far ahead.

"That's when you get down to individual medical records. For example, remember the hierarchy of doctors' opinions?"

Chris nodded.

"After you see what the substantive diagnosis is, you want to see what the treating doctor(s) say, because their opinion is given the most weight."

"OK, then what?"

"Next, find examining doctors, such as consultants or DDS CEs. See what they say."

"Is that it?"

"No. After you find the diagnosis, you want a third level screening to examine the medical records for limitations. This is a variation of the first screening, because you're attempting to (1) find treating doctors, (2) identify what limitations or restrictions they place on your client, and (3) ascertain the timeline." [See Figure 16–27.]

"Can I look at medical records by type?"

"Sure. Sometimes it's helpful to look at what the Social Security Administration CEs write first, because they tend to give the history of a claimant's medical condition. Then, look at the major hospitalizations, because hospitalizations are generally the most severe point in the history."

"Can we?"

"Sure, but I'm going to break it down by type of record in this sample case, so you can get a better idea of what different kinds of records actually look like."

"OK!"

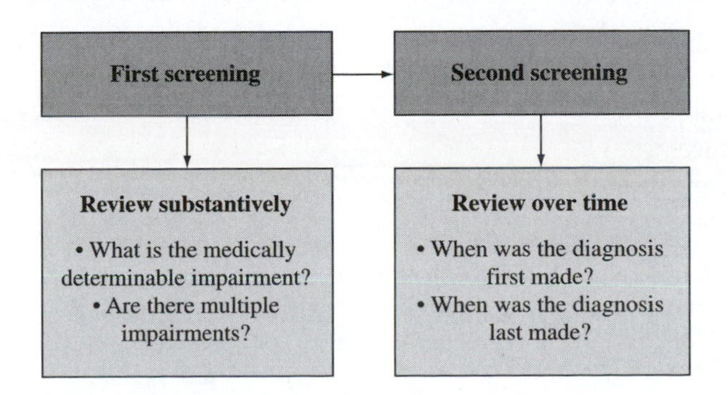

Figure 16–26 **Medical Records Are Screened for Substantive Information Over Time**

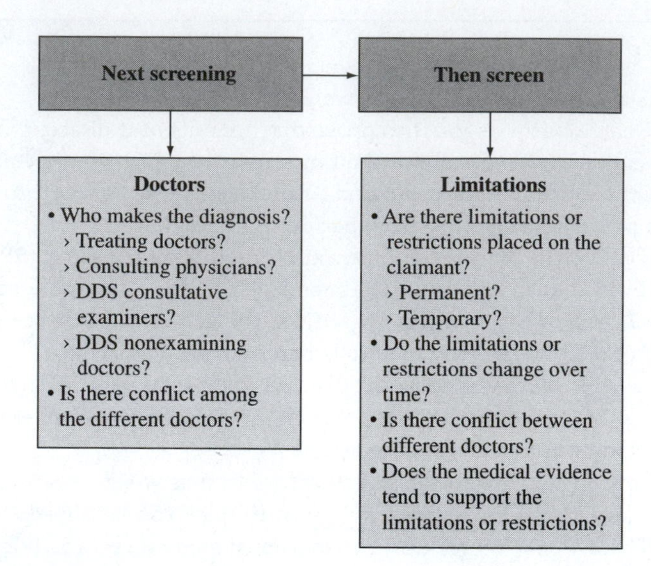

Figure 16–27 **Medical Records Are Screened for Information about Treating Physicians and Limitations of Function**

FRONT OF YOUR MIND QUESTIONS AND CONSIDERATIONS, 16.5

DDS OPINIONS

DDS opinions take the form of RFC assessments, physical, mental, or both. Essentially, the DDS physician reviews the claimant's medical records, including narrative reports of CEs, and prepares a written opinion. Taking the form of an RFC assessment, the opinion is expressed in terms of the physical and mental limitations that the DDS physician believes accurately describe the claimant's capability.

As the name implies, the DDS RFC assessment is the opinion of the DDS nonexamining physician completing the form. It addresses the claimant's ability to

- ❑ Lift;
- ❑ Carry;
- ❑ Sit; and
- ❑ Stand.

The RFC assessment also addresses postural limitations, including the ability to

- ❑ Climb;
- ❑ Balance;
- ❑ Stoop;
- ❑ Kneel;
- ❑ Crouch; and
- ❑ Crawl.

The RFC assessment asks the author to comment on

- ❑ Reaching; and
- ❑ Handling and fingering;

as well as

- ❑ Visual limitations;
- ❑ Communications limitations; and
- ❑ Environmental limitations.

Notably, the RFC assessment gives the author the opportunity to further explain the basis of his or her opinion, specifically asking for an assessment of the claimant's reported symptoms.

In effect, the Residual Functional Capacity assessment, when completed by a DDS nonexamining physician, constitutes the basis of the underlying DDS denial decision. This is often a good place to start a records review, because sometimes the DDS assessment becomes the basis of a step 5 determination. So, although the DDS examiner may conclude that the claimant's condition does not meet or equal a listing at step 3, it is possible that the RFC assessment may permit a decision at step 5. In such a case, for example, the claimant may have aged from a younger individual to an individual closely approaching advanced age, yielding a different result at the older age than when the "Grids" were originally applied by DDS. See Figure 16–28 for a sample RFC evaluation.

DDS-Ordered Consultative Examinations

The DDS-ordered consultative examination (CE) is a physical or mental examination conducted by a private physician under contract with the state to provide medical services in aid of a disability determination. Such exams may also be ordered by the Administrative Law Judge, before or after an administrative hearing.

Generally, such examinations are limited; they are not conducted for purposes of treatment but for evaluation. Each examination is accompanied by a narrative report, referred to within the administrative record as a CE. Generally, DDS orders such an examination when there is little medical information available or when a particular aspect of a claim has not yet been fully developed (explored and documented). Where possible, individual state DDS agencies contract with multiple physicians and psychologists, including specialists. The number of such doctors is not, of course, within DDS control because private physicians must volunteer to participate, giving their time for less money than they might earn privately. Consultative examinations take a common form. They include

- ❑ The claimant's history;
- ❑ Complaints and symptoms;
- ❑ Treatment and medications;
- ❑ Examination (physical or mental); and
- ❑ The physician's, psychiatrist's or psychologist's assessment or diagnosis.

DDS physicians are not employees of the Administration and, thus, do not generally have a bias for or against a claimant. Some doctors, however, develop various reputations, deserved, or not, but claimants do not usually have a choice who they see. If a consultative examination is refused by a claimant, such refusal may form the basis for either a negative inference or an outright denial for failure to cooperate. See, Title 20 CFR §404.1518.

Figure 16–29 shows the results of a mental examination. The usual DDS mental status examination is a basic (and, therefore, limited) inquiry into the claimant's essential mental well-being. Such exams are rarely detailed. They generally are of marginal value, although individuals and doctors vary. Here, the psychologist completes the assessment with a Global Assessment of Functioning (GAF), found within the DSM-IV, which lists various mental and emotional disorders.

GAF scores are plotted along a range and are estimates of functioning, both current and during the past year. GAF scores can reach to a maximum of 100 points. Generally, however, an individual with a rating of between 50 and 55 is said to be suffering from serious symptoms, with significant impairment vocationally. A score of 60 to 65 is said to reflect moderate impairment, and an individual with a score of 65 to 70 is considered mildly impaired. In Figure 16–29, a GAF of 60 coincides with a diagnosis of "Major Depression, moderate."

What's Important?

Consultative examinations, even mental exams, can be corroborative of (1) the claimant's allegations and (2) other medical records. In Figure 16–29, the psychologist notes that the claimant is very angry with his back and leg impairments, which corroborates the claimant's allegations about his leg, lending further credence to the SSA employee's observation that the claimant walked with a limp.

Because such exams ask the claimant to relate his or her history as well as symptoms, the exam presents an opportunity for a claimant to demonstrate consistency. The symptoms described to the consultative examiner should match those set forth in the underlying application(s) and reports. If they do not, the representative's

FORM APPROVED
OMB NO. 0960-0431

RESIDUAL PHYSICAL FUNCTIONAL CAPACITY ASSESSMENT

CLAIMANT:

SOCIAL SECURITY NUMBER:

NUMBERHOLDER (IF CDB CLAIM):

PRIMARY DIAGNOSIS:

SECONDARY DIAGNOSIS:

OTHER ALLEGED IMPAIRMENTS:

RFC ASSESSMENT IS FOR:

☐ Current Evaluation

☐ Date Last Insured: ____________ (Date)

☐ Date 12 Months After Onset: ____________ (Date)

☐ Other (Specify): ____________

Paperwork/Privacy Act Notice: The information requested on this form is authorized by Section 223 and Section 1633 of the Social Security Act. The information provided will be used in making a decision on this claim. Failure to complete this form may result in a delay in processing the claim. Information furnished on this form may be disclosed by the Social Security Administration to another person or governmental agency only with respect to Social Security programs and to comply with federal laws requiring the exchange of information between Social Security and other agencies.

TIME IT TAKES TO COMPLETE THIS FORM: We estimate that it will take you about 20 minutes to complete this form. This includes the time it will take to read the instructions, gather the necessary facts and fill out the form. If you have comments or suggestions on how long it takes to complete this form or on any other aspect of this form, write to the Social Security Administration, ATTN: Reports Clearance Officer, 1-A-21 Operations Bldg., Baltimore, MD 21235, and to the Office of Management and Budget, Paperwork Reduction Project (0960-0431), Washington, D.C. 20503.

I. LIMITATIONS:

For Each Section A - F

➡ Base your conclusions on **all evidence** in file (clinical and laboratory findings; symptoms; observations; lay evidence; reports of daily activities; etc.).

➡ Check the blocks which reflect your **reasoned judgment**.

➡ Describe how the **evidence substantiates your conclusions.** (Cite specific clinical and laboratory findings, observations, lay evidence, etc.).

➡ Ensure that you have requested:

- Apropriate treating and examining source statements regarding the individual's capacities (DI 22505.000ff. and DI 22510.000ff.) and that you have given appropriate **weight to treating source conclusions**. (See Section III.)
- Considered and responded to **any alleged limitations imposed by symptoms** (pain, fatigue, etc.) attributable, in your judgment, to a medically determinable impairment. Discuss your assessment of symptom - related limitations in the explanation for your conclusions in A - F below. (See also Section II.)
- Responded to all allegations of physical limitations or factors which can cause physical limitations.

➡ **Frequently** means occurring one-third to two-thirds of an 8-hour workday (cumulative, not continuous). **Occasionally** means occurring from very little up to one-third of an 8-hour workday (cumulative, not continuous).

FORM **SSA-4734-U8** (1/89)
Supersedes Forms SSA-4734-F4 (3-82)

Page 1

☐ Continued on Page 2

Figure 16–28 **Physical RFC Assessment**

(continued)

A. EXERTIONAL LIMITATIONS

☐ None established. (Proceed to section B.)

1. **Occasionally** lift and/or carry (including upward pulling) (maximum)—when less than one-third of the time or less than 10 pounds, explain the amount (time/pounds) in item 6.

   ☐ less than 10 pounds
   ☐ 10 pounds
   ☐ 20 pounds
   ☐ 50 pounds
   ☐ 100 pounds or more

2. **Frequently** lift and/or carry (including upward pulling) (maximum)—when less than two-thirds of the time or less than 10 pounds, explain the amount (time/pounds) in item 6.

   ☐ less than 10 pounds
   ☐ 10 pounds
   ☐ 25 pounds
   ☐ 50 pounds or more

3. Stand and/or walk (with normal breaks) for a total of—

   ☐ less than 2 hours in an 8-hour workday
   ☐ at least 2 hours in an 8-hour workday
   ☐ about 6 hours in an 8-hour workday

   ☐ medically required hand-held assistive device is necessary for ambulation

4. Sit (with normal breaks) for a total of—

   ☐ less than about 6 hours in an 8-hour workday
   ☐ about 6 hours in an 8-hour workday

   ☐ must periodically alternate sitting and standing to relieve pain or discomfort. (If checked, explain in 6.)

5. Push and/or pull (including operation of hand and/or foot controls)—

   ☐ unlimited, other than as shown for lift and/or carry
   ☐ limited in **upper** extremities (describe nature and degree)
   ☐ limited in **lower** extremities (describe nature and degree)

6. Explain how and why the evidence supports your conclusions in item 1 through 5. Cite the specific facts upon which your conclusions are based.

FORM **SSA-4734-U8** (1-89) Page 2 ☐ Continued on Page 3

(continued)

Figure 16–28 **Physical RFC Assessment *(continued)***

6. Continue (NOTE: MAKE ADDITIONAL COMMENTS IN SECTION IV)

B. POSTURAL LIMITATIONS

☐ None established. (Proceed to section C.)

	Frequently	Occasionally	Never
1. Climbing—ramp/stairs —ladder/rope/scaffolds →	☐	☐	☐
2. Balancing →	☐	☐	☐
3. Stooping →	☐	☐	☐
4. Kneeling →	☐	☐	☐
5. Crouching →	☐	☐	☐
6. Crawling →	☐	☐	☐

7. When less than two-thirds of the time for frequently or less than one-third for occasionally, fully describe and explain. Also explain how and why the evidence supports your conclusions in items 1 through 6. Cite the specific facts upon which your conclusions are based.

FORM SSA-4734-U8 (1-89) Page 3 ☐ Continued on Page 4

C. MANIPULATIVE LIMITATIONS

☐ **None established. (Proceed to section D.)**

	LIMITED	UNLIMITED
1. Reaching all directions (including overhead) →	☐	☐
2. Handling (gross manipulation) →	☐	☐
3. Fingering (fine manipulation) →	☐	☐
4. Feeling (skin receptors) →	☐	☐

5. Describe how the activities checked "limited" are impaired. Also, explain how and why the evidence supports your conclusions in item 1 through 4. Cite the specific facts upon which your conclusions are based.

D. VISUAL LIMITATIONS

☐ None established. (Proceed to section E.)

	LIMITED	UNLIMITED
1. Near acuity →	☐	☐
2. Far acuity →	☐	☐
3. Depth perception →	☐	☐
4. Accommodation →	☐	☐
5. Color vision →	☐	☐
6. Field of vision →	☐	☐

7. Describe how the faculties checked "limited" are impaired. Also explain how and why the evidence supports your conclusions in item 1 through 6. Cite the specific facts upon which your conclusions are based.

FORM **SSA-4734-U8** (1-89) Page 4 ☐ Continued on Page 5

(continued)

E. COMMUNICATIVE LIMITATIONS

☐ **None established. (Proceed to section F.)**

	LIMITED	UNLIMITED
1. Hearing	☐	☐
2. Speaking	☐	☐

3. Describe how the faculties checked "limited" are impaired. Also, explain how and why the evidence supports your conclusions in items 1 and 2. Cite the specific facts upon which your conclusions are based.

F. ENVIRONMENTAL LIMITATIONS

☐ **None established. (Proceed to section II.)**

	UNLIMITED	AVOID CONCENTRATED EXPOSURE	AVOID EVEN MODERATE EXPOSURE	AVOID ALL EXPOSURE
1. Extreme cold	☐	☐	☐	☐
2. Extreme heat	☐	☐	☐	☐
3. Wetness	☐	☐	☐	☐
4. Humidity	☐	☐	☐	☐
5. Noise	☐	☐	☐	☐
6. Vibration	☐	☐	☐	☐
7. Fumes, odors, dusts, gases, poor ventilation, etc.	☐	☐	☐	☐
8. Hazards (machinery, heights, etc.)	☐	☐	☐	☐

9. Describe how these environmental factors impair activities and identify hazards to be avoided. Also, explain how and why the evidence supports your conclusions in items 1 through 8. Cite the specific facts upon which your conclusions are based.

FORM **SSA-4734-U8** (1-89) Page 5 ☐ Continued on Page 6

9. Continue (NOTE: MAKE ADDITIONAL COMMENTS IN SECTION IV)

II. **SYMPTOMS**

For symptoms alleged by the claimant to produce physical limitations, and for which the following have not previously been addressed in section I, discuss whether:

A. The symptom(s) is attributable, in your judgment, to a medically determinable impairment.

B. The severity or duration of the symptom(s), in your judgment, is disproportionate to the expected severity or expected duration on the basis of the claimant's medically determinable impairment(s).

C. The severity of the symptom(s) and its alleged effect on function is consistent, in your judgment, with the total medical and nonmedical evidence, including statements by the claimant and others, observations regarding activities of daily living, and alterations of usual behavior or habits.

FORM **SSA-4734-U8** (1-89) Page 6 ☐ Continued on Page 7

(continued)

III. TREATING OR EXAMINING SOURCE STATEMENT(S)

A. Is a treating or examining source statement(s) regarding the claimant's physical capacities in file?

☐ **Yes**

☐ **No (Includes situations in which there was no source or when the source(s) did not provide a statement regarding the claimant's physical capacities.)**

B. If yes, are there treating/examining source conclusions about the claimant's limitations or restrictions which are significantly different from your findings?

☐ **Yes**

☐ **No**

C. If yes, explain why those conclusions are not supported by the evidence in file. (Cite the source's name and the statement date.)

☐ Continued on Page 8

IV. ADDITIONAL COMMENTS:

MEDICAL CONSULTANT'S SIGNATURE:	MEDICAL CONSULTANT'S CODE:	DATE:

FORM **SSA-4734-U8** (1-89)

STATE OF GRACE
Disability Determination Division
January 2

PSYCHOLOGICAL EVALUATION

History of Illness

Complaints and Symptoms

This 43-year-old male was seen for a mental status examination on December 19 as a result of his claim for disability benefits. The client states that he suffered a gunshot to the right leg, which occurred in October. He presents as depressed. He states his feelings are related both to his physical condition as well as his overall life status.

Treatment and Medications

The client was just released from prison where he had been prescribed Zoloft for depression and Motrin for his leg. He states that he now has no regular physician and is not now involved in psychotherapy or counselling. He says he has no money for such treatment.

Personal History

The client states he was born in New York City, New York; one of two children. He says that in general his childhood was good. In school his academic achievement suffered. He did below average work, until he finally quit school after repeating the seventh grade. He is only marginally literate, able to read and write only simple instructions. The client's past work was primarily in construction. His last job was as a general construction site laborer. He suffered a gunshot to the right leg in October and never returned to work after that time. He says he was unable to drive to work; and even if he could, he says he could not have done the type of activity that his job required of him.

Daily Functioning

Social Functioning

The client states that he does not get along with others. He states he has a difficult time being around people and prefers to be alone. He presented negatively, and would likely experience a good deal of difficulty in interpersonal relationships.

Personal Interests

The client states that he once enjoyed hunting and fishing, but no longer, primarily because of his physical impairment. Also, he notes that he used to enjoy his work, but is again, unable to continue due to physical problems. He stated that he feels very depressed and professes an inability to function.

Daily Activities

The client lives alone. On a typical day he reports that he does not sleep well because of pain and is up early at 6:00 a.m. He does very little once up, having instant coffee and watching television. He says he uses a cane when walking even short distances, even in his apartment. As a result, he indicates that he does not go into stores or walk very much. He reports he is limited in performing household chores, but does tinker with "odds and ends" through the course of the day. However, he spends most of the time watching television. He does indicate that he can perform all activities of personal care.

Mental Status Examination

Attitude and Behavior

The client presents himself in a reasonably appropriate manner, given his age and gender. His posture does seem uncomfortable and his gait was slow and limping.

He seems to have appropriate reality contact. His feelings of self-esteem are, however, significantly impaired; and he does not seem very well motivated. His self-insight is poor.

Figure 16–29 **Consultative Examination Report**

Stream of Mental Activity

The client is a relatively quiet individual, who has trouble at times expressing himself. However, his thoughts do not appear disorganized. He denies symptoms of psychosis and suicidal thoughts, but does acknowledge depression and an inability to maintain concentration, largely secondary to pain.

Emotional Reaction

The client's affect is flat. He also expresses anger at the Social Security Administration for denial of benefits.

Sensorium and Mental Capacity

Orientation

This person is well oriented to time and place.

Memory

Immediate: Able to repeat eight digits forward and four backward.
Recent: Able to recall all three objects presented.
Remote: Presidents Bush, Clinton, Reagan and Carter

Information

Cities: Tulsa, Dallas, Houston
Famous People: Bush, Reagan, O'Reilly
Current Events: Afghanistan, World Trade Center, Middle East

Abstract Thinking

Grass: "Where you're at isn't as good as on the other side of the hill."
Milk: Don't let the small things get to you.

Similarities and Differences

Orange/Apple: "They're both round."
Bush/Tree: "They both grow leaves."

Judgment

Envelope: "I'd let someone else pick it up and mail it."
Fire: "I'd scream and then start limping out."

Additional Information

This is a severely depressed individual, rather reserved, though he appears to possess adequate intelligence. He seems upset with his physical condition and with the Social Security Administration.

Diagnosis

Axis I **296.22** **Major Depression, moderate**
Axis II **No diagnosis**
Axis III **Right Leg impairments, pain**
Axis IV **Severity of psychosocial stressors: moderate to severe**
Axis V **Current GAF: 55**
Highest GAF in past year: 60

Claimant is capable of handling his own funds.

Signed,

Dr. T, Ph.D.
Licensed Clinical Psychologist

immediate questions should be whether there has been a change, or whether the client is confused or not telling the truth. If they do match, the representative should take advantage of the opportunity to point out the consistency to the judge, emphasizing the reliability of the records and the credibility of the claimant.

Finally, a consultative report holds potential to state limitations and restrictions, either directly or indirectly, by confirming the claimant's diagnosis and symptoms. All of this should be pointed out to the judge, either in an opening or closing statement at the administrative hearing.

Hospital Records

Hospital records can be voluminous. Of special import are the admissions report and the discharge summary. If surgery is performed, an operative report, together with one or more consultative reports,[2] should also be a part of the record. Generally, nursing chart notes need not be included, because they contain minimal information about the claimant's vital signs during the course of a hospital stay. This, of course, is a judgment call that must be made for each case. Vital signs may form the heart of a case and may become the focus of intense scrutiny.

Figure 16–30 shows a typical hospital admission from Acme General Hospital (a fictitious institution). An initial history and physical is taken,[3] as well as a brief medical history. A diagnosis is made, and a treatment plan is set forth. In this case, the claimant suffers from a gunshot wound, and bullet fragments are lodged in the hip. This is consistent with the claimant's continuing allegations of leg pain.

ACME GENERAL HOSPITAL

Pre-Admission Examination

Patient Name: ______________________________

Date of Admission: ________________

Room Number: __________

Attending Physician: ______________________________

HISTORY AND PHYSICAL: This 43-year-old male suffered a self-inflicted gunshot wound to the right leg on October 1, nicking the right femoral artery. The patient was maintained on I.V. antibiotics overnight and discharged with crutches. He returns today with significant right leg pain. Radiographs indicate a bullet fragment within the right fibula and a fracture of the right tibia, heretofore undetected. This is now documented by subsequent tomography. The patient is being admitted for exploration of the common peroneal nerve, along with removal of the bullet fragment.

PAST MEDICAL HISTORY: Usual childhood illnesses. A broken nose at age 12 and an injury to the low back at age 27 as a result of a MVA [motor vehicle accident].

PHYSICAL EXAMINATION: On examination today, this 5' 11" 195 pound male with a BP [blood pressure]g of 130/90, has a heart rate of 74 and regular. Respiratory rate is 22. Patient is a well-developed, well-nourished WM [white male] in no acute distress. HEENT: pupils equal, reactive to light. Lungs clear, heart regular rate and rhythm. Abdomen is soft. Extremities: There is an entrance and exit wound to the right lower extremity. There is peroneal palsy foot drop on the right.

DIAGNOSIS: Gunshot wound, right lower extremity with peroneal palsy, foot drop on the right.

PLAN: Patient scheduled for admission to ACME GENERAL HOSPITAL for removal of bullet fragment, exploration of the peroneal nerve. Possible complications of surgery include infection, bleeding, anesthetic risk, post-operative lower extremity pain (right), persistent nerve palsy. All explained to patient.

Dictated: / /

Transcribed: / /

Figure 16–30 **Hospital Record, with Diagnosis of Gunshot Wound**

INSTITUTIONAL RECORDS[4]

Institutional records can take many forms, from prison records to nursing home records. Figure 16–31 shows a prison medical record, which looks very much like a doctor's progress notes. Such records can be lengthy, reflecting in part the length of institutionalization or, as in this case, imprisonment. Institutional records can be particularly helpful, because they reflect the totality of care as well as some insight into the lifestyle of an individual. Institutional records, however, can be artificial in that they reflect life within what is often a highly structured environment.

Like medical progress notes, institutional records can be terse, and sometimes cryptic, reflecting institutional jargon. Nevertheless, such records can offer a complete picture of the individual, especially in a prison. The requirement that a medical condition be documented, and all reasonable treatment be afforded, ensures a potentially comprehensive record.

What's Important?

Institutional records (in this case, the exemplar prison record) yield the following information (corroborative of the claimant's claim in this example):

- ❑ The December 5 psychiatric notes comment on "severe problems of the right lower limb," noting that the inmate suffers from an "adjustment disorder with depressed mood";
- ❑ The June 10 consultation form reveals that the right leg is one inch shorter than the left in length, corroborative of the severe leg problems;
- ❑ The March 12 and May 21 progress notes reveal "asymmetry of hips," "foot drop," and "continuing pain";
- ❑ The January 8 progress note reveals "osteoarthritis of the right ankle and left hand";
- ❑ The November 4 progress note reveals a "brace on the right ankle";
- ❑ Progress notes throughout September reflect leg pain; and
- ❑ The April 15 progress note reveals an allergic reaction to an environmental agent within one hour of entering the print shop.

The institutional records in Figure 16–31 corroborate the claimant's allegations. However, the exemplar records also reveal the following information not corroborative of the claimant's claim (see Figure 16–32):

- ❑ A September 10 progress note indicates that the claimant was on the "rec. yard playing Ping-Pong jumping & moving with no apparent problems";
- ❑ A March 21 record comments that the patient is "into muscle building and bench presses >200 lbs.";
- ❑ The same note that comments on the environmental allergy to the print shop is also indicative of the fact that the claimant was willing and able to at least begin working there; and
- ❑ A March 1 progress note reveals that the claimant "Lifts wts. 300 lbs every other day" and has "No SOB [shortness of breath]."

See Figure 16–32, consisting of several pages, which are institutional records that *do not* corroborate the claimant's allegations.

This record then, like other medical records maintained over time, holds both good and bad news for the claim. It is not atypical of a record that has existed over a period of years. The key is to successfully interpret the significance of the positive and negative points. For example, the hypothetical claimant can bench press up to 300 pounds yet experiences pain from an old gunshot wound in his right leg, which is one inch shorter than his left. Arguably then, he has maintained his upper-body strength but cannot, because of the hip injury, stand and walk six out of eight hours a day and is, therefore, limited to sedentary work—this, notwithstanding the well-demonstrated upper-body strength.

As is clear from the regulations, however, the ability to engage in light, medium, or heavy work involves both the upper and lower body—requiring the ability to lift as well as stand and walk. Here, the hypothetical claimant can clearly lift but is not able to stand and walk.

What about the Ping-Pong? The note that reveals the claimant's ability to play Ping-Pong was made earlier in his incarceration. Arguably, his condition worsened since that point in time, as evidenced, for example, by increasing reports of pain. A claim as to increasing severe pain could be advanced later, but not credibly so at the earlier time. The foregoing synthesis of the medical records is the type of analysis necessary to any complex medical record containing both favorable and unfavorable information.

PRISON (Institutional) MEDICAL RECORD

PSYCHIATRIC PROGRESS NOTES

Inmate Name: ____

Prison Number: __________________

Date: ______________

Inmate is referred for complaints of inability to sleep, "nerves" and depression.

Forty-year-old white male has been incarcerated since February and was in County Jail for 6 months previous. He states he was charged with burglary and suffered a self-inflicted gunshot wound, when his weapon accidentally discharged upon arrest. No previous adult convictions.

He used to be a construction laborer. Divorced, with a seventh-grade education and marginal literacy. No history of previous psychiatric care. No history of suicidal ideation. He is 5'11" and weighs 195 pounds and takes no medications other than OTC pain killers for right lower extremity pain.

MENTAL STATUS EXAM: This is an unhappy middle age white male with mild psychomotor retardation and normal intelligence. Memory is intact. He says: "I am depressed and don't know what I am going to do." He says he is having a difficult time adjusting to being in prison. He is oriented in three spheres.

DIAGNOSIS:

AXIS I: **Adjustment disorder with Depressed Mood**

AXIS II: **None**

AXIS III: **Neuro-orthopedic problems, right lower extremity from a gunshot wound**

Recommendations: Continue Zoloft, 50 mg by mouth at bedtime. See again, three weeks.

Dr. Z, M.D., Psychiatrist

PRISON (Institutional) MEDICAL RECORD

Inmate Name: _____

Prison Number: _____

Date: _____

CONSULTATION FORM

Medical Problem: Drop foot, right sided.
Right Lower Extremity Pain.
Residual Nerve Damage, Gunshot Wound to Right Leg

Findings: Drop foot, right sided
Common Peroneal Nerve Injury
Right Leg Shorter than Left _ in

Laboratory or x-ray results: Right less than left _ in

Diagnosis: S/P [status post] GSW [gunshot wound] with common peroneal nerve injury on right and drop foot; leg length discrepancy

Treatment Recommended: Send to Orthopedic for right foot brace; right shoe buildup _″ heel and sole.

Medications recommended: OTC pain

Follow-up appointment: prn [as needed]

Date: / /

Consulting Physician: ______________________________

Figure 16–31 **Corroborative Report from an Institutional Center**

PRISON (Institutional) MEDICAL RECORD

Inmate Name: ____________________

Prison Number: ____________________

Date: ____________________

PROGRESS NOTES

3/23 S. Has foot/lower leg pain; antalgic gait\
A. Rt. leg shorter than left
A. Post-traumatic leg asymmetry secondary to GSW with foot drop.
B. Refer to orthopedic for foot brace

4/12 S. Fell on right leg
C. No swelling; tender to touch; some parathesias
A. Rt. leg pain
B. Motrin 800 mg, 1 bid x 10 days. Full sick bed x 5 days

4/20 S. Pt. fell yesterday on right leg
C. Motion is slow but good.
A. Right leg strain
B. X-ray right foot/leg

4/22 S. Swollen rt. ankle & right foot
C. Good pulses
A. Arthritis secondary to asymmetry
B. Request shoe evaluation
Cont. Motrin 88 mg., bid x 10 days

5/1 Psych. Pt. says Zoloft helps. Feels "more energy." Will try reducing dosage. Reduce to 30 mg. x 60 days

5/5 S. Renew Motrin 800 mg. bid 30 days

5/15 S. Having continuing pain in lower right extremity
C. Right lower extremity tender. No swelling
A. Sequelae pain in right lower leg from GSW
B. X-ray right lower leg and return 2 wks.

6/1 Ortho. called. Approved for orthopedic brace. Not an emergency. Will schedule for 6/8.

PRISON (Institutional) MEDICAL RECORD

Inmate Name: ____________________

Prison Number: ____________________

Date: ____________________

Acknowledgment of Receipt of Medical Care

I certify that I have received the following items:

– 1 walking cane in good condition

I will be responsible for the return of the foregoing equipment in good condition. Failure to return the foregoing equipment in good condition will result in a charge to my prison account.

Signed, ____________________
Inmate

PRISON (Institutional) MEDICAL RECORD

Inmate Name: ____________________

Prison Number: ____________________

Date: ____________________

MEDICAL EVALUATION

43-year-old white male with history of GSW to right leg resulting in damage to common peroneal nerve, with right drop foot and leg shortening. Bullet removed from tibia. Incarcerated for several months and receiving Motrin 800 mg for pain relief. Referred for evaluation - orthopedic - for orthosis for right foot drop and intermittent leg pain. Splint broke while playing Ping Pong. Inmate admits he does not use the orthotic device all the time. In addition, the inmate participates in muscle building program, bench presses 220# [pounds] and is attempting to increase walking time in prison exercise yard. He states that when the pain is bad he uses a cane. Right leg shorter by _ inch than left. Normal back examination with abnormal neurological findings in lower right extremity.

Recommendation: Continue MOTRIN 800 mg as needed; replace orthosis; measurements taken. Will call back when orthosis is ready. Inmate is to use at all times.

Inmate being reassigned to the copy shop.

Signed, Dr. N, M.D.

Figure 16–32 **Noncorroborative Report from an Institutional Center**

TREATING PHYSICIAN RECORDS

Because the regulations give the opinions of treating physicians greater weight than those of other doctors, these records are particularly important. Treating physician records include:

- ❑ Treatment or progress notes;
- ❑ Laboratory findings;
- ❑ Narrative reports;
- ❑ Medication prescriptions; and, where appropriate,
- ❑ Hospital or clinic records (e.g., records of the Veteran's Administration, etc.).

What's Important?

Treating physician records, if present, are critical to the success of any claim. Without treating physician records, records of consultative examinations must suffice. When there is a conflict between a treating physician and an examining physician (who is not a treating physician, such as a consultative examiner [CE]) the treating physician's opinion and conclusions, if supported by evidence over time, will be given controlling weight.[5] In other words, such records trump those of nontreating (such as DDS) physicians or CEs.

To this end, an effective representative, having reviewed the totality of the medical records, shall obtain, if possible, a RFC assessment from the treating physician. The physician should be asked to comment on the claimant's physical or mental limitations (depending on the nature of the treatment) during the entire course of treatment. All supporting records, including treatment records, laboratory records, and so forth, should be included.

Note, however, that medical records should not be withheld from the administrative record, even if they are unfavorable. Although some lawyers believe zealous advocacy demands submission of only those records that support a claim, others disagree with this practice. The reality of the hearing process is such that the absence of records will be noted. Once the absence of medical records becomes evident, the judge may well determine that their absence affects the claimant's credibility, which potentially imperils the claim. It is far more effective to ask the judge to examine the whole medical record, the good and the bad; this will engender both the claimant's and the representative's credibility.

In the exemplar records (see Figure 16–33), Dr. O (a fictitious doctor), in a March 19 letter, directly limits the claimant:

> **[D]ue to permanent partial disability, he would be unable to perform any heavy physical work and should be limited to a more sedentary type employment.**

Dr. F confirms this in a report of August 17 (see Figure 16–34):

> **The patient also has some parasthesias [numbness] in the leg and foot.**

Finally, Dr. M writes on a prescription pad on July 6 (see Figure 16–35):

> **I have treated [the claimant] 3× [three times] in the past 8 months for RLE condition. Based on my review of the clinic notes, he remains disabled.**

PRISON (Institutional) MEDICAL RECORD

Inmate Name: ____________________

Prison Number: ____________________

Date: ____________________

TO WHOM IT MAY CONCERN

RE: Inmate

Dear Sir or Madam:

This patient is presently incarcerated, having suffered a gunshot wound to the right lower leg with resultant damage to the common peroneal nerve causing right foot drop (palsy). A bullet fragment remains lodged in the right tibia.

As a result of the traumatic injury, the patient suffers from a permanent nerve palsy. He would, therefore, be unable to engage in prolonged standing and walking, lifting heavy weights and should be limited to a more sedentary type job.

If you need further information, please do not hesitate to contact me.

Sincerely,

Dr. O., M.D.

Figure 16–33 **Narrative Report of Treating Physician**

DOCTOR F., M.D.
123 Any street
Anyplace, USA 01234

Any date, 2002

Disability Determination Division
ANY STATE, USA

Re: Inmate

Dear Sir or Madam:

The named inmate was seen in my office to evaluate right leg and back pain. In October, the inmate suffered a gunshot wound to the right leg, causing a traumatic injury to the right common peroneal nerve. The patient developed a right drop foot and subsequent surgery was necessary to remove a bullet fragment located in the right tibia. Additionally, and as a result of the bullet wound and surgery, the patient now suffers from an asymmetry of gait as a result of the shortening by _ inch of his right leg when compared to the left. The inmate has suffered right leg pain for more than eighteen months as a result of the gunshot wound.

On examination, the patient has good range of motion of the back in lateral bending, flexion and only voices mild to moderate complaints when twisting. Because of the loss of height on the right, the patient's posture when standing is asymmetrical. Examination of the right lower extremity shows no active dorsi flexion of the foot, although plantar flexion appears without loss. Parasthesias on the right ankle and foot is noted to be intermittent. Reflexes and the knees and ankles were equal. Radiography of the lumbar spine was within normal limits. Radiography of the right tibia shows a bullet fragment remaining.

As a result of this examination, and review of pertinent medical records, I am of the opinion that the inmate will suffer a permanent foot drop on the right with attendant difficulty in gait and station. In addition, he will likely develop arthritis of the foot; and will likely require further surgical intervention in aid of the bullet fragment which remains. He should not be expected to engage in activity which will cause him to remain standing for long periods; nor should he be expected to engage in activity which will require that he walk for long periods.

Thank you for allowing me to see this very interesting patient.

Very truly yours,

Dr. F., M.D.

Figure 16–34 **Shorthand Note of Corroborating Treating Physician**

NAME Mr Inmate DATE ______

℞ I have treated Mr. Inmate 4 times in the past 10 months for right lower extremity condition as a result of a gunshot wound. Based on my review of the clinic notes, Mr. Inmate remains disabled and is unable to engage in work or worklike activity.

REFILL ________ X

Dr. M., M.D.

PHYSICAN (PLEASE PRINT)

DEA # ______

Dr. M.D

PHYSICAN (PLEASE PRINT)

Figure 16–35 **Additional Medical Evidence**

Although commenting directly on disability, a doctor who, in effect, "plays judge" by pronouncing the verdict, does little more than offer corroborating evidence. The doctor cannot, by offering such an opinion, decide the case. The disability decision is ultimately a legal decision, not a medical one. Such a writing, even by a treating physician, is of little value because it does not explain *why* the doctor reaches his or her conclusion. A "prescription pad verdict" from a treating physician cannot be viewed as "controlling," because it does not explain the basis for the legal/medical conclusion; it is not supported by substantial evidence; no other "Dr. M" treatment notes are part of the administrative record.

Finally, the exemplar record contains a Report of Contact with Dr. O, a treating physician. The ROC bears directly on the issue of disability because the subject of the conversation is a clarification of the claimant's limitations. Because this is from a treating physician and was obtained by the Social Security Administration, it will weigh heavily in the claimant's favor. (Dr. O explains why he limited the claimant to sedentary work.) See Figure 16–36.

REPORT OF CONTACT
(Use ink or typewriter)

ACCOUNT NUMBER AND SYMBOL

NAME OF WAGE EARNER OR SE PERSON

TO: NE MAT SE GL WN MAM
ODO DIO DDS

PERSON(S) CONTACTED AND ADDRESSES: ☐ WE OR SE PERSON ☐ OTHER *(Specify)*

DR. O

CONTACT MADE: ☐ DO ☐ BO ☐ CS ☐ HOME ☐ PHONE: ☐ OTHER

DATE OF CONTACT 4-10

SUBJECT EXERTIONAL LIMITATIONS

I called Dr. O to clarify his statement limiting this claimant to a "more sedentary type of employment." Dr. O said he meant that the patient should lift and carry no more than 10 pounds at a time and that standing and walking may be limited to about 2 hours in an 8 hour workday. The patient also requires use of a cane for long distances and over rough terrain.

According to Dr. O, these limitations are based on the fact that the patient has a marked postural abnormality which has been associated with chronic pain on weight-bearing.

SIGNATURE SSA Employee

DISTRICT OFFICE *(Name, Address & Code)*

☐ CR ☐ FR ☐ SR ☐ CLAIMS CLERICAL

☐ OTHER *(Specify)*

DATE OF REPORT 4-10

PAGE OF

Form SSA-5002 (8-81)

Printed on recycled paper

*U.S. GPO: 1995-398-915/29102

Figure 16–36 **Report of Contact**

LABORATORY FINDINGS

Laboratory findings are medical records reflecting the results of medical testing. They are important as objective evidence of the claimant's complaints. Such reports include

- Radiology (including X-rays, CT scans, MRIs, diskography, and so on);
- Blood chemistry;
- Doppler studies;
- EMG studies;
- EEG studies;
- Treadmill testing;
- EKG testing; and
- Other testing of specific bodily function.

The exemplar record contains a radiology consultation, in which the radiologist reviews X-rays of the right femur, the cervical spine, the lumbosacral spine (low back), and the left shoulder. This is typical of the objective testing part of a medical record. X-rays can confirm the presence of multiple metallic fragments about the right femur, corroborative of the old gunshot injury. See Figure 16–37, Radiology Consultation.

BACK TO CHRIS

"Wow!" Chris breathed, closing the sample file. "That's a lot of stuff."

"It looks like a lot, but it's really understandable once you know how to prioritize each of the different types of records," Steve replied.

"I can see that. Thanks for helping me get a handle on this. It'll be really useful!"

"You're welcome! Just remember, be prepared! And that means, getting all the records up to date *before* the administrative hearing. You don't want to further delay the process after your client has waited so long!"

"Gotcha!"

RADIOLOGY CONSULTATION

8/20

RIGHT FEMUR: AP and lateral views of the right femur show a considerable deformity of the proximal shaft indicating an old united fracture. Multiple metallic fragments are seen in the soft tissue surrounding the fracture.

CERVICAL SPINE: Multiple views of the cervical spine, including oblique projections, show no evidence of bone injury, arthritis or other significant abnormality.

IMPRESSION: Negative cervical spine.

LUMBOSACRAL SPINE: Antero-posterior, lateral and oblique projections of the lumbosacral spine show no abnormalities.

IMPRESSION: Negative lumbosacral spine.

LEFT SHOULDER: Films of the left shoulder reveal no evidence of bursitis, arthritis, or other bony abnormality.

Trans. 8-20

Figure 16–37 **Radiology Consultation**

FRONT OF YOUR MIND QUESTIONS AND CONSIDERATIONS, 16.6

FINAL NOTE ON ANALYSIS OF MEDICAL RECORDS

To be effective, the medical records must be complete and up-to-date. Complete records contain all medical records during the claimed period of disability. It may also be important to have records from prior to the beginning of the claimed period to show the existence of a condition that has worsened over time.

Up-to-date records should be as recent as one month prior to the actual hearing. Pragmatically, up-to-date records can date back three months. Records that end between six months and a year before the hearing are only marginally helpful, and no judge can effectively render a decision with such an information gap. Too much time has passed with little information about the claimant's ongoing condition. Good faith efforts must, therefore, be made well in advance of the hearing to secure complete and up-to-date medical records.

Having said that, the analysis of records is central to the theory formation of a case. By examining the medical records it can be determined whether a case can be made that a client's condition meets or medically equals a Listing. If it does not, the question becomes whether the records support a defined RFC assessment. The analytical process thus proceeds in logical fashion:

1. Identify the client's most significant impairment;
2. If possible, find the appropriate medical Listing; or the Listing that most closely approximates the client's impairment;
3. Examine the specific requirements of the Listings regarding symptoms, medical signs, and laboratory findings;
4. Ask whether the medical records contain all of the elements of the specific medical Listing. If yes, the next question is, Do all of the elements of the specific medical Listing occur within a defined twelve-month period? If yes, an argument can be made that the client's impairment meets a Listing. If no, it is still possible that the client's primary impairment is equivalent in medical severity to a Listed impairment;
5. Determine what the expected symptoms and limitations associated with the impairment at the Listing level are. Does the client suffer these or similar symptoms and impairments? If yes, his or her condition may equal a Listing, if

   A. He or she also suffers from additional impairment(s) that, when considered in combination with the primary impairment, produce symptoms and limitations that are the same or equivalent to those that would be suffered if he or she met the Listing; or

   B. He or she suffers from a symptom or limitation that, because of its individual severity, is equivalent to the Listed impairment globally; or

   C. The medical records document these conditions over the course of the claimed period of disability, or sufficiently so, to constitute substantial evidence of the same.

6. Ascertain whether the medical records provide evidence of the claimant's limitations;
7. Determine whether the evidence is direct or indirect:

   A. Direct evidence of the claimant's limitations or restrictions include a completed RFC form from a treating physician, a consultative physician, or a nonexamining DDS physician; a narrative report or letter from a physician discussing the claimant's restrictions; a chart or progress notes stating limitations or restrictions; physical therapy evaluation(s) that identify the claimant's capabilities; and vocational–rehabilitation evaluation(s) that identify the claimant's capabilities.

   B. Indirect evidence of the claimant's limitations or restrictions may be drawn from the treating records themselves. Remembering that physicians do not generally write for legal purposes (their records are for medical purposes, not disability purposes), you can infer certain basic restrictions without specific functional limitation statements from the doctor. For example, an individual who suffers amputation of multiple fingers on the dominant hand will not be able to engage in bilateral fine-motor manipulation. The limitation is self-evident. Similarly, an individual with severe degenerative arthritis of the right hip, whose right leg is one inch shorter than the left, and who alleges pain on prolonged standing will not be able to stand and walk six out of eight hours in a workday. Again, the limitation is self-evident. Indirect evidence is, to some degree, a result of the following formula: [Claimant's testimony of limitation] + [Medical evidence of an impairment related to the limitation complained of] = [Functional limitation]. Alternately, the claimant may not need to testify, even in the case of indirect evidence of a limitation: [Medical evidence of an impairment] (*is equivalent to, without further proof*) [Functional limitation].

Thus, review of the medical records should be undertaken with an eye toward the ultimate goal, keyed to an assessment using the five-step sequential process. When undertaking such a review, medical records should be cataloged using a proof matrix as discussed earlier in Chapter 12 (See Figure 12–4). Such a matrix should identify the recovery theory (meets a Listing, equals a Listing at step 3, "Grids" out at step 5, or using the "Grids" as a "framework") as well as the individual elements required, and then show which records support such a finding. Figure 16–38 illustrates an exemplar proof matrix for a back problem.

BACK TO CHRIS

"It's a lot like an investigator, isn't it? I mean, you generally know what you're searching for; it's a matter of seeing what's actually there."

Steve nodded. "Interestingly, legal educators list investigation as one of the fundamental skills a lawyer must have as part of the educational and professional training process. So, you're right on."

"It is, I must admit, a little intimidating."

"I'd be surprised if you didn't feel that way. This is new stuff. It's not simply health care and it's not only law. It's a combination of the two. It requires a synthesis of knowledge and an understanding of where the key points are. Fortunately, the five-step sequential evaluation is a pretty good guide. The bottom line is the more you do this the more apparent the process becomes. Don't be put off simply because it's new. Remember, you're talking about a human life."

Chris gulped quietly, then grinned. "I can do it."

"You can," Steve said, holding out the file.

Meets or Equals Medical Listing 1.04(b)								
Document	Diagnosis	Pain	Muscle Spasm	Range of Motion Limitation	Sensory Loss	Weakness	Reflex Loss	Radiation of Symptoms
Dr. "O"	Exhibit 3F	Exhibit 3F/ page 11	Exhibit 6F/ page 2					
X-ray	Exhibit 5F							
EMG					Exhibit 10F/ page 2			Exhibit 10F/ page 1
DR "Z"				Exhibit 7F/ page 1		Exhibit 7F/ page 2		
CE			Exhibit 11F/ page 1					
ACME Hospital							Exhibit 5F/ page 8	

Figure 16–38 **Proof Matrix of a Back Problem**

WHAT IF . . . ? SAMPLE PROBLEMS

WHAT IF . . .

What section of the six-part modular disability folder does the representative look to when examining medical records?

1. Section 1.
2. Section A.
3. Section F.
4. Section E.

Answer: All disability files are the same if compiled in the modular format. Earlier files, created before the six-part folder was adopted, are not sectioned, and contain exhibits in numerical sequence. The six-part modular disability folder contains sections A, B, D, E & F. A temporary holding section is not assigned a section designator. Section F contains direct medical documents. Section E contains disability related documents (such as school records, and so forth), but not medical records. The correct answer is 3.

What should I do if I check the file and find that some of the records I wish to submit to the judge are duplicates?

1. Purge all duplicate records from the materials you send the Office of Hearings and Appeals.
2. Do nothing. Submit everything. Let OHA sort it out.
3. Contact the paralegal specialist or attorney working with the judge and ask whether the documents should be submitted.
4. None of the above.

Answer: Before submitting documents to the Office of Hearings and Appeals, examine the official file and make sure that you are not submitting duplicates. Duplicate records are the bane of OHA. Because file space is at a premium, and because the judge's decision will identify specific exhibits in the administrative record, only one copy of a given document should be in the file. If you fail to purge your own duplicates, the judge will spend unnecessary time sorting through the documents at the hearing; and the process will become a distraction from the ultimate goal. You do not need to contact the paralegal specialist or attorney working with the judge because OHA's policy is firm: duplicate records are not to be included in a representative's submission if it can be avoided. The correct answer is 1.

---

[1]The materials used are fictitious and do not represent a particular person. These same materials—in more complete form—were originally used as part of a Social Security training program to train new attorneys and paralegal specialists coming into the agency.
[2]Different from a consultative examination, the consultative report is prepared by a consulting physician who advises the surgeon on the propriety of the proposed procedure(s).
[3]Note, on Figure 16–30, the term "HEENT" is medical shorthand for "Head, Eyes, Ears, Nose, Throat, Neck Exam."
[4]See Title § 404.1538 (2001).
[5]See Title 20 C.F.R. § 404.1527(d) (2001).

17

CHAPTER SEVENTEEN

The Appeals Council

HIGHLIGHTS

- ❑ The administrative appeal
- ❑ After the ALJ hearing

CHRIS

"I want to know more about the Appeals Council. What if we lose the case before the Administrative Law Judge? What then?"

"Good question," Steve answered. "Let's go into some more detail. There's a real possibility you might lose. Many of these cases depend to some degree on how credible the claimant is perceived to be because of the subjectivity of pain."

"So, if we lose, is that it?"

"Not at all. Remember the pyramid we looked at?"

"The one showing the complete disability process from start to finish?"

"That's the one." Steve pointed to the upper portion of the diagram. "After the hearing before the Administrative Law Judge, if you lose, you appeal to the Appeals Council of the Social Security Administration."

"What's that?"

"The Appeals Council consists of some twenty-five Administrative Appeals Judges, supported by Appeals Analysts. Their job is to review the decision of the Administrative Law Judge. If they affirm the decision, then the decision of the Administrative Law Judge becomes the final decision of the Commissioner. If they don't, they can either reverse the case and pay benefits, or, and this is the more likely scenario, they remand the case back to the Administrative Law Judge for further action."

"Almost like an appeals court, then?"

"Very similar, but with some notable differences. For example, it is extremely rare for the Appeals Council, which is located in Falls Church, Virginia, to hear oral argument. Almost everything, and I mean everything, is done in writing."

"Anything else?"

"Big time. They can review a favorable decision—one that the Administrative Law Judge reversed that the State agency denied—on their own motion. It's called 'own motion review.' "[1]

"That's weird. Even though nobody appeals, they can review the case anyway?"

"Tell me about it. Sometimes a component of the Social Security Administration, usually the Payment Center, may lodge a protest to an Administrative Law Judge's decision, and that will provoke an appeal."

"Wait a minute. Even though the government decides it's not going to appear at a hearing, it can later decide to object to a judge's decision, and that will push the case to the Appeals Council." Chris was puzzled. "I mean, how do you know that the government has objected?"

"You don't. The next thing that happens, instead of your client getting paid, is that the client gets a letter from the Appeals Council indicating that the judge's favorable decision is being reconsidered. Your client can opt, however, to receive payment anyway, with the understanding that she or he may have to repay it."

"That's got to be a shocker!"

"There have been cases where the news triggered a severe adverse response. One claimant, who unfortunately suffered from paranoid schizophrenia and almost had to be dragged to his hearing, was convinced the government was out to get him. The judge granted benefits, only to have the Appeals Council review the case on their own motion. The poor fellow was then absolutely certain of a government conspiracy and tried to commit suicide!"

"That's awful."

"We can never forget that we're dealing with human life. Even though the numbers may be big, each case you handle is still a life."

"Is the Appeals Council process a long one?"

"Unfortunately, it is. Sometimes it lasts more than a year; sometimes up to two plus years."

"Ouch! What happens to the claimant during this process?"

"He or she waits."

"Does the claimant get benefits in the meantime?"

"No. Unless the claimant was already receiving benefits and the question before the Administrative Law Judge was whether the Social Security Administration properly terminated benefits."

"What do you mean?"

"If a claimant was already receiving benefits, he or she can elect to continue to receive them even through the course of an appeal."

"What if the claimant loses the appeal?"

"Then he or she has been overpaid and owes the money to the government."

"Well, tell me more about the appeal to the Appeals Council."

"You got it."

FRONT OF YOUR MIND QUESTIONS AND CONSIDERATIONS, 17.1

MORE ABOUT THE APPEALS COUNCIL OF THE SOCIAL SECURITY ADMINISTRATION

When an appeal must be taken from the Administrative Law Judge, the claimant must make a request for review to the Appeals Council (AC) within sixty days of receipt of the adverse decision writing. See Figure 15–1. The Appeals Council may

- ❑ Dismiss the appeal;
- ❑ Deny the Request for Review;
- ❑ Grant the Request for Review;
- ❑ Grant the Request for Review and remand the case back to the Administrative Law Judge for further proceedings; or
- ❑ Grant the Request for Review and issue a decision itself.

See Title 20 C.F.R. § 404.967. The process is illustrated in Figure 17–1. The written request for review must be filed within sixty days after receiving notice of the hearing decision or dismissal with

- ❑ The Office of Hearings and Appeals local hearing office;
- ❑ The Veteran's Administration regional office in the Philippines; or
- ❑ The Railroad Retirement Board (if the claimant has ten years service in the railroad industry).

See Title 20 C.F.R. § 404.968.

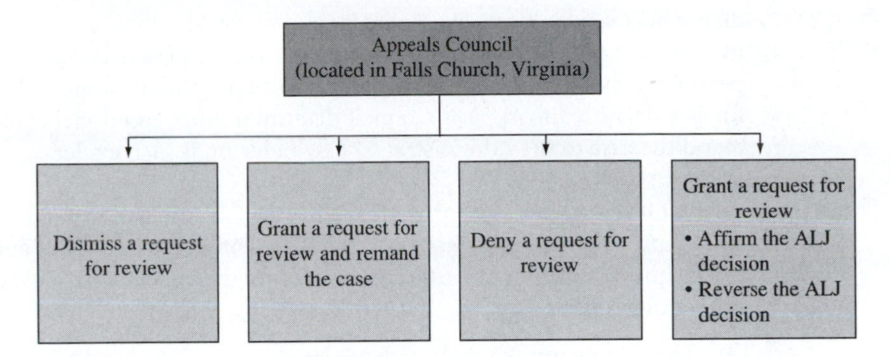

Figure 17–1 Possible Appeals Council Actions

An extension of time may be requested in writing and filed with the Appeals Council. It must specify the reasons an extension is being requested. To be successful, the claimant must demonstrate good cause for missing a deadline. The good cause standard is set forth at Title 20 C.F.R. § 404.911 and includes the following:

- Misleading Social Security Administration actions;
- Physical, mental, educational, communicative, or other limitations that prevent the claimant from meeting the deadline; or
- Additional information that was requested within the sixty-day time frame but that was not provided before the expiration of sixty days.

The Appeals Council reviews cases in the following instances:

- Abuse of discretion by the Administrative Law Judge;
- Error of law;
- Action, findings, or conclusion unsupported by substantial evidence; and
- A broad policy interest or procedural issue exists that may affect public interest.[2]

A Request for Review may be dismissed if

- The request is untimely; or
- The party to the proceeding dies and the record shows dismissal will not adversely affect any other person; or
- The request for dismissal is made by the party appealing.[3]

A dismissal is final and cannot be appealed.[4] If the claimant's appeal is dismissed, he or she must refile an application for disability benefits.

PROCEEDING BEFORE THE APPEALS COUNCIL

Proceeding before the Appeals Council involves more than simply filing a Request for Review. The representative must also provide the AC with the reason for the appeal. This usually requires the filing of a "brief," or an explication of the law and facts of the case, including the reason(s) the Administrative Law Judge's decision was in error.

On request, the Appeals Council will give the parties a "reasonable opportunity to file briefs."[5] Briefs may be filed with the Appeals Council by mail or by faxing to the specified "Branch" component handling the claimant's Request for Review. By regulation, the Appeals Council will hear new evidence that relates "to the period on or before the date of the administrative law judge hearing decision."[6] Such evidence must be material to the issues then before the AC. If the Appeals Council has indicated that the issues will be limited to specifically identified areas and the new evidence does not relate to such areas, the evidence likely is not material and will be disregarded.

As with any submission, either to the Administrative Law Judge or the Appeals Council, the number and extent of voluntary submissions should be carefully monitored. Simply submitting materials (such as newsletters, encyclopedia quotes, etc.) for the sake of documenting the record will probably have a deleterious, rather than a persuasive, effect. The Appeals Council decides thousands of cases each year. A case that includes material not directly related to the identified issues will be delayed—to the claimant's detriment. If the Appeals Council determines documents are not material or not new, they will be returned—again, causing further delay. If the Appeals Council determines that additional evidence is necessary, it may either remand the case to the Administrative Law Judge or, if such evidence can be obtained quickly, provide the evidence itself.

In filing a brief it is important to realize that this submission is likely the only opportunity to make a persuasive presentation. In other words, the representative has one shot and would be wise to make the best of it. The question is, how best to take advantage of the opportunity? Two principles should guide any submission to the Appeals Council:

- ❑ The submission should be well prepared; and
- ❑ The submission should be well presented.

Preparation

Preparation is key to any written submission alleging an erroneous decision by an Administrative Law Judge. It is important to articulate, in a single sentence if possible, the statement of error committed by the judge in reaching his or her decision. This is the theme of the appeal. The appeal should be framed in such a way as to overturn or remand the case. The Appeals Council must be persuaded of the validity and necessity of the appeal.

Persuasion is an adversarial art, requiring careful crafting of the issues and clear expression of the facts. The written decision must communicate effectively. The reader, on reviewing the document, must understand the following:

- ❑ The issue on which the appeal is taken;
- ❑ The desired outcome of the appeal; and
- ❑ The underlying law or fact(s) on which the appeal is based.

An effective brief usually does not exceed five to ten typewritten pages. In reality, it is harder to write shorter than it is to write longer. A short, well-written brief is far more persuasive than a long, rambling dissertation with little focus or direction. Following are the key elements to a well-prepared brief:

- ❑ *Introduction* A statement identifying the claimant, the representative, and a brief history of the underlying proceeding (what happened, when).
- ❑ *Statement of facts* A statement identifying the claimant's disabling condition; his or her education and previous work; followed by an overview of the medical diagnosis and treatment.
- ❑ *Statement of the issue(s)* A succinct explanation of the judge's ruling and why it was in error.
- ❑ *Analysis* A more detailed explanation of the judge's error. The analysis should draw on existing law as expressed by
    - ■ The Social Security Act;
    - ■ The regulations;
    - ■ Social Security Rulings;
    - ■ Case law;
    - ■ *HALLEX* (*Hearing and Litigation Law Manual*); and
    - ■ *POMS* (*Program Operations Manual System*).
- ❑ *Conclusion* A summary of the analysis, including the error, the law, and the desired result.

The analysis should present the theme of the appeal, setting forth in clear language how the judge's action(s) or decision violated law. (See Figure 17–2).

Once the theme of the appeal has been articulated, it must be determined whether the issues are addressed by (1) regulations, (2) Social Security Rulings, or (3) case law (preferably within the same circuit). If applicable, the pertinent regulation, ruling, or case, and the legal principle for which it stands should be identified. Then the judge's decision or action(s) that contravened the applicable regulation, ruling, or case should be presented. The proper course of action or decision should then be identified with an explanation as to why such action would have complied with the regulation, Ruling, or case.

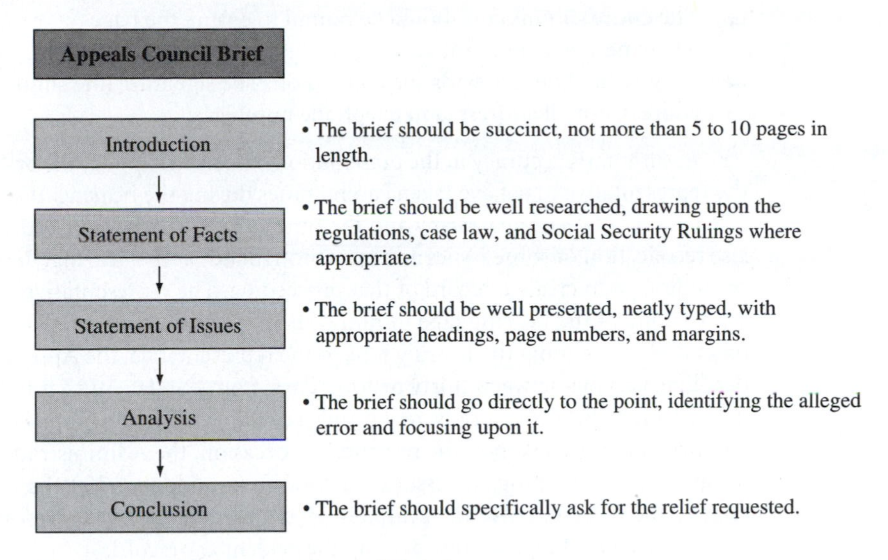

Figure 17–2 **Elements of an Appeals Council Brief**

Finally, a concise conclusion summarizes the alleged error, the governing law, and the desired result of the appeal.

Presentation

A brief can be detailed and well prepared yet fail to be persuasive because it is not readable. For example, avoid handwritten briefs at all costs. They are not persuasive because they are not professional. The manner of presentation detracts and distracts from the substance of the presentation. The presentation of material is as important as the substance. The hallmarks of a professional presentation include the following:

- ❑ A title page, table of contents, and table of authorities (these introductory pages are not included in the five-page limit);
- ❑ Proper captioning at the beginning of the brief on both the title page and the first page of the actual brief, for example

Before the Appeals Council of the Social Security Administration

In Re: The Claim of John Doe
Social Security Number ______________

Appeal From: Decision of the Honorable Joe Justice
U.S. Administrative Law Judge
Anytown, USA

- ❑ Clearly distinguished headings and subheadings, set in **bold** and <u>underlined;</u>
- ❑ Ample use of space. Do not crowd the brief. Use one-inch margins and double-spacing (except direct quotes more than one line in length). Single-space direct quotes and indent them on both sides, to center. Avoid long run-on paragraphs. No more than two discrete points should be made in a given paragraph. Allow two double-spaces between the end of one section and the heading for the next section;
- ❑ Page numbers, either at the bottom center or at the top right of the page;
- ❑ Proper case notations and citations including *italicizing* or <u>underlining</u> of case names;
- ❑ A transmittal letter, noting the attachment of the brief. *Note:* The appeals brief should not take the form of a letter;
- ❑ New evidence submitted as exhibits to the brief. Each exhibit should have a cover page, identifying the document(s) and giving the exhibit number, such as "Exhibit A." The exhibits should be included at the back of the brief;

- The entire submission should be bound to ensure the pages stay together. Avoid staples, especially where new evidence is attached; and
- A signature line following the conclusion. The signature line should contain the representative's name, address, e-mail address, and telephone number.

In summary, accuracy in the presentation of facts to support the brief's arguments is essential. Although the representative may have taken careful notes during the hearing, the passage of time and the handling of other cases between the hearing and the time a brief is prepared for the Appeals Council may hamper precise recollection of some issues and facts brought out at the hearing. Remember that the hearing is recorded on audiotape to create a record of that proceeding. The representative can request that the Appeals Council send a copy of the hearing tape to him or her. The tape request can be noted on the "Request for Review" form itself. In sending the hearing tape to the representative, the Appeals Council provides a notice giving a deadline, varying between thirty or forty days' from the date of that notice, for the submission of new evidence and the brief. Generally, requesting a copy of the hearing tape is advisable as a means to supplement handwritten notes taken at the hearing. On occasion, the Administrative Law Judge's decision recites testimony or makes findings on issues which were not addressed at the hearing. Review of the hearing tape enables the representative to accurately describe the misstated testimony or identify omissions by the Administrative Law Judge to fully develop the evidentiary record.

Take *A Trip to the Hard Drive* to view a complete sample Appeals Council brief.

A Trip to the Hard Drive, 17.1

Everyone's writing style is different. However, certain basics apply across the board. An effective brief must be persuasive. To be persuasive, a brief must be readily "digestible." It must be succinct, yet thorough; pithy, yet with sufficient explanation to lay a foundation on which the substantive merits of the appeal rest. An exemplar brief follows as a reference; it is not necessarily a document to copy verbatim.

Before the Appeals Council

Office of Hearings and Appeals
Social Security Administration
5107 Leesburg Pike
Falls Church, VA 22041

RE: John Doe Claimant
SSN: 000-00-0000

Appeal from: Decision of the Honorable Joe Justice
U.S. Administrative Law Judge
Anytown, USA

Ladies and Gentlemen:

MEMORANDUM BRIEF

The claimant, John Doe Claimant, by and through his representative of record, Chris Legal Professional, submits the following brief in support of his appeal.

The claimant filed applications for a period of disability, disability insurance benefits and supplemental security income benefits on February X, 1997, alleging a disability onset date of December XX, 1996. The applications and subsequent requests for reconsideration were denied. Administrative Law Judge (ALJ) Knott A. Clue held a hearing on the claim on July XX, 1998. He issued a decision denying benefits on October XX, 1998. The following error(s) were made by the ALJ in his decision:

1. The ALJ failed to properly evaluate the treating physician's opinion.

2. The ALJ failed to properly evaluate the claimant's credibility, and his finding is not supported by substantial evidence.
3. The ALJ's finding regarding the claimant's residual functional capacity is not supported by substantial evidence.
4. The ALJ failed to properly evaluate the claimant's ability to return to his past work at step 4.

ARGUMENT

1. The ALJ Failed to Properly Evaluate the Treating Physician's Opinion.

The claimant is required to present evidence that he is disabled. 20 C.F.R.§ 04.1512; 20 C.F.R. § 416.912. That evidence can include medical opinions about the nature and severity of his impairments, symptoms, and resulting limitations. 20 C.F.R. § 404.1527; 20 C.F.R. § 416.927.

The Administrative Law Judge must adopt a treating physician's medical opinion if it is well supported by medically accepted clinical and laboratory diagnostic techniques and not inconsistent with other substantial evidence. An opinion cannot be rejected just because it is not entitled to controlling weight. In most cases, it will still be entitled to the greatest weight and should still be adopted. 20 C.F.R. § 404.1527; 20 C.F.R. § 416.927; Social Security Ruling 96-2p.

Dr. Ima Quack has been the claimant's treating physician, having performed surgeries on the claimant's lumbar spine, knees, and shoulders. Dr. Quack provided her medical opinion on the claimant's residual functional capabilities on August X, 1998. (Exhibit 9F, pages 1–5)

[Here, summarize all of the treating physician's restrictions and limitations.]

The ALJ rejected Dr. Quack's opinion as inconsistent with her treatment records, which the ALJ characterized as giving positive reports on postsurgical recoveries on claimant's knee and shoulder. The ALJ based this characterization on two postsurgical follow-up visits on May X and XX, 1998, in which Dr. Quack noted the claimant's shoulder had "clean wounds" and "very little pain." The ALJ interpreted those brief notes to mean "very little pain" in the shoulder joint and not the incision site itself. Similarly, the ALJ interpreted Dr. Quack's report of the claimant's postsurgical condition of the knee as "OK" to mean restoration to normal functioning. The ALJ cannot rely on his subjective interpretation of the physician's treatment notes as a means to discredit that opinion.

The ALJ again substituted his own "medical expertise" and interpreted MRI reports that characterized the claimant's cervical spondylosis as "mild" to mean that Dr. Quack's evaluation of the severity and effects from claimant's pain was unsubstantiated. Rather than "playing doctor," the ALJ should have consulted a medical expert or recontacted Dr. Quack for an explanation. The ALJ's stated reasons for discrediting Dr. Quack's opinion are meritless, and those reasons do not constitute substantial evidence.

Moreover, the ALJ focused only on the evidence that he thought discredited Dr. Quack's opinion. The ALJ did not discuss the evidence that was consistent with, and supported, Dr. Quack's opinion.

[Here, give examples from the evidence that supported the treating physician's opinion.]

The ALJ's reasons for discrediting Dr. Quack's opinion are based on the ALJ's own subjective interpretation of the doctor's brief treatment notations and MRI findings, for which interpretation the ALJ was not medically qualified to make. The ALJ ignored evidence in the record that supported Dr. Quack's opinion and failed to obtain further development of the record, as required by the regulations and Social Security Ruling 96-2p, to clarify any discrepancies or ambiguities he found in the record. Accordingly, the ALJ's failure to properly consider the treating physician's opinion, consistent with the regulations and Social Security rulings, constitutes grounds to reverse and remand his decision.

2. The ALJ Failed to Properly Evaluate the Claimant's Credibility, and His Finding is Not Supported by Substantial Evidence.

The ALJ found the claimant's allegations of disabling pain were not substantiated by the medical evidence. The ALJ did not discuss in his decision any of the reasons why he did not find

(continued)

the claimant to be credible. The ALJ did not specify what medical evidence discredited the claimant's description of his pain and other symptoms or weigh that evidence against the rest of the evidence of record, including the claimant's testimony and the statements of the claimant's treating physicians.

The medical evidence consistently shows a basis for the claimant's pain and other symptoms. The ALJ did not weigh the medical evidence or articulate reasons to support his view that the claimant was not credible. Because the ALJ did not properly evaluate the claimant's credibility according to the standards set forth in the regulations and in Social Security Ruling 96-7p, reversal and remand of his decision is required.

3. The ALJ's Finding Regarding the Claimant's Residual Functional Capacity is Not Supported by Substantial Evidence.

The ALJ found that the claimant could perform light work activity, with a limited ability to reach in all directions with the right arm. In order to perform work at a light level of exertion, the claimant must be able to perform substantially all the activities required at that exertional level on a regular and continuing basis. Social Security Ruling 96-8p. Since the evidence shows that the claimant is incapable of sustaining even a sedentary level of exertion, the ALJ's RFC assessment is erroneous and not based on substantial evidence.

The ALJ's RFC assessment is not based on any objective medical evidence. Nothing in the medical record shows that the claimant has the capability to perform light work, which is defined as requiring "a good deal of walking and standing" for a total of at least six hours in an eight-hour workday. Light work activity can also entail jobs that involve sitting with some pushing and pulling of arm–hand or leg–foot controls, and that require the use of arms and hands to grasp, hold, and turn objects. Social Security Ruling 83-10. There is no evidence in the medical record to which the ALJ can point to support his conclusion that the claimant can perform light work. Dr. Quack, the claimant's treating physician, found that the claimant could only walk for up to 15 minutes at a time and stand for an hour at a time, with a maximum of two hours of standing and two hours of walking in an eight-hour workday, which is completely inconsistent with the ability to perform light work.

[Here discuss Dr. Quack's other restrictions that would prevent claimant from performing light work.]

The claimant's testimony likewise did not provide evidence to support the assessment of an ability to perform light work. The claimant testified that he could only walk for four to six blocks, stand for only an hour, and sit for only an hour, and that he is able to lift only ten pounds and with his left arm only. The claimant testified that, due to pain in his lumbar spine and knee, he lies down for an hour in both the morning and afternoon to relieve that pain. The claimant also testified that he continues to experience swelling in his left knee and elevates his left leg to relieve the swelling as needed once or twice a week.

The ALJ's RFC assessment failed to include side effects of dizziness, which the claimant testified that he experienced from his pain medication, Darvocet. The claimant testified that he took Darvocet every three to four hours for pain and that he could not drive when he took the Darvocet. The ALJ's conclusion that the claimant could perform light work is not supported by any of the evidence in the record. The ALJ did not explain the grounds on which he based his finding that the claimant could perform a level of light work, on a sustained basis, for five days a week, eight hours a day. The medical evidence, as well as the claimant's testimony, demonstrates that the claimant can perform work activities at a less than sedentary level of exertion. Additionally, the ALJ failed to include limitations associated with side effects of dizziness from the claimant's pain medication in his RFC assessment. For these reasons, the ALJ's RFC is legally flawed and not supported by the evidence, and his finding must be reversed and remanded for further consideration, consistent with the evidence of record.

4. The ALJ Failed to Properly Evaluate the Claimant's Ability to Return to His Past Work at Step 4.

At step 4 of the sequential evaluation process, the ALJ determined that the claimant could return to his "past work" and thus was not disabled. Review of the hearing tape shows that, while a vocational expert was present at the hearing, the ALJ made no inquiry at all of the vocational expert. The ALJ did not question either the vocational expert or the claimant regarding the claimant's performance of his past work.

Social Security Ruling 82-62 requires that the ALJ give "careful consideration" to the interaction between the impairment's limitations and the physical and mental demands of the past relevant work (PRW) to determine if the individual can still perform that work. The ALJ must make a "careful appraisal" and make specific findings of fact in three areas of concern: (1) the individual's RFC, (2) the physical and mental demands of the past job or occupation, and (3) that the individual's RFC would permit a return to his past job.

The ALJ failed to correlate his limited RFC with the duties of the claimant's past relevant work. The ALJ simply relied on his own interpretation of the claimant's past job duties rather than seeking expert testimony from the vocational expert. The ALJ's conclusion that the claimant could return to his past relevant work is not based on any evidence at all in the record, because the ALJ failed to develop that evidence as required by Ruling 82-62.

CONCLUSION

The ALJ failed to properly evaluate the opinion of the claimant's treating physician. The medical record establishes the existence of several medically determinable impairments that could reasonably be expected to produce the pain alleged by the claimant. The ALJ's finding that the claimant's allegations regarding his symptoms were not fully credible is legally flawed and not supported by substantial evidence. Further, the ALJ's finding that the claimant had a residual functional capacity to perform light work is completely unsupported by the evidence of record. Finally, the ALJ's finding that the claimant could return to his past work was not made in accordance with the three-step analysis set out in Social Security Ruling 82-62, and thus was legal error and was not supported by any evidence in the record.

Remand of this case is necessary to correct the legal errors committed by the ALJ and to permit a proper evaluation of the medical evidence in this case.

JOHN DOE CLAIMANT

by: Chris Legal Professional
The Busy Law Firm
Street Address
City, State, 12345
(123) 555-1234

BACK TO CHRIS

"That's pretty detailed."

"It has to be to be effective. A brief must list specific errors in order to be successful. You can't appeal simply because you don't like the result."

"That makes sense. So, what you're really saying is that the case isn't done when the hearing is finished?"

"That's right. It's even important following a hearing to make notes of the proceeding, and what you didn't like and what went well, so if an appeal is necessary, you have your thoughts readily available."

"Because I might forget?"

Steve smiled. "Not so much that as you might have more hearings. You want to be able to be as specific as you can in an appeal, so writing your thoughts down afterward can be a real benefit if you later have to do an appeal."

"OK. Anything else I need to know about the Appeals Council?"

"Just a couple of things."

FRONT OF YOUR MIND QUESTIONS AND CONSIDERATIONS, 17.2

The Administrative Law Judge can issue a recommended decision, which means the case goes to the Appeals Council with that decision. If a recommended decision is issued, the parties have twenty days from "the date that the recommended decision is mailed" to "file briefs or other written statements."[7] The Appeals Council will then review the case, adopting, rejecting, or modifying the Administrative Law Judge's recommended decision.[8]

Finally, it should be noted, that nothing prevents the claimant from filing a new application for Social Security disability benefits while the first application is on appeal. The catch is that if the appeal is denied, the denial acts as an administrative bar to the period adjudicated in the first case. The second case may only address time after the Administrative Law Judge's first decision. If no appeal is taken to an Administrative Law Judge, the earlier time may be addressed in a later decision if the judge reopens the earlier application. To do so, the judge must generally find "good cause," which is defined at Title 20 C.F.R. § 404.987 through § 404.989.

BACK TO CHRIS

"So the theme is, 'never give up' in a Social Security case?"

"That's pretty much it. If you believe your client is entitled to benefits nothing prevents you from refiling and appealing at the same time."

"Wow!"

WHAT IF . . . ? SAMPLE PROBLEMS

WHAT IF . . .

What if you lose the case before the Administrative Law Judge? What then?

1. Nothing. You lost, case closed. The end.
2. Ask the judge to re-open the case.
3. Within 60 days, file a "Request for Review" with the Appeals Council of the Social Security Administration. At the same time, consider filing a new claim for benefits with the Social Security Field Office.
4. File a complaint with the United States District Court seeking review of the Administrative Law Judge's decision.

Answer: ***Nothing prevents a request to reopen the decision; however, failure to timely file the "Request for Review" with the Appeals Council will preclude an appeal. The "Request for Review" must be filed within 60 days of receipt of notice of the Administrative Law Judge's decision. (20 C.F.R. § 404.966(c). Because the Appeals Council is the final step in the administrative adjudicatory process there is no right of immediate review by the federal district court. The correct answer is 3.***

What kind of paperwork should be provided to the Appeals Council?

1. The only thing the Appeals Council should have is the "Request for Review."
2. Beyond the "Request for Review," the representative should also provide the Appeals Council with a statement of the reason for the appeal. This usually takes the form of a brief, outlining the legal and factual issues and describing the errors committed by the Administrative Law Judge.
3. A complete copy of all exhibits should be mailed to the Appeals Council.
4. Retention of an expert, to testify or offer further written reports is critical.

Answer: ***While the "Request for Review" is the formal document initiating Appeals Council review, it should not be the only document submitted. A brief, consisting of an analysis of the facts and governing regulations should also be filed. It should point out to the Appeals Council legal or factual errors, omissions and pertinent case law. No further oral testimony is taken. Under limited circumstances "new" evidence may be received, provided it relates to the period on or before the Administrative Law Judge decision. 20 C.F.R. § 404.976(b). The correct answer is 2.***

---

[1]See Title 20 C.F.R. § 404.969 (2001), which provides that "anytime within sixty days after the date of a hearing decision or dismissal" the Appeals Council may decide on its own to review a case. Sometimes this is part of a random quality review of a case, or the Payment Center may have protested a decision entered by an Administrative Law Judge.

[2]Title 20 C.F.R. § 404.970 (2001).

[3]Title 20 C.F.R. § 404.971 (2001).

[4]Title 20 C.F.R. § 404.972 (2001).

[5]Title 20 C.F.R. § 404.975 (2001).

[6]Title 20 C.F.R. § 404.976(b) (2001).

[7]Title 20 C.F.R. § 404.977 (2001).

[8]See Title 20 C.F.R. § 404.979 (2001).

18

CHAPTER EIGHTEEN

Special Circumstances and Cases

HIGHLIGHTS

- ❑ Drug and alcohol addiction
- ❑ Reopening a prior case
- ❑ Overpayment

CHRIS

"Almost there Chris."

"I know. It's amazing how much information there is. And, I know that I still haven't uncovered all the wrinkles yet! That's what's exciting. There's a lot to know, and yet it will never be the same."

Steve agreed, sitting down at the small coffee table. Outside, the traffic blared, cars rushed, and people scurried to meet deadlines. A normal day in the city.

Steve and Chris ordered lunch and settled at a table. "Chris, before you meet with Mr. Carson, there are a couple of special circumstances I want to talk about, just so you're aware of them."

"OK. Not that we haven't talked about enough!" Chris chuckled in wonderment that there could still be more to discuss.

"I know. But, it's important that we at least touch the bases on these just in case you run into them."

"Shoot." Chris sipped a cold glass of ice tea expectantly.

"Three things," Steve held up three fingers. "First, drug and alcohol addiction. Second, reopening a prior file, and finally," Steve lowered the third finger, "overpayments."

"I heard a little about drug and alcohol. It used to be that you could actually be found disabled because of drug and alcohol use."

"That's right. But no more," Steve replied. "Here, let me show you while we're waiting for lunch."

FRONT OF YOUR MIND QUESTIONS AND CONSIDERATIONS, 18.1

DRUG AND ALCOHOL ADDICTION

On March 29, 1996, Congress passed Public Law 104-121, The Contract with America Advancement Act of 1996. The act revised §§ 223(d)(2) and 1614(a)(3) of the Social Security Act. Specifically, § 105 of the *Contract with America Advancement Act of 1996* provided that beginning March 29, 1996, individuals for whom drug addiction or alcoholism is a contributing factor, material to the determination that they are disabled, are no longer eligible for, or entitled to, disability benefits. The new legislation curtailed eligibility for disability benefits because of drug and/or alcohol addiction. Simply put, if an individual is found to be disabled, and if the individual drinks alcohol or drug user, the issue is whether the disability would remain if the individual were to cease the drug or alcohol use. With drug or alcohol use (DA&A), the disability inquiry proceeds as follows (see Figure 18–1):

- ❑ *Is the individual disabled?*
- ❑ If "Yes," the next question is, *Is there medical evidence of DA&A?*
- ❑ If "No," then the person is "disabled" and no further inquiry need be made.
- ❑ If the answer to the second question is "Yes," the next question is, *Would the person be disabled if drug or alcohol use stopped?*
- ❑ If "Yes," then drug or alcohol use is *not material* and the person is disabled.
- ❑ If "No," then drug or alcohol use is *material* and the person is determined, as a matter of law, to be not disabled.

For the Administrative Law Judge, the inquiry is twofold. First, the judge must determine whether the claimant is disabled—that is, she or he cannot, because of a medically determinable impairment, return to past work or perform other, less demanding work within the national or regional economies. Second, the judge must determine whether the use of alcohol or drugs (not otherwise prescribed or abused) contributes to the finding of disability.

For the judge, the decision ultimately boils down to a pragmatic inquiry: Will the claimant remain disabled even if drug or alcohol use is stopped? If the answer is affirmative, drug or alcohol use is not material. If the answer is negative, drug or alcohol use is material and benefits will be denied.

The ultimate question is, how does the judge decide? The danger is self-evident. The judge must rely on evidence that if drug or alcohol use ceased the claimant's disabling condition would remain. This is, intrinsically, a subject of medical expertise. If (as is often the case) a mental impairment accompanies the drug or alcohol use, a psychologist must offer testimony and present evidence that distinguishes the mental impairment from the effects of alcohol or drug use.

For the medical expert, the question is not as simple as inquiring whether the alcohol or drug use is material. Instead, the medical expert must carefully examine the entire medical record then before the judge and then make a professional judgement. The medical expert must consider: Would the claimant's limitations be as severe as they are (or even exist) if the claimant were to stop drug or alcohol use? If the judge makes this inquiry without the benefit of medical expertise, an argument on appeal is likely if benefits are denied. The

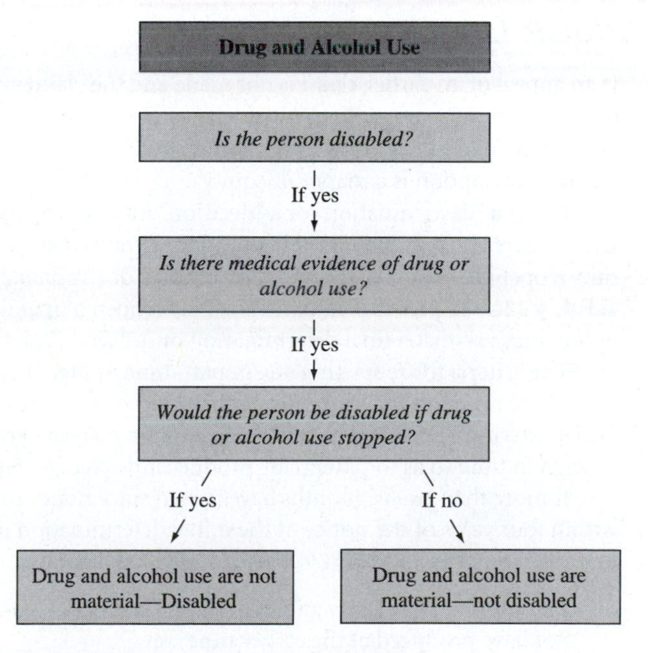

Figure 18–1 **Analysis of Drug or Alcohol Use and Disability**

basis of such an appeal is that the judge substituted his or her judgment for the evidence of record. In simple terms, the judge may not play doctor and make a decision that is, effectively, a medical opinion without evidence to support such a decision in the record. Thus, with a hearing for a client who has a history of drug or alcohol use, carefully consider making a formal request for a medical expert to be present, if one is not already scheduled to appear. The regulations make the process plain:

> **The key factor we will examine in determining whether drug addiction or alcoholism is a contributing factor material to the determination of disability is whether we would still find you disabled if you stopped using drugs or alcohol.[1]**

The process is one of parsing the alcohol or drug related limitations from those that are not so tainted:

> **In making this determination, we will evaluate which of your current physical and mental limitations . . . would remain if you stopped using drugs or alcohol and then determine whether any or all of your remaining limitations would be disabling.[2]**

BACK TO CHRIS

"Let me see if I understand. First, the judge makes a determination that the claimant is disabled, then has to decide whether the disability would remain if drug or alcohol use were stopped?"

"That's essentially right." Steve took a bite of his hamburger, pausing.

"But . . . ?" Chris prompted.

"The focus is on limitations. The question is more properly phrased, *Would the limitations remain at the same level of severity, or even exist, if drug use or drinking ceased?*"

"OK, that makes sense. So, if drinking or drug use stops, and the limitations become less severe, or even go away, the question is whether the claimant would be disabled, given his or her remaining limitations?"

"You've got it! Now let's talk about reopening."

FRONT OF YOUR MIND QUESTIONS AND CONSIDERATIONS, 18.2

REOPENING A PRIOR CASE

If an appeal of an earlier claim is not made and the claimant later files a successive application for disability benefits, it may be possible to revisit the earlier-denied determination. This option has limited application and is intended to remedy a prior administrative decision that may not have fully addressed the issues. Essentially, the option is a matter of equity.

Either a "determination" or a "decision" may be reopened. A determination is a conclusion by the state DDS; whereas a decision is that of an Administrative Law Judge or the Appeals Council. The regulation permits reopening on application of the claimant, or *sua sponte* (on the Administration's own motion). Title 20 C.F.R. § 404.987 provides in part, "We may reopen a final determination or decision on our own initiative, or you may ask that a final determination or decision . . . be reopened."

The criteria for reopening are, in part, time limited. Reopening may occur within twelve months of the date of the notice of the initial determination for any reason. Given the short period between the date of the initial determination and the mandated request, no reason need be stated—that is, the determination is close enough in time so as to potentially produce little change in the claimant's original medical condition.

If more than twelve months have passed since notice of the initial determination, reopening may occur within four years of the notice of the initial determination if there is good cause to do so. Good cause is defined at Title 20 C.F.R. § 404.989 to include the following:

- The submission of new and material evidence (evidence that the claimant was not aware of and could not have produced at the earlier time); or
- The existence of a clerical error in the computation or recomputation of benefits; or
- The fact that evidence used in making the first decision clearly shows that an error was made.

A change in the law, or legal interpretation, does not constitute good cause for retroactive reopening.

An earlier-decided claim also may be reopened at any time for a variety of other reasons, including the following:

- If the determination or decision was obtained by fraud or similar fault;
- If another person files a claim on the same earnings record and allowance of the claim will adversely affect the earlier decision;
- If a person, once thought dead, is found alive; or
- If the Railroad Retirement Board has awarded duplicate benefits on the same earnings record.[3]

This procedure is potentially beneficial to a claimant who has a prior history of filings and who alleges an onset date beyond the one-year period for which monetary benefits under Title II can be awarded. If the earlier application is reopened, the earlier date then becomes the date of determination, allowing, in effect, for benefits to be retroactive to the earlier time, even though it is beyond twelve months from the date of the most recent application. Figure 18–2 is illustrative.

BACK TO CHRIS

"You mean," exclaimed Chris, almost choking on the salad, "even if the claimant never follows through with an appearance to an Administrative Law Judge, the earlier application can be reopened and, if granted, benefits can be paid as if the earlier application were the one at issue?"

"Bingo," said Steve.

"Yikes! That could be a lot of money!"

"I knew of one case where the judge determined that the claimant receive a lump sum well into five figures because of that."

"And, a 25 percent fee?"

"Yes. Remember, however, it can only exceed $5,300 if you use the fee petition process."

"Who wouldn't?"

"Good point Chris. If the option is there for your client, you should at least try it.

"Great. Should we get back?"

"One last thing. Overpayments. . . . "

"What does that mean?"

"Let me tell you."

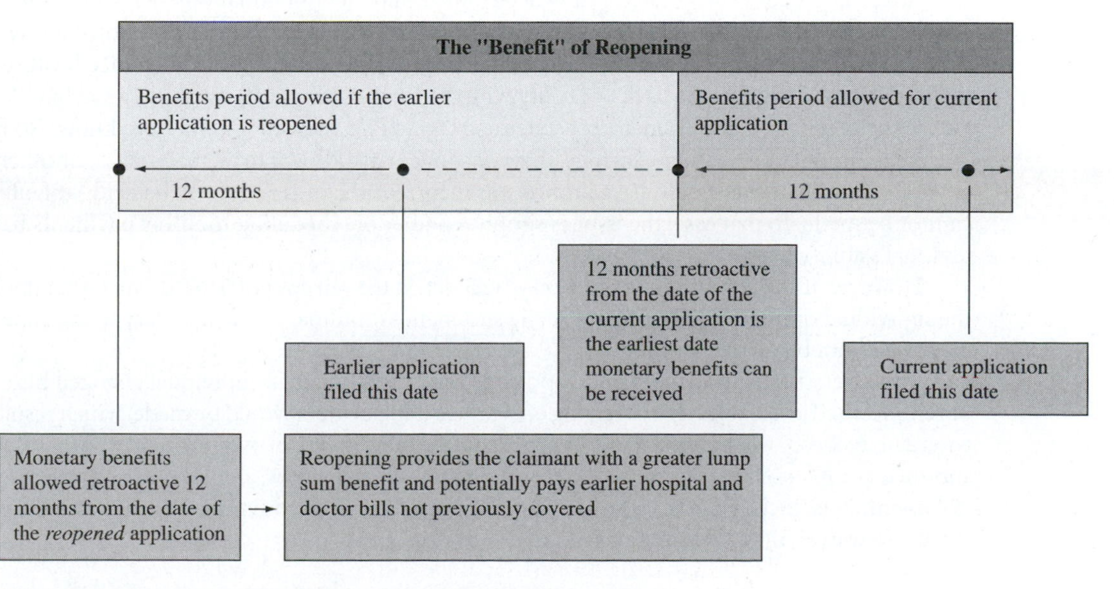

Figure 18–2 **Benefits of Reopening an Earlier-Denied Application**

FRONT OF YOUR MIND QUESTIONS AND CONSIDERATIONS, 18.3

OVERPAYMENTS

Consider the following situations.

- ❑ The Social Security Administration makes a mistake and pays a client too much money;
- ❑ A client elects to keep receiving benefits after being notified that Social Security believes he or she has medically improved and that the benefits he or she was receiving will be terminated;
- ❑ A client does not fully disclose all work during the claimed period of disability and the Social Security Administration later discovers this.

These are the difficult issues that sometimes give rise to a circumstance in which a client is paid too much money—and the government wants it back—an overpayment! When overpayment is determined, the Social Security Administration takes the following steps:

> **Whenever an initial determination is made that more than the correct amount of payment has been made, and we seek adjustment or recovery of the overpayment, the individual from whom we are seeking adjustment or recovery is immediately notified. The notice includes:**
> (a) **The overpayment amount and how and when it occurred;**
> (b) **A request for full, immediate refund . . .**
> . . .
> (e) **An explanation of the right to request waiver of adjustment or recovery and the automatic scheduling of a file review and pre-recoupment hearing (commonly referred to as a personal conference). . . .**[4]

Frequently, when an overpayment exists, the individual has no means of repaying the money. A request for a waiver of the overpaid amount is generally the first step taken. This requires completion of a Request for Waiver form Overpayment Recovery or Change in Repayment Rate (SSA-632-BK), as shown in Figure 18–3.

The Request for a Waiver requires complete disclosure of family and household finances, including expenses of all types, assets held, and income earned. A waiver is not automatic. Once a Request for Waiver is filed, all collection actions cease, and a personal conference is scheduled. At the conference "the individual and the individual's representative have the right to review the claims file and applicable law and regulations with the decision maker or another SSA representative who is prepared to answer questions."[5] The personal conference also provides an opportunity for witnesses to testify.[6] Documents may be submitted and legal positions articulated. The decision maker is not an Administrative Law Judge, but an employee of the Social Security Administration who was "not previously involved in the issue under review."[7]

A waiver can only be granted if it is determined that the individual was "without fault" in causing the overpayment. In making this determination, the administration is required to "consider all pertinent circumstance, including the individual's age and intelligence, and any physical, mental, educational, or linguistic limitations (including any lack of facility with the English language), the individual has."[8]

If the claimant made an incorrect statement "which he knew or should have known to be incorrect,"[9] "failed to furnish information which he knew or should have known to be material,"[10] or otherwise accepted payment that he or she should have known was incorrect, the individual will be held "at fault" and a waiver cannot be made. In that case, the issue is simply a matter of scheduling monthly payments based on the individual's ability to pay.

However, if the adjustment or recovery "will defeat the purpose of Title II" such that it will impoverish the individual or deprive her or him of daily sustenance ("ordinary and necessary living expenses"), the recovery will not be carried forward.[11]

If recovery is "against equity and good conscience," such that an individual changed his or her position or relinquished a valuable right in relying on a notice that payment would be made, which resulted in an overpayment, recovery will not be sought.[12] When seeking to overturn an overpayment, the representative should submit a complete statement of the claimant's income and expenses, all bills and any other pertinent financial documents, including tax records, if filed. The challenge is to convince the judge that the claimant is entitled to a waiver; or at the least, a reduced monthly payment.

SOCIAL SECURITY ADMINISTRATION

Form Approved
OMB No. 0960-0037

Request For Waiver Of Overpayment Recovery Or Change In Repayment Rate

We will use your answers on this form to decide if we can waive collection of the overpayment or change the amount you must pay us back each month. If we can't waive collection, we may use this form to decide how you should repay the money.

Please answer the questions on this form as completely as you can. We will help you fill out the form if you want. If you are filling out this form for someone else, answer the questions as they apply to that person.

FOR SSA USE ONLY	
ROAR Input	☐ Yes ☐ No
Input Date	
Waiver	☐ Approval ☐ Denial
SSI	☐ Yes ☐ No
AMT OF OP $	
PERIOD (DATES) OF OP	

1. A. Name of person on whose record the overpayment occurred:

____

B. Social Security Number

☐☐☐ — ☐☐ — ☐☐☐☐

C. Name of overpaid person(s) making this request and his/her Social Security Number(s):

____________________________ ☐☐☐ — ☐☐ — ☐☐☐☐

____________________________ ☐☐☐ — ☐☐ — ☐☐☐☐

____________________________ ☐☐☐ — ☐☐ — ☐☐☐☐

____________________________ ☐☐☐ — ☐☐ — ☐☐☐☐

2. Check any of the following that apply. (Also, Fill in the dollar amount in B, C, or D.)

A. ☐ The overpayment was not my fault and I cannot afford to pay the money back and/or it is unfair for some other reasons.

B. ☐ I cannot afford to use all of my monthly benefit to pay back the overpayment. However I can afford to have $________ withheld each month.

C. ☐ I am no longer receiving Supplement Security Income (SSI) payments. I want to pay back $________ each month instead of paying all of the money at once.

D. ☐ I am receiving SSI payments. I want to pay back $________ each month instead of paying 10% of my total income.

FORM **SSA-632-BK** (4-91) EF (8-99) Page 1

Figure 18–3 **Request for Waiver of Overpayment**

(continued)

Figure 18–3 **Request for Waiver of Overpayment *(continued)***

SECTION I-INFORMATION ABOUT RECEIVING THE OVERPAYMENT

3. A. Did you, as representative payee, receive the overpaid benefits to use for the beneficiary?

☐ Yes ☐ No (Skip to Question 4)

B. Name and address of the beneficiary

C. How were the overpaid benefits used?

4. If we are asking you to repay someone else's overpayment:

A. Was the overpaid person living with you when he/she was overpaid? ☐ Yes ☐ No

B. Did you receive any of the overpaid money? ☐ Yes ☐ No

C. Explain what you know about the overpayment AND why it was not your fault.

5. Why did you think you were due the overpaid money and why do you think you were not at fault in causing the overpayment or accepting the money?

6. A. Did you tell us about the change or event that made you overpaid? ☐ Yes ☐ No

If no, why didn't you tell us?

B. If yes, how, when and where did you tell us? If you told us by phone or in person, who did you talk with and what was said?

C. If you did not hear from us after your report, and/or your benefits did not change, did you contact us again? ☐ Yes ☐ No

7. A. Have we ever overpaid you before? ☐ Yes ☐ No

If yes, on what Social Security number? ☐☐☐—☐☐—☐☐☐☐

B. Why were you overpaid before? If the reason is similar to why you are overpaid now, explain what you did to try to prevent the present overpayment.

FORM **SSA-632-BK** (4-91) EF (8-99) Page 2

FOR SSA USE ONLY

NAME:

SSN:

SECTION II-YOUR FINANCIAL STATEMENT

You need to complete this section if you are asking us either to waive the collection of the overpayment or to change the rate at which we asked you to repay it. Please answer all questions as fully and as carefully as possible. We may ask to see some documents to support your statements, so you should have them with you when you visit our office.

EXAMPLES ARE:

- Current Rent or Mortgage Books
- Savings Passbooks
- Pay Stubs
- Your most recent Tax Return
- 2 or 3 recent utility, medical, charge card, and insurance bills
- Cancelled checks
- Similar documents for your spouse or dependent family members

Please write only whole dollar amounts-Round any cents to the nearest dollar. If you need more space for answers, use the "Remarks" section at the bottom of page 7.

9. A. Do you now have any of the overpaid checks or money in your possession (or in a savings or other type of account)?

☐ Yes Amount: $ ________ Return this amount to SSA
☐ No

B. Did you have any of the overpaid checks or money in your possession (or in a savings or other type of account) at the time you received the overpayment notice?

☐ Yes Amount: $ Answer Question 10.
☐ No

10. Explain why you believe you should not have to return this amount.

____

ANSWER 11 AND 12 ONLY IF THE OVERPAYMENT IS SUPPLEMENTAL SECURITY INCOME PAYMENTS (SSI). IF NOT, SKIP TO 13.

11. A. Did you lend or give away any property or cash after notification of the overpayment?

☐ Yes (Answer Part B)
☐ No (Go to question 12.)

B. Who received it, relationship (if any), description and value:

____

12. A. Did you receive or sell any property or receive any cash (other than earnings) after notification of this overpayment?

☐ Yes (Answer Part B)
☐ No (Go to Question 13.)

B. Describe property and sale price or amount of cash received:

____

13. A. Are you now receiving cash public assistance such as Supplemental Security Income (SSI) payments?

☐ Yes (Answer B and C and See note below)
☐ No

B. Name or kind of public assistance ______________________________

C. Claim Number ______________

IMPORTANT: If you answered "YES" to question 13, DO NOT answer any more questions on this form. Go to page 8, sign and date the form, and give your address and phone number(s). Bring or mail any papers that show you receive public assistance to your local Social Security office as soon as possible.

FORM **SSA-632-BK** (4-91) EF (8-99) Page 3

(continued)

Figure 18–3 **Request for Waiver of Overpayment *(continued)***

Members Of Household

14. List any person (child, parent, friend, etc.) who depends on you for support AND who lives with you.

NAME	AGE	RELATIONSHIP (If none, explain why the person is dependent on you)

Assets-Things You Have And Own

15. A. How much money do you and any person(s) listed in question 14 above have as cash on hand, in a checking account, or otherwise readily available? **$**

B. Does your name, or that of any other member of your household appear, either alone or with any other person, on any of the following?

TYPE OF ASSET	OWNER	BALANCE OR VALUE	PER MONTH	SHOW THE INCOME (Interest, dividends) EARNED EACH MONTH. (If none explain in spaces below) If paid quarterly, divide by 3.
SAVINGS (Bank, Savings and Loan, Credit Union)		$	$	
		$	$	
CERTIFICATES OF DEPOSIT (CD)		$	$	
INDIVIDUAL RETIREMENT ACCOUNT (IRA)		$	$	
MONEY OR MUTUAL FUNDS		$	$	
BONDS, STOCKS		$	$	
TRUST FUND		$	$	
CHECKING ACCOUNT		$	$	
OTHER (EXPLAIN)		$	$	
	TOTALS →	$	$	Enter the "Per Month" total on line (k) of question 19.

16. A. If you or a member of your household own a car, (other than the family vehicle), van, truck, camper, motorcycle, or any other vehicle or a boat, list below.

OWNER	YEAR, MAKE/MODEL	PRESENT VALUE	LOAN BALANCE (if any)	MAIN PURPOSE FOR USE
		$	$	
		$	$	
		$	$	

B. If you or a member of your household own any real estate (buildings or land), OTHER than where you live, or own or have an interest in, any business, property, or valuables, describe below.

OWNER	DESCRIPTION	MARKET VALUE	LOAN BALANCE (if any)	USAGE-INCOME (rent etc.)
		$	$	
		$	$	
		$	$	
		$	$	

FORM SSA-632-BK (4-91) EF (8-99) Page 4

Monthly Household Income

If paid weekly, multiply by 4.33 (4 1/3) to figure monthly pay. If paid every 2 weeks, multiply by 2.166 (2 1/6) If self-employed, enter 1/12 of net earnings. Enter monthly TAKE HOME amounts on line A of question 19 also.

17. A. Are you employed? ☐ YES (Provide information below) ☐ NO (Skip to B)

Employer name, address, and phone: (Write "self" if self-employed) — Monthly pay before deduction (Gross) $ — Monthly TAKE-HOME pay (NET) $

B. Is your spouse employed? ☐ YES (Provide information below) ☐ NO (Skip to C)

Employer(s) name, address, and phone: (Write "self" if self-employed) — Monthly pay before deduction (Gross) $ — Monthly TAKE-HOME pay (NET) $

C. Is any other person listed in Question 14 employed? ☐ YES ☐ NO (Go to Question 18) Name(s)

Employer(s) name, address, and phone: (Write "self" if self-employed) — Monthly pay before deduction (Gross) $ — Monthly TAKE-HOME pay (NET) $

18. A. Do you, your spouse or any dependent member of your household receive support or contributions from any person or organization? ☐ YES (Answer B) ☐ NO (Go to question 19)

B. How much money is received each month? $ (Show this amount on line (J) of question 19) — SOURCE

BE SURE TO SHOW **MONTHLY** AMOUNTS BELOW-If received weekly or every 2 weeks, read the instruction at the top of this page.

19.

INCOME FROM #17 AND #18 ABOVE AND OTHER INCOME TO YOUR		YOURS	✓	SPOUSE'S	✓	OTHER HOUSEHOLD MEMBERS	✓	SSA USE ONLY
A. TAKE HOME Pay (Net) (From #17 A, B, C, above)		$		$		$		
B. Social Security Benefits								
C. Supplemental Security Income (SSI)								
D. Pension(s) (VA, Military, Civil Service, Railroad, etc.)	TYPE							
	TYPE							
E. Public Assistance (Other than SSI)	TYPE							
F. Food Stamps (Show full face value of stamps received)								
G. Income from real estate (rent, etc.) (From question 16B)								
H. Room and/or Board Payments (Explain in remarks below)								
I. Child Support/Alimony								
J. Other Support (From #18 (B) above)								
K. Income From Assets (From question 15)								
L. Other (From any source, explain below)								
REMARKS	TOTALS	$		$		$		

GRAND TOTAL $

FORM **SSA-632-BK** (4-91) EF (8-99) Page 5

(continued)

MONTHLY HOUSEHOLD EXPENSES

If the expense is paid weekly or every 2 weeks, read the instruction at top of Page 5. Do NOT list an expense that is withheld from income (Such as Medical Insurance). Only take home pay is used to figure income.

Show "CC" as the expense amount if the expense (such as clothing) is part of CREDIT CARD EXPENSE SHOWN ON LINE (F).

20.	$ PER MONTH	SSA USE ONLY
A. Rent or Mortgage (If mortgage payment includes property or other local taxes, insurance, etc. DO NOT list again below.		
B. Food (Groceries (include the value of food stamps) and food at restaurants, work, etc.)		
C. Utilities (Gas, electric, telephone)		
D. Other Heating/Cooking Fuel (Oil, propane, coal, wood, etc.)		
E. Clothing		
F. Credit Card Payments (show minimum monthly payment allowed)		
G. Property Tax (State and local)		
H. Other taxes or fees related to your home (trash collection, water-sewer fees)		
I. Insurance (Life, health, fire, homeowner, renter, car, and any other casualty or liability policies)		
J. Medical-Dental (After amount, if any, paid by insurance)		
K. Car operation and maintenance (Show any car loan payment in (N) below)		
L. Other transportation		
M. Church-charity cash donations		
N. Loan, credit, lay-away payments (If payment amount is optional, show minimum)		
O. Support to someone NOT in household (Show name, age, relationship (if any) and address)		
P. Any expense not shown above (Specify)		
EXPENSE REMARKS Also explain any unusual or very large expenses, such as medical, college, etc.) — TOTAL	$	

FORM **SSA-632-BK** (4-91) EF (8-99) Page 6

INCOME AND EXPENSES COMPARISON

21. A. Monthly income (Write the amount here from the "Grand Total" of #19. → $

B. Monthly Expenses Write the amount here from the "Total" of #20. → $

C. Adjusted Household Expenses → + $25

D. Adjusted Monthly Expenses (Add (B) and (C)) → $

22. If your expenses (D) are more than your income (A), explain how you are paying your bills.

FOR SSA USE ONLY	
☐ INC. **EXCEEDS** ADJ EXPENSE	$ +
☐ INC LESS THAN ADJ EXPENSE	$ -

FINANCIAL EXPECTATION AND FUNDS AVAILABILITY

23. A. Do you, your spouse or any dependent member of your household expect your or their financial situation to change (for the better or worse) in the next 6 months? (For example: a tax refund, pay raise or full repayment

☐ YES (Explain on line below)
☐ NO

B. If there is an amount of cash on hand or in checking accounts shown in item 15A, is it being held for a special purpose?

No amount on hand
NO (Money available for any use)
YES (Explain on line below)

C. Is there any reason you CANNOT convert to cash the "Balance or Value" of any financial asset shown in item 15B.

☐ YES (Explain on line below)
☐ NO

D. Is there any reason you CANNOT SELL or otherwise convert to cash any of the assets shown in items 16A and B?

☐ YES (Explain on line below)
☐ NO

REMARKS SPACE-- If you are continuing an answer to a question, please write the number (and letter, if any) of the question first.

(MORE SPACE ON NEXT PAGE)

(continued)

Figure 18–3 **Request for Waiver of Overpayment *(continued)***

(REMARKS SPACE (Continued)

PENALTY CLAUSE, CERTIFICATION AND PRIVACY ACT STATEMENT

I know that anyone who makes or causes to be made a false statement of representation of material fact in an application or for use in determining a right to payment under the Social Security Act commits a crime punishable under Federal law and/or State law. I affirm that all information I have given in this document is true.

SIGNATURE OF OVERPAID PERSON OR REPRESENTATIVE PAYEE

SIGNATURE (First name, middle initial, last name) (Write ink) **SIGN HERE** ▶	DATE (Month, Day, Year) HOME TELEPHONE NUMBER (Include area code) WORK TELEPHONE NUMBER IF WE MAY CALL YOU AT WORK (Include area code)
MAILING ADDRESS (Number and street, Apt. No., P.O. Box, or Rural Route)	
CITY AND STATE ZIP CODE	ENTER NAME OF COUNTY (IF ANY) IN WHICH YOU NOW LIVE

Witnesses are required ONLY if this statement has been signed by mark (X) above. If signed by mark (X), two witnesses to the signing who know the individual must sign below, giving their full addresses.

SIGNATURE OF WITNESS	SIGNATURE OF WITNESS
ADDRESS (Number and street, City, State, and zip Code)	ADDRESS (Number and street, City, State, and zip Code)

About the Privacy Act

The Social Security Act (Sections 204, 1631(b), and 1870) and the Federal Coal Mine Health and Safety Act of 1969 allow us to collect the facts on this form. This form is voluntary. However, if you do not give us the facts we ask for, we may not be able to approve your waiver request. If we cannot collect the overpayment, we may ask the Justice Department to collect it.

Sometimes the law requires us to give out the facts on this form without your consent. We must give these facts to another person or government agency if Federal law requires that we do so or to do the research and audits needed to monitor and improve the programs we manage.

We may also give these facts to the Justice Department to investigate and prosecute violations of the Social Security Act or we may use the facts in computer matching programs. Matching programs compare our records with those of other Federal, State, or local government agencies. All the Agencies may use matching programs to find or prove that a person qualifies for benefits paid for or managed by the Federal government. Another use is to identify and collect overpayments or to collect overdue loans under these benefits programs.

Explanations about these and other reasons why information you provide us may be used or given out are available in Social Security offices. If you want to learn more about this, contact any Social Security office.

The **Paperwork Reduction Act of 1995** requires us to notify you that this information collection is in accordance with the clearance requirements of section 3507 of the Paperwork Reduction Act of 1995. We may not conduct or sponsor, and you are not required to respond to, a collection of information unless it displays a valid OMB control number. We estimate that it will take you about 25 minutes to complete this form. This includes the time it will take to read the instructions, gather the necessary facts and fill out the form.

FORM **SSA-632-BK** (4-91) EF (8-99)   Page 8

BACK TO CHRIS

"It sounds like the regulations try to be fair at least."

"They do offer a lot of latitude to look at all the circumstances."

"Is this something I need to think about?"

"Well, just keep it in the back of your mind, in case a former client contacts you and brings it up. SSA is a vast organization; it does a lot of things well, but mistakes happen. And unfortunately, sometimes our clients are not as understanding of the law as we would like. Mistakes happen on both sides."

"Just keep it in the back of my mind?"

"Just be aware of the possibility."

"Right."

WHAT IF . . . ? SAMPLE PROBLEMS

WHAT IF . . .

What if the claimant informs the representative that he has stopped drinking, even though the record indicates a long history of drug or alcohol use and does not otherwise indicate remission (cessation)?

1. First look for medical records which reflect the abstinence. If not, obtain a statement from the claimant's treating physician which documents the claimant's allegation that he is no longer drinking or using. The doctor should explain what medical findings support the conclusion.
2. Ask for a psychological consultative examination, with a complete battery of tests, including the Minnesota Multiphasic Personality Inventory (MMPI-2).
3. Have the claimant testify about prior drinking/use and cessation.
4. All of the above.

Answer: When faced with a drug and alcohol scenario a concerted effort should be made to persuade the judge that the behavior no longer continues. Alternately, where the behavior continues the issue is whether it is material and/or contributes to a finding of disability. In either case, a three-pronged approach is appropriate. Information from the treating physician, coupled with objective testing and the claimant's testimony will effectively present the issues. All three approaches must be taken to persuade the judge. The correct answer is 4.

If the Social Security Administration mistakenly deposits checks into your client's account and she believes them to be correctly credited to her and spends the money, and cannot now repay it, what is the correct action if the Social Security Administration now charges your client with an overpayment and seeks recovery?

1. Do nothing. The Social Security Administration is a behemoth agency and will eventually lose track of your client and its money;
2. Request a Hearing before an Administrative Law Judge within 60 days following SSA's determination. Assuming that an administrative application for waiver has been requested and denied, the challenge is to prove 1) SSA's mistake; 2) the claimant's reasonable and good faith reliance on SSA's representations; and 3) the claimant's financial inability to make repayment. This will require careful analysis of the communications between SSA and the claimant; a compilation of all bank records; and a listing of expenses and income for the claimant and his or her family.
3. Focus your attack on the Social Security Administration. If they are shown to be in error the claimant need not repay the money.
4. None of the above.

Answer: It is not sufficient to simply show SSA's error. Even in the face of an error the question is whether the claimant knew or should have known that the amounts deposited were incorrect. Once the claimant's "good faith" has been established, the next question is whether requiring repayment would defeat the purposes of Title II of the Social Security Act, to-wit whether repayment would impoverish the claimant. To prove these various issues in the claimant's favor requires a compilation of various records, including all communications between the claimant and SSA, as well as bank records and proof of income and expenses. The correct answer is 2.

[1]Title 20 C.F.R. § 404.1535(b) (2001).

[2]Ibid. Note, also, that as of this publication, SSA has taken the position that if use of drugs and/or alcohol cannot be separated from other limitations, DA&A is to be deteremined, as a matter of law, as not material.

[3]See Title 20 C.F.R. § 404.989(c) (2001).

[4]Title 20 C.F.R. § 404.502a (2001).

[5]Title 20 C.F.R. § 404.506(d) (2001).

[6]Title 20 C.F.R. § 404.506 (e).

[7]Title 20 C.F.R. § 404.506(f)(1).

[8]Title 20 C.F.R. § 404.507 (2001).

[9]Ibid.

[10]Ibid.

[11]Title 20 C.F.R. § 404.508 (2001).

[12]Title 20 C.F.R. § 404.509 (2001).

19

CHAPTER NINETEEN

The Administrative Law Judge Decision

HIGHLIGHTS

- ❑ The form of the Administrative Law Judge decision
- ❑ Comments on Hearing Office structure

CHRIS

"Hey Chris!"

Chris turned, saw Steve walking out of the elevator, and grinned, "I did it!"

"You had your hearing?"

"Yes."

"Well? How did it go?"

"It went pretty well. The judge asked me what my "legal theory" for recovery was, and not only was I able to answer in terms of the five-step sequential analysis but I was also able to give her exhibit numbers and cite to the regs!"

"That's great. What did Mr. Carson think?"

"He was nervous, naturally, but he and I met several times before the hearing. We went over new medical information and updated the record."

"So, you went to the Office of Hearings and Appeals and got a copy of the administrative record, I mean, the file?"

"I did that first, then reviewed it, then met with Mr. Carson to review medical records, and then scheduled a second meeting to go through a mock examination."

"Sounds like you did it all the right way."

"After learning from the best, how could I not?"

"Well, I don't know about that, but do you have any other questions?"

"The judge took the case under advisement. She said we could expect a decision within the month."

"That isn't too bad. It's normal for a judge not to tell you what her decision is at the hearing; though some judges will, regardless of whether it's favorable."

The pair stopped at the entrance to Steve's office. "I do have one question."

"Shoot," Steve prompted, glad of the delay. His desk was a disaster.

"I don't think we ever looked at a final decision from an Administrative Law Judge."

Steve's eyes went wide as he slapped his forehead. "I can hardly believe it. You definitely need to see several different forms. Of course, you're really only interested in analyzing a decision if it's unfavorable."

"That makes sense. I guess I don't need to appeal a favorable decision, do I?"

"Shouldn't," Steve pulled out a file drawer. "Here, I have several sample decisions, so you can at least see the format."

"Cool."

Steve passed Chris a sample decision [see Figure 19–1].

"Look at the form of the decision. Every formal decision is accompanied by a notice that informs the claimant of his or her right to an appeal. It specifically references an appeal to the Appeals Council using Form HA-520, the Request for Review form we discussed earlier."

"What about the decision itself?"

"Decisions vary in form, but they generally include common points."

"It looks like this decision doesn't really track the five-step sequential analysis, but instead it has several different general topics. Is that the way most of them are?"

"Unfortunately, yes. You have to understand, given the sheer volume of cases handled by the Office of Hearings and Appeals, it is generally rare for a judge to write his or her own decision in every case. Instead, attorney advisors and paralegal specialists do most of the decision writing."

"If I had a question about my case, either before the hearing or afterward, could I call the attorney advisor or paralegal specialist?"

"You could. The key is to know who the right person to contact is."

"You mean who works for the judge?"

"Yes and no. OHA is not like a court system. The judges do not run the shop. Instead, the administrative staff reports directly to the hearing office director (HOD) who, in turn, reports to the Hearing Office Chief Administrative Law Judge (HOCALJ). Each of the judges in the hearing office are assigned to a working group, usually denoted as Group A, Group B, and so forth."

"Sort of like sharing an administrative assistant, as we do here?"

"Sort of. Each hearing office has its own procedures, but generally administrative staff is assigned to a group and collectively supports the hearings process."

Chris wondered at the efficiency of such a process. "Same for the attorneys and paralegals?"

"In some offices they are assigned and work directly with a specific judge."

"That makes more sense to me—the lawyers and representatives know who to talk to, and the paralegal or attorney gets to know the way a particular judge does things."

"You'd think so, but this is the government—efficiency isn't necessarily the goal. Some judges work with several different paralegals and attorneys on a rotational basis, or even randomly, as cases are pulled out of a common drawer for writing."

"Sounds awfully confusing. Doesn't a judge have an administrative assistant?"

"It is confusing. No, the judges don't have administrative assistants, not even shared ones. But you can find out who to contact by simply asking the judge. You might get an answer."

"OK. What are the titles of the various administrative types?"

"There are *case technicians, senior case technicians, paralegal specialists,* and *attorneys*. The head of a group is the *group supervisor*."

"I heard something about *senior attorneys*?"

"Oh, right. Each group has a senior attorney whose primary task is to screen cases before hearings, as early in the process as possible, to determine whether a case can be decided in the claimant's favor without a formal hearing. A senior attorney may contact you after a case is filed, and before any notice of hearing is sent."

"About the decision . . . ?"

"Yes. If upon review the senior attorney believes the case can be decided in your client's favor he or she may call you if the case can be favorably decided using a later onset date than the one your client originally alleged."

Chris thought a moment.

"So, a senior attorney may not call either?"

"Correct. You'll generally get a call if they think the case can be decided favorably without a hearing."

Chris looked at the decision. "It looks like the major areas in a decision are *procedural history, issues, evaluation or analysis of the evidence,* and *findings*."

"That seems to be the standard OHA format. Many judges are trying to avoid the standard format, because it lends itself to too much boilerplate language, without enough actual analysis, and lulls the writer into creating lists of medical evidence without actually discussing the interrelationship between the evidence, the claimant's residual functional capacity, and the judge's decision."

"You're saying, read these carefully."

"Absolutely. Let me show you a different format, one that follows the five-step sequential analysis. This will give you a better idea of some of the possibilities." The pages flapped as Steve slid the next two sample decisions over to Chris [see Figures 19–2 and 19–3].

"You're showing me both *favorable* and *unfavorable* formats?"

"That's right, but notice the difference between the first and the second?"

"The first is much clearer and easier to follow. The judge's thinking is apparent at each step of the analysis."

"Exactly. That's why you should present your case the same way. Address each of the steps sequentially."

"The second decision still addresses procedural history and issues, just like the first decision."

"That's right. The procedural history tells the reader just that, where this case has been before the Administrative Law Judge decided it. It gives a sort of pedigree, as it were, of the case itself."

"OK."

"The issues are presented before the Administrative Law Judge at the hearing. If they are not accurate, an appeal is likely—indicating the Administrative Law Judge failed to address something she should have."

"That makes sense."

"Each of the steps in the analysis should address the facts of record. If a judge reaches a conclusion, without considering key facts, such as medical evidence or other exhibits, you may be able to appeal."

"You mean, if I lose?"

"Correct."

Chris paused, suddenly unsure what to do next. "What do I do now?"

"You mean now that the hearing is over?"

"Yes."

"Did you have to get any other evidence, medical records and the like?"

"No, we were up to date and had everything."

"Any further testing required, CEs, or tests your client was going to have done by his own doctor?"

"No. Again, it was all up to date."

"Sounds like you only have two things to do," Steve declared.

"What?" Chris asked.

"First, make notes about the major issues and discussions that took place during the hearing itself."

"Like what?"

"Areas of inquiry undertaken by the judge to begin with. But most importantly, the hypothetical questions the judge asked the vocational expert. You need to have a record of what was asked and what evidence was considered. This is important because if you lose, you're going to want to remember these issues for an appeal."

"That's good. Do you have a form?"

"Sure. It's pretty basic, but it jogs your memory." [See Figure 19–4.]

"What's the other thing I should do?"

"Get on with the next case! You did a great job here, and you shouldn't be hesitant to begin another."

"What about Mr. Carson?"

"Hopefully, you've told him what to expect from this point. Both of you have to wait. Mr. Carson should expect to wait from two weeks to several months before a final decision from the Administrative Law Judge."

"Why so long?"

"Unfortunately, the number of cases each judge must handle is significant. Even with attorneys and paralegal specialists helping, the delay can be substantial at times, particularly if additional evidence is needed."

"So, one step at a time, is that it?"

"That's it Chris. Like I said, you've done a fine job learning this material. Keep up the good work!"

SOCIAL SECURITY ADMINISTRATION

Refer to: **Office of Hearings and Appeals**

Date:

NOTICE OF DECISION—FULLY FAVORABLE

I have made the enclosed decision in your case. Please read this notice and the decision carefully.

This Decision Is Fully Favorable To You

Another office will process the decision and send you a letter about your benefits. Your local Social Security office or another office may first ask you for more information. If you do not hear anything for 60 days, contact your local office.

The Appeals Council May Review The Decision On Its Own Motion

The Appeals Council may decide to review my decision even though you do not ask it to do so. To do that, the Council must mail you a notice about its review within 60 days from the date shown above. Review at the Council's own motion could make the decision less favorable or unfavorable to you.

If You Disagree With The Decision

If you believe my decision is not fully favorable to you, or if you disagree with it for any reason, you may file an appeal with the Appeals Council.

How To File An Appeal

To file an appeal you or your representative must request the Appeals Council to review the decision. You must make the request in writing. You may use our Request for Review form, HA-520, or write a letter.

You may file your request at any local Social Security office or a hearing office. You may also mail your request right to the Appeals Council, Office of Hearings and Appeals, 5107 Leesburg Pike, Falls Church, VA 22041-3255. Please put the Social Security number shown above on any appeal you file.

Time To File An Appeal

To file an appeal, you must file your request for review **within 60 days** from the date you get this notice.

The Appeals Council assumes you got the notice 5 days after the date shown above unless you show you did not get it within the 5-day period. The Council will dismiss a late request unless you show you had a good reason for not filing it on time.

Time to Submit New Evidence

You should submit any new evidence you wish to the Appeals Council to consider **with** your request for review.

How An Appeal Works

Our regulations state the rules the Appeals Council applies to decide whether to review a case and in reviewing a case. These rules appear in the Code of Federal Regulations, Title 20, Chapter III, Part 404 (Subpart J) and Part 416 (Subpart N).

If you file an appeal, the Council will consider all of my decision, even the parts with which you agree. The Council **will** review your case if one of the reasons for review listed in our regulations exists. Sections 404.970 and 416.1470 of the regulations list these reasons.

Requesting review places the entire record of your case before the Council. Review can make any part of my decision more or less favorable or unfavorable to you.

On review, the Council may itself consider the issues and decide your case. The Council may also send it back to an Administrative Law Judge for a new decision.

If No Appeal And No Review On The Appeals Council's Own Motion

If you do not appeal and the Council does not review my decision on its own motion, you will not have a right to court review. My decision will be a final decision that can be changed only under special rules.

Do You Have Any Questions?

If you have any questions, you may call, write or visit any Social Security office. If you visit an office, please bring this notice and decision with you. The telephone number of the local office that serves your area is _______________. Its address is

Enclosures

cc:

Figure 19–1 **Exemplar Fully Favorable Decision—One Example**

NOTE TO PROCESSING CENTER
FURTHER ACTION NECESSARY

DEPARTMENT OF
HEALTH AND HUMAN SERVICES
Social Security Administration
OFFICE OF HEARINGS AND APPEALS

DECISION

IN THE CASE OF

____
(Claimant)

____
(Wage Earner)

CLAIM FOR

Period of Disability,
Disability Insurance Benefits, and
Supplemental Security Income

____
(Social Security Number)

I. PROCEDURAL HISTORY

A. The claimant filed his Title II application for disability insurance benefits on February ___, 19___ (protected filing date) (protective filing date), and his Title XVI application for supplemental security income on February ___, 19___ (protective filing date), alleging disability since February ___, 19___.

B. After proper notice, a hearing was held on January ___, 19___, in __________. The claimant personally appeared and testified, represented by Mr. __________, Attorney at Law.

C. Also testifying were Ms. __________, claimant's former spouse; and Mr. __________, qualified as a vocational expert.

II. ISSUES

A. The issues in this case are whether the claimant is under a disability as defined by the Social Security Act and if so, when his disability commenced, the duration of the disability, and whether the insured status requirements of the Act are met for the purpose of entitlement to a period of disability and disability insurance benefits.

III. EVALUATION OF THE EVIDENCE

A. After a thorough evaluation of the entire record, it is concluded that the claimant has been disabled since February ___, 19___, and met the insured status requirements of the Social Security Act on that date and thereafter, through the date of this decision.

B. The claimant was ___ years old on the date his disability began. The claimant has a college education, with a bachelors degree in Business Administration.

C. The claimant has not engaged in any substantial gainful activity since the disability onset date.

D. The claimant has the following impairments which are considered to be "severe" under the Social Security Act and Regulations:

1. diabetes mellitus;
2. chronic pancreatitis; and
3. constant pain associated with chronic pancreatitis.

E. These impairments prevent the claimant from

1. driving more than five (5) minutes at a time;
2. standing more than one (1) hour before becoming fatigued;

(continued)

3. sitting for more than one (1) hour before having to make significant postural changes:
4. lifting more than ten (10) pounds; and
5. concentrating and focusing on a given task.

F. Mr. __________ works with various __________ departments, including the __________.

G. Since that time he has had "odd" or "temporary" jobs, until he was finally only able to obtain unskilled general labor positions. He was finally forced to quit his last job as a delivery driver when his diabetes and pancreatitis caused him such difficulty with his vision as he could no longer safely read traffic control devices.

H. He was diagnosed with chronic pancreatitis in January 19___. Prior to that time Mr. __________ had been hospitalized two times over a one and one-half (1.5) year period.

1. He experienced significant weight loss (25–30 pounds) and suffered severe debilitating pain. (*See* "Exhibit 28," correspondence of Dr. __________, M.D., January ___, 19___.)
2. As a result of pancreatic failure, Mr. __________ now suffers severe diabetes; and must take pancreatic enzymes as well as insulin to control his blood sugar.
3. As a result of his deteriorating condition, brought on by a *past* history of alcohol abuse (Mr. __________ has not used alcohol for some time as of the date of the *Administrative Hearing*—"no apparent episodes of drinking in the past year"), Mr. __________ suffers "continuing, unrelenting, intractable pain in his abdomen". (*Id.*)
4. As a result of this pain, Mr. __________ must take a variety of medications, including morphine Contin, Tylenol #3, and Ibuprofen. These medications cause Mr. __________ to be groggy, render him unable to "think clearly" and suffer memory lapses.
5. As reported by his treating physician, Mr. __________ "has been unable to gain any further weight and continues to complain of chronic fatigue." As a consequence, Mr. __________ is unable to function for a majority of each day, being required to lay down by 10:00 each morning. He says of himself, "I'm a wreck; hurting; groggy and done for."

I. Mr. __________ testimony as to his inability to concentrate because of pain, and to engage in any significant activity because of chronic fatigue are credible, his testimony borne out by the report of his treating physician, Dr. __________ (*Id.*)

J. Mr. __________, qualified as a vocational expert, testified that the claimant could not return to his past employment and was prevented from doing so by reason of his inability to attend to even sedentary tasks before him.

1. Furthermore, Mr. __________ testified that an individual who was unable to concentrate because of the side effects of pain medication would be unable to perform even sedentary tasks.

K. Accordingly, the undersigned concludes that as a result of the combination of his impairments, including the side effects of his medications and constant, unrelenting, and intractable pain, Mr. __________ residual functional capacity for work is significantly less than that required for sedentary activity.[1]

L. The claimant's description of his limitations is consistent with the record when considered in its entirety. Mr. __________ cannot perform his past relevant work and does not have transferable skills to perform other work within his residual functional capacity.

M. Given the claimant's residual functional capacity, and the vocational factors of his age, education, and past relevant work experience, there are no jobs existing in significant numbers that the claimant is capable of performing. The claimant is under a disability as defined by the Social Security Act and Regulations.

IV. FINDINGS

After consideration of the entire record, the Administrative Law Judge makes the following findings:

1. The claimant met the insured status requirements of the Act on February ___ 19___. The claimant has not performed any substantial gainful activity since February ___, 19___.
2. The claimant's impairments which are considered to be "severe" under the Social Security Act are:
   a. diabetes mellitus;
   b. chronic pancreatitis; and
   c. constant pain associated with chronic pancreatitis.

[1]Residual functional capacity (RFC) is the maximum degree to which an individual retains the capacity for sustained performance of the physical/mental requirements of jobs. 20 C.F.R. 404.1545. RFC may also be defined as a multi-dimensional description of the work-related abilities which an individual retains in spite of medical impairments. 20 C.F.R. Pt. 404, Subpt. P, App. 1, Sec 12.00A.

3. The claimant's impairments do not meet or equal in severity the appropriate medical findings contained in 20 C.F.R. Part 404, Appendix 1 to Subpart P (Listing of Impairments).
4. The claimant's allegations are found to be credible.
5. The claimant's impairments prevent him from
   a. driving more than five (5) minutes at a time;
   b. standing more than one (1) hour before becoming fatigued;
   c. sitting for more than one (1) hour before having to make significant postural changes;
   d. lifting more than ten (10) pounds; and
   e. concentrating and focusing on a given task.
6. The claimant is unable to perform his past relevant work.
7. The claimant was ___ years old on the date disability began, which is defined as closely approaching advanced age. The claimant has a college education, with a bachelors degree in Business Administration.
8. The claimant does not have transferable skills to perform other work within his physical and mental residual functional capacity.
9. Based upon the claimant's residual functional capacity, and vocational factors, there are no jobs existing in significant numbers which he can perform. This finding is based upon Section 201.00(h) of the Medical–Vocational Guidelines, 20 C.F.R. Part 404, Appendix 2 to Subpart P.
10. The claimant has been under a disability as defined by the Social Security Act and Regulations since February ___, 19___.

V. DECISION

A. Based on the Title II application filed on February ___, 19___ (protected filing date), the claimant is entitled to a period of disability commencing February ___, 19___, and to disability insurance benefits under Sections 216(i) and 223 of the Social Security Act, respectively, and the claimant's disability has continued at least through the date of this decision.

B. It is the further decision of the Administrative Law Judge that based on the Title XVI application filed on February ___, 19___ (protected filing date), the claimant has been disabled since February ___, 19___, under Section 1614(a)(3)(A) of the Social Security Act, and the claimant's disability has continued through the date of this decision.

C. The Social Security Administration must also determine whether the claimant meets the income and resources and other eligibility requirements for supplemental security income payments, and if the claimant is eligible, the amount and the month(s) for which the claimant will receive payment.

D. The claimant will receive a notice from another office of the Social Security Administration when that office makes those determinations.

____

United States Administrative Law Judge

Date: __________________________

DECISION

(FAVORABLE)

IN THE CASE OF	**CLAIM FOR**
	Period of Disability and Disability Insurance Benefits and Supplemental Security Income Benefits Based on Disability
______________________ (Claimant)	______________________
______________________ (Wage Earner)	______________________ (Social Security Number)

I. PROCEDURAL HISTORY

A. The claimant filed his Title II *Application* for Disability Insurance Benefits on September ___, 19___, and his Title XVI *Application* for Supplemental Security Income on September ___, 19___ (protective filing date), alleging disability since October ___, 19___.

B. After proper notice, a hearing was held on November ___ 19___, in Tulsa, Oklahoma. The claimant personally appeared and testified, represented by Ms. __________, Attorney at Law.

C. Also testifying was Mr. __________, qualified as a vocational expert.

II. ISSUES

A. The issues in this case are:

1. Whether the claimant is under a disability as defined by the Social Security Act;
2. The date disability commenced;
3. The duration of the disability; and
4. Whether the insured status requirements of the Act are met for the purpose of entitlement to a period of disability and disability insurance benefits.

III. FINDINGS OF FACT AND CONCLUSIONS OF LAW

A. Upon review of the *Adminstrative Record,* together with the evidence adduced at the *Administrative Hearing,* the United States Administrative Law Judge, applying the **five-step sequential evaluation process** set forth at 20 CFR 404.1520 and 416.920, makes the following *Findings* in accord with the pertinent statutes, regulations and case law:

1. **Insured Status—20 CFR 404.130**

   a. The claimant, Mr./Ms. __________, met the insured status requirements of the Social Security Act (hereafter, the "Act") on October ___, 19___, the date he alleges he became unable to work.

   b. Mr./Ms. __________ continues to meet the requirements of insured status through December ___, 19___. (*See* "Exhibits __________.")

2. **Step One: Substantial Gainful Activity** ***(20 CFR 404.1520(b)/416.920(b))***

   a. Mr./Ms. __________ has not engaged in any substantial gainful activity since October ___, 19___.[1]

      1. Mr./Ms. __________ testified at the *Administrative Hearing* that he worked from June through August 19___ as a waiter and cook.

[1]See 20 CFR 404.1520(b) as regards the award of benefits under Title II of the Act; and at 20 CFR 416.920(b) as regards award of benefits under Title XVI of the Act.

"The term 'substantial gainful activity' is used to describe a level of work activity that is both substantial and gainful. Substantial work activity involves performance of significant physical or mental duties, or a combination of both, which are productive in nature. Gainful work activity is work performed for remuneration or profit; or work intended for profit, whether or not a profit is realized. For work activity to be substantial, it need not be performed on a full-time basis; work activity performed on a part-time basis may also be substantial." **See Social Security Handbook, *Section 603 (U.S. Social Security Administration, SSA Publication No. 65-008).***

Figure 19–2 **Exemplar Favorable Decision—A Second Example**

Step One: Substantial Gainful Activity *(continued)*

b. The undersigned finds, however, that this work does not constitute "substantial gainful activity. Mr./Ms. __________ worked on a temporary basis and did not earn enough money to constitute "substantial gainful activity."[2]

3. **Step Two: A "Severe" Impairment (20 CFR 404.1520(c)/416.920(c))**

a. The claimant's impairments, which **[in combination] [taken together],** are **[considered] [determined]** to be "severe" under the Act are:[3]

1. Gout;
2. Cluster headaches; and
3. Hypertension, poorly controlled and associated with occasional syncope. (See "Exhibits __________.") (See also 20 CFR 404.1520(c) and 416.920(c); 20 CFR 404.1521 and 416.921.)

b. Mr./Ms. __________ subjective complaints are found to be credible. (See 20 CFR 404.1529 and 416.929; together with Social Security Ruling ["SSR"] 95-5p.)

4. **Step Three: Listed Impairments (20 CFR 404.1520(d)/416.920(d))**

a. The claimant's impairments do not meet or equal the medical findings contained in 20 CFR Part 404, Appendix 1 to Subpart P (Listing of Impairments).

5. **Step Four: Residual Functional Capacity (20 CFR 404.1520(e)/416.920(e))**

a. Mr./Ms. __________ has a history of chronic cluster headaches over the past several years. These headaches worsened in 19___ (see "Exhibit ___," page ___), and are only partially responsive to medication.
b. Mr./Ms. __________ gout affects many of his joints, and particularly his left knee (see, "Exhibit ___," page ___).
c. Mr./Ms. __________ hypertension has not been consistently controlled (see "Exhibit ___," page ___), and he has occasional episodes of syncope associated with this lack of control (see "Exhibit ___," page ___).
d. Dr. __________, M.D., Mr./Ms. __________ treating physician, corroborates these findings, stating that Mr./Ms. __________ has not capacity for work (see "Exhibit ___," page ___).
e. As a result of his impairments, Mr./Ms. __________ is limited to performing a range of sedentary work. (See 20 CFR 404.1545 and 416.945.)

1. Specifically, Mr./Ms. __________ is restricted to a range of sedentary work because of the limitations on his ability to walk and stand due to gout; together with his inability to work at heights, around dangerous machinery, or to operate motor vehicles as a result of occasional syncope.

6. **Step Four: Past Relevant Work (20 CFR 404.1520(e)/416.920(e))**

a. Mr./Ms. __________ is unable to perform his past relevant work as a:

1. Cook;
2. Waiter; or
3. Janitor.

b. The foregoing jobs require more than sedentary exertion. (See "Exhibits __________," together with Mr./Ms.'s *Testimony,* as set forth in the *Record of the Administrative Hearing.*)

---

[2]"Certain earnings criteria have been established as reasonable indications of whether an employee is engaged in substantial gainful activity. Earnings after 1989 as an employee averaging:

A. Over $740 a month will ordinarily demonstrate that an individual is engaged in substantial gainful activity.
B. Formerly, less than $300 a month will ordinarily demonstrate that an individual has not engaged in substantial gainful activity. Now, less than $740 per month earnings are presumed not to be SGA.
C. Formerly, between $300 and $740 a month would have required that consideration be given to all circumstances related to the work activity." **See Social Security Handbook, *Section 620 (U.S. Social Security Administration, SSA Publication No. 65-008).*** Now, evidence to the contrary can be offered to rebut the presumption at $740 per month.

[3]"Severity" is not equivalent to a finding of "disability" under the Act. Rather, the term "severe" describes the nature of a physical or mental impairment and is defined as "any impairment or combination of impairments which significantly limits your physical or mental ability to do basic work activities." **See 20 CFR 404.1520(c).**

(continued)

Figure 19–2 **Exemplar Favorable Decision *(continued)***

7. **<u>Step Five:</u>** **<u>Other Work</u>**
   (20 CFR 404.1520(f)/416.920(f))
   a. Mr./Ms. __________ was ___ years old on the date he alleged he became disabled. He is closely approaching advanced age under Social Security Regulations (see 20 CFR 404.1563 and 416.963).
   b. Mr./Ms. __________ has a "limited" education. See "Exhibit ___," together with Mr./Ms. __________ *Testimony*, as set forth in the *Record of the Administrative Hearing.*
   c. In accord with the testimony of Mr. __________, qualified as a vocational expert, Mr./Ms. __________ does not have any acquired work skills which are transferable to the skilled or semi-skilled work activities of other work within his residual functional capacity.

8. **Conclusion**
   a. Mr./Ms. __________ has been under a disability as defined in the Act, as amended, since October ___, 19___.
      1. This conclusion is reached within the framework of Rule 201.10, Table No. 1 of Appendix 2, Subpart P. See also 20 CFR 404.1520(f) and 416.920(f)

IV. DECISION

In accord with the foregoing, the United States Administrative Law Judge enters the following *Decision:*

A. Based on the Title II *Application* filed on September ___, 19___, the claimant is entitled to a period of disability commencing October ___, 19___, and to disability insurance benefits under Sections 216(i) and 223, respectively.
   1. The claimant's disability has continued through at least the date of this *Decision.*
B. Based on the Title XVI *Application* filed on September ___, 19___ (protective filing date), the claimant has been disabled since October ___, 19___, under Section 1614()(3)(A) of the Act, and the claimant's disability has continued through the date of this *Decision.*
C. The Social Security Administration must also determine whether the claimant meets the income and resources and other eligibility requirements for Supplemental Security Income payments; and if the claimant is eligible, the amount and months(s) for which the claimant will receive payment.
D. The claimant will receive a notice from another office of the Social Security Administration when that office makes the foregoing determinations.

DONE THIS DAY,

____

United States Administrative Law Judge

____

Date

DECISION

(UNFAVORABLE)

IN THE CASE OF

____

(Claimant)

____

(Wage Earner)

CLAIM FOR

Period of Disability and
Disability Insurance Benefits

____

(Social Security Number)

I. PROCEDURAL HISTORY

A. The claimant filed his Title II *Application* for Disability Insurance Benefits on October ____, 19____, alleging disability since April ____, 19____.

B. After proper notice, a hearing was held on October ____, 19____, in Tulsa, Oklahoma. The claimant personally appeared and testified, represented by Ms. ___________, Attorney at Law.

C. Also testifying was Mr. ___________, qualified as a vocational expert.

II. ISSUES

A. The issues in this case are:

1. Whether the claimant is under a disability as defined by the Social Security Act (hereinafter, the "Act");
2. The date disability commenced;
3. The duration of the disability; and
4. Whether the claimant was disabled on or before June ____, 19____, the date he last met the disability insured status requirements of the Act.

III. FINDINGS OF FACT AND CONCLUSIONS OF LAW

A. Upon review of the *Administrative Record,* together with the evidence adduced at the *Administrative Hearing,* the United States Administrative Law Judge, applying the **five-step sequential evaluation process** set forth at 20 CFR 404.1520 and 416.920, makes the following *Findings* in accord with the pertinent statutes, regulations and case law:

1. **Insured Status—20 CFR 404.130**

   a. The claimant, Mr./Ms. ___________, met the insured status requirements of the Act on April ____, 19____, the date he alleges he became unable to work.

   b. Mr./Ms. ___________ continues to meet the requirements of insured status through June ____, 19____, but not thereafter. (See "Exhibits ___________.")

2. **Step One: Substantial Gainful Activity—20 CFR 404.1520(b)**

   a. Mr./Ms. ___________ has not engaged in any substantial gainful activity since April ____, 19____.[1]

[1]See 20 CFR 404.1520(b) as regards the award of benefits under Title II of the Act; and at 20 CFR 416.920(b) as regards award of benefits under Title XVI of the Act.

"The term 'substantial gainful activity' is used to describe a level of work activity that is both substantial and gainful. Substantial work activity involves performance of significant physical or mental duties, or a combination of both, which are productive in nature. Gainful work activity is work performed for remuneration or profit; or work intended for profit, whether or not a profit is realized. For work activity to be substantial, it need not be performed on a full-time basis; work activity performed on a part-time basis may also be substantial." **See Social Security Handbook, *Section 603 (U.S. Social Security Administration, SSA Publication No. 65-008).***

Figure 19–3 **Exemplar Unfavorable Decision**

(continued)

3. Step Two: A "Severe" Impairment—20 CFR 404.1520(c)

   a. The evidence establishes that on or before June ____, 19____, the claimant's impairments, which **[in combination] [taken together]**, are **[considered] [determined]** to be "severe" under the Act are:[2]

      1. Severe shoulder and back impairments;

         (a) Specifically, questionable small, left-sided disk herniation at level C3-4; minimal bulging at L3-4, with straightening at L4-5; together with overall degenerative changes;

      2. Congenital aortic coarctation; and
      3. Hypertension.

      (See "Exhibits ___________.") (See also 20 CFR 404.1520(c)).

   b. Mr./Ms. ___________ testimony regarding the severity of his symptoms, including pain, prior to expiration of his insured status on June ____, 19____, was generally not credible. (See 20 CFR 404.1529; together with Social Security Ruling ["SSR"] 95-5p.)

      1. The *Administrative Record* shows minimal objective findings and medical treatment until the latter part of 19____.
      2. This determination is consistent with the fact that the majority of Mr./Ms. ___________ complaints pertain to problems which arose after his insured status expired.
      3. Despite the alleged severity of his symptoms, he has consistently failed to follow his treating physician's recommendations for physical therapy. (See 20 CFR 404.1530(b)).

         a. The *Administrative Record* indicates that such therapy proved successful on at least two prior occasions in resolving his symptoms. (See "Exhibits ___________.")

         b. Mr./Ms. ___________ reportedly did not supplement his treatment with the prescribed home exercise program and was ultimately discharged from physical therapy due to his failure to attend on a regular basis. (See "Exhibits ___________.")

4. **Step Three: Listed Impairments—20 CFR 404.1520(d)**

   a. The claimant did not have an impairment or combination of impairments which met or equaled the medical findings contained in 20 CFR Part 404, Appendix 1 to Subpart P (Listing of Impairments) on or before June ____, 19____.

   b. During the period on or before June ____, 19____, the *Administrative Record* does not include evidence suggesting arthritis or significant degenerative factors.

   c. Furthermore, the *Administrative Record* does not show that Mr./Ms. ___________ had significant limitations of motion or muscles loss with muscle weakness and attendant sensory and reflex loss (see "Exhibits ___________").

   d. Mr./Ms. ___________ impairments, individually, or **[in combination] [taken together],** did not meet or equal the specific findings in Section 1.05C or any other Section of the Listings at 1.00.

   e. On or before June ____, 19____, the claimant's congenital aortic coarctation was asymptomatic.

   f. On or before June ____, 19____, the claimant's hypertension was determined to be borderline and controlled with low dose medication (see (5.)(),*supra*). The claimant's condition did not meet or equal any Listing in section 4.00.

5. **Step Four: Residual Functional Capacity—20 CFR 404.1520(e)**

   a. Following a motor vehicle accident on April ____, 19____, Mr./Ms. ___________ was diagnosed as having a "whiplash-type" injury, resulting in headaches and nausea, for which he was prescribed Tylenol 3 and st (see "Exhibit ___________").

   b. In November 19____, radiological testing, carried out because of pain, revealed a questionable small left-sided disc herniation at level C3-4, a straightening of the L4-5 disc, and mild overall degenerative changes.

---

[2]"Severity" is not equivalent to a finding of "disability" under the Act. Rather, the term "severe" describes the nature of a physical or mental impairment and is defined as "any impairment or combination of impairments which significantly limits your physical or mental ability to do basic work activities." See 20 CFR 404.1520(c).

c. Mr./Ms. __________ was referred to a physical therapy program, and reported feeling greatly improved after treatment.

d. Mr./Ms. __________ was discharged from physical therapy in March 19___, as a result of his failure to attend (see "Exhibits __________").

e. On December ___, 19___, claimant was involved in yet another motor vehicle accident. One week later he again sought treatment for a stiff neck and tightness in the back. Once again, he was referred for physical therapy.

f. The evidence thereafter reflects steady progress with respect to cervical pain and range of motion (see "Exhibits __________").

g. In February 19___, Mr./Ms __________ reported that he had not more pain, but only some stiffness and pulling which he felt was "tolerable." (See "Exhibit ___")

h. Dr. __________, the claimant's treating physician, noted some tenderness in the cervical spine and again prescribed Tylenol 3 (see "Exhibit ___").

i. The *Administrative Record* shows that the claimant's symptoms improved after each period of physical therapy and medication. It also reflects medical treatment until the latter part of 19___.

j. Based upon the minimal objective findings and the successful results of his treatment, Mr./Ms. __________ could, at a minimum:

   1. Lift and carry ten (10) pounds;
   2. Sit for six (6) hours each day without significant postural changes; and
   3. Stand for at least two (2) hours each day without significant postural changes, such as stooping or bending.

k. The claimant's congenital aortic coarctation and hypertension did not cause any additional exertional limitations prior to June ___, 19___.

   1. Although he has been informed that he *may* need an additional angioplasty when he reaches his forties, Mr./Ms. __________ condition has remained asymptomatic (see "Exhibit ___").
   2. The claimant's hypertension was completely controlled on low dosage medication for the period in question.

l. Dr. __________, a medical facilitator who works with fibromyalgia support groups, suggested that the claimant may have fibromyalgia. He further indicated that virtually any activity would exacerbate the claimant's *present* condition.

   1. However, Dr. __________ offers no evidence as regards the claimant's condition during the period in question (on or before June ___, 19___).
   2. Accordingly, the undersigned gives little weight to Dr. __________ opinion, given that the opinion post-dates Mr./Ms. __________ date last insured (June ___, 19___) by several years.
   3. Furthermore, Dr. __________ later opinion contradicts that of Dr. __________, claimant's treating physician, who expressly concluded that Mr./Ms. __________ symptoms do not fit the criteria of fibromyalgia (see "Exhibit ___").

m. After careful consideration of the objective evidence in the *Administrative Record,* and upon review of Mr./Ms. __________ testimony, including evidence of activities of daily living and medical treatment, the undersigned finds that on or before June ___, 19___, Mr./Ms. __________ was capable of performing the physical and exertional requirements of sedentary work.

6. **Step Four: Past Relevant Work—20 CFR 404.1520(e)/416.920(e)**

   a. Mr./Ms. __________ was unable to perform his past relevant work as a:

      1. Delivery man; or
      2. Mail clerk.
      (See Exhibit ___," together with Mr./Ms. __________ *Testimony,* as set forth in the *Record of the Administrative Hearing.*)

   b. The foregoing jobs required light to medium exertion, which exceed Mr./Ms. __________ residual functional capacity for sedentary work. (See "Exhibit ___," together with Mr./Ms. __________ *Testimony,* as set forth in the *Record of the Administrative Hearing.*)

(continued)

Figure 19–3 **Exemplar Unfavorable Decision** ***(continued)***

7. <u>Step Five:</u> <u>Other Work—20 CFR 404.1520(f)</u>
   a. As of June ___, 19___, Mr./Ms. __________ was ___ years old. He is a younger individual under Social Security Regulations (see 20 CFR 404.1563(b)).
   b. Mr./Ms. __________ had a high school education and had completed additional college level course work in computer science. (See "Exhibit ___," together with Mr./Ms. __________ *Testimony*, as set forth in the *Record of the Administrative Hearing*)
   [c. Mr. __________, qualified to testify as a vocational expert, testified that Mr./Ms. __________ could perform the following jobs within the national and regional economy:
      1. Surveillance monitor, with ___ positions in the region and ___ positions nationally;
      2. Sedentary cashier, with ___ positions in the region and ___ positions nationally; and
      3. Sedentary assembly work, with ___ positions in the region and ___ positions nationally.]
   [d. Each of these positions are at the sedentary exertional level.]
   [e. The undersigned finds that significant numbers of jobs exist in the regional and national economy which Mr./Ms. __________ can perform.]

8. <u>Conclusion</u>
   a. Mr./Ms. __________ was "not disabled" as disability is defined in the Act, on or before June ___, 19___.
      1. The conclusion is reached applying Rule 201.28, Table No. 1 of Appendix 2, Subpart P. See also 20 CFR 404.1520(f).

      or

      [2. This conclusion is reached at step 5 of the sequential evaluation process, there being significant numbers of jobs both within the regional and national economy that claimant can perform.]

IV. DECISION

A. Based on the *Application* filed on October ___, 19___, the claimant is not entitled to a period of disability or disability insurance benefits under Section 216(i) and 223, respectively, of the Social Security Act.

DONE THIS DAY,

____

United States Administrative Law Judge

____

Date

Hearing Notes

Section I

1. Claimant:
2. Date of hearing:
3. Judge:
4. Vocational expert:
5. Medical expert:
6. Other witnesses:

Section II

1. Posthearing medical records required:

2. Posthearing consultative examinations ordered:

3. Other evidence to obtain:

4. Need for a supplemental hearing? If so, why?

Section III

1. Notable Areas of Inquiry by the Judge of the Claimant

- ❑ Work:
- ❑ ADLs:
- ❑ Family:
- ❑ Friends:
- ❑ Medical symptoms:
- ❑ Restrictions/limitations:
- ❑ Other:

2. Notable Areas of Inquiry of the Medical Expert

- ❑ Diagnosis:
- ❑ Prognosis:
- ❑ Restrictions/limitations:
- ❑ Meet/equals listing:

3. Notable Areas of Inquiry of the Vocational Expert

- ❑ Past work:
- ❑ Transferrable skills:
- ❑ Hypos:

4. Notable Areas of Inquiry of Other Witnesses

Other Areas of Note

Figure 19–4 **Taking Notes of the Proceedings**

WHAT IF . . . ? SAMPLE PROBLEMS

WHAT IF . . .

What does the representative do after the hearing?

1. Nothing.
2. Make sure that you have good contact information from your client, so that you can stay in touch, particularly in an SSI case, where the fee must be collected directly from the claimant.
3. If no further action is required, the representative should make certain that hearing notes properly reflect the judge's inquiry, both to the claimant and to the Vocational Expert.
4. Both 1 and 2.

Answer: If there is no need to gather additional medical records, participate in post-hearing consultative examinations or submit a brief to the judge on a legal issue, the representative should prepare for an appeal, unless the judge has announced a favorable decision from the bench. In preparing for an appeal, ensure complete hearing notes, including notations of the judge's inquiry of the claimant and the Vocational Expert, making particular note of the hypothetical questions asked of the VE. It is also important to maintain a continuing relationship with your client; in case an appeal is necessary; or, if not, to ensure payment of the fee, especially if the claim is an SSI case. Fees are not withheld in an SSI case; and in the case of non-lawyer representatives, neither are they withheld in a Title II case. The correct answer is 4.

What if the judge issues a denial? Is there anything to be done short of an appeal?

1. No, nothing. Any appeal must be filed before the Appeals Council within 60 days of the judge's decision.
2. Request the judge reopen the decision while at the same time, filing an appeal.
3. Ask the judge to reconsider the decision.
4. File an application with the federal court for a writ of prohibition, prohibiting implementation of the administrative decision.

Answer: Federal regulation at Title 20 C.F.R. § 404.987 provides for reopening a determination or decision under defined circumstances. If an application to reopen is made within 12 months, the judge may do so "for any reason." 20 C.F.R. § 404.988(a). The strategy in the case of a denial is to make a formal request to reopen (not reconsider) while at the same time filing an appeal. Such a request should not be generic, but should specify the reasons for the request.

This request, while not mandated by regulation, nor required for an appeal, is nevertheless akin to, but does not take the place of an appeal. It should state specific legal and/or factual errors or oversights, cite governing regulation and law, and refer to exhibits in the administrative record. The request to reopen is an opportunity to avoid an appeal. It need not be responded to by the judge; and in many cases, will not be. Ideally, a request to reopen a denial decision should be submitted to the Administrative Law Judge within the first 60 days following receipt of the denial decision. If granted, any appeal to the Appeals Council can be withdrawn. Note, however, the making of a request to reopen does not toll the sixty-day time within which an appeal must otherwise be taken. The correct answer is 2.

20

CHAPTER TWENTY

Internet Resources

HIGHLIGHTS

- The SSA Web site
- Other sites

CHRIS

Chris pondered the laptop screen and finally decided to key the words "social security" into the search engine.

"Wow." A number of hits came up. "Which one do I choose?"

Clicking almost randomly on various sites, Chris hit on **www.ssa.gov.**

"Hey! The official Web site for the Social Security Administration. "Well, that seems like the logical place to start." Chris scrolled through the Web site.

A TRIP TO THE HARD DRIVE, 20.1

The SSA Web site provides a wealth of important information and resources. For a general overview of the Social Security Administration and its programs go to **www.ssa.gov.** Following are additional resource sites linked to the SSA site.

- **www.ssa.gov/history/law.html** Provides a history of the Social Security Administration and its various programs
- **www.ssa.gov/enews/last/html** Provides the latest news from the Social Security Administration
- **www.ssa.gov/disability** Addresses Title II Disability Insurance Benefits
- **www.ssa.gov/notices/supplemental-security-income/** Provides information about Title XVI, Supplemental Security Income Benefits
- **www.ssa.gov/disability/3368/** Provides information regarding completion of the disability report form, considered the foundation of the disability application, including all instructions and requirements
- **www.ssa.gov/representation** Special site important for representatives that provides forms for fee agreements and fee petitions, as well as general information for representatives. These forms can be downloaded for ease of use or reference.
- **www.ssa.gov/online/forms/html** Provides a variety of forms
- **www.ssa.gov/oha/index.html** Provides information about the Social Security's Office of Hearings and Appeals. Many forms can also be downloaded from this site.
- **www.ssa.gov/foia/bluebook/app_f.htm** Provides a list of all regional and local OHA offices regionally, as opposed to alphabetically
- **www.ssa.gov/payee** Provides information about representative payees

Back to Chris

"That's a lot of sites!"

Steve walked into Chris's office, peering at the computer screen. "You're at ssa.gov?"

"Yes. And there's a lot here."

"That's a good reference point. But don't forget about some of the private sites."

"For Social Security?"

"Absolutely. Here, let me show you." Steve sat down at the keyboard.

A Trip to the Hard Drive, 20.2

Various Web sites address Social Security issues, including a number of sites maintained by private practitioners. Because all such sites cannot be listed here—and because we cannot know the full content of such private sites—they are not included. However, one important location that contains links to other resources is maintained by the National Organization of Social Security Claimant's Representatives or NOSSCR (pronounced, noss-cur). NOSSCR is a professional organization dedicated to education and advocacy on behalf of those who represent claimants before the Social Security Administration. Its Web address is **www.nosscr.org.** Following are additional Web site resources.

- **www.socsec.org** The Social Security Network, a private organization, provides a broad view of Social Security policy and directions
- **www.asaging.org** The American Association on Aging provides general information and links to both Social Security and disability issues, but more from a perspective of policy than practice
- **www.aapd-dc.org** The American Association of People with Disabilities is dedicated to the dissemination of information about Social Security and disability issues generally
- **www.ssas.com/connect** SSAS Connect is a site rife with talk, comment, gossip, complaints, information, and individual opinion, all related to SSA disability.

Back to Chris

"Pretty wild! There are a lot of sites!"

Steve nodded. "But remember, you have to determine the merits of each site based on your own research and information. Just because something's on the Internet doesn't necessarily mean its accurate."

"Thanks for the leads. It certainly gives one pause for thought—and plenty to explore!"

"Good luck!" said Steve, grinning as he made his way back to his office. *Chris will do just fine,* he thought.

Appendix A

Glossary of Terms

Highlights

- ❑ Definitions
- ❑ Acronyms

A bewildering series of terms and acronyms pepper Social Security disability practice. What follows is a Glossary of General Disability Terms, a list of Common Medical Acronyms and Abbreviations, and a Childhood Disability Glossary. These terms have been compiled by both the Social Security Administration and the authors.

A-1

Appendix A–1

General Disability Glossary

Abandonment A term used internally to refer to the dismissal of a request for hearing on the basis of the claimant's, or the claimant's representative's, failure to appear at the time and place of the scheduled hearing, without the Administrative Law Judge finding good cause for such failure to appear.

Acceptable medical sources 20 C.F.R. § 404.1513(a) and 20 C.F.R. § 416.913(a) define these as (1) licensed physicians; (2) licensed osteopaths; (3) licensed or certified psychologists; (4) licensed optometrists for the measurement of visual acuity and visual fields; and (5) persons authorized to send SSA a copy or summary of the medical records of a hospital, clinic, sanatarium, medical institution, or health care facility.

Access The release of a record to the individual to whom it pertains, or to the parent of a minor, or the legal guardian of an incompetent person when the parent or guardian is acting on behalf of his or her ward.

Acquiescence Ruling (AR) A published Social Security Ruling that explains how the Administration will apply a decision of a federal court of appeals to other similar cases within the circuit when the decision is at variance with SSA's national policy in adjudicating claims.

Adjudicated Something that has been ruled on, judged, arbitrated, or decided.

Adjustment The process whereby SSA withholds all or part of the benefit payments due an overpaid person, other persons receiving Title II benefits on the same account, or an eligible spouse under Title XVI.

Alleged Onset Date (AOD) See "onset".

Administrative Appeals Judge An attorney who is a member of the Appeals Council, the Executive Director of the Appeals Council, or the Director of the Office of Civil Actions.

Administrative Law Judge (ALJ) A qualified attorney, appointed by the Federal Office of Personnel Management and serving in SSA's Office of Hearings and Appeals, who conducts impartial hearings and makes decisions on appealed determinations involving retirement, survivors, disability, health insurance, black lung, and supplemental security income benefits.

Administrative Procedures Act (APA) Legislation enacted in 1946 which established and defined the role of Hearing Examiners (Referees) now, Adminstrative Law Judges, and also provided explicit powers to Hearing Officers concerning the conduct of hearings. It also guarantees the Hearing Officer's right to decisional independence by limiting the agency review to its own post-decision motion review.

Administrative review process The steps of reconsideration, hearing, and Appeals Council review, which may follow the initial determination made on a claim.

Advanced age By regulatory definition (20 C.F.R § 404.1563(d) and § 416.963(d), an individual age 55 and older.

Adverse party A person who makes a showing in writing that his or her rights may be adversely affected by a decision, or a person an ALJ determines on his/her own initiative may have his or her rights adversely affected, and thus has a right to a hearing.

Affidavit A sworn statement in writing made under oath or on affirmation before an authorized magistrate or officer.

Affirmation An action deciding that the previous favorable or unfavorable determination or decision made at a lower adjudicative level will not be changed.

ALJ file Also known as the hearing office file, it maintains a record of correspondence activity of a case. It is kept in the hearing office for at least one year following the last correspondence in a fully favorable case and for at least two years following the last correspondence in a denial case.

Allowance decision A decision that results in an outcome fully favorable, or partially favorable, to the claimant.

Annual earnings test A provision of the Social Security Act that limits the amount of money a person can earn and still collect all his or her Social Security Benefits; it affects people under the age of 70 who collect Social Security retirement, dependents, or survivors' benefits.

Appeals Council (AC) A group of attorneys SSA employs as Adminstrative Appeals Judges, who have the authority to deny or dismiss a claimant's request for review of the ALJ's decision or order, or grant the request and either issue a decision or remand the case to an ALJ. The AC may, on its own initiative, review an ALJ's decision and may recommend action to be taken on a claim when a claimant files a civil action. Incoming appeals are assigned to an AC member on the basis of geographic jurisdiction and rotational distribution.

Appeals Council remands Cases which the Appeals Council returns to the ALJ hearing level for further action or consideration.

Applicant The person who files an application for benefits for himself or herself or on behalf of someone else.

Application An application for benefits on a form prescribed by the Administration.

Approaching advanced age By regulatory definition (20 C.F.R. § 404.1563 and § 416.963), an individual age 50 to 54.

Approaching retirement age By regulatory definition (20 C.F.R. § 404.1563 and § 416.963), an individual age 60 to 64.

Authorized representative An individual appointed in writing by another individual to represent the latter individual before SSA and who has been accepted by SSA to act as an authorized representative (SSA Form 1696).

Auxiliary An individual entitled to benefits on another person's Social Security earnings record, such as a wife, husband, child, widow/widower, parent, and so on.

Average Indexed Monthly Earnings (AIME) Earnings for the year 1951 up to and including the second year before the year of first eligibility for Social Security benefits or death, whichever comes first, which are indexed (i.e., adjusted to put them in proportion to the earnings level of all workers for those years).

Average Monthly Earnings (AME) Actual employees' earnings (wages) employers report, or net earnings from self-employment individuals report as self-employment income for Social Security purposes.

Basic work activities The abilities and aptitudes necessary to do most jobs. 20 C.F.R. § 404.1521 and § 416.921 give examples, which include:

(1) Physical functions, such as walking, standing, sitting, lifting, pushing, pulling, reaching, carrying, or handling;
(2) Capacities for seeing, hearing, and speaking;
(3) Understanding, carrying out, and remembering simple instructions;
(4) Use of judgment;
(5) Responding appropriately to supervision, co-workers, and usual work situations; and
(6) Dealing with changes in a routine work setting.

Benefits Any payments made to or on behalf of an eligible individual under the SSA, SSI, Health Insurance, and Black Lung programs. SSI payments also include any federally administered state supplementary programs.

Black Lung benefits Monthly cash benefits payable to a coal miner (or his widow) who is (or was) totally disabled by pneumoconiosis resulting from employment in the nation's coal mines and who has filed a timely application for benefits under the Federal Coal Mine Health and Safety Act of 1969, as amended.

Blind child (BC) An individual under age 18, who files for benefits based on blindness under Title XVI of the Social Security Act (SSI).

Blind individual (BI) An individual, age 18 or older, who files for benefits based on blindness under Title XVI of the Act (SSI).

Blind spouse (BS) An individual, age 18 or older, who files for benefits based on blindness under Title XVI of the Act (SSI), and is the spouse of an eligible individual.

Body habitus A term used in Social Security Ruling 96-8p to mean natural body build, physique, constitution, size, and weight, insofar as they are unrelated to the individual's medically determinable impairment(s) and related symptoms.

Brief A statement of a client's case made out for the instruction of counsel in a trial of law; an outline of an argument on behalf of the client dealing with facts and points of law and presented to a trial or appellate court.

Broad world of work Work which exists at all exertional levels, and may include skilled, semiskilled, and unskilled work, as defined in Social Security Ruling 83–10.

Central office SSA headquarters in Baltimore, Maryland.

Cessation or cessation date The date a claimant's disability ends.

Child's insurance benefits Title II Social Security benefits based on the record of a parent, payable to a child who meets certain statutory and regulatory requirements.

Civil action A court action or suit filed in federal district court against the government claiming benefits under the Social Security Act.

Claim file A case folder generally containing an application and documentation supporting a claim for benefits.

Claimant A person who files an application for Social Security benefits, or the person on whose behalf a claim is filed; or one who seeks other relief (i.e., relief from repayment of an overpayment).

Claims representative (CR) The Social Security representative who is responsible for interviewing claimants and processing their Social Security applications and handling related matters in SSA field and branch offices.

Closed period of disability (CPOD) A period of disability where the beginning and ending dates are established at the time the claim is adjudicated.

Closed record A record into which no further evidence may be introduced.

Code of Federal Regulations (CFR) A codification of the general and permanent rules that the executive departments and agencies of the federal government publish in the *Federal Register.*

Collateral estoppel The rule, generally relevant to the filing of concurrent applications under Titles II and XVI disability programs, that conflicting findings and conclusions may not be made concerning a claimant's rights to benefits on the same issue(s) arising under different titles of the law.

Comparability test A comparison of the ability to perform substantial gainful activity requiring skills and abilities comparable to those a claimant used in any substantial gainful activity which he or she performed regularly and for a substantial period of time; applicable to blind claimants receiving Social Security benefits who are age 55 or older.

Computation year To determine Social Security cash benefit amounts, the years of the highest earnings are selected from the "base years" or the years after 1950 up to the year in which the first month of entitlement to retirement or disability insurance benefits occurs; for a survivor's claim, the "base years" include the year of the worker's death.

Conclusory Arriving at a conclusion without the support of a rationale based on credible evidence.

Concurrent claims Claims (which are evidenced by application forms) under different programs of the Social Security Act, having similar issues, such as Social Security disability and supplemental security income disability, which are processed simultaneously.

Consolidated hearing A hearing to decide benefit rights under two different parts of the Social Security Act, both administered by the Administration.

Consultative examination (CE) A physical or mental examination or test purchased for the claimant at Social Security's request and expense from a physician or psychologist of record, or from an independent source.

Continuing Disability Review (CDR) Re-examination of an individual's impairment(s) to determine whether he or she continued to be disabled and entitled to disability benefits.

Controlling weight The weight given to a medical opinion from a treating source that must be adopted when the following criteria are present:

(1) the opinion is from a treating source;

(2) the opinion must be a medical opinion;

(3) the treating source's medical opinion is well-supported by medically acceptable clinical and laboratory diagnostic techniques; and

(4) the treating source's medical opinion is not inconsistent with the other substantial evidence in the case record.

See 20 C.F.R. § 404.1527(d)(2) and § 416.927(d)(2) and Social Security Ruling 96–2p.

Countable income Cash and in-kind, earned and unearned income, which is used to determine the monthly SSI benefit amount—the greater the countable income, the less the monthly payment. There are a number of exclusions to countable income specified in the Act. Regulations include a standard disregard of $65 per month of earned income and $20 per month unearned income, other than in-kind support and maintenance and income based on need.

Court remand Any court action returning a case to an administrative or lower judicial level.

Credibility The degree to which an individual's statements about pain or other symptoms and their functional effects can be believed and accepted as true in determining whether an individual is disabled. When evaluating the credibility of an individual's statements, the adjudicator must consider the entire case record and give specific reasons for the weight given to the individual's statements. See Social Security Ruling 96–7p.

Currently insured Having at least six quarters of coverage during the thirteen-quarter period ending with the quarter in which an individual dies, most recently became entitled to disability insurance benefits, or became entitled to retirement insurance benefits.

Date Last Met (DLM) or Date Last Insured (DLI) Last day and month of the last calendar quarter in which the claimant last meets the earnings requirements for Title II disability insurance benefits.

Decision A written statement of the applicable issues, law, facts, rationale, findings, and conclusions in a case decided by an Administrative Law Judge, the Appeals Council, or a district court.

Deemed valid marriage A situation where a claimant will be deemed to be the insured's spouse, if, in good faith, he or she went through a marriage ceremony with the wage earner that would have resulted in a valid marriage except for a legal impediment.

Denial A refusal of the benefits or action claimed or requested.

De novo review A new and independent examination of a Social Security claim by an Administrative Law Judge.

Determination Outcome of a case at the initial and reconsideration levels.

***Dictionary of Occupational Titles* (DOT)** A publication of the U.S. Department of Labor that provides basic occupational information. The DOT groups jobs into "occupations" based on their similarities and define the structure and content of all listed occupations. The DOT is used as a vocational resource in determining functions of past relevant work (at step 4) and other work (step 5). See Social Security Ruling 00–4p regarding the ALJ's correlation of the vocational expert's testimony with the DOT.

Dire need The claimant is, or soon will be, without food, medicine, or shelter.

Disability The inability to engage in any substantial gainful activity by reason of any medically determinable physical or mental impairment which can be expected to result in death or which has lasted or can be expected to last for a continuous period of not less than twelve months.

Disability Determination Services (DDS) or Disability Determination Unit (DDU) A federally funded agency of a state which makes disability and blindness determinations in Social Security and SSI disability claims.

Disability Insurance Benefits (DIB) Benefits paid to disabled individuals, their spouses, and their dependents, under Title II of the Act.

DIB after death An application for disability insurance benefits on behalf of a deceased worker.

Disabled adult child (DAC) Benefits payable to a Title II insured wage earner's child who meets the requirements for child's insurance benefits under that Title and was disabled prior to age 22.

Disabled child (DC) An individual under age 18, who files for disability under Title XVI of the Act (SSI).

Disabled spouse (DS) An individual who filed for benefits based on disability under Title XVI of the Act (SSI) and who is the spouse of an eligible individual.

Disabled Widow(er) Benefits (DWB) A claim for, or an individual who applies for, disability benefits on the earnings of a deceased spouse.

Dismissal Disposition of a case without consideration of, or action on, the substantive issues (keeping the previous determination or decision in effect).

Disposition The conclusion of an action by an Administrative Law Judge or the Appeals Council which includes issuance of an ALJ or AC decision, or order of dismissal, a denial of a request for review, or an AC remand.

Docket A list of cases awaiting hearing or disposition.

Duration The requirement that a disability must have lasted or be expected to last at least twelve continuous months, or result in death.

Earnings record Official record of an individual's wage and self-employment income on which Social Security taxes are paid; or, in some instances, income or activity on which gratuitous wage credits are based.

Earnings requirement The requirement that a person has worked a specified minimum amount or period of time in Social Security covered employment and/or self-employment to be eligible for benefits.

Effectuation The process of putting into effect the action directed by a determination or decision.

End organs Heart, brain, eyes (retina), and kidneys.

End-stage renal A stage of kidney impairment that appears irreversible and permanent and requires a regular course of dialysis or kidney transplantation to maintain life.

Entitled One who has applied for and has proven his or her right to Title II benefits for a period of time; under Title XVI an individual who is aged, blind, or disabled who has filed an application and meets all other requirements to receive SSI benefits.

Environmental restrictions Restrictions that result in an inability to tolerate some physical feature(s) of the work setting that occurs in certain industries or types of work, such as an inability to tolerate dust or fumes, cold or hot temperatures, or loud noises.

Escalated claim A claim that is brought up to the hearing level before lower-level determinations are made in order to process the claim as one claim with a claim already at the hearing level. Both claims must present the same claim for decision.

Evidence Any record or document submitted to, or obtained by, SSA relating to the individual's claim for benefits. Evidence includes, but is not limited to, (1) objective medical evidence such as medical signs and laboratory findings; (2) other evidence from medical sources, such as medical history, opinions, and statements about treatment; (3) statements the individual or others make about the individual's impairment(s), restrictions, daily activities, efforts to work, or any other relevant statements the individual makes to medical sources during the course of treatment or to SSA employees during interviews, in letters, or in testimony during administrative hearings; (4) information from other sources such as public and private social welfare agencies, observations by non-medical sources, and other practitioners; (5) decisions by any governmental or nongovernmental agency about whether the individual is disabled or blind; or (6) at the ALJ and AC levels, certain findings other than the ultimate determination about whether the individual is disabled, made by DDS medical or psychological consultants and other program physicians or psychologists, and opinions expressed by medical advisors based on their review of the evidence in the individual's case record. See 20 C.F.R. § 404.1512(b) and § 416.912(b); 20 C.F.R. § 404.1513(e) and § 416.913(e); Social Security Ruling 96–6p.

Exertional capacity This addresses an individual's limitations and restrictions of physical strength and defines the individual's remaining abilities to perform each of seven strength demands: standing, walking, sitting, lifting, carrying, pushing, and pulling. Each function should be considered separately. See Social Security Rulings 83–10 and 96–8p.

Exertional limitations Impairment-caused limitations are classified as exertional if they affect an individual's ability to meet strength demands of jobs (sitting, standing, walking, lifting, carrying, pushing, and pulling). See 20 C.F.R. § 404.1569a(a) & (b) and § 416.969a(a) & (b), Social Security Rulings 83–10 and 96–4p.

Exhibit list List of documents contained in a claim filed which an Administrative Law Judge or Appeals Council enters into the case record and will consider in issuing a decision.

Expert witness Generally a medical expert (physician or psychologist) or vocational expert who testifies at a hearing or provides responses to written interrogatories.

Father's insurance benefits Benefits payable to the widower of an insured individual who has in his care a child of the insured who is under age 16 or disabled, who is entitled to the child's benefits.

Favorable decision or determination A determination or decision which results in an outcome fully or partially favorable (advantageous) to the claimant.

Federal Benefit Rate (FBR) The monthly payment rate for an SSI benefit recipient or couple; the figure from which countable income, if any, is subtracted to determine the amount of the federal SSI benefit.

Federal Register A publication that provides a uniform system for making available to the public proposal and final regulations and legal notices issued by federal agencies.

Federal Insurance Contributions Act (FICA) The law requiring that Social Security taxes (FICA) be paid on wages and self-employment income and which fund the Social Security and Medicare programs.

Framework of rule An adjudication standard for disability evaluation provided in the regulatory Medical–Vocational guidelines; applies when one or more factors do not precisely conform to the requirements of a particular rule (i.e., a claimant with combined exertional and non-exertional limitations or a work capacity falling between two exertional levels). A framework decision generally departs from the result directed by the Medical-Vocational Rule.

Freedom of Information Act (FOIA) The federal law that requires all agencies to publish certain items of information in the *Federal Register,* including descriptions of organizations, substantive rules of general applicability, statements of function, and so on; to make available for public inspection and copying certain other items of information, including statements of policy and interpretations not published in the *Federal Register,* administrative staff manuals and instructions to staff, and so on; and to make available information to any member of the public upon specific request for that information unless one of nine exceptions apply (see 5 U.S.C. § 552).

Frequent Refers to work-related activities occurring from one-third to two-thirds of the time (i.e., up to six hours) in an eight-hour work day. See Social Security Ruling 83–10.

Full range of work All or substantially all occupations existing at an exertional level. See Social Security Ruling 83–10.

Fully favorable decision A decision which results in an outcome fully consistent with that requested by the claimant.

Fully insured Having one quarter of coverage, whenever acquired, for each calendar year elapsing after the later of 1950 or the year of attaining age 21, and ending with the earliest year in which the worker attains retirement age, becomes disabled, or dies.

Good cause Condition which may be found to exist if a request for reconsideration, hearing, review by the Appeals Council, or the request for filing a civil action in a federal district court is not filed within the appropriate time limit and such failure is the result of untoward circumstances, or the claimant's confusion as to the law resulting from amendments to the Act or other legislation, or fault or misleading action of the Administration. The decision as to whether or not to find "good cause" is made by the office responsible for making the reconsideration, by the Administrative Law Judge, or the Appeals Council, depending upon which component has jurisdiction of the case.

An Administrative Law Judge will find good cause for changing the time or place of the claimant's hearing, and will reschedule the hearing if the reason for the claimant's failure to appear at the scheduled hearing is supported by the evidence and is consistent with the regulations.

Good cause is also a term applied to the legal basis (reason) on which a determination or decision may be reopened within four years (or two years in SSI cases) from the date of the initial determination notice. A finding of good cause to reopen a determination or decision will be made if (1) new and material evidence is furnished, (2) there was a clerical error in the computation of benefits, or (3) the evidence on which the determination or decision was made clearly shows on its face that there was an error. See Title 20 C.F.R. §404.989.

Grant review Agreement by the Appeals Council to review an ALJ's decision or dismissal order pursuant to the claimant's request.

"Grid" A term used to refer to the table of Medical–Vocational rules found in Appendix 2, Subpart P of Title 20 of the Code of Federal Regulations.

Health Care Financing Administration (HCFA) The agency responsible for administering the Medicare program. SSA assists HCFA in some areas of this process, including processing claims for entitlement to Medicare and related appeals under Parts A and B for Medicare.

Hearing A hearing held before an Administrative Law Judge when the party or parties to the hearing and/or the representative (if any) appear and testify.

Hearing office (HO) The local Office of Hearings and Appeals office responsible for processing requests for a hearing, akin to a "presiding" or "chief" judge in a court.

Hearing Office Chief ALJ (HOCALJ) An ALJ in charge of the entire hearing office operation.

Hearing Office Director (HOD) A hearing office employee who assists the HOCALJ in administrative functions and manages the hearing office support staff.

***Hearings, Appeals, and Litigation Law Manual* (HALLEX)** The operations and procedures manual for processing and adjudicating claims at the Office of Hearings and Appeals and Appeals Council levels of adjudication.

Husband's insurance benefits Social Security benefits payable to the husband or divorced husband of an individual entitled to retirement or disability insurance benefits.

Hypothetical A question posed to an expert witness based on assumed findings by the Administrative Law Judge on a claimant's medical condition, functional limitations, and/or vocational factors.

Impairment Related Work Expenses (IRWE) The reasonable cost to a disability beneficiary or recipient of certain items and services needed and used by him or her to work, which may be deducted from earnings when determining whether he or she is engaging in substantial gainful activity, and also in determining the amount of countable earned income for SSI disability recipients.

Income and resources (I & R) In SSI cases, an individual's income (in cash and in-kind) and assets.

In-kind income Income which is not in the form of cash or negotiable instruments as compensation for employment (i.e., real property, food, clothing, room, and board).

In-kind support and maintenance Unearned income in the form of food, clothing, or shelter that is given to an individual or that an individual receives because someone else pays for it.

Insured status A basic factor of entitlement to benefits under Title II of the Act, used to determine whether an individual has sufficient work coverage to be insured for benefits; the basic factor in determining entitlement to retirement insurance benefits, auxiliary benefits, and survivor's benefits.

Interrogatories Questions put to a person (usually a medical expert or a vocational expert) in writing which require a written response.

Laboratory findings Medical findings that are anatomical, physiological, or psychological phenomena which can be shown by the use of medically acceptable laboratory diagnostic techniques, such as chemical tests, electrophysiological studies (electrocardiogram, electroencephalogram), X-rays, and psychological tests. See 20 C.F.R. § 404.1528(c) and § 416.928(c).

Light work Work that involves lifting no more than twenty pounds at a time with frequent lifting or carrying of objects weighing up to ten pounds. Even though the weight lifted may be very little, a job is in this category when it requires a good deal of walking or standing (generally, six out of an eight-hour work day) or when it involves sitting most of the time with some pushing or pulling of arm or leg controls. To be considered capable of performing a full or wide range of light work, an individual must have the ability to do substantially all of these activities. If someone can do light work, the determination will be that he or she can also do sedentary work, unless there are additional limiting factors, such as loss of fine dexterity or inability to sit for long periods of time. See 20 C.F.R. § 404.1567(b) and § 416.967(b).

Limited education By regulatory definition (20 C.F.R. § 404.1564(b)(3) and § 416.964(b)(3), a formal education at a seventh through eleventh grade level.

Listing of Impairments (Listings) Certain severe medical descriptions and conditions, found in

Appendix 1, Subpart P, of Part 404 of Title 20 of the Code of Federal Regulations.

Lump Sum Death Payment (LSDP) A payment made upon the death of a person who was fully and currently insured under the Social Security system; the intended purpose of the payment is to help defray burial expenses.

Marginal education By regulatory definition (20 C.F.R. § 404.1564(b)(2) and § 416.964(b)(2)), a formal education at a sixth-grade level or less.

Medicaid A provision of Title XIX of the Act which provides assistance with certain costs of medical care based on an individual's needs, administered by states.

Medical expert (ME) A medical doctor, osteopath, podiatrist, optometrist, or clinical psychologist under contractual agreement with the Office of Hearings and Appeals to provide expert advice or medical opinions to the Administrative Law Judge in individual disability cases at the hearing level.

Medical opinion A statement from a physician, psychologist, or other acceptable medical source that reflects a judgment about the nature and severity of an individual's impairment(s), including the individual's symptoms, diagnosis, and prognosis; what the individual can still do despite impairment(s); and the individual's physical and mental restrictions. See 20 C.F.R. § 404.1527(a)(2) and § 416.927(a)(2).

Medical source statement (MSS) A statement about what the individual can still do despite his or her impairment(s) based on the medical source's findings. The statement should describe, but is not limited to, physical capabilities for sitting, standing, walking, lifting, carrying, handling objects, hearing, speaking, and traveling; and mental capabilities, such as the ability to understand, carry out and remember instructions, and to respond appropriately to supervision, co-workers, and work pressures in a work setting. See 20 C.F.R. § 404.1513(b)(6) and (c)(1 &2) and § 416.913(b)(6) and (c)(1&2), and Social Security Ruling 96–5p.

Medical–Vocational Rules (Guidelines or "grids") The Medical–Vocational rules in Appendix 2 to Subpart P of Title 20 of the Code of Federal Regulations, which direct findings of "disabled" or "not disabled" on the basis of residual functional capacity, age, education, and previous work experience; applicable to cases that cannot be evaluated on medical consideration alone but where the claimant has a severe medical impairment, is not working, and is not able to perform past relevant work.

Medically acceptable A term from the Act used in several regulations to describe objective medical evidence. It is used in Social Security Ruling 96–2p to mean that the clinical and laboratory diagnostic techniques that the medical source uses are in accordance with the medical standards that are generally accepted within the medical community as the appropriate techniques to establish the existence and severity of an impairment.

Medically determinable impairment An impairment that results from anatomical, physiological, or psychological abnormalities which can be shown by medically acceptable clinical and laboratory diagnostic techniques.

Medically equivalent Terminology used in Social Security when medical findings are at least equal in severity and duration to an impairment listed in the Listings of Impairments in Appendix 1, Subpart P of Title 20 of the Code of Federal Regulations.

Medicare Health insurance protection provided to eligible beneficiaries under the Act and administered by the Health Care Financing Administration; includes hospital insurance protection (Part A) and medical insurance protection (Part B).

Medium work Work that involves lifting no more than fifty pounds at a time with frequent lifting or carrying of objects weighing up to twenty-five pounds. If someone can do medium work, he or she is determined to be able to also do light and sedentary work. See 20 C.F.R. § 404.1567(c) and § 416.967(c); Social Security Ruling 83–10.

Mother's insurance benefits Benefits payable to the widow of the insured individual who has in her care a child of the insured who is entitled to child's benefits and is under age 16 or is disabled.

Net Earnings from Self-Employment (NESE) The figure derived from the gross income of an individuals' trade or business less the allowable deductions attributed to the trade or business plus any distributive share of income (or loss) from a trade or business carried on by a partnership of which the person is a member.

No show Failure to appear at the time and place of a scheduled hearing.

Non-examining sources An acceptable medical source who provides evidence about individuals not examined or treated. All evidence from a non-examining source is opinion evidence. See 20 C.F.R. § 404.1527(f) and § 416.927(f).

Non-exertional capacity Considers all work-related limitations and restrictions that do not depend on an individual's physical strength which are not reflected in the seven strength demands such as sitting, standing, walking, and so on. Abilities assessed as non-exertional include postural activities (stooping, bending, climbing, and so on), manipulative (reaching, handling, fingering, and so on), visual (seeing), communicative (hearing and speaking), and mental (understanding and remembering instructions and responding appropriately to supervision). In addition to these activities, it also considers the ability to tolerate various environmental factors, such as dust and fumes, temperature extremes, and so on. See Social Security Ruling 96–8p.

Non-exertional limitation Any impairment-caused limitations of function which directly affect capacity to perform work activities other than the seven primary strength activities. When the limitations and restrictions imposed by an individual's impairment(s) and related symptoms, such as pain, affect only the individual's ability to meet the demands of jobs other than strength demands, the individual is considered to have only non-exertional limitations or restrictions. Examples of non-exertional limitations or restrictions include difficulties in functioning because of anxiety, depression, or nervousness; difficulty maintaining concentration and attention; difficulties with vision or hearing; difficulties in performing postural or manipulative functions; and difficulties in tolerating some physical feature of certain work settings involving dust, fumes, or temperature extremes. See 20 C.F.R. § 404.1569a(c) and § 416.969a(c), and Social Security Rulings 83–10 and 96–4p.

Not inconsistent A term used to indicate that a well-supported treating source opinion need not be supported directly by all of the other evidence (i.e., it does not have to be consistent with all the other evidence as long as there is no other substantial evidence in the case record that establishes or suggests that the opinion should not be adopted without further question. See 20 C.F.R. § 404.1527(d) and § 416.927(d), and Social Security Ruling 96–2p.

Not severe impairment An impairment or combination of impairments is "not severe" if it does not significantly limit an individual's physical or mental ability to do basic work activities (i.e., it must be a slight abnormality (or a combination of slight abnormalities) that has no more than a minimal effect on the ability to do basic work activities). See 20 C.F.R. § 404.1521(a) and § 416.921(a), and Social Security Rulings 85–28 and 96–3p.

Number holder (NH) The individual upon whom a Social Security record or claim is based; a person assigned a Social Security number; a wage earner.

Objective medical evidence Evidence obtained from the application of medically acceptable clinical and laboratory diagnostic techniques. See 20 C.F.R. § 404.1512(b)(1) and § 416.912(b)(1); 20 C.F.R. § 1529(a) & (c)(2), and § 416.929(a) & (c)(2).

Occasionally Refers to work-related activities occurring from very little up to one-third of the time (i.e., up to two hours) in an eight-hour work day. See Social Security Ruling 83–10.

Occupation A grouping of numerous individual "jobs" with similar duties. Within occupations (e.g., "carpenter") there may be variations among jobs performed for different employers (e.g., "rough carpenter"). See Social Security Ruling 96–9p.

Occupational base The approximate number of occupations that an individual has the residual functional capacity to perform considering all exertional and non-exertional limitations. The occupational base considered in each vocational rule consists of those unskilled occupations identified at the exertional level in question and may be enhanced by the addition of specific skilled or semi-skilled occupations that an individual can perform by reason of his or her education or work experience. The regulations take note of approximately 2,500 medium, light, and sedentary occupations; 1,600 light and sedentary occupations; and 200 sedentary occupations. Each occupation represents numerous jobs in the national economy. See Social Security Rulings 83–10 and 96–9p.

Office of General Counsel (OGC) Social Security Administration employees (attorneys) who are responsible for recommending appropriate action to the Department of Justice and for preparing a response to the complaint for the U.S. Attorney in cases in which a civil action is filed.

Office of Hearings and Appeals (OHA) The SSA component responsible for hearing and deciding appeals under the Act and processing requests for review of ALJ decisions and dismissal orders.

On-the-record decision (OTR) A decision based on the written case record without any personal appearance or submission of other evidence by the claimant at a hearing.

One-half support A situation where an individual's contribution amounts equal or exceed one-half of another person's ordinary living cost, and any income that other person has available for support purposes is one-half or less of his or her ordinary living costs.

Onset The date that a period of disability begins, or is alleged by the claimant (AOD) to have begun.

Order to show good cause A notice sent to a claimant asking him or her to provide an explanation for failure to appear at a scheduled hearing.

Other evidence May include statements or reports from the individual, the individual's treating or examining physician or psychologist, and others about the individual's medical history, diagnosis, prescribed treatment, daily activities, efforts to work, and any other evidence showing how his or her impairment(s) and any related symptoms affect his or her ability to work. See 20 C.F.R. § 404.1512(b)(2)-(6) and § 416.912(b)(2)-(6); 20 C.F.R. § 404.1513(b)(1),(4)(5) & (e) and § 416.913(b)(1),(4)(5) & (e).

Other sources Sources of evidence other than acceptable medical sources. See 20 C.F.R. § 404.1513(e) and § 416.913(e).

Overpayment An excess payment; the amount an individual received for any period which exceeds the total amount which should have been paid for that period.

Own initiative Appeals Council review of a hearing decision on its own initiative without an appeal being filed by a party to the hearing.

Parent's insurance benefits Benefits payable to the parent of an insured individual who was providing at least one-half support of the parent.

Partially favorable decision A decision which results in an outcome not fully congruent with that requested by the claimant, such as the finding of a later disability onset date than that alleged.

Past due benefits The sums of benefits which have accumulated from the date of entitlement to the date of payment on a claim.

Past Relevant Work (PRW) Work that an individual performed within the past fifteen years before the time of adjudication (or before the date last insured for disability) which was performed for a sufficient period of time for the individual to learn the job and which constituted substantial gainful activity. See Social Security Rulings 82–61 and 82–62.

Period of disability (POD) In Title II cases, a continuous period of time in which an individual is disabled, which begins on the date of onset established by SSA and ends with the month of termination or at other times specified and outlined in Subpart D of Title 20 of the Code of Federal Regulations.

Preferred evidence of age The best evidence of age; a birth certificate, hospital birth record, or religious record recorded before age 5.

Prescribed period The period of time during or before which a widow(er) must be found disabled in order to qualify for disability benefits.

Primary insurance amount (PIA) A basic figure computed from an individual's Social Security earnings, by one of several methods computed by law, that is used to determine the actual monthly payment an individual and his or her family receive if entitled to benefits under Title II of the Act.

Prior file A file that has been adjudicated previously.

Privacy Act The law which protects the privacy of individuals in information collection by placing restraints on government record keeping, providing individuals access to their records maintained in a system of records, and limiting disclosure of information to protect the individual (5 U.S.C. 552a).

Pro se Without counsel or representation.

Processing centers SSA centers which house claims files and are responsible for payment of Title II retirement, survivors, and disability benefits as well as a variety of other functions essential to maintaining the beneficiary rolls.

Professional qualifications (PQ) Relevant background and credentials of an individual furnishing evidence or expert testimony, usually a medial doctor, doctor of osteopathy, licensed clinical psychologist, or vocational expert.

Proffer To offer for review, with an opportunity to respond to the material offered.

Program Operations Manual System (POMS) The working manual containing operating and procedural guidelines for SSA field offices, disability determination services, and program service centers, as well as other operations components.

Program policy statements (PPS) Statements issued by SSA to clarify policy on specific issues.

Program service centers (PSC) Offices responsible for maintaining claims files, processing claims which cannot be processed in the field office, and processing post-entitlement actions in retirement and survivor claims.

Protected groups An Equal Employment Opportunity term referring to women, African Americans, Asians, American Indians, Hispanics, and handicapped individuals.

Protective filing A statement of intent (or that can be construed as intent) to file an application for benefits, the date of which can be used as a filing date.

Psychiatric Review Technique Form (PRTF) A form attached to a disability determination at the state agency level, or to a hearing decision which documents the signs, symptoms, and functional limitations of mental impairments. In 2001, SSA revised its regulations so that an ALJ is no longer required to attach the PRTF to his or her decision, but the ALJ must state the conclusions about the claimant's mental functioning he or she has reached and must discuss the evidence on which he or she relied in reaching those conclusions in the decision.

Quarter and calendar quarter A period of three calendar months ending on March 31, June 30, September 30, and December 31.

Quarter of Coverage (QC) The basic unit of coverage used in determining a worker's insured status.

Query To request information about a case from a computerized data system (verb); the computerized request for information (noun).

Rationale That portion of the decision which sets forth the reasons for the Administrative Law Judge's findings on the relevant issues and ultimate decision.

Readily transferable skills Skills which require little or no vocational adjustment in terms of tools, work processes, work setting, or the industry.

Recipient An individual who receives SSI payments.

Reconsideration The level of administrative appeals following an initial determination.

Recovery Collection of an overpayment by requiring an individual to refund the incorrect payment(s).

Recusation The process by which an Administrative Law Judge is disqualified (or disqualifies himself or herself) in an individual case, usually because of bias or conflict of interest.

Re-entitlement period Beginning December 1, 1980, a period of up to thirty-six months, in addition to the nine month trial work period, during which a disabled claimant may continue to test his or her ability to work; after the third month the claimant will be paid benefits only for months in which substantial gainful activity was not performed; if substantial gainful activity is discontinued during this period, benefits may be resumed without a new application and new disability determination.

Regional office (RO) The office responsible for SSA operations in several states.

Remand To send back for further action or consideration (verb); an order or other notice returning a case to a lower review level (noun).

Remote site A location, geographically separate from a hearing office, where hearings are held.

Reopening Changing the final decision of the Commissioner on a previous determination or decision.

Representative payee An individual or organization selected by SSA to receive benefits on behalf of a beneficiary.

Request for Hearing (RH) A request for a hearing before an Administrative Law Judge following denial at the reconsideration level.

Request for Review (RR) A request for review of an Administrative Law Judge's decision by the Appeals Council.

Res judicata "A decided thing"—the doctrine which states a claim will not be readjudicated if it involves the same person, the same facts, and the same issues which have been previously decided.

Residual functional capacity (RFC) An assessment of what a claimant can do in a work setting in spite of functional limitations and environmental restrictions imposed by his or her medical determinable impairment(s). RFC is the maximum degree to which the claimant retains the capacity for sustained performance of the physical or mental requirements of work on a regular, day-to-day basis (eight hours a day, five days a week, or an equivalent work schedule). See 20 C.F.R. § 404.1545 and § 416.945, and Social Security Rulings 83–10, 96–8p, and 96–9p.

Retirement and Survivor's Insurance Benefits (RSI) Social Security benefits payable to retired and disabled individuals, their auxiliaries, and survivors.

Retirement Insurance Benefits (RIB) Social Security benefits payable to individuals who are at least age 62, have applied for benefits, and are fully insured.

Reversal A decision which allows a previously decided claim, or denies a previously allowed claim—a decision which is changed in a case so that it is different from the previous decision.

Sedentary work Work that involves lifting no more than ten pounds at a time with frequent lifting or carrying of articles like docket files, ledgers, and small tools. Although a sedentary job is defined as one which involves sitting, a certain amount of walking and standing is often necessary in carrying out job duties. Jobs are sedentary if walking and standing are required occasionally (generally, only two hours out of an eight-hour work day) and other sedentary criteria are met. See 20 C.F.R. § 404.1567(a) and § 416.967(a), and Social Security Ruling 96–9p.

Selected Characteristics of Occupations (SCO) Published by the U.S. Department of Labor to provide more detailed occupational data than that contained in the *Dictionary of Occupational Titles,* Fourth Edition (DOT). Data on specific vocational training time, physical demands, and environmental conditions are listed for each occupation defined in the DOT.

Self-employment income The amount of an individual's net earnings from self-employment income subject to Social Security tax and counted for Social Security benefit purposes.

Senior ALJ A retired ALJ returned to temporary service who holds hearings and issues decisions and dismissals on requests for hearings.

Sequential evaluation process A step-by-step approach used to evaluate a disability claim.

Severe impairment An impairment or combination of impairments that significantly limits physical or mental abilities to do basic work activities. At step 2 of the sequential evaluation process, an impairment or combination of impairments is considered "severe" if it significantly limits an individual's physical or mental abilities to do one or more basic work activities. See 20 C.F.R. § 404.1520(c) and § 416.920(c), and Social Security Ruling 96–3p.

Signs Anatomical, physiological, or psychological abnormalities which can be observed apart from the individual's statements (symptoms). Signs must be shown through the use of medically acceptable clinical diagnostic techniques. Psychiatric signs are medically demonstrable phenomena which indicate specific abnormalities of behavior, affect, thought, memory, orientation, and contact with reality. They must also be shown by observable facts that can be medically described and evaluated. See 20 C.F.R. § 404.1528(b) and § 416.928(b).

Skill A knowledge of a work activity which requires the exercise of significant judgment that goes beyond the carrying out of simple job duties and is acquired through performance of an occupation which is above the unskilled level (requires more than thirty days to learn). It is practical and familiar knowledge of the principles and processes of an art, science, or trade, combined with the ability to apply them in practice in a proper and approved manner. This includes activities such as making precise measurements, reading blueprints, and setting up and operating complex machinery. See 20 C.F.R. § 404.1568 and § 416.968, and Social Security Rulings 82–41 and 83–10.

Social Security Number (SSN) The number which SSA uses to track earnings while an individual is working and to track benefits once he/she is receiving Social Security benefits.

Social Security regulations Regulations published by the Commissioner of the Social Security Administration to implement the Act.

Social Security Rulings (SSR) Precedent setting, final opinions, and orders and statements of policy and interpretation issued by the Commissioner of the Social Security Administration.

State agency That organization in a state which has been designated by the state to carry out the disability determination function for the federal Social Security program.

Statutory blindness A legal definition of blindness under the Act which requires the clinical findings described in the Listing of Impairments.

Subpoena A writ commanding a person designated in it to appear in court under a penalty for failure. An ALJ (or the Appeals Council) may, on his or her own initiative or at the request of a party, issue subpoenas for the appearance and testimony of witnesses and for the production of books, records, correspondence, papers, or other documents that are material to an issue at the hearing. See Title 20 C.F.R. § 404.950.

Substantial evidence Term describing the quality of evidence. Substantial evidence is "more than a mere scintilla. It means such relevant evidence as a reasonable mind might accept as adequate to support a conclusion." See Social Security Ruling 96–2p.

Substantial gainful activity (SGA) Work that involves doing significant and productive physical or mental duties and which is done (or intended to be done) for pay or profit. Work may be "substantial" even if it is done on a part-time basis or if the individual does less, or has less responsibility than when he or she worked before. Work activity is "gainful" if it is the kind of work usually done for profit, whether or not a profit is realized. See 20 C.F.R. § 404.1510 and § 416.910, § 404.1572 and § 416.972.

Supplemental Security Income (SSI) A program administered by the Administration and financed by general revenue funds; provides monthly payments to aged, blind, or disabled individuals with low income and few assets.

Surviving divorced spouse's benefits Benefits payable to the surviving divorced spouse of an individual who dies fully insured.

Survivor benefits Benefits payable to certain family members when an individual insured under Title II dies.

Symptoms The individual's own description of his or her physical or mental impairments. A "symptom" is not a medically determinable physical or mental impairment and no symptom by itself can establish the existence of such an impairment or be the basis for a finding of disability. See 20 C.F.R. § 404.1528(a) and § 416.928(a), and Social Security Ruling 96–4p.

Technical dismissals A dismissal where the case fails to meet certain technical requirements, such as timely filing of the appeal. Technical dismissals are identified in the prehearing screening process in order to reduce case processing time.

Teleservice centers (TSC) SSA centers which serve as the primary telephone answering point for general inquiries and reports from the public and SSA beneficiaries.

Temporary instructions *HALLEX* instructions that apply only for a limited time period or that address special situations or communicate information that will later be incorporated in other divisions of *HALLEX*.

TERI case A case where the claimant is terminally ill. These cases are time managed by the hearing office, on an expedited basis.

Termination Non-payment of benefits due to the end of entitlement.

Title II That part of the Act pertaining to retirement, survivors, and disability insurance benefits derived from an earned right to entitlement.

Title XVI That part of the Act pertaining to Supplemental Security Income payments for the aged, blind, and disabled.

Title XVIII That part of the Act pertaining to health insurance benefits (Medicare) for the aged and disabled.

Trait In vocational evaluation, an aptitude as opposed to a skill.

Transferability In vocational evaluation, for disability purposes, the ability to apply work skills learned in one job to meet the requirements of another job.

Transferable skills Skills obtained from performing a past relevant job(s) which can be applied to meet the requirements of other skilled or semiskilled jobs that fall within the individual's residual function capacity. Transferable skills are distinct from those learned recently in school which may serve as a basis for direct entry into skilled work. Skills cannot be transferred to unskilled work. See 20 C.F.R. § 404.1568 and § 416.968, and Social Security Rulings 82–41 and 83–10.

Treating source The individual's own physician or psychologist who has provided medical treatment or evaluation and who has or had an ongoing treatment relationship with the individual. Generally, an ongoing treatment relationship is established by the medical evidence showing the individual sees or has seen the physician or psychologist with a frequency consistent with accepted medical practice for the type of treatment and evaluation required for the individual's medical condition(s). If the individual's relationship with a physician or psychologist is not based on a need for treatment but solely on a need to obtain a report in support of the claim for disability, the physician or psychologist will be considered a consulting, rather than treating, physician or psychologist. See 20 C.F.R. § 404.1502 and § 416.902.

Trial work period (TWP) A period of nine months (not necessarily consecutive) in which a Social Security disability beneficiary may test his or her ability to work without jeopardizing entitlement to benefits. See Title 20 C.F.R. 8404.1585 and 404.1592.

Unskilled work Work which needs little or no judgment to do; simple duties that can be learned on the job in a short period of time. The jobs may or may not require considerable strength. For example, jobs are considered unskilled if the primary work duties are handling, feeding, and offbearing (that is, placing or removing materials from machines which are automatic or operated by others) or machine tending; a person can usually learn to do the job in thirty days; and little specific vocational preparation and judgment are needed. See 20 C.F.R. § 404.1568 and § 416.968, and Social Security Rulings 82–41 and 83–10.

Unsuccessful Work Attempt (UWA) Work for up to six months which had to be terminated because of the complained-of impairment(s). See Title 20 C.F.R. § 1574 (c).

Vacate Nullify, declare legally void.

Vocational expert (VE) A consultant or specialist on job placement and occupational requirements who, at the request of the ALJ, provides an opinion regarding skill and exertional levels of various jobs, transferability of skills, and jobs a claimant for disability could or could not perform, based on the ALJ's proposed findings on RFC, other limitations, and vocational factors.

Wage earner (WE) A Social Security account number holder who has had earnings credited under the Social Security system or who has a claim filed under his or her Social Security number.

Waiting period A period of five full, consecutive calendar months following an established onset date for disability in which no disability benefits are payable—applicable to Title II benefits only.

Waiver of overpayment An action under regulatory provisions excusing the repayment of an overpayment of benefits.

Widow(er)'s insurance benefits Benefits payable to the widow or widower of an individual who dies fully insured.

Wife's insurance benefits Social Security benefits payable to the wife and divorced wife of a person entitled to retirement or disability insurance benefits.

Withdrawal Action by a claimant and/or his or her representative to further pursue an application or appeal.

Work experience Skills and abilities an individual has acquired through work he or she had done that show the type of work he or she may be expected to do. See 20 C.F.R. § 404.1565(a) and § 416.965(a).

Younger individual By regulatory definition (20 C.F.R. § 404.1563(b) and § 416.963(b)), an individual age 18 through 49.

A-2

Appendix A-2

Common Medical Acronyms and Abbreviations

AB	asthmatic bronchitis
abd, abdom	abdomen, abdominal
abn, abnorm	abnormal
ABP	arterial blood pressure
abs feb	in the absence of fever
AC	acromioclavicular; or air conduction
ac	before meals
acc	accident; or accommodation; or according
accom	accommodation (eye)
ACP	aspirin, caffeine, phenacetin
ACVD	acute cardiovascular disease
AD	right atrium; or right ear
ADL	activities of daily life
adm	admission or admit
ADR	adverse drug reaction
AE	above elbow
AF	atrial fibrillation or atrial flutter
AHD	antihypertensive drug
AI	aortic insufficiency; or atrial insufficiency
AID	acute infectious disease
AJ	ankle jerk
AK	above knee
AKA	above knee amputation
alc	alcohol
alk	alkaline
AMI	acute myocardial infarction
ANA	antinuclear antibodies
ANF	antinuclear factor
AOD	arterial occlusive disease
aort reg	aortic regurgitation
aort sten	aortic stenosis
AP	anteroposterior; or appendix, appendectomy; or arterial pressure
ap	before dinner
A&P	anterior and posterior; or auscultation and palpation
AP&L or AP&Lat	anteroposterior and lateral (X-ray)
AR	aortic regurgitation
ARD	acute respiratory distress
ARF	acute renal failure
AS	ankylosing spondylitis; or aortic stenosis; or arteriosclerosis; or atrial stenosis; or left ear
ASA	acetylsalicylic acid (aspirin)
ASCVD	arteriosclerotic cardiovascular disease
ASD	atrioseptal defect
ASHD	arteriosclerotic heart disease
ATB	atrial tachycardia with block
ATR	Achilles tendon reflex
AU	both ears together; or each ear
AV	atrioventricular
BA	brachial artery; or bronchial asthma
B/A	backache
BB	both bones; or buffer base
BBB	bundle branch block
bd	twice a day
BE	barium enema; or base excess; or below elbow
bib	drink
bid	twice daily
bil or bilat	bilateral
bil or bili	bilirubin
bin	two times a night
BJ	biceps jerk
B&J	bone and joint
BK	below knee
BL or bl or bleed	blood loss; or bleeding
BM	bone marrow; or bowel movement; or basal metabolism
BO	body odor
BP	birthplace; or bedpan; or blood pressure
BS	bowel sounds; or breath sounds
BSO	bilateral salpingo-oophorectomy
BT	bedtime; or bladder tumor; or body temperature; or brain tumor
BUN	blood urea nitrogen
BV	blood volume
BW	birth weight; or body weight
BX	biopsy
CA or Ca	cancer or carcinoma; or cardiac arrest; or chronological age; or coronary artery
CAB	coronary artery bypass
CABG	coronary artery bypass graft
CAD	coronary artery disease
cath	catheter, catheterize
CB	chronic bronchitis
CBC	complete blood count

CBD	closed bladder drainage; or common bile duct
CC	chief complaint; or critical condition; or current complaint
CCF	congestive cardiac failure
CCI	chronic coronary insufficiency
C Cr	creatinine clearance
CD	cardiovascular disease; or convulsive disorder; or Crohn's disease
CF	chest and left lung; or complement fixation; or cystic fibrosis
CHD	coronary heart disease
CHF	congestive heart failure
CHO or CH2O or COH	carbohydrate
chr or chron	chronic
cn	tomorrow night
CNS	central nervous system
CO	carbon monoxide; or cardiac output
C/O	complains of
COLD or COPD	chronic obstructive lung disease; or chronic obstructive pulmonary disease
CP	capillary pressure; or cerebral palsy; or constant pressure; or cor pulmonale
CPB	cardiopulmonary bypass
CPR	cardiac and pulmonary rehabilitation; or cardiopulmonary resuscitation
CR	chest and right arm; or closed reduction; or colon resection; or conditioned response
CSF	cerebrospinal fluid
CTS	carpal tunnel syndrome
CVA	cardiovascular accident; or cerebrovascular accident
db or dB	decibel
DBP	diastolic blood pressure
DC	discharge, discharged; or discontinue
DI	diabetes insipidus
DM	diabetes mellitus
DT	delirium tremens
DTR	deep tendon reflexes
D&V	diarrhea and vomiting
DVT	deep venous thrombosis
Dx	diagnosis
ECG	electrocardiograph or electrocardiogram
EEG	electroencephalogram or electroencephalography
EENT	eye, ear, nose, and throat
EJ	elbow jerk
EKG	electrocardiogram
EOM	extraocular movements
ET	endotrachial; or exercise treadmill (test)
ETOH	ethyl alcohol
FA	femoral artery; or first aid; or folic acid; or forearm
FB	fingerbreadth; or foreign body
FEV	forced expiratory volume
FEV1	volume of gas forcefully expired in one second

FN	finger to nose (coordination test)
FOB	fiberoptic broncheoscopy
FRJM	full range of joint movement
FROM	full range of motion
FU	follow-up
FVC	forced vital capacity
fx or Fx	fracture
GB	gall bladder
GHQ	general health questionnaire
GI	gastrointestinal
grav	pregnant
GSW	gun shot wound
HBP	high blood pressure
HBV	hepatitis B virus
hct	hematocrit
hd	at bedtime
HEENT	head, ears, eyes, nose, and throat
HF	heart failure; or high frequency
HHD	hypertensive heart disease
HNP	herniated nucleus pulposus
hpn or HPN	hypertension
HR	heart rate
HSV	herpes simplex virus
hx	history
IBS	irritable bowel syndrome
JJ	jaw jerk
KJ	knee jerk
KUB	kidney, ureter, and bladder
LAD	left anterior descending (heart artery)
LB	low back
LBP	low back pain; or low blood pressure
LCA	left coronary artery
LD	learning disabled; or lethal dose; or perception of light difference
LE	left eye; or lower extremity (leg); or lupus erythematosus
LFT	liver function test
LLE	left lower extremity
LLQ	left lower quadrant
LOC	level of consciousness or loss of consciousness
LOM	limitation of motion; or loss of movement
LP	latent period; or light perception; or low pressure; or lumbar puncture
LS	lumbosacral
LUE	left upper extremity (arm)
LUQ	left upper quadrant
MBC	maximum breathing capacity
MBP	mean blood pressure
MCPH	metacarpophalangeal
MCR	metabolic clearance rate
MD	muscular dystrophy
ME	middle ear
MFB	metallic foreign body
MG	myasthenia gravis
MI	mental illness; or mitral insufficiency; or myocardial infarction
mm	muscles

MMPI Minnesota Multiphasic Personality Inventory
MNCV motor nerve conduction velocity
MOM milk of magnesia
MP metacarpophalangeal; or metatarsophalangeal
MR mentally retarded; or metabolic rate; or mitral regurgitation
MS mitral stenosis; or morphine sulfate; or multiple sclerosis; or muscle strength
MSG monosodium glutamate
MSL midsternal line
MSU midstream specimen of urine
MT tympanic membrane
NAD no apparent distress; or no acute distress; or no appreciable distress
NAS no added salt
NBM nothing by mouth
NC no change; or noncontributory
N/C no complaints
NED no evidence of disease
NHL non-Hodgkin's lymphoma
NM neuromuscular
nn nerves
NSA no significant abnormality
NSC not service connected
NSR normal sinus rhythm
NTG nitroglycerine
N&V; NVD nausea and vomiting; nausea, vomiting, and diarrhea
NWB non-weight bearing
NYD not yet diagnosed
OA occiput anterior; or old age; or osteoarthritis
OBS organic brain syndrome
OD overdose; or right eye; or open drop (anesthesia); or occupational disease
O&E observation and examination
OGTT oral glucose tolerance test
OHD organic heart disease
OL left eye
OM occupational medicine; or otitis media
OOB out of bed
ORIF open reduction with internal fixation
os left eye; or mouth
OT occupational therapy; orotracheal
OTC over the counter (non-prescribed)
OU both eyes together; or each eye
PA pernicious anemia; or physician's assistant; or posterioanterior; or psychoanalyst or psychoanalysis; or pulmonary artery
P&A percussion and auscultation
PAB premature atrial beats
para number of pregnancies
PAT paroxysmal atrial tachycardia
Pb presbyopia
pCO2 partial pressure of carbon dioxide
PCP peripheral coronary pressure
PDE paroxysmal dyspnea on exertion
PDR Physicians' Desk Reference (book)
PE pharyngoesophageal; or physical examination; or probable error; or pulmonary embolism
PERRLA pupils equal, round, react to light and accommodation
PF platelet factor; or pulmonary function
pH measure of alkalinity and acidity
PH past history or personal history
PID pelvic inflammatory disease
PIF peak inspiratory flow
PIP proximal interphalangeal
PKU phenylketonuria
PN peripheral neuropathy: or practical nurse; or percussion note
PND paroxysmal nocturnal dyspnea; or post nasal drip
PNS peripheral nervous system
pO2 partial pressure of oxygen
PRF progressive renal failure
prn whenever necessary
PT physical therapy; or prothrombin time
PUD peptic ulcer disease
PVC premature ventricular contractions
PVD peripheral vascular disease
PWB partial weight bearing
PX or Px physical examination or prognosis
RA repeat action (drugs); or rheumatoid arthritis; or right arm; or right atrium; or right auricle
RBB right bundle branch
RBC red blood count
RBF renal blood flow
RCA right coronary artery
RD Raynaud's disease; or respiratory disease; or retinal detachment
RE right eye
REM rapid eye movement
RF relative flow (rate); or rheumatoid factor
RH right hand
RHD rheumatic heart disease
RLE right lower extremity
RLQ right lower quadrant
RMSF Rocky Mountain spotted fever
R/O rule out
ROM range of motion
ROS review of systems
RPA right pulmonary artery
RUE right upper extremity
RUQ right upper quadrant
RV residual volume
Rx prescription; or take; or treatment
SCD service connected disability
SCT sickle cell trait

SF spinal fluid; or synovial fluid
SI sacroiliac; or saturation index; or seriously ill
SIG sigmoidoscope, or sigmoidoscopy
SIJ sacroiliac joint
SIW self-inflicted wound
SLE systemic lupus erythematosus
SLR straight leg raising
SM systolic murmur
SO salpingo oophorectomy
SOB shortness of breath
sx signs; or symptoms
TAH total abdominal hysterectomy
TENS transcutaneous electrical nerve stimulator
TH thyroid hormone
TIA transient ischemic attack
TMJ temporomandibular joint
TSH thyroid stimulating hormone
tx treatment
UA uric acid; or urinanalysis
UC ulcerative colitis
UCD usual childhood diseases
UE upper extremity
UPQ upper left quadrant
URI upper respiratory infection
URQ upper right quadrant
UTI urinary tract infection
VA visual acuity
vent fib ventricular fibrillation
VF ventricular fibrillation; or ventricular flutter; or visual field
VOD vision, right eye
VOS vision, left eye
VPB ventricular premature beat
VRI viral respiratory infection
VSD ventricular septal defect
VT ventricular tachycardia
WB weight bearing; or whole blood
WH well-healed
WNL within normal limits
x or X times or multiplied by
XR X-ray
y/o years old
↑ (up arrow) increase
↓ (down arrow) decrease
> greater than
< less than

Appendix A-3

Childhood Disability Glossary

Activities of daily living (ADL) Activities that involve continuity of purpose and action, and goal or task orientation; that is, the practical implementation of skills mastered at earlier ages. Ordinarily most important indicators of functional limitations in children ages 3 to 16, but may be used for younger children.

Adaptations Assistive devices, appliances, or technology used to improve functioning or ameliorate impairment(s) effects (e.g., eyeglasses, hand/foot splints, custom-made tools or utensils).

Adult A person age 18 or older.

Age-appropriate activities Activities a child is expected to be able to do given his or her age. May be described in terms of achievement of developmental milestones, activities of daily living, or work-related activities.

Behaviors In infants—physical and emotional responses to stimuli; in children—concentration, persistence, and pace.

Child A person who has not attained age 18.

Children In general use, plural of "child." As an age category, from age 3 to attainment of age 18.

Childhood disability evaluation Comprehensive assessment form usually completed by an authorized medical source, evaluating whether the child's impairment "meets," "equals," or "functionally equals" a listed impairment.

Chronological age The period elapsed from the time of birth.

Cognition Ability to learn through perception, reasoning, or intuition, and to retain, use, and manifest acquired knowledge in action or communication.

Communication With respect to language—ability to receive, comprehend, and express messages in an age-appropriate manner in order to meet needs or obtain/convey information. With respect to speech—audibility, intelligibility, and efficiency.

Concentration, persistence, and pace Ability to sustain focus on, and attention to, an activity/task, and to perform the activity or complete the task at a reasonable (or age-appropriate) rate.

Corrected chronological age Chronological age (CA) adjusted for prematurity. Corrected CA = CA minus number of weeks of prematurity.

Developmental milestones Expected principal developmental achievements at particular points in time. Ordinarily most important indicators of functioning for children from birth to age 3, but may be used for older children, especially preschool children.

Domains Broad areas of development or functioning that can be identified in infancy and traced throughout growth and maturation into adulthood. *Developmental domains* generally apply for newborns, infants, toddlers, and preschool children. *Functional domains* generally apply for school-age children and adolescents.

Extreme limitation For children not yet 3 years of age, functioning at a level that is one-half or less of chronological age. For any child under 18, a standard score of 3 deviations or more from the mean on a comprehensive standardized test. See Title 20 C.F.R. §416.926a(3).

Gestational age The age of a child based on the date of conception. May be calculated from the first day of the mother's last menstrual period, or based on certain physical signs at birth using scoring systems designed for this purpose.

Indvidualized education plan/program (IEP) A specially tailored school curriculum designed to accomodate the special needs of children requiring special education.

Individualized functional assessment (IFA) Assessment of the impact of a child's impairment(s) on his or her functioning.

Low birth weight infant Infant weighing less than 2,500 grams (about 5 1/2 pounds) at birth. There are special rules for low birth weight infants weighing less than 2,000 grams.

Marked limitation For newborns, infants, and toddlers—functioning at more than one-half but not more than two-thirds of chronological age in one developmental domain or behavior. For children—more than "moderate" but less than "extreme" limitation. Limitation interferes *seriously* with ability to function independently, appropriately, and effectively in an age-appropriate manner and, when applicable, on a sustained basis.

Moderate limitation For newborns, infants and toddlers—functioning at more than two-thirds but not more than three-quarters of chronological age in one domain or behavior. For children—more than "mild" but less than "marked" limitation. Limitation interferes *considerably* with ability to function independently, appropriately, and effectively in an age-appropriate manner and, when applicable, on a sustained basis.

Motor ability Ability to use one's body and extremities in gross and fine motions to relate to the physical environment and serve one's own or others' physical needs or purposes.

Newborn and young infants Birth to attainment of age 1.

Older adolescent Child age 16 to attainment of age 18.

Older infants and toddlers Age 1 to attainment of age 3.

Personal/behavioral patterns Age-appropriate activities and behaviors entailed in self-help, self-regulation, self-improvement, self-protection, and self-control.

Premature infant An infant born at less than thirty-seven weeks of gestation (also referred to as a preterm baby).

Preschool child Child age 3 to attainment of age 6.

Responsiveness to stimuli Physical and emotional behaviors in reaction to visual, auditory, or tactile stimulation. The term normally applies to the evaluation of newborns and young infants.

School-age child Child age 6 to attainment of age 12.

Small for gestational age (SGA) Birth weight at least two standard deviations (approximately the third percentile) below the average weight for the gestational age.

Social ability Ability to form, develop, and sustain relationships with other people on a personal and social basis in an age-appropriate manner, to respond appropriately within one's own social role or to the social roles of others, and to conduct oneself according to the manners and moves of one's social group.

Structured or highly supportive settings Environments specially planned or designed to improve the ability to function and/or ammeliorate other effects of the child's impairment(s) (e.g., a residential or outpatient treatment facility; a classroom in which the child is accommodated; a home in which family members make extraordinary adjustments to accommodate the child's impairment[s]).

Substantial loss of deficit Used to describe a disabling degree of functional restriction in an older adolescent. Not a precise number, percentage, or other quantitative measure, it represents an inability to meet any one of the basic mental demands of unskilled work, or any one of the basic physical demands of at least sedentary work.

Time spent in therapy Frequent and/or ongoing therapy (e.g., physical therapy, special nursing services, psychological counseling). May interfere with child's age-appropriate functioning.

Young adolescent Child age 12 to attainment of age 16.

APPENDIX B

Social Security Rulings

The Social Security Administration promulgates Rulings, which are policy statements, governing the interpretation of implementing regulations. Appendix B presents significant Rulings. It was originally compiled by U.S. Administrative Law Judge Paul Conaway (Denver, Colorado, Office of Hearings and Appeals) for training purposes. These materials are used with Judge Conaway's permission, for which the authors are grateful.

OUTLINE OF SIGNIFICANT SOCIAL SECURITY RULINGS

1. SSR 82-40: The vocational relevance of past work performed in a foreign country
2. SSR 82-41: Work skills and their transferability
3. SSR 82-52: Duration of the impairment
4. SSR 82-57: Loss of speech
5. SSR 82-59: Failure to follow prescribed treatment
6. SSR 82-60: Evaluation of drug addiction and alcoholism
7. SSR 82-61: Past relevant work—the particular job or the occupation as generally performed
8. SSR 82-62: A disability claimant's capacity to do past relevant work, in general
9. SSR 82-63: Medical–vocational profiles showing an inability to make an adjustment to other work
10. SSR 83-10: Determining capability to do other work—the medical–vocational rules of Appendix 2
11. SSR 83-11: Capability to do other work—the exertionally based medical–vocational rules met
12. SSR 83-12: Capability to do other work—the medical–vocational rules as a framework for evaluating exertional limitations within a range of work or between ranges of work
13. SSR 83-14: Capability to do other work—the medical–vocational rules as a framework for evaluating a combination of exertional and nonexertional impairments
14. SSR 83-20: Onset of disability
15. SSR 83-21: Person convicted of a felony
16. SSR 83-33: Determining whether work is substantial gainful activity—employees
17. SSR 83-34: Determining whether work is substantial gainful activity—self-employed persons
18. SSR 83-35: Averaging of earnings in determining whether work is substantial gainful activity
19. SSR 83-46c: Inability to perform previous work—administrative notice under the Medical–Vocational Guidelines of the existence of other work
20. SSR 84-25: Determination of substantial gainful activity if substantial work activity is discontinued or reduced—unsuccessful work attempt
21. SSR 85-15: Capability to do other work—the medical–vocational rules as a framework for evaluating solely nonexertional impairments
22. SSR 85-16: Residual functional capacity for mental impairments
23. SSR 85-28: Medical impairments that are not severe
24. SSR 86-8: The sequential evaluation process
25. SSR 87-6: The role of prescribed treatment in the evaluation of epilepsy
26. SSR 87-11c: Loss of use of limb prevents performance of past work—"employability" immaterial in determining ability to do other work

27. SSR 87-19c: Evaluation of claimant's subjective complaints and credibility—applicability of the medical–vocational guidelines
28. SSR 88-1c: Appeal from administration's refusal to reopen prior final decision
29. SSR 88-3c: Validity of the severity of impairment regulation
30. SSR 90-5c: Interpreting the statutory blindness provision
31. SSR 91-5p: Mental incapacity and good cause for missing the deadline to request review
32. SSR 91-7c: SSI disability standard for children
33. AR 92-2(6): In disability cessations, the adjudicator must decide through the date of the decision, rather than through the date of initial cessation determination
34. AR 92-6(10): Entitlement to trial work period before approval of an award for benefits and before twelve months have elapsed since onset of disability
35. SSR 93-2p: Evaluation of human immunodeficiency virus infection
36. SSR 94-1c: Illegal activity as substantial gainful activity
37. SSR 95-1p: Good cause for missing deadline to request administrative review
38. SSR 95-2c: Authority of Appeals Council to dismiss a request for hearing for a reason for which the Administrative Law Judge could have dismissed the request—res judicata
39. SSR 96-1p: Application by the Social Security Administration of federal circuit court and district court decisions
40. SSR 96-2p: Giving controlling weight to treating source medical opinions
41. SSR 96-3p: Considering allegations of pain and other symptoms in determining whether a medically determinable impairment is severe
42. SSR 96-4p: Symptoms, medically determinable physical and mental impairments, and exertional and nonexertional limitations
43. SSR 96-5p: Medical source opinions on issues reserved to the commissioner
44. SSR 96-6p: Consideration of administrative findings of fact by state agency medical and psychological consultants and other program physicians and psychologists at the Administrative Law Judge and Appeals Council levels of administrative review; medical equivalence
45. SSR 96-7p: Evaluation of symptoms in disability claims: assessing the credibility of an individual's statements
46. SSR 96-8p: Assessing residual functional capacity in initial claims
47. SSR 96-9p: Determining capability to do other work—implications of a residual functional capacity for less than a full range of sedentary work
48. SSR 97-2p: Prehearing case review by Disability Determination Service
49. SSR 99-2p: Evaluating cases involving chronic fatigue syndrome (CFS)
50. SSR 99-3p: Evaluation of disability and blindness in initial claims for individuals age sixty-five or older
51. SSR 00-1c: Claims filed under both the Social Security Act and the Americans with Disabilities Act
52. SSR 00-2p: Evaluation of claims involving the issue of "similar fault" in the providing of evidence
53. SSR 00-3p: Evaluation of obesity
54. SSR 00-4p: Use of vocational expert and vocational specialist evidence, and other reliable occupational information in disability decisions

Significant Social Security Rulings

Pursuant to 20 CFR Section 402.35(b)(1), Social Security Rulings are binding on all components of the Social Security Administration and are to be relied upon as precedents in adjudicating cases.

This list of Rulings is focused on disability claims. For example, there are no overpayment Rulings. Overpayment cases are fairly infrequent, and their individual facts rarely have broad applicability to other cases. This [appendix] does not attempt to summarize every topic addressed in each Ruling. The emphasis is on selected important items that are useful, or even critical, to correct decision making. . . . Rulings which merely repeat well-established case law are not discussed in detail. . . . All Tenth Circuit acquiescence Rulings relating to disability are included. Acquiescence Ruling from other circuits have been omitted, with the exception of AR 92-2(6).

1. *SSR 82-40: The vocational relevance of past work performed in a foreign country*

Work performed in a foreign country can be past relevant work. There is no requirement that a comparable job exist in the U.S. economy.

This Ruling was upheld in the case of *Han v. Bowen,* 882 F.2d 1453 (9th Cir. 1989). The claimant's past work was as an herbal pharmacy clerk in Vietnam. No such job exists in the United States.

The statute and regulations are silent on the definition of "previous work." The Social Security Administration's interpretation of the statute and regulations will be upheld "unless they are plainly erroneous or inconsistent with the Act or regulations." The ALJ determined that the job was light exertion and semiskilled. The claimant retained the physical capacity for such work.

2. *SSR 82-41: Work skills and their transferability*
This Ruling expands on §§ 404.1568 and 416.968. It further defines a skill as "knowledge of a work activity which requires the exercise of significant judgment that goes beyond the carrying out of simple job duties and is acquired through performance of an occupation which is above the unskilled level (requires more than thirty days to learn). It is practical and familiar knowledge of the principles and processes of an art, science, or trade combined with the ability to apply them. . . ."

The difference between a skill and a "trait" or "ability" is set forth. Traits are inherent abilities such as alertness, coordination, manual dexterity, etc. Skills are learned knowledge such as reading blueprints, making precise measurements, operating complex machinery, etc.

3. *SSR 82-52: Duration of the impairment*
This Ruling focuses on the twelve-month duration requirement. "Tacking" of successive and unrelated impairments, each of which do not meet the twelve-month duration requirement, is not permitted. For example, assume an individual had two unrelated incapacitating impairments. If the first lasted nine months, and the other developed six months after the onset of the first and lasted seven months, the duration requirement is not met, despite thirteen months of total disability.

If the first impairment meets the duration requirement, and a second impairment begins before the first one ends, the second impairment does not have to also last twelve months, since the individual has already met the duration requirement.

Where only the second impairment meets the duration requirement, onset of disability is the first day that the second impairment became disabiling.

Return to work at SGA levels prior to twelve months requires denial of the claim at step 1, subject to finding an unsuccessful work attempt. In that event, the original denial can be reopened.

Per the case of *Walker v. Secretary of Health and Human Services,* 942 F.2d 1257 (10th Cir. 1991) and AR 92-6(10), SSA must evaluate a trial work period, if the following conditions are met. The return to SGA must occur after the five-month waiting period. If there is a return to SGA prior to twelve months, so long as the disability was expected to last at least twelve months, a trial work period must be considered. If the claimant remained medically disabled at least twelve months, then a trial work period must be awarded. The claim cannot simply be denied at step 1. A full review of the claim using the sequential analysis must be made without consideration of the wages earned.

It should be noted that four other circuits have issued similar decisions. See *McDonald v. Bowen,* 818 F.2d 559 (7th Cir. 1986), AR 88-3(7); *Newton v. Chater,* 92 F.3d 688 (8th Cir. 1996), AR 98-1(8); *Salamalekis v. Commissioner of Social Security,* 221 F.3d 828 (6th Cir. 2000), AR 00-5(6); and *Walton v. Apfel,* 235 F.3d 184 (4th Cir. 2000), cert. granted sub nom *Massanari v. Walton,* 70 U.S.L.W. 3232 (U.S. Sept. 25, 2001)(No. 00-1937). As can be seen from the citation, the *Walton* case has been accepted for decision by the U.S. Supreme Court.

Effective 8/10/00, 404.1592(d) was revised to incorporate many of the provisions of this Ruling. The regulation did not attempt to rescind the various acquiescence Rulings mentioned previously. Clearly, the conflict between the Ruling, regulation, and circuit case law will be resolved by the U.S. Supreme Court.

4. *SSR 82-57: Loss of speech*
Evaluation must take into account the intensity of speech (audibility), ability to articulate (intelligibility), and rate of speech and ease of flow (functional efficiency).

5. *SSR 82-59: Failure to follow prescribed treatment*
This Ruling follows the regulations at 404.1530 and 416.930. In addition, it clarifies "justifiable cause" for refusing recommended treatment. The most important items are

- **a.** Fear of surgery—if a treating source indicates that the claimant's fear is so great that he is not a "satisfactory candidate for surgery," then justifiable excuse exists.
- **b.** Cannot afford treatment—there must be documentation that free community resources are not available.
- **c.** Conflict between treating sources—if any treating source recommends against the treatment, then justifiable cause is shown.

6. *SSR 82-60: Evaluation of drug addiction and alcoholism*
There is nothing of great significance in this Ruling. The applicable case law gives the best guidance. The Ruling stresses that "loss of volitional control" is the essence of the diagnosis of addiction. However, a finding of addiction does not necessarily equate to a finding of disability. An addict or alcoholic can still be capable of SGA. Note that recent statutes and regulations (404.1535 and 416.935) require a denial of benefits if drug addiction and/or alcoholism is a "contributing factor material to the determination of disability."

7. *SSR 82-61: Past relevant work—the particular job or the occupation as generally performed*
The regulations were not specific as to the definition of "past relevant work." This is the Ruling that gives authority to the concept that PRW is both the job as the claimant actually performed it *and* the "functional demands and job duties of the occupation as generally required by employers throughout the national economy."

See AR 90-3(4). In the Fourth Circuit, a vocational expert can only testify at step 5. Elsewhere, a vocational expert can also testify regarding step 4, that is, ability to return to past relevant work.

8. *SSR 82-62: A disability claimant's capacity to do past relevant work, in general*
For work to constitute past relevant work, it must meet three requirements:

- **a.** It must qualify as "substantial gainful activity."
- **b.** Duration—this refers to the length of time for the individual to acquire the job experience needed for average performance in the job.
- **c.** Recency—work must have been performed within fifteen years of the date of adjudication, or fifteen years prior to the DLI in Title II claims, if said fifteen years is earlier.

A denial based on ability to engage in past relevant work must contain findings of fact as to the RFC, the physical and mental demands of the past job, and that the individual's RFC permits a return to PRW.

9. *SSR 82-63: Medical–vocational profiles showing an inability to make an adjustment to other work*

This Ruling relates to two specific medical–vocational profiles that lead to awards, which are outside of the Grids. They are

a. Work experience limited to arduous unskilled physical labor—404.1562 and 416.962 direct an award if the claimant has only a marginal education (six or lower) and work experience limited to thirty-five years or more of arduous unskilled labor. Note that arduous work does not require that it was at heavy exertion. If a "great deal of stamina or activity such as repetitive bending and lifting at a very fast pace" was required, then lighter exertion can be arduous.
b. Age fifty-five or more, limited education or less, and "no work experience"—for exertional impairments, Grids 203.10 (medium), 202.01 (light), and 201.01 (sedentary) direct that a person age fifty-five or more, with a limited or less education (less than twelve), and no PRW is disabled. In effect, the finding of a severe impairment alone, with this profile, dictates that there are no jobs in significant numbers in the U.S. economy at step 5. Per Grid 204.00, the ability to do the full range of heavy work is not consistent with a severe impairment.

This Ruling extends this policy to *nonexertional* impairments. "Generally," the only medical issue with this vocational profile is whether there is a severe impairment. If so, an award is appropriate.

This Ruling does not give any guidance as to when it would not apply. "Generally" is not defined, and no examples of appropriate cases for denial are given.

Also, "no" does not necessarily mean "no." If the "work activity performed within this fifteen year period does not (on the basis of job content, recency, or duration) enhance present work capability," then it is equivalent to "no" work experience. No guidance is given as to how to make such a determination.

10. *SSR 83-10: Determining capability to do other work—the medical–vocational rules of Appendix 2*

This is clearly the most important SSR. It is essential for use of the Grid regs. The following items are of particular importance:

a. Exertional capability under the Grids is for "maximum sustained work capability," that is, the highest functional level a person can perform on a regular work basis. It is the ability to "perform sustained work on a regular basis at the particular level of exertion."
b. Stooping is defined as "a type of bending in which a person bends his or her body downward and forward by bending the spine at the waist. Flexibility of the knees as well as the torso is important for this activity."
c. Sedentary work is defined. There is "no significant stooping." Note this is less than occasionally or less than two hours in an eight-hour day. Also, "most unskilled sedentary jobs require good use of the hands and fingers for repetitive hand–finger actions." Therefore, unless a claimant has good bilateral hand and arm use for repetitive motions, he is not capable of most sedentary jobs.
d. Light work is defined. Occasional stooping is required, but not frequent. Again, good bilateral upper-extremity use is required, but less fine activities than sedentary work.
e. Medium work is defined. Frequent bending and stooping are required. Again, bilateral upper-extremity use is required, but not for finer activities.
f. Full range of work is "all or substantially all occupations existing at an exertional level." The Grid regs are predicated on the ability to perform the *full range* of work at a given exertional level. See § 201.00(h).
g. Age is not mechanically applied under the Grids in borderline situations. If a claimant is close to a new age (example given is 54 and 11 months), can apply age 55 grid.
h. Education is not necessarily the grade level achieved. One can raise or lower the education based on the person's present level of reasoning, communication, and arithmetical ability. Also, can look to work skills and responsibilities, daily activities, hobbies, and testing to modify grade level.

11. *SSR 83-11: Capability to do other work—the exertionally based medical–vocational rules met*

a. Can apply Grid only if rule is "exactly met."
b. If rule not exactly met, then can use Grid as a "framework for decision making."
c. Grids assume an absence of any nonexertional limitation.
d. A given RFC for a full range of work requires ability to do all or substantially all the "primary strength activities" of that exertional level. "All or substantially all" means "essentially all" rather than "in the main" or "for the most part."

This definition of "substantially all" would apply to the language in SSR 83-10 defining full range of work as all or substantially all of the *occupations* at a given exertional level.

12. *SSR 83-12: Capability to do other work—the medical–vocational rules as a framework for evaluating exertional limitations within a range of work or between ranges of work*

a. Where an RFC is between two rules which direct opposite conclusions, i.e., at higher exertion "not disabled" and at lower "disabled," need to consider erosion of the higher-level occupational base. If it is "slightly reduced," then not disabled. If it is "significantly reduced," then disabled.
b. Adjudicator can consult vocational resources, such as the *DOT*, etc. pursuant to 20 CFR 404.1566 and 414.966, to assess erosion of the occupational base. In "more complex cases" a vocational expert would be needed. Obviously, the safest course of action is to always have a vocational expert assess the erosion of the occupational base and whether significant numbers of jobs still exist.

However, this Ruling, the cited regulations, and the case of *Sanchez v. Secretary of Health and Human Services,* 812 F. 509 (9th Cir. 1987) establish that the ALJ has authority to take notice of information in the *DOT* without utilization of a vocational expert. For example, to establish how the claimant's PRW is "generally performed" in the U.S. economy, the ALJ could rely on the *DOT.*

c. Alternate sitting and standing—if a person must alternate sitting and standing, [he or she is] not capable of the full range of either sedentary or light work. Some professional and managerial jobs allow a person to sit or stand at will. However, unskilled jobs ordinarily do not permit this. Most jobs "have ongoing work processes which require that a worker be in a certain place or posture for at least a certain lenth of time to accomplish a certain task." VE testimony is necessary to assess erosion of occupational base.

d. Loss of use of an upper extremity—this is inconsistent with the full range of any level of work. VE testimony is necessary to assess erosion of occupational base.

13. *SSR 83-14: Capability to do other work—the medical–vocational rules as a framework for evaluating a combination of exertional and nonexertional impairments*

First evaluate the exertional impairment alone. If a determination of disabled can be made, then award under the Grid. If not, then assess the nonexertional impairment. The question is whether the nonexertional impairment significantly erodes the exertional occupational base. In "clear" cases, the ALJ can make this determination. Obviously, the safe course of action is to utilize a vocational expert.

Again, stooping is defined. Crouching is defined as "bending the body downward and forward by bending both the legs and spine." Frequent bending, both stooping and crouching, is required in most medium, heavy, and very heavy jobs.

14. *SSR 83-20: Onset of disability*

In disabilities of a nontraumatic nature, the onset date of disability may be critical to the determination of the case. All relevant evidence should be considered including the claimant's allegations, work history, medical evidence, and other evidence. Other evidence may be obtained from family members, friends, and former employers. However, the medical evidence serves as the primary element in the onset determination. When the alleged onset and date last worked are far in the past and adequate medical records are not available, the onset date must be inferred from the medical and other evidence. An ALJ should obtain testimony from a medical expert, if an informed judgment cannot be based on the evidence of record.

15. *SSR 83-21: Person convicted of a felony*

Benefits are suspended while incarcerated for a felony. In addition

a. Any physical or mental impairment, which arises or is aggravated (but only to the extent of the aggravation) in connection with the commission of a felony (for which the person is convicted) after 10/19/80, shall not be considered in the determination of disability during the lifetime of the individual. This is a permanent exclusion of the impairment. For example, if a burglar is shot in the arm and has an amputation, for purposes of adjudication, he has "2 arms."

b. Any impairment arising or aggravated during imprisonment for a felony conviction after 10/19/80 will be excluded for purposes of benefit payments. However, the claimant can still be granted a disability freeze and period of disability without benefits. The mere fact that the impairment first occurs or is aggravated during confinement is sufficient for exclusion. There is no need to show a causal relationship between the conditions of the confinement and the impairment.

According to the Ruling, this only applies in Title II cases, not SSI. Also see 404.1506. There is no corresponding SSI regulation.

16. *SSR 83-33: Determining whether work is substantial gainful activity—employees*

Effective August 10, 2000, provisions of this Ruling were clarified and incorporated in 404.1574(a) and 416.974(a). However, the Ruling was not rescinded.

a. This Ruling clarifies "subsidized" work situations. An employer may, because of a benevolent attitude, pay wages in excess of the worth of the services performed. If so, the excess is regarded as a subsidy rather than earnings. The following factors indicate a strong possibility of a subsidy: sheltered employment, childhood disability, mental impairment, marked discrepancy between the amount paid and the value of the services, unusual help from others in performing the work, and government sponsored job training.

b. Impairment related work expenses are discussed. Far more information is provided in the regulations 404.1576 and 416.976.

c. 404.1574 and 416.974 state monetary amounts of earnings that create presumptions that earnings are or are not SGA. Prior to the new regulations effective January 1, 2001, for earnings that are between the primary and secondary amounts, one must look to two tests. The "test of comparability" asks whether the work is comparable to that of unimpaired individuals in the community engaged in the same or similar occupations as their means of livelihood. The "test of worth" asks whether the employee's work is clearly worth more than the primary amount in the regulation. Any reasonable doubt under these two tests should be resolved (generally) in favor of the claimant by finding no SGA.

d. Work activity for blind claimants is also discussed.

17. *SSR 83-34: Determining whether work is substantial gainful activity—self-employed persons*

This Ruling clarified 404.1575 and 416.975 prior to 8/10/00. Effective 8/10/00, the provisions of this Ruling were incorporated into the regulations. However, the Ruling was not rescinded.

SGA determinations for self-employed persons requires a comparison of pre-AOD activities and income with the post-AOD period of time. There should be an explanation and documentation as to the alleged decline in business, perhaps the replacement of the owner's services by new employees. Three tests are used: the test of significant services and substantial income, the test of comparable work, and the test of worth. Work activity for blind claimants is also discussed.

18. *SSR 83-35: Averaging of earnings in determining whether work is substantial gainful activity*

The provisions of this Ruling were added to the regulations as 404.1574a and 416.974a effective 8/10/00. However, the Ruling was not rescinded.

Earnings are generally averaged over the period of time in which work was performed. This is particularly required when earnings and work activity varies (greatly) from month to month. For example, persons working on commission may have great variation in their earnings, which do not necessarily relate to the amount of services performed in a given month. This is also often true in self-employment situations. However, earnings are averaged over separate periods of time if there is a change in SGA presumptive levels or a significant change in work patterns or earnings occurs.

19. *SSR 83-46c: Inability to perform previous work—administrative notice under the Medical–Vocational Guidelines of the existence of other work*

This is the case of *Heckler v. Campbell,* 461 U.S. 458 (1983). The U.S. Supreme Court upholds the Grid regulations. There is no need to use a VE, if the Grids (exactly) apply.

20. *SSR 84-25: Determination of substantial gainful activity if substantial work activity is discontinued or reduced—unsuccessful work attempt*

Prior to 8/10/00, the regulations provided scant guidance regarding unsuccessful work attempts. However, as of 8/10/00, this Ruling was incorporated into §§ 404.1573, 404.1574, 404.1575, 416.973, 416.974, and 416.975 of the regulations. However, the Ruling was not rescinded.

This Ruling provides guides for analysis of unsuccessful work attempts.

- **a.** Before there can be an UWA, there must be a "significant break in the continuity of a person's work." The break must occur "because of the impairment or the removal of special conditions related to the impairment that are essential to the further performance of work."
- **b.** "Special conditions" may be evidenced by sheltered workshop, special assistance from other employees, irregular hours or frequent rest periods, special equipment, assistance from others for preparation for or transportation to work, lower standards of productivity or efficiency, family relationship, or other altruistic reason.
- **c.** The break can be work which is "discontinued" or reduced below SGA levels.
- **d.** Work is "discontinued" if the person was out of work for at least thirty consecutive days or was forced to change to another type of work or another employer.
- **e.** One can have multiple successive UWAs, as long as each one meets the standards above and the duration requirements below.
- **f.** Duration requirements
  - **1.** Three months or less—work must end because of the Impairment or removal of special conditions.
  - **2.** Between three months and six months—same as above and
    - **a.** Frequent absences due to impairment, or
    - **b.** Work must have been unsatisfactory due to impairment, or
    - **c.** Work during period of temporary remission, or
    - **d.** Work done under special conditions.
  - **3.** More than six months—cannot be UWA regardless of why it ended or was reduced below SGA.

21. *SSR 85-15: Capability to do other work—the medical–vocational rules as a framework for evaluating solely nonexertional impairments*

The title of this Ruling implies that the Grids can be used as a framework. However, the Ruling itself clearly states that they cannot be used for nonexertional impairments. If there are no exertional impairments, there is unlimited exertional capacity. If PRW has already been eliminated at step 4, then the question remains as to whether the nonexertional impairment significantly erodes the occupational base. Unless it can be determined that the nonexertional impairment does not have a significant impact on the full range of work, a vocational expert is needed to assess whether a significant number of jobs are available. The first step is to assess the effect of the nonexertional impairment on the broad range of work and then to assess the additional effects of age, education, and work experience.

- **a.** Mental impairments

Mental impairments are the most common nonexertional impairment. Where a claimant's mental impairment prevents return to PRW or transferability of acquired job skills, the final question is whether the claimant can perform unskilled competitive employment.

"The basic mental demands of competitive, remunerative, unskilled work include the abilities (on a sustained basis) to understand, carry out, and remember simple instructions; to respond appropriately to supervision, coworkers, and usual work situations; and to deal with changes in a routine work setting."

A substantial loss of ability to meet *any* of these basic work related activities would severely limit the occupational base. It would justify a finding of disability, even if the claimant had favorable factors of age, education, or work experience.

Four examples are provided. The first is a very young person, university education, and highly skilled work experience. With only a "substantial loss of ability to respond appropriately to supervision, coworkers, and usual work situations," a finding of disability would be appropriate.

- **b.** Postural–manipulative impairment
  - **1.** Climbing and balancing—where there is only "some limitation" in climbing and balancing, it does not have a significant impact on the broad world of work.
  - **2.** Stooping, kneeling, crouching, and crawling—again states (as in SSR 83-10 and 83-14) that stooping and crouching are frequently required in medium and greater work. Kneeling and crawling are a relatively rare activity, even in arduous work. Limitations in kneeling and crawling have little significance in the broad world of work.
- **c.** Reaching, handling, fingering, and feeling—nothing new. Need a VE to assess vocational effect.
- **d.** Visual impairments—even if a visual impairment eliminates jobs requiring very good vision (such as working with small objects or reading small print), as long as the person can handle and work with rather large objects and has the visual fields to avoid ordinary hazards in a workplace, there are a substantial number of jobs remaining at all exertional levels.
- **e.** Environmental restrictions—a person with a seizure disorder, who is restricted only from being on unprotected elevations and near dangerous moving machinery, does not have a significant effect on work that exists at all exertional levels.

Where a person must avoid "excessive amounts" of noise or pulmonary irritants (dust, fumes, etc.), the effect on the broad world of work is minimal.

22. *SSR 85-16: Residual functional capacity for mental impairments*

If a mental impairment is severe, then there is a significant restriction in the ability to perform some basic work-related activity. If the mental impairment does not meet or equal a listing, it is mandatory to determine a mental RFC and proceed to step 4 or 5 in the sequential evaluation.

Relevant, reliable information from third-party sources "such as social workers, previous employers, family members, and staff members of halfway houses, mental health centers, and community centers, may be valuable in assessing an individual's level of activities of daily living." Along with 404.1513 and 416.913 regarding "acceptable medical sources," this limits the ambit of "medical opinions" which can be accepted from social workers, etc.

23. *SSR 85-28: Medical impairments that are not severe*

This Ruling clarifies 404.1521 and 416.921.

a. Even with the Social Security Reform Act of 1984, the severity step based on medical considerations alone is still applied.
b. An impairment can only be determined not severe "when medical evidence establishes only a slight abnormality or a combination of slight abnormalities which would have no more than a minimal effect on an individual's ability to work . . . i.e., the person's impairment(s) has no more than a minimal effect on his or her physical or mental ability(ies) to perform basic work activities."
c. The combined effect of all the impairments must be assessed to make the severity determination. One cannot assess the severity of each impairment separately and determine that separately they are not severe.
d. Great care should be exercised in applying the not severe concept. It should only be used when the medical evidence clearly shows no severe impairment.

24. *SSR 86-8: The sequential evaluation process*
The sequential evaluation process is set forth. When a decision can be made at any step, evaluation under a subsequent step is unnecessary.

25. *SSR 87-6: The role of prescribed treatment in the evaluation of epilepsy*
a. Only a small percentage of epileptics, who receive appropriate medical treatment, are incapable of SGA.
b. Appropriate medical treatment requires close rapport and an ongoing relationship with a physician to closely monitor anticonvulsant medications.
c. If a claimant does not have an "ongoing treatment relationship," for whatever reason, it is unreasonable to assume that the seizures cannot be controlled. Therefore, the impairment cannot meet or equal a listing, regardless of the frequency of seizures.
d. The issue of failure to follow prescribed medical treatment must be addressed.
e. In every case, the record of anticonvulsant blood levels is required before an award can be made.

26. *SSR 87-11c: Loss of use of limb prevents performance of past work—"employability" immaterial in determining ability to do other work*
This Ruling adopts the Court's opinion in *Odle v. Secretary of Health and Human Services,* 788 F.2d 1158 (6th Cir. 1985). A man who had lost the use of his left hand and arm was unable to perform PRW. Based on testimony of a vocational expert, the ALJ determined that significant numbers of other jobs were available. The ALJ was correct in not accepting the opinion of a second VE that the claimant was unable to engage in SGA because he was "unemployable" based on the VE's experience in job placement. "Employability" is not the issue. The correct standard is the "ability" to perform work.

27. *SSR 87-19c: Evaluation of claimant's subjective complaints and credibility—applicability of the Medical–Vocational Guidelines*
This Ruling adopts the district court's opinion in *Rodrigues v. Heckler,* 1A Unempl. Ins. Rep. (CCH)17,011 (S.D. Cal. July 31, 1986). The claimant testified to seizures and blackouts that, if credible, would clearly disable him. The ALJ determined that the subjective complaints were exaggerated, and he was not "wholly credible." The court affirmed based on substantial evidence. This case gives excellent examples of the types of findings required by an ALJ to support a determination that subjective complaints are not credible. The ALJ noted the following:
a. There were no objective findings to substantiate the impairment.
b. Several treating physicians expressed doubts regarding the diagnosis and the frequency of claimant's reported seizures.
c. Due to pending litigation under the Jones Act, the claimant had little motivation to work.
d. The claimant had given contradictory statements to various physicians and in his testimony regarding the following:
   1. He told one doctor he had worked as a "nautical navigator," when he had only been an ordinary fisherman.
   2. The claimant gave widely varied accounts regarding his education (fourth grade in Portugal, high school in the United States, and university in Mexico).
   3. Claimant told one doctor that his seizures prevented him from driving since his accident, but he told another doctor that he had two seizures while driving.
   4. The medical histories contain ever-increasing reports as to the length of time the claimant was unconscious following his accident (fifteen minutes, twenty minutes, forty-five minutes, and finally three hours).

28. *SSR 88-1c: Appeal from administration's refusal to reopen prior final decision*
Section 404.988(a) provides that an initial determination may be reopened within twelve months of said notice "for any reason." The claimant argued, and some circuits have held, that this imposes a mandatory duty on SSA to reopen any prior claim, if a new application is filed within twelve months of the notice of initial denial. This Ruling adopts the decision in *Monger v. Bowen,* 817 F.2d 15 (4th Cir. 1987), which determines that the twelve month reopening regulation is *discretionary.* SSA may reopen for any reason, but it is in its discretion to refuse reopening. Otherwise, the sixty-day limit on requesting reconsideration would be meaningless.

29. *SSR 88-3c: Validity of the severity of impairment regulation*
This is the Supreme Court decision in *Bowen v. Yuckert,* 482 U.S. 137 (1987), which upheld the severity of impairment regulation after the Social Security Reform Act of 1984. Step 2 is a "de minimis" test. The medical evidence is reviewed to see if there is an impairment severe enough to "interfere with ability to work."

30. *SSR 90-5c: Interpreting the statutory blindness provision*
This Ruling is the decision in *Adams v. Sullivan,* 872 F.2d 926 (9th Cir. 1989), cert. denied, 493 U.S. 851, 110 S. Ct. 151 (1989). The statutory blindness definition is strictly applied. The claimant argued that her vision and additional neurological impairment was more severe than the effects of the statutory definition. The court rejected the attempt to create an "equivalency" standard.

31. *SSR 91-5p: Mental incapacity and good cause for missing the deadline to request review*
a. A claimant establishes good cause for late filing due to mental incapacity if he "lacked the mental capacity to understand the procedures for requesting review."
b. The claimant must also show that he "had no one legally responsible for prosecuting the claim (e.g., a parent of a claimant who is a minor, legal guardian, attorney, or other legal representative)."

c. The ALJ must consider the following factors:

- ❑ Inability to read or write;
- ❑ Lack of facility with the English language;
- ❑ Limited education;
- ❑ Any mental or physical condition which limits the claimant's ability to do things for him/herself.

d. If these substantive criteria are satisfied, the time limits in the reopening regulations do not apply. Regardless of how much time has passed since the prior administrative action, the claimant can extend the deadline for requesting review.

e. The ALJ must resolve any reasonable doubt in favor of the claimant.

32. *SSR 91-7c: SSI disability standard for children*

This is the U.S. Supreme Court's decision in *Sullivan v. Zebley,* 493 U.S. 521 (1990). The Court invalidates the prior Social Security regulations in SSI child disability claims. It was improper for SSA to apply a meets or equals criteria alone in assessing child disability. Note that this Ruling has been changed by the 1996 laws revising the childhood disability standard.

33. *AR 92-2(6): In disability cessations, the adjudicator must decide through the date of the decision, rather than through the date of initial cessation determination*

This acquiescence Ruling responds to a Sixth Circuit decision in *Difford v. Secretary of Health and Human Services,* 910 F.2d 1316 (6th Cir. 1990). The claimant's disability benefits were terminated due to medical improvement. The ALJ affirmed the termination as of the date the disability was determined to have ceased. However, the ALJ did not address the issue of disability from the date of the cessation up through the date of the ALJ decision. The court held that disability must be assessed up to the date of the decision being made.

This acquiescence Ruling is important, in that, it establishes Social Security policy regarding cessations (outside of the Sixth Circuit). In a cessation determination, an ALJ must only evaluate the issue of disability as of the date of the cessation. An ALJ is not required to evaluate the issue of disability up through the date of the ALJ's decision. This logically makes sense, in that, if the cessation determination is correct, the claimant must file a new application to obtain further benefits.

This Social Security policy was affirmed in the decision of *Johnson v. Apfel,* 191 F.3d 770 (7th Cir. 1999). The court specifically rejected the *Difford* decision.

34. *AR 92-6(10): Entitlement to trial work period before approval of an award for benefits and before twelve months have elapsed since onset of disability*

This Ruling acquiesces to the decision in *Walker v. Secretary of Health and Human Services,* 943 F.2d 1257 (10th Cir. 1991). The claimant returned to work at substantial gainful activity within twelve months of his alleged onset date of disability. The ALJ denied the (Title II) claim, at step 1, based on SGA. The claimant argued that his disability continued despite SGA and that he was entitled to a trial work period. Social Security policy is that if, prior to an award, a claimant returns to work demonstrating the ability to engage in SGA prior to twelve months, the claim must be denied. The court overturned this decision, as long as the claimant's return to work was after the five-month waiting period, and the claimant's disability was expected to last twelve continuous months or more.

See the prior discussion regarding SSR 82-52 and 404.1592(d)(effective 8/10/00). Numerous other circuits have also adopted this holding. The matter is currently pending before the U.S. Supreme Court for ultimate resolution.

For Title XVI cases, the same rule applies except there is no requirement relating to a waiting period. Pursuant to Public Law 87-642, effective July 1, 1987, the trial work provisions are no longer applicable in SSI disability cases. Such income places the person in § 1619 status, rather than a trial work period. This Ruling still applies in order to place the person in 1619 status.

35. *SSR 93-2p: Evaluation of human immunodeficiency virus infection*

The duration requirement in HIV listing cases is clarified. If a person has documented HIV infection per 14.00D3 or 114.00D3 and meets or equals one of the listed criteria in listing 14.08 or 114.08, there is no need to assess duration. The impairment is considered permanent or expected to result in death.

36. *SSR 94-1c: Illegal activity as substantial gainful activity*

This Ruling adopts the decision in *Dotson v. Shalala,* 1 F.3d 571 (7th Cir. 1993). The court held that $200 to $300 per day from "hustling and stealing" was SGA. The court rejected the claimant's argument that his subsequent purchase of drugs should count as impairment-related work expenses to reduce his income below SGA. The court also rejects a vague "Catch 22" argument. If the claimant testifies that he uses less than $500 per month in drugs, then he doesn't have an uncontrollable addiction. However, if the claimant testifies to a large habit, then he must "rob, cheat, or steal" greater than $500 per month, which is SGA. Either way, his case can be denied.

The new amendments to 42 U.S.C. 423(d)(4) regarding alcoholism and drug addiction make it clear by statute that illegal activity can be SGA.

37. *SSR 95-1p: Good cause for missing deadline to request administrative review*

This parallels the holding in AR 92-7(9). The Ruling applies to initial and reconsideration decisions prior to 7/1/91. Those on or after 7/1/91 are covered by § 205(b) of the Social Security Act, as amended by Public Law 101-508. Good cause for failure to file a timely request for reconsideration or hearing can be found if

a. The claimant received a defective notice prior to 7/1/91 that stated that if he failed to file an appeal, he could "file another application at any time."

b. There is a presumption of a defective notice in all Title II notices after 8/31/77 and prior to 3/1/90. In all other cases, there must be actual proof of a defective notice provided by the claimant or in the Social Security file.

c. The claimant must provide an "acceptable explanation" that the failure to appeal was based on the absence of language explaining that the failure to appeal would result in a final decision. The ALJ should consider

- ❑ The claimant's explanation;
- ❑ The claimant' mental condition;
- ❑ The claimant's ability in the English language;
- ❑ How much time has elapsed before the claimant filed a new claim or appeal;
- ❑ Whether the claimant was represented by a nonattorney. Normally, representation by an attorney bars a claimant from relief.

38. *SSR 95-2c: Authority of Appeals Council to dismiss a request for hearing for a reason for which the Administrative Law Judge could have dismissed the request—res judicata*

This Ruling adopts the decision in the case of *Harper v. Secretary of Health and Human Services*, 978 F.2d 260 (6th Cir. 1992). The claimant filed multiple applications for disability benefits. Her fifth application was filed after a final decision was rendered after her date last insured. The ALJ could have dismissed the request for hearing on the grounds of res judicata. Instead, he held a hearing on the merits and denied the claim. The claimant appealed. The Appeals Council vacated the decision stating that the final decision on the fourth application was res judicata. The court upholds the appeals council's authority to vacate an ALJ's decision and dismiss the claim on grounds of res judicata.

The following nine SSRs (96-1p through 96-9p) implement SSA's process unification initiatives. All of the Rulings were effective July 2, 1996.

39. *SSR 96-1p: Application by the Social Security Administration of federal circuit court and district court decisions*

Unless and until an Acquiescence Ruling is issued determining that a final circuit court holding conflicts with the agency's interpretation of the act or regulations, SSA decision makers are bound by SSA's nationwide policy, rather than the court's holding, in adjudicating other claims within that court's jurisdiction.

The regulations already provide a procedure for claimants who are denied in the interim between a circuit court's opinion and the issuance of an AR. The claimant, upon request, can have the claim readjudicated with immediate application of the AR without the necessity of appeal.

SSA does not acquiesce in decisions of federal district courts, unless the court directs otherwise, such as in class actions.

40. *SSR 96-2p: Giving controlling weight to treating source medical opinions*

A medical opinion of an acceptable treating medical source, about the nature and severity of the claimant's impairments, that is well supported by medically acceptable findings, and which is not inconsistent with *any* other substantial evidence in the claim must be given controlling weight. It must be accepted by the adjudicator to decide the claim. Portions of a treating source opinion may be controlling, while other portions are not.

A medical opinion from an acceptable treating medical source that is either not well supported or inconsistent with some other substantial evidence can still be entitled to the greatest weight, but it is not controlling. The adjudicator can accept or reject it.

An adjudicator must always give good and specific reasons for the weight given to a treating source's medical opinion.

This Ruling is nothing new to ALJs. Repeated opinions of the federal courts have required specific reasons for rejecting the opinions of treating physicians. However, this Ruling has a profound effect on DDS, which has historically relied on a "lack of objective medical evidence" to reject treating opinions. Also, see SSR 96-7p, which requires reasons for rejecting a claimant's subjective complaints.

41. *SSR 96-3p: Considering allegations of pain and other symptoms in determining whether a medically determinable impairment is severe*

There is nothing new in this Ruling. There must be a medically determinable physical or mental impairment that reasonably could cause *some* degree of the symptoms alleged. If the symptoms have anything more than a minimal effect on an individual's ability to do basic work activities, then the adjudicator must find a severe impairment.

42. *SSR 96-4p: Symptoms, medically determinable physical and mental impairments, and exertional and nonexertional limitations*

The Act requires a medically determinable physical or mental impairment. An impairment must result from anatomical, physiological, or psychological abnormalities that can be shown by medically acceptable clinical and laboratory diagnostic techniques. A symptom is not a "medically determinable physical or mental impairment." It cannot be the basis for a finding of a medically determinable impairment, no matter how many symptoms there are or how genuine the individual's complaints may appear to be, unless there are medical signs and laboratory findings demonstrating a medically determinable impairment.

In the absence of a medically determinable impairment, an individual must be found "not disabled" at step 2 (no severe impairment).

Once a medically determinable impairment is established that could reasonably produce *some* pain or other symptoms, allegations about the intensity and persistence of the symptoms must be considered with both the objective medical evidence and all other evidence in the file.

Symptoms are neither exertional nor nonexertional. They can cause limitations that are exertional or nonexertional or both. This determines whether the Grids may be used to direct a decision or as a framework for decision making.

43. *SSR 96-5p: Medical source opinions on issues reserved to the commissioner*

Certain issues are reserved to the Commissioner. They are

a. Whether an impairment meets or equals a listing.
b. What is the RFC.
c. Whether the RFC permits a return to past relevant work.
d. How the vocational factors or age, education, and work experience apply.
e. Whether the claimant is "disabled."

Treating source opinions on these issues must never be ignored. However, they are never entitled to controlling weight or any special significance. The decision must discuss the weight given to such opinions.

Examples include statements that the claimant is "disabled," "unable to work," or is "capable of sedentary work." An adjudicator cannot assume that the medical source is aware of the definition of such terms as "sedentary" or "light."

A medical source statement is a medical opinion, while the RFC is the adjudicator's ultimate finding as to what the claimant is able to do despite his limitations.

Assessments by state agency medical and psychological consultants constitute expert medical opinion evidence by nonexamining physicians and psychologists. These opinions must be addressed in the ALJ's decision.

If evidence does not support a treating source's opinion on any issue reserved to the Commissioner and the adjudicator cannot ascertain the basis of the opinion from the record, the adjudicator must make a reasonable effort to recontact the source for clarification of the reasons for the opinion. This Ruling is a restatement of prior policy. Regulation 404.1512 indicates that SSA will recontact a treating source when the evidence from the treating or other medical source is "inadequate for us to determine whether you are disabled."

44. *SSR 96-6p: Consideration of administrative findings of fact by state agency medical and psychological consultants and other program physicians and psychologists at the Administrative Law Judge and Appeals Council levels of administrative review; medical equivalence*

Findings of fact made by state agency medical and psychological consultants must be treated as expert opinion evidence of nonexamining sources by the ALJ. The opinion should be evaluated considering all the factors set out in the regulations for opinion evidence. The ALJ may not ignore these opinions and must explain the weight given to these opinions in the decision. Also see 404.1527(f).

In some cases, the state agency opinion may be given greater weight than the opinion of the treating source. An example is when a state agency doctor has more detailed and comprehensive information than was available to the treating source, combined with a medical report from a specialist (i.e., CE report) in the particular impairment.

The signature of the state agency physician or psychologist on the 831 form ensures that consideration was given to whether an impairment equals (and by inference whether it meets) a listing at the initial and reconsideration level. Note that 404.1527(f)(1) specifically states that the state agency physicians consider whether a person meets or equals the listings.

An ALJ cannot find medical equivalence without an updated opinion of a medical expert.

45. *SSR 96-7p: Evaluations of symptoms in disability claims: assessing the credibility of an individual's statements*

This Ruling supercedes SSR 95-5p. There is very little new for ALJ's than what has long been established by case law. The Ruling is a profound change in how DDS evaluates claims. An adjudicator must give specific reasons for the finding on credibility regarding subjective complaints. The decision must articulate what weight was given to the claimant's statements. The assessment cannot be made based on an intangible or intuitive notion about a claimant's credibility. It is not sufficient to simply make a statement that "credibility has been evaluated" or that "the allegations are not credible." Subjective complaints cannot be rejected *solely* on the basis of a lack of objective medical evidence, but this is one factor to be considered. An adjudicator can accept all, part, or none of the claimant's statements as credible.

An adjudicator must consider the observations of any SSA personnel who interviewed the claimant in person or by phone. If a state agency doctor opines about a claimant's credibility, the ALJ must consider the opinion and explain the weight given to it.

Guidelines for evaluating credibility (i.e., types of specific reasons) are provided.

When additional information is needed to assess credibility, the adjudicator must make every reasonable effort to obtain available information that could shed light on the credibility of the individual's statements.

46. *SSR 96-8p: Assessing residual functional capacity in initial claims*

RFC is an assessment of a claimant's ability to do sustained work-related physical and mental activities in a work setting on a regular and continuing basis (eight hours per day and five days per week, or an equivalent work week). At step 4, an RFC for part-time work that meets the criteria for past relevant work (recency, duration, and SGA) is sufficient for a finding of not disabled.

The Act requires that disability be due to a medically determinable physical or mental impairment. Therefore, factors of age and body habitus (height, weight, size, physique), insofar as they are unrelated to an impairment, may not be considered in determining the RFC.

RFC is the most a person can do, not the least. At step 5, it is in error to express the RFC at the lowest level that would still direct a finding of not disabled.

A footnote indicates that only in the Fourth Circuit has the SSA issued an acquiescence Ruling, AR 94-2(4), accepting that res judicata requires acceptance of an RFC from a prior application in the absence of "new and material evidence." SSA's policy is that a second ALJ is not bound by a prior RFC if it covers a new period of time. However, since this SSR 96-8p was issued, another acquiescence Ruling has been issued. In the Ninth Circuit, factual findings are res judicata in a subsequent claim in the absence of "changed circumstances." See *Chavez v. Bowen*, 844 F.2d 691 (9th Cir. 1988); *Lester v. Chater*, 81 F.3d 821 (9th Cir. 1995); and AR 97-4(9).

The "B" and "C" sections of the PRTF are not a mental RFC assessment but are used to evaluate listing severity at step 3. At steps 4 and 5, a more detailed assessment is necessary.

In determining RFC, the adjudicator must evaluate the combined effect of all impairments, even nonsevere impairments.

The RFC assessment requires a narrative discussion to support each conclusion, resolve all material inconsistencies or ambiguities, and explain why the opinion of a medical source was not adopted.

47. *SSR 96-9p: Determining capability to do other work—implications of a residual functional capacity for less than a full range of sedentary work*

An RFC for less than a full range of sedentary work reflects very serious limitations and is expected to be relatively rare. A finding of less than sedentary does not necessarily equate to a finding of disabled. If past relevant work is eliminated, an RFC of less than sedentary may still permit the performance of jobs which exist in significant numbers in the U.S. economy. At the hearing level, this would clearly require a VE.

The erosion of the sedentary range of jobs caused by various limitations is discussed. They are lifting/carrying and pushing/pulling; standing and walking; sitting; alternate sitting and standing; medically required handheld assistive device; postural limitations; manipulative limitations; visual limitations; communicative limitations; environmental restrictions; and mental limitations.

SSR 97-2p: Prehearing case review by Disability Determination Service

Effective 8/8/97, OHA has authority to remand disability cases to DDS for a new determination when new medical evidence is received at a hearing if all the following criteria are met:

a. The claim is for disability benefits under Title II or SSI, and the issue to be determined is "disability."

b. A hearing has not been held.
c. SSA received additional medical evidence after the date of the reconsideration determination.
d. The additional evidence is not duplicative and was not a result of SSA development.
e. SSA has not previously returned the case to DDS for a prehearing case review.

SSR 99-2p: Evaluating cases involving chronic fatigue syndrome (CFS)

Chronic fatigue syndrome is a medically determinable impairment, and it can be a basis for a finding of "disability." Per the Centers for Disease Control criteria, such a diagnosis can be established by a patient's complaints alone, after all other alternative medical and psychiatric causes have been excluded. However, per the Social Security Act and regulations, an individual cannot establish a medically determinable impairment, or [his or her] disability, by subjective complaints alone. The Ruling lists numerous medical signs, laboratory findings, and mental findings that are sufficient to establish a medically determinable impairment. Some examples are swollen lymph nodes; persistent muscle tenderness on repeated examinations, including the presence of positive tender points; an elevated antibody titer to Epstein–Barr virus; etc. The list of objective findings in the Ruling is not all inclusive, so other findings can be used.

A footnote states that there is considerable overlap of symptoms between CFS and Fibromyalgia Syndrome (FMS). The American College of Rheumatology criteria for FMS includes a minimum number of tender points. Even if the minimum number of tender points is not sufficient to establish FMS, this finding may still be used to establish CFS. By inference, it is clear from this Ruling that fibromyalgia is also a medically determinable impairment, which can be the basis for a finding of disability.

SSR 99-3p: Evaluation of disability and blindness in initial claims for individuals age sixty-five or older

Per statutory changes, for most noncitizens, SSI benefits are no longer payable based on age alone. Even though age sixty-five or more, the individual must establish that [he or she is] disabled. The Social Security regulations and Grids are premised on the evaluation of disability for persons less than sixty-five. This Ruling provides the evaluation procedures for individuals age sixty-five or older.

It is not likely that many of these cases will reach the OHA level. The number of noncitizen disability claims, for persons sixty-five or more, cannot be very numerous. Also, given the strong bias in the regulations, Rulings, and Grids for findings of disability for elderly, less educated, and illiterate persons, it is anticipated that the vast majority of these claims will be paid by DDS. Therefore, no analysis of the Ruling will be made in this appendix.

SSR 00-1c: Claims filed under both the Social Security Act and the Americans with Disabilities Act

This Ruling is based on the Supreme Court's decision in *Cleveland v. Policy Management Systems Corp.*, 119 S.Ct. 1597 (1999). This case resolved the conflict among the circuits regarding the interplay of claims under the Americans with Disabilities Act (ADA) and claims for Social Security disability. In this case, the claimant filed for Social Security disability asserting that she was disabled. Later, she filed an ADA claim requesting reasonable accommodations and stating that she was capable of performing the "essential functions" of her job. In her ADA claim, it was held by the lower court that she had taken inconsistent positions. Her earlier filing for disability benefits estopped her from asserting her claim under the ADA.

The Supreme Court reversed. It held that the two claims are not necessarily inconsistent. It noted that the SSA does not take "reasonable accommodations" under the ADA into account when assessing disability. In a disability claim, a claimant can be entitled to a presumption of disability, by meeting a listing, and still maintain employment. Also, disabled persons may test their ability to work and still receive benefits through a trial work period and extended period of disability. Finally, a person's condition may change over time, so a statement about disability at the time of the disability application may not reflect the person's capabilities at the time of the ADA determination.

It is the plaintiff's burden in an ADA action to provide an explanation as to the apparent contradiction between a disability claim and an ADA claim. This is a question of fact to be resolved. The mere fact that simultaneous claims were made does not estop the plaintiff from asserting a claim under the ADA.

Obviously, by inference, the converse is true. In a Social Security claim, the fact that the claimant also filed under the ADA does not, in and of itself, defeat the disability claim. It is a fact to consider, along with all other evidence of record.

SSR 00-2p: Evaluation of claims involving the issue of "similar fault" in the providing of evidence

The Social Security Independence and Program Improvements Act of 1994, Public Law 103-296 mandated a redetermination of individual's entitlement to benefits if there was a reason to believe that fraud or similar fault was involved in the individual's application for such benefits. In regard to new claims, when determining eligibility, SSA "shall disregard any evidence, if there is reason to believe that fraud or similar fault was involved in the providing of such evidence." "Similar fault" is involved, if an incorrect or incomplete statement that is material to the determination is knowingly made, or information that is material to the determination is knowingly concealed. Fraud is different in that it includes an element of intent to defraud.

A finding of "similar fault" may be made, based on a preponderance of the evidence, if the person knew that the evidence was false or incomplete. A finding of "similar fault" regarding a given material fact may be used as evidence of "similar fault" regarding other evidence from the same source.

A finding of "similar fault" regarding some evidence does not direct a denial of the claim. A person may still be found disabled based on the remaining evidence.

53. *SSR 00-3p: Evaluation of Obesity*
Effective 10/25/99, listing 9.09 regarding obesity was deleted. This Ruling provides guidance on the evaluation of claims involving obesity in the absence of the listing. Obesity is a medically determinable impairment. Obesity alone can be a basis for a finding of "disability." Obesity can be used in conjunction with another listing, such as 12.05 or 112.05, for a determination of "meets" a

listing. In such a case, obesity would be an additional and significant work-related limitation of function. Also, obesity can be used as part of an "equals" determination. Obesity, by itself, could be functionally equivalent to the requirements of another listing, such as 1.03. Obesity could substitute for arthritis and the associated criteria, when it markedly limits the individual's ability to walk and stand. Also, if a combination of impairments, including obesity, is equivalent in severity to a listed impairment, an "equals" determination may be made. Even if an individual does not meet or equal a listing, the limiting effects of obesity must be assessed with all other evidence of record in determining the residual functional capacity. Of course, this can lead to a determination of disability at step 5 of the sequential evaluation.

SSR 00-4p: Use of vocational expert and vocational specialist evidence, and other reliable occupational information in disability decisions

This Ruling results from the decision in *Haddock v. Apfel,* 196 F.3d 1084 (10th Cir. 1999). The ALJ denied the claim at step 5. Given the claimant's age a finding of transferable skills was necessary. The VE identified transferable skills from the claimant's past skilled work to four semiskilled jobs (payroll clerk, parts clerk, materials lister, and inventory clerk). In providing numbers for the jobs, he lumped all four together and stated that there were "many thousands of these jobs" in the regional and national economies.

On appeal, it was established that three of the jobs given by the VE were inconsistent either with the skill or exertional requirements stated in the *DOT.* Only the job of payroll clerk was consistent with the *DOT.* However, it was impossible to tell the numbers of this specific job, given the VE's failure to provide numbers for each separate job. It was held that the ALJ's decision was not based on substantial evidence. The court held that the *DOT* does not "trump" all VE testimony. However, in deciding a case at step 5, the ALJ must

a. Correlate a VE's testimony with the *DOT,* that is, ask if it is consistent with the *DOT.*
b. If the job is not consistent with the *DOT,* a reasonable explanation of the discrepancy must be provided. It would most likely require an explanation by the VE for the source of his information. This duty rests with the ALJ based on the shifting of the burden of proof.
c. Numbers for each job should be given separately and not lumped together. On appeal, if any job should be found invalid, substantial evidence may exist given specific numbers for the remaining jobs.

Following this decision, the SSA issued AR00-3(10) on 6/20/00. SSA did not dispute that the ALJ's decision in *Haddock* was erroneous, in that, the ALJ failed to resolve the conflict between the VE's opinion and the *DOT.* However, this acquiescence Ruling stated that the *Haddock* decision differed from Social Security policy. An ALJ must resolve conflicts in the record. This includes conflicts between a VE's opinion and job information in the *DOT.* When there is a conflict, the VE should be asked to explain the reason his or her opinion differs from the *DOT* and the basis for the opinion. It is then up to the ALJ to resolve the conflict and explain it in the decision. However, SSA policy does not place an affirmative duty on the ALJ to ask a VE, as a preliminary step, whether his or her opinion is consistent with the *DOT.*

AR00-3(10) clearly was consistent with long established Social Security policy. Unless a claimant can establish that, in fact, there is a conflict between the VE's opinion and the *DOT,* no basis for appeal should exist. In effect, if an ALJ makes a perfectly valid denial of a claim based on VE testimony that is *not* inconsistent with the *DOT,* the claim should not be remanded on appeal, simply because the ALJ failed to ask if the VE's opinion was consistent with the *DOT.* With this acquiescence Ruling, at least in all circuits outside of the Tenth Circuit, an appeal of an ALJ denial could not be prefaced *solely* on the fact that the ALJ failed to ask a VE if his or her testimony was consistent with the *DOT.*

Effective 12/4/00, the SSA rescinded AR00-3(10) and issued SSR 00-4p. SSR 00-4p adopts the entire rationale of the *Haddock* decision. Therefore, in all disability claims, an ALJ has an affirmative duty to ask a VE, as a preliminary step, whether his or her opinion is consistent with the *DOT.* It appears that if an ALJ makes a perfectly valid denial of a claim based on VE testimony that is *not* inconsistent with the *DOT,* the claim will be subject to remand, if the ALJ simply failed to ask if the VE's opinion was consistent with the *DOT.*

APPENDIX C

Administrative Actions

Appendix C contains the Social Security Administration's compilation of administrative actions constituting an initial determination for which review is available by an Administrative Law Judge. The form reflects actions under Title II (Disability Insurance Benefits), Title XVI (Supplemental Security Income Benefits), and Title XVIII (Medicare).

Note: These lists cover the vast majority of administrative actions that are initial determinations. However, they are not all inclusive.

TITLE II

1. Entitlement or continuing entitlement to benefits;
2. Reentitlement to benefits;
3. The amount of benefit;
4. A recomputation of benefit;
5. A reduction in disability benefits because benefits under a workers' compensation law was also received;
6. A deduction from benefits on account of work;
7. A deduction from disability benefits because of claimant's refusal to accept rehabilitation services;
8. Termination of benefits;
9. Penalty deductions imposed because of failure to report certain events;
10. Any overpayment or underpayment of benefits;
11. Whether an overpayment of benefits must be repaid;
12. How an underpayment of benefits due a deceased person will be paid;
13. The establishment or termination of a period of disability;
14. A revision of an earnings record;
15. Whether the payment of benefits will be made, on the claimant's behalf to a representative payee, unless the claimant is under age 18 or legally incompetent;
16. Who will act as the payee if SSA determines that representative payment will be made;
17. An offset of benefits because the claimant previously received Supplemental Security Income payments for the same period;
18. Whether completion of or continuation for a specified period of time in an appropriate vocational rehabilitation program will significantly increase the likelihood that the claimant will not have to return to the disability benefit rolls and thus, whether the claimant's benefits may be continued even though the claimant is not disabled; and
19. Nonpayment of benefits because of claimant's confinement in a jail, prison, or other penal institution or correctional facility for conviction of a felony.

TITLE XVI

1. Eligibility for, or the amount of, Supplemental Security Income benefits;
2. Suspension, reduction, or termination of Supplemental Security Income benefits;
3. Whether an overpayment of benefits must be repaid;
4. Whether payments will be made, on claimant's behalf to a representative payee, unless the claimant is under age 18, legally incompetent, or determined to be a drug addict or alcoholic;
5. Who will act as payee if SSA determines that representative payment will be made;

6. Imposing penalties for failing to report important information;
7. Drug addiction or alcoholism;
8. Whether claimant is eligible for special SSI cash benefits;
9. Whether claimant is eligible for special SSI eligibility status;
10. Claimant's disability; and
11. Whether completion of or continuation for a specified period of time in an appropriate vocational rehabilitation program will significantly increase the likelihood that claimant will not have to return to the disability benefit rolls and thus, whether claimant's benefits may be continued even though he or she is not disabled.

Note: Every redetermination which gives an individual the right of further review constitutes an initial determination.

TITLE XVIII

1. Entitlement to hospital insurance benefits and to enrollment for supplementary medical insurance benefits;
2. Disallowance (including denial of application for HIB and denial of application for enrollment for SMIB);
3. Termination of benefits (including termination of entitlement to HI and SMI).

APPENDIX D

Modular Folder Documents

Appendix D contains the Social Security Administration's compilation of the various documents and their placement within the six-part modular disability folder (MDF).

DOCUMENTS RECEIVED/GENERATED BY HEARING OFFICE

The following is a list (in alphabetical order) of documents received or generated by the hearing office subsequent to request for hearing and the section of the MDF in which they are filed.

Document	Part
Briefs	Part E
Case History, HOTS	Part A
Cassette (Hearing) and Cassette Envelope	Part A
Certificates	
Birth	Part D
Death	Part D
Congressional Inquiries and Responses	Part D
Correspondence	
Disability Related	Part E
Not Disability Related	Part D
Decision/Dismissal	
ALJ	Part A
Senior Attorney	Part A
Earnings, Proof of (certified earnings record, employer statement, W2, tax return, DEQY/SEQY)	
Evidence	
*Request for Additional Medical	Part C Part E
Fees	
Agreement or Contract	Part B
Order or Authorization	Part A
Petition, Form SSA-1560	Part B
Hearing	
Acknowledgment of Request/Attachments	Part B
Continuance of Hearing	Part B
Notice of Hearing (claimant, representative, ME, VE)	Part B
Waiver of Right to Appear	Part B
Individualized Functional Assessment (IFAs)	
Completed by DDS Physician	Part E
Completed by treating physician	Part F
Information, Release of Form SSA-827	Part E
Interrogatories	
Medical Expert (ME)	Part F
Vocational Expert (VE)	Part E
Printouts, Systems Screen (not pertinent)	Part C
Professional Qualification Statements (PQs)	
Attached to Notice of Hearing (ME/VE)	Part B
Attached to Medical Evidence	Part F
Attached to SSA 831-833	Part A
Proffer	
ME, Request and Response	Part F
VE, Request and Response	Part E
Psychiatric Review Technique (PRT) Form	
Completed by DDS Physician	Part E
Completed by ALJ/Senior Attorney	Part A
Completed by Treating Physician	Part F
Queries	Part C
Questionnaires, Disability	
Activities of Daily Living (ADL)	Part E
Claimant's Medication	Part E

***Request will be placed in Part C, Current Development/Temporary, pending receipt of evidence. If the evidence is not received, the original request and documentation regarding follow-up attempts should be transferred to Part E, Disability Related Development and Documentation, prior to release of the file.**

Document	Location
Recent Medical Treatment	Part E
Work History	Part E
Reports of Contact	
Disability Related	Part E
Not Disability Related	Part D
Representative	
Appointment of SSA-1696	Part B
Withdrawal of Representative	Part B
Resume (see Professional Qualification Statements)	
Substitute Party Form	Part B
Workers' Compensation Information	Part D

DOCUMENTS RECEIVED/GENERATED BY APPEALS COUNCIL

Note: The Appeals Council will continue to use an appeals file (AF) to house its working papers.

Document	Location
Additional Evidence	
Briefs	Part F
Nonmedical	Part D
Briefs	Part E
Cassette	
Cassettes	Part A
Cassette Envelopes	Part A
Search Requests	
Certifications	Part A
Congressional Correspondence	
Inquiries	Part D
Interim Responses	AF
Final Responses	Part D
(Other) Correspondence	
Disability Related	Part E
Not Disability Related	Part D
Interim Correspondence	
Dispositions	
Decision by AC	Part A
Dismissal by AC	Part A
Notice Denying R/R	Part B
Remand by AC	Part B
Fees	
Agreement or Contract	Part B
Order or Authorization	Part A
Petition	Part B
MSS Comments	
Made AC Exhibit	Part E
Not Made AC Exhibit	
Order Entering Exhibits	Part D
PRTF	
(Part of AC Decision)	Part A
Representative	
Notice of Appointment	Part B
Withdrawal	Part B
Request for Review	Part B
Substitute Party Form	Part B

Index